PLAYFAIR
CRICKET

EDITED BY BILL FRINDALL

All statistics by the Editor unless otherwise credited

PLAYFAIR CRICKET COMPETITION 1991
TEST CRICKET QUIZ
£1500 TO BE WON

PLUS NATWEST FINAL TICKETS AND HOSPITALITY
PLUS 25 CONSOLATION PRIZES

First Prize   £500 + overnight accommodation (B and B) at the Regents Park Hilton Hotel (opposite Lord's) on 6 and 7 September + TWO tickets to the 1991 NatWest Trophy Final + NatWest hospitality.

Second Prize £400 + TWO tickets to the 1991 NatWest Trophy Final

Third Prize £300 + TWO tickets to the 1991 NatWest Trophy Final

Fourth Prize £200

Fifth Prize £100

Consolation prizes
Senders of the next 25 correct entries will each receive a copy of THE GOLDEN AGE OF CRICKET by George Plumptre and published by Queen Anne Press at £14.95

Closing date for entries is 12.00 noon on 31 July 1991

Winning entries will be drawn by the Man of the Match Adjudicator at one of the NatWest semi-finals played on Wednesday 14 August.

PLAYFAIR CRICKET COMPETITION 1991

TEST CRICKET QUIZ

ENTRY FORM

Please PRINT your answers in the spaces provided and answer every question.

1 Who is the only visiting captain to lead his team to victory in a Bridgetown Test? ....

2 Which was the 64th GROUND (not town/city) to stage a Test match? ....

3 Who is the only batsman to play over 100 consecutive Test innings without a duck? ....

4 Who holds the record for the most successive matches as a Test captain? ....

5 How many runs did Graham Gooch score in Test cricket during the calendar year of 1990? ....

6 Who was the first wicket-keeper to make five stumpings in a Test innings? ....

7 Who was the first batsman in Test cricket to hit four consecutive balls for six? ....

8 The first triple century in Test cricket was scored in the West Indies – by whom? ....

9 Who equalled the Test record by catching five batsmen in an innings in November 1989? ....

10 Who is the only umpire to have stood in more Tests than 'Dickie' Bird? ....

Your name and address:

....

....

....

Your daytime telephone number: ....

Post to: PLAYFAIR CRICKET COMPETITION, Special Events, Corporate Affairs Department, National Westminster Bank PLC, 1st Floor, 2 Broadgate, London EC2M 2AD.

Entries must be received before noon on 31 July 1991. All-correct entries will go into the prize-winning draw on 14 August and an announcement detailing all prize-winners will appear in the October edition of *The Cricketer* magazine. A list of winners is available on request by writing to Mrs B.J.Quinn at the above address and enclosing a stamped addressed envelope.

Rules: All entries must be on this official form. Proof of posting is not proof of entry. The decision of the editor regarding the answers to this quiz shall be final and binding; no correspondence may be entered into.

3

1990 PLAYFAIR CRICKET COMPETITION
TEST CRICKET QUIZ ANSWERS

1	Who captained India in their first official Test match?	C.K.NAYUDU
2	Which was the 62nd GROUND to stage a Test match?	BELLERIVE OVAL
3	Who was the first batsman to score 5,000 runs in Test cricket?	J.B.HOBBS
4	Where was the shortest completed Test match (5 hours 53 minutes) staged?	MELBOURNE
5	How many runs did Mark Taylor score in Test cricket during the calendar year of 1989?	1,219
6	Who was the first wicket-keeper to complete the Test double (1,000 runs/100 dismissals)?	W.A.S.OLDFIELD
7	Who captured New Zealand's first Test wicket with his very first ball?	M.HENDERSON
8	What is the most expensive Test career bowling average?	294.00
9	Who achieved the only hat-trick for England against Australia in England?	J.T.HEARNE
10	Which English GROUND has lost most complete days of Test cricket to rain?	OLD TRAFFORD

There were 130 sets of correct answers out of a total of 594 entries. The winners were drawn by Trevor Bailey (Essex and England) and Glen Emanuel (Manager, Special Events, National Westminster Bank) after the 1990 NatWest Trophy semi-final between Lancashire and Middlesex at Old Trafford.

First Prize:	£500 + two nights accommodation + two tickets to include hospitality at the 1990 NatWest Trophy Final	J.P.CHEESLEY (Shoreham)
Second Prize:	£400 + two tickets to the 1990 NatWest Trophy Final	G.LARSEN (Caernarfon)
Third Prize:	£300 + two tickets to the 1990 NatWest Trophy Final	J.N.BIRD (Loughborough)
Fourth Prize:	£200	I.ROBERTS (Edinburgh)
Fifth Prize:	£100	C.J.MANN (Croydon)

25 Runners-up: each received a copy of *Three Men At The Match.*

F.Austin (Castle Donington)	M.G.Konstant (Bristol)
F.Beale (Folkestone)	T.Myrling (Huntingdon)
J.Bray (Mirfield)	A.T.Parker (Newark)
C.Brough (Luton)	Mrs S.J.Porter (Portishead)
J.Browne (Gloucester)	C.M.Spencer (Gloucester)
Julia Consterdine (London SW11)	S.T.Taylor (Liverpool)
P.Flintoft (Middlesbrough)	J.H.Thomas (Llandovery)
J.Hebron (Guisborough)	M.Thomas (Great Yarmouth)
N.Hodgson (London SE5)	A.R.Wilde (Norwich)
G.Hotten (London E4)	N.W.Williams (Neath)
S.A.Humphreys (Watford)	A.Williamson (Maidenhead)
N.A.Johns (Weymouth)	A.Youngman (Sutton)
R.Keighley (Halifax)	

EDITORIAL PREFACE

Refusing to do things by halves, last season the TCCB dramatically transformed the balance between batsman and bowler by simultaneously flattening both the ball and the playing surface. With the 25-point pitches penalty hovering over the Championship like the sword of Damocles, the high-seamed ball outlawed and few clouds around to encourage swing or swerve, batsmen were transported back to the Elysian fields of the 1930s. Despite the bowlers' protests, virtually the same conditions will apply this season. Will 1991 become another Year of the Bat? Certainly Graham Gooch will be hoping for a repeat of the summer which yielded the highest first-class aggregate (2,746) since the Championship was substantially reduced in 1969, including an unprecedented tally of 1,058 runs in the six Test matches.

The mighty West Indies attack is unlikely to be daunted by the current regulations. Back by demand of cricket's exchequer after an interval of just three seasons, they may find sterner opposition than in 1988. Now under stable leadership, hand injuries permitting, England's revamped team have been hardened by the experience of hard-fought campaigns overseas. Crucially, they can at last call upon the supreme batting talent of Graeme Ashley Hick, whose ever-growing list of records includes that of being the youngest to score 50 first-class hundreds.

After the five-match series for the Wisden Trophy (which West Indies have held since 1973), the international season will continue with Sri Lanka's third Test outing at Lord's. There, after an extraordinary period of confinement, the Nursery End should be able to display its new-born Compton and Edrich stands. Should Middlesex retain the Britannic Assurance title, Lord's will also be the scene of a unique international finale to the season in the form of a four-day challenge match against the winners of Australia's Sheffield Shield competition.

Pressure from stockists has resulted in another price increase; their previous profit simply did not justify shelf space. Even so, *Playfair*, the world's largest-selling cricket publication, remains well below the average price of 256-page paperbacks. For those who prefer a more substantial binding, we have introduced a cased edition.

My congratulations and thanks are due to the National Westminster Bank on extending their sponsorship of both the NatWest Trophy and this publication for at least three years. We wish Glen Emanuel a long and busy retirement and welcome Barbara Quinn, who succeeds him as Manager, Special Events. My thanks also go to Tony Brown and Kate Jenkins of the TCCB, to John Jameson of MCC, to David Armstrong of the MCCA, and to all the county administrations and scorers for their invaluable and ready assistance. I am especially grateful to Ian Marshall for ensuring that masses of typescript (plus one micro floppy disc) have been safely transformed into this 44th edition and to Christine Forrest for her expert proof scrutiny.

BILL FRINDALL
January 1991

NEW ZEALAND v INDIA (1st Test)

Played at Lancaster Park, Christchurch, on 2, 3, 4, 5 February 1990.
Toss: New Zealand.   Result: NEW ZEALAND won by 10 wickets.
Debuts: India – S.L.V.Raju, A.S.Wassan.

NEW ZEALAND

T.J.Franklin c Prabhakar b Kapil Dev	20		
*J.G.Wright b Raju	185		
A.H.Jones c Raju b Hirwani	52		
M.D.Crowe lbw b Raju	24		
M.J.Greatbatch b Wassan	46		
K.R.Rutherford b Kapil Dev	69		
J.G.Bracewell b Hirwani	0		
†D.S.Smith lbw b Raju	9		
R.J.Hadlee c Hirwani b Prabhakar	28		
M.C.Snedden lbw b Kapil Dev	3	(1) not out	1
D.K.Morrison not out	1	(2) not out	1
Extras (B3, LB12, NB7)	22		
Total	**459**	(0 wickets)	**2**

INDIA

W.V.Raman lbw b Hadlee	0	c Jones b Morrison	96
N.S.Sidhu lbw b Morrison	51	absent hurt	–
S.V.Manjrekar c Jones b Hadlee	5	b Hadlee	4
*M.Azharuddin lbw b Hadlee	48	b Bracewell	30
S.L.V.Raju c Crowe b Snedden	31	(8) c Smith b Snedden	21
S.R.Tendulkar c Smith b Morrison	0	c Smith b Bracewell	24
M.Prabhakar c Smith b Snedden	1	(2) b Snedden	40
Kapil Dev c Snedden b Morrison	4	(7) lbw b Hadlee	25
†K.S.More c Smith b Morrison	1	(5) b Hadlee	11
A.S.Wassan c Smith b Morrison	2	(9) not out	24
N.D.Hirwani not out	1	(10) c Bracewell b Hadlee	0
Extras (B5, LB5, NB10)	20	(B6, LB2, NB13)	21
Total	**164**		**296**

INDIA	O	M	R	W	O	M	R	W	FALL OF WICKETS				
										NZ	I	I	NZ
Kapil Dev	28.3	4	89	3					Wkt	1st	1st	2nd	2nd
Prabhakar	38	8	114	1	0.5	0	2	0	1st	26	0	80	–
Wassan	25	3	95	1					2nd	141	27	85	–
Raju	35	12	86	3					3rd	182	88	135	–
Hirwani	29	9	60	2					4th	307	146	160	–
NEW ZEALAND									5th	374	146	206	–
Hadlee	14	1	45	3	22.5	3	69	4	6th	375	148	242	–
Morrison	16	2	75	5	19	0	94	1	7th	394	153	254	–
Bracewell	3	0	14	0	20	4	45	2	8th	448	158	289	–
Snedden	12.5	4	20	2	25	5	59	2	9th	454	161	296	–
Rutherford					5	1	21	0	10th	459	164	—	–

Umpires: R.S.Dunne (2) and S.J.Woodward (21).   Test No. 1137/29

NEW ZEALAND v INDIA (2nd Test)

Played at McLean Park, Napier, on 9‡, 10, 11, 12, 13‡ February 1990.
Toss: India.   Result: MATCH DRAWN.
Debuts: Nil.

(‡ no play)

INDIA

W.V.Raman lbw b Hadlee	0
M.Prabhakar c Smith b Hadlee	95
S.V.Manjrekar c Smith b Morrison	42
*M.Azharuddin b Morrison	33
D.B.Vengsarkar c Smith b Morrison	0
S.R.Tendulkar c Wright b Morrison	88
Kapil Dev lbw b Hadlee	4
†K.S.More c Franklin b Snedden	73
S.L.V.Raju not out	3
A.S.Wassan b Morrison	0
N.D.Hirwani not out	1
Extras (LB5, NB14)	19
Total (9 wickets declared)	358

NEW ZEALAND

T.J.Franklin c Kapil Dev b Wassan	50
*J.G.Wright not out	113
A.H.Jones not out	4
M.D.Crowe	
M.J.Greatbatch	
K.R.Rutherford	
†I.D.S.Smith	did not bat
R.J.Hadlee	
J.G.Bracewell	
M.C.Snedden	
D.K.Morrison	
Extras (B5, LB3, W1, NB2)	11
Total (1 wicket)	178

NEW ZEALAND	O	M	R	W
Hadlee	35	11	73	3
Morrison	38	8	98	5
Snedden	42	10	104	1
Bracewell	22	2	50	0
Rutherford	9	0	28	0
INDIA				
Prabhakar	13	3	25	0
Kapil Dev	14	4	30	0
Wassan	15	2	48	1
Hirwani	18	7	40	0
Raju	11	4	27	0

FALL OF WICKETS

	I	NZ
Wkt	1st	1st
1st	0	149
2nd	92	–
3rd	150	–
4th	152	–
5th	210	–
6th	218	–
7th	346	–
8th	356	–
9th	356	–
10th	–	–

Umpires: B L Aldridge (6) and S J Woodward (22).   Test No. 1138/30

NEW ZEALAND v INDIA (3rd Test)

Played at Eden Park, Auckland, on 22, 23, 24, 25, 26 February 1990.
Toss: India.   Result: MATCH DRAWN.
Debuts: New Zealand – S.A.Thomson; India – Gursharan Singh.

NEW ZEALAND

T.J.Franklin c Tendulkar b Wassan	4	lbw b Prabhakar	2
*J.G.Wright c Gursharan b Kapil Dev	3	c Wassan b Hirwani	74
A.H.Jones c More b Prabhakar	19	not out	170
M.D.Crowe c More b Wassan	24	lbw b Hirwani	113
M.J.Greatbatch b Wassan	4	c Gursharan b Wassan	43
K.R.Rutherford c Prabhakar b Wassan	20	c More b Hirwani	8
S.A.Thomson c More b Kapil Dev	22	not out	43
R.J.Hadlee b Hirwani	87		
†I.D.S.Smith lbw b Prabhakar	173		
M.C.Snedden c More b Prabhakar	22		
D.K.Morrison not out	0		
Extras (LB9, NB4)	13	(B4, LB14, NB12)	30
Total	**391**	(5 wickets declared)	**483**

INDIA

W.V.Raman c Franklin b Hadlee	8	not out	72
M.Prabhakar lbw b Snedden	36	not out	63
S.V.Manjrekar b Morrison	16		
D.B.Vengsarkar c Smith b Morrison	47		
*M.Azharuddin c Rutherford b Thomson	192		
S.R.Tendulkar c Smith b Morrison	5		
Gursharan Singh c and b Thomson	18		
Kapil Dev c Jones b Hadlee	22		
†K.S.More lbw b Morrison	50		
A.S.Wassan b Morrison	53		
N.D.Hirwani not out	0		
Extras (B1, LB11, W1, NB22)	35	(LB9, NB5)	14
Total	**482**	(0 wickets)	**149**

INDIA	O	M	R	W	O	M	R	W
Kapil Dev	29.2	6	85	2	31	4	101	0
Prabhakar	29.2	3	123	3	38	6	118	1
Wassan	16.4	1	108	4	25	5	80	1
Hirwani	17	1	66	1	46	11	143	3
Raman					19	10	23	0
NEW ZEALAND								
Hadlee	30	8	123	2	4	1	9	0
Morrison	30	3	145	5	7	1	34	0
Snedden	26	4	110	1	12	1	29	0
Thomson	18.3	3	92	2	9	1	30	0
Jones					9	1	28	0
Rutherford					3	0	10	0
Greatbatch					1	1	0	0

FALL OF WICKETS

Wkt	NZ 1st	I 1st	NZ 2nd	I 2nd
1st	8	15	7	–
2nd	29	65	155	–
3rd	29	71	334	–
4th	51	215	396	–
5th	64	223	406	–
6th	85	263	–	–
7th	131	308	–	–
8th	234	396	–	–
9th	370	482	–	–
10th	391	482	–	–

Test No. 1139/31

Umpires: B.L.Aldridge (7) and R.S.Dunne (3).

NEW ZEALAND v INDIA 1989-90

NEW ZEALAND – BATTING AND FIELDING

	M	I	NO	HS	Runs	Avge	100	50	Ct/St
J.G.Wright	3	4	1	185	375	125.00	2	1	1
A.H.Jones	3	4	2	170*	245	122.50	1	1	3
I.D.S.Smith	3	2	0	173	182	91.00	1	–	11
R.J.Hadlee	3	2	0	87	115	57.50	–	1	–
M.D.Crowe	3	3	0	113	161	53.66	1	–	1
K.R.Rutherford	3	3	0	69	97	32.33	–	1	1
M.J.Greatbatch	3	3	0	46	93	31.00	–	–	–
T.J.Franklin	3	4	0	50	76	19.00	–	1	2
M.C.Snedden	3	3	1	22	26	13.00	–	–	1
D.K.Morrison	3	3	3	1*	2	–	–	–	–

Also played (two Tests): J.G.Bracewell 0 (1 ct); *(one Test):* S.A.Thomson 22, 43* (1 ct).

NEW ZEALAND – BOWLING

	O	M	R	W	Avge	Best	5wI	10wM
R.J.Hadlee	105.5	24	319	12	26.58	4-69	–	–
D.K.Morrison	110	14	446	16	27.87	5-75	3	–
M.C.Snedden	117.5	24	322	6	53.66	2-20	–	–

Also bowled: J.G.Bracewell 45-6-109-2; M.J.Greatbatch 1-1-0-0; A.H.Jones 9-1-28-0; K.R.Rutherford 17-1-59-0; S.A.Thomson 27.3-4-122-2.

INDIA – BATTING AND FIELDING

	M	I	NO	HS	Runs	Avge	100	50	Ct/St
M.Azharuddin	3	4	0	192	303	75.75	1	–	–
M.Prabhakar	3	5	1	95	235	58.75	–	2	2
W.V.Raman	3	5	1	96	176	44.00	–	2	–
K.S.More	3	4	0	73	135	33.75	–	2	5
S.R.Tendulkar	3	4	0	88	117	29.25	–	1	1
S.L.V.Raju	2	3	1	31	55	27.50	–	–	1
A.S.Wassan	3	4	1	53	79	26.33	–	1	1
D.B.Vengsarkar	2	2	0	47	47	23.50	–	–	–
S.V.Manjrekar	3	4	0	42	67	16.75	–	–	–
Kapil Dev	3	4	0	25	55	13.75	–	–	1
N.D.Hirwani	3	4	3	1*	2	2.00	–	–	1

Played in one Test: Gursharan Singh 18 (2 ct); N.S.Sidhu 51.

INDIA – BOWLING

	O	M	R	W	Avge	Best	5wI	10wM
A.S.Wassan	81.4	11	331	7	47.28	4-108	–	–
N.D.Hirwani	110	28	309	6	51.50	3-143	–	–
Kapil Dev	102.5	18	305	5	61.00	3-89	–	–
M.Prabhakar	119.1	20	382	5	76.40	3-123	–	–

Also bowled: S.L.V.Raju 46-16-113-3; W.V.Raman 19-10-23-0.

WEST INDIES v ENGLAND (1st Test)

Played at Sabina Park, Kingston, Jamaica, on 24, 25, 26, 28‡ February, 1 March 1990.
Toss: West Indies. Result: ENGLAND won by 9 wickets.
Debuts: England – N.Hussain, A.J.Stewart.   (‡ no play)

WEST INDIES

C.G.Greenidge run out	32	c Hussain b Malcolm	36
D.L.Haynes c and b Small	36	b Malcolm	14
R.B.Richardson c Small b Capel	10	lbw b Fraser	25
C.A.Best c Russell b Capel	4	c Gooch b Small	64
C.L.Hooper c Capel b Fraser	20	c Larkins b Small	8
*I.V.A.Richards lbw b Malcolm	21	b Malcolm	37
†P.J.L.Dujon not out	19	b Malcolm	15
M.D.Marshall b Fraser	0	not out	8
I.R.Bishop c Larkins b Fraser	0	c Larkins b Small	3
C.A.Walsh b Fraser	6	b Small	2
B.P.Patterson b Fraser	0	run out	2
Extras (B9, LB3, NB4)	16	(B14, LB10, W1, NB1)	26
Total	**164**		**240**

ENGLAND

*G.A.Gooch c Dujon b Patterson	18	c Greenidge b Bishop	8
W.Larkins lbw b Walsh	46	not out	29
A.J.Stewart c Best b Bishop	13	not out	0
A.J.Lamb c Hooper b Walsh	132		
R.A.Smith c Best b Bishop	57		
N.Hussain c Dujon b Bishop	13		
D.J.Capel c Richardson b Walsh	5		
†R.C.Russell c Patterson b Walsh	26		
G.C.Small lbw b Marshall	4		
A.R.C.Fraser not out	2		
D.E.Malcolm lbw b Walsh	0		
Extras (B23, LB12, W1, NB12)	48	(LB1, NB3)	4
Total	**364**	(1 wicket)	**41**

ENGLAND	O	M	R	W	O	M	R	W	FALL OF WICKETS				
Small	15	6	44	1	22	6	58	4		WI	E	WI	E
Malcolm	16	4	49	4	21.3	2	77	4	Wkt	1st	1st	2nd	2nd
Fraser	20	8	28	5	14	4	31	1	1st	62	40	26	35
Capel	13	4	31	2	15	1	50	0	2nd	81	60	69	–
WEST INDIES									3rd	92	116	87	–
									4th	92	288	112	–
Patterson	18	2	74	1	3	1	11	0	5th	124	315	192	–
Bishop	27	5	72	3	7.3	2	17	1	6th	144	315	222	–
Marshall	18	3	46	1					7th	144	325	222	–
Walsh	27.2	4	68	5	6	0	12	0	8th	150	339	227	–
Hooper	6	0	28	0					9th	164	364	237	–
Richards	9	1	22	0					10th	164	364	240	–
Best	4	0	19	0									

Umpires: L.H.Barker (12) and S.Bucknor (2).   Test No. 1140/96

The 2nd Test at Bourda, Georgetown, Guyana, scheduled for 9, 10, 11, 13, 14 March, was abandoned without a ball being bowled.

WEST INDIES v ENGLAND (3rd Test)

Played at Queen's Park Oval, Port-of-Spain, Trinidad, on 23, 24, 25, 27, 28 March 1990.

Toss: England.   Result: MATCH DRAWN.
Debuts: West Indies – E.A.Moseley.

WEST INDIES

C.G.Greenidge	c Stewart b Malcolm	5	lbw b Fraser		42
*D.L.Haynes	c Lamb b Small	0	c Lamb b Malcolm		45
R.B.Richardson	c Russell b Fraser	8	c Gooch b Small		34
C.A.Best	c Lamb b Fraser	10	lbw b Malcolm		0
†P.J.L.Dujon	lbw b Small	4	b Malcolm		0
A.L.Logie	c Lamb b Fraser	98	c Larkins b Malcolm		20
C.L.Hooper	c Russell b Capel	32	run out		10
E.A.Moseley	c Russell b Malcolm	0	c Lamb b Malcolm		26
C.E.L.Ambrose	c Russell b Malcolm	7	c Russell b Fraser		18
I.R.Bishop	b Malcolm	16	not out		15
C.A.Walsh	not out	8	lbw b Malcolm		1
Extras	(LB4, NB7)	11	(B2, LB13, W1, NB12)		28
Total		**199**			**239**

ENGLAND

*G.A.Gooch	c Dujon b Bishop	84	retired hurt		18
W.Larkins	c Dujon b Ambrose	54	c Dujon b Moseley		7
A.J.Stewart	c Dujon b Ambrose	9	c Bishop b Walsh		31
A.J.Lamb	b Bishop	32	lbw b Bishop		25
R.A.Smith	c Dujon b Moseley	5	lbw b Walsh		2
R.J.Bailey	c Logie b Moseley	0	b Walsh		0
D.J.Capel	c Moseley b Ambrose	40	not out		17
†R.C.Russell	c Best b Walsh	15	not out		5
G.C.Small	lbw b Bishop	0			
A.R.C.Fraser	c Hooper b Ambrose	11			
D.E.Malcolm	not out	0			
Extras	(B10, LB9, W3, NB16)	38	(B2, LB7, NB6)		15
Total		**288**	**(5 wickets)**		**120**

ENGLAND	O	M	R	W	O	M	R	W	FALL OF WICKETS				
										WI	E	WI	E
Small	17	4	41	2	21	8	56	1	Wkt	1st	1st	2nd	2nd
Malcolm	20	2	60	4	26.2	4	77	6	1st	5	112	96	27
Fraser	13.1	2	41	3	24	4	61	2	2nd	5	152	100	74
Capel	15	2	53	1	13	3	30	0	3rd	22	195	100	79
WEST INDIES									4th	27	214	100	85
Ambrose	36.2	8	59	4	6	0	20	0	5th	29	214	142	106
Bishop	31	6	69	3	10	1	31	1	6th	92	214	167	
Walsh	22	5	45	1	7	0	27	3	7th	93	243	200	
Hooper	18	5	26	0					8th	103	244	200	
Moseley	30	5	70	2	10	2	33	1	9th	177	284	234	
									10th	199	288	239	

Umpires: L.H.Barker (13) and C.E.Cumberbatch (10).   Test No. 1141/97

C.G.Greenidge deputised as wicket-keeper for a period during the first innings.
G.A.Gooch retired at 37-1 in the second innings.

WEST INDIES v ENGLAND (4th Test)

Played at Kensington Oval, Bridgetown, Barbados, on 5, 6, 7, 8, 10 April 1990.
Toss: England.   Result: WEST INDIES won by 164 runs.
Debuts: Nil.

WEST INDIES

C.G.Greenidge	c Russell b DeFreitas	41	lbw b Small	3
D.L.Haynes	c Stewart b Small	0	c Malcolm b Small	109
R.B.Richardson	c Russell b Small	45	lbw b DeFreitas	39
C.A.Best	c Russell b Small	164		
*I.V.A.Richards	c Russell b Capel	70	(4) c Small b Capel	12
A.L.Logie	c Russell b Capel	31	(5) lbw b DeFreitas	48
†P.J.L.Dujon	b Capel	31	(8) not out	15
M.D.Marshall	c Lamb b Small	4	(7) c Smith b Small	7
C.E.L.Ambrose	not out	20	c Capel b DeFreitas	1
I.R.Bishop	run out	10	not out	11
E.A.Moseley	b DeFreitas	4	(6) b Small	5
Extras	(LB8, NB18)	26	(LB12, W1, NB4)	17
Total		**446**	(8 wickets declared)	**267**

ENGLAND

A.J.Stewart	c Richards b Moseley	45	c Richards b Ambrose	37
W.Larkins	c Richardson b Bishop	0	c Dujon b Bishop	0
R.J.Bailey	b Bishop	17	c Dujon b Ambrose	6
*A.J.Lamb	lbw b Ambrose	119	(6) c Dujon b Moseley	10
R.A.Smith	b Moseley	62	(7) not out	40
N.Hussain	lbw b Marshall	18	(8) lbw b Ambrose	0
D.J.Capel	c Greenidge b Marshall	2	(9) lbw b Ambrose	6
†R.C.Russell	lbw b Bishop	7	(5) b Ambrose	55
P.A.J.DeFreitas	c and b Ambrose	24	(10) lbw b Ambrose	0
G.C.Small	not out	1	(4) lbw b Ambrose	0
D.E.Malcolm	b Bishop	12	lbw b Ambrose	4
Extras	(B14, LB9, W3, NB25)	51	(B8, LB9, W1, NB15)	33
Total		**358**		**191**

ENGLAND	O	M	R	W	O	M	R	W	FALL OF WICKETS				
										WI	E	WI	E
Malcolm	33	6	142	0	10	0	46	0	Wkt	1st	1st	2nd	2nd
Small	35	5	109	4	20	1	74	4	1st	6	1	13	1
DeFreitas	29.5	5	99	2	22	2	69	3	2nd	69	46	80	10
Capel	24	5	88	3	16	1	66	1	3rd	108	75	109	10
WEST INDIES									4th	227	268	223	71
Bishop	24.3	4	70	4	20	7	40	1	5th	291	297	228	97
Ambrose	25	2	82	0	22.4	10	45	8	6th	395	301	239	166
Moseley	28	3	114	2	19	3	44	1	7th	406	308	239	173
Marshall	23	6	55	2	18	8	31	0	8th	411	340	239	181
Richards	9	4	14	0	10	5	11	0	9th	431	340	–	181
Richardson					2	1	3	0	10th	446	358	–	191

Umpires: D.M. Archer (23) and L.H. Barker (14).   Test No. 1142/98

WEST INDIES v ENGLAND (5th Test)

Played at Recreation Ground, St John's, Antigua, on 12, 14, 15, 16 April 1990.
Toss: England.   Result: WEST INDIES won by an innings and 32 runs.
Debuts: Nil.

ENGLAND

A.J.Stewart	c Richards b Walsh	27		c Richardson b Bishop	8
W.Larkins	c Hooper b Ambrose	30		b Ambrose	10
R.J.Bailey	c Dujon b Bishop	42	(4)	c Dujon b Bishop	8
*A.J.Lamb	c Richards b Ambrose	37	(5)	b Baptiste	35
R.A.Smith	lbw b Walsh	12	(6)	retired hurt	8
N.Hussain	c Dujon b Bishop	35	(7)	c Dujon b Bishop	34
D.J.Capel	c Haynes b Bishop	10	(8)	run out	1
†R.C.Russell	c Dujon b Bishop	7	(9)	c Richardson b Ambrose	24
P.A.J.DeFreitas	lbw b Bishop	21	(10)	c Greenidge b Ambrose	0
G.C.Small	lbw b Walsh	8	(3)	b Ambrose	4
D.E.Malcolm	not out	0		not out	1
Extras	(B5, LB11, NB15)	31		(B1, LB8, W1, NB11)	21
Total		**260**			**154**

WEST INDIES

C.G.Greenidge	run out	149
D.L.Haynes	c Russell b Small	167
R.B.Richardson	c Russell b Malcolm	34
C.L.Hooper	b Capel	1
*I.V.A.Richards	c Smith b Malcolm	1
A.L.Logie	c Lamb b DeFreitas	15
†P.J.L.Dujon	run out	25
E.A.E.Baptiste	c Russell b Malcolm	9
C.E.L.Ambrose	c DeFreitas b Capel	5
I.R.Bishop	not out	14
C.A.Walsh	b Malcolm	8
Extras	(LB5, NB13)	18
Total		**446**

WEST INDIES	O	M	R	W	O	M	R	W
Bishop	28.1	6	84	5	14	2	36	3
Ambrose	29	5	79	2	13	7	22	4
Walsh	21	4	51	3	10	1	40	0
Baptiste	13	4	30	0	10	1	47	1
ENGLAND								
Small	31	3	123	1				
Malcolm	34.5	3	126	4				
Capel	28	1	118	2				
DeFreitas	27	4	74	1				

FALL OF WICKETS			
	E	WI	E
Wkt	1st	1st	2nd
1st	42	298	16
2nd	101	357	20
3rd	143	358	33
4th	167	359	37
5th	167	382	86
6th	195	384	96
7th	212	415	148
8th	242	417	148
9th	259	433	154
10th	260	446	–

Umpires: D.M.Archer (24) and A.E.Weekes (4).   Test No. 1143/99

R.A.Smith retired hurt at 61-4 in the second innings.

WEST INDIES v ENGLAND 1989-90

WEST INDIES – BATTING AND FIELDING

	M	I	NO	HS	Runs	Avge	100	50	Ct/St
D.L.Haynes	4	7	0	167	371	53.00	2	–	1
C.A.Best	3	5	0	164	242	48.40	1	1	3
C.G.Greenidge	4	7	0	149	308	44.00	1	–	3
A.L.Logie	3	5	0	98	212	42.40	–	1	1
I.V.A.Richards	3	5	0	70	141	28.20	–	1	4
R.B.Richardson	4	7	0	45	195	27.85	–	–	4
P.J.L.Dujon	4	7	2	31	109	21.80	–	–	15
I.R.Bishop	4	7	3	16	69	17.25	–	–	1
C.L.Hooper	3	5	0	32	71	14.20	–	–	3
C.E.L.Ambrose	3	5	1	20*	51	12.75	–	–	1
E.A.Moseley	2	4	0	26	35	8.75	–	–	1
M.D.Marshall	2	4	1	8*	19	6.33	–	–	–
C.A.Walsh	3	5	1	8*	25	6.25	–	–	–

Played in one Test: E.A.E.Baptiste 9; B.P.Patterson 0, 2 (1 ct).

WEST INDIES – BOWLING

	O	M	R	W	Avge	Best	5wI	10wM
C.E.L.Ambrose	132	32	307	20	15.35	8-45	1	1
I.R.Bishop	162.1	37	419	21	19.95	5-84	1	–
C.A.Walsh	93.2	14	243	12	20.25	5-68	1	–
E.A.Moseley	87	13	261	6	43.50	2-70	–	–

Also bowled: E.A.E.Baptiste 23-5-77-1; C.A.Best 4-0-19-0; C.L.Hooper 24-5-54-0;
M.D.Marshall 59-17-132-3; B.P.Patterson 21-3-85-1; I.V.A.Richards 28-10-47-0;
R.B.Richardson 2-1-3-0.

ENGLAND – BATTING AND FIELDING

	M	I	NO	HS	Runs	Avge	100	50	Ct/St
A.J.Lamb	4	7	0	132	390	55.71	2	–	7
G.A.Gooch	2	4	1	84	128	42.66	–	1	2
R.A.Smith	4	7	2	62	186	37.20	–	2	2
W.Larkins	4	8	1	54	176	25.14	–	1	4
A.J.Stewart	4	8	1	45	170	24.28	–	–	2
R.C.Russell	4	7	1	55	139	23.16	–	1	14
N.Hussain	3	5	0	35	100	20.00	–	–	1
D.J.Capel	4	7	1	40	81	13.50	–	–	2
A.R.C.Fraser	2	2	1	11	13	13.00	–	–	–
R.J.Bailey	3	6	0	42	73	12.16	–	–	–
P.A.J.DeFreitas	2	4	0	24	45	11.25	–	–	1
D.E.Malcolm	4	6	3	12	17	5.66	–	–	1
G.C.Small	4	6	1	8	17	3.40	–	–	3

ENGLAND – BOWLING

	O	M	R	W	Avge	Best	5wI	10wM
A.R.C.Fraser	71.1	18	161	11	14.63	5-28	1	–
G.C.Small	161	33	505	17	29.70	4-58	–	–
D.E.Malcolm	161.4	21	577	19	30.36	6-77	1	1
P.A.J.DeFreitas	78.5	11	242	6	40.33	3-69	–	–
D.J.Capel	124	17	436	9	48.44	3-88	–	–

NEW ZEALAND v AUSTRALIA (Only Test)

Played at Basin Reserve, Wellington, on 15, 16, 17, 18, 19 March 1990.
Toss: Australia.   Result: NEW ZEALAND won by 9 wickets.
Debuts: Nil.

AUSTRALIA

M.A.Taylor lbw b Morrison	4	lbw b Hadlee	5
G.R.Marsh b Morrison	4	c Rutherford b Bracewell	41
D.C.Boon lbw b Hadlee	0	c Smith b Bracewell	12
*A.R.Border b Morrison	1	(5) not out	78
D.M.Jones c Wright b Snedden	20	(6) lbw b Morrison	0
S.R.Waugh b Hadlee	25	(7) c Greatbatch b Hadlee	25
†I.A.Healy b Snedden	0	(8) c Rutherford b Bracewell	10
P.L.Taylor c Wright b Hadlee	29	(4) c Smith b Morrison	87
G.D.Campbell lbw b Hadlee	4	b Bracewell	0
C.G.Rackemann not out	6	b Bracewell	1
T.M.Alderman b Hadlee	4	st Smith b Bracewell	1
Extras (LB6, NB7)	13	(LB6, NB3)	9
Total	**110**		**269**

NEW ZEALAND

T.J.Franklin c Marsh b P.L.Taylor	28	c Healy b Campbell	18
*J.G.Wright b Healy b Alderman	36	not out	117
A.H.Jones c and b Border	18	not out	33
M.C.Snedden b Alderman	23		
M.J.Greatbatch c Healy b P.L.Taylor	16		
K.R.Rutherford c Healy b P.L.Taylor	12		
J.J.Crowe lbw b Alderman	9		
R.J.Hadlee lbw b Campbell	18		
†I.D.S.Smith c M.A.Taylor b Campbell	19		
J.G.Bracewell not out	1		
D.K.Morrison c M.A.Taylor b Alderman	12		
Extras (B2, LB5, NB3)	10	(B2, LB10, NB1)	13
Total	**202**	**(1 wicket)**	**181**

NEW ZEALAND	O	M	R	W	O	M	R	W	FALL OF WICKETS				
										A	NZ	A	NZ
Hadlee	16.2	5	39	5	25	3	70	2	Wkt	1st	1st	2nd	2nd
Morrison	10	4	22	3	24	8	58	2	1st	4	48	27	53
Snedden	15	2	33	2	25	5	46	0	2nd	9	89	54	–
Rutherford	2	0	8	0					3rd	9	89	91	–
Bracewell	2	1	2	0	34.2	11	85	6	4th	12	111	194	–
Jones					1	0	4	0	5th	38	123	194	–
AUSTRALIA									6th	44	150	232	–
Alderman	29	9	46	4	14	8	27	0	7th	70	151	261	–
Rackemann	32	17	42	0	15	4	39	0	8th	87	152	261	–
P.L.Taylor	33	19	44	3	11	3	39	0	9th	103	171	267	–
Campbell	21	3	51	2	7	2	23	1	10th	110	202	269	–
Border	6	3	12	1	10.4	5	27	0					
Jones					6	3	14	0					

Umpires: R.S.Dunne (4) and S.J.Woodward (23).   Test No. 1144/26

ENGLAND v NEW ZEALAND (1st Test)

Played at Trent Bridge, Nottingham, on 7, 8, 9, 11, 12 June 1990.
Toss: New Zealand. Result: MATCH DRAWN.
Debuts: New Zealand – M.W.Priest.

NEW ZEALAND

T.J.Franklin b Malcolm	33		not out	22
*J.G. Wright c Stewart b Small	8		c Russell b Small	1
A.H.Jones c Stewart b Malcolm	39		c Russell b DeFreitas	13
M.D.Crowe b DeFreitas	59			
M.J.Greatbatch b Hemmings	1			
M.W.Priest c Russell b DeFreitas	26			
M.C.Snedden c Gooch b Small	0			
J.G.Bracewell c Gooch b Small	28			
R.J.Hadlee b DeFreitas	0			
†I.D.S.Smith not out	2			
D.K.Morrison lbw b DeFreitas	0	(4)	not out	0
Extras (B1, LB10, W1)	12			
Total	**208**		**(2 wickets)**	**36**

ENGLAND

*G.A.Gooch lbw b Hadlee	0
M.A.Atherton c Snedden b Priest	151
A.J.Stewart c Smith b Hadlee	27
A.J.Lamb lbw b Hadlee	0
R.A.Smith c Smith b Bracewell	55
N.H.Fairbrother c Franklin b Snedden	19
†R.C.Russell c Snedden b Morrison	28
P.A.J.DeFreitas lbw b Bracewell	14
G.C.Small c Crowe b Hadlee	26
E.E.Hemmings not out	13
D.E.Malcolm not out	4
Extras (B2, LB3, NB3)	8
Total (9 wickets declared)	**345**

ENGLAND	O	M	R	W	O	M	R	W	FALL OF WICKETS			
Small	29	9	49	2	6	2	14	1		NZ	E	NZ
Malcolm	19	7	48	2	7	2	22	0	Wkt	1st	1st	2nd
Hemmings	19	6	47	1	2	2	0	0	1st	16	0	8
DeFreitas	22	6	53	5	2	2	0	1	2nd	75	43	36
NEW ZEALAND									3rd	110	45	–
Hadlee	33	6	89	4					4th	121	141	–
Morrison	22	3	96	1					5th	170	168	–
Snedden	36	17	54	1					6th	174	260	–
Bracewell	35	8	75	2					7th	191	302	–
Priest	12	4	26	1					8th	191	306	–
									9th	203	340	–
									10th	208	–	–

Umpires: H.D.Bird (43) and J.H.Hampshire (6).   Test No. 1145/67

ENGLAND v NEW ZEALAND (2nd Test)

Played at Lord's, London, on 21, 22, 23, 25, 26 June 1990.
Toss: New Zealand.   Result: MATCH DRAWN.
Debuts: Nil.

ENGLAND

*G.A.Gooch	c and b Bracewell	85	b Hadlee		37
M.A.Atherton	b Morrison	0	c Bracewell b Jones		54
A.J.Stewart	lbw b Hadlee	54	c sub (M.W.Priest) b Bracewell		42
A.J.Lamb	lbw b Snedden	39	not out		84
R.A.Smith	c Bracewell b Morrison	64	hit wicket b Bracewell		0
N.H.Fairbrother	c Morrison b Bracewell	2	not out		33
†R.C.Russell	b Hadlee	13			
P.A.J.DeFreitas	c Franklin b Morrison	38			
G.C.Small	b Morrison	3			
E.E.Hemmings	b Hadlee	0			
D.E.Malcolm	not out	0			
Extras	(LB13, W1, NB22)	36	(B8, LB8, NB6)		22
Total		**334**	(4 wickets declared)		**272**

NEW ZEALAND

T.J.Franklin	c Russell b Malcolm	101
*J.G.Wright	c Stewart b Small	98
A.H.Jones	c Stewart b Malcolm	49
M.D.Crowe	c Russell b Hemmings	1
M.J.Greatbatch	b Malcolm	47
K.R.Rutherford	c Fairbrother b Malcolm	0
Sir R.J.Hadlee	b Hemmings	86
J.G.Bracewell	run out (DeFreitas/Russell)	4
†I.D.S.Smith	c Small b Malcolm	27
M.C.Snedden	not out	13
D.K.Morrison	not out	2
Extras	(B12, LB15, W2, NB5)	34
Total	(9 wickets declared)	**462**

NEW ZEALAND	O	M	R	W	O	M	R	W	FALL OF WICKETS			
										E	NZ	E
Hadlee	29	5	113	3	13	2	32	1	Wkt	1st	1st	2nd
Morrison	18.4	4	64	4	16	0	81	0	1st	3	185	68
Snedden	21	4	72	1					2nd	151	278	135
Bracewell	21	3	72	2	34	13	85	2	3rd	178	281	171
Jones					12	3	40	1	4th	216	284	175
Rutherford					3	0	18	0	5th	226	285	–
ENGLAND									6th	255	408	–
Malcolm	43	14	94	5					7th	319	415	–
Small	35	4	127	1					8th	322	425	–
DeFreitas	35.4	1	122	0					9th	332	448	–
Hemmings	30	13	67	2					10th	334	–	–
Gooch	13	7	25	0								
Atherton	1	1	0	0								

Umpires: M.J.Kitchen (1) and D.R.Shepherd (10).   Test No. 1146/68

ENGLAND v NEW ZEALAND (3rd Test)

Played at Edgbaston, Birmingham, on 5, 6, 7, 9, 10 July 1990.
Toss: New Zealand.   Result: ENGLAND won by 114 runs.
Debuts: England – C.C.Lewis; New Zealand – A.C.Parore.

ENGLAND

*G.A.Gooch c Hadlee b Morrison	154	b Snedden	30
M.A.Atherton lbw b Snedden	82	c Rutherford b Bracewell	70
A.J.Stewart c Parore b Morrison	9	lbw b Bracewell	15
A.J.Lamb c Parore b Hadlee	2	st Parore b Bracewell	4
R.A.Smith c Jones b Bracewell	19	c and b Hadlee	14
N.H.Fairbrother lbw b Snedden	2	lbw b Bracewell	3
†R.C.Russell b Snedden	43	c sub (J.J.Crowe) b Hadlee	0
C.C.Lewis c Rutherford b Bracewell	32	c Parore b Hadlee	1
G.C.Small not out	44	not out	11
E.E.Hemmings c Parore b Hadlee	20	b Hadlee	0
D.E.Malcolm b Hadlee	0	lbw b Hadlee	0
Extras (B4, LB15, NB9)	28	(LB6, NB4)	10
Total	**435**		**158**

NEW ZEALAND

T.J.Franklin c Smith b Hemmings	66	lbw b Malcolm	5
*J.G.Wright c Russell b Malcolm	24	c Smith b Lewis	46
A.H.Jones c Russell b Malcolm	2	c Gooch b Small	40
M.D.Crowe lbw b Lewis	11	lbw b Malcolm	25
M.J.Greatbatch b Hadlee	45	c Atherton b Hemmings	22
K.R.Rutherford c Stewart b Hemmings	29	c Lamb b Lewis	18
Sir R.J.Hadlee c Atherton b Hemmings	8	b Malcolm	13
J.G.Bracewell b Hemmings	25	(9) c Atherton b Malcolm	0
†A.C.Parore not out	12	(8) c Lamb b Lewis	20
M.C.Snedden lbw b Hemmings	2	not out	21
D.K.Morrison b Hemmings	1	b Malcolm	6
Extras (B9, LB11, W2, NB2)	24	(LB9, W1, NB4)	14
Total	**249**		**230**

NEW ZEALAND	O	M	R	W	O	M	R	W	FALL OF WICKETS				
										E	NZ	E	NZ
Hadlee	37.5	8	97	3	21	3	53	5	Wkt	1st	1st	2nd	2nd
Morrison	26	7	81	2	3	1	29	0	1st	170	45	50	25
Snedden	35	9	106	3	9	0	32	1	2nd	193	67	87	85
Bracewell	42	12	130	2	16	5	38	4	3rd	198	90	99	111
Jones	1	0	2	0					4th	245	161	129	125
ENGLAND									5th	254	163	136	155
Small	18	7	44	0	16	5	56	1	6th	316	185	141	163
Malcolm	25	7	59	3	24.4	8	46	5	7th	351	223	146	180
Lewis	19	5	51	1	22	3	76	3	8th	381	230	157	180
Hemmings	27.3	10	58	6	29	13	43	1	9th	435	243	158	203
Atherton	9	5	17	0					10th	435	249	158	230

Umpires: J.W.Holder (8) and B.J.Meyer (22).   Test No. 1147/69

ENGLAND v NEW ZEALAND 1990

ENGLAND – BATTING AND FIELDING

	M	I	NO	HS	Runs	Avge	100	50	Ct/St
M.A.Atherton	3	5	0	151	357	71.40	1	3	3
G.A.Gooch	3	5	0	154	306	61.20	1	1	3
G.C.Small	3	4	2	44*	84	42.00	–	–	1
A.J.Lamb	3	5	1	84*	129	32.25	–	1	2
R.A.Smith	3	5	0	64	152	30.40	–	2	2
A.J.Stewart	3	5	0	54	147	29.40	–	1	5
P.A.J.DeFreitas	2	2	0	38	52	26.00	–	–	–
R.C.Russell	3	4	0	43	84	21.00	–	–	7
N.H.Fairbrother	3	5	1	33*	59	14.75	–	–	1
E.E.Hemmings	3	4	1	20	33	11.00	–	–	–
D.E.Malcolm	3	4	2	4*	4	2.00	–	–	–

Played in one Test: C.C.Lewis 32, 1.

ENGLAND – BOWLING

	O	M	R	W	Avge	Best	5wI	10wM
D.E.Malcolm	118.4	38	269	15	17.93	5-46	2	–
E.E.Hemmings	107.3	44	215	10	21.50	6-58	1	–
P.A.J.DeFreitas	59.4	9	175	6	29.16	5-53	1	–
G.C.Small	104	27	290	5	58.00	2-49	–	–

Also bowled: M.A.Atherton 10-6-17-0; G.A.Gooch 13-7-25-0; C.C.Lewis 41-8-127-4.

NEW ZEALAND – BATTING AND FIELDING

	M	I	NO	HS	Runs	Avge	100	50	Ct/St
T.J.Franklin	3	5	1	101	227	56.75	1	1	2
J.G.Wright	3	5	0	98	177	35.40	–	1	–
I.D.S.Smith	2	2	1	27	29	29.00	–	–	2
M.J.Greatbatch	3	4	0	47	115	28.75	–	–	–
A.H.Jones	3	5	0	49	143	28.60	–	–	1
Sir R.J.Hadlee	3	4	0	86	107	26.75	–	1	2
M.D.Crowe	3	4	0	59	96	24.00	–	1	1
M.C.Snedden	3	4	2	21*	36	18.00	–	–	2
K.R.Rutherford	2	3	0	29	47	15.66	–	–	2
J.G.Bracewell	3	4	0	28	57	14.25	–	–	3
D.K.Morrison	3	5	2	6	9	3.00	–	–	1

Played in one Test: A.C.Parore 12*, 20 (4 ct, 1 st); M.W.Priest 26.

NEW ZEALAND – BOWLING

	O	M	R	W	Avge	Best	5wI	10wM
Sir R.J.Hadlee	133.5	24	384	16	24.00	5-53	1	–
J.G.Bracewell	148	41	400	12	33.33	4-38	–	–
M.C.Snedden	101	30	264	6	44.00	3-106	–	–
D.K.Morrison	85.4	15	351	7	50.14	4-64	–	–

Also bowled: A.H.Jones 13-3-42-1; M.W.Priest 12-4-26-1; K.R Rutherford 3-0-18-0.

ENGLAND v INDIA (1st Test)

Played at Lord's, London, on 26, 27, 28, 30, 31 July 1990.
Toss: India.   Result: ENGLAND won by 247 runs.
Debuts: England – J.E.Morris.

ENGLAND

*G.A.Gooch b Prabhakar	333	c Azharuddin b Sharma	123
M.A.Atherton b Kapil Dev	8	c Vengsarkar b Sharma	72
D.I.Gower c Manjrekar b Hirwani	40	not out	32
A.J.Lamb c Manjrekar b Sharma	139	c Tendulkar b Hirwani	19
R.A.Smith not out	100	b Prabhakar	15
J.E.Morris not out	4		
R.C.Russell			
†C.C.Lewis			
E.E.Hemmings } did not bat			
A.R.C.Fraser			
D.E.Malcolm			
Extras (B2, LB21, W2, NB4)	29	(LB11)	11
Total (4 wickets declared)	653	(4 wickets declared)	272

INDIA

R.J.Shastri c Gooch b Hemmings	100	c Russell b Malcolm	12
N.S.Sidhu c Morris b Fraser	30	c Morris b Fraser	1
S.V.Manjrekar c Russell b Gooch	18	c Russell b Malcolm	33
D.B.Vengsarkar c Russell b Fraser	52	c Russell b Hemmings	35
*M.Azharuddin b Hemmings	121	c Atherton b Lewis	37
S.R.Tendulkar b Lewis	10	c Gooch b Fraser	27
M.Prabhakar c Lewis b Malcolm	25	lbw b Lewis	8
Kapil Dev not out	77	c Lewis b Hemmings	7
†K.S.More c Morris b Fraser	8	lbw b Fraser	16
S.K.Sharma c Russell b Fraser	0	run out (Gooch)	38
N.D.Hirwani lbw b Fraser	0	not out	0
Extras (LB1, W4, NB8)	13	(B3, LB1, NB6)	10
Total	454		224

INDIA	O	M	R	W	O	M	R	W	FALL OF WICKETS				
										E	I	E	I
Kapil Dev	34	5	120	1	10	0	53	0	Wkt	1st	1st	2nd	2nd
Prabhakar	43	6	187	1	11.2	2	45	1	1st	14	63	204	9
Sharma	33	5	122	1	15	0	75	2	2nd	141	102	207	23
Shastri	22	0	99	0	7	0	38	0	3rd	449	191	250	63
Hirwani	30	1	102	1	11	0	50	1	4th	641	241	272	114
ENGLAND									5th	–	288	–	127
Malcolm	25	1	106	1	10	0	65	2	6th	–	348	–	140
Fraser	39.1	9	104	5	22	7	39	3	7th	–	393	–	158
Lewis	24	3	108	1	8	1	26	2	8th	–	430	–	181
Gooch	6	3	26	1					9th	–	430	–	206
Hemmings	20	3	109	2	21	2	79	2	10th	–	454	–	224
Atherton					1	0	11	0					

Umpires: H.D.Bird (44) and N.T.Plews (4).   Test No. 1148/76

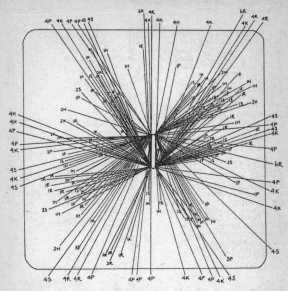

PAVILION END

BOWLER	SYMBOL	BALLS	RUNS						TOTAL
			1	2	3	4	5	6	
KAPIL DEV	K	114	18	3	·	12	·	·	72
PRABHAKAR	P	126	21	1	2	14	·	·	85
SHARMA	S	93	16	3	·	9	·	·	58
SHASTRI	R	79	22	4	·	5	3	·	68
HIRWANI	H	73	30	4	·	3	·	·	50
TOTALS		485	107	15	2	43	3	3	333

GRAHAM GOOCH
v INDIA at LORD'S
26·27 JULY 1990

333 RUNS
485 BALLS
627 MINUTES

© BILL FRINDALL 1990

21

ENGLAND v INDIA (2nd Test)

Played at Old Trafford, Manchester, on 9, 10, 11, 13, 14 August 1990.
Toss: England. Result: MATCH DRAWN.
Debuts: India – A.Kumble. ‡(C.J.Adams)

ENGLAND

*G.A.Gooch	c More b Prabhakar	116	c More b Prabhakar	7
M.A.Atherton	c More b Hirwani	131	lbw b Kapil Dev	74
D.I.Gower	c Tendulkar b Kapil Dev	38	b Hirwani	16
A.J.Lamb	c Manjrekar b Kumble	38	b Kapil Dev	109
†R.C.Russell	c More b Hirwani	8	(7) not out	16
R.A.Smith	not out	121	(5) not out	61
J.E.Morris	b Kumble	13	(6) retired hurt	15
C.C.Lewis	b Hirwani	3		
E.E.Hemmings	lbw b Hirwani	19		
A.R.C.Fraser	c Tendulkar b Kumble	1		
D.E.Malcolm	b Shastri	13		
Extras	(B2, LB9, W1, NB6)	18	(LB15, NB7)	22
Total		**519**	**(4 wickets declared)**	**320**

INDIA

R.J.Shastri	c Gooch b Fraser	25	b Malcolm	12
N.S.Sidhu	c Gooch b Fraser	13	c sub‡ b Fraser	0
S.V.Manjrekar	c Smith b Hemmings	93	c sub‡ b Hemmings	50
D.B.Vengsarkar	c Russell b Fraser	6	b Lewis	32
*M.Azharuddin	c Atherton b Fraser	179	c Lewis b Hemmings	11
S.R.Tendulkar	c Lewis b Hemmings	68	not out	119
M.Prabhakar	c Russell b Malcolm	4	(8) not out	67
Kapil Dev	lbw b Lewis	0	(7) b Hemmings	26
†K.S.More	b Fraser	6		
A.Kumble	run out (Morris)	2		
N.D.Hirwani	not out	15		
Extras	(B5, LB4, NB12)	21	(B17, LB3, NB6)	26
Total		**432**	**(6 wickets)**	**343**

INDIA	O	M	R	W	O	M	R	W	FALL OF WICKETS				
Kapil Dev	13	2	67	1	22	4	69	2		*E*	*I*	*E*	*I*
Prabhakar	25	2	112	1	18	1	80	1	Wkt	1st	1st	2nd	2nd
Kumble	43	7	105	3	17	3	65	0	1st	225	26	15	4
Hirwani	62	10	174	3	15	0	52	1	2nd	292	48	46	35
Shastri	17.5	2	50	1	9	0	39	0	3rd	312	57	180	109
ENGLAND									4th	324	246	248	109
Malcolm	26	3	96	1	14	5	59	1	5th	366	358	–	127
Fraser	35	5	124	5	21	5	81	1	6th	392	364	–	183
Hemmings	29.2	8	74	2	31	10	75	3	7th	404	365	–	–
Lewis	13	1	61	1	20	3	86	1	8th	434	396	–	–
Atherton	16	3	68	0	4	0	22	0	9th	459	401	–	–
									10th	519	432	–	–

Umpires: J.H.Hampshire (7) and J.W.Holder (9).   Test No. 1149/77

J.E.Morris retired hurt at 290-4 in the second innings.

ENGLAND v INDIA (3rd Test)

Played at Kennington Oval, London, on 23, 24, 25, 27, 28 August 1990.
Toss: India.   Result: MATCH DRAWN.
Debuts: England – N.F.Williams.

INDIA

R.J.Shastri	c Lamb b Malcolm	187
N.S.Sidhu	c Russell b Fraser	12
S.V.Manjrekar	c Russell b Malcolm	22
D.B.Vengsarkar	c and b Atherton	33
*M.Azharuddin	c Russell b Williams	78
M.Prabhakar	lbw b Fraser	28
S.R.Tendulkar	c Lamb b Williams	21
Kapil Dev	st Russell b Hemmings	110
†K.S.More	not out	61
A.S.Wassan	b Hemmings	15
N.D.Hirwani	not out	2
Extras	(B7, LB8, W6, NB16)	37
Total	(9 wickets declared)	606

ENGLAND

*G.A.Gooch	c Shastri b Hirwani	85	c Vengsarkar b Hirwani	88
M.A.Atherton	c More b Prabhakar	7	lbw b Kapil Dev	86
N.F.Williams	lbw b Prabhakar	38		
D.I.Gower	lbw b Wassan	8	(3) not out	157
J.E.Morris	c More b Wassan	7	(4) c More b Wassan	32
A.J.Lamb	b Kapil Dev	7	(5) c Shastri b Kapil Dev	52
R.A.Smith	c Manjrekar b Shastri	57	(6) not out	7
†R.C.Russell	run out (Wassan)	35		
E.E.Hemmings	c Vengsarkar b Prabhakar	51		
A.R.C.Fraser	c More b Prabhakar	0		
D.E.Malcolm	not out	15		
Extras	(B8, LB9, W4, NB9)	30	(B16, LB22, W5, NB12)	55
Total		340	(4 wickets declared)	477

ENGLAND	O	M	R	W	O	M	R	W	FALL OF WICKETS			
										I	*E*	*E*
Malcolm	35	7	110	2					*Wkt*	*1st*	*1st*	*2nd*
Fraser	42	17	112	2					1st	16	18	176
Williams	41	5	148	2					2nd	61	92	251
Gooch	12	1	44	0					3rd	150	111	334
Hemmings	36	3	117	2					4th	289	120	463
Atherton	7	0	60	1					5th	335	139	–
INDIA									6th	368	231	–
Kapil Dev	25	7	70	1	24	5	66	2	7th	478	233	–
Prabhakar	32.4	9	74	4	25	8	56	0	8th	552	295	–
Wassan	19	3	79	2	18	2	94	1	9th	576	299	–
Hirwani	35	12	71	1	59	18	137	1	10th	–	340	–
Shastri	12	2	29	1	28	2	86	0				

Umpires: N.T.Plews (5) and D.R.Shepherd (11).   Test No. 1150/78

ENGLAND v INDIA 1990

ENGLAND – BATTING AND FIELDING

	M	I	NO	HS	Runs	Avge	100	50	Ct/St
R.A.Smith	3	6	4	121*	361	180.50	2	2	1
G.A.Gooch	3	6	0	333	752	125.33	3	2	4
D.I.Gower	3	6	2	157*	291	72.75	1	–	–
M.A.Atherton	3	6	0	131	378	63.00	1	3	3
A.J.Lamb	3	6	0	139	364	60.66	2	1	2
E.E.Hemmings	3	2	0	51	70	35.00	–	1	–
R.C.Russell	3	3	1	35	59	29.50	–	–	11/1
D.E.Malcolm	3	2	1	15*	28	28.00	–	–	–
J.E.Morris	3	5	2	32	71	23.66	–	–	3
A.R.C.Fraser	3	2	0	1	1	0.50	–	–	–

Also played (two Tests): C.C.Lewis 3 (4 ct); *(one Test)* N.F.Williams 38.

ENGLAND – BOWLING

	O	M	R	W	Avge	Best	5wI	10wM
A.R.C.Fraser	159.1	41	460	16	28.75	5-104	2	–
E.E.Hemmings	137.2	26	454	11	41.27	3-75	–	–
C.C.Lewis	65	8	281	5	56.20	2-26	–	–
D.E.Malcolm	110	16	436	7	62.28	2-65	–	–

Also bowled: M.A.Atherton 28-3-161-1; G.A.Gooch 18-4-70-1; N.F.Williams 41-5-148-2.

INDIA – BATTING AND FIELDING

	M	I	NO	HS	Runs	Avge	100	50	Ct/St
M.Azharuddin	3	5	0	179	426	85.20	2	1	1
R.J.Shastri	3	5	0	187	336	67.20	2	–	2
S.R.Tendulkar	3	5	1	119*	245	61.25	1	1	3
Kapil Dev	3	5	1	110	220	55.00	1	1	–
S.V.Manjrekar	3	5	0	93	216	43.20	–	2	4
M.Prabhakar	3	5	1	67*	132	33.00	–	1	–
D.B.Vengsarkar	3	5	0	52	158	31.60	–	1	3
K.S.More	3	4	1	61*	91	30.33	–	1	8
N.D.Hirwani	3	4	3	15*	17	17.00	–	–	–
N.S.Sidhu	3	5	0	30	56	11.20	–	–	–

Played in one Test: A.Kumble 2; S.K.Sharma 0, 38; A.S.Wassan 15.

INDIA – BOWLING

	O	M	R	W	Avge	Best	5wI	10wM
Kapil Dev	128	23	445	7	63.57	2-66	–	–
N.D.Hirwani	212	41	586	9	65.11	4-174	–	–
M.Prabhakar	155	28	554	8	69.25	4-74	–	–

Also bowled: A.Kumble 60-10-170-3; S.K.Sharma 43-5-197-3; R.J.Shastri 95.5-6-341-2; A.S.Wassan 37-5-173-3.

PAKISTAN v NEW ZEALAND (1st Test)

Played at National Stadium, Karachi, on 10, 11, 12, 14, 15 October 1990.
Toss: Pakistan. Result: PAKISTAN won by an innings and 43 runs.
Debuts: New Zealand – G.E.Bradburn, C.Pringle, D.J.White.

NEW ZEALAND

T.J.Franklin	c Salim Yousuf b Waqar	16	b Wasim	0
D.J.White	c Salim Yousuf b Wasim	9	b Wasim	18
M.J.Greatbatch	c and b Ijaz	43	lbw b Aaqib	21
*M.D.Crowe	c Ramiz b Waqar	7	not out	68
K.R.Rutherford	b Aaqib	79	lbw b Aaqib	0
D.N.Patel	lbw b Waqar	2	lbw b Wasim	19
D.K.Morrison	lbw b Wasim	4 (9)	b Wasim	0
G.E.Bradburn	not out	11 (7)	c Salim Yousuf b Waqar	2
†I.D.S.Smith	lbw b Wasim	4 (8)	b Waqar	14
C.Pringle	b Waqar	0	lbw b Qadir	20
W.Watson	lbw b Wasim	0	lbw b Waqar	11
Extras	(B5, LB11, W2, NB3)	21	(B7, LB9, NB5)	21
Total		**196**		**194**

PAKISTAN

Ramiz Raja	c Crowe b Bradburn	78
Shoaib Mohammad	not out	203
Salim Malik	c Rutherford b Pringle	43
*Javed Miandad	lbw b Morrison	27
Wasim Akram	run out	28
Ijaz Ahmed	b Watson	9
†Salim Yousuf	c Crowe b Morrison	13
Abdul Qadir	not out	6
Tausif Ahmed		
Waqar Younis	} did not bat	
Aaqib Javed		
Extras	(B3, LB11, W1, NB11)	26
Total	(6 wickets declared)	**433**

PAKISTAN	O	M	R	W	O	M	R	W
Wasim	29.5	12	44	4	24	5	60	3
Waqar	22	7	40	4	15.4	9	39	3
Aaqib	16	4	37	1	12	1	45	2
Qadir	7	1	32	0	10	2	32	1
Tausif	5	0	18	0	1	0	0	0
Ijaz	5	0	9	1				
NEW ZEALAND								
Morrison	28.3	5	86	2				
Pringle	25	3	68	1				
Watson	40	8	125	1				
Bradburn	17	3	56	1				
Patel	24	6	62	0				
Crowe	6	1	22	0				

FALL OF WICKETS			
	NZ	P	NZ
Wkt	1st	1st	2nd
1st	28	172	4
2nd	37	239	23
3rd	51	288	56
4th	167	360	57
5th	174	384	96
6th	181	413	103
7th	181	–	119
8th	194	–	120
9th	195	–	173
10th	196	–	194

Umpires: Feroze Butt (1) and Mahboob Shah (20).

Test No. 1151/30

PAKISTAN v NEW ZEALAND (2nd Test)

Played at Gaddafi Stadium, Lahore, on 18, 19, 20, 22, 23 October 1990.
Toss: New Zealand. Result: PAKISTAN won by 9 wickets.
Debuts: Nil.

NEW ZEALAND

T.J.Franklin c Wasim b Salim Jaffer	11		c S.Yousuf b S.Jaffer	25
D.J.White c Salim Yousuf b Wasim	3		b Waqar	1
M.J.Greatbatch b Waqar	11		b Waqar	6
*M.D.Crowe c Salim Malik b Aaqib	20		not out	108
K.R.Rutherford lbw b Wasim	23	(6)	lbw b Waqar	60
D.N.Patel b Waqar	4	(7)	c S.Yousuf b S.Jaffer	7
G.E.Bradburn lbw b Salim Jaffer	8	(8)	c sub (A.Sohail) b Waqar	14
†I.D.S.Smith c Salim Yousuf b Qadir	33	(9)	c Salim Jaffer b Qadir	8
C.Pringle c Ramiz b Waqar	9	(10)	b Waqar	7
D.K.Morrison c Salim Yousuf b Qadir	0	(5)	b Waqar	7
W.Watson not out	0		lbw b Waqar	0
Extras (B5, LB13, W5, NB15)	38		(B17, LB10, NB17)	44
Total	**160**			**287**

PAKISTAN

Ramiz Raja c Greatbatch b Watson	48	c Crowe b Morrison	11
Shoaib Mohammad b Morrison	105	not out	42
Salim Malik lbw b Watson	6	not out	19
*Javed Miandad c Smith b Bradburn	43		
Ijaz Ahmed c Greatbatch b Watson	86		
†Salim Yousuf c Rutherford b Pringle	33		
Wasim Akram c Bradburn b Watson	1		
Waqar Younis b Watson	17		
Salim Jaffer not out	10		
Aaqib Javed c Crowe b Watson	7		
Abdul Qadir did not bat			
Extras (B4, LB1, NB12)	17	(LB1, W1, NB3)	5
Total (9 wickets declared)	**373**	**(1 wicket)**	**77**

PAKISTAN	O	M	R	W	O	M	R	W	FALL OF WICKETS				
										NZ	P	NZ	P
Wasim	16	3	43	2	9	4	15	0		1st	1st	2nd	2nd
Waqar	15	7	20	3	37.5	11	86	7	Wkt	1st	1st	2nd	2nd
Salim Jaffer	12	2	37	2	25	8	62	2	1st	7	98	10	27
Aaqib	13	2	37	1	21	9	40	0	2nd	30	117	18	—
Qadir	3	1	5	2	19	4	43	1	3rd	39	132	57	—
Shoaib					2	0	8	0	4th	79	246	74	—
Ijaz					2	0	6	0	5th	99	317	206	—
NEW ZEALAND									6th	103	337	228	—
Morrison	29	9	103	1	8	2	36	1	7th	143	342	264	—
Pringle	31	6	112	1	7	4	10	0	8th	147	363	277	—
Watson	36	10	78	6	0	0	12	0	9th	154	373	287	—
Patel	16	5	43	0	3	0	13	0	10th	160	—	287	—
Bradburn	13	4	32	1									
White					0.3	0	5	0					

Umpires: Athar Zaidi (1) and Salim Badar (2).

Test No. 1152/31

PAKISTAN v NEW ZEALAND (3rd Test)

Played at Iqbal Stadium, Faisalabad, on 26, 28, 29, 30, 31 October 1990.
Toss: New Zealand. Result: PAKISTAN won by 65 runs.
Debuts: Nil.

‡ (A.C.Parore)

PAKISTAN

Ramiz Raja c Smith b Pringle	20		lbw b Watson	16
Shoaib Mohammad c Crowe b Pringle	15		c sub‡ b Pringle	142
Salim Malik c Smith b Pringle	4	(4)	c and b Crowe	71
*Javed Miandad c Smith b Pringle	25	(5)	c Bradburn b Pringle	55
Ijaz Ahmed c Horne b Watson	5	(6)	c Horne b Pringle	6
†Salim Yousuf c Morrison b Watson	14	(3)	c Crowe b Pringle	13
Naved Anjum c Smith b Pringle	10		b Morrison	22
Tausif Ahmed c Rutherford b Pringle	1		not out	12
Waqar Younis b Pringle	0		c Rutherford b Morrison	4
Salim Jaffer lbw b Watson	0		b Morrison	2
Aaqib Javed not out	0		c sub‡ b Morrison	4
Extras (LB3, NB5)	8		(B1, LB8, NB5)	14
Total	**102**			**357**

NEW ZEALAND

T.J.Franklin b Waqar	25		c Ijaz b Aaqib	12
P.A.Horne c Ramiz b Salim Jaffer	0		lbw b Waqar	12
M.J.Greatbatch c Salim Yousuf b Waqar	8	(4)	b Aaqib	0
*M.D.Crowe c Tausif b Salim Jaffer	31	(5)	c Salim Yousuf b Waqar	10
K.R.Rutherford b Waqar	0	(6)	c S.Yousuf b S.Jaffer	25
D.N.Patel lbw b Waqar	0	(7)	c S.Yousuf b S.Jaffer	45
D.K.Morrison c Shoaib b Waqar	25	(3)	c Salim Yousuf b Aaqib	0
†I.D.S.Smith c Salim Malik b Tausif	61	(9)	c and b Waqar	21
G.E.Bradburn c Salim Yousuf b Waqar	18	(8)	not out	30
C.Pringle not out	24		c Salim Yousuf b Waqar	0
W.Watson lbw b Waqar	2		lbw b Waqar	2
Extras (B12, LB8, NB3)	23		(B10, LB5, W1, NB4)	20
Total	**217**			**177**

NEW ZEALAND	O	M	R	W	O	M	R	W	FALL OF WICKETS			
										P	NZ	P	NZ
Morrison	9	3	18	0	29.5	3	105	4					
Pringle	16	4	52	7	43	13	100	4	Wkt	1st	1st	2nd	2nd
Watson	15.3	5	29	3	44	23	77	1	1st	35	36	33	23
Patel					6	0	21	0	2nd	37	37	61	25
Crowe					11	5	22	1	3rd	42	37	192	28
Bradburn					6	1	23	0	4th	65	37	309	31
PAKISTAN									5th	82	89	314	45
Waqar	30.2	13	76	7	23.5	9	54	5	6th	92	166	321	64
Aaqib	10	5	24	0	17	1	57	3	7th	98	171	349	148
Naved	6	4	13	0					8th	102	178	349	171
Salim Jaffer	20	5	47	2	18	4	51	2	9th	102	207	353	171
Tausif	10	2	37	1					10th	102	217	357	177

Umpires: Athar Zaidi (2) and Salim Badar (3).   Test No. 1153/32

In New Zealand's first innings, P.A.Horne (0) retired hurt at 7-0 and resumed at 166-6.
In Pakistan's second innings, P.A.Horne kept wicket from 106th to 110th over, and
A.C.Parore (sub) kept wicket after lunch (from 116th over) to the end of the
innings.

PAKISTAN v NEW ZEALAND AVERAGES

PAKISTAN – BATTING AND FIELDING

	M	I	NO	HS	Runs	Avge	100	50	Ct/St
Shoaib Mohammad	3	5	2	203*	507	169.00	3	–	1
Javed Miandad	3	4	0	55	150	37.50	–	1	–
Salim Malik	3	5	1	71	143	35.75	–	1	2
Ramiz Raja	3	5	0	78	173	34.60	–	1	3
Ijaz Ahmed	3	4	0	86	106	26.50	–	1	2
Salim Yousuf	3	4	0	33	73	18.25	–	–	15
Wasim Akram	2	2	0	28	29	14.50	–	–	1
Tausif Ahmed	2	2	1	12*	13	13.00	–	–	1
Salim Jaffer	2	3	1	10*	12	12.00	–	–	1
Waqar Younis	3	3	0	17	17	5.66	–	–	1
Aaqib Javed	3	3	1	7	11	5.50	–	–	–

Also played: Abdul Qadir (2 Tests) 6*; Naved Anjum (1 Test) 10, 22.

PAKISTAN – BOWLING

	O	M	R	W	Avge	Best	5wI	10wM
Waqar Younis	144.4	51	315	29	10.86	7-76	3	2
Wasim Akram	78.5	24	162	10	16.20	4-44	–	–
Salim Jaffer	75	19	197	8	24.62	2-37	–	–
Abdul Qadir	39	8	112	4	28.00	2-5	–	–
Aaqib Javed	89	22	240	7	34.28	3-57	–	–

Also bowled: Ijaz Ahmed 7-0-15-1; Naved Anjum 6-4-13-0; Shoaib Mohammad 2-0-8-0; Tausif Ahmed 16-2-57-1.

NEW ZEALAND – BATTING AND FIELDING

	M	I	NO	HS	Runs	Avge	100	50	Ct/St
M.D.Crowe	3	6	2	106*	244	61.00	1	1	7
K.R.Rutherford	3	6	0	79	187	31.16	–	2	4
I.D.S.Smith	3	6	0	61	141	23.50	–	1	5
G.E.Bradburn	3	6	2	30*	83	20.75	–	–	2
T.J.Franklin	3	6	0	25	89	14.83	–	–	–
M.J.Greatbatch	3	6	0	43	89	14.83	–	–	2
D.N.Patel	3	6	0	45	77	12.83	–	–	–
C.Pringle	3	6	1	24*	60	12.00	–	–	–
D.J.White	2	4	0	18	31	7.75	–	–	–
D.K.Morrison	3	6	0	25	36	6.00	–	–	1
W.Watson	3	6	1	11	15	3.00	–	–	–

Played in one Test: P.A.Horne 0, 12 (2 ct).

NEW ZEALAND – BOWLING

	O	M	R	W	Avge	Best	5wI	10wM
C.Pringle	122	30	342	13	26.30	7-52	1	1
W.Watson	137.3	46	321	11	29.18	6-78	1	–
D.K.Morrison	104.2	22	348	8	43.50	4-105	–	–

Also bowled: G.E.Bradburn 36-8-111-2; M.D.Crowe 17-6-44-1; D.N.Patel 49-11-139-0; D.J.White 0.3-0-5-0.

PAKISTAN v WEST INDIES (1st Test)

Played at National Stadium, Karachi, on 15, 16, 17, 19, 20 November 1990.
Toss: West Indies. Result: PAKISTAN won by 8 wickets.
Debuts: Pakistan – Zahid Fazal.

WEST INDIES

C.G.Greenidge lbw b Waqar	3	st Salim Yousuf b Qadir	11
*D.L.Haynes lbw b Wasim	117	c Salim Yousuf b Waqar	47
R.B.Richardson st S.Yousuf b Mushtaq	26	lbw b Waqar	11
C.A.Best c Ramiz b Mushtaq	1	lbw b Mushtaq	8
C.L.Hooper lbw b Waqar	8	lbw b Wasim	0
A.L.Logie c Salim Yousuf b Wasim	25	not out	58
†P.J.L.Dujon c Miandad b Waqar	17	b Shoaib	1
M.D.Marshall b Waqar	13	b Wasim	21
C.E.L.Ambrose lbw b Waqar	2	lbw b Waqar	0
I.R.Bishop c Salim Yousuf b Wasim	22	b Waqar	0
C.A.Walsh not out	6	b Wasim	0
Extras (B6, LB6, NB9)	21	(B10, LB8, NB6)	24
Total	261		181

PAKISTAN

Shoaib Mohd c Richardson b Marshall	86	not out	32
Ramiz Raja b Bishop	0	lbw b Walsh	7
Zahid Fazal c Logie b Ambrose	0	c Richardson b Walsh	12
Javed Miandad c Dujon b Bishop	7		
Salim Malik c Dujon b Marshall	102	(4) not out	30
*Imran Khan not out	73		
†Salim Yousuf b Ambrose	5		
Wasim Akram c Richardson b Walsh	9		
Mushtaq Ahmed b Richardson b Ambrose	3		
Abdul Qadir c Dujon b Ambrose	0		
Waqar Younis c Hooper b Bishop	5		
Extras (B7, LB14, W1, NB26)	48	(LB8, NB9)	17
Total	345	(2 wickets)	98

PAKISTAN	O	M	R	W	O	M	R	W	FALL OF WICKETS				
										WI	P	WI	P
Wasim	23.3	1	61	3	20.3	6	39	3	Wkt	1st	1st	2nd	2nd
Waqar	22	0	76	5	17	3	44	4	1st	4	2	47	15
Qadir	20	2	56	0	8	1	22	1	2nd	77	16	85	56
Mushtaq	18	3	56	2	15	5	38	1	3rd	81	27	86	–
Shoaib					6	1	15	1	4th	96	201	90	–
Salim Malik					1	0	5	0	5th	151	281	111	–
WEST INDIES									6th	178	298	127	–
Ambrose	34	7	78	4	2	0	4	0	7th	200	313	166	–
Bishop	27.2	3	81	3					8th	204	318	174	–
Marshall	24	5	48	2	5	1	8	0	9th	243	318	174	–
Walsh	19	0	50	1	12	2	27	2	10th	261	345	181	–
Hooper	28	6	65	0	11	2	30	0					
Best	1	0	2	0									

Umpires: Khizer Hayat (23) and Riazuddin (1).　　　　Test No. 1154/26

PAKISTAN v WEST INDIES (2nd Test)

Played at Iqbal Stadium, Faisalabad, on 23, 24, 25 November 1990.
Toss: Pakistan. Result: WEST INDIES won by 7 wickets.
Debuts: Pakistan – Moin Khan, Saeed Anwar.

PAKISTAN

Saeed Anwar c Best b Ambrose	0		lbw b Bishop		0
Shoaib Mohammad c Dujon b Bishop	7		b Ambrose		15
Zahid Fazal run out	32		b Bishop		5
Javed Miandad c Dujon b Walsh	7	(6)	c Dujon b Ambrose		9
Salim Malik c Richardson b Bishop	74	(4)	b Marshall		71
*Imran Khan lbw b Walsh	3	(7)	c Dujon b Marshall		0
Wasim Akram run out	4	(8)	run out		0
†Moin Khan c Greenidge b Ambrose	24	(5)	c Logie b Walsh		32
Akram Raza b Bishop	5		b Marshall		0
Mushtaq Ahmed not out	2		not out		5
Waqar Younis c Dujon b Bishop	1		c Dujon b Marshall		3
Extras (LB3, NB8)	11		(LB4, NB10)		14
Total	**170**				**154**

WEST INDIES

C.G.Greenidge lbw b Waqar	12	(4)	lbw b Wasim	10
*D.L.Haynes lbw b Akram Raza	7	(1)	c Akram Raza b Wasim	0
R.B.Richardson c Saeed b Akram Raza	44		not out	70
C.A.Best c Moin b Waqar	6	(2)	b Wasim	7
C.L.Hooper lbw b Waqar	5		not out	33
A.L.Logie c Moin b Waqar	12			
†P.J.L.Dujon lbw b Wasim	9			
M.D.Marshall b Wasim	20			
C.E.L.Ambrose b Waqar	15			
I.R.Bishop lbw b Wasim	0			
C.A.Walsh not out	14			
Extras (B8, LB20, NB11)	39		(B4, LB2, NB4)	10
Total	**195**		**(3 wickets)**	**130**

WEST INDIES	O	M	R	W	O	M	R	W	FALL OF WICKETS				
Bishop	17.2	6	47	4	11	1	53	2		*P*	*WI*	*P*	*WI*
Ambrose	17	3	47	2	13	4	32	2	*Wkt*	*1st*	*1st*	*2nd*	*2nd*
Walsh	10	1	38	2	9	0	32	1	1st	1	26	0	0
Marshall	8	1	30	0	4.2	0	24	4	2nd	15	78	10	11
Hooper	2	1	5	0	3	1	9	0	3rd	29	101	38	34
PAKISTAN									4th	76	101	127	–
Wasim	17	1	63	3	12	0	46	3	5th	91	108	145	–
Waqar	16	3	46	5	9	2	41	0	6th	99	121	146	–
Akram Raza	19	4	52	2	7.2	1	37	0	7th	146	143	146	–
Mushtaq	4	1	6	0	1	1	0	0	8th	157	162	146	–
									9th	169	162	146	–
									10th	170	195	154	–

Umpires: Khizer Hayat (24) and Riazuddin (2).   Test No. 1155/27

PAKISTAN v WEST INDIES (3rd Test)

Played at Gaddafi Stadium, Lahore, on 6, 7, 8, 10, 11 December 1990.
Toss: West Indies. Result: MATCH DRAWN.
Debuts: Pakistan – Masood Anwar; West Indies – B.C.Lara.

WEST INDIES

C.G.Greenidge lbw b Imran	21	c Zahid b Waqar	1
*D.L.Haynes c Moin b Imran	3	c Shoaib b Masood	12
R.B.Richardson lbw b Wasim	5	c Aamer b Imran	6
B.C.Lara c Aamer b Qadir	44	c Salim b Imran	5
C.L.Hooper c Zahid b Masood	134	run out	49
A.L.Logie lbw b Waqar	16	lbw b Wasim	59
†P.J.L.Dujon st Moin b Masood	0	c Moin b Wasim	3
M.D.Marshall b Wasim	27	b Wasim	11
C.E.L.Ambrose lbw b Wasim	0	lbw b Wasim	0
I.R.Bishop c Moin b Wasim	9	not out	1
C.A.Walsh not out	5	lbw b Wasim	0
Extras (B8, LB12, NB10)	30	(B14, LB4, NB8)	26
Total	**294**		**173**

PAKISTAN

Aamer Malik b Bishop	3		c Logie b Ambrose	0
Shoaib Mohammad b Bishop	0	(3)	b Bishop	49
Zahid Fazal c Haynes b Ambrose	13	(7)	b Walsh	6
Ramiz Raja c Logie b Ambrose	6	(2)	b Walsh	41
Salim Malik c Greenidge b Bishop	8		b Bishop	0
*Imran Khan c Logie b Ambrose	17		not out	58
Wasim Akram b Ambrose	38	(8)	not out	21
†Moin Khan c Logie b Ambrose	7			
Masood Anwar c Logie b Bishop	2	(4)	c Lara b Hooper	37
Abdul Qadir lbw b Bishop	1			
Waqar Younis not out	0			
Extras (B4, LB12, W1, NB10)	27		(LB4, NB26)	30
Total	**122**		**(6 wickets)**	**242**

PAKISTAN	O	M	R	W	O	M	R	W	FALL OF WICKETS				
										WI	P	WI	P
Imran	6	0	22	2	13	5	32	2	Wkt	1st	1st	2nd	2nd
Wasim	24	4	61	4	9	0	28	5	1st	13	2	1	0
Waqar	17	0	57	1	8	0	32	1	2nd	24	11	13	90
Qadir	18	1	75	1	4	0	19	0	3rd	37	33	27	107
Masood	13.5	3	59	2	13	1	43	1	4th	132	34	47	110
Shoaib					1	0	1	0	5th	185	48	154	177
WEST INDIES									6th	186	93	155	187
Ambrose	20	5	35	5	20.4	5	43	1	7th	247	108	172	–
Bishop	19.2	7	41	5	23	6	59	2	8th	249	120	172	–
Marshall	5	2	8	0	19	5	48	0	9th	278	121	173	–
Walsh	5	1	22	0	19	3	53	2	10th	294	122	173	–
Hooper					15	4	35	1					

Umpires: Khizer Hayat (25) and Riazuddin (3). Test No. 1156/28
Aamer Malik kept wicket on the third day while West Indies scored 128-4 in 34 overs.

PAKISTAN v WEST INDIES AVERAGES

PAKISTAN – BATTING AND FIELDING

	M	I	NO	HS	Runs	Avge	100	50	Ct/St
Salim Malik	3	6	1	102	285	57.00	1	2	1
Imran Khan	3	5	2	73*	151	50.33	–	2	–
Shoaib Mohammad	3	6	1	86	189	37.80	–	1	1
Moin Khan	2	3	0	32	63	21.00	–	–	5/1
Wasim Akram	3	5	1	38	72	18.00	–	–	–
Ramiz Raja	2	4	0	41	54	13.50	–	–	1
Zahid Fazal	3	6	0	32	75	12.50	–	–	2
Mushtaq Ahmed	2	3	2	5*	10	10.00	–	–	–
Javed Miandad	2	3	0	9	23	7.66	–	–	1
Waqar Younis	3	4	1	5	9	3.00	–	–	–
Abdul Qadir	2	2	0	1	1	0.50	–	–	–

Played in one Test: Aamer Malik 3, 0 (2 ct); Akram Raza 5, 0 (1 ct); Masood Anwar 2, 37; Saeed Anwar 0, 0 (1 ct); Salim Yousuf 5 (3 ct, 2 st).

PAKISTAN – BOWLING

	O	M	R	W	Avge	Best	5wI	10wM
Imran Khan	19	5	54	4	13.50	2-22	–	–
Wasim Akram	106	12	298	21	14.19	5-28	2	–
Waqar Younis	89	8	296	16	18.50	5-46	2	–
Mushtaq Ahmed	38	10	100	3	33.33	2-56	–	–
Masood Anwar	26.5	4	102	3	34.00	2-55	–	–

Also bowled: Abdul Qadir 50-4-172-2; Akram Raza 26.2-5-89-2; Salim Malik 1-0-5-0; Shoaib Mohammad 7-1-16-1.

WEST INDIES – BATTING AND FIELDING

	M	I	NO	HS	Runs	Avge	100	50	Ct/St
C.L. Hooper	3	6	1	134	229	45.00	1	–	7
A.L.Logie	3	5	1	59	170	42.50	–	2	7
D.L.Haynes	3	6	0	117	198	33.00	1	–	1
R.B.Richardson	3	6	1	70*	162	32.40	–	1	5
M.D.Marshall	3	5	0	27	92	18.40	–	–	–
C.A.Walsh	3	5	3	14*	25	12.50	–	–	–
C.G.Greenidge	3	6	0	21	58	9.66	–	–	2
I.R.Bishop	3	5	1	22	32	8.00	–	–	–
P.J.L.Dujon	3	5	0	17	30	6.00	–	–	9
C.A.Best	2	4	0	8	22	5.50	–	–	1
C.E.L.Ambrose	3	5	0	15	17	3.40	–	–	–

Played in one Test: B.C.Lara 44, 5 (1 ct).

WEST INDIES – BOWLING

	O	M	R	W	Avge	Best	5wI	10wM
C.E.L.Ambrose	106.4	24	239	14	17.07	5-35	1	–
I.R.Bishop	105	23	302	16	18.87	5-41	1	–
M.D.Marshall	65.2	14	166	6	27.66	4-24	–	–
C.A.Walsh	74	7	222	8	27.75	2-27	–	–

Also bowled: C.A.Best 1-0-2-0; C.L.Hooper 59-14-144-1.

INDIA v SRI LANKA (Only Test)

Played at Sector 16 Stadium, Chandigarh, on 23, 24, 25, 27 November 1990.
Toss: India. Result: INDIA won by an innings and 8 runs.
Debuts: Sri Lanka – M.S.Atapattu.

INDIA

R.J.Shastri c De Silva b Warnaweera	88	
M.Prabhakar lbw b Warnaweera	31	
S.V.Manjrekar lbw b Madurasinghe	39	
D.B.Vengsarkar lbw b Ratnayake	7	
*M.Azharuddin c Labrooy b Madurasinghe	23	
S.R.Tendulkar lbw b Madurasinghe	11	
Kapil Dev c De Silva b Warnaweera	4	
†K.S.More not out	37	
S.L.V.Raju lbw b Ratnayake	14	
G.Sharma lbw b Ratnayake	0	
N.D.Hirwani run out	0	
Extras (B5, LB10, NB19)	34	
Total	**288**	

SRI LANKA

R.S.Mahanama c More b Kapil Dev	1	c More b Kapil Dev	48
M.A.R.Samarasekera lbw b Prabhakar	13	c More b Prabhakar	5
A.P.Gurusinha not out	52	c Sharma b Prabhakar	0
P.A.De Silva b Raju	5	lbw b Hirwani	7
*A.Ranatunga b Raju	1	c Azharuddin b Raju	42
†H.P.Tillekeratne b Raju	0 (7)	c Shastri b Kapil Dev	55
M.S.Atapattu c More b Raju	0 (6)	lbw b Kapil Dev	0
R.J.Ratnayake lbw b Raju	0	lbw b Raju	0
G.F.Labrooy b Sharma	0	b Kapil Dev	0
A.W.R.Madurasinghe run out	2	b Prabhakar	11
K.P.J.Warnaweera b Raju	0	not out	0
Extras (B1, LB2, NB5)	8	(B5, LB15, NB10)	30
Total	**82**		**198**

SRI LANKA	O	M	R	W	O	M	R	W	FALL OF WICKETS			
										I	*SL*	*SL*
Ratnayake	21.5	3	60	3					Wkt	*1st*	*1st*	*2nd*
Labrooy	12	1	59	0					1st	58	4	14
Warnaweera	46	17	90	3					2nd	134	34	14
Ranatunga	5	2	4	0					3rd	158	50	47
Madurasinghe	26	6	60	3					4th	208	54	110
INDIA									5th	210	54	110
Kapil Dev	8	3	14	1	29.4	15	36	4	6th	220	54	135
Prabhakar	9	0	27	1	15	4	43	3	7th	240	60	135
Raju	17.5	13	12	6	36	25	25	2	8th	276	65	136
Sharma	17	5	26	1	20	7	39	0	9th	276	77	196
Hirwani					20	9	34	1	10th	288	82	198

Umpires: S.B.Kulkarni (1) and R.S.Rathore (1).   Test No. 1157/8

AUSTRALIA v ENGLAND (1st Test)

Played at Woolloongabba, Brisbane, on 23, 24, 25 November 1990.
Toss: Australia. Result: AUSTRALIA won by 10 wickets.
Debuts: Nil

‡ (P.E.Cantrell)

ENGLAND

M.A.Atherton lbw b Reid	13		b Alderman	15
W.Larkins c Healy b Hughes	12		lbw b Reid	0
D.I.Gower c Healy b Reid	61		b Hughes	27
*A.J.Lamb c Hughes b Matthews	32		lbw b Alderman	14
R.A.Smith b Reid	7	(6)	c Taylor b Alderman	1
A.J.Stewart lbw b Reid	4	(7)	c sub‡ b Alderman	6
†R.C.Russell c and b Alderman	16	(5)	lbw b Waugh	15
C.C.Lewis c Border b Hughes	20		lbw b Alderman	14
G.C.Small not out	12		c Alderman b Hughes	15
A.R.C.Fraser c Healy b Alderman	1		c sub‡ b Alderman	0
D.E.Malcolm c Waugh b Hughes	5		not out	0
Extras (B1, LB7, NB3)	11		(LB3, NB4)	7
Total	**194**			**114**

AUSTRALIA

G.R.Marsh lbw b Fraser	9	not out	72
M.A.Taylor c Lewis b Fraser	10	not out	67
D.C.Boon lbw b Small	18		
*A.R.Border c Atherton b Small	9		
D.M.Jones c Small b Lewis	17		
S.R.Waugh c Smith b Small	1		
G.R.J.Matthews c Small b Malcolm	35		
†I.A.Healy c Atherton b Lewis	22		
M.G.Hughes c Russell b Fraser	9		
B.A.Reid b Lewis	0		
T.M.Alderman not out	0		
Extras (B1, LB10, NB11)	22	(B3, LB2, W3, NB10)	18
Total	**152**	**(0 wickets)**	**157**

AUSTRALIA	O	M	R	W	O	M	R	W	FALL OF WICKETS				
										E	A	E	A
Alderman	18	5	44	2	22	7	47	6	*Wkt*	*1st*	*1st*	*2nd*	*2nd*
Reid	18	3	53	4	14	3	40	1	1st	23	22	0	–
Hughes	19	5	39	3	12.1	5	17	2	2nd	43	35	42	–
Waugh	7	2	20	0	4	2	7	1	3rd	117	49	46	–
Matthews	16	8	30	1	1	1	0	0	4th	123	60	60	–
ENGLAND									5th	134	64	78	–
Malcolm	17	2	45	1	9	5	22	0	6th	135	89	84	–
Fraser	21	6	33	3	14	2	49	0	7th	167	135	93	–
Small	16	4	34	3	15	2	36	0	8th	181	150	112	–
Lewis	9	0	29	3	6	0	29	0	9th	187	150	114	–
Atherton					2	0	16	0	10th	194	152	114	–

Umpires: A.R.Crafter (30) and P.J.McConnell (17).

Test No. 1158/270

AUSTRALIA v ENGLAND (2nd Test)

Played at Melbourne Cricket Ground on 26, 27, 28, 29, 30 December 1990.
Toss: England. Result: AUSTRALIA won by 8 wickets.
Debuts: England – P.C.R.Tufnell.

ENGLAND

*G.A.Gooch lbw b Alderman	20	c Alderman b Reid	58
M.A.Atherton c Boon b Reid	0	c Healy b Reid	4
W.Larkins c Healy b Reid	64	c Healy b Reid	54
R.A.Smith c Healy b Hughes	30	c Taylor b Reid	8
D.I.Gower c and b Reid	100	c Border b Matthews	0
A.J.Stewart c Healy b Reid	79	c Marsh b Reid	8
†R.C.Russell c Healy b Hughes	15	c Jones b Matthews	0
P.A.J.DeFreitas c Healy b Reid	3	lbw b Reid	0
A.R.C.Fraser c Jones b Alderman	24	c Taylor b Reid	0
D.E.Malcolm c Taylor b Reid	6	lbw b Matthews	1
P.C.R.Tufnell not out	0	not out	0
Extras (LB2, NB9)	11	(B7, LB3, NB6)	16
Total	**352**		**150**

AUSTRALIA

G.R.Marsh c Russell b DeFreitas	36	not out	79
M.A.Taylor c Russell b DeFreitas	61	c Atherton b Malcolm	5
D.C.Boon c Russell b Malcolm	28	(4) not out	94
*A.R.Border c Russell b Fraser	62		
D.M.Jones c Russell b Fraser	44		
S.R.Waugh b Fraser	19		
G.R.J.Matthews lbw b Fraser	5	(3) c Atherton b Fraser	1
†I.A.Healy c Russell b Fraser	5		
M.G.Hughes lbw b Malcolm	4		
T.M.Alderman b Fraser	0		
B.A.Reid not out	3		
Extras (B4, LB12, NB16)	32	(B4, LB12, NB2)	18
Total	**306**	(2 wickets)	**197**

AUSTRALIA	O	M	R	W	O	M	R	W	FALL OF WICKETS				
Alderman	30.4	7	86	2	10	2	19	0		*E*	*A*	*E*	*A*
Reid	39	8	97	6	22	12	51	7	*Wkt*	*1st*	*1st*	*2nd*	*2nd*
Hughes	29	7	83	2	9	4	26	0	1st	12	63	17	9
Matthews	27	8	65	0	25	9	40	3	2nd	30	133	103	10
Waugh	6	2	19	0	7	6	4	0	3rd	109	149	115	–
ENGLAND									4th	152	224	122	–
Malcolm	25.5	4	74	2	23	7	52	1	5th	274	266	147	–
Fraser	39	10	82	6	20	4	33	1	6th	303	281	148	–
Tufnell	21	5	62	0	24	12	36	0	7th	307	289	148	–
DeFreitas	25	5	69	2	16	3	46	0	8th	324	298	148	–
Atherton	2	1	3	0	3	0	14	0	9th	344	302	150	–
									10th	352	306	150	–

Umpires: A.R.Crafter (31) and P.J.McConnell (18).   Test No. 1159/271

AUSTRALIA v ENGLAND (3rd Test)

Played at Sydney Cricket Ground on 4, 5, 6, 7, 8 January 1991.
Toss: Australia. Result: MATCH DRAWN.
Debuts: Nil.

AUSTRALIA

G.R.Marsh c Larkins b Malcolm	13	(2)	c Stewart b Malcolm	4
M.A.Taylor c Russell b Malcolm	11	(1)	lbw b Hemmings	19
D.C.Boon c Atherton b Gooch	97	(4)	c Gooch b Tufnell	29
*A.R.Border b Hemmings	78	(5)	c Gooch b Tufnell	20
D.M.Jones st Russell b Small	60	(6)	c and b Tufnell	0
S.R.Waugh c Stewart b Malcolm	48	(7)	c Russell b Hemmings	14
G.R.J.Matthews c Hemmings b Tufnell	128	(8)	b Hemmings	19
†I.A.Healy c Small b Hemmings	35	(3)	c Smith b Tufnell	69
C.G.Rackemann b Hemmings	1		b Malcolm	9
T.M.Alderman not out	26		c Gower b Tufnell	1
B.A.Reid c Smith b Malcolm	0		not out	5
Extras (B5, LB8, NB8)	21		(LB16)	16
Total	**518**			**205**

ENGLAND

*G.A.Gooch c Healy b Reid	59		c Border b Matthews	54
M.A.Atherton c Boon b Matthews	105	(6)	not out	3
W.Larkins run out	11		lbw b Border	0
R.A.Smith c Healy b Reid	18	(5)	not out	10
D.I.Gower c Marsh b Reid	123	(2)	c Taylor b Matthews	36
A.J.Stewart lbw b Alderman	91	(4)	run out	7
†R.C.Russell not out	30			
G.C.Small lbw b Alderman	10			
E.E.Hemmings b Alderman	0			
P.C.R.Tufnell not out	5			
D.E.Malcolm did not bat				
Extras (B1, LB8, NB8)	17		(LB1, NB2)	3
Total (8 wickets declared)	**469**		**(4 wickets)**	**113**

ENGLAND	O	M	R	W	O	M	R	W
Malcolm	45	12	128	4	6	1	19	2
Small	31	5	103	1	2	1	6	0
Hemmings	32	7	105	3	41	9	94	3
Tufnell	30	6	95	1	37	18	61	5
Gooch	14	3	46	1				
Atherton	5	0	28	0	3	1	9	0
AUSTRALIA								
Alderman	20.1	4	62	3	4	0	29	0
Reid	35.1	9	79	3				
Rackemann	25.5	5	89	0	3	0	20	0
Matthews	58	16	145	1	9	2	26	2
Border	19	5	45	0	9	1	37	1
Waugh	14	3	40	0				

FALL OF WICKETS

	A	E	A	E
Wkt	1st	1st	2nd	2nd
1st	21	95	21	84
2nd	38	116	29	84
3rd	185	156	81	100
4th	226	295	129	100
5th	292	394	129	–
6th	347	426	166	–
7th	442	444	166	–
8th	457	444	189	–
9th	512	–	192	–
10th	518	–	205	–

Umpires: A.R.Crafter (32) and P.J.McConnell (19).

Test No. 1160/272

AUSTRALIA v ENGLAND (4th Test)

Played at Adelaide Oval on 25, 26, 27, 28, 29 January 1991.
Toss: Australia. Result: MATCH DRAWN.
Debuts: Australia – M.E.Waugh.

AUSTRALIA

G.R.Marsh	c Gooch b Small	37	(2)	c Gooch b Small	0
M.A.Taylor	run out (Smith/Small)	5	(1)	run out (Gower)	4
D.C.Boon	c Fraser b Malcolm	49		b Tufnell	121
*A.R.Border	b DeFreitas	12	(7)	not out	83
D.M.Jones	lbw b DeFreitas	0	(4)	lbw b Malcolm	8
M.E.Waugh	b Malcolm	138	(5)	b Malcolm	23
G.R.J.Matthews	c Stewart b Gooch	65	(8)	not out	34
†I.A.Healy	c Stewart b DeFreitas	1			
C.J.McDermott	not out	42			
M.G.Hughes	lbw b Small	1	(6)	c Gooch b Fraser	30
B.A.Reid	c Lamb b DeFreitas	5			
Extras	(B2, LB23, W2, NB4)	31		(B1, LB7, W1, NB2)	11
Total		**386**		**(6 wickets declared)**	**314**

ENGLAND

*G.A.Gooch	c Healy b Reid	87		c Marsh b Reid	117
M.A.Atherton	lbw b McDermott	0		c Waugh b Reid	87
A.J.Lamb	c Healy b McDermott	0		b McDermott	53
R.A.Smith	c and b Hughes	53	(5)	not out	10
D.I.Gower	c Hughes b McDermott	11	(4)	lbw b Hughes	16
†A.J.Stewart	c Healy b Reid	11		c Jones b McDermott	9
P.DeFreitas	c Matthews b McDermott	45		not out	19
G.C.Small	b McDermott	1			
A.R.C.Fraser	c Healy b Reid	2			
D.E.Malcolm	c Healy b Reid	2			
P.C.R.Tufnell	not out	0			
Extras	(B1, LB3, NB13)	17		(B5, LB9, W1, NB9)	24
Total		**229**		**(5 wickets)**	**335**

ENGLAND	O	M	R	W	O	M	R	W	FALL OF WICKETS				
										A	*E*	*A*	*E*
Malcolm	38	7	104	2	21	0	87	1	*Wkt*	*1st*	*1st*	*2nd*	*2nd*
Fraser	23	6	48	0	26	3	66	1	1st	11	10	1	203
Small	34	10	92	2	18	3	64	1	2nd	62	11	8	246
DeFreitas	26.2	6	56	4	23	6	61	1	3rd	104	137	25	287
Tufnell	5	0	38	0	16	3	28	1	4th	104	160	64	287
Gooch	9	2	23	1					5th	124	176	130	297
AUSTRALIA									6th	295	179	240	–
Reid	29	9	53	4	23	5	59	2	7th	298	198	–	–
McDermott	26.3	3	97	5	27	5	106	2	8th	358	215	–	–
Hughes	22	4	62	1	14	3	52	1	9th	373	219	–	–
Waugh	4	1	13	0	1	0	4	0	10th	386	229	–	–
Matthews					31	7	100	0					

Umpires: L.J.King (4) and T.A.Prue (3).　　　　　　　　　　**Test No. 1161/273**

AUSTRALIA v ENGLAND (5th Test)

Played at W.A.C.A. Ground, Perth, on 1, 2, 3, 5 February 1991.
Toss: England. Result: AUSTRALIA won by 9 wickets.
Debuts: Nil.

ENGLAND

*G.A.Gooch c Healy b McDermott	13	c Alderman b Hughes	18
M.A.Atherton c Healy b McDermott	27	c Boon b Hughes	25
A.J.Lamb c Border b McDermott	91	lbw b McDermott	5
R.A.Smith c Taylor b McDermott	58	lbw b Alderman	43
D.I.Gower not out	28	c Taylor b Alderman	5
†A.J.Stewart lbw b McDermott	2	c Healy b McDermott	7
P.A.J.DeFreitas c Marsh b McDermott	5	c Healy b Alderman	5
P.J.Newport c Healy b McDermott	0	not out	40
G.C.Small c Boon b Hughes	0	c Taylor b Hughes	4
P.C.R.Tufnell c Healy b Hughes	0	c Healy b Hughes	8
D.E.Malcolm c Marsh b McDermott	7	c Jones b McDermott	6
Extras (B1, LB6, W1, NB5)	13	(B5, LB5, NB6)	16
Total	**244**		**182**

AUSTRALIA

G.R.Marsh c Stewart b Small	1	(2)	not out	63
M.A.Taylor c Stewart b Malcolm	12	(1)	c Stewart b DeFreitas	19
D.C.Boon c Stewart b Malcolm	64		not out	30
*A.R.Border lbw b DeFreitas	17			
D.M.Jones b Newport	34			
M.E.Waugh c Small b Malcolm	26			
G.R.J.Matthews not out	60			
†I.A.Healy c Lamb b Small	42			
C.J.McDermott b Tufnell	25			
M.G.Hughes c Gooch b Tufnell	0			
T.M.Alderman lbw b DeFreitas	7			
Extras (B2, LB8, W1, NB8)	19		(LB5, W2, NB1)	8
Total	**307**		**(1 wicket)**	**120**

AUSTRALIA	O	M	R	W	O	M	R	W	FALL OF WICKETS				
Alderman	22	5	66	0	22	3	75	3		E	A	E	A
McDermott	24.4	2	97	8	19.3	2	60	3	Wkt	1st	1st	2nd	2nd
Hughes	17	3	49	2	20	7	37	4	1st	27	1	41	39
Waugh	1	0	9	0					2nd	50	44	49	–
Matthews	2	0	16	0					3rd	191	90	75	–
ENGLAND									4th	212	113	80	–
Malcolm	30	4	94	3	9	0	40	0	5th	220	161	114	–
Small	23	5	65	2	10	5	24	0	6th	226	168	118	–
DeFreitas	16.5	2	57	2	6.2	0	29	1	7th	226	230	125	–
Newport	14	0	56	1	6	0	22	0	8th	227	281	134	–
Tufnell	7	1	25	2					9th	227	283	144	–
									10th	244	307	182	–

Umpires: S.G.Randell (8) and C.D.Timmins (2).   Test No. 1162/274

AUSTRALIA v ENGLAND

AUSTRALIA – BATTING AND FIELDING

	M	I	NO	HS	Runs	Avge	100	50	Ct/St
D.C.Boon	5	9	2	121	530	75.71	1	3	4
G.R.J.Matthews	5	7	2	128	353	70.60	1	2	1
M.E.Waugh	2	3	0	138	187	62.33	1	–	1
A.R.Border	5	7	1	83*	281	46.83	–	3	4
G.R.Marsh	5	10	3	79*	314	44.85	–	3	5
I.A.Healy	5	7	0	69	175	25.00	–	1	24
M.A.Taylor	5	10	1	67*	213	23.66	–	2	8
D.M.Jones	5	7	0	60	163	23.28	–	1	4
S.R.Waugh	3	4	0	48	82	20.50	–	–	1
T.M.Alderman	4	5	2	26*	34	11.33	–	–	4
M.G.Hughes	4	5	0	30	44	8.80	–	–	3
B.A.Reid	4	5	2	13	4.33	4.33	–	–	1

Also played: C.J.McDermott (*2 Tests*) 42*, 25; C.G.Rackemann (*1 Test*) 1, 9.

AUSTRALIA – BOWLING

	O	M	R	W	Avge	Best	5wI	10wM
B.A.Reid	180.1	49	432	27	16.00	7-51	2	1
C.J.McDermott	97.4	12	360	18	20.00	8-97	2	1
M.G.Hughes	142.1	38	365	15	24.33	4-37	–	–
T.M.Alderman	148.5	33	428	16	26.75	6-47	1	–
G.R.J.Matthews	169	51	422	7	60.28	3-40	–	–

Also bowled: A.R.Border 28-6-82-1; C.G.Rackemann 28.5-5-109-0; M.E.Waugh 6-1-26-0; S.R.Waugh 38-15-90-1.

ENGLAND – BATTING AND FIELDING

	M	I	NO	HS	Runs	Avge	100	50	Ct/St
G.A.Gooch	4	8	0	117	426	53.25	1	4	6
D.I.Gower	5	10	1	123	407	45.22	2	1	1
A.J.Lamb	3	6	0	91	195	32.50	–	2	2
M.A.Atherton	5	10	1	105	279	31.00	1	1	5
R.A.Smith	5	10	2	58	238	29.75	–	2	3
W.Larkins	3	6	0	64	141	23.50	–	2	1
A.J.Stewart	5	10	0	91	224	22.40	–	2	8
R.C.Russell	3	5	1	30*	77	19.25	–	–	9/1
P.A.J.DeFreitas	3	6	1	45	77	15.40	–	–	–
G.C.Small	4	6	1	15	42	8.40	–	–	4
P.C.R.Tufnell	4	6	4	8	13	6.50	–	–	1
A.R.C.Fraser	3	5	0	24	27	5.40	–	–	1
D.E.Malcolm	5	7	1	7	27	4.50	–	–	–

Also played (*1 Test*): E.E.Hemmings 0 (1 ct); C.C.Lewis 20, 14 (1 ct); P.J.Newport 0, 40*.

ENGLAND – BOWLING

	O	M	R	W	Avge	Best	5wI	10wM
A.R.C.Fraser	143	31	311	11	28.27	6-82	1	–
P.A.J.DeFreitas	113.3	22	318	10	31.80	4-56	–	–
E.E.Hemmings	73	16	199	6	33.16	3-94	–	–
P.C.R.Tufnell	140	45	345	9	38.33	5-61	1	–
D.E.Malcolm	223.5	42	665	16	41.56	4-128	–	–
G.C.Small	149	33	424	9	47.11	3-34	–	–

Also bowled: M.A.Atherton 15-2-70-0; G.A.Gooch 23-5-69-2; C.C.Lewis 15-0-58-3; P.J.Newport 20-0-78-1.

THE 1990 FIRST-CLASS SEASON
STATISTICAL HIGHLIGHTS

HIGHEST INNINGS TOTALS (28 of 500 or more)

863†	Lancashire v Surrey	The Oval
761-6d	Essex v Leicestershire	Chelmsford
707-9d	Surrey v Lancashire	The Oval
653-4d	England v India (1st Test)	Lord's
648	Surrey v Kent	Canterbury
636-6d	Northamptonshire v Essex	Chelmsford
613-6d	Surrey v Essex	The Oval
606-9d	India v England (3rd Test)	The Oval
600-8d	Hampshire v Sussex	Southampton
592-6d	Northamptonshire v Essex	Northampton
574	Gloucestershire v Yorkshire	Cheltenham
558-6d	Lancashire v Oxford University	Oxford
551-8d	Gloucestershire v Worcestershire	Bristol
539	Essex v Surrey	The Oval
535-2d	Somerset v Glamorgan	Cardiff
525-9d	Somerset v Sussex	Hove
521	Gloucestershire v Northamptonshire	Northampton
520-9d	Worcestershire v Somerset	Taunton
520	Leicestershire v Essex	Chelmsford
519	England v India (2nd Test)	Manchester
517	Surrey v Hampshire	Southampton
514-4d	Worcestershire v Glamorgan	Abergavenny
514-5d	Derbyshire v Kent	Chesterfield
512-6d	Indians v Minor Counties	Trowbridge
510-5d	Middlesex v Nottinghamshire	Lord's
508-9d	Essex v Kent	Chelmsford
506-7d	Sri Lankans v Hampshire	Southampton
500-5d	Somerset v Sussex	Taunton

† The second-highest total in County Championship matches.

HIGHEST FOURTH INNINGS TOTALS

493-6	Glamorgan v Worcestershire (set 495)	Abergavenny
446-8	Hampshire v Gloucestershire (set 445)	Southampton

LOWEST INNINGS TOTALS

50†	Northamptonshire v Derbyshire	Northampton
72	Derbyshire v Gloucestershire	Derby
96	Warwickshire v Worcestershire	Worcester
99	Middlesex v Derbyshire	Derby

† Three men absent.

MATCH AGGREGATES OF 1400 RUNS

Runs-Wkts

1650-19	Surrey v Lancashire	The Oval
1641-16	Glamorgan v Worcestershire	Abergavenny
1614-30	England v India (2nd Test)	Manchester
1603-28	England v India (1st Test)	Lord's
1530-19	Essex v Leicestershire	Chelmsford
1509-36	Somerset v Worcestershire	Taunton
1451-29	Kent v Surrey	Canterbury
1430-17	Glamorgan v Somerset	Cardiff
1423-23	England v India (3rd Test)	The Oval

FIRST TO INDIVIDUAL TARGETS

1000 RUNS	S.J.Cook	Somerset	June 7
2000 RUNS	S.J.Cook	Somerset	August 4
100 WICKETS	No instance; the highest aggregate was 94 by N.A.Foster (Essex).		

DOUBLE HUNDREDS (32)

M.W.Alleyne	256	Gloucestershire v Northamptonshire	Northampton
R.J.Bailey	204*	Northamptonshire v Sussex	Northampton
P.D.Bowler	210	Derbyshire v Kent	Chesterfield
B.C.Broad	227*	Nottinghamshire v Kent	Tunbridge Wells
K.R.Brown	200*	Middlesex v Nottinghamshire	Lord's
S.J.Cook	313*	Somerset v Glamorgan	Cardiff
P.A.De Silva	221*	Sri Lankans v Hampshire	Southampton
N.H.Fairbrother (2)	366‡	Lancashire v Surrey	The Oval
	203*	Lancashire v Warwickshire	Coventry
A.Fordham	206*	Northamptonshire v Yorkshire	Leeds
G.A.Gooch (2)	215	Essex v Leicestershire	Chelmsford
	333‡	England v India (1st Test)	Lord's
I.A.Greig	291	Surrey v Lancashire	The Oval
D.L.Haynes (2)	220*	Middlesex v Essex	Ilford
	255*	Middlesex v Sussex	Lord's
G.A.Hick	252*	Worcestershire v Glamorgan	Abergavenny
S.G.Hinks	234	Kent v Middlesex	Canterbury
A.J.Lamb	235	Northamptonshire v Yorkshire	Leeds
W.Larkins	207	Northamptonshire v Essex	Northampton
A.J.Moles	224*	Warwickshire v Glamorgan	Swansea
M.D.Moxon	218*	Yorkshire v Sussex	Eastbourne
P.J.Prichard	245	Essex v Leicestershire	Chelmsford
D.A.Reeve	202*	Warwickshire v Northamptonshire	Northampton
R.T.Robinson	220*	Nottinghamshire v Yorkshire	Nottingham
P.M.Roebuck	201*	Somerset v Worcestershire	Worcester
J.P.Stephenson	202*	Essex v Somerset	Bath
C.J.Tavaré	219	Somerset v Sussex	Hove
N.R.Taylor	204	Kent v Surrey	Canterbury
D.M.Ward (2)	263	Surrey v Kent	Canterbury
	208	Surrey v Essex	The Oval
M.E.Waugh (2)	204	Essex v Gloucestershire	Ilford
	207*	Essex v Yorkshire	Middlesbrough

† The second-highest first-class score by an Englishman.
‡ Ground record for all matches.

THREE HUNDRED RUNS IN A DAY

		Day		
N.H.Fairbrother	311*	3	Lancashire v Surrey	The Oval

HUNDRED BEFORE LUNCH

		Day		
B.C.Broad	101*	1	Nottinghamshire v Kent	Tunbridge Wells
N.H.Fairbrother	100*†	3	Lancashire v Surrey	The Oval
I.A.Greig	145*	2	Surrey v Lancashire	The Oval
D.L.Haynes	102*	1	Middlesex v Sussex	Lord's
	110*	1	Middlesex v Yorkshire	Leeds
A.A.Metcalfe	107*	1	Yorkshire v Gloucestershire	Cheltenham
D.A.Reeve	102*	2	Warwickshire v Cambridge U	Cambridge
R.A.Smith	127*	2	Hampshire v Sussex	Southampton

† Scored 100 or more in each session – 100, 108, 103.

HUNDREDS IN THREE CONSECUTIVE INNINGS

K.J.Barnett	107 v Glos, 123 v Sussex, 109 v Lancs	Derby/Hove/Liverpool
G.A.Gooch	177 v Lancs, 333 and 123 v India	Colchester/Lord's
M.R.Ramprakash	146* v Somerset, 100* and 125 v Kent	Uxbridge/Canterbury
I.V.A.Richards	111 and 118* v Essex, 127 v Notts	Southend/Worksop

HUNDRED IN EACH INNINGS OF A MATCH (12)

C.W.J.Athey	108* 122	Gloucestershire v Warwickshire	Bristol
G.A.Gooch (2)	333 123	England v India (1st Test)	Lord's
	The record individual aggregate in a Test match.		
	174 126	Essex v Northamptonshire	Northampton
M.J.Greatbatch	168* 128*	World XI v Indians	Scarborough
D.L.Haynes	181 129	Middlesex v New Zealanders	Lord's
G.A.Hick	252* 100*	Worcestershire v Glamorgan	Abergavenny
A.A.Metcalfe	194* 107	Yorkshire v Nottinghamshire	Nottingham
H.Morris	110 102*	Glamorgan v Nottinghamshire	Worksop
J.E.Morris	122 109	Derbyshire v Somerset	Taunton
M.R.Ramprakash	100* 125	Middlesex v Kent	Canterbury
I.V.A.Richards	111 118*	Glamorgan v Essex	Southend
N.R.Taylor	204 142	Kent v Surrey	Canterbury

FASTEST HUNDRED (WALTER LAWRENCE TROPHY)

| T.M.Moody | 36 balls | Warwickshire v Glamorgan | Swansea |

In 26 minutes and including 7 sixes and 11 fours. The fastest hundred in first-class cricket but achieved against 'soft' bowling.

HUNDRED ON FIRST-CLASS DEBUT

| J.J.B.Lewis | 116* | Essex v Surrey | The Oval |

HUNDRED ENTIRELY WITH THE AID OF A RUNNER

| M.P.Speight | 131 | Sussex v Glamorgan | Hove |

500 RUNS WITHOUT BEING DISMISSED

G.A.Hick (Worcestershire) 645: 171*, 69*, 252*, 100*, 53.
Hick scored seven successive fifties (also 12 in consecutive 13 innings).

FIFTY BOUNDARIES IN AN INNINGS

| N.H.Fairbrother 52 (5 sixes, 47 fours) Lancashire v Surrey | The Oval |

MOST SIXES OFF SUCCESSIVE BALLS

FOUR†: Kapil Dev (off E.E.Hemmings) India v England (1st Test) Lord's
THREE: M.R.Ramprakash (off C.J.Tavaré) Middx v Somerset Uxbridge
† The first instance in Test matches.

CARRYING BAT THROUGH COMPLETED INNINGS

| N.E.Briers | 157*† | Leicestershire (359) v Nottinghamshire | Leicester |
| P.M.Roebuck | 114* | Somerset (270) v Warwickshire | Taunton |

† One man retired hurt.

RECORD SEQUENCE OF FIRST-CLASS INNINGS WITHOUT SCORING

M.A.Robinson (Northamptonshire) 12: 0, 0*, 0*, 0*, 0*, 0*, 0, 0, 0, 0*, 0*, 0.

FIRST-WICKET PARTNERSHIP OF 200 IN EACH INNINGS

227 220 G.A.Gooch/J.P.Stephenson, Essex v Northants Northampton
Only the third instance in all first-class cricket.

FIRST-WICKET PARTNERSHIP OF 100 IN EACH INNINGS

| 145 | 170 | T.J.Boon/N.E.Briers, Leicestershire v Essex | Chelmsford |
| 140 | 256 | A.R.Butcher/H.Morris, Glamorgan v Worcestershire | Abergavenny |

OTHER NOTABLE PARTNERSHIPS
First Wicket
321	D.J.Bicknell/G.S.Clinton, Surrey v Northamptonshire	The Oval
306	D.L.Haynes/M.A.Roseberry, Middlesex v Essex	Ilford
292	V.P.Terry/T.C.Middleton, Hampshire v Northamptonshire	Bournemouth
264	V.P.Terry/C.L.Smith, Hampshire v Oxford University	Oxford
256	D.J.Bicknell/D.M.Ward, Surrey v Oxford University	Oxford
256	A.R.Butcher/H.Morris, Glamorgan v Worcestershire	Abergavenny
255*	A.R.Butcher/H.Morris, Glamorgan v Kent	Swansea
251	R.J.Shastri/N.S.Sidhu, Indians v Gloucestershire	Bristol

Second Wicket
403†	G.A.Gooch/P.J.Prichard, Essex v Leicestershire	Chelmsford
366†	S.G.Hinks/N.R.Taylor, Kent v Middlesex	Canterbury
264	T.S.Curtis/G.A.Hick, Worcestershire v Somerset	Taunton
258	P.M.Roebuck/A.N.Hayhurst, Somerset v Worcestershire	Worcester

Third Wicket
413†	D.J.Bicknell/D.M.Ward, Surrey v Kent	Canterbury
393†	A.Fordham/A.J.Lamb, Northamptonshire v Yorkshire	Leeds
364†	M.A.Atherton/N.H.Fairbrother, Lancashire v Surrey	The Oval
308	G.A.Gooch/A.J.Lamb, England v India (1st Test)	Lord's
293*	A.A.Metcalfe/P.E.Robinson, Yorkshire v Derbyshire	Scarborough
285*	S.J.Cook/C.J.Tavaré, Somerset v Glamorgan	Cardiff
268	M.R.Benson/G.R.Cowdrey, Kent v Essex	Maidstone
264	G.A.Hick/D.B.D'Oliveira, Worcestershire v Glamorgan	Abergavenny
256	D.I.Gower/R.A.Smith, Hampshire v Sussex	Southampton

Fourth Wicket
285	B.C.Broad/D.W.Randall, Nottinghamshire v Kent	Tunbridge Wells
263	P.A.De Silva/H.P.Tillekeratne, Sri Lankans v Hampshire	Southampton
258	S.G.Hinks/G.R.Cowdrey, Kent v Leicestershire	Leicester
256	C.J.Tavaré/R.J.Harden, Somerset v New Zealanders	Taunton

Sixth Wicket
226	D.B.D'Oliveira/S.J.Rhodes, Worcestershire v Lancashire	Manchester

Seventh Wicket
229	K.M.Curran/R.C.Russell, Gloucestershire v Somerset	Bristol

Eighth Wicket
205†	I.A.Greig/M.P.Bicknell, Surrey v Lancashire	The Oval

Ninth Wicket
183†	C.J.Tavaré/N.A.Mallender, Somerset v Sussex	Hove

Tenth Wicket
116	G.Yates/P.J.W.Allott, Lancashire v Nottinghamshire	Nottingham
107	G.Miller/S.J.Base, Derbyshire v Yorkshire	Chesterfield

† County record.

EIGHT OR MORE WICKETS IN AN INNINGS

| G.D.Harrison | 9-113 | Ireland v Scotland | Edinburgh |
| C.A.Walsh | 8-58 | Gloucestershire v Northamptonshire | Cheltenham |

TEN OR MORE WICKETS IN A MATCH (13)

C.E.L.Ambrose	12-155	Northamptonshire v Leicestershire	Leicester
J.G.Bracewell	12-227	New Zealanders v Combined Univs	Cambridge
R.P.Davis	10-142	Kent v Leicestershire	Dartford
N.A.Foster	11-76	Essex v Surrey	Chelmsford
M.Frost	10-82	Glamorgan v Gloucestershire	Bristol
D.A.Graveney	10-104	Gloucestershire v Sussex	Bristol
C.C.Lewis	10-119	Leicestershire v Glamorgan	Cardiff
M.D.Marshall (2)	10-107	Hampshire v Derbyshire	Portsmouth
	11-92	Hampshire v Glamorgan	Pontypridd
M.M.Patel	10-148	Kent v Leicestershire	Dartford
R.A.Pick	10-184	Nottinghamshire v Leicestershire	Leicester
C.A.Walsh	11-99	Gloucestershire v Northamptonshire	Cheltenham
Waqar Younis	11-128	Surrey v Warwickshire	The Oval

HAT-TRICKS

D.V.Lawrence	Gloucestershire v Nottinghamshire	Nottingham
S.M.McEwan	Worcestershire v Leicestershire	Leicester
P.A.Smith	Warwickshire v Sussex	Eastbourne

WICKET WITH FIRST BALL IN FIRST-CLASS CRICKET

| J.E.R.Gallian | Lancashire v Oxford University | Oxford |

SIX OR MORE WICKET-KEEPING DISMISSALS IN AN INNINGS

R.J.Blakey	(6 ct)	Yorkshire v Sussex	Eastbourne
C.P.Metson (2)	(6 ct)	Glamorgan v Hampshire	Southampton
	(6 ct)	Glamorgan v Warwickshire	Birmingham
P.A.Nixon	(5 ct, 1 st)	Leicestershire v Glamorgan	Hinckley
K.J.Piper	(5 ct, 1 st)	Warwickshire v Someret	Taunton

NINE OR MORE WICKET-KEEPING DISMISSALS IN A MATCH

| R.J.Blakey | (9 ct) | Yorkshire v Sussex | Eastbourne |

1000 RUNS AND 50 WICKETS

K.M.Curran	Gloucestershire	1267 runs and 64 wickets
A.I.C.Dodemaide	Sussex	1001 runs and 61 wickets
G.D.Rose	Somerset	1000 runs and 53 wickets

FIFTY EXTRAS IN AN INNINGS

B	LB	W	NB		
71	33	26	2	10	Nottinghamshire v Leicestershire	Leicester
56	15	26	11	4	Nottinghamshire v Worcestershire	Worcester
55	16	22	5	12	England v India (3rd Test)	The Oval
54	10	29	2	13	Northamptonshire v Essex	Chelmsford
50	11	12	9	18	Kent v Leicestershire	Leicester

HAYNES BOOSTS MIDDLESEX

Middlesex, thrice winners in the Eighties, won the first County Championship of the Nineties by the convincing margin of 31 points. They clinched the title 15 minutes before tea on the penultimate day of the most protracted first-class season of all time when they completed an innings victory over the wooden spoonists, Sussex.

Those Hove celebrations were the richly deserved reward for the coaching expertise of Don Bennett, the aggressive captaincy of Mike Gatting, the shrewd backing of his henchman John Emburey, and their magnificent support from the best balanced team in the country. The previous winter's lure of the rand proved vital to the Metropolitans' fortunes, ensuring as it did that Gatting and Emburey could not be poached by England.

Equally crucial was the contribution of Desmond Haynes. Apart from scoring 2,036 runs and launching the innings with a flying start more often than not, he proved to be a marvellous mentor and inspiration to the younger players. Mike Roseberry, Keith Brown and Mark Ramprakash all paid testimony to his influence; all enjoyed their most productive seasons, each exceeding 1,300 runs in the Britannic Assurance competition.

Philip Tufnell was the season's revelation. With his mane shorn and his approach moved nearer the stumps, he provided the perfect foil for Emburey and at last filled the void caused by the retirement of Phil Edmonds. No other spinning duo could rival their combined haul of 122 Championship wickets. Augmented by the quicker men – Angus Fraser, Neil Williams, Norman Cowans and the 1991 beneficiary, Simon Hughes – they provided an impressive attack. Their tally of ten victories was two more than any other side and their only defeat caused their victors, Derbyshire, to be fined 25 points for an imperfect pitch.

By late August the Championship was a two-horse race, with Essex four points ahead as they each faced their last three matches. Erratic Northamptonshire virtually settled the issue by winning the first of those encounters after amassing the highest total in their history for the second time in successive games – both against Essex. Then came the injury to Graham Gooch and the end of their aspirations. The loss of their captain for half the programme must have been a severe drain despite the unique spirit in their dressing room. Neil Foster (94) came closest to taking 100 wickets with the flat ball and Mark Waugh exceeded 2,000 runs. If four batsmen from the same county (Gooch, Waugh, Stephenson and Prichard) have ever before scored Championship double centuries in the same season, I have not managed to find them. Not even Middlesex in 1947 could equal that.

BRITANNIC ASSURANCE
COUNTY CHAMPIONSHIP 1990
FINAL TABLE

Win = 16 points

		P	W	L	D	Bonus Points Bat	Bonus Points Bowl	Total Points
1	MIDDLESEX (3)	22	10	1	11	73	55	288
2	Essex (2)	22	8	2	12	73	56	257
3	Hampshire (6)	22	8	4	10	67	48	243
4	Worcestershire (1)	22	7	1	14	70	58	240
5	Warwickshire (8)	22	7	7	8	55	64	231
6	Lancashire (4)	22	6	3	13	65	56	217
7	Leicestershire (13)	22	6	7	9	61	53	210
8	Glamorgan (17)	22	5	6	11	64	48	192
9	Surrey (12)	22	4	3	15	54	64	190
10	Yorkshire (16)	22	5	9	8	52	55	187
11	Northamptonshire (5)	22	4	9	9	61	60	185
12	Derbyshire (6)	22	6	7	9	58	52	181
13	Gloucestershire (9)	22	4	7	11	51	58	173
13	Nottinghamshire (11)	22	4	8	10	51	58	173
15	Somerset (14)	22	3	4	15	73	45	166
16	Kent (15)	22	3	6	13	69	35	152
17	Sussex (10)	22	3	9	10	51	44	143

1989 final positions are shown in brackets.

Surrey's total includes eight points for levelling the scores in a drawn match.
Derbyshire were penalised 25 points for a sub-standard pitch at Derby.

SCORING OF POINTS

(a) For a win, 16 points, plus any points scored in the first innings.

(b) In a tie, each side to score eight points, plus any points scored in the first innings.

(c) If the scores are equal in a drawn match, the side batting in the fourth innings to score eight points, plus any points scored in the first innings.

(d) **First Innings Points** (awarded only for performances **in the first 100 overs** of each first innings and retained whatever the result of the match).

    (i) A maximum of four batting points to be available as under:-

        150 to 199 runs — 1 point
        200 to 249 runs — 2 points
        250 to 299 runs — 3 points
        300 runs or over — 4 points

    (ii) A maximum of four bowling points to be available as under:-

        3 to 4 wickets taken — 1 point
        5 to 6 wickets taken — 2 points
        7 to 8 wickets taken — 3 points
        9 to 10 wickets taken — 4 points

(e) If play starts when less than eight hours playing time remains and a one innings match is played, no first innings points shall be scored. The side winning on the one innings to score 12 points.

(f) A County which is adjudged to have prepared a pitch unsuitable for First-Class Cricket shall be liable to have 25 points deducted from its aggregate of points under the procedure agreed by the TCCB in December 1988.

(g) The side which has the highest aggregate of points gained at the end of the season shall be the Champion County. Should any sides in the Championship table be equal on points, the side with most wins will have priority.

COUNTY CHAMPIONS

The English County Championship was not officially constituted until December 1889. Prior to that date there was no generally accepted method of awarding the title; although the 'least matches lost' method existed, it was not consistently applied. Rules governing playing qualifications were not agreed until 1873, and the first unofficial points system was not introduced until 1888.

Recent research has produced a list of champions dating back to 1826, but at least seven different versions exist for the period from 1864 to 1889 (see *The Wisden Book of Cricket Records*). Only from 1890 can any authorised list of county champions commence.

From 1977 to 1983 the Championship was sponsored by Schweppes. BRITANNIC ASSURANCE have been its benefactors since 1984.

1890	Surrey	1930	Lancashire	1970	Kent
1891	Surrey	1931	Yorkshire	1971	Surrey
1892	Surrey	1932	Yorkshire	1972	Warwickshire
1893	Yorkshire	1933	Yorkshire	1973	Hampshire
1894	Surrey	1934	Lancashire	1974	Worcestershire
1895	Surrey	1935	Yorkshire	1975	Leicestershire
1896	Yorkshire	1936	Derbyshire	1976	Middlesex
1897	Lancashire	1937	Yorkshire	1977	Kent / Middlesex
1898	Yorkshire	1938	Yorkshire		
1899	Surrey	1939	Yorkshire	1978	Kent
1900	Yorkshire	1946	Yorkshire	1979	Essex
1901	Yorkshire	1947	Middlesex	1980	Middlesex
1902	Yorkshire	1948	Glamorgan	1981	Nottinghamshire
1903	Middlesex	1949	Middlesex / Yorkshire	1982	Middlesex
1904	Lancashire			1983	Essex
1905	Yorkshire	1950	Lancashire / Surrey	1984	Essex
1906	Kent			1985	Middlesex
1907	Nottinghamshire	1951	Warwickshire	1986	Essex
1908	Yorkshire	1952	Surrey	1987	Nottinghamshire
1909	Kent	1953	Surrey	1988	Worcestershire
1910	Kent	1954	Surrey	1989	Worcestershire
1911	Warwickshire	1955	Surrey	1990	Middlesex
1912	Yorkshire	1956	Surrey		
1913	Kent	1957	Surrey		
1914	Surrey	1958	Surrey		
1919	Yorkshire	1959	Yorkshire		
1920	Middlesex	1960	Yorkshire		
1921	Middlesex	1961	Hampshire		
1922	Yorkshire	1962	Yorkshire		
1923	Yorkshire	1963	Yorkshire		
1924	Yorkshire	1964	Worcestershire		
1925	Yorkshire	1965	Worcestershire		
1926	Lancashire	1966	Yorkshire		
1927	Lancashire	1967	Yorkshire		
1928	Lancashire	1968	Yorkshire		
1929	Nottinghamshire	1969	Glamorgan		

LANCASHIRE'S UNIQUE DOUBLE

Lancashire's victory over Northamptonshire in this tenth NatWest Trophy final was achieved by the emphatic margin of seven wickets; a humiliation made more withering by a little matter of 14.2 unused overs. The county of the red rose thus became not only the first to win both Lord's finals in the same season but, added to their four Gillette Cup triumphs, the first to win five September finals.

It was no coincidence that their veteran captain, David Hughes, has featured in all those five matches. His role of specialist guru-cum-motivator who is rarely required to bat or bowl could be accommodated only in a side bursting with talented specialists and all-rounders. His new two-year contract, with another testimonial in 1992, is well merited.

Once Allan Lamb had completed a full hand of lost tosses in the 1990 NatWest competition, a damp pitch dictated the course of this 60-over final. Sadly for the crowd's entertainment, the adjudicator's task was greatly simplified by a devastating spell of seam bowling by Phillip DeFreitas. Using the conditions superbly to gain sharp lateral movement and occasionally awkward bounce, he removed the first five batsmen for 15 runs in 35 balls. Only Joel Garner, with 6 for 29 in 1979, has surpassed the Lancashire bowler's 5 for 26 in these finals.

Although David Capel, ignoring medical advice and the pain of a double fracture to his left little finger, led a brave rearguard action for 39 overs, the eventual total of 171 was unlikely to challenge Lancashire's lengthy batting list. It might have done if Curtly Ambrose had not nullified his valiant innings of 48 by muffing a simple mid-on catch when Neil Fairbrother had scored just 6. While Michael Atherton relished the role of anchorman, Fairbrother pulled and drove his way to a 49-ball fifty, saluting all corners of the ground with arms and bat aloft like the Bradman take-off in *Bodyline*.

Perhaps NatWest, having agreed to continue their sponsorship for three years with an option on a further two, should propose a rise in over rates so that the dreaded 10.30am start becomes unnecessary.

GILLETTE CUP WINNERS

1963	Sussex	1969	Yorkshire	1975	Lancashire
1964	Sussex	1970	Lancashire	1976	Northamptonshire
1965	Yorkshire	1971	Lancashire	1977	Middlesex
1966	Warwickshire	1972	Lancashire	1978	Sussex
1967	Kent	1973	Gloucestershire	1979	Somerset
1968	Warwickshire	1974	Kent	1980	Middlesex

NATWEST BANK TROPHY WINNERS

1981	Derbyshire	1985	Essex	1989	Warwickshire
1982	Surrey	1986	Sussex	1990	Lancashire
1983	Somerset	1987	Nottinghamshire		
1984	Middlesex	1988	Middlesex		

1990 NATWEST TROPHY FINAL

LANCASHIRE v NORTHAMPTONSHIRE

Played at Lord's, London, on 1 September.
Toss: Lancashire. Result: LANCASHIRE won by 7 wickets.
Match Award: P.A.J.DeFreitas (adjudicator: F.S.Trueman).

NORTHAMPTONSHIRE	Runs	Mins	Balls	6s	4s	Fall
A.Fordham lbw b DeFreitas	5	24	15	–	1	2-19
N.A.Felton c Allott b DeFreitas	4	6	4	–	1	1-8
W.Larkins c Hegg b DeFreitas	7	25	24	–	–	3-20
*A.J.Lamb lbw b DeFreitas	8	33	17	–	1	5-39
R.J.Bailey c Hegg b DeFreitas	7	17	15	–	1	4-38
D.J.Capel run out (Allott)	36	152	100	–	5	8-126
R.G.Williams b Watkinson	9	22	14	–	2	6-56
†D.Ripley b Watkinson	13	64	60	–	2	7-87
C.E.L.Ambrose run out (Wasim Akram)	48	89	94	–	5	9-166
N.G.B.Cook b Austin	9	38	17	–	–	10-171
M.A.Robinson not out	3	4	3	–	–	
Extras (B1, LB10, W9, NB2)	22					
Total (60 overs; 247 minutes)	171					

LANCASHIRE	Runs	Mins	Balls	6s	4s	Fall
G.D.Mendis c Ripley b Capel	14	63	62	–	–	2-28
G.Fowler c Cook b Robinson	7	37	26	–	–	1-16
M.A.Atherton not out	38	132	103	–	5	
N.H.Fairbrother c Ambrose b Williams	81	89	68	2	9	3-142
M.Watkinson not out	24	15	18	2	2	
*D.P.Hughes						
Wasim Akram						
P.A.J.DeFreitas ⎫						
†W.K.Hegg ⎬ did not bat						
I.D.Austin						
P.J.W.Allott ⎭						
Extras (LB4, W2, NB3)	9					
Total (45.4 overs; 171 minutes)	173-3					

LANCASHIRE	O	M	R	W
Allott	12	3	29	0
DeFreitas	12	5	26	5
Wasim Akram	12	0	35	0
Watkinson	12	1	29	2
Austin	12	4	41	1
NORTHAMPTONSHIRE				
Ambrose	10	1	23	0
Robinson	9	2	26	1
Cook	10.4	2	50	0
Capel	9	0	44	1
Williams	7	0	26	1

Umpires: J.W.Holder and D.R.Shepherd.

THE NATWEST BANK TROPHY 1990

FIRST ROUND 27, 28 June	SECOND ROUND 11 July	QUARTER-FINALS 1 August	SEMI-FINALS 15, 17 August	FINAL 1 September
DERBYSHIRE†	Derbyshire†			
Shropshire		LANCASHIRE†		
LANCASHIRE†	LANCASHIRE			
Durham			LANCASHIRE†	
GLOUCESTERSHIRE†	GLOUCESTERSHIRE†			
Lincolnshire		Gloucestershire (£3,000)		
Oxfordshire†	Kent			LANCASHIRE (£24,000)
KENT				
Berkshire	MIDDLESEX†			
MIDDLESEX†		MIDDLESEX†		
Wiltshire†	Surrey			
SURREY			Middlesex (£6,000)	
Dorset	GLAMORGAN†			
GLAMORGAN†		Glamorgan (£3,000)		
Ireland†	Sussex			
SUSSEX				
Staffordshire	NORTHAMPTONSHIRE†			
NORTHAMPTONSHIRE†		NORTHAMPTONSHIRE†		
Buckinghamshire†	Nottinghamshire			
NOTTINGHAMSHIRE			NORTHAMPTONSHIRE	
Devon†	Somerset†			
SOMERSET		Worcestershire (£3,000)		Northamptonshire (£12,000)
Suffolk†	WORCESTERSHIRE			
WORCESTERSHIRE				
Hertfordshire†	Warwickshire			
WARWICKSHIRE		Yorkshire (£3,000)		
Norfolk	YORKSHIRE†			
YORKSHIRE†			Hampshire (£6,000)	
Scotland	Essex†			
ESSEX†		HAMPSHIRE†		
Leicestershire†	HAMPSHIRE			
HAMPSHIRE				

†Home team.   Winning teams are in capitals. Amounts in brackets show prize-money won by that county.

Congratulations Lancashire on winning the 1990 NatWest Trophy

NATWEST BANK TROPHY
PRINCIPAL RECORDS 1963–1990
(Including The Gillette Cup)

Highest Total	413-4	Somerset v Devon	Torquay	1990
Highest Total in a Final	317-4	Yorkshire v Surrey	Lord's	1965
Highest Total by a Minor County	261-8	Dorset v Glam	Swansea	1990
Highest Total Batting Second	326-9	Hampshire v Leics	Leicester	1987
Highest Total to Win Batting 2nd	307-5	Hampshire v Essex	Chelmsford	1990
Lowest Total	39	Ireland v Sussex	Hove	1985
Lowest Total in a Final	118	Lancashire v Kent	Lord's	1974
Lowest Total to Win Batting First	98	Worcs v Durham	Chester-le-St	1968
Highest Score	206 A.I.Kallicharran	Warwicks v Oxon	Birmingham	1984
HS (Minor County)	132 G.Robinson	Lincs v Northumb	Jesmond	1971
Hundreds	191 have been scored in GC (93) and NWT (98) matches			
Fastest Hundred	36 balls – G.D.Rose	Somerset v Devon	Torquay	1990

Highest Partnerships for each Wicket

1st	242*	M.D.Moxon/A.A.Metcalfe	Yorks v Warwicks	Leeds	1990
2nd	286	I.S.Anderson/A.Hill	Derbys v Cornwall	Derby	1986
3rd	209	P.Willey/D.I.Gower	Leics v Ireland	Leicester	1986
4th	234*	D.Lloyd/C.H.Lloyd	Lancs v Glos	Manchester	1978
5th	166	M.A.Lynch/G.R.J.Roope	Surrey v Durham	The Oval	1982
6th	105	G.St A.Sobers/R.A.White	Notts v Worcs	Worcester	1974
7th	160*	C.J.Richards/I.R.Payne	Surrey v Lincs	Sleaford	1983
8th	83	S.N.V.Waterton/D.A.Hale	Oxon v Glos	Oxford	1989
9th	87	M.A.Nash/A.E.Cordle	Glamorgan v Lincs	Swansea	1974
10th	81	S.Turner/R.E.East	Essex v Yorkshire	Leeds	1982

Best Bowling

8-21	M.A.Holding	Derbys v Sussex	Hove	1988
8-31	D.L.Underwood	Kent v Scotland	Edinburgh	1987
7-15	A.L.Dixon	Kent v Surrey	The Oval	1967
7-15	R.P.Lefebvre	Somerset v Devon	Torquay	1990
7-30	P.J.Sainsbury	Hants v Norfolk	Southampton	1965
7-32	S.P.Davis	Durham v Lancs	Chester-le-St	1983
7-33	R.D.Jackman	Surrey v Yorkshire	Harrogate	1970
7-37	N.A.Mallender	Northants v Worcs	Northampton	1984

Hat-Tricks

J.D.F.Larter	Northants v Sussex	Northampton	1963
D.A.D.Sydenham	Surrey v Cheshire	Hoylake	1964
R.N.S.Hobbs	Essex v Middlesex	Lord's	1968
N.M.McVicker	Warwicks v Lincs	Birmingham	1971
G.S.Le Roux	Sussex v Ireland	Hove	1985
M.Jean-Jacques	Derbyshire v Notts	Derby	1987
J.F.M.O'Brien	Cheshire v Derbys	Chester	1988

Most Wicket-Keeping Dismissals

6 (5 ct, 1 st)	R.W.Taylor	Derbys v Essex	Derby	1981
6 (4 ct, 2 st)	T.Davies	Glamorgan v Staffs	Stone	1986

Most Catches in the Field

4	A.S.Brown	Glos v Middlesex	Bristol	1963
4	G.Cook	Northants v Glam	Northampton	1972
4	C.G.Greenidge	Hants v Cheshire	Southampton	1981
4	D.C.Jackson	Durham v Northants	Darlington	1984
4	T.S.Smith	Herts v Somerset	St Albans	1984
4	H.Morris	Glam v Scotland	Edinburgh	1988

Most Match Awards: 8 – C.H.Lloyd (Lancs); 7 – G.A.Gooch (Essex), Imran Khan (Worcs/Sussex), C.L.Smith (Hants), P.Willey (Northants/Leics), B.Wood (Lancs/Cheshire).

1990 BENSON AND HEDGES CUP FINAL

LANCASHIRE v WORCESTERSHIRE

Played at Lord's, London, on 14 July.
Toss: Worcestershire. Result: LANCASHIRE won by 69 runs.
Match Award: M. Watkinson (adjudicator: R.B.Simpson).

LANCASHIRE	Runs	Mins	Balls	6s	4s	Fall
G.D.Mendis c Neale b Botham	19	36	31	–	2	1-27
G.Fowler c Neale b Newport	11	24	17	–	2	2-33
M.A.Atherton run out (Lampitt)	40	123	105	–	1	4-135
N.H.Fairbrother b Lampitt	11	25	19	–	2	3-47
M.Watkinson c and b Botham	50	87	79	–	7	5-136
Wasim Akram c Radford b Newport	28	33	21	2	1	6-191
P.A.J.DeFreitas b Lampitt	28	36	30	–	2	7-199
I.D.Austin run out (Rhodes)	17	19	12	–	2	8-231
†W.K.Hegg not out	31	18	17	1	3	
*D.P.Hughes not out	1	3	2	–	–	
P.J.W.Allott did not bat						
Extras (LB4, NB1)	5					
Total (55 overs; 209 minutes)	241-8 closed					

WORCESTERSHIRE	Runs	Mins	Balls	6s	4s	Fall
T.S.Curtis c Hegg b Wasim	16	52	52	–	1	1-27
M.J.Weston b Watkinson	19	75	43	–	2	3-41
G.A.Hick c Hegg b Wasim	1	16	12	–	–	2-38
D.B.D'Oliveira b Watkinson	23	50	45	–	1	4-81
I.T.Botham b DeFreitas	38	92	73	–	3	7-114
*P.A.Neale b Austin	0	5	5	–	–	5-87
†S.J.Rhodes lbw b Allott	5	34	21	–	–	6-112
N.V.Radford not out	26	56	40	–	1	
R.K.Illingworth lbw b DeFreitas	16	31	21	–	–	8-154
P.J.Newport b Wasim	3	10	12	–	–	9-164
S.R.Lampitt b Austin	4	5	6	–	1	10-172
Extras (LB9, W8, NB4)	21					
Total (54 overs; 221 minutes)	172					

WORCESTERSHIRE	O	M	R	W
Newport	11	1	47	2
Botham	11	0	49	2
Lampitt	11	3	43	2
Radford	8	1	41	0
Illingworth	11	0	41	0
Hick	3	0	16	0
LANCASHIRE				
Allott	10	1	22	1
DeFreitas	11	2	30	2
Wasim	11	0	30	3
Watkinson	11	0	37	2
Austin	11	1	44	2

Umpires: J.H.Hampshire and N.T.Plews.

1990 BENSON AND HEDGES CUP

ZONAL POINTS TABLE

	P	W	L	NR	Pts	Run Rate
GROUP A						
WORCESTERSHIRE	4	3	1	–	6	72.77
GLAMORGAN	4	3	1	–	6	69.46
Kent	4	2	1	1	5	71.71
Warwickshire	4	1	3	–	2	63.58
Gloucestershire	4	–	3	1	1	67.77
GROUP B						
SOMERSET	4	3	1	–	6	85.46
MIDDLESEX	4	3	1	–	6	74.86
Derbyshire	4	2	2	–	4	77.34
Sussex	4	2	2	–	4	78.94
Minor Counties	4	0	4	–	0	66.43
GROUP C						
LANCASHIRE	4	3	–	1	7	67.84
SURREY	4	2	2	–	4	75.30
Yorkshire	4	2	2	–	4	62.08
Hampshire	4	1	2	1	3	75.45
Combined Universities	4	1	3	–	2	61.91
GROUP D						
ESSEX	4	3	–	1	7	82.35
NOTTINGHAMSHIRE	4	3	1	–	6	63.44
Leicestershire	4	1	2	1	3	62.33
Scotland	4	1	3	–	2	66.66
Northamptonshire	4	1	3	–	2	60.60

FINAL ROUNDS

QUARTER-FINALS 30 May	SEMI-FINALS 13 June	FINAL 14 July
WORCESTERSHIRE† Glamorgan (£3,000)	WORCESTERSHIRE	Worcestershire (£12,000)
Essex† NOTTINGHAMSHIRE (£3,000)	Nottinghamshire† (£6,000)	
LANCASHIRE† Surrey (£3,000)	LANCASHIRE†	LANCASHIRE (£24,000)
SOMERSET† Middlesex (£3,000)	Somerset (£6,000)	

†Home team.   Winning teams are in capitals.   Prize-money in brackets.

BENSON AND HEDGES CUP
PRINCIPAL RECORDS 1972–1990

Highest Total		350-3	Essex v Comb Univs	Chelmsford	1979
Highest Total Batting Second } **Highest Losing Total**		303-7	Derbys v Somerset	Taunton	1990
Lowest Total		56	Leics v Minor C	Wellington	1982
Highest Score	198* G.A.Gooch		Essex v Sussex	Hove	1982
Hundreds	188 have been scored in Benson and Hedges Cup matches				
Fastest Hundred	62 min – M.A.Nash		Glamorgan v Hants	Swansea	1976

Highest Partnerships for each Wicket

1st	252	V.P.Terry/C.L.Smith	Hants v Comb Us	Southampton	1990
2nd	285*	C.G.Greenidge/D.R.Turner	Hants v Minor C (S)	Amersham	1973
3rd	269*	P.M.Roebuck/M.D.Crowe	Somerset v Hants	Southampton	1987
4th	184*	D.Lloyd/B.W.Reidy	Lancashire v Derbys	Chesterfield	1980
5th	160	A.J.Lamb/D.J.Capel	Northants v Leics	Northampton	1986
6th	121	P.A.Neale/S.J.Rhodes	Worcs v Yorkshire	Worcester	1988
7th	149*	J.D.Love/C.M.Old	Yorks v Scotland	Bradford	1981
8th	109	R.E.East/N.Smith	Essex v Northants	Chelmsford	1977
9th	83	P.G.Newman/M.A.Holding	Derbyshire v Notts	Nottingham	1985
10th	80*	D.L.Bairstow/M.Johnson	Yorkshire v Derbys	Derby	1981

Most Wickets	7-12 W.W.Daniel	Middx v Minor C (E)	Ipswich	1978
	7-22 J.R.Thomson	Middx v Hampshire	Lord's	1981
	7-32 R.G.D.Willis	Warwicks v Yorks	Birmingham	1981

Hat-Tricks	G.D.McKenzie	Leics v Worcs	Worcester	1972
	K.Higgs	Leics v Surrey	Lord's	1974
	A.A.Jones	Middlesex v Essex	Lord's	1977
	M.J.Procter	Glos v Hampshire	Southampton	1977
	W.Larkins	Northants v Comb Us	Northampton	1980
	E.A.Moseley	Glamorgan v Kent	Cardiff	1981
	G.C.Small	Warwicks v Leics	Leicester	1984
	N.A.Mallender	Somerset v Comb Us	Taunton	1987
	W.K.M.Benjamin	Leics v Notts	Leicester	1987
	A.R.C.Fraser	Middx v Sussex	Lord's	1988

Most Wicket-Keeping Dismissals

8 (8ct)	D.J.S.Taylor	Somerset v Comb Us	Taunton	1982

Most Catches in the Field

5	V.J.Marks	Comb Us v Kent	Oxford	1976

Most Match Awards: 18 G A Gooch (Essex); 11 T E Jesty (Hants/Surrey/Lancs), B.Wood (Lancs/Derbys); 10 J.C.Balderstone (Leics), M.W Gatting (Middx).

BENSON AND HEDGES CUP WINNERS

1972	Leicestershire	1979	Essex	1986	Middlesex
1973	Kent	1980	Northamptonshire	1987	Yorkshire
1974	Surrey	1981	Somerset	1988	Hampshire
1975	Leicestershire	1982	Somerset	1989	Nottinghamshire
1976	Kent	1983	Middlesex	1990	Lancashire
1977	Gloucestershire	1984	Lancashire		
1978	Kent	1985	Leicestershire		

REFUGE ASSURANCE LEAGUE 1990
FINAL TABLE

		P	W	L	NR	Pts	Away Wins	Runs/ 100 bl
1	**DERBYSHIRE** (5)	16	12	3	1	50	6	87.35
2	Lancashire (1)	16	11	3	2	48	7	100.18
3	Middlesex (9)	16	10	5	1	42	5	95.40
4	Nottinghamshire (4)	16	10	5	1	42	4	89.31
5	Hampshire (6)	16	9	5	2	40	4	88.82
6	Yorkshire (11)	16	9	6	1	38	4	83.60
	Surrey (6)	16	9	6	1	38	3	90.39
8	Somerset (10)	16	8	8	–	32	4	91.25
	Gloucestershire (16)	16	7	7	2	32	2	87.80
10	Worcestershire (2)	16	7	8	1	30	4	84.96
	Kent (11)	16	7	8	1	30	3	85.94
12	Essex (3)	16	6	9	1	26	3	90.56
13	Sussex (11)	16	5	9	2	24	2	85.90
14	Warwickshire (14)	16	5	10	1	22	2	80.69
15	Glamorgan (16)	16	4	11	1	18	2	84.20
	Leicestershire (14)	16	4	11	1	18	1	76.59
17	Northamptonshire (6)	16	3	12	1	14	1	86.40

1989 final positions are shown in brackets.

When two or more counties finish with an equal number of points, the first four places are decided by (a) most wins, (b) most away wins, (c) runs per 100 balls.

The top four counties qualified for the Refuge Assurance Cup semi-finals.

REFUGE ASSURANCE CUP

SEMI-FINALS (5 September)

DERBYSHIRE beat Nottinghamshire by 22 runs at Derby.
MIDDLESEX beat Lancashire by 45 runs at Manchester.

FINAL (16 September)

MIDDLESEX beat Derbyshire by 5 wickets at Birmingham.

JOHN PLAYER LEAGUE CHAMPIONS

1969	Lancashire	1975	Hampshire	1981	Essex
1970	Lancashire	1976	Kent	1982	Sussex
1971	Worcestershire	1977	Leicestershire	1983	Yorkshire
1972	Kent	1978	Hampshire	1984	Essex
1973	Kent	1979	Somerset	1985	Essex
1974	Leicestershire	1980	Warwickshire	1986	Hampshire

REFUGE ASSURANCE LEAGUE CHAMPIONS

1987	Worcestershire	1989	Lancashire	1990	Derbyshire
1988	Worcestershire				

REFUGE ASSURANCE LEAGUE

PRINCIPAL RECORDS 1969–1990
(Including the John Player League)

Highest Total	360-3	Somerset v Glam	Neath	1990
Highest Total Batting Second	301-6	Warwicks v Essex	Colchester	1982
Lowest Total	23	Middlesex v Yorks	Leeds	1974
Highest Score 176	G.A.Gooch	Essex v Glamorgan	Southend	1983
Hundreds	368 have been scored in Sunday League matches			
Fastest Hundred 46 balls	G.D.Rose	Somerset v Glam	Neath	1990

Highest Partnerships for each Wicket

1st 239	G.A.Gooch/B.R.Hardie	Essex v Notts	Nottingham	1985
2nd 273	G.A.Gooch/K.S.McEwan	Essex v Notts	Nottingham	1983
3rd 223	S.J.Cook/G.D.Rose	Somerset v Glam	Neath	1990
4th 219	C.G.Greenidge/C.L.Smith	Hampshire v Surrey	Southampton	1987
5th 185*	Asif Din/B.M.McMillan	Warwicks v Essex	Chelmsford	1986
6th 121	C.P.Wilkins/A.J.Borrington	Derbys v Warwicks	Chesterfield	1972
7th 132	K.R.Brown/N.F.Williams	Middx v Somerset	Lord's	1988
8th 95*	D.Breakwell/K.F.Jennings	Somerset v Notts	Nottingham	1976
9th 105	D.G.Moir/R.W.Taylor	Derbyshire v Kent	Derby	1984
10th 57	D.A.Graveney/J.B.Mortimore	Glos v Lancashire	Tewkesbury	1973

Most Wickets	8-26	K.D.Boyce	Essex v Lancashire	Manchester	1971
	7-15	R.A.Hutton	Yorkshire v Worcs	Leeds	1969
	7-39	A.Hodgson	Northants v Somerset	Northampton	1976
	7-41	A.N.Jones	Sussex v Notts	Nottingham	1986

Four Wkts in Four Balls A.Ward   Derbyshire v Sussex   Derby   1970

Hat-Tricks (19): Derbyshire – A.Ward (1970), C.J.Tunnicliffe (1979); Essex – K.D.Boyce (1971); Glamorgan – M.A.Nash (1975), A.E.Cordle (1979), G.C.Holmes (1987); Gloucestershire – K.M.Curran (1989); Hampshire – J.M.Rice (1975), M.D.Marshall (1981); Kent – R.M.Ellison (1983); Leicestershire – G.D.McKenzie (1972); Northamptonshire – A.Hodgson (1976); Nottinghamshire – K.Saxelby (1987); Somerset – R.Palmer (1970), I.V.A.Richards (1982); Sussex – A.Buss (1974); Warwickshire – R.G.D.Willis (1973), W.Blenkiron (1974); Yorkshire – P.W.Jarvis (1982).

Most Economical Analysis

O	M	R	W				
8	8	0	0	B.A.Langford	Somerset v Essex	Yeovil	1969

Most Expensive Analyses

O	M	R	W				
7.5	0	89	3	G.Miller	Derbys v Glos	Gloucester	1984
8	0	88	1	E.E.Hemmings	Notts v Somerset	Nottingham	1983

Most Wicket-Keeping Dismissals

7 (6 ct, 1 st)   R.W.Taylor   Derbyshire v Lancs Manchester   1975

Most Catches in the Field

5   J.M.Rice   Hants v Warwicks Southampton 1978

MINOR COUNTIES CHAMPIONSHIP 1990

FINAL TABLE

		Played	Won	Lost	Won 1st Inns	Tied 1st Inns	Lost 1st Inns	No Result	Bonus Points	Total Points
EASTERN DIVISION										
Hertfordshire	NW	9	3	2a	3	–	1	–	34	77
Lincolnshire	NW	9	2	2a	2	–	3	–	36	68
Staffordshire	NW	9	3	1	2	–	2	1	24	65
Bedfordshire	NW	9	3	1	2	–	2	1	22	63
Durham	NW	9	1	–	6	–	2	–	33	63
Norfolk	NW	9	2	1	1	–	5	–	33	61
Cambridgeshire	NW	9	1	2a	3	1	2	–	31	57
Suffolk		9	2	3a	1	–	3	–	24	53
Cumberland		9	–	2	5	1	1	–	30	48
Northumberland		9	–	3a	1	–	5	–	23	34
WESTERN DIVISION										
Berkshire	NW	9	3	1c	3	–	2	–	26	69
Oxfordshire	NW	9	2	1a	4	–	2	–	26	63
Shropshire	NW	9	2	–	4	–	3	–	25	60
Buckinghamshire	NW	9	2	–	4	–	3	–	25	60
Dorset	NW	9	2	3b	–	–	4	–	27	57
Devon	NW	9	–	1a	7	–	1	–	32	57
Wiltshire		9	1	3b	3	–	1	1	24	53
Wales		9	1	2	1	–	5	–	28	46
Cheshire		9	1	–	2	–	5	1	16	40
Cornwall		9	1	4	1	–	3	–	17	33

a   1st innings points in 1 match lost.
b   1st innings points in 2 matches lost.
c   tie on 1st innings in 1 match lost.
NW Qualified for the 1991 NatWest Trophy.

Where points are equal, priority is given to the County winning the greater number of completed matches. Where this number also is equal, priority is decided according to the nett batting averages.

1990 CHAMPIONSHIP FINAL

Played at Wardown Park, Luton, on 9 September.
Toss: Hertfordshire. Result: HERTFORDSHIRE won by 7 wickets.

BERKSHIRE

M.G.Lickley	c Ligertwood b Merry	15
G.E.Loveday	c Ligertwood b Smith	42
G.T.Headley	not out	50
D.J.M.Mercer	c and b Smith	0
*M.L.Simmons	run out	6
P.J.Oxley	c MacLaurin b Surridge	31
T.P.Todd	not out	3
M.G.Stear		
†M.E.Stevens	did not bat	
J.H.Jones		
P.J.Lewington		
Extras	(B1, LB16, W5, NB2)	24
Total	(55 overs; 5 wickets)	171

HERTFORDSHIRE

N.P.G.Wright	c Stevens b Jones	45
J.D.Carr	c Simmons b Jones	16
A.Needham	c Oxley b Lewington	29
N.R.C.MacLaurin	not out	52
B.G.Evans	not out	18
†D.G.Ligertwood		
D.M.Smith		
E.P.Neal	did not bat	
W.G.Merry		
*D.Surridge		
G.A.R.Harris		
Extras	(B4, LB5, W2, NB1)	12
Total	(52.5 overs; 3 wickets)	172

HERTFORDSHIRE	O	M	R	W	FALL OF WICKETS		
Harris	10	1	36	0	*Wkt*	*B*	*H*
Merry	11	2	36	1	1st	25	23
Neal	2	0	12	0	2nd	88	81
Surridge	10	1	31	1	3rd	88	118
Needham	11	3	24	0	4th	97	–
Smith	11	3	15	2	5th	167	–
BERKSHIRE					6th	–	–
Jones	10.5	3	35	2	7th	–	–
Headley	5	3	10	0	8th	–	–
Stear	10	2	31	0	9th	–	–
Dodd	7	1	30	0	10th	–	–
Lewington	11	3	30	1			
Oxley	9	0	27	0			

Umpires: P.Adams and T.V.Wilkins.

MINOR COUNTIES CHAMPIONS

1895	Norfolk	1926	Durham	1962	Warwickshire II
	Durham	1927	Staffordshire	1963	Cambridgeshire
	Worcestershire	1928	Berkshire	1964	Lancashire II
1896	Worcestershire	1929	Oxfordshire	1965	Somerset II
1897	Worcestershire	1930	Durham	1966	Lincolnshire
1898	Worcestershire	1931	Leicestershire II	1967	Cheshire
1899	Northamptonshire	1932	Buckinghamshire	1968	Yorkshire II
	Buckinghamshire	1933	Undecided	1969	Buckinghamshire
	Glamorgan	1934	Lancashire II	1970	Bedfordshire
1900	Durham	1935	Middlesex II	1971	Yorkshire II
	Northamptonshire	1936	Hertfordshire	1972	Bedfordshire
1901	Durham	1937	Lancashire II	1973	Shropshire
1902	Wiltshire	1938	Buckinghamshire	1974	Oxfordshire
1903	Northamptonshire	1939	Surrey II	1975	Hertfordshire
1904	Northamptonshire	1946	Suffolk	1976	Durham
1905	Norfolk	1947	Yorkshire II	1977	Suffolk
1906	Staffordshire	1948	Lancashire II	1978	Devon
1907	Lancashire II	1949	Lancashire II	1979	Suffolk
1908	Staffordshire	1950	Surrey II	1980	Durham
1909	Wiltshire	1951	Kent II	1981	Durham
1910	Norfolk	1952	Buckinghamshire	1982	Oxfordshire
1911	Staffordshire	1953	Berkshire	1983	Hertfordshire
1912	In abeyance	1954	Surrey II	1984	Durham
1913	Norfolk	1955	Surrey II	1985	Cheshire
1920	Staffordshire	1956	Kent II	1986	Cumberland
1921	Staffordshire	1957	Yorkshire II	1987	Buckinghamshire
1922	Buckinghamshire	1958	Yorkshire II	1988	Cheshire
1923	Buckinghamshire	1959	Warwickshire II	1989	Oxfordshire
1924	Berkshire	1960	Lancashire II	1990	Hertfordshire
1925	Buckinghamshire	1961	Somerset II		

1990 MINOR COUNTIES CHAMPIONSHIP

LEADING BATTING AVERAGES
(Qualifications: 8 innings, average 37.00)

		I	NO	HS	Runs	Avge
J.Abrahams	Shropshire	13	4	113*	765	85.00
M.R.Davies	Shropshire	15	7	114*	628	78.50
A.Needham	Herts	13	2	130*	750	68.18
P.Burn	Durham	13	4	105	582	64.66
M.G.Lickley	Berkshire	16	3	122*	838	64.46
A.S.Patel	Durham	12	4	103*	512	64.00
D.R.Turner	Wiltshire	17	3	125*	887	63.35
S.N.V.Waterton	Oxon	17	3	123*	883	63.07
G.W.Ecclestone	Cambs	10	2	111	487	60.87
G.K.Brown	Durham	11	4	110*	417	59.57
D.Cartledge	Staffs	13	2	141*	626	56.90
M.J.Roberts	Bucks	18	1	124	921	54.17
K.N.Foyle	Wiltshire	11	4	87*	373	53.28
S.T.Crawley	Cheshire	17	4	107	671	51.61
I.Cockbain	Cheshire	12	0	106	590	49.16
S.J.Dean	Staffs	14	2	101*	587	48.91
R.Swann	Beds	14	2	135*	584	48.66
B.G.Evans	Herts	9	3	113*	292	48.66

		I	NO	HS	Runs	Avge
N.J.C.Gandon	Lincs	14	4	103	476	47.60
J.A.Claughton	Dorset	10	4	81	283	47.16
S.Burrow	Bucks	17	1	86	743	46.44
M.P.Briers	Beds	10	0	124	451	45.10
N.A.Riddell	Durham	9	2	92	314	44.85
N.J.Archer	Staffs	8	3	58*	224	44.80
A.J.Pugh	Devon	16	3	100*	582	44.76
J.A.Benn	N'land	18	1	129	760	44.70
J.Foster	Shropshire	14	2	123*	533	44.41
N.P.G.Wright	Herts	13	2	113	486	44.18
K.G.Rice	Devon	14	2	93*	528	44.00
J.R.Moyes	C'land	13	3	137	437	43.70
T.A.Lester	Oxon	16	5	98*	471	42.81
T.Parton	Shropshire	16	4	119	506	42.16
R.A.Milne	Cambs	11	1	134*	421	42.10
N.A.Folland	Devon	16	3	109*	542	41.69
J.D.Love	Lincs	14	1	103*	537	41.30
S.M.Clements	Suffolk	14	2	137	483	40.25
G.S.Calway	Dorset	18	0	121	721	40.05
P.A.C.Bail	Wiltshire	11	0	119	437	39.72
A.C.Puddle	Wales	18	5	100*	512	39.38
G.E.Loveday	Berkshire	16	0	110	626	39.12
D.B.Storer	Lincs	15	2	100	497	38.23
K.J.C.Thomas	Cornwall	12	1	108*	414	37.63
C.J.Rogers	Norfolk	15	2	75	487	37.46
T.J.A.Scriven	Bucks	16	4	79*	445	37.08

LEADING BOWLING AVERAGES
(Qualifications: 20 wickets, average 30.00)

		O	M	R	W	Avge
A.S.Patel	Durham	119.5	35	318	21	15.14
D.Surridge	Herts	224.4	69	488	29	16.82
S.Turner	Cambs	286.5	79	727	40	18.17
A.C.Jelfs	Lincs	158.5	36	488	25	19.52
P.J.Kippax	Durham	220.4	75	531	26	20.42
N.R.Taylor	Dorset	165	39	497	24	20.70
A.Greasley	Cheshire	140.1	32	471	22	21.40
I.L.Pont	Lincs	150.5	26	569	26	21.88
G.Edmunds	Shropshire	270.4	68	807	36	22.41
J.H.Shackleton	Dorset	290.3	78	759	33	23.00
R.A.Evans	Oxon	258.5	71	713	31	23.00
K.A.Arnold	Oxon	267.1	67	767	33	23.24
M.D.Woods	C'land	242.1	83	704	30	23.46
S.Burrow	Bucks	194	34	648	27	24.00
D.J.Makinson	C'land	267.2	69	700	29	24.13
R.Kingshott	Norfolk	279.4	69	878	35	25.08
A.Akhtar	Cambs	208.3	55	579	23	25.17
J.P.Taylor	Staffs	280.3	66	811	32	25.34
A.Smith	Wales	187.2	46	584	23	25.39
C.Stone	Dorset	221.5	46	664	26	25.53
J.C.M.Lewis	Norfolk	189	30	703	27	26.03
J.Abrahams	Shropshire	168.5	35	610	23	26.52
M.C.Woodman	Devon	286	68	784	29	27.03
I.J.Curtis	Oxon	197.1	49	641	23	27.86
C.C.Lovell	Cornwall	175.3	18	732	25	29.28
T.J.A.Scriven	Bucks	200	45	706	24	29.41

SECOND XI CHAMPIONSHIP 1990
RAPID CRICKETLINE FINAL TABLE

	P	W	L	D	T	Bonus Points Bat	Bowl	Total Points
1 SUSSEX (14)	16	9	1	6	–	45	39	228
2 Glamorgan (10)	16	7	3	6	–	34	56	202
3 Surrey (16)	16	5	1	9	1	40	54	182
4 Nottinghamshire (7)	16	6	4	6	–	32	53	181
5 Kent (3)	16	5	2	9	–	43	46	169
6 Middlesex (1)	16	4	3	9	–	45	43	152
7 Warwickshire (2)	16	4	3	9	–	39	46	149
8 Lancashire (15)	16	3	5	8	–	43	48	139
9 Essex (12)	16	3	3	10	–	39	49	136
10 Worcestershire (17)	16	2	3	10	1	43	51	134
11 Hampshire (6)	16	2	5	9	–	45	44	129
12 Northamptonshire (5)	16	3	4	9	–	40	35	123
13 Derbyshire (4)	16	2	8	6	–	33	44	109
14 Gloucestershire (11)	16	2	5	9	–	33	36	101
15 Somerset (13)	16	1	2	13	–	41	40	97
16 Leicestershire (8)	16	–	1	15	–	43	47	90
17 Yorkshire (9)	16	1	6	9	–	33	40	89

Win = 16 points; Tie = 8 points.
1989 final positions are shown in brackets.
Hampshire's total includes 8 points for levelling the scores in a drawn match.

RAPID CRICKETLINE CHAMPIONSHIP PLAYER OF THE SEASON:
R.J.Bartlett (Somerset)

SECOND XI CHAMPIONS

1959 Gloucestershire	1970 Kent	1981 Hampshire
1960 Northamptonshire	1971 Hampshire	1982 Worcestershire
1961 Kent	1972 Nottinghamshire	1983 Leicestershire
1962 Worcestershire	1973 Essex	1984 Yorkshire
1963 Worcestershire	1974 Middlesex	1985 Nottinghamshire
1964 Lancashire	1975 Surrey	1986 Lancashire
1965 Glamorgan	1976 Kent	1987 Kent/Yorkshire
1966 Surrey	1977 Yorkshire	1988 Surrey
1967 Hampshire	1978 Sussex	1989 Middlesex
1968 Surrey	1979 Warwickshire	1990 Sussex
1969 Kent	1980 Glamorgan	

COUNTY BENEFICIARIES 1991

Derbyshire	—	Northamptonshire	—
Essex	D.E.East	Nottinghamshire	B.N.French
Glamorgan	G.C.Holmes	Somerset	—
Gloucestershire	P.W.Romaines	Surrey	M.A.Lynch
Hampshire	M.C.J.Nicholas	Sussex	A.C.S.Pigott
Kent	M.R.Benson	Warwickshire	—
Lancashire	G.Fowler	Worcestershire	—
Leicestershire	—	Yorkshire	K.Sharp
Middlesex	S.P.Hughes		

THE FIRST-CLASS COUNTIES
HONOURS, REGISTER, RECORDS
AND 1990 AVERAGES

Records are complete to the end of the 1990 English season (21 September).

ABBREVIATIONS

General

*	not out/unbroken partnership	f-c	first-class
b	born	HS	Highest Score
BB	Best innings bowling analysis	LOI	Limited-Overs Internationals
Cap	Awarded 1st XI County Cap	Tests	Official Test Matches
Tours	Overseas tours involving first-class appearances		

Awards

BHC	Benson and Hedges Cup 'Gold' Award
NWT	NatWest Trophy/Gillette Cup 'Man of the Match' Award
Wisden 1990	One of Wisden Cricketers' Almanack's Five Cricketers of 1990
YC 1990	Cricket Writers' Club Young Cricketer of 1990

Competitions

BHC	Benson and Hedges Cup
GC	Gillette Cup
NWT	NatWest Trophy
RAL	Refuge Assurance League

Playing Categories

LB	Bowls right-arm leg-breaks
LF	Bowls left-arm fast
LFM	Bowls left-arm fast-medium
LHB	Bats left-handed
LM	Bowls left-arm medium pace
LMF	Bowls left-arm medium-fast
OB	Bowls right-arm off-breaks
RHB	Bats right-handed
RM	Bowls right-arm medium pace
RMF	Bowls right-arm medium-fast
RF	Bowls right-arm fast
RSM	Bowls right-arm slow-medium
SLA	Bowls left-arm leg-breaks
WK	Wicket-keeper

Education

BHS	Boys' High School
BS	Boys' School
C	College
CE	College of Education
CFE	College of Further Education
CHE	College of Higher Education
CPE	College of Physical Education
CS	Comprehensive School
GS	Grammar School
HS	High School
LSE	London School of Economics
RGS	Royal Grammar School
S	School
SFC	Sixth Form College
SS	Secondary School
TC	Technical College
TGS	Technical Grammar School
THS	Technical High School
U	University

Teams (see also p 166)

Cav	Cavaliers	NSW	New South Wales
DHR	D.H.Robins' XI	OFS	Orange Free State
DN	Duke of Norfolk's XI	PIA	Pakistan International Airlines
EC	English Counties XI	RW	Rest of the World XI
GW	Griqualand West	SAB	South African Breweries XI
Int	International XI	SAU	South African Universities
IW	International Wanderers	Z	Zimbabwe (Rhodesia)

DERBYSHIRE

Formation of Present Club: 4 November 1870
Colours: Chocolate, Amber and Pale Blue
Badge: Rose and Crown
Championships: (1) 1936
NatWest Trophy/Gillette Cup Winners: (1) 1981
Benson and Hedges Cup Winners: (0) Finalists 1978, 1988
Sunday League Champions: (1) 1990
Match Awards: NWT 29; BHC 48

Chief Executive: R.J.Lark, County Ground, Nottingham Road, Derby DE2 6DA
(☎ 0332-383211)
Captain: K.J.Barnett
Scorer: S.W.Tacey

ADAMS, Christopher John (Repton S), b Whitwell 6 May 1970. 6'0". RHB, OB. Debut 1988. HS 111* v CU (Cambridge) 1990. BAC HS 101 v Yorks (Scarborough) 1990. BB 1-5. **NWT:** HS 0. **BHC:** HS 44 Minor C (Wellington) 1990. **RAL:** HS 58* v Warwks (Derby) 1990.

BARNETT, Kim John (Leek HS), b Stoke-on-Trent, Staffs 17 Jul 1960. 6'1". RHB, LB. Debut 1979. Cap 1982. Captain 1983-. Boland 1982-88. Staffordshire 1976. Wisden 1988. **Tests: 4** (1988 to 89); HS 80 v A (Leeds) 1989. LOI: 1. Tours: SA 1989-90 (Eng XI); NZ 1979-80 (DHR); SL 1985-86 (Eng B). 1000 runs (8); most - 1734 (1984). HS 239* v Leics (Leicester) 1988. BB 6-115 v Yorks (Bradford) 1985. Awards: NWT 2; BHC 8. **NWT:** HS 88 v Middx (Derby) 1983. BB 6-24 v Cumberland (Kendal) 1984. **BHC:** HS 115 v Glos (Derby) 1987. BB 1-10. **RAL:** HS 131* v Essex (Derby) 1984. BB 3-39 v Yorks (Chesterfield) 1979.

BASE, Simon John (Fish Hoek HS, Cape Town), b Maidstone, Kent 2 Jan 1960. 6'2". RHB, RMF. W Province 1981-84. Boland 1987-88. Border 1989-90. Derbyshire debut 1988. Cap 1990. HS 58 v Yorks (Chesterfield) 1990. 50 wkts (1): 60 (1989). BB 7-60 v Yorks (Chesterfield) 1989. **NWT:** HS 4. BB 2-49 Gm v Sussex (Hove) 1986. **BHC:** HS 15* v Somerset (Taunton) 1990. BB 3-33 v Minor C (Wellington) 1990. **RAL:** HS 19 Gm v Kent (Swansea) 1987. BB 4-28 v Sussex (Hove) 1990.

BISHOP, Ian Raphael (Belmont SS), b Port-of-Spain, Trinidad 24 Oct 1967. Nephew of R.J. (Trinidad 1986-87). 6'5". RHB, RF. Trinidad 1986-90. Derbyshire debut 1989. Cap 1990. **Tests (WI): 8** (1988-89 to 1989-90); HS 30* v I (P-of-S); BB 6-87 v I (Bridgetown). LOI (WI): 26. Tour (WI): E 1988; A 1988-89. HS 103* v Yorks (Scarborough) 1990. 50 wkts (1): 59 (1990). BB 6-39 WI v Kent (Canterbury) 1988. D BB 6-67 v Leics (Leicester) 1989. **RAL:** HS 16* and BB 1-51 v Worcs (Worcester) 1989.

BOWLER, Peter Duncan (Educated at Canberra, Australia), b Plymouth, Devon 30 Jul 1963. 6'1". RHB, OB. Leicestershire 1986 – first to score hundred on f-c debut for Leics (100* and 62 v Hants). Tasmania 1986-87. Derbyshire debut 1988 scoring 155* v CU at Cambridge – first to score hundreds on debut for two counties. Cap 1989. 1000 runs (3): 1725 (1988). HS 210 v Kent (Chesterfield) 1990. BB 2-1 v Leics (Chesterfield) 1989. **NWT:** HS 46 v Cheshire (Chester) 1988. **BHC:** HS 109 v Somerset (Taunton) 1990. BB 1-15. **RAL:** HS 71 v Hants (Derby) 1989. BB 2-29 v Leics (Derby) 1988.

BROWN, Andrew Mark (Aldercar CS; SE Derbyshire C), b Heanor 6 Nov 1964. 5'9". LHB, OB. Debut 1985 – no appearances 1987-88. HS 139* v Northants (Chesterfield) 1990. **RAL:** HS 2*.

CORK, Dominic Gerald (St Joseph's C, Stoke-on-Trent), b Newcastle-under-Lyme, Staffs 7 Aug 1971. 6'2". RHB, RFM. Debut 1990. Staffs 1989-90. HS 7. BB 1-4.

GOLDSMITH, Steven Clive (Simon Langton GS, Canterbury), b Ashford, Kent 19 Dec 1964. 5'10". RHB, RM. Kent 1987. Derbyshire debut 1988. 1000 runs (1): 1071 (1988). HS 89 v Kent (Chesterfield) 1988. BB 2-105 v Essex (Derby) 1990. Award: BHC 1. **NWT:** HS 21 and BB 1-20 v Lancs (Derby) 1990. **BHC:** HS 45* and BB 3-38 v Minor C (Wellington) 1990. **RAL:** HS 61 v Middx (Repton) 1988.

GRIFFITH, Frank Alexander (Beaconsfield HS; Wm Morris HS; Haringey Cricket C), b Whipps Cross, Essex 15 Aug 1968. 6'0". RHB, RM. Debut 1988. HS 37 v Northants (Northampton) 1988. BB 4-47 v Lancs (Manchester) 1988. **BHC:** HS 10 v Notts (Nottingham) 1989. **RAL:** HS 9. BB 2-14 v Kent (Canterbury) 1989.

JEAN-JACQUES, Martin (Aylestone SS, London), b Soufriere, Dominica 2 Jul 1960. 6'0". RHB, RMF. Debut 1986. Buckinghamshire 1983-85. HS 73 v Yorks (Sheffield) 1986 (on debut, sharing Derbys record 10th-wkt stand of 132 with A.Hill). BB 8-77 v Kent (Derby) 1986. **NWT:** HS 16 v Surrey (Derby) 1986. BB 3-23 v Cambs (Wisbech) 1987. **BHC:** HS 2*. BB 3-22 v Notts (Nottingham) 1987. **RAL:** HS 15 v Somerset (Derby) 1987. BB 3-36 v Worcs (Worcester) 1986.

KRIKKEN, Karl Matthew (Rivington & Blackrod HS & SFC), b Bolton, Lancs 9 Apr 1969. Son of B.E. (Lancs and Worcs 1966-69). 5'9". RHB, WK. GW 1988-89. Derbyshire debut 1989. HS 77* v Somerset (Taunton) 1990. **RAL:** HS 16 v Middx (Lord's) 1989.

MALCOLM, Devon Eugene (Richmond C, Sheffield), b Kingston, Jamaica 22 Feb 1963. 6'2". RHB, RF. Debut 1984. Cap 1989. Tests: 11 (1989 to 1990); HS 15* v I (Oval) 1990; BB 6-77 v WI (P-of-S) 1989-90. LOI: 2. Tour: WI 1989-90. HS 51 v Surrey (Derby) 1989. 50 wkts (2); most – 56 (1988). BB 6-68 v Warwks (Derby) 1988. Award: BHC 1. **NWT:** HS 6. BB 3-54 v Lancs (Derby) 1990. **BHC:** HS 5. BB 5-27 v Middx (Derby) 1988. **RAL:** HS 16 v Northants (Finedon) 1986. BB 4-21 v Surrey (Derby) 1989 and v Leics (Knypersley) 1990.

MORRIS, John Edward (Shavington CS; Dane Bank CFE), b Crewe, Cheshire 1 Apr 1964. 5'10". RHB, RM. Debut 1982. Cap 1986. GW 1988-89. Tests: 3 (1990); HS 32 v I (Oval) 1990. 1000 runs (5); most –1739 (1986). HS 191 v Kent (Derby) 1986. BB 1-13. Award: NWT 1. **NWT:** HS 94* v Salop (Chesterfield) 1990. **BHC:** HS 123 v Somerset (Taunton) 1990. **RAL:** HS 134 v Somerset (Taunton) 1990.

MORTENSEN, Ole Henrek (Brondbyoster S; Abedore C, Copenhagen), b Vejle, Denmark 29 Jan 1958. 6'3". RHB, RFM. Debut 1983. Cap 1986. Denmark 1975-82. HS 74* v Yorks (Chesterfield) 1987. 50 wkts (1): 55 (1987). BB 6-27 v Yorks (Sheffield) 1983. Hat-trick 1987. Awards: NWT 2. **NWT:** HS 11 v Surrey (Derby) 1986. BB 6-14 v Ire (Derby) 1989. **BHC:** HS 3*. BB 3-17 v Leics (Chesterfield) 1986. **RAL:** HS 11 v Worcs (Worcester) 1989. BB 4-10 v Leics (Chesterfield) 1985.

O'GORMAN, Timothy Joseph Gerard (St George's C, Weybridge; Durham U), b Woking, Surrey 15 May 1967. Grandson of J.G.O'Gorman (Surrey 1927). 6'2". RHB, OB. Debut 1987. HS 124 v Glos (Cheltenham) 1989. **BHC:** HS 43 Comb Us v Glam (Cardiff) 1988. **RAL:** HS 46* v Yorks (Chesterfield) 1989.

ROBERTS, Bruce (Peterhouse; Prince Edward S, Salisbury), b Lusaka, N Rhodesia 30 May 1962. 6'2". RHB, RM, WK. Transvaal 1982-89. Derbyshire debut 1984. Cap 1986. 1000 runs (3); most – 1643 (1987). HS 184 v Sussex (Chesterfield) 1987. BB 5-68 Transvaal B v N Transvaal B (Johannesburg) 1986-87. BAC BB 4-77 v Essex (Ilford) 1984. Awards: BHC 2. NWT: HS 64* v Worcs (Worcester) 1989. BB 2-73 v Leics (Leicester) 1984. BHC: HS 100 v Northants (Derby) 1987. BB 2-47 v Minor C (Shrewsbury) 1984. RAL: HS 101* v Sussex (Hove) 1987. BB 4-29 v Lancs (Derby) 1984.

SADIQ, Zahid Asa (Rutlish S), b Nairobi, Kenya 6 May 1965. 5'11". RHB. Surrey 1988-89. HS 64 Sy v CU (Oval) 1988 (on debut). BAC HS 37 Sy v Somerset (W-s-M) 1988. BHC: HS 9. RAL: HS 53 Sy v Leics (Oval) 1988.

WARNER, Allan Esmond (Tabernacle S, St Kitts), b Birmingham 12 May 1957. 5'7". RHB, RFM. Worcestershire 1982-84. Derbyshire debut 1985. Cap 1987. HS 91 v Leics (Chesterfield) 1986. BB 5-27 Wo v Glam (Worcester) 1984. D BB 5-51 v Essex (Colchester) 1985. Awards: NWT 1. NWT: HS 32 v Kent (Canterbury) 1987. BB 4-39 v Salop (Chesterfield) 1990. BHC: HS 24* Wo v Derbys (Worcester) 1982. BB 4-36 v Notts (Nottingham) 1987. RAL: HS 68 v Hants (Heanor) 1986. BB 5-39 v Worcs (Knypersley) 1985.

NEWCOMER

AZHARUDDIN, Mohammad (Nizam C; Osmania U), b Hyderabad, India 8 Feb 1963. 5'11". RHB, LB. Hyderabad 1981-90. Wisden 1990. **Tests** (I): 40 (1984-85 to 1990, 6 as captain); HS 199 v SL (Kanpur) 1986-87. LOI (I): 106. Tours (I) (C=captain): E 1986, 1990C; A 1985-86; WI 1988-89; NZ 1989-90C; P 1989-90; SL 1985-86; Z 1983-84 (Young Ind). 1000 runs (0+2); most – 1104 (1989-90). HS 226 S Zone v C Zone (Jamadoba) 1983-84. BB 2-33 Hyderabad v Andhra (Hyderabad) 1987-88.

DEPARTURES

KUIPER, Adrian Paul (Diocesan C; Stellenbosch U), b Johannesburg, South Africa 24 Aug 1959. 5'11". Brother of J.L. (SAU 1973-74). RHB, RMF. W Province 1977-90. SAU 1978-81. Derbyshire 1990. HS 161* W Province v Natal (Durban) 1989-90. D HS 68 v NZ (Derby) 1990. BAC HS 48 v Lancs (Derby) 1990. BB 6-55 W Province v N Transvaal (Pretoria) 1983-84. D BB 4-69 v Lancs (Liverpool) 1990. Award: BHC 1. NWT: HS 49 and BB 1-20 v Salop (Chesterfield) 1990. BHC: HS 106* and BB 3-71 v Middx (Derby) 1990. RAL: HS 62* v Northants (Northampton) 1990. BB 3-50 v Lancs (Manchester) 1990.

MAHER, Bernard Joseph Michael (Abbotsfield CS; Bishopshalt GS; Loughborough U), b Hillingdon, Middx 11 Feb 1958. 5'10". RHB, WK. Derbyshire 1981-90 (cap 1987). HS 126 v NZ (Derby) 1986. BAC HS 121* v Leics (Derby) 1988. BB 2-69 v Glam (Abergavenny) 1986. NWT: HS 44 v Hants (Derby) 1988. BHC: HS 50 v Northants (Derby) 1987. RAL: HS 78 v Lancs (Manchester) 1987.

MILLER, Geoffrey (Chesterfield GS), b Chesterfield, Derbys 8 Sep 1952. 6'1". RHB, OB. Derbyshire 1973-86 and 1990 (cap 1976; captain 1979-81; benefit 1985). Natal 1983-84. Essex 1987-89 (cap 1988). YC 1976. Tests: 34 (1976 to 1984); HS 98* v P (Lahore) 1977-78; BB 5-44 v A (Sydney) 1978-79. LOI: 25. Tours: A 1976-77, 1978-79, 1979-80, 1982-83; WI 1980-81; NZ 1977-78; I and SL 1976-77; P 1977-78. HS 130 v Lancs (Manchester) 1984. 50 wkts (4); most – 87 (1977, 1984). BB 8-70 v Leics (Coalville) 1982. Awards: BHC 4. NWT: HS 59* v Worcs (Worcester) 1978. BB 3-23 Ex v Wilts (Chelmsford) 1988. BHC: HS 88* v Minor C (Derby) 1982. BB 3-23 v Surrey (Derby) 1979. RAL: HS 84 v Somerset (Chesterfield) 1980. BB 4-22 v Yorks (Huddersfield) 1978.

DERBYSHIRE 1990

RESULTS SUMMARY

	Place	Won	Lost	Drew	Abandoned
Britannic Assurance Championship	12th	6	7	9	
All First-class Matches		7	8	9	
Refuge Assurance League	1st	12	3		1
NatWest Bank Trophy	2nd Round				
Benson and Hedges Cup	3rd in Group B				

BRITANNIC ASSURANCE CHAMPIONSHIP AVERAGES

BATTING AND FIELDING

Cap		M	I	NO	HS	Runs	Avge	100	50	Ct/St
1986	J.E.Morris	16	26	4	157*	1353	61.50	6	6	8
1982	K.J.Barnett	22	36	5	141	1572	50.70	5	8	14
1989	P.D.Bowler	21	37	4	210	1408	42.66	3	7	15
–	T.J.G.O'Gorman	6	11	1	100	393	39.30	1	3	3
–	A.M.Brown	7	11	1	139*	379	37.90	1	1	6
1986	B.Roberts	22	35	7	124*	1038	37.07	2	4	23
1976	G.Miller	13	13	7	47*	208	34.66	–	–	4
1990	I.R.Bishop	12	15	4	103*	326	29.63	1	–	2
–	C.J.Adams	21	32	3	101	800	27.58	1	5	22
1990	S.J.Base	13	13	2	58	215	19.54	–	2	4
–	A.P.Kuiper	10	15	0	48	288	19.20	–	–	9
–	K.M.Krikken	21	28	2	77*	426	16.38	–	1	58/3
–	S.C.Goldsmith	11	16	1	34	216	14.40	–	–	7
–	M.Jean-Jacques	10	11	4	25	80	11.42	–	–	2
1989	D.E.Malcolm	9	6	2	20*	44	11.00	–	–	–
1986	O.H.Mortensen	11	11	9	5*	20	10.00	–	–	5
1987	A.E.Warner	14	19	2	59	160	9.41	–	1	2

Also played (1 match each): D.G.Cork 7; F.A.Griffith 1; Z.A.Sadiq 0.

BOWLING

	O	M	R	W	Avge	Best	5wI	10w-M
I.R.Bishop	395.3	91	1087	59	18.42	6-71	3	–
O.H.Mortensen	301.2	88	764	32	23.87	4-22	–	–
D.E.Malcolm	277.4	44	947	30	31.56	4-63	–	–
K.J.Barnett	267.1	42	720	19	37.89	4-49	–	–
S.J.Base	414.3	68	1402	35	40.05	6-105	2	–
A.E.Warner	393.3	67	1330	33	40.30	3-56	–	–
G.Miller	427.2	94	1285	31	41.45	6-45	1	–
M.Jean-Jacques	261.3	33	983	19	51.73	6-60	1	–

Also bowled: C.J.Adams 8-0-36-1; P.D.Bowler 8-0-56-1; D.G.Cork 24-6-70-0;
S.C.Goldsmith 112-19-347-7; F.A.Griffith 11-2-20-1; A.P.Kuiper 108.3-25-325-9;
J.E.Morris 20-0-123-1; B.Roberts 7-0-26-0.

The First-Class Averages (pp 166–181) give the records of Derbyshire players in
all first-class county matches (their other opponents being the New Zealanders
and Cambridge U.), with the exception of:
D.E.Malcolm 10-7-2-20*-44-8.80-0-0-0ct. 289.4-45-983-30-32.76-4/63.
J.E.Morris 17-27-4-157*-1373-59.69-6-6-9ct. 27-0-170-1-170.00-1/17.

DERBYSHIRE RECORDS

FIRST-CLASS CRICKET

Highest Total	For 645		v Hampshire	Derby	1898
	V 662		by Yorkshire	Chesterfield	1898
Lowest Total	For 16		v Notts	Nottingham	1879
	V 23		by Hampshire	Burton upon T	1958
Highest Innings	For 274	G.A.Davidson	v Lancashire	Manchester	1896
	V 343*	P.A.Perrin	for Essex	Chesterfield	1904

Highest Partnership for each Wicket

1st	322	H.Storer/J.Bowden	v Essex	Derby	1929
2nd	349	C.S.Elliott/J.D.Eggar	v Notts	Nottingham	1947
3rd	291	P.N.Kirsten/D.S.Steele	v Somerset	Taunton	1981
4th	328	P.Vaulkhard/D.Smith	v Notts	Nottingham	1946
5th	203	C.P.Wilkins/I.R.Buxton	v Lancashire	Manchester	1971
6th	212	G.M.Lee/T.S.Worthington	v Essex	Chesterfield	1932
7th	241*	G.H.Pope/A.E.G.Rhodes	v Hampshire	Portsmouth	1948
8th	182	A.H.M.Jackson/W.Carter	v Leics	Leicester	1922
9th	283	A.Warren/J.Chapman	v Warwicks	Blackwell	1910
10th	132	A.Hill/M.Jean-Jacques	v Yorkshire	Sheffield	1986

Best Bowling	For 10-40	W.Bestwick	v Glamorgan	Cardiff	1921
(Innings)	V 10-47	T.F.Smailes	for Yorkshire	Sheffield	1939
Best Bowling	For 17-103	W.Mycroft	v Hampshire	Southampton	1876
(Match)	V 16-101	G.Giffen	for Australians	Derby	1886

Most Runs – Season	2,165	D.B.Carr	(av 48.11)		1959
Most Runs – Career	20,516	D.Smith	(av 31.41)		1927-1952
Most 100s – Season	8	P.N.Kirsten			1982
Most 100s – Career	32	K.J.Barnett			1979-1990
Most Wkts – Season	168	T.B.Mitchell	(av 19.55)		1935
Most Wkts – Career	1,670	H.L.Jackson	(av 17.11)		1947-1963

LIMITED-OVERS CRICKET

Highest Total	NWT	365-3		v Cornwall	Derby	1986
	BHC	303-7		v Somerset	Taunton	1990
	RAL	292-9		v Worcs	Knypersley	1985
Lowest Total	NWT	79		v Surrey	The Oval	1967
	BHC	102		v Yorkshire	Bradford	1975
	RAL	61		v Hampshire	Portsmouth	1990
Highest Innings	NWT	153	A.Hill	v Cornwall	Derby	1986
	BHC	123	J.E.Morris	v Somerset	Taunton	1990
	RAL	134	J.E.Morris	v Somerset	Taunton	1990
Best Bowling	NWT	8-21	M.A.Holding	v Sussex	Hove	1988
	BHC	6-33	E.J.Barlow	v Glos	Bristol	1978
	RAL	6-7	M.Hendrick	v Notts	Nottingham	1972

ESSEX

Formation of Present Club: 14 January 1876
Colours: Blue, Gold and Red
Badge: Three Seaxes above Scroll bearing 'Essex'
Championships: (4) 1979, 1983, 1984, 1986
NatWest Trophy/Gillette Cup Winners: (1) 1985
Benson and Hedges Cup Winners: (1) 1979
Sunday League Champions: (3) 1981, 1984, 1985
Match Awards: NWT 31; BHC 63

Secretary/General Manager: P.J.Edwards, County Cricket Ground, New Writtle Street, Chelmsford CM2 0PG (☎ 0245 252420)
Captain: G.A.Gooch
Scorer: C.F.Driver
1991 Beneficiary: D.E.East

ANDREW, Stephen Jon Walter (Milton Abbey S; Portchester SS), b London 27 Jan 1966. 6'3". RHB, RMF. Hampshire 1984-89. Essex debut 1990. HS 35 v Northants (Chelmsford) 1990. BB 7-92 H v Glos (Southampton) 1987. Ex BB 5-55 v Yorks (Middlesbrough) 1990. Awards: BHC 2. **NWT:** HS 0*. BB 2-34 v Scot (Chelmsford) 1990. **BHC:** HS 4*. BB 5-24 H v Essex (Chelmsford) 1987. **RAL:** HS 5. BB 4-50 H v Middx (Southampton) 1988.

BODEN, David Jonathan Peter (Alleynes HS, Stone; Stafford CFE), b Eccleshall, Staffs 26 Nov 1970. 6'3". RHB, RMF. Middlesex 1989. HS – . BB 4-11 M v OU (Oxford) 1989 - on debut. Awaiting BAC debut; no 1st XI appearances for Essex - joined staff 1990.

BUTLER, Keith Andrew (Dagenham Priory CS), b Camden Town, London 20 Jan 1971. 5'8". RHB, RM. Debut 1989. HS 10* v CU (Cambridge) 1989. Awaiting BAC debut.

CHILDS, John Henry (Audley Park SMS, Torquay), b Plymouth, Devon 15 Aug 1951. LHB, SLA. Gloucestershire 1975-84 (cap 1977). Essex debut 1985. Cap 1986. Devon 1973-74. Wisden 1986. **Tests:** 2 (1988); HS 2*; BB 1-13. HS 34* Gs v Notts (Cheltenham) 1982. Ex HS 34 v NZ (Chelmsford) 1986. 50 wkts (5); most – 89 (1986). BB 9-56 Gs v Somerset (Bristol) 1981. Ex BB 8-58 v Glos (Colchester) 1986. Awards: BHC 1. **NWT:** HS 14* Gs v Hants (Bristol) 1983. BB 2-15 Gs v Ire (Dublin) 1981. **BHC:** HS 10 Gs v Somerset (Bristol) 1979. BB 3-36 Gs v Glam (Bristol) 1982. **RAL:** HS 16* Gs v Warwks (Bristol) 1981. BB 4-15 Gs v Northants (Northampton) 1976.

EAST, David Edward (Hackney Downs S; E Anglia U), b Clapton 27 Jul 1959. 5'9". RHB, WK. Debut 1981. Cap 1982. Benefit 1991. HS 134 v Glos (Ilford) 1988. Set world f-c record by catching the FIRST eight wickets to fall in an innings (v Somerset at Taunton 1985 on his 26th birthday). Award: NWT 1. **NWT:** HS 28 v Northumb (Jesmond) 1986. **BHC:** HS 33 v Glos (Chelmsford) 1984. **RAL:** HS 43 v Derbys (Derby) 1982.

FOSTER, Neil Alan (Philip Morant CS), b Colchester 6 May 1962. 6'3". RHB, RFM. Debut 1980. Cap 1983. YC 1983. Wisden 1987. **Tests:** 28 (1983 to 1989); HS 39 v P (Lahore) 1987-88 and 39 v A (Manchester) 1989; BB 8-107 v P (Leeds) 1987. LOI: 48. Tours: A 1986-87, 1987-88; SA 1989-90 (Eng XI); WI 1985-86; NZ

FOSTER – continued:
1983-84, 1987-88; Ind/SL 1984-85; P 1983-84, 1987-88. HS 101 v Leics (Chelmsford) 1990. 50 wkts (8) inc 100 wkts (1): 105 (1986). BB 8-107 (Tests). Ex BB 7-33 v Warwks (Chelmsford) 1987. Awards: NWT 1; BHC 2. **NWT:** HS 26 v Worcs (Chelmsford) 1987. BB 4-9 v Northumb (Jesmond) 1987. **BHC:** HS 37* v Somerset (Taunton) 1987. BB 5-32 v Surrey (Oval) 1985. **RAL:** HS 44 v Worcs (Colchester) 1989. BB 5-17 v Derbys (Derby) 1986.

FRASER, Alastair Gregory James (Gayton HS, John Lyon S, Harrow; Harrow Weald SFC), b Edgware, Middx 17 Oct 1967. Brother of A.R.C. (Middlesex and England). 6'1". RHB, RFM. Middlesex 1986-89. HS 19* M v Warwks (Uxbridge) 1986. BB 3-46 M v NZ (Lord's) 1986. BAC BB 2-12 M v Lancs (Lord's) 1986. **RAL:** HS 2*. BB 1-19. No f-c appearances for Essex – joined staff 1990.

GARNHAM, Michael Anthony (Camberwell GS, Melbourne; Scotch C, Perth; Barnstaple GS; N Devon SFC; East Anglia U), b Johannesburg, SA 20 Aug 1960. 5'10". RHB, WK. Gloucestershire 1979. Leicestershire 1980-85 and 1988. Essex debut 1989. Cap 1990. Cambridgeshire 1986-88. HS 100 Le v OU (Oxford) 1985. Ex HS 91 v Northants (Northampton) 1989. Awards: NWT 1; BHC 1. **NWT:** HS 110 Cambs v Warwks (Birmingham) 1988. **BHC:** HS 55 Le v Derbys (Leicester) 1982. **RAL:** HS 79* Le v Lancs (Leicester) 1982.

GOOCH, Graham Alan (Norlington Jr HS), b Leytonstone 23 Jul 1953. 6'0". RHB, RM. Debut 1973. Cap 1975. Captain 1986-87, 1989-. Benefit 1985. W Province 1982-84. Wisden 1979. Tests: 81 (1975 to 1990, 10 as captain); HS 333 and record match aggregate of 456 v I (Lord's) 1990; BB 2-12 v I (Delhi) 1981-82. LOI: 85. Tours (C=captain): A 1978-79, 1979-80; SA 1981-82 (SAB); WI 1980-81, 1985-86, 1989-90C; I 1979-80, 1981-82; P 1987-88; SL 1981-82. 1000 runs (14+1) inc 2000 runs (4); most – 2746 (1990). HS 333 (Tests). Ex HS 275 v Kent (Chelmsford) 1988. Shared Essex record stand of 403 for 2nd wkt with P.J. Prichard v Leics (Chelmsford) 1990. BB 7-14 v Worcs (Ilford) 1982. Awards: NWT 7; BHC 18 (record). **NWT:** HS 144 v Hants (Chelmsford) 1990. BB 3-31 v Warwks (Birmingham) 1986. **BHC:** HS 198* v Sussex (Hove) 1982. BB 3-24 v Sussex (Hove) 1982. **RAL:** HS 176 v Glam (Southend) 1983. BB 4-33 v Worcs (Chelmsford) 1984.

HUSSAIN, Nasser (Forest S, Snaresbrook; Durham U), b Madras, India 28 Mar 1968. Brother of M. (Worcs 1985). 5'11". RHB, LB. Debut 1987. Cap 1989. YC 1989. Tests: 3 (1989-90); HS 35 v WI (St John's) 1989-90. LOI: 2. Tour: WI 1989-90. HS 197 v Surrey (Oval) 1990. Award: BHC 1. **NWT:** HS 24 v Somerset (Taunton) 1989. **BHC:** HS 118 Comb Us v Somerset (Taunton) 1989. **RAL:** HS 66* v Yorks (Middlesbrough) 1990.

ILOTT, Mark Christopher (Francis Combe S, Garston), b Watford, Herts 27 Aug 1970. 6'0½". LHB, LMF. Debut 1988. Hertfordshire 1987-88. HS 42* v Kent (Chelmsford) 1990. BB 5-34 v Derbys (Derby) 1990. **NWT:** BB 1-45. **RAL:** HS 6 and BB 2-24 v Yorks (Middlesbrough) 1990.

KNIGHT, Nicholas Verity (Felsted S; Loughborough U), b Watford, Herts 28 Nov 1969. 6'0". LHB. Joined staff 1990 – no 1st XI appearances. **BHC:** HS 16 Comb Us v Hants (Southampton) 1990.

LEWIS, Jonathan James Benjamin (King Edward VI S, Chelmsford; Roehampton IHE), b Isleworth, Middlesex 21 May 1970. 5'9½". RHB, RSM. Debut 1990 scoring 116* v Surrey (Oval). HS 116* (above).

70

MILLER, Craig Aston (Bedfords Park S; City & East London C), b Wanstead 24 Apr 1971. 5'11". RHB, RFM. Joined staff 1990 – no 1st XI appearances.

PRICHARD, Paul John (Brentwood HS), b Billericay 7 Jan 1965. 5'10". RHB. Debut 1984. Cap 1986. 1000 runs (3); most – 1407 (1990). HS 245 v Leics (Chelmsford) 1990, sharing Essex record stand of 403 for 2nd wkt with G.A.Gooch. Awards: BHC 2. **NWT:** HS 94 v Oxon (Chelmsford) 1985. **BHC:** HS 107 v Scot (Glasgow) 1990. **RAL:** HS 103* v Lancs (Manchester) 1986.

PRINGLE, Derek Raymond (Felsted S; Fitzwilliam C, Cambridge), b Nairobi, Kenya 18 Sep 1958. Son of D.J. (East Africa). 6'4½". RHB, RMF. Debut 1978. Cap 1982. Cambridge U 1979-82 (blue 1979-80-81; capt 1982). **Tests:** 21 (1982 to 1989); HS 63 v I (Lord's) 1986; BB 5-95 v WI (Leeds) 1988. LOI: 26. Tours: A 1982-83; SL 1985-86 (Eng B); Z 1989-90 (Eng A). HS 128 v Kent (Chelmsford) 1988. 50 wkts (6); most – 94 (1989). BB 7-18 v Glam (Swansea) 1989. Awards: NWT 2; BHC 4. **NWT:** HS 80* v Wilts (Chelmsford) 1988. BB 5-12 v Oxon (Chelmsford) 1985. **BHC:** HS 77* v Scot (Glasgow) 1990. BB 5-35 v Lancs (Chelmsford) 1984. **RAL:** HS 81* v Warwks (Birmingham) 1985. BB 5-41 v Glos (Southend) 1985.

SEYMOUR, Adam Charles (Millfield S), b Royston, Cambs 7 Dec 1967. 6'2". LHB. Debut 1988. HS 89 v CU (Cambridge) 1990. BAC HS 10* v Hants (Southampton) 1990.

SHAHID, Nadeem (Ipswich S), b Karachi, Pakistan 23 Apr 1969. 6'0". RHB, LB. Debut 1989. Suffolk 1988. 1000 runs (1): 1003 (1990). HS 125 v Lancs (Colchester) 1990. BB 3-91 v Surrey (Oval) 1990. **RAL:** HS 31 v Sussex (Chelmsford) and v Yorks (Middlesbrough) 1990.

STEPHENSON, John Patrick (Felsted S; Durham U), b Stebbing 14 Mar 1965. 6'1". RHB, RM. Debut 1985. Cap 1989. Boland 1988-89. **Tests:** 1 (1989); HS 25 v A (Oval) 1989. Tour: Z 1989-90 (Eng A). 1000 runs (2); most – 1887 (1990). HS 202* v Somerset (Bath) 1990. BB 3-22 Eng A v Zimbabwe (Bulawayo) 1989-90. Ex BB 2-18 v CU (Cambridge) 1989. BAC BB 2-41 v Surrey (Oval) 1989. Award: BHC 1. **NWT:** HS 55 v Warwks (Birmingham) 1986. BB 1-24. **BHC:** HS 75 Comb Us v Somerset (Taunton) 1987. BB 3-22 v Northants (Northampton) 1990. **RAL:** HS 109 v Lancs (Colchester) 1990. BB 3-27 v Middx (Chelmsford) 1989.

SUCH, Peter Mark (Harry Carlton CS, Ex Leake, Notts), b Helensburgh, Dunbartonshire 12 Jun 1964. 5'11". RHB, OB. Nottinghamshire 1982-86. Leicestershire 1987-89. Essex debut 1990. HS 27 v Middx (Ilford) 1990. BB 6-123 Nt v Kent (Nottingham) 1983. Ex BB 3-34 v Yorks (Middlesbrough) 1990. **BHC:** BB 3-50 Nt v Scot (Glasgow) 1985. **RAL:** HS 8*. BB 2-43 v Sussex (Chelmsford) 1990.

TOPLEY, Thomas Donald (Royal Hospital S, Holbrook, Suffolk), b Canterbury, Kent 25 Feb 1964. Brother of P.A. (Kent 1972-75). 6'3". RHB, RMF. Surrey (v CU) and Essex debuts 1985. Cap 1988. GW 1987-88. Norfolk 1984-85. MCC Cricket Staff. HS 66 v Yorks (Leeds) 1987. 50 wkts (2); most – 77 (1989). BB 7-75 v Derbys (Chesterfield) 1988. Awards: NWT 1; BHC 1. **NWT:** HS 15* v Worcs (Chelmsford) 1987. BB 4-21 v Northumb (Jesmond) 1987. **BHC:** HS 10* v Notts (Chelmsford) 1990. BB 4-22 v Surrey (Chelmsford) 1988. **RAL:** HS 23 v Middx (Lord's) 1988. BB 6-33 v Notts (Colchester) 1988.

NEWCOMER and DEPARTURES – see p 154.

ESSEX 1990

RESULTS SUMMARY

	Place	Won	Lost	Drew	Abandoned
Britannic Assurance Championship	2nd	8	2	12	
All First-class Matches		9	2	13	
Refuge Assurance League	12th	6	9		1
NatWest Bank Trophy	2nd Round				
Benson and Hedges Cup	Quarter-Finalist				

BRITANNIC ASSURANCE CHAMPIONSHIP AVERAGES

BATTING AND FIELDING

Cap		M	I	NO	HS	Runs	Avge	100	50	Ct/St
1975	G.A.Gooch	11	18	2	215	1586	99.12	7	5	8
1989	M.E.Waugh	21	32	6	207*	2009	77.26	8	7	18
1974	B.R.Hardie	11	15	5	125	650	65.00	2	3	7
1989	J.P.Stephenson	22	37	7	202*	1525	50.83	2	12	14
–	N.Shahid	18	27	7	125	964	48.20	1	6	22
1986	P.J.Prichard	20	30	3	245	1276	47.25	4	4	8
1989	N.Hussain	14	21	2	197	714	37.57	1	2	14
1990	M.A.Garnham	22	26	7	84*	589	31.00	–	2	45/1
1982	D.R.Pringle	15	13	2	84	318	28.90	–	1	7
1983	N.A.Foster	22	22	2	101	530	26.50	1	2	13
–	P.M.Such	10	5	3	27	44	22.00	–	–	2
1988	T.D.Topley	7	4	1	23	55	18.33	–	–	5
–	M.C.Ilott	8	10	2	42*	123	15.37	–	–	1
–	S.J.W.Andrew	16	15	7	35	119	14.87	–	–	1
1986	J.H.Childs	21	16	5	26	123	11.18	–	–	7

Also played: (1 match each): J.J.B.Lewis 116* (1 ct); A.W.Lilley (cap 1986) 1; A.C.Seymour (2 matches) 10*, 0, 4*.

BOWLING

	O	M	R	W	Avge	Best	5wI	10wM
N.A.Foster	819.2	175	2502	94	26.61	6-32	6	1
D.R.Pringle	325.3	82	927	29	31.96	5-66	1	–
T.D.Topley	178	26	557	16	34.81	4-67	–	–
P.M.Such	252.3	58	682	18	37.88	3-34	–	–
M.C.Ilott	289.1	60	951	25	38.04	5-34	1	–
S.J.W.Andrew	449	67	1763	43	41.00	5-55	1	–
J.H.Childs	595.1	189	1435	25	57.40	4-56	–	–
M.E.Waugh	183	33	731	12	60.91	5-37	–	–

Also bowled: G.A.Gooch 35-8-125-0; B.R.Hardie 1-0-16-0; N.Hussain 4-1-29-0; A.W.Lilley 1-0-7-0; P.J.Prichard 1.4-0-11-0; N.Shahid 106.2-18-413-7; J.P. Stephenson 96-22-383-3.

The First-Class Averages (pp 166–181) give the records of Essex players in all first-class county matches (their other opponents being the New Zealanders and Cambridge U.), with the exception of N.Shahid, whose full county figures are as above, and:

G.A.Gooch 12-19-3-215-1688-105.50-8-5-9ct. 35-8-125-0.
N.Hussain 15-22-2-197-715-35.75-1-2-15ct. 12-2-62-0.
J.P.Stephenson 24-39-7-202*-1730-54.06-3-13-15ct. 111-24-451-4-112.75-1/16.

ESSEX RECORDS

FIRST-CLASS CRICKET

Highest Total	For	761-6d	v	Leics	Chelmsford	1990
	V	803-4d	by	Kent	Brentwood	1934
Lowest Total	For	30	v	Yorkshire	Leyton	1901
	V	14	by	Surrey	Chelmsford	1983
Highest Innings	For	343* P.A.Perrin	v	Derbyshire	Chesterfield	1904
	V	332 W.H.Ashdown	for	Kent	Brentwood	1934

Highest Partnership for each Wicket

1st	270	A.V.Avery/T.C.Dodds	v	Surrey	The Oval	1946
2nd	403	G.A.Gooch/P.J.Prichard	v	Leics	Chelmsford	1990
3rd	343	P.A.Gibb/R.Horsfall	v	Kent	Blackheath	1951
4th	298	A.V.Avery/R.Horsfall	v	Worcs	Clacton	1948
5th	287	C.T.Ashton/J.O'Connor	v	Surrey	Brentwood	1934
6th	{206	J.W.H.T.Douglas/J.O'Connor	v	Glos	Cheltenham	1923
	{206	B.R.Knight/R.A.G.Luckin	v	Middlesex	Brentwood	1962
7th	261	J.W.H.T.Douglas/J.Freeman	v	Lancashire	Leyton	1914
8th	263	D.R.Wilcox/R.M.Taylor	v	Warwicks	Southend	1946
9th	251	J.W.H.T.Douglas/S.N.Hare	v	Derbyshire	Leyton	1921
10th	218	F.H.Vigar/T.P.B.Smith	v	Derbyshire	Chesterfield	1947

Best Bowling	For	10-32	H.Pickett	v	Leics	Leyton	1895
(Innings)	V	10-40	E.G.Dennett	for	Glos	Bristol	1906
Best Bowling	For	17-119	W.Mead	v	Hampshire	Southampton	1895
(Match)	V	17-56	C.W.L.Parker	for	Glos	Gloucester	1925

Most Runs – Season	2,559	G.A.Gooch	(av 67.34)		1984
Most Runs – Career	29,434	K.W.R.Fletcher	(av 36.88)		1962-1988
Most 100s – Season	{9	J.O'Connor			1934
	{9	D.J.Insole			1955
Most 100s – Career	71	J.O'Connor			1921-1939
Most Wkts – Season	172	T.P.B.Smith	(av 27.13)		1947
Most Wkts – Career	1,610	T.P.B.Smith	(av 26.68)		1929-1951

LIMITED-OVERS CRICKET

Highest Total	NWT	386-5		v	Wiltshire	Chelmsford	1988
	BHC	350-3		v	Comb Univs	Chelmsford	1979
	RAL	310-5		v	Glamorgan	Southend	1983
Lowest Total	NWT	100		v	Derbyshire	Brentwood	1965
	BHC	100		v	Hampshire	Chelmsford	1987
	RAL	69		v	Derbyshire	Chesterfield	1974
Highest Innings	NWT	144	G.A.Gooch	v	Hampshire	Chelmsford	1990
	BHC	198*	G.A.Gooch	v	Sussex	Hove	1982
	RAL	176	G.A.Gooch	v	Glamorgan	Southend	1983
Best Bowling	NWT	5-8	J.K.Lever	v	Middlesex	Westcliff	1972
	BHC	5-13	J.K.Lever	v	Middlesex	Lord's	1985
	RAL	8-26	K.D.Boyce	v	Lancashire	Manchester	1971

GLAMORGAN

Formation of Present Club: 6 July 1888
Colours: Blue and Gold
Badge: Gold Daffodil
Championships: (2) 1948, 1969
NatWest Trophy/Gillette Cup Winners: (0) Finalists 1977
Benson and Hedges Cup Winners: (0) Semi-Finalists 1988
Sunday League Champions: (0) Fifth 1988
Match Awards: NWT 24; BHC 39

Secretary: G.R.Stone, Sophia Gardens, Cardiff, CF1 9XR (☎ 0222-343478)
Captain: A.R.Butcher
Scorer: B.T.Denning
1991 Beneficiary: G.C.Holmes

BARWICK, Stephen Royston (Cwrt Sart CS; Dwr-y-Felin CS), b Neath 6 Sep 1960. 6'2". RHB, RMF. Debut 1981. Cap 1987. HS 30 v Hants (Bournemouth) 1988. 50 wkts (2); most – 64 (1989). BB 8-42 v Worcs (Worcester) 1983. Awards: BHC 1. **NWT:** HS 6. BB 4-14 v Hants (Bournemouth) 1981. **BHC:** HS 18 v Kent (Canterbury) 1984. BB 4-11 v Minor C (Swansea) 1985. **RAL:** HS 48* v Worcs (Worcester) 1989. BB 4-23 v Yorks (Cardiff) 1987.

BASTIEN, Steven (St Bonaventure S, Forest Gate; Haringey Cricket C), b Stepney, London 13 Mar 1963 (of Dominican parents). 6'1". RHB, RMF. Debut 1988. HS 36* v Warwicks (Birmingham) 1988 (his first innings). BB 6-75 v Worcs (Worcester) 1990. **BHC:** HS 7. **RAL:** HS 1. BB 1-21.

BUTCHER, Alan Raymond (Heath Clark GS), b Croydon, Surrey 7 Jan 1954. Brother of I.P. (Leics 1980-87 and Glos 1988-90) and M.S. (Surrey 1982). 5'8½". LHB, SLA/LM. Surrey 1972-86 (cap 1975; benefit 1985). Glamorgan debut/cap 1987. Captain 1989-. Wisden 1990. **Tests:** 1 (1979); HS 20 v India (Oval) 1979. **LOI:** 1. Tours: WI 1982-83 (Int); I 1980-81 (Overseas XI). 1000 runs (11) inc 2000 (1): 2116 (1990). HS 216* Sy v CU (Cambridge) 1980. BAC HS 188 Sy v Sussex (Hove) 1978. Gm HS 171* v Warwicks (Birmingham) 1989. BB 6-48 Sy v Hants (Guildford) 1972. Gm BB 3-35 v Middx (Cardiff) 1987. Awards: NWT 3; BHC 6. **NWT:** HS 104* v Middx (Lord's) 1990. BB 1-27. **BHC:** HS 95 v Glos (Cardiff) 1990. BB 4-36 Sy v Middx (Lord's) 1985. **RAL:** HS 113* Sy v Warwicks (Birmingham) 1978. BB 5-19 Sy v Glos (Bristol) 1975.

CANN, Michael James (St Illtyds C, Cardiff; Swansea U), b Cardiff 4 July 1965. 5'9". LHB, OB. Debut 1986. OFS B 1989-90 (captain). HS 138 OFS B v GW (Virginia) 1989-90 on debut in SA. Gm HS 109 v Somerset (Cardiff) 1989. BB 3-30 v Middx (Abergavenny) 1989. **NWT:** HS 2*. BB 3-40 v Staffs (Cardiff) 1989. **BHC:** HS 46 Comb Us v Somerset (Taunton) 1987. BB 1-1. **RAL:** HS 5.

COTTEY, Phillip Anthony (Bishopston CS, Swansea), b Swansea 2 Jun 1966. 5'4". RHB. Debut 1986. 1000 runs (1): 1001 (1990). HS 156 v OU (Oxford) 1990. BAC HS 125 v Leics (Hinckley) 1990. BB 1-49. **NWT:** HS 27 v Sussex (Cardiff) 1990. **BHC:** HS 68 v Hants (Southampton) 1989. **RAL:** HS 50* v Notts (Nottingham) 1990.

CROFT, Robert Damien Bale (St John Lloyd Catholic CS; W Glam IHE), b Morriston 25 May 1970. 5'10½". RHB, OB. Debut 1989. HS 91* v Worcs (Abergavenny) 1990. BB 3-10 v Derbys (Cardiff) 1990. **NWT:** HS 26 v Middx (Lord's) 1990. **RAL:** HS 31 v Notts (Nottingham) 1990. BB 1-39.

DALE, Adrian (Chepstow CS; Swansea U), b Germiston, SA 24 Oct 1968 (to UK at 6 mths). 5'11½". RHB, RM. Debut 1989. HS 92 v Essex (Southend) 1990. BB 3-21 v Ind (Swansea) 1990. BAC BB 1-41. **NWT:** HS 10 v Hants (Cardiff) 1989. BB 2-32 v Staffs (Cardiff) 1989. **BHC:** HS 40 Comb Us v Surrey (Oxford) 1990. BB 3-24 Comb Us v Surrey (Cambridge) 1989. **RAL:** HS 67* v Derbys (Heanor) 1989. BB 3-35 v Worcs (Swansea) 1990.

DAVIES, Mark (Cwrt Sart CS; Neath Tertiary C), b Neath 18 Apr 1969. 5'6". RHB, SLA. Debut 1990. MCC staff. HS 5*.

DENNIS, Simon John (Scarborough C), b Scarborough, Yorks 18 Oct 1960. Nephew of F. (Yorkshire 1928-33) and Sir Leonard Hutton (Yorkshire and England 1934-55). 6'1". RHB, LFM. Yorkshire 1980-88 (cap 1983). Glamorgan debut 1989. OFS 1982-83. Tour: WI 1986-87 (Yorks). HS 53* Y v Notts (Nottingham) 1984. Gm HS 38 v Derbys (Derby) 1989. 50 wkts (1): 52 (1983). BB 5-35 Y v Somerset (Sheffield) 1981. Gm BB 5-76 v Leics (Cardiff) 1990. **NWT:** HS 14 Yv Salop (Telford) 1984. BB 2-45 Y v Northants (Leeds) 1983. **BHC:** HS 10 Y v Warwicks (Birmingham) 1984. BB 3-41 Y v Northants (Bradford) 1984. **RAL:** HS 16* (twice for Yorks). BB 3-19 Y v Hants (Middlesbrough) 1981.

DERRICK, John (Blaengwawr CS), b Cwmaman 15 Jan 1963. 6'1". RHB, RM. Debut 1983. Cap 1988. MCC Cricket Staff. HS 78* v Derbys (Abergavenny) 1986. BB 6-54 v Leics (Leicester) 1988. **NWT:** HS 4. BB 4-14 v Scot (Edinburgh) 1985. **BHC:** HS 42 v Kent (Cardiff) 1985. BB 4-53 v Comb Us (Cardiff) 1988. **RAL:** HS 26 v Northants (Northampton) 1983 and 26 v Kent (Maidstone) 1986. BB 5-32 v Middx (Lord's) 1987.

FROST, Mark (Alexander HS, Tipton; St Peter's S, Wolverhampton; Durham U), b Barking, Essex 21 Oct 1962. 6'2". RHB, RMF. Surrey 1988-89. Glamorgan debut 1990. Staffordshire 1987. HS 12 v Warwks (Birmingham) 1990. 50 wkts (1): 59 (1990). BB 5-40 Sy v Leics (Leicester) 1989 and 5-40 (10-82 match) v Glos (Bristol) 1990. Award: BHC 1. **NWT:** BB 3-50 v Dorset (Swansea) 1990. **BHC:** HS 3. BB 4-25 v Worcs (Worcester) 1990. **RAL:** HS 6. BB 4-30 v Northants (Northampton) 1990.

HEMP, David Lloyd (Olchfa CS; Millfield S; W Glamorgan C), b Bermuda 8 Nov 1970. 6'0". LHB, RM. UK resident since 1976. No 1st XI appearances – joined staff 1990.

HOLMES, Geoffrey Clark (West Denton HS), b Newcastle-upon-Tyne, Northumb 16 Sep 1958. 5'10". RHB, RM. Debut 1978. Cap 1985. Benefit 1991. Border 1989-90. MCC Cricket Staff. 1000 runs (3); most – 1129 (1985). HS 182 Border v W Province B (East London) 1989-90. Gm HS 125* v Somerset (Cardiff) 1990. BB 5-38 v Essex (Colchester) 1988. Awards: NWT 2. **NWT:** HS 57 v Cheshire (Cardiff) 1987. BB 5-24 v Scot (Edinburgh) 1985. **BHC:** HS 70 v Somerset (Taunton) 1985. BB 3-26 v Minor C (Swansea) 1985. **RAL:** HS 73 v Warwicks (Birmingham) 1984. BB 5-2 v Derbys (Ebbw Vale) 1984.

JAMES, Stephen Peter (Monmouth S; Swansea U; Hughes Hall, Cambridge), b Lydney, Glos 7 Sep 1967. 6'0". RHB. Debut 1985. Cambridge U 1989-90; blue 1989-90. 1000 runs (1): 1000 (1990). HS 151* CU v Warwicks (Cambridge) 1989. Gm HS 106 v OU (Oxford) 1987 – sharing Glam record 2nd-wkt stand of 249 with H.Morris. BAC HS 53 v Surrey (Oval) 1989. NWT: HS 26 v Cheshire (Cardiff) 1987. BHC: HS 65 Comb Us v Worcs (Worcester) 1989. RAL: HS 13 v Hants (Cardiff) 1989.

MAYNARD, Matthew Peter (David Hughes S, Anglesey), b Oldham, Lancs 21 Mar 1966. 5'10½". RHB, RM. Debut 1985 scoring 102 out of 117 in 87 min v Yorks (Swansea), reaching 100 with 3 sixes off successive balls. Cap 1987. YC 1988. Tests: 1 (1988); HS 10 v WI (Oval) 1988. Tour: SA 1989-90 (Eng XI). 1000 runs (5): most - 1626 (1987). HS 191* v Glos (Cardiff) 1989. BB 3-21 v OU (Oxford) 1987. BAC BB 1-25. Awards: BHC 4. NWT: HS 64 v Surrey (Oval) 1988. BHC: HS 115 v Comb Us (Cardiff) 1988. RAL: HS 100 v Lancs (Colwyn Bay) 1990.

METSON, Colin Peter (Enfield GS; Stanborough S, Welwyn Garden City; Durham U), b Goffs Oak, Herts 2 Jul 1963. 5'5½". RHB, WK. Middlesex 1981-86. Glamorgan debut/cap 1987. HS 96 M v Glos (Uxbridge) 1984. Gm HS 81 v Yorks (Cardiff) 1987. NWT: HS 9. BHC: HS 23 v Kent (Swansea) 1990. RAL: HS 30* v Hants (Bournemouth) 1990.

MORRIS, Hugh (Blundell's S), b Cardiff 5 Oct 1963. 5'8". LHB, RM. Debut 1981. Cap 1986. Captain 1986-89. 1000 runs (4) inc 2000 (1): 2276 – inc 10 hundreds – both Gm records (1990). HS 160* v Derbys (Cardiff) 1990. Shared Glam record 2nd-wkt stand of 249 with S.P.James v OU (Oxford) 1987. BB 1-6. BAC BB 1-45. Awards: NWT 1; BHC 3. NWT: HS 154* v Staffs (Cardiff) 1989. BHC: HS 143* v Hants (Southampton) 1989. BB 1-14. RAL: HS 100 v Derbys (Ebbw Vale) 1986.

RICHARDS, Isaac Vivian Alexander (Antigua GS), b St John's, Antigua 7 Mar 1952. 5'11". RHB, OB. Leeward Is 1971-90 (capt 1981-90). Somerset 1974-86 (cap 1974; benefit 1982). Glamorgan debut/cap 1990. Queensland 1976-77. Wisden 1976. Tests (WI): 111 (1974-75 to 1989-90, 40 as captain); HS 291 v Eng (Oval) 1976; BB 2-17 v P (P-of-S) 1987-88. LOI (WI): 179. Tours (WI) (C= captain): Eng 1976, 1980, 1984, 1988; A 1975-76, 1979-80, 1981-82, 1984-85, 1986-87C, 1988-89C; NZ 1986-87C; I 1974-75, 1983-84, 1987-88C; P 1974-75, 1980-81, 1986-87C; SL 1974-75. 1000 runs (13+3) inc 2000 (1): 2161 (1977). HS 322 (Sm record) v Warwicks (Taunton) 1985. Shared record Somerset 8th-wkt stand of 172 with I.T.Botham v Leics (Leicester) 1983. BB 5-88 WI v Queensland (Brisbane) 1981-82. BAC BB 4-36 Sm v Derbys (Chesterfield) 1986. Gm BB 2-27 v Sussex (Hove) 1990. Awards: NWT 6; BHC 6. NWT: HS 139* Sm v Warwicks (Taunton) 1978. BB 3-15 Somerset v Beds (Bedford) 1982. BHC: HS 132* Sm v Surrey (Lord's) 1981. BB 3-38 v Warwks (Birmingham) 1990. RAL: HS 126* Sm v Glos (Bristol Imp) 1975. BB 6-24 Sm v Lancs (Manchester) 1983.

ROBERTS, Martin Leonard (Helston CS), b Mullion, Cornwall 12 Apr 1966. 6'1". RHB, WK. Debut 1985. Cornwall 1983-84. HS 25 v SL (Ebbw Vale) 1990. BAC HS 13 v Lancs (Colwyn Bay) 1990. RAL: HS 12* v Sussex (Hove) 1990.

SHASTRI, Ravishankar Jayadritha (Don Bosco HS, Bombay), b Bombay, India 27 May 1962. 6'3". RHB, SLA. Bombay 1979-90 (capt 1987-88). Glamorgan debut 1987. Cap 1988. **Tests** (I): 72 (1980-81 to 1990 – 1 as captain); HS 187 v E (Oval) 1990; BB 5-75 v P (Nagpur) 1983-84. LOI (I): 123. Tours (I): E 1982, 1986, 1990; A 1985-86; WI 1982-83, 1988-89; NZ 1980-81; P 1982-83, 1984-85, 1989-90; SL 1985-86. 1000 runs (1+1); most – 1027 (1983-84). HS 200* Bombay v Baroda (Bombay) 1984-85 (including 6 sixes off one over and 200 in 113 min – world records). Gm HS 157 v Somerset (Cardiff) 1988. BB 9-101 Bombay v Rest (Indore) 1981-82. Gm BB 7-49 v Lancs (Swansea) 1988. Award: NWT 1. **NWT:** HS 59* v Surrey (Oval) 1988. BB 5-13 v Scot (Edinburgh) 1988. **BHC:** HS 55 v Hants (Southampton) 1988. BB 1-17. **RAL:** HS 92 and BB 3-33 v Middx (Merthyr Tydfil) 1989.

SMITH, Ian (Ryton CS), b Chopwell, Co Durham 11 Mar 1967. 6'2". RHB, RM. Debut 1985. HS 116 v Kent (Canterbury) 1989. BB 3-48 v Hants (Cardiff) 1989. **NWT:** HS 33 v Hants (Cardiff) 1989. BB 1-18. **BHC:** HS 21 v Worcs (Worcester) 1990. BB 1-21. **RAL:** HS 56* v Warwicks (Aberystwyth) 1989. BB 3-22 v Hants (Cardiff) 1989.

WATKIN, Steven Llewellyn (Cymer Afan CS; S Glamorgan CHE), b Maesteg 15 Sep 1964. 6'3". RHB, RMF. Debut 1986. Cap 1989. Tour: Z 1989-90 (Eng A). HS 31 v Leics (Leicester) 1989. 50 wkts (2); most – 94 (1989). BB 8-59 v Warwicks (Birmingham) 1988. **NWT:** HS 6*. BB 3-18 v Sussex (Cardiff) 1990. **BHC:** HS 6. BB 2-29 v Kent (Cardiff) 1989. **RAL:** HS 28* v Somerset (Taunton) 1989. BB 5-23 v Warwks (Birmingham) 1990.

NEWCOMER

FOSTER, Daren Joseph (Somerset S; Southgate TS; Haringey Cricket C), b Tottenham, London 14 Mar 1966. 5'9". RHB, RFM. Somerset 1986-89. HS 20 Sm v Hants (Southampton) 1988. BB 4-46 Sm v Worcs (Worcester) 1988. **NWT:** HS 0. BB 1-15. **BHC:** HS 0. BB 2-26 Sm v Yorks (Leeds) 1989. **RAL:** HS 8*. BB 4-26 Sm v Glos (Bath) 1989.

DEPARTURES

ANTHONY, Hamish Arbeb Gervais (Urlings Secondary S), b Urlings Village, Antigua 16 Jan 1971. 6'5". RHB, RFM. Leeward Is 1989-90. Glamorgan 1990. HS 39 v Lancs (Colwyn Bay) 1990. BB 5-40 LI v Jamaica (Kingston) 1989-90. Gm BB 3-95 v Ind (Swansea) 1990. BAC BB 2-70 v Warwks (Birmingham) 1990.

COWLEY, Nigel Geoffrey (Dutchy Manor SS, Mere), b Shaftesbury, Dorset 1 Mar 1953. 5'7". RHB, OB. Hampshire 1974-89 (cap 1978; benefit 1988). Glamorgan debut 1990. Dorset 1972. 1000 runs (1): 1042 (1984). HS 109* H v Somerset (Taunton) 1977. Gm HS 76 v Kent (Swansea) 1990. BB 6-48 H v Leics (Southampton) 1982. Gm BB 3-84 v Lancs (Colwyn Bay) 1990. Award: NWT 1. **NWT:** HS 63* H v Glos (Bristol) 1979. BB 5-24 H v Norfolk (Norwich) 1984. **BHC:** HS 59 H v Glos (Southampton) 1977. BB 3-39 H v Sussex (Bournemouth) 1982. **RAL:** HS 74 H v Warwicks (Birmingham) 1981. BB 4-42 H v Surrey (Portsmouth) 1983.

POOK, Robert Neil (Chafford CS), b Rainham 9 Feb 1967. 5'10". RHB, RM. Essex (1 match) 1988. Glamorgan (1 match) 1990. MCC Cricket Staff. HS 6.

GLAMORGAN 1990

RESULTS SUMMARY

	Place	Won	Lost	Drew	Abandoned
Britannic Assurance Championship	8th	5	6	11	
All First-class Matches		5	6	15	
Refuge Assurance League	15th	4	11		1
NatWest Bank Trophy	Quarter-Finalist				
Benson and Hedges Cup	Quarter-Finalist				

BRITANNIC ASSURANCE CHAMPIONSHIP AVERAGES

BATTING AND FIELDING

Cap		M	I	NO	HS	Runs	Avge	100	50	Ct/St
1990	I.V.A.Richards	18	28	5	164*	1425	61.95	7	3	8
1987	A.R.Butcher	21	39	5	151*	2044	60.11	6	14	8
1986	H.Morris	22	41	4	160*	1914	51.72	8	9	12
1987	M.P.Maynard	19	34	5	125*	1306	45.03	2	10	13
–	R.D.B.Croft	14	23	10	91*	570	43.84	–	3	2
–	N.G.Cowley	13	16	4	76	523	43.58	–	6	8
–	I.Smith	6	8	1	112*	293	41.85	1	2	1
1985	G.C.Holmes	7	10	3	125*	260	37.14	1	–	1
–	P.A.Cottey	17	30	5	125	816	32.64	2	4	9
–	M.J.Cann	5	8	0	64	180	22.50	–	2	2
–	A.Dale	7	11	0	92	179	16.27	–	1	6
1987	C.P.Metson	22	26	4	34	302	13.72	–	–	58
1989	S.L.Watkin	22	22	7	25*	170	11.33	–	–	5
–	S.Bastien	10	9	3	12	47	7.83	–	–	–
–	M.Frost	18	17	7	12	40	4.00	–	–	2
–	S.J.Dennis	12	8	1	6	23	3.28	–	–	3
–	S.P.James	3	6	0	7	10	1.66	–	–	1

Also played: H.A.G.Anthony (2 matches) 39, 0, 13; S.R.Barwick (3 matches – cap 1987) 0*, 2*; M.L.Roberts (1 match) 13.

BOWLING

	O	M	R	W	Avge	Best	5wI	10wM
S.Bastien	274.5	47	1075	35	30.71	6-75	2	–
M.Frost	509.1	63	1919	56	34.26	5-40	2	1
S.L.Watkin	731.1	118	2489	61	40.80	5-100	1	–
S.J.Dennis	283	53	957	20	47.85	5-76	1	–
R.D.B.Croft	357.1	76	1126	23	48.95	3-10	–	–
N.G.Cowley	296.3	58	851	11	77.36	3-84	–	–

Also bowled: H.A.G.Anthony 62-13-207-5; S.R.Barwick 124.4-27-396-5; A.R.Butcher 25.3-2-153-1; M.J.Cann 35.3-3-162-1; P.A.Cottey 18-0-116-1; A.Dale 51-8-187-0; G.C.Holmes 21-3-85-1; M.P.Maynard 20-1-150-0; H.Morris 6-0-62-0; I.V.A.Richards 137-26-426-5; I.Smith 33-3-157-1.

The First-Class Averages (pp 166–181) give the records of Glamorgan players in all first-class county matches (their other opponents being the Indians, the Sri Lankans and Oxford U. – twice), with the exception of:
S.P.James 5-10-0-47-79-7.90-0-0-4ct. Did not bowl.
S.L.Watkin 23-24-8-25*-173-10.81-0-0-6ct. 767.1-130-2629-65-40.44-5/100-1-0.

GLAMORGAN RECORDS

FIRST-CLASS CRICKET

Highest Total	For	587-8d	v Derbyshire	Cardiff	1951
	V	653-6d	by Glos	Bristol	1928
Lowest Total	For	22	v Lancashire	Liverpool	1924
	V	33	by Leics	Ebbw Vale	1965
Highest Innings	For	287* D.E.Davies	v Glos	Newport	1939
	V	313* S.J.Cook	for Somerset	Cardiff	1990

Highest Partnership for each Wicket

1st	330	A.Jones/R.C.Fredericks	v Northants	Swansea	1972
2nd	249	S.P.James/H.Morris	v Oxford U	Oxford	1987
3rd	313	D.E.Davies/W.E.Jones	v Essex	Brentwood	1948
4th	306*	Javed Miandad/Younis Ahmed	v Australians	Neath	1985
5th	264	M.Robinson/S.W.Montgomery	v Hampshire	Bournemouth	1949
6th	230	W.E.Jones/B.L.Muncer	v Worcs	Worcester	1953
7th	195*	W.Wooller/W.E.Jones	v Lancashire	Liverpool	1947
8th	202	D.Davies/J.J.Hills	v Sussex	Eastbourne	1928
9th	203*	J.J.Hills/J.C.Clay	v Worcs	Swansea	1929
10th	143	T.Davies/S.A.B.Daniels	v Glos	Swansea	1982

Best Bowling	For	10-51	J.Mercer	v Worcs	Worcester	1936
(Innings)	V	10-18	G.Geary	for Leics	Pontypridd	1929
Best Bowling	For	17-212	J.C.Clay	v Worcs	Swansea	1937
(Match)	V	16-96	G.Geary	for Leics	Pontypridd	1929

Most Runs – Season	2,276	H.Morris	(av 55.51)		1990
Most Runs – Career	34,056	A.Jones	(av 33.03)		1957-1983
Most 100s – Season	10	H.Morris			1990
Most 100s – Career	52	A.Jones			1957-1983
Most Wkts – Season	176	J.C.Clay	(av 17.34)		1937
Most Wkts – Career	2,174	D.J.Shepherd	(av 20.95)		1950-1972

LIMITED-OVERS CRICKET

Highest Total	NWT	318-4	v Staffs	Cardiff	1989
	BHC	302-6	v Comb Univs	Cardiff	1988
	RAL	277-6	v Derbyshire	Ebbw Vale	1984
Lowest Total	NWT	76	v Northants	Northampton	1968
	BHC	68	v Lancashire	Manchester	1973
	RAL	42	v Derbyshire	Swansea	1979
Highest Innings	NWT	154* H.Morris	v Staffs	Cardiff	1989
	BHC	143* H.Morris	v Hampshire	Southampton	1989
	RAL	130* J.A.Hopkins	v Somerset	Bath	1983
Best Bowling	NWT	5-13 R.J.Shastri	v Scotland	Edinburgh	1988
	BHC	5-17 A.H.Wilkins	v Worcs	Worcester	1978
	RAL	6-29 M.A.Nash	v Worcs	Worcester	1975

GLOUCESTERSHIRE

Formation of Present Club: 1871
Colours: Blue, Gold, Brown, Silver, Green and Red
Badge: Coat of Arms of the City and County of Bristol
Championships (since 1890): (0) Second 1930, 1931, 1947, 1959, 1969, 1986
NatWest Trophy/Gillette Cup Winners: (1) 1973
Benson and Hedges Cup Winners: (1) 1977
Sunday League Champions: (0) Second 1988
Match Awards: NWT 33; BHC 39

Secretary: P.G.M.August, Phoenix County Ground, Nevil Road, Bristol BS7 9EJ (☎ 0272-245216)
Captain: A.J.Wright
Scorer: B.H.Jenkins
1991 Beneficiary: P.W.Romaines

ALLEYNE, Mark Wayne (Harrison C, Barbados; Cardinal Pole S, London E9; Haringey Cricket C), b Tottenham, London 23 May 1968. 5'10". RHB, RM. Debut 1986. Cap 1990. Tour: SL 1986-87 (Glos). HS 256 v Northants (Northampton) 1990. BB 4-48 v Glam (Bristol) 1988. NWT: HS 9*. BB 5-30 v Lincs (Gloucester) 1990. BHC: HS 36 v Derbys (Derby) 1987. BB 5-27 v Comb Us (Bristol) 1988. RAL: HS 49* v Derbys (Heanor) 1988. BB 3-25 v Essex (Chelmsford) 1990.

ATHEY, Charles William Jeffrey (Stainsby SS; Acklam Hall HS), b Middlesbrough, Yorks 27 Sep 1957. 5'9½". RHB, RM. Yorkshire 1976-83 (cap 1980). Gloucestershire debut 1984. Cap 1985. Captain 1989. Benefit 1990. Tests: 23 (1980 to 1988); HS 123 v P (Lord's) 1987. LOI: 31. Tours: A 1986-87, 1987-88; SA 1989-90 (Eng A); WI 1980-81; NZ 1979-80 (DHR), 1987-88; P 1987-88; SL 1985-86 (Eng B). 1000 runs (8); most – 1812 (1984). HS 184 Eng B v Sri Lanka (Galle) 1985-86. Gs HS 171* v Northants (Northampton) 1986. BB 3-3 v Hants (Bristol) 1985. Awards: NWT 3; BHC 5. NWT: HS 115 Y v Kent (Leeds) 1980. BB 1-18. BHC: HS 95 v Northants (Northampton) 1987. BB 4-48 v Comb Us (Bristol) 1984. RAL: HS 121* v Worcs (Moreton) 1985. BB 5-35 Y v Derbys (Chesterfield) 1981.

BALL, Martyn Charles John (King Edmund SS; Bath CFE), b Bristol 26 Apr 1970. 5'8". RHB, OB. Debut 1988. HS 17* v Hants (Portsmouth) 1989. BB 4-53 v Kent (Maidstone) 1989. NWT: BB 3-42 v Lancs (Gloucester) 1989. RAL: HS 4. BB 1-17.

BARNES, Stuart Neil (Beechen Cliff S, Bath), b Bath, Somerset 27 Jun 1970. 6'1". RHB, RM. Debut 1990. HS 12* v Ind (Bristol) 1990. BAC HS 6. BB 4-51 v CU (Cambridge) 1990. BAC BB 2-10 v Derbys (Derby) 1990. NWT: HS 0. BB 1-64. RAL: HS 11* v Sussex (Hove) 1989. BB 3-39 v Surrey (Cheltenham) 1990.

BELL, Robert Malcolm (Truro S), b St Mary's, Isles of Scilly 26 Feb 1969. 6'5". RHB, RM. Debut 1990. Cornwall 1990. HS 0*. BB 2-38 v Worcs (Worcester) 1990.

HODGSON, Geoffrey Dean (Nelson Thomlinson CS, Wigton; Loughborough U), b Carlisle, Cumberland 22 Oct 1966. 6'1". RHB. Debut 1989. Cumberland 1984-88 (cap 1987 when aged 20 – county record). Warwickshire (RAL only) 1987. 1000 runs (1): 1320 (1990). HS 126 v Z (Bristol) 1990. BAC HS 109 v Worcs (Bristol) 1990. NWT: HS 52 v Lancs (Manchester) 1990. BHC: HS 1. RAL: HS 39 v Northants (Moreton) 1989.

LAWRENCE, David Valentine (Linden S), b Gloucester 28 Jan 1964. 6'2". RHB, RF. Debut 1981. Cap 1985. YC 1985. **Tests:** 1 (1988) HS 4 and BB 2-74 v SL (Lord's) 1988. Tours: SL 1985-86 (Eng B); 1986-87 (Glos). HS 65* v Glam (Swansea) 1987. 50 wkts (4); most – 85 (1985). BB 7-47 v Surrey (Cheltenham) 1988. Hat-trick 1990. Awards: NWT 1; BHC 1. **NWT:** HS 2*. BB 4-36 v Berks (Reading) 1986. **BHC:** HS 22* v Scot (Bristol) 1985. BB 5-48 v Hants (Bristol) 1984. **RAL:** HS 21* v Leics (Leicester) 1986. BB 5-18 v Somerset (Bristol) 1990.

LLOYDS, Jeremy William (Blundell's S), b Penang, Malaya 17 Nov 1954. 6'0". LHB, OB. Somerset 1979-84 (cap 1982). OFS 1983-88. Gloucestershire debut/cap 1985. MCC Cricket Staff. Tour: SL 1986-87 (Glos). 1000 runs (3); most – 1295 (1986). HS 132* Sm v Northants (Northampton) 1982. Gs HS 130 v Glam (Swansea) 1988. BB 7-88 Sm v Essex (Chelmsford) 1982. Gs BB 7-134 v Somerset (Bath) 1989. **NWT:** HS 73* v Lincs (Gloucester) 1990. BB 2-35 v Berks (Reading) 1986. **BHC:** HS 53* v Warwks (Bristol) 1990. BB 3-21 v Glam (Swansea) 1986. **RAL:** HS 65 v Yorks (Leeds) 1989. BB 2-1 Sm v Hants (Taunton) 1981.

MILBURN, Edward Thomas (King Edward VI C, Nuneaton), b Nuneaton 15 Sep 1967. 6'1½". RHB, RM. Warwickshire 1987. Gloucestershire debut 1990. HS 35 v Ind (Bristol) 1990. BAC HS 24 Wa v Hants (Birmingham) 1987. BB 3-43 v Ind (Bristol) 1990. BAC BB 1-26. **BHC:** BB 1-23. **RAL:** HS 5*. BB 2-34 v Surrey (Cheltenham) 1990.

PRITCHARD, Neil Michael Albert (Marlwood S; Swansea U), b Thornbury 4 Jul 1967. 5'10". RHB. Awaiting f-c debut. RAL debut 1989. **RAL:** HS 9.

ROMAINES, Paul William (Leeholm S), b Bishop Auckland, Co Durham 25 Dec 1955. 6'0". RHB, occ OB. Northants 1975-76. Gloucestershire debut 1982. Cap 1983. Benefit 1991. GW 1984-85. Durham 1977-81. Tour: SL 1986-87 (Glos). 1000 runs (3); most – 1844 (1984). HS 186 v Warwks (Nuneaton) 1982. BB 3-42 v Surrey (Oval) 1985. Awards: BHC 2. **NWT:** HS 82 v Hants (Bristol) 1983. **BHC:** HS 125 v Notts (Bristol) 1985. **RAL:** HS 105 v Northants (Northampton) 1985.

RUSSELL, Robert Charles (**Jack**) (Archway CS), b Stroud 15 Aug 1963. 5'8½". LHB, WK, occ OB. Debut 1981. Cap 1985. Wisden 1989. **Tests:** 17 (1988 to 1990); HS 128* v A (Manchester) 1989. LOI: 17. Tours: WI 1989-90; P 1987-88; SL 1986-87 (Glos). HS 128* (Tests). Gs HS 120 v Somerset (Bristol) 1990. Award: BHC 1. **NWT:** HS 42* v Lancs (Gloucester) 1989. **BHC:** HS 46* v Glam (Cardiff) 1990. **RAL:** HS 108 v Worcs (Hereford) 1986.

WALSH, Courtney Andrew (Excelsior HS), b Kingston, Jamaica 30 Oct 1962. 6'5½". RHB, RF. Jamaica 1981-90. Gloucestershire debut 1984. Cap 1985. Wisden 1986. **Tests (WI):** 37 (1984-85 to 1989-90); HS 30* v A (Melbourne) 1988-89; BB 6-62 v I (Kingston) 1988-89. LOI (WI): 88. Tours (WI): Eng 1984, 1988; A 1984-85, 1986-87, 1988-89; NZ 1986-87; I 1987-88; P 1986-87; Z 1983-84 (Young WI). HS 63* v Yorks (Cheltenham) 1990. 50 wkts (5) inc 100 wickets (1): 118 (1986). BB 9-72 v Somerset (Bristol) 1986. Award: NWT 1. **NWT:** HS 25* v Berks (Reading) 1986. BB 6-21 v Kent (Bristol) 1990. **BHC:** HS 28 v Comb Us (Bristol) 1989. BB 2-19 v Scot 1985. **RAL:** HS 35 v Glam (Cardiff) 1986. BB 4-19 v Kent (Cheltenham) 1987.

WILLIAMS, Richard Charles James (Millfield S), b Southmead, Bristol 8 Aug 1969. 5'8". LHB, WK. Debut 1990. HS 50* v Ind (Bristol) 1990. BAC HS 44* v Northants (Cheltenham) 1990.

WRIGHT, Anthony John (Alleyn's GS), b Stevenage, Herts 27 Jun 1962. 6'0". RHB, RM. Gloucestershire debut 1982. Cap 1987. Captain 1990-. Tour: SL 1986-87 (Glos). 1000 runs (3); most – 1268 (1988). HS 161 v Glam (Bristol) 1987. BB 1-16. Award: NWT 1. **NWT:** HS 92 v Lincs (Gloucester) 1990. **BHC:** HS 97 v Worcs (Bristol) 1990. **RAL:** HS 81 v Kent (Moreton) 1988 and 81 v Leics (Leicester) 1989.

NEWCOMERS

BABINGTON, Andrew Mark (Reigate GS; Borough Road PE College), b Middlesex Hospital, London 22 Jul 1963. 6'2". LHB, RFM. Sussex 1986-90. HS 20 Sx v Glam (Hove) 1990. BB 5-37 Sx v Lancs (Liverpool) 1989. Hat-trick 1988. **NWT:** HS 4*. BB 3-53 Sx v Leics (Hove) 1989. **BHC:** HS 9. BB 4-29 Sx v Surrey (Hove) 1988. **RAL:** HS 1*. BB 4-48 Sx v Worcs (Hove) 1989.

GILBERT, David Robert (Marist Brothers S, Eastwood), b Darlinghurst, Sydney, Australia 29 Dec 1960. 6'1". RHB, RFM. NSW 1983-88. Tasmania 1988-90. Lincolnshire 1984. **Tests** (A): 9 (1985 to 1986-87); HS 15 v NZ (Christchurch) 1985-86; BB 3-48 v NZ (Perth) 1985-86. LOI (A): 14. Tours (A): Eng 1985; NZ 1985-86; I 1986-87; Z 1985-86 (Young A), 1987-88 (NSW). HS 117 Aus v Delhi (Baroda) 1986-87. BB 7-43 Young Aus v Zimbabwe (Harare) 1985-86.

HARDY, Jonathan James Ean (Canford S), b Nakaru, Kenya 2 Oct 1960. 6'3½". LHB. Hampshire 1984-85. Somerset 1986-90 (cap 1987). W Province 1987-90. 1000 runs (1): 1089 (1987). HS 119 Sm v Glos (Taunton) 1987. Award: NWT 1. **NWT:** HS 100 Sm v Durham (Darlington) 1988. **BHC:** HS 109 Sm v Derbys (Taunton) 1990. **RAL:** HS 94* Sm v Essex (Taunton) 1987.

SCOTT, Richard John (Queen Elizabeth S, Bournemouth), b Bournemouth, Hants 2 Nov 1963. 5'11". LHB, RM. Hampshire 1988-90. Dorset 1981-85. HS 107* H v SL (Southampton) 1988. BAC HS 77 H v Leics (Bournemouth) 1989. BB 2-5 H v Middx (Bournemouth) 1990. **NWT:** HS 22 H v Middx (Southampton) 1989. **BHC:** HS 69 H v Sussex (Hove) 1989. **RAL:** HS 116* H v Yorks (Southampton) 1989. BB 2-8 H v Worcs (Worcester) 1990.

DEPARTURES

BAINBRIDGE, Philip (Hanley HS; Stoke-on-Trent SFC; Borough Road CE), b Sneyd Green, Stoke-on-Trent, Staffs 16 Apr 1958. 5'10". RHB, RM. Gloucestershire 1977-90 (cap 1981; benefit 1989). Wisden 1985. Tours: SL 1986-87 (Glos); Z 1984-85 (EC). 1000 runs (8); most – 1644 (1985). HS 169 v Yorks (Cheltenham) 1988. BB 8-53 v Somerset (Bristol) 1986. Awards: NWT 1; BHC 2. **NWT:** HS 89 v Leics (Leicester) 1988. BB 3-49 v Scot (Bristol) 1983. **BHC:** HS 96 v Hants (Southampton) 1988. BB 3-21 v Notts (Gloucester) 1981. **RAL:** HS 106* v Somerset (Bristol) 1986. BB 5-22 v Middx (Lord's) 1987.

BUTCHER, Ian Paul (John Ruskin HS), b Farnborough, Kent 1 Jul 1962. Brother of A.R. (Surrey, Glam and England) and M.S. (Surrey 1982). 6'0". RHB, RM. Leicestershire 1980-87 (cap 1984). Gloucestershire 1988-90. 1000 runs (2); most – 1349 (1984). HS 139 Le v Notts (Leicester) 1983. Gs HS 105* v Kent (Maidstone) 1989. **NWT:** HS 81 Le v Northants (Northampton) 1984. BB 1-6. **BHC:** HS 103* Le v Minor C (Leicester) 1986. **RAL:** HS 71 Le v Northants (Leicester) 1982.

CURRAN, K.M. – see NORTHAMPTONSHIRE.

GRAVENEY, D.A. – see SOMERSET.

Continued on p 154.

GLOUCESTERSHIRE 1990

RESULTS SUMMARY

	Place	Won	Lost	Drew	Abandoned
Britannic Assurance Championship	13th	4	7	11	
All First-class Matches		5	7	13	
Refuge Assurance League	8th	7	7		2
NatWest Bank Trophy	Quarter-Finalist				
Benson and Hedges Cup	5th in Group A				

BRITANNIC ASSURANCE CHAMPIONSHIP AVERAGES

BATTING AND FIELDING

Cap		M	I	NO	HS	Runs	Avge	100	50	Ct/St
1985	C.W.J.Athey	21	32	6	131	1384	53.23	3	8	18
1985	K.M.Curran	22	32	8	144*	1261	52.54	3	5	15
1990	M.W.Alleyne	11	17	0	256	763	44.88	2	2	9
1981	P.Bainbridge	18	25	2	152	1019	44.30	2	4	4
1985	R.C.Russell	11	16	1	120	651	43.40	2	3	27
1985	J.W.Lloyds	21	29	10	93	704	37.05	–	3	15
–	G.D.Hodgson	21	34	2	109	1059	33.09	1	9	10
1983	P.W.Romaines	5	7	1	61	177	29.50	–	1	2
1985	C.A.Walsh	19	19	3	63*	464	29.00	–	3	6
–	I.P.Butcher	9	13	3	102	280	28.00	1	–	–
1976	A.W.Stovold	2	4	0	74	104	26.00	–	1	–
1987	A.J.Wright	22	36	3	112	809	24.51	1	4	21
–	R.C.J.Williams	7	7	3	44*	82	20.50	–	–	22/4
1976	D.A.Graveney	12	12	4	46*	100	12.50	–	–	5
–	M.C.J.Ball	3	5	0	15	39	7.80	–	–	2
1985	D.V.Lawrence	20	21	3	29	124	6.88	–	–	6
–	S.N.Barnes	7	7	1	6	11	1.83	–	–	2

Also played: R.M.Bell (2 matches) 0, 0*; K.B.S.Jarvis (1 match) 0*, 1*;
E.T.Milburn (1 match) 0, 3*; P.A.Owen (3 matches) 1, 1; G.A.Tedstone (4 matches)
13, 6, 23 (3 ct).

BOWLING

	O	M	R	W	Avge	Best	5wI	10wM
M.W.Alleyne	77	23	254	11	23.09	3-23	–	–
C.A.Walsh	584.1	98	1961	70	28.01	8-58	3	1
K.M.Curran	561.3	105	1839	60	30.65	5-63	1	–
D.V.Lawrence	418.3	45	1679	50	33.58	5-51	2	–
D.A.Graveney	462.4	125	1145	29	39.48	5-45	3	1
J.W.Lloyds	314.5	52	1175	24	48.95	4-11	–	–

Also bowled: C.W.J.Athey 36.5-9-104-2; P.Bainbridge 137.4-24-426-9; M.C.J.Ball
34-7-114-0; S.N.Barnes 138-25-388-8; R.M.Bell 44-7-114-3; K.B.S.Jarvis 12-1-61-1;
E.T.Milburn 7-1-34-0; P.A.Owen 57-7-239-4; G.A.Tedstone 2-1-1-0; A.J.Wright
0.5-0-7-0.

The First-Class Averages (pp 166–181) give the records of Gloucestershire players in
all first-class county matches (their other opponents being the Indians, the
Zimbabweans and Cambridge U.), with the exception of R.C.Russell, whose full
county figures are as above, and:
D.V.Lawrence 22-23-3-35-159-7.95-0-0-7ct. 472.2-52-1874-56-33.46-5/51-2-0.

GLOUCESTERSHIRE RECORDS

FIRST-CLASS CRICKET

Highest Total	For	653-6d		v Glamorgan	Bristol	1928
	V	774-7d		by Australians	Bristol	1948
Lowest Total	For	17		v Australians	Cheltenham	1896
	V	12		by Northants	Gloucester	1907
Highest Innings	For	318*	W.G.Grace	v Yorkshire	Cheltenham	1876
	V	296	A.O.Jones	for Notts	Nottingham	1903

Highest Partnership for each Wicket

1st	395	D.M.Young/R.B.Nicholls	v Oxford U	Oxford	1962
2nd	256	C.T.M.Pugh/T.W.Graveney	v Derbyshire	Chesterfield	1960
3rd	336	W.R.Hammond/B.H.Lyon	v Leics	Leicester	1933
4th	321	W.R.Hammond/W.L.Neale	v Leics	Gloucester	1937
5th	261	W.G.Grace/W.O.Moberley	v Yorkshire	Cheltenham	1876
6th	320	G.L.Jessop/J.H.Board	v Sussex	Hove	1903
7th	248	W.G.Grace/E.L.Thomas	v Sussex	Hove	1896
8th	239	W.R.Hammond/A.E.Wilson	v Lancashire	Bristol	1938
9th	193	W.G.Grace/S.A.P.Kitcat	v Sussex	Bristol	1896
10th	131	W.R.Gouldsworthy/J.G.Bessant	v Somerset	Bristol	1923

Best Bowling	For	10-40	E.G.Dennett	v Essex	Bristol	1906
(Innings)	V	10-66	A.A.Mailey	for Australians	Cheltenham	1921
		10-66	K.Smales	for Notts	Stroud	1956
Best Bowling	For	17-56	C.W.L.Parker	v Essex	Gloucester	1925
(Match)	V	15-87	A.J.Conway	for Worcs	Moreton-in-M	1914

Most Runs – Season	2,860	W.R.Hammond (av 69.75)		1933
Most Runs – Career	33,664	W.R.Hammond (av 57.05)		1920-1951
Most 100s – Season	13	W.R.Hammond		1938
Most 100s – Career	113	W.R.Hammond		1920-1951
Most Wkts – Season	222	T.W.J.Goddard (av 16.80)		1937
	222	T.W.J.Goddard (av 16.37)		1947
Most Wkts – Career	3,170	C.W.L.Parker (av 19.43)		1903-1935

LIMITED-OVERS CRICKET

Highest Total	NWT	327-7		v Berkshire	Reading	1966
	BHC	300-4		v Comb Univs	Oxford	1982
	RAL	272-4		v Middlesex	Lord's	1983
		272-7		v Northants	Northampton	1990
Lowest Total	NWT	82		v Notts	Bristol	1987
	BHC	62		v Hampshire	Bristol	1975
	RAL	49		v Middlesex	Bristol	1978
Highest Innings	NWT	158	Zaheer Abbas	v Leics	Leicester	1983
	BHC	154*	M.J.Procter	v Somerset	Taunton	1972
	RAL	131	Sadiq Mohd	v Somerset	Bristol (Imp)	1975
Best Bowling	NWT	6-21	C.A.Walsh	v Kent	Bristol	1990
	BHC	6-13	M.J. Proctor	v Hampshire	Southampton	1977
	RAL	6-52	D.J.Shepherd	v Kent	Bristol	1975

HAMPSHIRE

Formation of Present Club: 12 August 1863
Colours: Blue, Gold and White
Badge: Tudor Rose and Crown
Championships: (2) 1961, 1973
NatWest Trophy/Gillette Cup Semi-Finalists: (7) 1966, 1976, 1983, 1985, 1988, 1989, 1990
Benson and Hedges Cup Winners: (1) 1988
Sunday League Champions: (3) 1975, 1978, 1986
Match Awards: NWT 43; BHC 46

Chief Executive: A.F.Baker, County Ground, Northlands Road, Southampton SO9 2TY (☎ 0703-333788)
Captain: M.C.J.Nicholas
Scorer: V.H. Isaacs
1991 Beneficiary: M.C.J.Nicholas

AYLING, Jonathan Richard (Portsmouth GS), b Portsmouth 13 Jun 1967. 6'4". RHB, RM. Debut 1988. Took wicket of D.A.Polkinghorne (OU) with first ball in f-c cricket. HS 88* v Lancs (Liverpool) 1988. BB 4-57 v Glos (Gloucester) 1988. **NWT:** HS 29 v Leics (Leicester) 1990. BB 3-30 v Yorks (Southampton) 1990. **BHC:** HS 14 v Lancs (Southampton) 1990. BB 2-22 v Lancs (Manchester) 1990. **RAL:** HS 47* v Worcs (Worcester) 1990. BB 4-37 v Notts (Southampton) 1990.

AYMES, Adrian Nigel (Bellemoor SM, Southampton), b Southampton 4 Jun 1964. 6'0". RHB, WK. Debut 1987. HS 75* v Glam (Pontypridd) 1990. **RAL:** HS 15* v Yorks (Leeds) 1990.

BAKKER, Paul-Jan (Hugo De Groot C, The Hague), b Vlaardingen, Holland 19 Aug 1957. 5'11". RHB, RMF. Debut 1986. Cap 1989. HS 22 v Yorks (Southampton) 1989. 50 wkts (1): 77 (1989). BB 7-31 v Kent (Bournemouth) 1987. **NWT:** HS 3*. BB 3-34 v Worcs (Worcester) 1988. **BHC:** BB 2-19 v Comb Us (Oxford) 1986. **RAL:** HS 9. BB 5-17 v Derbys (Derby) 1989.

CONNOR, Cardigan Adolphus (The Valley SS, Anguilla; Langley C, Berkshire), b The Valley, Anguilla 24 Mar 1961. 5'9". RHB, RFM. Debut 1984. Cap 1988. Buckinghamshire 1979-83. HS 46 v Derbys (Portsmouth) 1990. 50 wkts (3); most – 62 (1984). BB 7-31 v Glos (Portsmouth) 1989. **NWT:** HS 13 v Yorks (Southampton) 1990. BB 4-73 v Northants (Southampton) 1990. **BHC:** HS 5*. BB 4-19 v Sussex (Hove) 1989. **RAL:** HS 19 v Glos (Trowbridge) 1989. BB 4-11 v Derbys (Portsmouth) 1990.

COX, Rupert Michael FIENNES- (Bradfield C), b Guildford, Surrey 20 Aug 1967. 5'9". LHB, OB. Debut 1990. HS 104* v Worcs (Worcester) 1990 – in second match. **RAL:** HS 2*.

FLINT, Darren Peter John (Queen Mary's SFC), b Basingstoke 14 Jun 1970. 6'0". RHB, SLA. No 1st XI appearances – joined staff 1990.

GOWER, David Ivon (King's S, Canterbury; London U), b Tunbridge Wells, Kent 1 Apr 1957. 6'0". LHB, OB. Leicestershire 1975-89 (cap 1977; captain 1984-86, 1988-89; benefit 1987). Hampshire debut/cap 1990. Wisden 1978. YC 1978. **Tests:** 109 (1978 to 1990, 32 as captain); HS 215 v A (Birmingham) 1985; BB 1-1. LOI: 109. Tours (C=captain): A 1978-79, 1979-80, 1982-83, 1986-87; WI 1980-81, 1985-86C, 1989-90; NZ 1983-84; I 1979-80, 1981-82, 1984-85C; P 1983-84; SL 1977-78 (DHR), 1981-82, 1984-85C. 1000 runs (10); most – 1530 (1982). HS 228 Le v Glam (Leicester) 1989. H HS 145 v Sussex (Southampton) 1990. Shared record Leics 2nd-wkt stand of 289* with J.C.Balderstone v Essex (Leicester) 1981. BB 3-47 Le v Essex (Leicester) 1977. Awards: NWT 5; BHC 1. **NWT:** HS 156 Le v Derbys (Leicester) 1984. **BHC:** HS 114* Le v Derbys (Derby) 1980. **RAL:** HS 135* Le v Warwks (Leicester) 1977.

JAMES, Kevan David (Edmonton County HS), b Lambeth, London 18 Mar 1961. 6'0". LHB, LMF. Middlesex 1980-84. Wellington 1982-83. Hampshire debut 1985. Cap 1989. Shared record Hants 8th-wkt stand of 227 with T.M.Tremlett v Somerset (Taunton) 1989. HS 162 v Glam (Cardiff) 1989. BB 6-22 v Australians (Southampton) 1985. BAC BB 5-25 v Glos (Southampton) 1988. **NWT:** HS 42 v Glam (Cardiff) 1989. BB 3-22 v Dorset (Southampton) 1987. **BHC:** HS 45 v Essex (Chelmsford) 1989. BB 3-31 v Middx 1987 and v Glam 1988. **RAL:** HS 66 v Glos (Trowbridge) 1989. BB 4-23 v Lancs (Southampton) 1986.

MARSHALL, Malcolm Denzil (Parkinson CS, Barbados), b St Michael, Barbados 18 Apr 1958. 5'11". RHB, RF. Barbados 1977-90 (capt 1987-88). Hampshire debut 1979. Cap 1981. Benefit 1987. Wisden 1982. **Tests** (WI): 68 (1978-79 to 1989-90); HS 92 v I (Kanpur) 1983-84; BB 7-22 v Eng (Manchester) 1988. LOI (WI): 113. Tours (WI): Eng 1980, 1984, 1988; A 1979-80, 1981-82, 1984-85, 1988-89; NZ 1979-80, 1986-87; I 1978-79, 1983-84; P 1980-81, 1986-87; SL 1978-79; Z 1981-82 (Young WI). HS 117 v Yorks (Leeds) 1990. 50 wkts (8+4) inc 100 wkts (2); most – 134 (1982). 2 hat-tricks: 1978-79 (Barbados), 1983 (4 wkts in 5 balls). BB 8-71 v Worcs (Southampton) 1982. Award: NWT 1. **NWT:** HS 77 v Northants (Southampton) 1990. BB 4-15 v Kent (Canterbury) 1983. **BHC:** HS 34 v Essex (Chelmsford) 1987. BB 4-26 v Kent (Canterbury) 1983. **RAL:** HS 46 v Leics 1982 and v Middx 1990. BB 5-13 v Glam (Portsmouth) 1979.

MARU, Rajesh Jamandass (Rook's Heath HS, Harrow; Pinner SFC), b Nairobi, Kenya 28 Oct 1962. 5'6". RHB, SLA. Middlesex 1980-82. Hampshire debut 1984. Cap 1986. Tour: Z 1980-81 (Middx). HS 74 v Glos (Gloucester) 1988. 50 wkts (4); most – 73 (1985). BB 8-41 v Kent (Southampton) 1988. **NWT:** HS 22 v Yorks (Southampton) 1990. BB 3-46 v Leics (Leicester) 1990. **BHC:** HS 9. BB 3-46 v Comb Us (Southampton) 1990. **RAL:** HS 12* v Kent (Canterbury) 1990. BB 3-30 v Leics (Leicester) 1988.

MIDDLETON, Tony Charles (Montgomery of Alamein S, and Peter Symonds SFC, Winchester), b Winchester 1 Feb 1964. 5'10½". RHB, SLA. Debut 1984. Cap 1990. 1000 runs (1): 1238 (1990). HS 127 v Kent (Canterbury) 1990. BB 1-13. **RAL:** HS 72 v Surrey (Southampton) 1990.

NICHOLAS, Mark Charles Jefford (Bradfield C), b London 29 Sep 1957. Grandson of F.W.H. (Essex 1912-29). 5'11". RHB, RM. Debut 1978. Cap 1982. Captain 1985-. Benefit 1991. Tours (C=captain): SL 1985-86C (Eng B); Z 1984-85C (EC), 1989-90 (Eng A). 1000 runs (7); most – 1559 (1984). HS 206* v OU (Oxford) 1982. BAC HS 158 v Lancs (Portsmouth) 1984. BB 6-37 v Somerset (Southampton) 1989.

Award: BHC 1. **NWT:** HS 71 v Surrey (Oval) 1989. BB 2-39 v Berks (Southampton) 1985. **BHC:** HS 74 v Glam (Southampton) 1985. BB 4-34 v Minor C (Reading) 1985. **RAL:** HS 108 v Glos (Bristol) 1984. BB 4-30 v Glos (Trowbridge) 1989.

PARKS, Robert James (Eastbourne GS; Southampton Inst of Technology), b Cuckfield, Sussex 15 Jun 1959. Son of J.M. (Sussex, Somerset and England 1949-76) and grandson of J.H. (Sussex and England 1924-52). 5'8". RHB, WK. Debut 1980. Cap 1982. Tour: Z 1984-85 (EC). Held 10 catches in match v Derbys (Portsmouth) 1981. HS 89 v CU (Cambridge) 1984. BAC HS 80 v Derbys (Portsmouth) 1986. Award: BHC 1. **NWT:** HS 27* v Yorks (Southampton) 1990. **BHC:** HS 23* v Somerset (Taunton) 1988. **RAL:** HS 38* v Essex (Portsmouth) 1987.

SHINE, Kevin James (Maiden Erlegh CS), b Bracknell, Berkshire 22 Feb 1969. 6'2½". RHB, RMF. Debut 1989. Berkshire 1986. HS 26* v Middx (Lord's) 1989. BB 4-52 v Yorks (Leeds) 1990. **BHC:** HS 0. BB 4-68 v Surrey (Oval) 1990.

SMITH, Christopher Lyall ('Kippy') (Northlands HS, Durban), b Durban, South Africa 15 Oct 1958. Brother of R.A. and grandson of Dr V.L.Shearer (Natal). 5'10". RHB, OB. Natal 1977-83. Glamorgan 1979. Hampshire debut 1980. Cap 1981. Benefit 1990. Wisden 1983. **Tests:** 8 (1983 to 1986); HS 91 v NZ (Auckland) 1983-84; BB 2-31 v NZ (Nottingham) 1983. **LOI:** 4. Tours: NZ 1983-84; P 1983-84; SL 1985-86 (Eng B). 1000 runs (9) inc 2000 (1): 2000 (1985). HS 217 v Warwks (Birmingham) 1987 – sharing record Hants 1st-wkt stand of 347 with V.P.Terry. BB 5-69 v Sussex (Southampton) 1988. Awards: NWT 7; BHC 3. **NWT:** HS 159 v Cheshire (Chester) 1989. BB 3-32 v Berks (Southampton) 1985. **BHC:** HS 154* v Comb Us (Southampton) 1990. **RAL:** HS 95 v Leics (Basingstoke) 1984. BB 2-3 v Glos (Bristol) 1984.

SMITH, Robin Arnold (Northlands HS), b Durban, South Africa 13 Sep 1963. Brother of C.L. and grandson of Dr V.L.Shearer (Natal). 5'11". RHB, LB. Natal 1980-83. Hampshire debut 1982. Cap 1985. Wisden 1989. **Tests:** 18 (1988 to 1990); HS 143 v A (Manchester) 1989. **LOI:** 20. Tour: WI 1989-90. 1000 runs (5); most – 1577 (1989). HS 209* v Essex (Southend) 1987. BB 2-11 v Surrey (Southampton) 1985. Awards: NWT 3; BHC 2. **NWT:** HS 125* v Surrey (Oval) 1989. BB 2-13 v Berks (Southampton) 1985. **BHC:** HS 155* v Glam (Southampton) 1989. **RAL:** HS 131 v Notts (Nottingham) 1989.

TERRY, Vivian Paul (Millfield S), b Osnabruck, W Germany 14 Jan 1959. 6'0". RHB, RM. Debut 1978. Cap 1983. **Tests:** 2 (1984); HS 8. Tour: Z 1984-85 (EC). 1000 runs (7); most – 1382 (1987). HS 190 v Sri Lankans (Southampton) 1988. BAC HS 180 v Derbys (Derby) 1990. Shared record Hants 1st-wkt stand of 347 with C.L.Smith v Warwks (Birmingham) 1987. Awards: NWT 3; BHC 3. **NWT:** HS 165* v Berks (Southampton) 1985. **BHC:** HS 134 v Comb Us (Southampton) 1990. **RAL:** HS 142 v Leics (Southampton) 1986.

TREMLETT, Timothy Maurice (Bellemoor SM; Richard Taunton SFC, Southampton), b Wellington, Somerset 26 Jul 1956. Son of M.F. (Somerset and England 1947-60). 6'2". RHB, RMF. Debut 1976. Cap 1983. Tours: SL 1985-86 (Eng B); Z 1984-85 (EC). HS 102* v Somerset (Taunton) 1985 – sharing record Hants 8th-wkt stand of 227 with K.D.James. 50 wkts (4); most – 75 (1985). BB 6-53 v Somerset (W-s-M) 1983. Awards: BHC 2. **NWT:** HS 43* v Leics (Leicester) 1987. BB 4-38 v Kent (Canterbury) 1987. **BHC:** HS 36* v Kent (Southampton) 1986. BB 4-30 v Surrey (Oval) 1986. **RAL:** HS 35 v Worcs (Worcester) 1984. BB 5-28 v Kent (Canterbury) 1985.

TURNER, Ian John (Cowplain SS; Southdown C), b Denmead 18 Jul 1968. 6'1". RHB, SLA. Debut 1989. HS 14 v OU (Oxford) 1990. BAC HS 9*. BB 3-20 v Glam (Southampton) 1989.

UDAL, Shaun David (Cove CS), b Farnborough 18 Mar 1969. Grandson of G.F. (Middx 1932 and Leics 1946). 6'2". RHB, OB. Debut 1989. HS 28* v Surrey (Southampton) 1990. BB 4-139 v SL (Southampton) 1990. BAC BB 4-144 v Sussex (Arundel) 1990. **RAL:** HS 2*. BB 2-36 v Worcs (Worcester) 1990.

WOOD, Julian Ross (Leighton Park S, Reading), b Winchester 21 Nov 1968. 5'8". LHB, RM. Debut 1989. MCC Cricket Staff. HS 96 v Northants (Northampton) 1989. BB 1-5. **NWT:** HS 3*. **BHC:** 43* v Yorks (Southampton) 1990. **RAL:** HS 66 v Notts (Nottingham) 1989.

NEWCOMERS

AAQIB JAVED, b Sheikhupura, Pakistan 5 Aug 1972. RHB, RFM. Debut 1984-85 when aged 12yr 76d. Lahore Division 1984-87. PACO 1989-90. **Tests** (P): 2 (1988-89 and 1989-90); HS 0 (pair) and BB 2-47 v A (Melbourne) 1989-90. LOI (P): 34. Tours (P): A 1988-89, 1989-90; NZ 1988-89. HS 32* PACO v PIA (Lahore) 1989-90. BB 3-15 Lahore Div v Faisalabad (Sialkot) 1984-85 – on debut.

TAYLOR, Neil Raymond (Arnewood CS), b Boscombe, Hants 9 Feb 1964. 6'0". RHB, RMF. Debut for Minor Counties 1990. Middlesex 1990. Dorset 1987-90. HS 0. BB 3-44 M v Hants (Bournemouth) 1990. **NWT:** (Dorset) HS 7. **BHC:** HS 3 and BB 3-52 Minor C v Derbys (Wellington) 1990. **RAL:** HS 5*. BB 1-16.

THURSFIELD, Martin John (Boldon CS), b South Shields, Co Durham 14 Dec 1971. 6'3". RHB, RM. Middlesex 1990. MCC cricket staff. HS -. BB 1-24.

DEPARTURES

JOSEPH, Linden Anthony (St Ambers S, Georgetown), b Georgetown, Guyana 8 Jan 1969. 6'1". RHB, RF. Debut (Demerara) 1986-87. Guyana 1986-90. Hampshire 1990. Tour: Z 1989-90 (WI B). HS 69* v OU (Oxford) 1990. BB 4-43 Guyana v Trinidad (Pointe-a-Pierre) 1988-89. H BB 2-28 v Ind (Southampton) 1990. BAC HS 43* and BB 2-128 v Worcs (Worcester) 1990.

SCOTT, R.J. – see GLOUCESTERSHIRE.

HAMPSHIRE 1990

RESULTS SUMMARY

	Place	Won	Lost	Drew	Abandoned
Britannic Assurance Championship	3rd	8	4	10	
All First-class Matches		9	4	12	
Refuge Assurance League	5th	9	5		2
NatWest Bank Trophy	Semi-Finalist				
Benson and Hedges Cup	4th in Group C				

BRITANNIC ASSURANCE CHAMPIONSHIP AVERAGES

BATTING AND FIELDING

Cap		M	I	NO	HS	Runs	Avge	100	50	Ct/St
–	L.A.Joseph	4	4	3	43*	83	83.00	–	–	1
1983	T.M.Tremlett	8	5	3	78	143	71.50	–	1	1
1985	R.A.Smith	11	18	4	181	897	64.07	4	3	7
–	A.N.Aymes	4	7	3	75*	255	63.75	–	2	7
1981	C.L.Smith	20	35	7	132*	1678	59.92	3	12	11
1990	T.C.Middleton	16	28	3	127	1216	48.64	5	5	8
–	R.M.F.Cox	3	6	2	104*	186	46.50	1	–	1
1981	M.D.Marshall	18	24	3	117	962	45.80	2	6	7
–	J.R.Ayling	7	9	2	62*	288	41.14	–	2	2
1983	V.P.Terry	19	31	3	165	1084	38.71	3	4	21
1990	D.I.Gower	14	21	1	145	684	34.20	1	2	14
1986	R.J.Maru	22	18	2	59	513	32.06	–	3	25
1982	M.C.J.Nicholas	20	30	8	78*	670	30.45	–	5	7
–	S.D.Udal	6	5	2	28*	65	21.66	–	–	2
1982	R.J.Parks	18	19	9	36*	203	20.30	–	–	46/4
1988	C.A.Connor	19	9	3	46	119	19.83	–	–	9
1989	P-J.Bakker	14	9	4	20	95	19.00	–	–	3
–	R.J.Scott	6	10	2	71	144	18.00	–	1	4

Also played: K.D.James (1 match – cap 1989) 50, 104*; K.J.Shine (6 matches) did
not bat (1 ct); I.J.Turner (4 matches) 1, 0* (2 ct); J.R.Wood (2 matches) 17, 11 (1 ct).

BOWLING

	O	M	R	W	Avge	Best	5wI	10wM
M.D.Marshall	554.2	142	1381	72	19.18	7-47	4	2
P-J.Bakker	371.2	86	1195	33	36.21	5-101	1	–
C.A.Connor	462.1	77	1623	44	36.88	5-96	1	–
T.M.Tremlett	120.5	30	393	10	39.30	3-33	–	–
R.J.Maru	720.1	178	2087	53	39.37	6-97	1	–
K.J.Shine	129.4	17	501	12	41.75	4-52	–	–
J.R.Ayling	135.2	35	454	10	45.40	2-48	–	–
S.D.Udal	191.3	35	746	16	46.62	4-144	–	–

Also bowled: K.D.James 28-8-74-1; L.A.Joseph 82-12-406-5; T.C.Middleton
1-0-10-0; M.C.J.Nicholas 54.2-7-209-2; R.J.Scott 36.4-5-165-5; C.L.Smith 22-8-76-3;
R.A.Smith 0.3-0-5-0; V.P.Terry 1-0-19-0; I.J.Turner 108.2-28-326-7.

The First-Class Averages (pp 166–181) give the records of Hampshire players in all
first-class county matches (their other opponents being the Indians, the Sri Lankans
and Oxford U.), with the exception of:
    D.I.Gower 17-26-3-145-972-42.26-2-3-17ct. Did not bowl.
    R.A.Smith 12-19-4-181-941-62.73-4-3-8ct. 0.3-0-5-0.

HAMPSHIRE RECORDS

FIRST-CLASS CRICKET

Highest Total	For	672-7d		v	Somerset	Taunton	1899
	V	742		by	Surrey	The Oval	1909
Lowest Total	For	15		v	Warwicks	Birmingham	1922
	V	23		by	Yorkshire	Middlesbrough	1965
Highest Innings	For	316	R.H.Moore	v	Warwicks	Bournemouth	1937
	V	302*	P.Holmes	for	Yorkshire	Portsmouth	1920

Highest Partnership for each Wicket

1st	347	V.P.Terry/C.L.Smith	v	Warwicks	Birmingham	1987
2nd	321	G.Brown/E.I.M.Barrett	v	Glos	Southampton	1920
3rd	344	C.P.Mead/G.Brown	v	Yorks	Portsmouth	1927
4th	263	R.E.Marshall/D.A.Livingstone	v	Middlesex	Lord's	1970
5th	235	G.Hill/D.F.Walker	v	Sussex	Portsmouth	1937
6th	411	R.M.Poore/E.G.Wynyard	v	Somerset	Taunton	1899
7th	325	G.Brown/C.H.Abercrombie	v	Essex	Leyton	1913
8th	227	K.D.James/T.M.Tremlett	v	Somerset	Taunton	1985
9th	230	D.A.Livingstone/A.T.Castell	v	Surrey	Southampton	1962
10th	192	H.A.W.Bowell/W.H.Livsey	v	Worcs	Bournemouth	1921

Best Bowling	For	9-25	R.M.H.Cottam	v	Lancashire	Manchester	1965
(Innings)	V	10-46	W.Hickton	for	Lancashire	Manchester	1870
Best Bowling	For	16-88	J.A.Newman	v	Somerset	Weston-s-Mare	1927
(Match)	V	17-119	W.Mead	for	Essex	Southampton	1895

Most Runs – Season	2,854	C.P.Mead	(av 79.27)		1928
Most Runs – Career	48,892	C.P.Mead	(av 48.84)		1905-1936
Most 100s – Season	12	C.P.Mead			1928
Most 100s – Career	138	C.P.Mead			1905-1936
Most Wkts – Season	190	A.S.Kennedy	(av 15.61)		1922
Most Wkts – Career	2,669	D.Shackleton	(av 18.23)		1948-1969

LIMITED-OVERS CRICKET

Highest Total	NWT	371-4		v	Glamorgan	Southampton	1975
	BHC	321-1		v	Minor C(S)	Amersham	1973
	RAL	292-1		v	Surrey	Portsmouth	1983
Lowest Total	NWT	98		v	Lancashire	Manchester	1975
	BHC	94		v	Glamorgan	Swansea	1973
	RAL	43		v	Essex	Basingstoke	1972
Highest Innings	NWT	177	C.G.Greenidge	v	Glamorgan	Southampton	1975
	BHC	173*	C.G.Greenidge	v	Minor C(S)	Amersham	1973
	RAL	172	C.G.Greenidge	v	Surrey	Southampton	1987
Best Bowling	NWT	7-30	P.J.Sainsbury	v	Norfolk	Southampton	1965
	BHC	5-13	S.T.Jefferies	v	Derbyshire	Lord's	1988
	RAL	6-20	T.E.Jesty	v	Glamorgan	Cardiff	1975

KENT

Formation of Present Club: 1 March 1859
Substantial Reorganisation: 6 December 1870
Colours: Maroon and White
Badge: White Horse on a Red Ground
Championships: (6) 1906, 1909, 1910, 1913, 1970, 1978
Joint Championship: (1) 1977
NatWest Trophy/Gillette Cup Winners: (2) 1967, 1974
Benson and Hedges Cup Winners: (3) 1973, 1976, 1978
Sunday League Champions: (3) 1972, 1973, 1976
Match Awards: NWT 41; BHC 61

Secretary: S.T.W.Anderson OBE, MC, St Lawrence Ground, Canterbury,
CT1 3NZ (☎ 0227-456886)
Captain: M.R.Benson
Scorer: J.Foley
1991 Beneficiary: M.R.Benson

BENSON, Mark Richard (Sutton Valence S), b Shoreham, Sussex 6 Jul 1958.
5'10". LHB, OB. Debut 1980. Cap 1981. Captain 1991. Benefit 1991. **Tests:** 1
(1986); HS 30 v I (Birmingham) 1986. LOI: 1. 1000 runs (9); most – 1725 (1987).
HS 162 v Hants (Southampton) 1985. BB 2-55 v Surrey (Dartford) 1986. Awards:
NWT 2; BHC 2. **NWT:** HS 113* v Warwks (Birmingham) 1984. **BHC:** HS 118 v
Glam (Swansea) 1990. **RAL:** HS 97 v Surrey (Oval) 1982.

COWDREY, Christopher Stuart (Tonbridge S), b Farnborough 20 Oct 1957.
Brother of G.R., son of M.C. (Kent and England 1950-76), grandson of E.A.
(Europeans). 6'1". RHB, RM. Kent 2nd XI debut when aged 15. Debut 1977. Cap
1979. Captain 1985-90. Benefit 1989. **Tests:** 6 (1984-85 to 1988, 1 as captain); HS
38 v I (Delhi) 1984-85; BB 2-65 v I (Madras) 1984-85. LOI: 3. **Tours:** SA 1989-90
(Eng XI); NZ 1979-80 (DHR); Ind/SL 1984-85; SL 1977-78 (DHR). 1000 runs (4);
most – 1364 (1983). HS 159 v Surrey (Canterbury) 1985. BB 5-46 v Hants (Canterbury) 1988. Awards: NWT 3; BHC 6. **NWT:** HS 122* v Essex (Chelmsford) 1983.
BB 4-36 v Hants (Canterbury) 1983. **BHC:** HS 114 v Sussex (Canterbury) 1977. BB
4-14 v Sussex (Canterbury) 1987. **RAL:** HS 95 v Worcs (Canterbury) 1983. BB 5-28
v Leics (Canterbury) 1984.

COWDREY, Graham Robert (Tonbridge S; Durham U), b Farnborough
27 Jun 1964. Brother of C.S., son of M.C. (Kent and England 1950-76), grandson
of E.A. (Europeans). 5'11". RHB, RM. Debut 1984. Cap 1988. 1000 runs (1): 1576
(1990). HS 145 v Essex (Chelmsford) 1988. BB 1-5. Award: BHC 1. **NWT:** HS 37
v Glos (Bristol) 1990. BB 2-19 v Warwks (Canterbury) 1988. **BHC:** HS 69 v
Sussex (Canterbury) 1987. BB 1-6. **RAL:** HS 102* v Leics (Folkestone) 1989. BB
4-15 v Essex (Ilford) 1987.

DAVIS, Richard Peter (King Ethelbert's S, Birchington; Thanet TC), b Westbrook,
Margate 18 Mar 1966. 6'3". RHB, SLA. Debut 1986. Cap 1990. HS 67 v Hants
(Southampton) 1989. 50 wkts (1): 73 (1990). BB 6-40 v CU (Cambridge) 1990.
BAC BB 6-59 v Sussex (Folkestone) 1990. **NWT:** HS 12 v Glos (Bristol) 1990.
BB 3-19 v Bucks (Canterbury) 1988. **BHC:** HS 0*. BB 2-33 v Sussex (Hove) 1988.
RAL: HS 16 v Notts (Nottingham) 1989. BB 5-52 v Somerset (Bath) 1989.

DOBSON, Mark Christopher (Simon Langton GS), b Canterbury 24 Oct 1967.
5'10". RHB, SLA. Debut 1989. HS 52 and BB 2-20 v Glam (Canterbury) 1989.
RAL: HS 21 v Glos (Maidstone) 1989.

EALHAM, Mark Alan (Stour Valley SS, Chartham), b Willesborough, Ashford 27 Aug 1969. Son of A.G.E. (Kent). 5'9". RHB, RMF. Debut 1989. HS 45 v Lancs (Manchester) 1989. BB 2-33 v Middx (Lord's) 1990. **BHC:** HS 17* v Glam (Swansea) 1990. BB 4-57 v Worcs (Worcester) 1990. **RAL:** HS 29* v Glam (Llanelli) 1990. BB 3-26 v Derbys (Canterbury) 1989.

ELLISON, Richard Mark (Tonbridge S; Exeter U), b Willesborough, Ashford 21 Sep 1959. Brother of C.C. (Cambridge U). 6'2". LHB, RMF. Debut 1981. Cap 1983. Tasmania 1986-87. Wisden 1985. **Tests:** 11 (1984 to 1986); HS 41 v SL (Lord's) 1984; BB 6-77 v A (Birmingham) 1985. LOI: 14. Tours: SA 1989-90 (Eng XI); WI 1985-86; Ind/SL 1984-85. HS 108 v OU (Oxford) 1984. BAC HS 98 v Notts (Nottingham) 1985. 50 wkts (4); most – 71 (1988). BB 7-75 v Notts (Dartford) 1988. Awards: NWT 1; BHC 5. **NWT:** HS 49* v Warwks (Birmingham) 1984. BB 4-19 v Cheshire (Canterbury) 1983. **BHC:** HS 72 v Middx (Lord's) 1984. BB 4-28 v Glam (Canterbury) 1984. **RAL:** HS 84 v Glos (Canterbury) 1984. BB 4-25 v Hants (Canterbury) 1983.

FLEMING, Matthew Valentine (St Aubyns S, Rottingdean; Eton C), b Maclesfield, Cheshire 12 Dec 1964. 5'11½". RHB, RM. Debut 1989. Cap 1990. Army and Combined Services. HS 102 v Notts (Tunbridge W) 1990. BB 3-65 v Sussex (Hove) 1990. **NWT:** HS 12 v Warwks (Canterbury) 1989. BB 2-4 v Oxon (Oxford) 1990. **BHC:** HS 28 v Hants (Southampton) 1989. BB 2-58 v Notts (Nottingham) 1989. **RAL:** HS 37 v Northants (Canterbury) 1989. BB 3-26 v Leics (Folkestone) 1989.

HINKS, Simon Graham (St George's S, Gravesend), b Northfleet 12 Oct 1960. 6'2". LHB, RM. Debut 1982. Cap 1985. 1000 runs (3); most – 1588 (1990). HS 234 v Middx (Canterbury) 1990 – sharing Kent record 2nd-wkt stand of 366 with N.R.Taylor. BB 2-18 v Notts (Nottingham) 1989. Awards: NWT 1; BHC 1. **NWT:** HS 95 v Surrey (Canterbury) 1985. **BHC:** HS 85 v Sussex (Canterbury) 1987. BB 1-15. **RAL:** HS 99 v Glam (Maidstone) 1986. BB 1-3.

IGGLESDEN, Alan Paul (Churchill S, Westerham), b Farnborough 8 Oct 1964. 6'6". RHB, RFM. Debut 1986. Cap 1989. W Province 1987-88. **Tests:** 1 (1989); HS 2* and BB 2-91 v A (Oval). Tour: Z 1989-90 (Eng A). HS 41 and BB 6-34 v Surrey (Canterbury) 1988. 50 wkts (2); most – 56 (1989). **NWT:** HS 12* v Oxon (Oxford) 1990. BB 3-54 v Derbys (Canterbury) 1990. **BHC:** HS 5*. BB 3-43 v Hants (Southampton) 1989. **RAL:** HS 13* v Glos (Cheltenham) 1987. BB 5-13 v Sussex (Hove) 1989.

KELLEHER, Daniel John Michael (St Mary's GS, Sidcup; Erith TC), b Southwark, London 5 May 1966. Nephew of H.R.A. (Surrey 1955, Northants 1956-58). 6'1". RHB, RMF. Debut 1987. HS 53* v Derbys (Dartford) 1989. BB 6-109 v Somerset (Bath) 1987. **NWT:** HS 21 and BB 3-16 v Oxon (Oxford) 1990. **BHC:** HS 11* v Notts (Nottingham) 1989. BB 1-23. **RAL:** HS 19 v Notts (Nottingham) 1987. BB 2-25 (twice in 1987).

LLONG, Nigel James (Ashford North S), b Ashford 11 Feb 1969. 6'0". LHB, OB. Debut 1990. HS –. **RAL:** HS 0*. BB 1-20.

LONGLEY, Jonathan Ian (Tonbridge S; Durham U), b New Brunswick, New Jersey, USA 12 Apr 1969. 5'7". RHB. Debut 1989. HS 17 v Essex (Southend) 1989. **BHC:** HS 49 Comb Us v Somerset (Taunton) 1989. **RAL:** HS 57 v Middx (Lord's) 1989.

MARSH, Steven Andrew (Walderslade SS; Mid-Kent CFE), b Westminster, London 27 Jan 1961. 5'10". RHB, WK. Debut 1982. Cap 1986. HS 120 v Essex (Chelmsford) 1988. BB 2-20 v Warwks (Birmingham) 1990. **NWT:** HS 24* v Middx (Lord's) 1988. **BHC:** HS 41* v Essex (Canterbury) 1989. **RAL:** HS 53 v Middx (Lord's) 1989.

MERRICK, Tyrone Anthony (All Saints S, Antigua), b St John's, Antigua 10 Jun 1963. 6'1". RHB, RFM. Leeward Is 1982-89. Warwickshire 1987-89 (cap 1988). Kent debut 1990. Tour (WI B). Z 1986-87. HS 74* Wa v Glos (Birmingham) 1987. K HS 35 v Notts (Tunbridge W) 1990. 50 wkts (2); most – 65 (1988). BB 7-45 (13-115 match) Wa v Lancs (Birmingham) 1987. K BB 4-66 v Middx (Lord's) 1990. Hat-trick 1988. **NWT:** HS 13 Wa v Cambs (Birmingham) 1988. BB 2-36 Wa v Kent (Canterbury) 1988. **BHC:** HS 14 v Worcs (Worcester) 1990. BB 4-24 Wa v Leics (Leicester) 1988. **RAL:** HS 59 Wa v Northants (Birmingham) 1987. BB 4-24 v Essex (Chelmsford) 1990.

PATEL, Minal Mahesh (Dartford GS; Erith TC), b Bombay, India 7 Jul 1970. 5'9". RHB, SLA. Debut 1989. HS 41* v Northants (Northampton) 1990. BB 6-57 v Leics (Dartford) 1990. **NWT:** BB 2-29 v Oxon (Oxford) 1990.

PENN, Christopher (Dover GS), b Dover 19 Jun 1963. 6'1". LHB, RFM. Debut 1982. Cap 1987. HS 115 v Lancs (Manchester) 1984. 50 wkts (1): 81 (1988). BB 7-70 v Middx (Lord's) 1988. **NWT:** HS 5. BB 3-30 v Warwks (Canterbury) 1988. **BHC:** HS 24* v Northants (Northampton) 1989. BB 4-34 v Surrey (Canterbury) 1982. **RAL:** HS 40 v Sussex (Maidstone) 1982. BB 4-15 v Glos (Maidstone) 1989.

TAYLOR, Neil Royston (Cray Valley THS), b Orpington 21 Jul 1959. 6'1". RHB, OB. Debut 1979 scoring 110 and 11 v SL at Canterbury. Cap 1982. 1000 runs (7); most – 1979 (1990). HS 204 v Surrey (Canterbury) 1990. Shared in Kent record 2nd-wkt stand of 366 with S.G.Hinks v Middx (Canterbury) 1990. BB 2-20 v Somerset (Canterbury) 1985. Awards: BHC 7. **NWT:** HS 85 v Derbys (Canterbury) 1987. BB 3-29 v Dorset (Canterbury) 1989. **BHC:** HS 137 v Surrey (Oval) 1988. **RAL:** HS 95 v Hants (Canterbury) 1990.

WARD, Trevor Robert (Hextable CS, nr Swanley), b Farningham 18 Jan 1968. 5'11". RHB, OB. Debut 1986. Cap 1989. 1000 runs (1): 1257 (1989). HS 175 v Hants (Bournemouth) 1990. BB 2-48 v Worcs (Canterbury) 1990. Awards: NWT 1; BHC 1. **NWT:** HS 83 and BB 1-58 v Dorset (Canterbury) 1989. **BHC:** HS 94 v Worcs (Worcester) 1990. **RAL:** HS 80 v Derbys (Chesterfield) 1990. BB 3-20 v Glam (Canterbury) 1989.

WELLS, Vincent John (Sir William Nottidge S, Whitstable), b Dartford 6 Aug 1965. 6'0". RHB, WK. Debut 1988. HS 58 v Hants (Bournemouth) 1990. BB 5-43 v Leics (Leicester) 1990. Award: NWT 1. **NWT:** 100* v Oxon (Oxford) 1990. **BHC:** HS 15* v Middx (Canterbury) 1988. **RAL:** HS 16 v Worcs (Canterbury) 1990. BB 3-17 v Somerset (Canterbury) 1988.

WREN, Timothy Neil, b Folkestone 26 Mar 1970. 6'3". RHB, LM. Debut 1990. HS 16 v Essex (Chelmsford) 1990. BB 2-78 v Worcs (Canterbury) 1990. **RAL:** BB 1-31.

DEPARTURE

De VILLIERS, Petrus Stephanus ('Fanie') (Sasolburg HS; Pretoria Teachers' C), b Vereeniging, South Africa 13 Oct 1964. RHB, RFM. N Transvaal 1985-90. Kent 1990. HS 46* NT v OFS (Verwoerdburg) 1988-89. K HS 37 v Sussex (Folkestone) 1990. BB 6-47 NT v W Province (Cape Town) 1988-89. K BB 6-70 v Middx (Canterbury) 1990. **NWT:** HS 14 and BB 1-29 v Glos (Bristol) 1990. **BHC:** HS 0. BB 2-37 v Glam (Swansea) 1990. **RAL:** HS 10 and BB 1-17 v Warwks (Birmingham) 1990.

KENT 1990

RESULTS SUMMARY

	Place	Won	Lost	Drew	Abandoned
Britannic Assurance Championship	16th	3	6	13	
All First-class Matches		4	7	13	
Refuge Assurance League	10th	7	8		1
NatWest Bank Trophy	2nd Round				
Benson and Hedges Cup	3rd in Group A				

BRITANNIC ASSURANCE CHAMPIONSHIP AVERAGES

BATTING AND FIELDING

Cap		M	I	NO	HS	Runs	Avge	100	50	Ct/St
1982	N.R.Taylor	20	35	4	204	1752	56.51	5	10	8
1988	G.R.Cowdrey	20	36	5	135	1471	47.45	3	8	8
1981	M.R.Benson	14	23	1	159	1029	46.77	5	3	5
1990	M.V.Fleming	17	30	5	102	940	37.60	1	5	6
1983	R.M.Ellison	13	18	6	81	444	37.00	–	3	5
1985	S.G.Hinks	22	41	0	234	1484	36.19	4	5	8
1979	C.S.Cowdrey	11	21	4	107*	599	35.23	2	2	9
1986	S.A.Marsh	22	34	8	114*	867	33.34	1	5	46/4
1989	T.R.Ward	15	28	1	175	863	31.96	2	5	14
–	V.J.Wells	8	15	0	58	352	23.46	–	2	8
–	P.S.de Villiers	12	15	3	37	264	22.00	–	–	6
1990	R.P.Davis	22	32	3	59	504	17.37	–	2	24
1987	C.Penn	6	6	2	23*	66	16.50	–	–	1
–	M.M.Patel	9	12	5	41*	104	14.85	–	2	
1989	A.P.Igglesden	13	17	9	24	105	13.12	–	–	5
–	D.J.M.Kelleher	5	8	0	44	101	12.62	–	2	2
–	T.A.Merrick	5	7	2	35	60	12.00	–	–	1
–	T.N.Wren	5	5	2	16	23	7.66	–	–	2

Also played: M.C.Dobson (1 match) 0, 6; M.A.Ealham (2 matches) 0, 13*.

BOWLING

	O	M	R	W	Avge	Best	5wI	10wM
V.J.Wells	85	19	257	12	21.41	5-43	1	–
T.A.Merrick	146.2	31	376	13	28.92	4-66	–	–
A.P.Igglesden	306	42	1093	30	36.43	4-79	–	–
P.S.de Villiers	304.5	58	992	25	39.68	6-70	1	–
R.P.Davis	839.1	202	2648	65	40.73	6-59	4	1
M.M.Patel	297.5	72	836	20	41.80	6-57	2	1
R.M.Ellison	260.5	45	869	19	45.73	4-76	–	–
M.V.Fleming	360.5	81	994	18	55.22	3-65	–	–

Also bowled: M.R.Benson 8-2-46-1; C.S.Cowdrey 57-12-173-4; G.R.Cowdrey 3.3-0-32-0; M.C.Dobson 3.1-1-7-0; M.A.Ealham 34.2-5-120-3; S.G.Hinks 15-2-60-2; D.J.M.Kelleher 112.5-20-398-7; S.A.Marsh 8.4-0-36-2; C.Penn 158-33-535-9; N.R.Taylor 21-5-57-1; T.R.Ward 53-6-225-4; T.N.Wren 122-14-489-6.

The First-Class Averages (pp 166–181) give the records of Kent players in all first-class county matches (their other opponents being the Indians and Cambridge U.), with the exception of:

M.R.Benson 15-24-1-159-1119-48.65-5-4-5ct. 8-2-46-1-46.00-1/14.

KENT RECORDS

FIRST-CLASS CRICKET

Highest Total	For	803-4d		v Essex	Brentwood	1934
	V	676		by Australians	Canterbury	1921
Lowest Total	For	18		v Sussex	Gravesend	1867
	V	16		by Warwicks	Tonbridge	1913
Highest Innings	For	332	W.H.Ashdown	v Essex	Brentwood	1934
	V	344	W.G.Grace	for MCC	Canterbury	1876

Highest Partnership for each Wicket

1st	283	A.E.Fagg/P.R.Sunnucks	v	Essex	Colchester	1938
2nd	366	S.G.Hinks/N.R.Taylor	v	Middlesex	Canterbury	1990
3rd	321*	A.Hearne/J.R.Mason	v	Notts	Nottingham	1899
4th	297	H.T.W.Harding/A.F.Chapman	v	Hampshire	Southampton	1926
5th	277	F.E.Woolley/L.E.G.Ames	v	New Zealand	Canterbury	1931
6th	284	A.P.F.Chapman/G.B.Legge	v	Lancashire	Maidstone	1927
7th	248	A.P.Day/E.Humphreys	v	Somerset	Taunton	1908
8th	157	A.L.Hilder/A.C.Wright	v	Essex	Gravesend	1924
9th	161	B.R.Edrich/F.Ridgway	v	Sussex	Tunbridge W	1949
10th	235	F.E.Woolley/A.Fielder	v	Worcs	Stourbridge	1909

Best Bowling	For	10-30	C.Blythe	v Northants	Northampton	1907
(Innings)	V	10-48	C.H.G.Bland	for Sussex	Tonbridge	1899
Best Bowling	For	17-48	C.Blythe	v Northants	Northampton	1907
(Match)	V	17-106	T.W.J.Goddard	for Glos	Bristol	1939

Most Runs – Season	2,894	F.E.Woolley	(av 59.06)		1928
Most Runs – Career	47,868	F.E.Woolley	(av 41.77)		1906-1938
Most 100s – Season	{10	F.E.Woolley			1928
	{10	F.E.Woolley			1934
Most 100s – Career	122	F.E.Woolley			1906-1938
Most Wkts – Season	262	A.P.Freeman	(av 14.74)		1933
Most Wkts – Career	3,340	A.P.Freeman	(av 17.64)		1914-1936

LIMITED-OVERS CRICKET

Highest Total	NWT	359-4		v Dorset	Canterbury	1989
	BHC	293-6		v Somerset	Taunton	1985
	RAL	290-4		v Lancashire	Manchester	1987
Lowest Total	NWT	60		v Somerset	Taunton	1979
	BHC	73		v Middlesex	Canterbury	1979
	RAL	83		v Middlesex	Lord's	1984
Highest Innings	NWT	129*	B.W.Luckhurst	v Durham	Canterbury	1974
	BHC	143	C.J.Tavaré	v Somerset	Taunton	1985
	RAL	142	B.W.Luckhurst	v Somerset	Weston-s-Mare	1970
Best Bowling	NWT	8-31	D.L.Underwood	v Scotland	Edinburgh	1987
	BHC	5-21	B.D.Julien	v Surrey	The Oval	1973
	RAL	6-9	R.A.Woolmer	v Derbyshire	Chesterfield	1979

LANCASHIRE

Formation of Present Club: 12 January 1864
Colours: Red, Green and Blue.
Badge: Red Rose.
Championships (since 1890): (7) 1897, 1904, 1926, 1927, 1928, 1930, 1934
Joint Championship: (1) 1950
NatWest Trophy/Gillette Cup Winners: (5) 1970, 1971, 1972, 1975, 1990
Benson and Hedges Cup Winners: (2) 1984, 1990
Sunday League Champions: (3) 1969, 1970, 1989
Match Awards: NWT 53; BHC 49

Secretary: C.D.Hassell, Old Trafford, Manchester M16 0PX (☎ 061-848 7021)
Captain: D.P.Hughes
Scorer: W.Davies
1991 Beneficiary: G.Fowler

ALLOTT, Paul John Walter (Altrincham GS; Durham U; b Altrincham, Cheshire 14 Sep 1956. 6'4". RHB, RFM. Debut 1978. Cap 1981. Benefit 1990. Wellington 1986-87. Cheshire 1976. **Tests:** 13 (1981 to 1985); HS 52* v A (Manchester) 1981 – on debut. BB 6-61 v WI (Leeds) 1981. LOI: 13. Tours: WI 1982-83 (Int), 1986-87 (Lancs); Ind/SL 1981-82, 1984-85; Z 1988-89 (Lancs). HS 88 v Hants (Southampton) 1987. 50 wkts (5); most – 85 (1981). BB 8-48 v Northants (Northampton) 1981. Awards: NWT 1; BHC 1. **NWT:** HS 19* v Worcs (Worcester) 1980. BB 4-28 v Leics (Leicester) 1986. **BHC:** HS 23* v Notts (Liverpool) 1986. BB 3-15 v Warwks (Lord's) 1984. **RAL:** HS 43 v Warwks (Manchester) 1988. BB 4-28 v Kent (Manchester) 1985.

ATHERTON, Michael Andrew (Manchester GS; Downing C, Cambridge), b Manchester 23 Mar 1968. 5'11". RHB, LB. CU 1987-89 (blue 1987-88-89; captain 1988-89). Lancashire debut 1987. Cap 1989. YC 1990. Wisden 1990. **Tests:** 8 (1989 to 1990); HS 151 v NZ (Nottingham) 1990. LOI: 2. Tour: Z 1989-90 (Eng A). 1000 runs (3); most – 1924 (1990). Scored 1193 in season of f-c debut. HS 191 v Surrey (Oval) 1990 – sharing in Lancs record 3rd-wkt stand of 364 with N.H. Fairbrother. BB 6-78 v Notts (Nottingham) 1990. Award: NWT 1. **NWT:** HS 55 v Derbys (Derby) 1990. BB 2-15 v Glos (Manchester) 1990. **BHC:** HS 74 v Surrey (Manchester) 1990. BB 4-42 Comb Us v Somerset (Taunton) 1989. **RAL:** HS 111 v Essex (Colchester) 1990. BB 3-33 v Notts (Nottingham) 1990.

AUSTIN, Ian David (Haslingden HS), b Haslingden 30 May 1966. 5'10". LHB, RM. Debut 1987. Cap 1990. Tour: Z 1988-89 (Lancs). HS 64 v Derbys (Manchester) 1988. BB 5-79 v Surrey (Oval) 1988. **NWT:** HS 13* v Derbys (Derby) 1990. BB 3-36 v Durham (Manchester) 1990. **BHC:** HS 80 v Worcs (Worcester) 1987 (on county debut). BB 4-25 v Surrey (Manchester) 1990. **RAL:** HS 41 v Derbys (Manchester) 1988. BB 4-28 v Derbys (Leek) 1989.

CRAWLEY, John Paul (Manchester GS; now at Trinity C, Cambridge U), b Maldon, Essex 21 Sep 1971. Brother of M.A. (see NOTTS). 6'1". RHB, RM. Debut 1990. HS 76* v Zimbabweans (Manchester) 1990 (on debut).

DeFREITAS, Phillip Anthony Jason (Willesden HS, London), b Scotts Head, Dominica 18 Feb 1966. 6'0". RHB, RFM. UK resident since 1976. Leicestershire 1985-88 (cap 1986). Lancashire debut 1989. Cap 1989. MCC Cricket Staff. **Tests:** 17 (1986-87 to 1990); HS 40 v A (Brisbane) 1986-87; BB 5-53 v NZ (Nottingham)

1990. LOI: 52. Tours: A 1986-87; WI 1989-90; NZ 1987-88; P 1987-88; Z 1988-89 (Lancs). HS 113 Le v Notts (Worksop) 1988. La HS 102 v OU (Oxford) 1990. 50 wkts (4); most – 94 (1986). BB 7-21 v Middx (Lord's) 1989. Awards: NWT 3; BHC 1. NWT: HS 69 Le v Lancs (Leicester) 1986. BB 5-13 v Cumberland (Kendal) 1989. BHC: HS 75* v Hants (Manchester) 1990. BB 4-13 v Scot (Perth) 1989. RAL: HS 37 Le v Derbys (Derby) 1988. BB 4-20 Le v Middx and v Worcs 1986.

DERBYSHIRE, Nicholas Alexander (Ampleforth C; London U); b Ramsbottom 11 Sep 1970. 5'11½". RHB, RFM. No 1st XI appearances – joined staff 1990.

FAIRBROTHER, Neil Harvey (Lymm GS), b Warrington 9 Sep 1963. 5'8". LHB, LM. Debut 1982. Cap 1985. **Tests:** 7 (1987 to 1990); HS 33* v NZ (Lord's) 1990. LOI: 11. Tours: NZ 1987-88; P 1987-88. 1000 runs (7); most – 1740 (1990). HS 366 v Surrey (Oval) 1990, including 311 in a day and 100 or more in each session, and sharing in Lancs record 3rd-wkt stand of 364 with M.A.Atherton. BB 2-91 v Notts (Manchester) 1987. Awards: NWT 4; BHC 5. NWT: HS 93* v Leics (Leicester) 1986. BHC: HS 116* v Scot (Manchester) 1988. RAL: HS 116* v Notts (Nottingham) 1988.

FITTON, John Dexter (Redbrook HS; Oulder Hill S), b Littleborough 24 Aug 1965. 5'10". LHB, OB. Debut 1987. HS 44 v A (Manchester) 1989. BAC HS 43 v Surrey (Manchester) 1989. BB 6-59 v Yorks (Manchester) 1988. RAL: HS 0. BB 1-25.

FOWLER, Graeme (Accrington GS; Durham U), b Accrington 20 Apr 1957. 5'9½". LHB, RM. Debut 1979. Cap 1981. Benefit 1991. **Tests:** 21 (1982 to 1984-85); HS 201 v I (Madras) 1984-85. LOI: 26. Tours: A 1982-83; WI 1982-83 (Int); NZ 1983-84; Ind/SL 1984-85; P 1983-84; Z 1988-89 (Lancs). 1000 runs (8); most – 1800 (1987). HS 226 v Kent (Maidstone) 1984. BB 2-34 v Warwks (Manchester) 1986. Awards: NWT 2; BHC 2. NWT: HS 122 v Glos (Bristol) 1984. BHC: HS 97 v Northants (Manchester) 1983. RAL: HS 112 v Kent (Canterbury) 1986.

GALLIAN, Jason Edward Riche (Pittwater House S, Sydney), b Manly, Sydney, Australia 25 Jun 1971. 6'0". RHB, RM. Debut 1990 taking the wicket of D.A.Hagan (OU) with his first ball. Unregistered player on scholarship visit and eligible for friendly and 2nd XI matches only. Captained Australia YC v England YC 1989-90 scoring 158* in 1st 'Test'. HS 17* and BB 1-50 v OU (Oxford) 1990.

HEGG, Warren Kevin (Unsworth HS, Bury; Stand C, Whitefield), b Whitefield 23 Feb 1968. 5'8". RHB, WK. Debut 1986. Cap 1989. Tours: WI 1986-87 (Lancs); Z 1988-89 (Lancs). HS 130 v Northants (Northampton) 1987. Held 11 catches (equalling world f-c match record) v Derbys (Chesterfield) 1989. NWT: HS 29 v Glos (Gloucester) 1989. BHC: HS 31* v Worcs (Lord's) 1990. RAL: HS 24* v Essex (Colchester) 1990.

HUGHES, David Paul (Newton-le-Willows GS), b Newton-le-Willows 13 May 1947. 5'11". RHB, SLA. Debut 1967. Cap 1970. Captain 1987-. Benefit 1981. Tasmania 1975-77. Wisden 1987. Tours: SA 1972-73 (DHR); WI 1986-87 (Lancs); Z 1988-89 (Lancs). 1000 runs (2); most – 1303 (1982). HS 153 v Glam (Manchester) 1983. 50 wkts (4); most – 82 (1970, 1971). BB 7-24 v OU (Oxford) 1970. BAC BB 7-77 v Essex (Ilford) 1975. Awards: NWT 1; BHC 1. NWT: HS 71 v Durham (Chester-le-St) 1983. BB 4-61 v Somerset (Manchester) 1972. BHC: HS 52 v Derbys (Manchester) 1981. BB 5-23 v Minor C (W) (Watford) 1978. RAL: HS 92 v Kent (Maidstone) 1984. BB 6-29 v Somerset (Manchester) 1977.

IRANI, Ronald (Smithills CS, Bolton), b Leigh 26 Oct 1971. 6'3". RHB, RM. Debut 1990. HS –. BB 1-12. Awaiting BAC debut.

JESTY, Trevor Edward (Privet County SS, Gosport), b Gosport, Hants 2 Jun 1948. 5'8½". RHB, RM. Hampshire 1966-84 (cap 1971; benefit 1982). Surrey 1985-87 (cap 1985; captain 1985). Lancashire debut 1988. Cap 1989. Border 1973-74. GW 1974-76, 1980-81. Canterbury 1979-80. Wisden 1982. LOI: 10. Tours: WI 1982-83 (Int); Z 1988-89 (Lancs). 1000 runs (10); most – 1645 (1982). HS 248 H v CU (Cambridge) 1984. La HS 98 v Kent (Maidstone) 1990. 50 wkts (2); most – 52 (1981). BB 7-75 H v Worcs (Southampton) 1976. La BB 1-20. Awards: NWT 6: BHC 11. **NWT:** HS 118 H v Derbys (Derby) 1980. BB 6-46 H v Glos (Bristol) 1979. **BHC:** HS 105 H v Glam (Swansea) 1977. BB 5-39 v Leics (Leicester) 1988. **RAL:** HS 166* H v Surrey (Portsmouth) 1983. BB 6-20 H v Glam (Cardiff) 1976.

LLOYD, Graham David (Hollins County HS), b Accrington 1 Jul 1969. Son of D. (Lancs and England 1965-83). 5'9". RHB, RM. Debut 1988. HS 117 v Notts (Worksop) 1989. **NWT:** HS 36 v Derbys (Derby) 1990. **RAL:** HS 100* v Kent (Maidstone) 1990.

MARTIN, Peter James (Danum S, Doncaster), b Accrington 15 Nov 1968. 6'4". RHB, RFM. Debut 1989. HS 21 and BB 4-68 v Notts (Nottingham) 1990.

MENDIS, Gehan Dixon (St Thomas C, Colombo; Brighton, Hove & Sussex GS; Durham U), b Colombo, Ceylon 24 Apr 1955. 5'9". RHB, RM. Sussex 1974-85 (cap 1980). Lancashire debut/cap 1986. Tours: WI 1982-83 (Int), 1986-87 (Lancs); P 1981-82 (Int); Z 1988-89 (Lancs). 1000 runs (11); most – 1756 (1985). HS 209* Sx v Somerset (Hove) 1984. La HS 203* v Middx (Manchester) 1987. BB 1-65. Awards: NWT 4; BHC 4. **NWT:** HS 141* Sx v Warwks (Hove) 1980. **BHC:** HS 109 Sx v Glos (Hove) 1980. **RAL:** HS 125* Sx v Glos (Hove) 1981.

ORRELL, Timothy Michael (Bury Church HS; Stand C, Whitefield; Salford U), b Prestwich, Manchester 25 Nov 1967. 6'0". RHB, RM. **BHC:** HS 15 Comb Us v Yorks (Leeds) 1990. No 1st XI appearances for Lancashire.

SPEAK, Nicholas Jason (Parrs Wood HS, Manchester), b Manchester 21 Nov 1966. 6'0". RHB, RM/OB. Debut v Jamaica (Kingston) 1986-87. Tour: WI 1986-87 (Lancs). HS 138 v Z (Manchester) 1990. BAC HS 64 v Essex (Lytham) 1989. BB 1-26. **RAL:** HS 13 v Glos (Manchester) 1987.

STANWORTH, John (Chadderton GS), b Oldham 30 Sep 1960. 5'10". RHB, WK. Debut 1983. Cap 1989. HS 50* v Glos (Bristol) 1985. **NWT:** HS 0. **BHC:** HS 8*. **RAL:** HS 4*.

TITCHARD, Stephen Paul (Lymm County HS; Priestley C), b Warrington 17 Dec 1967. 6'3". RHB, RM. Debut 1990. HS 80 v Zimbabweans (Manchester) 1990 – on debut.

WASIM AKRAM (Islamia C), b Lahore, Pakistan 3 Jun 1966. 6'3". LHB, LF. PACO 1984-86. Lahore Whites 1985-86. Lancashire debut 1988. Cap 1989. **Tests** (P): 32 (1984-85 to 1989-90); HS 123 v A (Adelaide) 1989-90; BB 6-62 v A (Melbourne) 1989-90. LOI (P): 97. Tours (P): E 1987; A 1988-89, 1989-90; WI 1987-88; NZ 1984-85; I 1986-87; SL 1984-85 (P U-23), 1985-86. HS 123 (Tests). La HS 116* v Somerset (Manchester) 1988. 50 wkts (1): 63 (1989). BB 7-42 World XI v MCC

(Scarborough) 1989. La BB 7-53 v Northants (Northampton) 1988. Hat-trick 1988.
NWT: HS 19 v Cumberland (Kendal) 1989. BB 4-27 v Lincs (Manchester) 1988.
BHC: HS 52 v Northants (Northampton) 1989. BB 5-27 v Scot (Perth) 1989. **RAL:** HS 50 v Glam (Colwyn Bay) 1990. BB 4-19 v Yorks (Scarborough) 1990.

WATKINSON, Michael (Rivington and Blackrod HS, Horwich), b Westhoughton 1 Aug 1961. 6'1". RHB, RMF. Debut 1982. Cap 1987. Cheshire 1982. HS 138 v Yorks (Manchester) 1990. 50 wkts (2); most – 55 (1989). BB 7-25 v Sussex (Lytham) 1987. Awards: NWT 1; BHC 2. **NWT:** HS 90 and BB 3-14 v Glos (Manchester) 1990. **BHC:** HS 70* v Derbys (Liverpool) 1988. BB 4-39 v Notts (Manchester) 1983. **RAL:** HS 58 v Sussex (Hove) 1988. BB 5-46 v Warwks (Manchester) 1990.

YATES, Gary (Manchester GS), b Ashton-under-Lyne 20 Sep 1967. 6'0". RHB, OB. Debut 1990. HS 106 v Notts (Nottingham) 1990 – on BAC debut. BB 4-94 v SL (Manchester) 1990. BAC BB 2-69 v Notts (Nottingham) 1990.

DEPARTURES

BRAMHALL, Stephen (Stockholm CHS; Newcastle U), b Warrington 26 Nov 1967. 6'1" RHB, WK. Lancashire 1990. Cheshire 1988-90. HS 1*. BAC HS 0*.

CRAWLEY, M.A. – see NOTTINGHAMSHIRE.

FOLLEY, Ian (Mansfield HS; Colne C), b Burnley 9 Jan 1963. 5'9½". RHB, SLA. Lancashire 1982-90 (cap 1987). Tours: WI 1986-87 (Lancs); Z 1988-89 (Lancs). HS 69 v Yorks (Manchester) 1985. 50 wkts (2); most – 74 (1987). BB 7-15 (12-57 match) v Warwks (Southport) 1987. **NWT:** HS 3*. BB 2-10 v Lancs (Chester-le-St) 1983. **BHC:** HS 11* v Notts (Nottingham) 1982. BB 4-18 v Middx (Lord's) 1982. **RAL:** HS 19 v Northants (Tring) 1987. BB 3-23 v Glos (Manchester) 1987.

PATTERSON, Patrick (Happy Grove HS; Wolmer's HS), b Portland, Jamaica 15 Sep 1961. 6'2½". RHB, RF. Jamaica 1982-90. Lancashire 1984-90 (cap 1987). **Tests** (WI): 18 (1985-86 to 1989-90); HS 21* v I (Bombay) 1987-88; BB 5-24 v I (Delhi) 1987-88. LOI (WI): 31. Tours (WI): Eng 1988; A 1988-89; NZ 1986-87; I 1987-88; P 1986-87. HS 29 v Northants (Northampton) 1987. 50 wkts (1): 52 (1987). BB 7-24 Jamaica v Guyana (Kingston) 1985-86. La BB 7-49 v OU (Oxford) 1985. BAC BB 6-40 v Warwks (Birmingham) 1987. **NWT:** HS 4. BB 1-69. **BHC:** HS 15* v Leics (Manchester) 1985. BB 3-31 v Scot (Perth) 1986. **RAL:** HS 3*. BB 3-25 v Essex (Chelmsford) 1987.

WATERTON, Stuart Nicholas Varney (Gravesend S; LSE), b Dartford, Kent 6 Dec 1960. 5'11½". RHB, WK. Kent 1980-85. Northamptonshire 1986-87. Lancashire 1990. Oxfordshire 1989-90. HS 58* Nh v Worcs (Northampton) 1986. La HS 3. Award: NWT 1. **NWT:** HS 92 Oxon v Glos (Oxford) 1989. **BHC:** HS 6. **RAL:** HS 28 Nh v Essex (Colchester) 1986.

LANCASHIRE 1990

RESULTS SUMMARY

	Place	Won	Lost	Drew	Abandoned
Britannic Assurance Championship	6th	6	3	13	
All First-class Matches		6	3	16	
Refuge Assurance League	2nd	11	3		2
NatWest Bank Trophy	Winners				
Benson and Hedges Cup	Winners				

BRITANNIC ASSURANCE CHAMPIONSHIP AVERAGES

BATTING AND FIELDING

Cap		M	I	NO	HS	Runs	Avge	100	50	Ct/St
1985	N.H.Fairbrother	17	24	6	366	1544	85.77	3	9	18
1989	M.A.Atherton	12	18	4	191	1053	75.21	4	6	16
1986	G.D.Mendis	21	35	6	180	1551	53.48	4	8	16
1989	T.E.Jesty	17	24	6	98	785	43.61	–	7	6
1989	W.K.Hegg	20	21	6	100*	617	41.13	1	2	47/2
1989	P.A.J.DeFreitas	15	17	3	100*	506	36.14	1	2	5
1987	M.Watkinson	18	22	2	138	706	35.30	1	4	8
1990	I.D.Austin	11	12	5	58	238	34.00	–	1	–
1981	G.Fowler	21	35	6	126	938	32.34	2	2	13
–	G.D.Lloyd	11	15	1	70	434	31.00	–	4	7
1981	P.J.W.Allott	13	6	2	55*	114	28.50	–	1	10
1970	D.P.Hughes	18	17	7	57	237	23.70	–	1	13
–	J.D.Fitton	14	11	5	25*	114	19.00	–	–	4
–	P.J.Martin	9	6	3	21	42	14.00	–	–	5
1989	Wasim Akram	7	10	0	32	117	11.70	–	–	2
–	N.J.Speak	3	4	0	30	41	10.25	–	–	2
1987	B.P.Patterson	10	4	1	4*	5	1.66	–	–	2

Also played: (1 match each): S.Bramhall 0* (1 ct, 1 st); J.P.Crawley did not bat; S.N.V.Waterton 3 (4 ct); G.Yates (2 matches) 106.

BOWLING

	O	M	R	W	Avge	Best	5wI	10wM
M.A.Atherton	356.3	85	1111	42	26.45	6-78	3	–
M.Watkinson	503.2	120	1572	47	33.44	5-65	3	–
B.P.Patterson	281.4	45	1015	29	35.00	4-52	–	–
P.A.J.DeFreitas	408.5	96	1219	33	36.93	6-39	1	–
P.J.Martin	240.3	46	750	20	37.50	4-68	–	–
D.P.Hughes	280.4	61	918	24	38.25	4-25	–	–
Wasim Akram	191	43	594	15	39.60	3-76	–	–
P.J.W.Allott	266	77	730	18	40.55	4-23	–	–
I.D.Austin	208.1	64	536	10	53.60	3-42	–	–
J.D.Fitton	428.4	86	1365	14	97.50	3-69	–	–

Also bowled: G.Fowler 4.1-2-33-1; T.E.Jesty 8-3-27-1; G.D.Lloyd 2.1-0-22-0; G.Yates 51-12-117-3.

The First-Class Averages (pp 166–181) give the records of Lancashire players in all first-class county matches (their other opponents being the Sri Lankans, the Zimbabweans and Oxford U.), with the exception of W.K.Hegg, whose full county figures are as above, and:

M.A.Atherton 13-19-4-191-1170-78.00-5-6-17ct. 395.3-95-1220-44-27.72-6/78-3-0.
M.A.Crawley 1-2-0-48-90-45.00-0-0-0ct. 14-3-25-0.
P.A.J.DeFreitas 16-18-3-102-608-40.53-2-2-7ct. 429.5-100-1265-34-37.20-6/39-1-0.
N.H.Fairbrother 19-27-6-366-1681-80.04-4-9-19ct. 7-0-29-0.

LANCASHIRE RECORDS

FIRST-CLASS CRICKET

Highest Total	For	863		v	Surrey	The Oval	1990
	V	707-9d		by	Surrey	The Oval	1990
Lowest Total	For	25		v	Derbyshire	Manchester	1871
	V	22		by	Glamorgan	Liverpool	1924
Highest Innings	For	424	A.C.MacLaren	v	Somerset	Taunton	1895
	V	315*	T.W.Hayward	for	Surrey	The Oval	1898

Highest Partnership for each Wicket

1st	368	A.C.MacLaren/R.H.Spooner	v	Glos	Liverpool	1903
2nd	371	F.B.Watson/G.E.Tyldesley	v	Surrey	Manchester	1928
3rd	364	M.A.Atherton/N.H.Fairbrother	v	Surrey	The Oval	1990
4th	324	A.C.MacLaren/J.T.Tyldesley	v	Notts	Nottingham	1904
5th	249	B.Wood/A.Kennedy	v	Warwicks	Birmingham	1975
6th	278	J.Iddon/H.R.W.Butterworth	v	Sussex	Manchester	1932
7th	245	A.H.Hornby/J.Sharp	v	Leics	Manchester	1912
8th	158	J.Lyon/R.M.Ratcliffe	v	Warwicks	Manchester	1979
9th	142	L.O.S.Poidevin/A.Kermode	v	Sussex	Eastbourne	1907
10th	173	J.Briggs/R.Pilling	v	Surrey	Liverpool	1885

Best Bowling	For	10-46	W.Hickton	v	Hampshire	Manchester	1870
(Innings)	V	10-40	G.O.B.Allen	for	Middlesex	Lord's	1929
Best Bowling	For	17-91	H.Dean	v	Yorkshire	Liverpool	1913
(Match)	V	16-65	G.Giffen	for	Australians	Manchester	1886

Most Runs – Season	2,663	J.T.Tyldesley	(av 56.02)	1901
Most Runs – Career	34,222	G.E.Tyldesley	(av 45.20)	1909-1936
Most 100s – Season	11	C.Hallows		1928
Most 100s – Career	90	G.E.Tyldesley		1909-1936
Most Wkts – Season	198	E.A.McDonald	(av 18.55)	1925
Most Wkts – Career	1,816	J.B.Statham	(av 15.12)	1950-1968

LIMITED-OVERS CRICKET

Highest Total	NWT	372-5		v	Glos	Manchester	1990
	BHC	317-5		v	Scotland	Manchester	1988
	RAL	268-3		v	Surrey	The Oval	1990
Lowest Total	NWT	59		v	Worcs	Worcester	1963
	BHC	82		v	Yorkshire	Bradford	1972
	RAL	71		v	Essex	Chelmsford	1987
Highest Innings	NWT	131	A.Kennedy	v	Middlesex	Manchester	1978
	BHC	124	C.H.Lloyd	v	Warwicks	Manchester	1981
	RAL	134*	C.H.Lloyd	v	Somerset	Manchester	1970
Best Bowling	NWT	5-13	P.A.DeFreitas	v	Cumberland	Kendal	1989
	BHC	6-10	C.E.H.Croft	v	Scotland	Manchester	1982
	RAL	6-29	D.P.Hughes	v	Somerset	Manchester	1977

LEICESTERSHIRE

Formation of Present Club: 25 March 1879
Colours: Dark Green and Scarlet
Badge: Gold Running Fox on Green Ground
Championships: (1) 1975
NatWest Trophy/Gillette Cup Semi-Finalists: (2) 1977, 1987
Benson and Hedges Cup Winners: (3) 1972, 1975, 1985
Sunday League Champions: (2) 1974, 1977
Match Awards: NWT 28; BHC 52

Chief Executive: F.M.Turner. **Secretary:** K.P.Hill, County Ground, Grace Road, Leicester LE2 8AD (☎ 0533-831880)
Captain: N.E.Briers
Scorer: G.R.Blackburn

BENSON, Justin David Ramsay (The Leys S, Cambridge), b Dublin, Ireland 1 Mar 1967. 6'2". RHB, RM. Debut 1988. Cambridgeshire 1984-87. HS 106 v Ind (Leicester) 1990. BAC HS 86 v Northants (Northampton) 1990. BB 1-44. Award: NWT 1. **NWT:** HS 85 Cambs v Yorks (Leeds) 1986. **BHC:** HS 43 v Notts (Nottingham) 1990. **RAL:** HS 67 v Surrey (Oval) 1990. BB 2-33 v Kent (Leicester) 1990.

BOON, Timothy James (Edlington CS, Doncaster), b Doncaster, Yorks 1 Nov 1961. 6'0". RHB, RM. Debut 1980. Cap 1986. Tour: Z 1980-81 (Leics). 1000 runs (5); most – 1539 (1990). HS 144 v Glos (Leicester) 1984. Shared record Leics 4th-wkt stand of 290* with P.Willey v Warwks (Leicester) 1984. BB 3-40 v Yorks (Leicester) 1986. **NWT:** HS 24 v Salop (Telford) 1989. **BHC:** HS 84 v Northants (Leicester) 1990. **RAL:** HS 97 v Kent (Leicester) 1990.

BRIERS, Nigel Edwin (Lutterworth GS; Borough Road CE), b Leicester 15 Jan 1955. 6'0". RHB, RM. Debut 1971 (aged 16yr 103d – youngest Leicestershire player). Cap 1981. Captain 1990-. Benefit 1990. Tour: Z 1980-81 (Leics). 1000 runs (7); most – 1996 (1990). HS 201* v Warwks (Birmingham) 1983. Shared record Leics 5th-wkt stand of 233 with R.W.Tolchard v Somerset (Leicester) 1979. BB 4-29 v Derbys (Leicester) 1985. Awards: BHC 3. **NWT:** HS 59 v Wilts (Swindon) 1984. BB 2-6 v Worcs (Leicester) 1979. **BHC:** HS 93* v Scot (Leicester) 1990. BB 1-26. **RAL:** HS 119* v Hants (Bournemouth) 1981. BB 3-29 v Middx (Leicester) 1984.

COBB, Russell Alan (Trent C), b Leicester 18 May 1961. 5'11". RHB, SLA. Debut 1980. Cap 1986. Natal B 1988-89. Tours: NZ 1979-80 (DHR); Z 1980-81 (Leics). 1000 runs (1): 1092 (1986). HS 91 v Northants (Leicester) 1986. Award: NWT 1. **NWT:** HS 66* v Oxon (Leicester) 1987. **BHC:** HS 22 v Warwks (Leicester) 1986. **RAL:** HS 24 v Worcs (Leicester) 1981.

GIDLEY, Martyn Ian (Loughborough GS), b Loughborough 30 Sep 1968. 6'1". LHB, OB. Debut 1989. HS 73 v Glam (Cardiff) 1990. BB 1-23 v Notts (Nottingham) 1989. **BHC:** HS 20* v Notts (Nottingham) 1990. **RAL:** HS 14* v Worcs (Leicester) 1990. BB 3-45 v Surrey (Oval) 1990.

HAWKES, Christopher James (Loughborough GS), b Loughborough 14 Jul 1972. 6'3". LHB, SLA. Debut 1990. HS 3.

HEPWORTH, Peter Nash, b Ackworth, Yorks 4 May 1967. 6'1". RHB, OB. Debut 1988. HS 55* v Derbys (Derby) 1990. **RAL:** HS 38 v Sussex (Leicester) 1988.

LEWIS, Clairmonte Christopher (Willesden HS, London), b Georgetown, Guyana 14 Feb 1968. 6'2½". RHB, RFM. Debut 1987. Cap 1990. **Tests**: 3 (1990); HS 32 and BB 3-76 v NZ (Birmingham) 1990 – on debut. LOI: 7. Tour: WI 1989-90 (part). HS 189* v Essex (Chelmsford) 1990. 50 wkts (1): 56 (1990). BB 6-22 v OU (Oxford) 1988. BAC BB 6-55 v Glam (Cardiff) 1990. **NWT**: HS 53 v Glos (Leicester) 1988. BB 2-32 v Suffolk (Leicester) 1988. **BHC**: HS 23* v Lancs (Manchester) 1989. BB 3-41 v Lancs (Leicester) 1988. **RAL**: HS 93* v Essex (Leicester) 1990. BB 4-13 v Essex (Leicester) 1988.

MILLNS, David James (Garibaldi CS), b Clipstone, Notts 27 Feb 1965. 6'3". LHB, RMF. Nottinghamshire 1988-89. Leicestershire debut 1990. HS 10* v Kent (Dartford) 1990. BB 6-63 v Northants (Leicester) 1990. **RAL**: HS 0*. BB 2-47 v Kent (Leicester) 1990.

MULLALLY, Alan David (Educated in Perth, Aus), b Southend-on-Sea, Essex 12 Jul 1969. 6'3½". RHB, LFM. W Australia 1987-90. Hampshire (1 match) 1988. Leicestershire debut 1990. HS 34 WA v Tasmania (Perth) 1989-90. Le HS 29 v Hants (Leicester) 1990. BB 4-59 v Yorks (Sheffield) 1990. **NWT**: BB 2-55 v Hants (Leicester) 1990. **BHC**: BB 1-28. **RAL**: HS 10* v Hants (Leicester) 1990. BB 2-20 v Glos (Gloucester) 1990.

NIXON, Paul Andrew (Ullswater HS, Penrith), b Carlisle, Cumberland 21 Oct 1970. 6'0". LHB, WK. Debut 1989. Cumberland 1987. MCC Cricket Staff. HS 46 v Surrey (Oval) 1990. **NWT**: HS 12 v Hants (Leicester) 1990. **RAL**: HS 10 v Hants (Leicester) 1990.

PARSONS, Gordon James (Woodside County SS, Slough), b Slough, Bucks 17 Oct 1959. 6'1". LHB, RMF. Leicestershire 1978-85 and 1989 (cap 1984). Warwickshire 1986-88 (cap 1987). Boland 1983-85. GW 1985-87. OFS 1988-90. Buckinghamshire 1977. Tours: NZ 1979-80 (DHR); Z 1980-81 (Leics). HS 76 Boland v N Province B (Cape Town) 1984-85. Le HS 69 v Glos (Leicester) 1989. 50 wkts (2); most – 67 (1984). BB 9-72 Boland v Transvaal B (Johannesburg) 1984-85. Le BB 6-11 v OU (Oxford) 1985. BAC BB 6-75 v Surrey (Oval) 1990. Awards: BHC 2. **NWT**: HS 23 v Northants (Northampton) 1984. BB 2-11 v Wilts (Swindon) 1984. **BHC**: HS 63* and BB 4-12 v Scot (Leicester) 1989. **RAL**: HS 26* Wa v Derbys (Birmingham) 1987. BB 4-19 v Essex (Harlow) 1982.

POTTER, Laurie (Kelmscott HS, Perth, Aus), b Bexleyheath, Kent 7 Nov 1962. 6'1". RHB, SLA. Kent 1981-85. Leicestershire debut 1986. Cap 1988. GW 1984-86 (captain 1985-86). OFS 1987-88. 1000 runs (2); most – 1093 (1989). HS 165* GW v Border (East London) 1984-85. Leics HS 121* v Notts (Leicester) 1989. BB 4-52 GW v Boland (Stellenbosch) 1985-86. Leics BB 3-37 v Glam (Leicester) 1986. Award: BHC 1. **NWT**: HS 45 Kent v Essex (Chelmsford) 1982. BB 1-28. **BHC**: HS 112 and BB 2-70 v Minor C (Leicester) 1986. **RAL**: HS 105 v Derbys (Leicester) 1986. BB 4-9 Kent v Derbys (Folkestone) 1985.

ROSEBERRY, Andrew (Durham S), b Sunderland, Co Durham 2 Apr 1971. 6'0". Younger brother of M.A. (Middlesex). RHB, RM. No 1st XI appearances – joined staff 1990.

SMITH, Benjamin Francis (Kibworth HS), b Corby, Northants 3 Apr 1972. 5'9". RHB, RM. Debut 1990. HS 15* v Glam (Hinckley) 1990. **RAL**: HS 29 v Warwks (Birmingham) 1990.

TENNANT, Lloyd (Shellfield CS), b Walsall, Staffs 9 Apr 1968. 5'11". RHB, RMF. Debut 1986. HS 12* v Sussex (Leicester) 1986. BB 1-0. **RAL**: HS 17* v Somerset (Leicester) 1988. BB 3-25 v Somerset (Leicester) 1986.

WHITAKER, John James (Uppingham S), b Skipton, Yorks 5 May 1962. 5'10". RHB, OB. Debut 1983. Cap 1986. Wisden 1986. YC 1986. **Tests:** 1 (1986-87); HS 11 v A (Adelaide) 1986-87. LOI: 2. Tours: A 1986-87; Z 1989-90 (Eng A). 1000 runs (7); most – 1767 (1990). HS 200* v Notts (Leicester) 1986. BB 1-41. Awards: NWT 1; BHC 1. **NWT:** HS 155 v Wilts (Swindon) 1984. **BHC:** HS 73* v Warwks (Birmingham) 1985. **RAL:** HS 132 v Glam (Swansea) 1984.

WHITTICASE, Philip (Crestwood CS, Kingswinford), b Marston Green, Solihull 15 Mar 1965. 5'8". RHB, WK. Debut 1984. Cap 1987. HS 71 v Somerset (Hinckley) 1988. **NWT:** HS 32 v Lancs (Leicester) 1986. **BHC:** HS 45 v Notts (Nottingham) 1990. **RAL:** HS 38 v Northants (Leicester) 1990.

WILLEY, Peter (Seaham SS) b Sedgefield, Co Durham 6 Dec 1949. 6'1". RHB, OB. Northamptonshire 1966-83 (cap 1971; benefit 1981). Leicestershire debut/cap 1984. Captain 1987. E Province 1982-85. **Tests:** 26 (1976-86); HS 102* v WI (St John's) 1980-81; BB 2-73 v WI (Lord's) 1980. LOI: 26. Tours: A 1979-80; SA 1972-73 (DHR), 1981-82 (SAB); WI 1980-81, 1985-86; I 1979-80; SL 1977-78 (DHR). 1000 runs (10); most – 1783 (1982). HS 227 Nh v Somerset (Northampton) 1976 – sharing record Northants 4th-wkt stand of 370 with R.T.Virgin. Le HS 177 v OU (Oxford) 1990. Shared record Leics 4th-wkt stand of 290* with T.J.Boon v Warwks (Leicester) 1984. 50 wkts (3); most – 52 (1979). BB 7-37 Nh v OU (Oxford) 1975. BAC BB 6-17 Nh v Sussex (Eastbourne) 1982. Le BB 6-43 v Hants (Leicester) 1985. Awards: NWT 7; BHC 7. **NWT:** HS 154 v Hants (Leicester) 1987. BB 3-33 v Derbys (Leicester) 1984. **BHC:** HS 88* v Nh (Leicester) 1984. BB 3-12 Nh v Minor C (E) (Horton) 1977. **RAL:** HS 107 Nh v Warwks 1975 and 107 v Hants 1976. BB 4-37 v Somerset (Leicester) 1986.

NEWCOMER

MAGUIRE, John Norman (Cavendish Road State HS; Queensland Institute of Technology), b Murwillumbah, NSW, Australia 15 Sep 1956. RHB, RFM. Queensland 1977-85. E Province 1989-90. **Tests** (A): 3 (1983-84); HS 15* v WI (St John's) 1983-84; BB 4-57 v WI (Kingston) 1983-84. LOI (A): 23. Tours (A): SA 1985-86 (Aus XI), 1986-87 (Aus XI); WI 1983-84. HS 65* EP v N Transvaal (Verwoerdburg) 1989-90. **BB** 7-46 Aus XI v EP (Pt Elizabeth) 1986-87 – inc hat-trick.

DEPARTURES

AGNEW, Jonathan Philip (Uppingham S), b Macclesfield, Cheshire 4 Apr 1960. 6'3½". RHB, RFM. Leicestershire 1978-90 (cap 1984; Wisden 1987). **Tests:** 3 (1984 to 1985); HS 5; BB 2-51 v WI (Oval) 1984. LOI: 3. Tours: I 1984-85; SL 1985-86 (Eng B); Z 1980-81 (Leics). HS 90 v Yorks (Scarborough) 1987. 50 wkts (7) inc 100 wkts (1): 101 (1987). BB 9-70 v Kent (Leicester) 1985. Award: BHC 1. **NWT:** HS 8*. BB 3-31 v Oxon (Leicester) 1987. **BHC:** HS 23* v Warwks (Leicester) 1984. BB 5-30 v Glos (Bristol) 1987. **RAL:** HS 23* v Notts (Nottingham) 1987. BB 4-25 v Glos (Leicester) 1989. Cricket correspondent of *Today*.

BENJAMIN, Winston Keithroy Matthew (All Saints S, Antigua), b St John's, Antigua 31 Dec 1964. 6'3". RHB, RFM. Debut (Rest of World XI) 1985. Leicestershire 1986-90 (cap 1989). Leeward Is 1985-90. Cheshire 1985. **Tests** (WI): 8 (1987-88 to 1988-89); HS 40* v P (Bridgetown) 1987-88; BB 4-52 v Eng (Oval) 1988. LOI (WI): 47. Tours (WI): I 1988; A 1986-87, 1988-89; I 1987-88; P 1986-87. HS 101* v Derbys (Leicester) 1990. 50 wkts (1): 69 (1989). BB 7-54 (inc hat-trick) v A (Leicester) 1989. Award: BHC 1. **NWT:** HS 17 v Sussex (Hove) 1988. BB 3-23 v Glos (Bristol) 1986. **BHC:** HS 21 v Northants (Northampton) 1987. BB 5-17 v Minor C (Leicester) 1986. **RAL:** HS 41* v Essex (Chelmsford) 1989. BB 4-19 v Lancs (Leicester) 1986.

Continued on p 155.

LEICESTERSHIRE 1990

RESULTS SUMMARY

	Place	Won	Lost	Drew	Abandoned
Britannic Assurance Championship	7th	6	7	9	
All First-class Matches		6	7	11	
Refuge Assurance League	15th	4	11		1
NatWest Bank Trophy	1st Round				
Benson and Hedges Cup	3rd in Group D				

BRITANNIC ASSURANCE CHAMPIONSHIP AVERAGES

BATTING AND FIELDING

Cap		M	I	NO	HS	Runs	Avge	100	50	Ct/St
1981	N.E.Briers	22	43	3	176	1846	46.15	4	11	7
1986	J.J.Whitaker	22	42	4	116	1575	41.44	3	7	12
1990	C.C.Lewis	13	21	5	189*	632	39.50	1	2	11
1986	T.J.Boon	22	43	4	138	1522	39.02	2	11	12
1989	W.K.M.Benjamin	11	13	2	101*	382	34.72	1	3	3
1988	L.Potter	22	36	5	109*	1028	33.16	1	7	22
–	P.N.Hepworth	4	8	2	55*	185	30.83	–	1	1
–	J.D.R.Benson	16	24	6	86	525	29.16	–	2	9
1984	P.Willey	20	37	6	112	892	28.77	1	4	10
–	M.I.Gidley	4	5	1	73	113	28.25	–	1	2
–	P.A.Nixon	17	20	6	46	379	27.07	–	–	44/1
1988	G.J.F.Ferris	5	6	0	35	104	17.33	–	–	–
–	J.P.Agnew	22	26	5	46*	257	12.23	–	–	5
1984	G.J.Parsons	8	12	2	20	101	10.10	–	–	3
–	A.D.Mullally	18	18	6	29	113	9.41	–	–	3
1987	P.Whitticase	5	7	2	11*	39	7.80	–	–	13
–	D.J.Millns	8	10	5	10*	23	4.60	–	–	3

Also played: (1 match each): C.J.Hawkes 3, 2* (1 ct); B.F.Smith 15* (1 ct);
L.B.Taylor (cap 1981) did not bat.

BOWLING

	O	M	R	W	Avge	Best	5wI	10wM
D.J.Millns	164.1	20	568	25	22.72	6-63	1	–
G.J.Parsons	247.5	56	821	31	26.48	6-75	2	–
C.C.Lewis	411.2	80	1238	44	28.13	6-55	2	1
W.K.M.Benjamin	260.3	60	769	27	28.48	5-73	2	–
A.D.Mullally	464.2	116	1351	37	36.51	4-59	–	–
J.P.Agnew	612	108	2196	59	37.22	5-54	5	–
P.Willey	377.4	101	1016	20	50.80	2-7	–	–

Also bowled: J.D.R.Benson 35.5-1-145-1; T.J.Boon 3.5-0-25-0; G.J.F.Ferris
101.2-16-404-9; M.I.Gidley 61-15-228-0; C.J.Hawkes 14-3-40-0; L.Potter
169-39-583-6; L.B.Taylor 9-1-34-0.

The First-Class Averages (pp 166–181) give the records of Leicestershire players in
all first-class county matches (their other opponents being the Indians and Oxford
U.), with the exception of:
C.C.Lewis 14-23-5-189*-661-36.72-1-2-11ct. 430.2-86-1289-47-27.42-6/55-2-1.

LEICESTERSHIRE RECORDS

FIRST-CLASS CRICKET

Highest Total	For	701-4d		v Worcs	Worcester	1906
	V	761-6d		by Essex	Chelmsford	1990
Lowest Total	For	25		v Kent	Leicester	1912
	V	{ 24		by Glamorgan	Leicester	1971
		{ 24		by Oxford U	Oxford	1985
Highest Innings	For	252*	S.Coe	v Northants	Leicester	1914
	V	341	G.H.Hirst	for Yorks	Leicester	1905

Highest Partnership for each Wicket

1st	390	B.Dudleston/J.F.Steele	v Derbyshire	Leicester	1979
2nd	289*	J.C.Balderstone/D.I.Gower	v Essex	Leicester	1981
3rd	316*	W.Watson/A.Wharton	v Somerset	Taunton	1961
4th	290*	P.Willey/T.J.Boon	v Warwicks	Leicester	1984
5th	233	N.E.Briers/R.W.Tolchard	v Somerset	Leicester	1979
6th	262	A.T.Sharpe/G.H.S.Fowke	v Derbyshire	Chesterfield	1911
7th	206	B.Dudleston/J.Birkenshaw	v Kent	Canterbury	1969
8th	164	M.R.Hallam/C.T.Spencer	v Essex	Leicester	1964
9th	160	W.W.Odell/R.T.Crawford	v Worcs	Leicester	1902
10th	228	R.Illingworth/K.Higgs	v Northants	Leicester	1977

Best Bowling	For	10-18	G.Geary	v Glamorgan	Pontypridd	1929
(Innings)	V	10-32	H.Pickett	for Essex	Leyton	1895
Best Bowling	For	16-96	G.Geary	v Glamorgan	Pontypridd	1929
(Match)	V	16-102	C.Blythe	for Kent	Leicester	1909

Most Runs – Season	2,446	L.G.Berry	(av 52.04)		1937
Most Runs – Career	30,143	L.G.Berry	(av 30.32)		1924-1951
Most 100s – Season	{7	L.G.Berry			1937
	{7	W.Watson			1959
	{7	B.F.Davison			1982
Most 100s – Career	45	L.G.Berry			1924-1951
Most Wkts – Season	170	J.E.Walsh	(av 18.96)		1948
Most Wkts – Career	2,130	W.E.Astill	(av 23.19)		1906-1939

LIMITED-OVERS CRICKET

Highest Total	NWT	354-7		v Wiltshire	Swindon	1984
	BHC	327-4		v Warwicks	Coventry	1972
	RAL	291-5		v Glamorgan	Swansea	1984
Lowest Total	NWT	56		v Northants	Leicester	1964
	BHC	56		v Minor C	Wellington	1982
	RAL	36		v Sussex	Leicester	1973
Highest Innings	NWT	156	D.I.Gower	v Derbyshire	Leicester	1984
	BHC	158*	B.F.Davison	v Warwicks	Coventry	1972
	RAL	152	B.Dudleston	v Lancashire	Manchester	1975
Best Bowling	NWT	6-20	K.Higgs	v Staffs	Longton	1975
	BHC	6-35	L.B.Taylor	v Worcs	Worcester	1982
	RAL	6-17	K.Higgs	v Glamorgan	Leicester	1973

MIDDLESEX

Formation of Present Club: 2 February 1864
Colours: Blue
Badge: Three Seaxes
Championships (since 1890): (9) 1903, 1920, 1921, 1947, 1976, 1980, 1982, 1985, 1990
Joint Championships: (2) 1949, 1977
NatWest Trophy/Gillette Cup Winners: (4) 1977, 1980, 1984, 1988
Benson and Hedges Cup Winners: (2) 1983, 1986
Sunday League Champions: (0) Second 1982
Match Awards: NWT 46; BHC 47

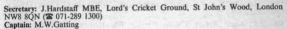

Secretary: J.Hardstaff MBE, Lord's Cricket Ground, St John's Wood, London NW8 8QN (☎ 071-289 1300)
Captain: M.W.Gatting
Scorer: H.P.H.Sharp
1991 Beneficiary: S.P.Hughes

BARNETT, Alexander Anthony (William Ellis S), b Malaga, Spain, 11 Sep 1970. Great nephew of C.J. (Glos and England 1929-53). 5'11". RHB, SLA. Debut 1988. HS 10 v Sussex (Hove) 1988. No appearances 1989-90.

BROWN, Keith Robert (Chace S, Enfield), b Edmonton 18 Mar 1963. Brother of G.K. (Middlesex 1986). 5'11". RHB, WK, RSM. Debut 1984. Cap 1990. MCC Cricket Staff. 1000 runs (1): 1505 (1990). HS 200* v Notts (Lord's) 1990. BB 2-7 v Glos (Bristol) 1987. Award: NWT 1. **NWT:** HS 103* v Surrey (Uxbridge) 1990. **BHC:** HS 56 v Minor C (Lord's) 1990. **RAL:** HS 102 v Somerset (Lord's) 1988.

COWANS, Norman George (Park High SS, Stanmore), b Enfield St Mary, Jamaica 17 Apr 1961. 6'3". RHB, RF. Debut 1980. Cap 1984. YC 1982. MCC Cricket Staff. **Tests:** 19 (1982-83 to 1985); HS 36 v A (Perth) 1982-83; BB 6-77 v A (Melbourne) 1982-83. LOI: 23. Tours: A 1982-83; NZ 1983-84; I 1984-85; P 1983-84; SL 1984-85, 1985-86 (Eng B); Z 1980-81 (Middx). HS 66 v Surrey (Lord's) 1984. 50 wkts (6); most – 73 (1984, 1985). BB 6-31 v Leics (Leicester) 1985. Awards: NWT 1; BHC 1. **NWT:** HS 12* v Lancs (Lord's) 1984. BB 4-24 v Yorks (Leeds) 1986. **BHC:** HS 12 v Derbys (Derby) 1990. BB 4-33 v Lancs (Lord's) 1983. **RAL:** HS 27 v Notts (Lord's) 1990. BB 4-44 v Sussex (Hove) 1982.

DOWNTON, Paul Rupert (Sevenoaks S; Exeter U), b Farnborough, Kent 4 Apr 1957. Son of G.C. (Kent 1948). 5'10". RHB, WK, OB. Kent 1977-79 (cap 1979). Middlesex debut 1980. Cap 1981. Benefit 1990. **Tests:** 30 (1980-81 to 1988); HS 74 v I (Delhi) 1984-85. LOI: 28. Tours: WI 1980-81, 1985-86; NZ 1977-78; Ind/SL 1984-85; P 1977-78; Z 1980-81 (Middx). 1000 runs (1): 1120 (1987). HS 126* v OU (Oxford) 1986. BAC HS 120 v Lancs (Manchester) 1990. BB 1-4. Award: NWT 1. **NWT:** HS 69 v Hants (Uxbridge) 1989. **BHC:** HS 80* v Hants (Southampton) 1987. **RAL:** HS 70 v Notts (Nottingham) 1985.

ELLCOCK, Ricardo McDonald (Welches S, Combermere, Barbados; Malvern C), b Bridgetown, Barbados 17 Jun 1965. 5'11". RHB, RF. Barbados 1983-84. Worcestershire 1982-88. Middlesex debut 1989. HS 45* Wo v Essex (Worcester) 1984. M HS 9. BB 5-35 v Yorks (Leeds) 1989. **NWT:** HS 6. BB 4-43 v Notts (Uxbridge) 1989. **BHC:** HS 12 and BB 2-45 Wo v Notts (Nottingham) 1984. **RAL:** HS 13 v Somerset (W-s-M) 1989. BB 4-43 v Kent (Canterbury) 1983.

EMBUREY, John Ernest (Peckham Manor SS), b Peckham, London 20 Aug 1952. 6'2". RHB, OB. Debut 1973. Cap 1977. Wisden 1983. W Province 1982-84. Benefit 1986. **Tests:** 60 (1978 to 1989, 2 as captain); HS 75 v NZ (Nottingham) 1986; BB 7-78 v A (Sydney) 1986-87. LOI: 58. Tours: A 1978-79, 1979-80, 1986-87, 1987-88; SA 1981-82 (SAB), 1989-90 (Eng XI); WI 1980-81, 1985-86; NZ 1987-88; I 1979-80, 1981-82; P 1987-88; SL 1977-78 (DHR), 1981-82; Z 1980-81 (Middx). HS 133 v Essex (Chelmsford) 1983. 50 wkts (12) inc 100 wkts (1): 103 (1983). BB 7-27 (12-66 match) v Glos (Cheltenham) 1989. Awards: NWT 1; BHC 6. **NWT:** HS 36* v Lancs (Manchester) 1978. BB 3-11 v Sussex (Lord's) 1989. **BHC:** HS 50 v Kent (Lord's) 1984. BB 4-22 v Notts (Lord's) 1986. **RAL:** HS 50 v Lancs (Blackpool) 1988. BB 5-36 v Warwks (Lord's) 1983.

FARBRACE, Paul (Geoffrey Chaucer S, Canterbury), b Ash, Kent 7 Jul 1967. 5'10". RHB, WK. Kent 1987-89. Middlesex debut 1990. HS 79 v CU (Cambridge) 1990. BAC HS 75* K v Yorks (Canterbury) 1987. **NWT:** HS 17 v Berks (Lord's) 1990. **RAL:** HS 3.

FRASER, Angus Robert Charles (Gayton HS, Harrow), b Billinge, Lancs 8 Aug 1965. Brother of A.G.J. (see ESSEX). 6'5". RHB, RFM. Debut 1984. Cap 1988. **Tests:** 8 (1989 to 1990); HS 29 v A (Nottingham) 1989; BB 5-28 v WI (Kingston) 1989-90. LOI: 13. Tour: WI 1989-90. HS 92 v Surrey (Oval) 1990. 50 wkts (3); most – 92 (1989). BB 7-77 v Kent (Canterbury) 1989. **NWT:** HS 19 v Durham (Darlington) 1989. BB 4-34 v Yorks (Leeds) 1988. **BHC:** HS 13* v Essex (Lord's) 1988. BB 3-39 (inc hat-trick) v Sussex (Lord's) 1988. **RAL:** HS 30* v Kent (Canterbury) 1988. BB 4-28 v Glam (Lord's) 1990.

GATTING, Michael William (John Kelly HS), b Kingsbury 6 Jun 1957. 5'10". RHB, RM. Debut 1975. Cap 1977. Captain 1983-. Benefit 1988. YC 1981. Wisden 1983. OBE 1987. **Tests:** 68 (1977-78 to 1989, 23 as captain); HS 207 v I (Madras) 1984-85; BB 1-14. LOI: 85. Tours (C=captain): A 1986-87C, 1987-88C; SA 1989-90C (Eng XI); WI 1980-81, 1985-86; NZ 1977-78, 1983-84, 1987-88C; Ind/SL 1981-82, 1984-85; P 1977-78, 1983-84, 1987-88C; Z 1980-81 (Middx). 1000 runs (12+1) inc 2000 (1): 2257 (1984). HS 258 v Somerset (Bath) 1984. BB 5-34 v Glam (Swansea) 1982. Awards: NWT 5; BHC 10. **NWT:** HS 132* v Sussex (Lord's) 1989. BB 2-14 (twice). **BHC:** HS 143* v Sussex (Hove) 1985. BB 4-49 v Sussex (Lord's) 1984. **RAL:** HS 124* v Leics (Leicester) 1990. BB 4-30 v Glos (Bristol) 1989.

HABIB, Aftab (Millfield S), b Reading, Berks 7 Feb 1972. 5'11". RHB, RMF. No 1st XI appearances – joined staff 1990.

HAYNES, Desmond Leo (Barbados Academy; Federal HS), b Holder's Hill, Barbados 15 Feb 1956. 5'11". RHB, RM/LBG. Barbados 1976-90. Middlesex debut/cap 1989. Scotland (BHC) 1983. Wisden 1990. **Tests (WI):** 89 (1977-78 to 1989-90, 1 as captain); HS 184 v Eng (Lord's) 1980; BB 1-2. LOI (WI): 174. Tours: E 1980, 1984, 1988; A 1979-80, 1981-82, 1984-85, 1986-87, 1988-89; NZ 1979-80, 1986-87; I 1983-84, 1987-88; P 1980-81, 1986-87; Z 1981-82 (WI B). 1000 runs (2+3) inc 2000 (1): 2346 (1990). HS 255* v Sussex (Lord's) 1990. BB 1-2 (Tests). M BB 1-18. Awards: NWT 1; BHC 3. **NWT:** HS 149* v Lancs (Manchester) 1990. **BHC:** HS 131 v Sussex (Hove) 1990. **RAL:** HS 107* v Lancs (Manchester) 1990.

HUGHES, Simon Peter (Latymer Upper S, Hammersmith; Durham U), b Kingston upon Thames, Surrey 20 Dec 1959. 5'10". RHB, RFM. Debut 1980. Cap 1981. Benefit 1991. N Transvaal 1982-83. Tours: I 1980-81 (Overseas XI); Z 1980-81 (Middx). HS 53 v CU (Cambridge) 1988. BAC HS 47 v Warwks (Uxbridge) 1986. 50 wkts (2); most – 63 (1986). BB 7-35 v Surrey (Oval) 1986. Award: NWT 1. **NWT:** HS 11 and BB 4-20 v Durham (Darlington) 1989. **BHC:** HS 22 v Somerset (Taunton) 1990. BB 4-34 v Somerset (Lord's) 1987. **RAL:** HS 22* v Surrey (Lord's) 1985. BB 5-23 v Worcs (Worcester) 1989.

HUTCHINSON, Ian James Frederick (Shrewsbury S), b Welshpool, Montgomerys, 31 Oct 1964. 6'1". RHB, RMF. Debut 1988. Shropshire 1984-86. MCC Cricket Staff. Scored 204 off 124 balls (14 sixes) before lunch for Cross Arrows 1985. HS 201* v OU (Oxford) 1989. BAC HS 177 v Kent (Uxbridge) 1989. **NWT:** HS 1. **RAL:** HS 22* v Lancs (Lord's) 1987.

KEECH, Matthew (Northumberland Park S), b Hampstead 21 Oct 1970. 6'0". RHB, RM. No 1st XI appearances – joined staff 1990.

POOLEY, Jason Calvin (Acton HS), b Hammersmith 8 Aug 1969. 6'0". LHB, OB. Debut 1989. HS 14 v Kent (Canterbury) 1989. **RAL:** HS 6.

RADFORD, Toby Alexander (St Bartholomew's S, Newbury), b Caerphilly, Glam 3 Dec 1971. 5'10". RHB, OB. No 1st XI appearances – joined staff 1990.

RAMPRAKASH, Mark Ravin (Gayton HS, Harrow; Harrow Weald SFC), b Bushey, Herts 5 Sep 1969. 5'9". RHB, RM. Debut 1987. Cap 1990. 1000 runs (2); most – 1541 (1990). HS 146* v Somerset (Uxbridge) 1990. BB 1-17. Award: NWT 1. **NWT:** HS 104 v Surrey (Uxbridge) 1990. **BHC:** HS 44 v Sussex (Hove) 1990. **RAL:** HS 147* v Worcs (Lord's) 1990. BB 1-5.

ROSEBERRY, Michael Anthony (Durham S), b Houghton-le-Spring, Co Durham 28 Nov 1966. 6'1". RHB, RM. Debut 1986. Cap 1990. 1000 runs (1): 1593 (1990). HS 135 v Essex (Ilford) 1990. BB 1-1. **NWT:** HS 48 v Surrey (Uxbridge) and v Glam (Lord's) 1990. **BHC:** HS 38 v Somerset (Taunton) 1990. **RAL:** HS 83* v Sussex (Hastings) 1989.

TAYLOR, Charles William (Spendlove S, Charlbury), b Banbury, Oxon 12 Aug 1966. 6'5½". LHB, LMF. Debut 1990. Oxfordshire 1986 and 1990. HS 13 v Notts (Nottingham) 1990. BB 5-33 v Yorks (Leeds) 1990.

TUFNELL, Philip Clive Roderick (Highgate S), b Barnet, Herts 29 Apr 1966. 6'0". RHB, SLA. Debut 1986. Cap 1990. MCC Cricket Staff. HS 37 v Leics (Leicester) and v Yorks (Leeds) 1990. 50 wkts (2); most – 74 (1990). BB 6-60 v Kent (Canterbury) 1987. Award: NWT 1. **NWT:** BB 3-29 v Herts (Lord's) 1988. **BHC:** HS 7*. BB 1-42. **RAL:** HS 13* v Glam (Merthyr Tydfil) 1989. BB 1-25.

WEEKES, Paul Nicholas (Homerton House SS, Hackney), b Hackney, London 8 Jul 1969. 5'10". LHB, OB. Debut 1990. MCC Cricket Staff. HS 51 v Sussex (Lord's) 1990. BB 2-115 v Somerset (Uxbridge) 1990. **RAL:** HS 29* v Yorks (Scarborough) 1990.

WILLIAMS, Neil FitzGerald (Acland Burghley CS), b Hope Well, St Vincent 2 Jul 1962. 5'11". RHB, RFM. Debut 1982. Cap 1984. Windward Is 1982-83 and 1989-90. Tasmania 1983-84. MCC Cricket Staff. Tests: 1 (1990); HS 38 and BB 2-148 v I (Oval) 1990. Tour: Z 1984-85 (EC). HS 69* v Hants (Lord's) 1989. 50 wkts (3); most – 63 (1983). BB 7-55 EC v Z (Harare) 1984-85. M BB 7-61 v Kent (Lord's) 1990. Award: BHC 1. **NWT:** HS 10 v Northumb (Jesmond) 1984. BB 4-36 v Derbys (Derby) 1983. **BHC:** HS 29* v Surrey (Lord's) 1985. BB 3-16 v Comb Us (Cambridge) 1982. **RAL:** HS 43 v Somerset (Lord's) 1988. BB 4-39 v Surrey (Oval) 1988.

NEWCOMER

SIMS, Robin Jason, b Hillingdon 22 Nov 1970. LHB, WK. MCC Cricket Staff. Held long-leg catch as substitute to dismiss A.R.Border in Lord's Test 1989. Scored 278 (15 sixes) for Ickenham in 1990 Cockspur Cup.

DEPARTURES – see p 155.

MIDDLESEX 1990

RESULTS SUMMARY

	Place	Won	Lost	Drew	Abandoned
Britannic Assurance Championship	1st	10	1	11	
All First-class Matches		10	1	13	
Refuge Assurance League	3rd	10	5		1
NatWest Bank Trophy	Semi-Finalist				
Benson and Hedges Cup	Quarter-Finalist				

BRITANNIC ASSURANCE CHAMPIONSHIP AVERAGES

BATTING AND FIELDING

Cap		M	I	NO	HS	Runs	Avge	100	50	Ct/St
1989	D.L.Haynes	22	37	5	255*	2036	63.62	6	7	14
1977	M.W.Gatting	22	36	7	170*	1685	58.10	4	9	19
1990	K.R.Brown	22	33	7	200*	1416	54.46	5	8	27
1990	M.R.Ramprakash	22	38	8	146*	1327	44.23	4	5	6
1990	M.A.Roseberry	22	40	3	135	1497	40.45	3	10	21
1977	J.E.Emburey	22	31	7	111*	698	29.08	1	2	31
1981	P.R.Downton	15	23	1	63	530	24.09	–	3	40/2
1988	A.R.C.Fraser	12	11	2	92	213	23.66	–	1	3
1990	P.C.R.Tufnell	20	20	9	37	235	21.36	–	–	7
1984	N.F.Williams	19	22	3	55*	390	20.52	–	2	4
1981	S.P.Hughes	15	17	5	23*	109	9.08	–	–	3
–	P.Farbrace	7	7	2	17*	45	9.00	–	–	15/2
1984	N.G.Cowans	16	16	6	31	81	8.10	–	–	3

Also played: C.W.Taylor (2 matches) 13, 0*; N.R.Taylor (1 match) 0 (1 ct); M.J.Thursfield (1 match) did not bat; P.N.Weekes (2 matches) 51, 2 (1 ct).

BOWLING

	O	M	R	W	Avge	Best	5wI	10wM
A.R.C.Fraser	436.5	103	1073	41	26.17	6-30	2	–
N.F.Williams	469.1	88	1430	49	29.18	7-61	2	–
N.G.Cowans	415	115	1127	36	31.30	5-67	1	–
J.E.Emburey	902	254	1911	57	33.52	5-32	2	–
P.C.R.Tufnell	948.5	254	2389	65	36.75	6-79	2	–
S.P.Hughes	333	60	1121	28	40.03	5-101	1	–

Also bowled: K.R.Brown 6-2-49-0; P.R.Downton 1.1-0-4-1; M.W.Gatting 45-18-113-7; D.L.Haynes 35-7-113-2; M.R.Ramprakash 34-5-147-2; M.A.Roseberry 11-3-74-1; C.W.Taylor 47.5-7-139-6; N.R.Taylor 14-5-44-3; M.J.Thursfield 17-4-45-1; P.N.Weekes 54-8-183-3.

The First-Class Averages (pp 166–181) give the records of Middlesex players in all first-class county matches (their other opponents being the New Zealanders and Cambridge U.), with the exception of A.R.C.Fraser and N.R.Taylor, whose full county figures are as above, and:

N.G.Cowans 17-16-6-31-81-8.10-0-0-3ct. 442-119-1208-38-31.78-5/67-1-0.
P.C.R.Tufnell 22-21-9-37-271-22.58-0-0-8ct. 1029.5-279-2622-74-35.43-6/79-2-0.
N.F.Williams 20-23-3-55*-410-20.50-0-2-4ct. 489.1-93-1470-52-28.26-7/61-2-0.

110

MIDDLESEX RECORDS

FIRST-CLASS CRICKET

Highest Total	For	642-3d	v Hampshire	Southampton	1923
	V	665	by W Indians	Lord's	1939
Lowest Total	For	20	v MCC	Lord's	1864
	V	31	by Glos	Bristol	1924
Highest Innings	For	331* J.D.B.Robertson	v Worcs	Worcester	1949
	V	316* J.B.Hobbs	for Surrey	Lord's	1926

Highest Partnership for each Wicket

1st	367*	G.D.Barlow/W.N.Slack	v Kent	Lord's	1981
2nd	380	F.A.Tarrant/J.W.Hearne	v Lancashire	Lord's	1914
3rd	424*	W.J.Edrich/D.C.S.Compton	v Somerset	Lord's	1948
4th	325	J.W.Hearne/E.H.Hendren	v Hampshire	Lord's	1919
5th	338	R.S.Lucas/T.C.O'Brien	v Sussex	Hove	1895
6th	227	C.T.Radley/F.J.Titmus	v S Africans	Lord's	1965
7th	271*	E.H.Hendren/F.T.Mann	v Notts	Nottingham	1925
8th	182*	M.H.C.Doll/H.R.Murrell	v Notts	Lord's	1913
9th	160*	E.H.Hendren/T.J.Durston	v Essex	Leyton	1927
10th	230	R.W.Nicholls/W.Roche	v Kent	Lord's	1899

Best Bowling	For	10-40	G.O.B.Allen	v Lancashire	Lord's	1929
(Innings)	V	9-38	R.C.Glasgow†	for Somerset	Lord's	1924
Best Bowling	For	{16-114	G.Burton	v Yorkshire	Sheffield	1888
		{16-114	J.T.Hearne	v Lancashire	Manchester	1898
(Match)	V	16-109	C.W.L.Parker	for Glos	Cheltenham	1930

Most Runs – Season	2,669	E.H.Hendren	(av 83.41)	1923
Most Runs – Career	40,302	E.H.Hendren	(av 48.81)	1907-1937
Most 100s – Season	13	D.C.S.Compton		1947
Most 100s – Career	119	E.H.Hendren		1907-1937
Most Wkts – Season	158	F.J.Titmus	(av 14.63)	1955
Most Wkts – Career	2,361	F.J.Titmus	(av 21.27)	1949-1982

LIMITED-OVERS CRICKET

Highest Total	NWT	296-4	v Lancashire	Manchester	1990
	BHC	303-7	v Northants	Northampton	1977
	RAL	290-6	v Worcs	Lord's	1990
Lowest Total	NWT	41	v Essex	Westcliff	1972
	BHC	73	v Essex	Lord's	1985
	RAL	23	v Yorkshire	Leeds	1974
Highest Innings	NWT	158 G.D.Barlow	v Lancashire	Lord's	1984
	BHC	143* M.W.Gatting	v Sussex	Hove	1985
	RAL	147* M.Ramprakash	v Worcs	Lord's	1990
Best Bowling	NWT	6-15 W.W.Daniel	v Sussex	Hove	1980
	BHC	7-12 W.W.Daniel	v Minor C (E)	Ipswich	1978
	RAL	6-6 R.W.Hooker	v Surrey	Lord's	1969

† R.C.Robertson-Glasgow

111

NORTHAMPTONSHIRE

Formation of Present Club: 31 July 1878
Colours: Maroon
Badge: Tudor Rose
Championships: (0) Second 1912, 1957, 1965, 1976
NatWest Trophy/Gillette Cup Winners: (1) 1976
Benson and Hedges Cup Winners: (1) 1980
Sunday League Champions: (0) Fourth 1974
Match Awards: NWT 35; BHC 36

Chief Executive: S.P.Coverdale, County Ground, Wantage Road, Northampton, NN1 4TJ (☎ 0604-32917)
Captain: A.J.Lamb
Scorers: B.H.Clarke and A.Kingston

AMBROSE, Curtly Elconn Lynwall (All Saints Village SS), b Swetes Village, Antigua 21 Sep 1963. Cousin of R.M.Otto (Leeward Is). 6'7". LHB, RF. Leeward Is 1985-90. Northamptonshire debut 1989. Cap 1990. **Tests** (WI): 20 (1987-88 to 1989-90); HS 44 v A (Melbourne) 1988-89; BB 8-45 v E (Bridgetown) 1989-90. **LOI** (WI): 37. **Tours** (WI): Eng 1988; A 1988-89. HS 59 WI v Sussex (Hove) 1988. Nh HS 55* v Leics (Leicester) 1990. 50 wkts (1): 61 (1990). BB 8-45 (Tests). Nh BB 7-89 v Leics (Leicester) 1990. **NWT:** HS 48 v Lancs (Lord's) 1990. BB 3-31 v Suffolk (Bury St E) 1989. **BHC:** HS 17* v Kent (Northampton) 1989. BB 3-19 v Leics (Leicester) 1990. **RAL:** HS 13* v Sussex (Hove) 1989. BB 3-15 v Notts (Finedon) 1989.

BAILEY, Robert John (Biddulph HS), b Biddulph, Staffs 28 Oct 1963. 6'3". RHB, OB. Debut 1982. Cap 1985. Staffordshire 1980. YC 1984. **Tests:** 4 (1988 to 1989-90); HS 43 v WI (Oval) 1988. **LOI:** 4. **Tour:** WI 1989-90. 1000 runs (7); most – 1987 (1990). HS 224* v Glam (Swansea) 1986. BB 3-27 v Glam (Wellingborough) 1988. **Awards:** NWT 1; BHC 5. **NWT:** HS 86* v Somerset (Taunton) 1989. BB 3-47 v Notts (Northampton) 1990. **BHC:** HS 134 v Glos (Northampton) 1987. BB 1-22. **RAL:** HS 125* v Derbys (Derby) 1987. BB 3-23 v Leics (Leicester) 1987.

CAPEL, David John (Roade CS), b Northampton 6 Feb 1963. 5'11". RHB, RMF. Debut 1981. Cap 1986. E Province 1985-86. **Tests:** 15 (1987 to 1989-90); HS 98 v P (Karachi) 1987-88; BB 3-88 v WI (Bridgetown) 1989-90. **LOI:** 23. **Tours:** A 1987-88; WI 1989-90; NZ 1987-88; P 1987-88. 1000 runs (3); most – 1311 (1989). HS 134 EP v W Province (Port Elizabeth) 1986-87. Nh HS 126 v Sussex (Hove) 1989. 50 wkts (3); most – 63 (1986). BB 7-46 v Yorks (Northampton) 1987. **Awards:** NWT 3. **NWT:** HS 101 v Notts (Northampton) 1987. BB 4-29 v Leics (Leicester) 1987. **BHC:** HS 97 v Yorks (Lord's) 1987. BB 4-29 v Warwks (Birmingham) 1984. **RAL:** HS 121 v Glam (Northampton) 1990. BB 4-30 v Yorks (Middlesbrough) 1982.

COOK, Nicholas Grant Billson (Lutterworth GS), b Leicester 17 June 1956. 6'0". RHB, SLA. Leicestershire 1978-85 (cap 1982). Northamptonshire debut 1986. Cap 1987. **Tests:** 15 (1983 to 1989); HS 31 v A (Oval) 1989; BB 6-65 (11-83 match) v P (Karachi) 1983-84. **LOI:** 3. **Tours:** NZ 1979-80 (DHR), 1983-84; P 1983-84, 1987-88; SL 1985-86 (Eng B); Z 1980-81 (Leics), 1984-85 (EC). HS 75 Le v Somerset (Taunton) 1980. Nh HS 64 v Lancs (Manchester) 1987. 50 wkts (8); most – 90 (1982). BB 7-63 Le v Somerset (Taunton) 1982. Nh BB 6-56 v Essex (Chelmsford) 1988 and v Lancs (Southport) 1989. **NWT:** HS 13 v Middx (Northampton) 1986. BB 4-24 v Ire (Northampton) 1987. **BHC:** HS 23 Le v Warwks (Leicester) 1984. BB 3-35 v Kent (Northampton) 1989. **RAL:** HS 13* (5 times). BB 3-20 v Kent (Canterbury) 1989.

FELTON, Nigel Alfred (Millfield S; Loughborough U), b Guildford, Surrey 24 Oct 1960. 5'8". LHB, OB. Somerset 1982-88 (cap 1986). Northamptonshire debut 1989. Cap 1990. 1000 runs (3); most – 1538 (1990). HS 173* Sm v Kent (Taunton) 1983. Nh HS 122 v Glam (Northampton) 1990. BB 1-48. Award: NWT 1. NWT: HS 87 Sm v Kent (Taunton) 1984. BHC: HS 50 Sm v Hants (Taunton) 1988. RAL: HS 96 Sm v Essex (Chelmsford) 1986.

FORDHAM, Alan (Bedford Modern S; Durham U), b Bedford 9 Nov 1964. 6'1". RHB, RM. Debut 1986. Cap 1990. Bedfordshire 1982-85. 1000 runs (1): 1767 (1990). HS 206* v Yorks (Leeds) 1990 – sharing in Northants record 3rd-wkt stand of 393 with A.J.Lamb. BB 1-25. Nh 2nd XI record score: 236 (158 balls) v Worcs (Kidderminster) 1989. Award: NWT 1. NWT: HS 130 v Staffs (Northampton) 1990. BHC: HS 67 v Notts (Nottingham) 1990. RAL: HS 74 v Essex (Chelmsford) 1990.

HUGHES, John Gareth (Sir Christopher Hatton SS, Wellingborough; now at Sheffield City Polytechnic), b Wellingborough 3 May 1971. 6'1". RHB, RM. Debut 1990. HS 2. BB 2-57 v Derbys (Chesterfield) 1990. RAL: HS 1*.

LAMB, Allan Joseph (Wynberg HS; Abbotts C) b Langebaanweg, Cape Province, SA 20 Jun 1954. 5'8". RHB, RM. W Province 1972-82. OFS 1987-88. Northamptonshire debut/cap 1978. Benefit 1988. Captain 1989-. Wisden 1980. Tests: 67 (1982 to 1990, 2 as captain); HS 139 v I (Lord's) 1990; BB 1-6. LOI: 99. Tours: A 1982-83, 1986-87; WI 1985-86, 1989-90; NZ 1983-84; Ind/SL 1984-85; P 1983-84. 1000 runs (9) inc 2000 (1): 2049 (1981). HS 294 OFS v E Province (Bloemfontein) 1987-88 – sharing record SA 5th-wkt stand of 355 with J.J.Strydom. Nh HS 235 v Yorks (Leeds) 1990 – sharing in Northants record 3rd-wkt stand of 393 with A.Fordham. BB 1-1. Awards: NWT 2; BHC 8. NWT: HS 103 v Suffolk (Bury St E) 1989. BB 1-4. BHC: HS 126* v Kent (Canterbury) 1987. BB 1-11. RAL: HS 132* v Surrey (Guildford) 1985.

LARKINS, Wayne (Bushmead SS, Eaton Socon), b Roxton, Beds 22 Nov 1953. 5'11". RHB, RM. Debut 1972. Cap 1976. Benefit 1986. E Province 1982-84. Tests: 10 (1979-80 to 1989-90); HS 54 v WI (P-of-S) 1989-90. LOI: 18. Tours: A 1979-80; SA 1981-82 (SAB); WI 1989-90; I 1979-80, 1980-81 (Overseas XI). 1000 runs (11); most – 1863 (1982). HS 252 v Glam (Cardiff) 1983. BB 5-59 v Worcs (Worcester) 1984. Awards: NWT 2; BHC 5. NWT: HS 121* v Essex (Chelmsford) 1987. BB 2-38 v Glos (Bristol) 1985. BHC: HS 132 v Warwks (Birmingham) 1982. BB 4-37 v Comb Us (Northampton) 1980. RAL: HS 172* v Warwks (Luton) 1983. BB 5-32 v Essex (Ilford) 1978.

LOYE, Malachy Bernhard (Moulton S), b Northampton 27 Sep 1972. 6'2". RHB, OB. No 1st XI appearances – joined staff 1990.

MONTGOMERIE, Richard Robert (Rugby S), b Rugby, Warwks 3 Jul 1971. 5'10". RHB, OB. No 1st XI appearances – joined staff 1990.

NOON, Wayne Michael (Caistor S), b Grimsby, Lincs 5 Feb 1971. 5'9". RHB, WK. Debut 1989. Worcs 2nd XI debut when aged 15yr 199d. HS 37 v A (Northampton) 1989. BAC HS 2. RAL: HS 21 v Surrey (Oval) 1990.

PENBERTHY, Anthony Leonard (Camborne CS), b Troon, Cornwall 1 Sep 1969. 6'1". LHB, RM. Debut 1989. Cornwall 1987-89. HS 101* v CU (Cambridge) 1990. BAC HS 83 v Essex (Chelmsford) 1990. BB 4-91 v Warwks (Northampton) 1990. Dismissed M.A.Taylor with his first ball in f-c cricket. BHC: HS 10 v Notts (Nottingham) 1990. RAL: HS 35 v Notts (Finedon) 1989. BB 3-26 v Essex (Northampton) 1989.

RIPLEY, David (Royds SS, Leeds), b Leeds, Yorks 13 Sep 1966. 5'9". RHB, WK. Debut 1984. Cap 1987. HS 134* v Yorks (Scarborough) 1986. BB 2-89 v Essex (Ilford) 1987. Award: BHC 1. **NWT:** HS 27* v Durham (Darlington) 1984. **BHC:** HS 33 v Derbys (Derby) 1987. **RAL:** HS 36* v Hants (Southampton) 1986.

ROBERTS, Andrew Richard, b Kettering 16 Apr 1971. 5'5". RHB, LB. Debut 1989. HS 8*. BB 2-123 v Glos (Cheltenham) 1990.

SNAPE, Jeremy Nicholas (Denstone C), b Stoke-on-Trent, Staffs 27 Apr 1973. 5'8½". RHB, OB. No 1st XI appearances – joined staff 1990.

STANLEY, Neil Alan (Bedford Modern S), b Bedford 16 May 1968. 6'2". RHB, RM. Debut 1988. Bedfordshire 1987. HS 75 v Leics (Leicester) 1989. **BHC:** HS 8. BB 1-3. **RAL:** HS 18 v Warwks (Birmingham) 1988.

THOMAS, John Gregory (Cwmtawe HS; Cardiff CE), b Trebanos, Glam 12 Aug 1960. 6'3". RHB, RF. Glamorgan 1979-88 (cap 1986). Border 1983-87. E Province 1987-89. Northamptonshire debut 1989. **Tests:** 5 (1985-86 to 1986); HS 31* v WI (P-of-S) 1985-86; BB 4-70 v WI (Bridgetown) 1985-86. LOI: 3. Tours: SA 1989-90 (Eng XI); WI 1985-86. HS 110 Gm v Warwks (Birmingham) 1988. Nh HS 48 v Somerset (Taunton) 1990. 50 wkts (1): 67 (1989). BB 7-75 v Glam (Northampton) 1990. Awards: NWT 1; BHC 1. **NWT:** HS 34 Gm v Cheshire (Cardiff) 1987. BB 5-17 Gm v Sussex (Cardiff) 1985. **BHC:** HS 32 Gm v Kent 1987 and Nh v Scot 1990. BB 4-38 Gm v Hants (Southampton) 1985. **RAL:** HS 37 Gm v Notts (Nottingham) 1983. BB 5-38 Gm v Warwks (Cardiff) 1983.

WALKER, Alan (Shelley HS), b Emley, Yorks 7 Jul 1962. 5'11". LHB, RFM. Debut 1983. Cap 1987. HS 41* v Warwks (Birmingham) 1987. 50 wkts (1): 54 (1988). BB 6-50 v Lancs (Northampton) 1986. Award: NWT 1. **NWT:** HS 7. BB 4-7 v Ire (Northampton) 1987. **BHC:** HS 15* v Notts (Nottingham) 1987. BB 4-46 v Glos (Northampton) 1985. **RAL:** HS 13 v Yorks (Tring) 1983. BB 4-21 v Worcs (Worcester) 1985.

WARREN, Russell John (Kingsthorpe Upper S), b Northampton 10 Sep 1971. 6'1". RHB, OB. No 1st XI appearances – joined staff 1990.

WILLIAMS, Richard Grenville (Ellesmere Port GS), b Bangor, Caernarvonshire 10 Aug 1957. 5'6½". RHB, OB. Debut 1974. Cap 1979. Benefit 1989. Tours: NZ 1979-80 (DHR); Z 1984-85 (EC). 1000 runs (6); most – 1262 (1980). HS 175* v Leics (Leicester) 1980. BB 7-73 v CU (Cambridge) 1980. BAC BB 6-65 v Glos (Northampton) 1990. Hat-trick 1980. Awards: NWT 1; BHC 4. **NWT:** HS 94 v Worcs (Northampton) 1984. BB 4-10 v Leics (Leicester) 1987. **BHC:** HS 83 v Yorks (Bradford) 1980. BB 4-41 v Glos (Northampton) 1987. **RAL:** HS 82 v Glos (Bristol) 1982. BB 5-30 v Warwks (Luton) 1983.

NEWCOMERS

BAPTISTE, Eldine Ashworth Elderfield (All Saints SS, Liberta), b Liberta, Antigua 12 Mar 1960. 6'1". RHB, RFM. Kent 1981-87 (cap 1983). Leeward Is 1981-90. **Tests** (WI): 10 (1983-84 to 1989-90); HS 87* v Eng (Birmingham) 1984; BB 3-31 v Eng (Manchester) 1984. LOI (WI): 43. Tours (WI): Eng 1984; A 1984-85; I 1983-84, 1987-88; Z 1986-87 (WI B). HS 136* K v Eng (Birmingham) 1984. BB 8-76 K v Warwicks (Birmingham) 1987. Awards: NWT 1; BHC 1. **NWT:** HS 22 K v Warwicks (Canterbury) 1985. BB 5-20 K v Hants (Canterbury) 1983. **BHC:** HS 43* K v Somerset (Taunton) 1985. BB 5-30 K v Glam (Cardiff) 1985. **RAL:** HS 60 K v Warwicks (Canterbury) 1985. BB 4-22 K v Surrey (Canterbury) 1986.

CURRAN, Kevin Malcolm (Marandellas HS), b Rusape, S Rhodesia 7 Sep 1959. Son of K.P. (Rhodesia 1947-54). 6'1". RHB, RMF. Zimbabwe 1980-88. Natal 1988-89. Gloucestershire 1985-90 (cap 1985). LOI (Z): 11. Tours (Z): E 1982; SL 1983-84. 1000 runs (5); most – 1353 (1986). HS 144* Gs v Sussex (Bristol) 1990. 50 wkts (3); most – 65 (1988). BB 7-47 Natal v Transvaal (Johannesburg) 1988-89. BAC BB 7-54 Gs v Leics (Gloucester) 1988. Awards: NWT 2; BHC 2. **NWT:** HS 58* Gs v Leics (Leicester) 1988. BB 4-34 Gs v Northants (Bristol) 1985. BHC: HS 57 Gs v Derbys (Derby) 1987. BB 4-41 Gs v Notts (Bristol) 1989. **RAL:** HS 92 Gs v Northants (Northampton) 1990. BB 5-15 Gs v Leics (Gloucester) 1988.

DEPARTURES

BROWN, Simon John (Boldon CS), b Cleadon, Co Durham 29 Jun 1969. 6'3". RHB, LFM. Northamptonshire 1987-90. HS 25* v Glos (Northampton) 1988. BB 3-20 v OU (Oxford) 1988. BAC BB 2-11 v Glam (Swansea) 1987. **RAL:** HS 3*. BB 3-26 v Leics (Leicester) 1990.

COOK, Geoffrey (Middlesbrough HS), b Middlesbrough, Yorks 9 Oct 1951. 6'0". RHB, SLA. Northamptonshire 1971-90 (capt 1975; captain 1981-88; benefit 1985). E Province 1978-81. **Tests:** 7 (1981-82 to 1982-83); HS 66 v I (Manchester) 1982. LOI: 6. Tours: A 1982-83; Ind/SL 1981-82. 1000 runs (12); most – 1759 (1981). HS 203 v Yorks (Scarborough) 1988. Shared record Northants 2nd-wkt stand of 344 with R.J.Boyd-Moss v Lancs (Northampton) 1986. BB 3-47 Eng XI v S Australia (Adelaide) 1982-83. BAC BB 1-7. Awards: NWT 5; BHC 3. **NWT:** HS 130 v Salop (Telford) 1985. **BHC:** HS 108 v Glos (Northampton) 1987. **RAL:** HS 98 v Lancs (Northampton) 1985.

DAVIS, Winston Walter (Emmanuel HS, St Vincent), b Sion Hill, St Vincent 18 Sep 1958. RHB, RF. Combined Is/Windward Is 1979-90 (capt 1987-88). Glamorgan 1982-84. Northamptonshire 1987-90 (cap 1987). Tasmania 1985-86. **Tests** (WI): 15 (1982-83 to 1987-88); HS 77 v Eng (Manchester) 1984; BB 4-19 v NZ (Kingston) 1984-85. LOI (WI): 35; BB 7-51 v A (Leeds) 1983 – LOI world record. Tours (WI): Eng 1984; A 1984-85; I 1983-84, 1987-88; Z 1981-82 (Young WI). HS 77 (Tests). BAC HS 50 Gm v Notts (Nottingham) 1984. Nh HS 47 v Hants (Bournemouth) 1990. 50 wkts (5); most – 73 (1988). BB 7-52 v Sussex (Northampton) 1988. Award: BHC 1. **NWT:** HS 14* v Ire (Northampton) 1987. BB 3-26 Gm v Norfolk (Norwich) 1983. **BHC:** HS 15* v Derbys (Derby) 1987. BB 5-29 Gm v Middx (Cardiff) 1984. **RAL:** HS 34 v Middx (Luton) 1988. BB 4-24 Gm v Derbys (Derby) 1982.

GOVAN, James Walter (Dunfermline HS; Napier C, Edinburgh), b Dunfermline, Fife 6 May 1966. 5'6". RHB, OB. Scotland 1987-89. Northamptonshire 1989-90. HS 17 (thrice). BB 5-54 Scot v Ire (Dumfries) 1988. Nh BB 2-12 v CU (Cambridge) 1990. BAC BB 2-49 v Essex (Northampton) 1989. **NWT:** HS 0 and BB 2-29 Scot v Glam (Edinburgh) 1988. **BHC:** HS 30 and BB 1-55 v Scot (Northampton) 1990. **RAL:** HS 9* and BB 3-23 v Essex (Northampton) 1989.

ROBINSON, M.A. - see YORKSHIRE.

WILD, Duncan James (Northampton GS), b Northampton 28 Nov 1962. Son of J. (Northamptonshire 1953-61). 5'11½". LHB, RM. Northamptonshire 1980-90 (cap 1986). HS 144 v Lancs (Southport) 1984. BB 4-4 v CU (Cambridge) 1986. BAC HS 4-18 v Notts (Nottingham) 1990. Award: BHC 1. **NWT:** HS 38 v Warwks (Northampton) 1989. BB 3-43 v Surrey (Northampton) 1987. **BHC:** HS 48 v Warwks (Northampton) 1984. BB 4-32 v Notts (Northampton) 1988. **RAL:** HS 91 v Derbys (Northampton) 1988. BB 5-7 v Derbys (Finedon) 1986.

NORTHAMPTONSHIRE 1990

RESULTS SUMMARY

	Place	Won	Lost	Drew	Abandoned
Britannic Assurance Championship	11th	4	9	9	
All First-class Matches		4	9	11	
Refuge Assurance League	17th	3	12		1
NatWest Bank Trophy	Finalist				
Benson and Hedges Cup	5th in Group D				

BRITANNIC ASSURANCE CHAMPIONSHIP AVERAGES

BATTING AND FIELDING

Cap		M	I	NO	HS	Runs	Avge	100	50	Ct/St
1978	A.J.Lamb	10	16	3	235	1040	80.00	4	3	5
1985	R.J.Bailey	22	37	8	204*	1965	67.75	7	9	16
1990	A.Fordham	22	38	2	206*	1653	45.91	4	8	22
1990	N.A.Felton	20	35	2	122	1484	44.96	4	9	18
1986	D.J.Capel	17	27	5	113	904	41.09	2	6	15
1987	D.Ripley	20	27	6	109*	634	30.19	1	2	28/6
1976	W.Larkins	15	25	0	207	701	28.04	2	2	8
1979	R.G.Williams	16	24	4	96	482	24.10	–	3	6
–	A.L.Penberthy	11	16	2	83	334	23.85	–	3	8
1975	G.Cook	8	11	1	49	200	20.00	–	–	2
1990	C.E.L.Ambrose	14	17	5	55*	203	16.91	–	1	1
1987	W.W.Davis	8	6	0	47	96	16.00	–	–	2
–	J.G.Thomas	11	11	2	48	131	14.55	–	–	7
1987	N.G.B.Cook	17	17	7	30	133	13.30	–	–	9
–	J.G.Hughes	4	7	0	2	4	0.57	–	–	–
1990	M.A.Robinson	17	16	10	1	3	0.50	–	–	4

Also played: S.J.Brown (3 matches) 2, 4*; J.W.Govan (2 matches) 17, 4, 17; W.M.Noon (2 matches) 2, 2 (4 ct, 1 st); A.R.Roberts (2 matches) 5, 0, 0 (1 ct); D.J.Wild (1 match – cap 1986) 17, 0.

BOWLING

	O	M	R	W	Avge	Best	5wI	10wM
C.E.L.Ambrose	483.4	124	1353	58	23.32	7-89	5	1
D.J.Capel	234	51	711	25	28.44	5-74	1	–
N.G.B.Cook	507.1	159	1320	40	33.00	5-44	2	–
R.G.Williams	417.3	116	1165	31	37.58	4-94	–	–
J.G.Thomas	288.2	49	1098	28	39.21	7-75	1	–
A.L.Penberthy	196	23	768	19	40.42	4-91	–	–
M.A.Robinson	520.1	97	1794	38	47.21	3-47	–	–
R.J.Bailey	168.2	29	604	11	54.90	3-82	–	–
W.W.Davis	216.5	26	747	12	62.25	3-28	–	–

Also bowled: S.J.Brown 52-7-221-4; N.A.Felton 19-1-113-1; A.Fordham 9-0-39-1; J.W.Govan 33-5-120-3; J.G.Hughes 66-12-293-3; W.Larkins 10-1-45-0; A.R.Roberts 63-14-207-3; D.J.Wild 12.5-4-42-0.

The First-Class Averages (pp 166–181) give the records of Northamptonshire players in all first-class county matches (their other opponents being the New Zealanders and Cambridge U.), with the exception of:
A.J.Lamb 11-18-3-235-1103-73.53-4-3-5ct. Did not bowl.

NORTHAMPTONSHIRE RECORDS

FIRST-CLASS CRICKET

Highest Total	For	636-6d	v Essex	Chelmsford	1990
	V	670-9d	by Sussex	Hove	1921
Lowest Total	For	12	v Glos	Gloucester	1907
	V	33	by Lancashire	Northampton	1977
Highest Innings	For	300	R.Subba Row v Surrey	The Oval	1958
	V	333	K.S.Duleepsinhji for Sussex	Hove	1930

Highest Partnership for each Wicket

1st	361	N.Oldfield/V.Broderick	v Scotland	Peterborough	1953
2nd	344	G.Cook/R.J.Boyd-Moss	v Lancashire	Northampton	1986
3rd	393	A.Fordham/A.J.Lamb	v Yorkshire	Leeds	1990
4th	370	R.T.Virgin/P.Willey	v Somerset	Northampton	1976
5th	347	D.Brookes/D.W.Barrick	v Essex	Northampton	1952
6th	376	R.Subba Row/A.Lightfoot	v Surrey	The Oval	1958
7th	229	W.W.Timms/F.A.Walden	v Warwicks	Northampton	1926
8th	164	D.Ripley/N.G.B.Cook	v Lancashire	Manchester	1987
9th	156	R.Subba Row/S.Starkie	v Lancashire	Northampton	1955
10th	148	B.W.Bellamy/J.V.Murdin	v Glamorgan	Northampton	1925

Best Bowling	For	10-127	V.W.C.Jupp	v Kent	Tunbridge W	1932
(Innings)	V	10-30	C.Blythe	for Kent	Northampton	1907
Best Bowling	For	15-31	G.E.Tribe	v Yorkshire	Northampton	1958
(Match)	V	17-48	C.Blythe	for Kent	Northampton	1907

Most Runs – Season	2,198	D.Brookes	(av 51.11)	1952
Most Runs – Career	28,980	D.Brookes	(av 36.13)	1934-1959
Most 100s – Season	8	R.A.Haywood		1921
Most 100s – Career	67	D.Brookes		1934-1959
Most Wkts – Season	175	G.E.Tribe	(av 18.70)	1955
Most Wkts – Career	1,097	E.W.Clark	(av 21.31)	1922-1947

LIMITED-OVERS CRICKET

Highest Total	NWT	360-2	v Staffs	Northampton	1990
	BHC	300-9	v Derbyshire	Derby	1987
	RAL	306-2	v Surrey	Guildford	1985
Lowest Total	NWT	62	v Leics	Leicester	1974
	BHC	85	v Sussex	Northampton	1978
	RAL	41	v Middlesex	Northampton	1972
Highest Innings	NWT {	130	G.Cook	v Shropshire	Telford	1985
		130	A.Fordham	v Staffs	Northampton	1990
	BHC	134	R.J.Bailey	v Glos	Northampton	1987
	RAL	172*	W.Larkins	v Warwicks	Luton	1983
Best Bowling	NWT	7-37	N.A.Mallender	v Worcs	Northampton	1984
	BHC	5-21	Sarfraz Nawaz	v Middlesex	Lord's	1980
	RAL	7-39	A.Hodgson	v Somerset	Northampton	1976

NOTTINGHAMSHIRE

Formation of Present Club: March/April 1841
Substantial Reorganisation: 11 December 1866
Colours: Green and Gold
Badge: County Badge of Nottinghamshire
Championships (since 1890): (4) 1907, 1929, 1981, 1987
NatWest Trophy/Gillette Cup Winners: (1) 1987
Benson and Hedges Cup Winners: (1) 1989
Sunday League Champions: (0) Second 1984, 1987
Match Awards: NWT 31; BHC 53

Secretary: B.Robson, Trent Bridge, Nottingham NG2 6AG (☎ 0602-821525)
Captain: R.T.Robinson
Scorer: L.Beaumont
1991 Beneficiary: B.N.French

AFFORD, John Andrew (Spalding GS; Stamford CFE), b Crowland, Lincs 12 May 1964. 6'1½". RHB, SLA. Debut 1984. Cap 1990. Tour: Z 1989-90 (Eng A). HS 22* v Leics (Nottingham) 1989. 50 wkts (1): 53 (1989). BB 6-81 v Kent (Nottingham) 1986. Award: BHC 1. **NWT:** HS 2*. BB 3-32 v Herts (Hitchin) 1989. **BHC:** HS 1*. BB 4-38 v Kent (Nottingham) 1989. **RAL:** HS 0*. BB 2-39 v Glam (Nottingham) 1990.

BROAD, Brian Christopher (Colston's S, Bristol; St. Paul's C, Cheltenham), b Knowle, Bristol 29 Sep 1957. 6'4". LHB, RM. Gloucestershire 1979-83 (cap 1981). Nottinghamshire debut/cap 1984. OFS 1985-86 (captain). **Tests:** 25 (1984 to 1989); HS 162 v A (Perth) 1986-87. LOI: 34. Tours: A (1986-87, 1987-88; SA 1989-90 (Eng XI); NZ 1987-88; P 1987-88; Z 1984-85 (EC). 1000 runs (8) inc 2000 (1): 2226 (1990). HS 227* v Kent (Tunbridge W) 1990. BB 2-14 Gs v WI (Bristol) 1980. Nt BB 2-23 v Derbys (Derby) 1984. Awards: NWT 4; BHC 2. **NWT:** HS 115 v Bucks (Marlow) 1990. **BHC:** HS 122 v Derbys (Derby) 1984. BB 2-73 v Lancs (Nottingham) 1984. **RAL:** HS 106* v Surrey (Nottingham) 1990. BB 3-46 Gs v Worcs (Bristol) 1982.

COOPER, Kevin Edwin (Hucknall National SS), b Hucknall 27 Dec 1957. 6'1". LHB, RFM. Debut 1976. Cap 1980. Benefit 1990. HS 46 v Middx (Nottingham) 1985. 50 wkts (8) inc 100 wkts (1): 101 (1988). BB 8-44 v Middx (Lord's) 1984. Awards: NWT 1; BHC 2. **NWT:** HS 11 v Glos (Nottingham) 1982. BB 4-49 v Warwks (Nottingham) 1985. **BHC:** HS 25* v Lancs (Manchester) 1983. BB 4-9 v Yorks (Nottingham) 1989. **RAL:** HS 31 v Glos (Nottingham) 1984. BB 4-25 v Hants (Nottingham) 1976.

EVANS, Kevin Paul (Colonel Frank Seely S), b Calverton 10 Sep 1963. Elder brother of R.J. (Notts 1987-90). 6'2". RHB, RMF. Debut 1984. Cap 1990. HS 100* v Somerset (W-s-M) 1990. BB 4-50 v CU (Cambridge) 1990. BAC BB 4-57 v Lancs (Southport) 1990. **NWT:** HS 10 v Devon (Exmouth) 1986. BB 4-30 v Kent (Nottingham) 1986. **BHC:** HS 31* v Northants (Northampton) 1988. BB 3-36 v Worcs (Worcester) 1988. **RAL:** HS 30 v Kent (Canterbury) 1990. BB 4-28 v Derbys (Nottingham) 1989.

FIELD-BUSS, Michael Gwyn (Wanstead HS), b Mtarfa, Malta 23 Sep 1964. 5'10". RHB, OB. Essex 1987. Nottinghamshire debut 1989. HS 34* Ex v Middx (Lord's) 1987. Nt HS 6*. BB 4-33 v Somerset (Nottingham) 1989. **RAL:** HS 5.

FRENCH, Bruce Nicholas (The Meden CS), b Warsop 13 Aug 1959. 5'6". RHB, WK. Debut 1976 (aged 16yr 287d). Cap 1980. Benefit 1991. **Tests:** 16 (1986 to 1987-88); HS 59.v P (Manchester) 1987. LOI: 13. Tours: A 1986-87, 1987-88; SA 1989-90 (Eng XI); WI 1985-86; NZ 1987-88; Ind/SL 1984-85; P 1987-88. HS 105* v Derbys (Derby) 1990. Award: BHC 1. **NWT:** HS 49 v Staffs (Nottingham) 1985. **BHC:** HS 48* v Worcs (Nottingham) 1984. **RAL:** HS 37 v Glos (Bristol) 1985.

HEMMINGS, Edward Ernest (Campion S), b Leamington Spa, Warwks 20 Feb 1949. 5'10". RHB, OB. Warwickshire 1966-78 (cap 1974). Nottinghamshire debut 1979. Cap 1980. Benefit 1987. **Tests:** 15 (1982 to 1990); HS 95 v A (Sydney) 1982-83; BB 6-58 v NZ (Birmingham) 1990. LOI: 28. Tours: A 1982-83, 1987-88; SA 1974-75 (DHR); WI 1982-83 (Int), 1989-90; NZ 1987-88; P 1981-82 (Int), 1987-88. HS 127* v Yorks (Worksop) 1982. 50 wkts (14); most – 94 (1984). BB 10-175 Int XI v WI XI (Kingston) 1982-83. Nt BB 7-23 v Lancs (Nottingham) 1983. 2 hat-tricks: 1977 (Wa), 1984. Awards: NWT 1; BHC 1. **NWT:** HS 31* v Staffs (Nottingham) 1985. BB 3-27 v Warwks (Nottingham) 1985. **BHC:** HS 61* Wa v Leics (Birmingham) 1974. BB 4-47 v Glos (Bristol) 1989. **RAL:** HS 44* Wa v Kent (Birmingham) 1971. BB 5-22 Wa v Notts (Birmingham) 1974.

JOHNSON, Paul (Grove CS, Balderton), b Newark 24 Apr 1965. 5'7". RHB, RM. Debut 1982. Cap 1986. 1000 runs (4); most – 1518 (1990). HS 165* v Northants (Nottingham) 1990. BB 1-9. BAC BB 1-14. Awards: NWT 1; BHC 1. **NWT:** HS 101* v Staffs (Nottingham) 1985. **BHC:** HS 104* v Essex (Chelmsford) 1990. **RAL:** HS 114 v Warwks (Birmingham) 1990.

MARTINDALE, Duncan John Richardson (Lymm GS; Trent Polytechnic), b Harrogate, Yorks 13 Dec 1963. 5'11". RHB, OB. Debut 1985. HS 138 v CU (Cambridge) 1990. HS 108* v Northants (Nottingham) 1990. **BHC:** HS 0. **NWT:** HS 47 v Herts (Hitchin) 1989. **RAL:** HS 53 v Northants (Finedon) 1989.

MIKE, Gregory Wentworth (Claremont CS), b Nottingham 14 Jul 1966. 6'0". RHB, RMF. Debut 1989. HS 56* and BB 2-62 v CU (Cambridge) 1989 (on debut). BAC HS 18* v Lancs (Nottingham) 1990. BAC BB 1-59. **BHC:** HS 29 v Kent (Nottingham) 1989. **RAL:** HS 25* v Kent (Nottingham) 1989. BB 3-30 v Glos (Nottingham) 1990.

NEWELL, Michael (West Bridgford CS), b Blackburn, Lancs 25 Feb 1965. 5'8". RHB, LB. Debut 1984. Cap 1987. 1000 runs (1): 1054 (1987). HS 203* v Derbys (Derby) 1987. BB 2-38 v SL (Nottingham) 1988. BAC BB 1-0. **NWT:** HS 60 v Derbys (Derby) 1987. **BHC:** HS 39 v Somerset (Taunton) 1989. **RAL:** HS 109* v Essex (Southend) 1990.

PICK, Robert Andrew (Alderman Derbyshire CS; High Pavement SFC), b Nottingham 19 Nov 1963. 5'10". LHB, RMF. Debut 1983. Cap 1987. Wellington 1989-90. HS 63 v Warwks (Nuneaton) 1985. 50 wkts (2); most – 51 (1990). BB 7-128 v Leics (Leicester) 1990. Awards: NWT 1; BHC 1. **NWT:** HS 34* v Sussex (Hove) 1983. BB 5-22 v Glos (Bristol) 1987. **BHC:** HS 4. BB 4-42 v Northants (Nottingham) 1987. **RAL:** HS 24 v Yorks (Hull) 1986. BB 4-32 v Glos (Moreton) 1987.

POLLARD, Paul Raymond (Gedling CS), b Carlton, Nottingham, 24 Sep 1968. 5'11". LHB, RM. Debut 1987. 1000 runs (1): 1064 (1989). HS 153 v CU (Cambridge) 1989. BAC HS 142 v Kent (Dartford) 1988. **NWT:** HS 23 v Middx (Uxbridge) 1989. **BHC:** HS 77 v Kent (Nottingham) 1989. **RAL:** HS 123* v Surrey (Oval) 1989.

RANDALL, Derek William (Sir Frederick Milner SS), b Retford 24 Feb 1951. 5'9". RHB, RM. Debut 1972. Cap 1973. Benefit 1983. Wisden 1979. **Tests:** 47 (1976-77 to 1984); HS 174 v A (Melbourne) 1976-77. LOI: 49. Tours: A 1976-77, 1978-79, 1979-80, 1982-83; SA 1975-76 (DHR); NZ 1977-78, 1983-84; Ind/SL 1976-77; P 1977-78, 1983-84; Z 1985-86 (Eng B). 1000 runs (12) inc 2000 (1): 2151 (1985). HS 237 v Derbys (Nottingham) 1988. BB 3-15 v MCC (Lord's) 1982. BAC BB 3-43 v Sussex (Hove) 1984. Awards: NWT 3; BHC 6. **NWT:** HS 149* v Devon (Torquay) 1988. **BHC:** HS 103* v Minor C (N) (Nottingham) 1979. **RAL:** HS 123 v Yorks (Nottingham) 1987.

ROBINSON, Robert Timothy (Dunstable GS; High Pavement SFC; Sheffield U), b Sutton in Ashfield 21 Nov 1958. 6'0". RHB, RM. Debut 1978. Cap 1983. Captain 1988-. Wisden 1985. **Tests:** 29 (1984-85 to 1989); HS 175 v A (Leeds) 1985. LOI: 26. Tours: A 1987-88; SA 1989-90 (Eng XI); NZ 1987-88; WI 1985-86; Ind/SL 1984-85; P 1987-88. 1000 runs (8) inc 2000 (1): 2032 (1984). HS 220* v Yorks (Nottingham) 1990. BB 1-22. Awards: NWT 4; BHC 5. **NWT:** HS 139 v Worcs (Worcester) 1985. **BHC:** HS 120 v Scot (Glasgow) 1985. **RAL:** HS 116 v Derbys (Derby) 1990.

SAXELBY, Mark (Nottingham HS), b Worksop 4 Jan 1969. 6'3". LHB, RM. Younger brother of K. (Notts 1978-90). Debut 1989. **Tests:** HS 73 v CU (Cambridge) 1990. BAC HS 51 v Hants (Portsmouth) 1990. BB 2-25 v CU (Cambridge) 1989. BAC BB 1-21. **NWT:** HS 41 v Bucks (Marlow) 1990. **BHC:** HS 0. **RAL:** HS 34 v Derbys (Derby) 1990. BB 2-48 v Kent (Canterbury) 1990.

SCOTT, Christopher Wilmot (Robert Pattinson CS), b Thorpe-on-the-Hill, Lincs 23 Jan 1964. 5'8". RHB, WK. Debut 1981. Cap 1988. HS 78 v CU (Cambridge) 1983. BAC HS 69* v Warwks (Nottingham) 1986. Held 10 catches in match v Derbys (Derby) 1988. **BHC:** HS 18 v Northants (Northampton) 1988. **RAL:** HS 26 v Yorks (Nottingham) 1987.

STEPHENSON, Franklyn Dacosta (Samuel Jackson Prescod Polytechnic), b St James, Barbados 8 Apr 1959. 6'3½". RHB, RFM. Barbados 1981-82 and 1989-90. Tasmania 1981-82. Gloucestershire 1982-83. Nottinghamshire debut/cap 1988. Staffordshire 1980. Wisden 1988. Tour (WI XI): SA 1982-83, 1983-84. 1000 runs (1): 1018 (1988). HS 165 Barbados v Leeward Is (Basseterre) 1981-82. Nt HS 121 v Leics (Nottingham) 1990. 50 wkts (3) inc 100 wkts (1): 125 (1988). BB 8-47 (15-106 match) v Essex (Nottingham) 1989. Scored 111 and 117 and took 11-222 v Yorks (Nottingham) 1988. Double 1988. Award: BHC 1. **NWT:** HS 29 v Bucks (Marlow) 1990. BB 2-17 Gs v Notts (Nottingham) 1982. **BHC:** HS 98* v Worcs (Nottingham) 1990. BB 4-14 v Minor C (Nottingham) 1988. **RAL:** HS 69 v Hants (Nottingham) 1989. BB 4-23 v Surrey (Nottingham) 1988.

NEWCOMER

CRAWLEY, Mark Andrew (Manchester GS; Oriel C, Oxford), b Newton-le-Willows, Lancs 16 Dec 1967. 6'3". RHB, RM. OU 1987-90 (blue 1987-88-89-90; captain 1989). Lancashire 1990. HS 140 OU v CU (Lord's) 1987. La HS 48 v SL (Manchester) 1990. BB 6-92 OU v Glam (Oxford) 1990. Awaiting BAC debut. Award: BHC 1. **BHC:** HS 54 Comb Us v Glos (Bristol) 1989. BB 2-72 Comb Us v Worcs (Worcester) 1989.

DEPARTURES

EVANS, Russell John (Colonel Frank Seely S), b Calverton 1 Oct 1965. Younger brother of K.P. (Notts 1984-90). 6'0". RHB, RM. Nottinghamshire 1987-90. HS 50* v SL (Nottingham) 1988. BAC HS 11 v Worcs (Worcester) 1990. BB 3-40 v OU (Oxford) 1988. **RAL:** HS 20 v Hants (Nottingham) 1985.

Continued on p 156.

NOTTINGHAMSHIRE 1990

RESULTS SUMMARY

	Place	Won	Lost	Drew	Abandoned
Britannic Assurance Championship	13th	4	8	10	
All First-class Matches		4	8	13	
Refuge Assurance League	4th	10	5		1
NatWest Bank Trophy	2nd Round				
Benson and Hedges Cup	Semi-Finalist				

BRITANNIC ASSURANCE CHAMPIONSHIP AVERAGES

BATTING AND FIELDING

Cap		M	I	NO	HS	Runs	Avge	100	50	Ct/St
1984	B.C.Broad	22	43	2	227*	2226	54.29	9	3	7
1990	K.P.Evans	12	22	8	100*	638	45.57	1	3	9
1983	R.T.Robinson	22	43	5	220*	1693	44.55	4	8	12
1986	P.Johnson	19	36	2	165*	1294	38.05	2	8	13
1973	D.W.Randall	15	28	1	178	987	36.55	2	5	14
1987	M.Newell	12	23	1	89*	653	29.68	–	5	4
–	D.J.R.Martindale	14	24	3	108*	559	26.61	1	2	5
1988	F.D.Stephenson	19	33	6	121	715	26.48	1	3	5
–	P.R.Pollard	5	10	0	72	254	25.40	–	1	4
–	M.Saxelby	7	13	3	51	232	23.20	–	1	3
1980	E.E.Hemmings	11	14	4	83	230	23.00	–	1	2
1987	R.A.Pick	14	15	6	35	199	22.11	–	–	4
1980	B.N.French	22	34	9	105*	506	20.24	1	–	46/11
–	G.W.Mike	3	5	1	18*	45	11.25	–	–	3
1980	K.E.Cooper	20	25	5	35*	217	10.85	–	–	9
1984	K.Saxelby	4	6	0	20	42	7.00	–	–	3
1990	J.A.Afford	19	21	7	5	14	1.00	–	–	7

Also played: (1 match each): R.J.Evans 11, 4 (1 ct); M.G.Field-Buss 0, 0.

BOWLING

	O	M	R	W	Avge	Best	5wI	10wM
R.A.Pick	443.5	70	1507	48	31.39	7-128	1	1
F.D.Stephenson	592.4	90	2047	53	38.62	6-84	2	–
E.E.Hemmings	443.3	127	1175	30	39.16	5-99	1	–
K.P.Evans	292	60	1085	27	40.18	4-57	–	–
K.E.Cooper	667.4	141	2105	51	41.27	5-56	3	–
J.A.Afford	627	186	1804	38	47.47	4-137	–	–

Also bowled: M.G.Field-Buss 10-2-43-0; G.W.Mike 54.2-9-230-2; M.Newell 2.2-0-13-0; K.Saxelby 89-19-309-7; M.Saxelby 56.4-8-260-3.

The First-Class Averages (pp 166–181) give the records of Nottinghamshire players in all first-class county matches (their other opponents being the Sri Lankans, Cambridge U. and Oxford U.), with the exception of E.E.Hemmings, whose full county figures are as above, and:

P.Johnson 22-41-3-165*-1514-39.84-3-9-14ct. 1-0-1-0.

NOTTINGHAMSHIRE RECORDS

FIRST-CLASS CRICKET

Highest Total	For	739-7d		v Leics	Nottingham	1903
	V	706-4d		by Surrey	Nottingham	1947
Lowest Total	For	13		v Yorkshire	Nottingham	1901
	V	16		by Derbyshire	Nottingham	1879
		16		by Surrey	The Oval	1880
Highest Innings	For	312*	W.W.Keeton	v Middlesex	The Oval	1939
	V	345	C.G.Macartney	for Australians	Nottingham	1921

Highest Partnership for each Wicket

1st	391	A.O.Jones/A.Shrewsbury	v Glos	Bristol	1899
2nd	398	A.Shrewsbury/W.Gunn	v Sussex	Nottingham	1890
3rd	369	W.Gunn/J.R.Gunn	v Leics	Nottingham	1903
4th	361	A.O.Jones/J.R.Gunn	v Essex	Leyton	1905
5th	266	A.Shrewsbury/W.Gunn	v Sussex	Hove	1884
6th	303*	F.H.Winrow/P.F.Harvey	v Derbyshire	Nottingham	1947
7th	204	M.J.Smedley/R.A.White	v Surrey	The Oval	1967
8th	220	G.F.H.Heane/R.Winrow	v Somerset	Nottingham	1935
9th	165	W.McIntyre/G.Wootton	v Kent	Nottingham	1869
10th	152	E.B.Alletson/W.Riley	v Sussex	Hove	1911

Best Bowling	For	10-66	K.Smales	v Glos	Stroud	1956
(Innings)	V	10-10	H.Verity	for Yorkshire	Leeds	1932
Best Bowling	For	17-89	F.C.Matthews	v Northants	Nottingham	1923
(Match)	V	17-89	W.G.Grace	for Glos	Cheltenham	1877

Most Runs – Season	2,620	W.W.Whysall	(av 53.46)		1929
Most Runs – Career	31,592	G.Gunn	(av 35.69)		1902-1932
Most 100s – Season	9	W.W.Whysall			1928
	9	M.J.Harris			1971
	9	B.C.Broad			1990
Most 100s – Career	65	J.Hardstaff, jr			1930-1955
Most Wkts – Season	181	B.Dooland	(av 14.96)		1954
Most Wkts – Career	1,653	T.G.Wass	(av 20.34)		1896-1920

LIMITED-OVERS CRICKET

Highest Total	NWT	312-9		v Bucks	Marlow	1990
	BHC	296-6		v Kent	Nottingham	1989
	RAL	283-6		v Yorkshire	Nottingham	1987
Lowest Total	NWT	123		v Yorkshire	Scarborough	1969
	BHC	74		v Leics	Leicester	1987
	RAL	66		v Yorkshire	Bradford	1969
Highest Innings	NWT	149*	D.W.Randall	v Devon	Torquay	1988
	BHC	130*	C.E.B.Rice	v Scotland	Glasgow	1982
	RAL	123*	P.R.Pollard	v Surrey	The Oval	1989
Best Bowling	NWT	6-18	C.E.B.Rice	v Sussex	Hove	1982
	BHC	6-22	M.K.Bore	v Leics	Leicester	1980
		6-22	C.E.B.Rice	v Northants	Northampton	1981
	RAL	6-12	R.J.Hadlee	v Lancashire	Nottingham	1980

SOMERSET

Formation of Present Club: 18 August 1875
Colours: Black, White and Maroon
Badge: Somerset Dragon
Championships: (0) Third in 1892, 1958, 1963, 1966, 1981
NatWest Trophy/Gillette Cup Winners: (2) 1979, 1983
Benson and Hedges Cup Winners: (2) 1981, 1982
Sunday League Champions: (1) 1979
Match Awards: NWT 38; BHC 51

Chief Executive: P.W.Anderson, The County Ground, Taunton TA1 1JT
(☎ 0823-272946)
Captain: C.J.Tavaré
Scorer: D.A.Oldam

BARTLETT, Richard James (Taunton S), b Ash Priors 8 Oct 1966. 5'9". RHB, OB. Debut 1986 scoring 117* v OU (Oxford). HS 117* (above). BAC HS 102* v Kent (Canterbury) 1988. **BB:** 1-9 (twice). **NWT:** HS 85 v Hants (Southampton) 1988. **BHC:** HS 36 v Comb Us (Taunton) 1989. **RAL:** HS 55 v Lancs (Manchester) 1988 and 1990.

BURNS, Neil David (Moulsham HS, Chelmsford), b Chelmsford, Essex 19 Sep 1965. 5'10". LHB, WK. W Province B 1985-86. Essex 1986. Somerset debut/cap 1987. HS 166 v Glos (Taunton) 1990. **NWT:** HS 25* v Worcs (Taunton) 1990. **BHC:** HS 51 v Middx (Lord's) 1987. **RAL:** HS 58 v Sussex (Hove) 1990.

CLEAL, Matthew William (Preston CS, Yeovil), b Yeovil 23 Jul 1969. 6'2". RHB, RMF. Debut 1988. HS 30 v Leics (Taunton) 1989. BB 4-41 v WI (Taunton) 1988 (on debut). BAC BB 3-16 v Worcs (Worcester) 1988. **NWT:** HS 25 v Northants (Taunton) 1989. BB 1-42. **RAL:** HS 15 v Worcs (Worcester) 1989. BB 1-14.

COOK, Stephen James (Hyde Park HS; Witwatersrand U), b Johannesburg, SA 31 Jul 1953. 6'3". RHB. Transvaal 1972-90. Somerset debut/cap 1989. Wisden 1989. Has appeared in every international against unofficial touring teams since 1981-82; captain v English XI 1989-90. 1000 runs (2+2) inc 2000 (2); most – 2608 (1990). HS 313* v Glam (Cardiff) 1990. BB 2-25 v Derbys (Taunton) 1990. Award: BHC 1. **NWT:** HS 45 v Worcs (Taunton) 1990. **BHC:** HS 177 v Sussex (Hove) 1990. **RAL:** HS 136* v Glam (Neath) 1990.

FLETCHER, Ian (Millfield S), b Sawbridgeworth, Herts 31 Aug 1971. RHB, RM. Hertfordshire. No 1st XI appearances – joined staff 1990. **NWT:** (Herts) HS 1.

HALLETT, Jeremy Charles (Millfield S; now at Durham U), b Yeovil 18 Oct 1970. 6'2". RHB, RMF. Debut 1990. HS 0. BB 2-40 v Kent (Canterbury) 1990. **BHC:** BB 1-52. **RAL:** HS 4*. BB 3-41 v Glam (Neath) 1990.

HARDEN, Richard John (King's C, Taunton), b Bridgwater 16 Aug 1965. 5'11". RHB, SLA. Debut 1985. Cap 1989. C Districts 1987-88. 1000 runs (2); most – 1460 (1990). HS 115* v Northants (Luton) 1989. BB 2-7 CD v Canterbury (Blenheim) 1987-88. Sm BB 2-24 v Hants (Taunton) 1986. **NWT:** HS 17 v Lancs (Taunton) 1986. **BHC:** HS 53* v Minor C (Taunton) 1990. **RAL:** HS 73 v Derbys (Derby) 1987.

123

HAYHURST, Andrew Neil (Worsley Wardley HS; Eccles SFC; Leeds Polytechnic), b Davyhulme, Manchester 23 Nov 1962. 5'11". RHB, RM. Lancashire 1985-89. Somerset debut/cap 1990. Tours: WI 1986-87 (Lancs); Z 1988-89 (Lancs). 1000 runs (1): 1559 (1990). HS 170 v Sussex (Taunton) and v Yorks (Scarborough) 1990. BB 4-27 La v Middx (Manchester) 1987. Sm BB 3-58 v Sussex (Hove) 1990. Award: BHC 1. **NWT:** HS 51 v Devon (Torquay) 1990. BB 4-40 La v Leics (Leicester) 1986. **BHC:** HS 76 v Minor C (Taunton) 1990. BB 4-50 La v Worcs (Worcester) 1987. **RAL:** HS 84 La v Leics (Manchester) 1988. BB 4-37 La v Glam (Pontypridd) 1988 and Sm v Sussex (Hove) 1990.

LEFEBVRE, Roland Philippe (Montessori Lyceum, Rotterdam; Hague Accademie of Physiotherapy), b Rotterdam, Holland 7 Feb 1963. 6'1". RHB, RMF. Debut 1990. Holland 1983-90; ICC Trophy 1986 and 1990. HS 53 v Northants (Taunton) 1990. BB 5-30 v Glos (Taunton) 1990. **NWT:** BB 7-15 v Devon (Torquay) 1990. **BHC:** HS 37 v Middx (Lord's) 1990. BB 2-39 v Sussex (Hove) 1990. **RAL:** HS 28 v Yorks (Scarborough) 1990. BB 4-35 v Northants (Taunton) 1990.

MALLENDER, Neil Alan (Beverley GS), b Kirk Sandall, Yorks 13 Aug 1961. 6'0". RHB, RFM. Northamptonshire 1980-86 (cap 1984). Somerset debut/cap 1987. Otago 1983-90. HS 88 Otago v C Districts (Oamaru) 1984-85. Sm HS 87* v Sussex (Hove) 1990 – sharing in Somerset record 9th-wkt stand of 183 with C.J.Tavaré. 50 wkts (5); most – 56 (1983). BB 7-27 Otago v Auckland (Auckland) 1984-85. BAC BB 7-41 Nh v Derbys (Northampton) 1982. Sm BB 7-61 v Derbys (Taunton) 1987. Award: NWT 1. **NWT:** HS 11* Nh v Yorks (Leeds) 1983. BB 7-37 Nh v Worcs (Northampton) 1984. **BHC:** HS 16* v Hants (Taunton) 1988. BB 5-53 Nh v Leics (Northampton) 1986. **RAL:** HS 24 v Glos (Bristol) 1990. BB 5-34 Nh v Middx (Tring) 1981.

PRINGLE, Nicholas John (Taunton S), b Weymouth, Dorset 20 Sep 1966. 5'10½". RHB, RMF. MCC Cricket Staff. Debut 1986. HS 79 v Warwks (Birmingham) 1987. BB 2-35 v Glam (W-s-M) 1987. **NWT:** HS 17 v Hants (Southampton) 1988. **RAL:** HS 22 v Glam (W-s-M) 1987.

ROEBUCK, Peter Michael (Millfield S; Emmanuel C, Cambridge), b Oxford 6 Mar 1956. Brother of P.G.P. (CU, Glos and Glam 1983-88). 6'0". RHB, LB. Debut 1974. Cap 1978. Captain 1986-88. Benefit 1990. 2nd XI debut 1969 (aged 13). Cricket 1975-76-77; blue 1975-76-77. Wisden 1987. 1000 runs (9); most – 1702 (1984). HS 221* v Notts (Nottingham) 1986. Shared record Somerset 3rd-wkt stand of 319 with M.D.Crowe v Leics (Taunton) 1984. BB 6-50 CU v Kent (Canterbury) 1977. Sm BB 2-22 v Glam (Taunton) 1989. Awards: NWT 1; BHC 2. **NWT:** HS 102 v Essex (Taunton) 1989. BB 1-21. **BHC:** HS 120 v Comb Us (Taunton) 1987. BB 2-13 v Comb Us 1982 and v Middx 1990. **RAL:** HS 105 v Glos (Bath) 1983. BB 3-23 v Derbys (Derby) 1989.

ROSE, Graham David (Northumberland Park S, Tottenham), b Tottenham, London 12 Apr 1964. 6'4". RHB, RM. Middlesex 1985-86. Somerset debut 1987. Cap 1988. 1000 runs (1): 1000 (1990). HS 97* v Glam (Bath) 1990. 50 wkts (2); most – 57 (1988). BB 6-41 M v Worcs (Worcester) 1985 – on debut. Sm BB 6-47 v Warwks (Bath) 1988. Award: BHC 1. **NWT:** HS 110 v Devon (Torquay) 1990. BB 2-30 v Bucks (High Wycombe) 1987. **BHC:** HS 64 v Derbys (Taunton) 1990. BB 4-37 v Sussex (Hove) 1990. **RAL:** HS 148 v Glam (Neath) 1990. BB 4-28 v Derbys (Derby) 1987.

SWALLOW, Ian Geoffrey (Hoyland Kirk CS, Balk), b Barnsley, Yorks 18 Dec 1962. 5'7½". RHB, OB. Yorkshire 1983-89. HS 114 Y v MCC (Scarborough) 1987. BAC HS 64 Y v Derbys (Leeds) 1989. Sm HS 32 v Warwks (Taunton) 1990. BB 7-95 Y v Notts (Nottingham) 1987. Sm BB 3-88 v Lancs (Manchester) 1990. **NWT:** HS 17* Y v Surrey (Oval) 1989. **BHC:** HS 18 v Middx (Taunton) 1990. BB 2-32 v Minor C (Taunton) 1990. **RAL:** HS 31 v Yorks (Scarborough) 1990. BB 2-44 v Middx (Lord's) 1990.

TAVARÉ, Christopher James (Sevenoaks S; St John's, Oxford), b Orpington, Kent 27 Oct 1954. 6'1½". RHB, RM. Kent 1974-88 (cap 1978; captain 1983-84; benefit 1988). Oxford U 1975-77 (blue 1975-76-77). Somerset debut/cap 1989. Captain 1990-. **Tests:** 31 (1980 to 1989); HS 149 v I (Delhi) 1981-82. **LOI:** 29. Tours: A 1982-83; NZ 1983-84; Ind/SL 1981-82; P 1983-84. 1000 runs (14); most – 1770 (1981). HS 219 v Sussex (Hove) 1990 – sharing in Somerset record 9th-wkt stand of 183 with N.A.Mallender. BB 1-3. Awards: NWT 4; BHC 9. **NWT:** HS 162* v Devon (Torquay) 1990. **BHC:** HS 143 Kent v Somerset (Taunton) 1985. **RAL:** HS 136* Kent v Glos (Canterbury) 1978.

TOWNSEND, Gareth Terence John (Tiverton S; Birmingham U), b Tiverton, Devon 28 Jun 1968. 6'0". RHB. Debut 1990. HS 15 v Warwks (Birmingham) 1990.

TRUMP, Harvey Russell John (Millfield S), b Taunton 11 Oct 1968. 6'0". RHB, OB. Debut 1988. HS 48 v Notts (Taunton) 1988 (on debut). BB 4-17 v Kent (Canterbury) 1988. **NWT:** HS 0. BB 2-44 v Essex (Taunton) 1989. **RAL:** HS 4. BB 2-23 v Kent (Bath) 1989.

VAN TROOST, Adrianus Pelrus, b Schiedam, Holland 2 Oct 1972. RHB, RFM. No 1st XI appearances – joined staff 1990.

NEWCOMERS

GRAVENEY, David Anthony (Millfield S), b Bristol 2 Jan 1953. Son of J.K. (Glos 1947-64); nephew of T.W. (Glos, Worcs, Queensland and England). 6'4". RHB, SLA. Gloucestershire 1972-90 (cap 1976; captain 1981-88; benefit 1986). Tours: SA 1989-90 (Eng XI – manager); SL 1986-87 (Glos – capt). HS 119 Gs v OU (Oxford) 1980. BAC HS 105* Gs v Northants (Bristol) 1981. 50 wkts (5); most – 73 (1976). BB 8-85 Gs v Notts (Cheltenham) 1974. Hat-trick 1983. Awards: NWT 2. **NWT:** HS 44 Gs v Surrey (Bristol) 1973. BB 5-11 Gs v Ire (Dublin) 1981. **BHC:** HS 49* Gs v Somerset (Taunton) 1982. BB 3-13 Gs v Scot (Glasgow) 1983. **RAL:** HS 56* Gs v Notts (Bristol) 1985. BB 4-22 Gs v Hants (Lydney) 1974.

MacLEAY, Kenneth Hervey (Scotch C, Perth; W Australia U), b Bradford-on-Avon, Wilts 2 Apr 1959. 6'4". RHB, RM. W Australia 1981-90. LOI (A) 16 – inc 1983 World Cup in England. Tours: I 1989-90 (WA); Z 1982-83 (Young A). HS 114* WA v NSW (Perth) 1986-87. BB 6-93 WA v NSW (Perth) 1985-86.

DEPARTURES

HARDY, J.J.E. – see GLOUCESTERSHIRE.

JONES, A.N. – see SUSSEX.

SOMERSET 1990

RESULTS SUMMARY

	Place	Won	Lost	Drew
Britannic Assurance Championship	15th	3	4	15
All First-class Matches		3	5	16
Refuge Assurance League	8th	8	8	
NatWest Bank Trophy	2nd Round			
Benson and Hedges Cup	Semi-Finalist			

BRITANNIC ASSURANCE CHAMPIONSHIP AVERAGES

BATTING AND FIELDING

Cap		M	I	NO	HS	Runs	Avge	100	50	Ct/St
1989	S.J.Cook	22	38	6	313*	2432	76.00	8	11	10
1990	A.N.Hayhurst	21	33	7	170	1554	59.76	4	8	9
1989	R.J.Harden	22	29	7	104*	1257	57.13	2	11	18
1978	P.M.Roebuck	16	25	5	201*	1085	54.25	2	6	6
1989	C.J.Tavaré	22	30	4	219	1399	53.80	2	11	15
1988	G.D.Rose	22	26	9	97*	897	52.76	–	7	13
1987	J.J.E.Hardy	7	13	5	91	343	42.87	–	1	5
1987	N.D.Burns	22	31	9	166	863	39.22	1	4	43/1
1987	N.A.Mallender	19	10	3	87*	177	25.28	–	1	3
1987	A.N.Jones	20	9	5	41	100	25.00	–	–	4
–	I.G.Swallow	21	17	7	32	187	18.70	–	–	11
–	R.P.Lefebvre	16	16	3	53	214	16.46	–	1	8
–	G.T.J.Townsend	2	4	1	15	21	7.00	–	–	3
–	H.R.J.Trump	7	5	1	4*	11	2.75	–	–	3

Also played: R.J.Bartlett (1 match): 73, 12; J.C.Hallett (2 matches) 0.

BOWLING

	O	M	R	W	Avge	Best	5wI	10wM
N.A.Mallender	537.2	114	1555	51	30.49	5-46	2	–
G.D.Rose	530.4	93	1807	51	35.43	5-52	1	–
A.N.Jones	539.4	81	1990	52	38.26	6-75	2	–
R.P.Lefebvre	493.1	132	1258	30	41.93	5-30	1	–
A.N.Hayhurst	291.2	46	974	17	57.29	3-58	–	–
I.G.Swallow	642.1	150	2042	31	65.87	3-88	–	–

Also bowled: N.D.Burns 0.3-0-8-0; S.J.Cook 8-0-42-2; J.C.Hallett 40.2-7-135-4;
R.J.Harden 64-6-254-6; P.M.Roebuck 160.3-37-460-7; C.J.Tavaré 17.2-0-162-0;
H.R.J.Trump 164-41-520-9.

The First-Class Averages (pp 166–181) give the records of Somerset players in all
first-class county matches (their other opponents being the New Zealanders and
Oxford U.).

SOMERSET RECORDS

FIRST-CLASS CRICKET

Highest Total	For	675-9d	v Hampshire	Bath	1924
	V	811	by Surrey	The Oval	1899
Lowest Total	For	25	v Glos	Bristol	1947
	V	22	by Glos	Bristol	1920
Highest Innings	For	322 I.V.A.Richards	v Warwicks	Taunton	1985
	V	424 A.C.MacLaren	for Lancashire	Taunton	1895

Highest Partnership for each Wicket

1st	346	H.T.Hewett/L.C.H.Palairet	v Yorkshire	Taunton	1892
2nd	290	J.C.W.MacBryan/M.D.Lyon	v Derbyshire	Buxton	1924
3rd	319	P.M.Roebuck/M.D.Crowe	v Leics	Taunton	1984
4th	310	P.W.Denning/I.T.Botham	v Glos	Taunton	1980
5th	235	J.C.White/C.C.C.Case	v Glos	Taunton	1927
6th	265	W.E.Alley/K.E.Palmer	v Northants	Northampton	1961
7th	240	S.M.J.Woods/V.T.Hill	v Kent	Taunton	1898
8th	172	I.V.A.Richards/I.T.Botham	v Leics	Leicester	1983
9th	183	C.H.M.Greetham/H.W.Stephenson	v Leics	Weston-s-Mare	1963
	183	C.J.Tavaré/N.A.Mallender	v Sussex	Hove	1990
10th	143	J.J.Bridges/A.H.D.Gibbs	v Essex	Weston-s-Mare	1919

Best Bowling	For	10-49 E.J.Tyler	v Surrey	Taunton	1895
(Innings)	V	10-35 A.Drake	for Yorkshire	Weston-s-Mare	1914
Best Bowling	For	16-83 J.C.White	v Worcs	Bath	1919
(Match)	V	17-137 W.Brearley	for Lancashire	Manchester	1905

Most Runs – Season	2,761	W.E.Alley	(av 58.74)	1961
Most Runs – Career	21,142	H.Gimblett	(av 36.96)	1935-1954
Most 100s – Season	10	W.E.Alley		1961
Most 100s – Career	49	H.Gimblett		1935-1954
Most Wkts – Season	169	A.W.Wellard	(av 19.24)	1938
Most Wkts – Career	2,166	J.C.White	(av 18.02)	1909-1937

LIMITED-OVERS CRICKET

Highest Total	NWT	413-4	v Devon	Torquay	1990
	BHC	321-5	v Sussex	Hove	1990
	RAL	360-3	v Glamorgan	Neath	1990
Lowest Total	NWT	59	v Middlesex	Lord's	1977
	BHC	98	v Middlesex	Lord's	1982
	RAL	58	v Essex	Chelmsford	1977
Highest Innings	NWT	162* C.J.Tavaré	v Devon	Torquay	1990
	BHC	177 S.J.Cook	v Sussex	Hove	1990
	RAL	175* I.T.Botham	v Northants	Wellingborough	1986
Best Bowling	NWT	7-15 R.P.Lefebvre	v Devon	Torquay	1990
	BHC	5-14 J.Garner	v Surrey	Lord's	1981
	RAL	6-24 I.V.A.Richards	v Lancashire	Manchester	1983

SURREY

Formation of Present Club: 22 August 1845
Colours: Chocolate
Badge: Prince of Wales' Feathers
Championships (since 1890): (15) 1890, 1891, 1892, 1894, 1895, 1899, 1914, 1952, 1953, 1954, 1955, 1956, 1957, 1958, 1971. **Joint:** (1) 1950
NatWest Trophy/Gillette Cup Winners: (1) 1982
Benson and Hedges Cup Winners: (1) 1974
Sunday League Champions: (0) Fifth 1969, 1980
Match Awards: NWT 32; BHC 46

Secretary: D.G.Seward, Kennington Oval, London, SE11 5SS (☎ 071-582 6660)
Captain: I.A.Greig
Scorer: M.R.L.W.Ayers
1991 Beneficiary: M.A.Lynch

ALIKHAN, Rehan Iqbal ('Ray') (KCS, Wimbledon), b Westminster Hospital, London 28 Dec 1962. 6'1½". RHB, OB. Sussex 1986-88. PIA 1986-87. Surrey debut 1989. HS 138 v Essex (Oval) 1990. BB 2-19 Sx v WI (Hove) 1988. Sy/BAC BB 1-3. **NWT:** HS 41 Sx v Worcs (Worcester) 1986. **BHC:** HS 71 Sx v Glam (Swansea) 1987. **RAL:** HS 23 Sx v Essex (Chelmsford) 1987.

ATKINS, Paul David (Aylesbury GS), b Aylesbury, Bucks 11 Jun 1966. 6'1". RHB, OB. Debut 1988 v CU (Oval) scoring 114* and 8. Buckinghamshire 1985-90 (cap 1986). HS 114* (above). BAC HS 99 v Lancs (Southport) 1988. Award: NWT 1. **NWT:** HS 82 v Glam (Oval) 1988. **BHC:** HS 9. **RAL:** HS 2.

BICKNELL, Darren John (Robert Haining SS; Guildford TC), b Guildford 24 Jun 1967. Elder brother of M.P. 6'4". LHB, LM. Debut 1987. Cap 1990. Tour: Z 1989-90 (Eng A). 1000 runs (2); most – 1392 (1989). HS 186 v Kent (Canterbury) 1990 – sharing in Surrey record 3rd-wkt stand of 413 with D.M.Ward. BB 1-73. Awards: NWT 1; BHC 1. **NWT:** HS 135* v Yorks (Oval) 1989. **BHC:** HS 119 v Hants (Oval) 1990. **RAL:** HS 75 v Middx (Oval) 1990.

BICKNELL, Martin Paul (Robert Haining SS), b Guildford 14 Jan 1969. Younger brother of D.J. 6'3". RHB, RFM. Debut 1986. Cap 1989. Tour: Z 1989-90 (Eng A). HS 50* v Sussex (Hove) 1990. Shared in Surrey record 8th-wkt stand of 205 with I.A.Greig v Lancs (Oval) 1990. 50 wkts (3); most – 67 (1990). BB 9-45 CU (Oval) 1988. BAC BB 6-47 v Glos (Oval) 1989. **NWT:** HS 4*. BB 4-49 v Yorks (Oval) 1989. **BHC:** HS 27* v Lancs (Manchester) 1990. BB 3-29 v Yorks (Leeds) 1987. **RAL:** HS 13 v Northants (Tring) 1986. BB 4-14 Middx (Oval) 1990.

BOILING, James (Rutlish S, Merton; Durham U), b New Delhi, India 8 Apr 1968. 6'4". RHB, OB. Debut 1988. HS 15 v Glam (Oval) 1989. BB 3-40 v Lancs (Manchester) 1989. Award: BHC 1. **BHC:** HS 9*. BB 3-9 Comb Us v Surrey (Cambridge) 1989.

BROWN, Alistair Duncan (Caterham S), b 11 Feb 1970. RHB, occ LB, occ WK. Awaiting f-c debut. **RAL:** HS 56 v Leics (Oval) 1990.

BULLEN, Christopher Keith (Rutlish S, Merton), b Clapham 5 Nov 1962. 6'4½". RHB, OB. Debut 1982. Cap 1990. HS 65 v P (Oval) 1987. BAC HS 57 v Glos (Cheltenham) 1987. BB 6-119 v Middx (Lord's) 1987. Award: NWT 1. **NWT:** HS 93* v Wilts (Trowbridge) 1990. BB 2-55 v Middx (Oval) 1988. **BHC:** HS 35* and BB 2-14 v Comb Us (Cambridge) 1989. **RAL:** HS 28* v Middx (Lord's) 1989. BB 5-31 v Yorks (Oval) 1989.

BUTCHER, Mark Alan (Archbishop Tenison's S, Croydon), b 23 Aug 1972. Son of A.R. (Surrey, Glam and England). LHB, RM. No 1st XI appearances – joined staff 1990.

FELTHAM, Mark Andrew (Tiffin S), b St John's Wood, London 26 June 1963. 6'2½". RHB, RM. Debut 1983. Cap 1990. MCC Cricket Staff. HS 101 v Middx (Oval) 1990. 50 wkts (1): 56 (1988). BB 6-53 v Leics (Oval) 1990. Award: BHC 1. **NWT:** HS 19* v Hants (Oval) 1989. BB 2-27 v Cheshire (Birkenhead) 1986. **BHC:** HS 29 v Middx (Lord's) 1989. BB 5-28 v Comb Us (Cambridge) 1989. **RAL:** HS 61 v Warwks (Oval) 1990. BB 4-35 v Sussex (Guildford) 1986.

GREIG, Ian Alexander (Queen's S, Queenstown; Downing C, Cambridge), b Queenstown, SA 8 Dec 1955. Brother of A.W. (Border, Sussex, E Province and England 1965-78). 5'11½". RHB, RMF. Border 1974-75, 1979-80. GW 1975-76. Cambridge U 1977-79 (blue 1977-78-79; captain 1979). Sussex 1980-85 (cap 1981). Surrey debut/cap 1987. Captain 1987-. **Tests:** 2 (1982). HS 14 and BB 4-53 v P (Birmingham) 1982. 1000 runs (2); most – 1259 (1990). HS 291 v Lancs (Oval) 1990 – sharing in Surrey record 8th-wkt stand of 205 with M.P.Bicknell. 50 wkts (3); most – 76 (1981). BB 7-43 Sx v CU (Cambridge) 1981. BAC BB 6-21 Sx v Lancs (Hove) 1981. Sy BB 6-34 v CU (Cambridge) 1988. Awards: NWT 1; BHC 1. **NWT:** HS 82 and BB 4-31 Sx v Warwks (Birmingham) 1981. **BHC:** HS 51 and BB 5-35 Sx v Hants (Hove) 1981. **RAL:** HS 61* v Yorks (Oval) 1989. BB 5-30 v Kent (Oval) 1988.

KENDRICK, Neil Michael (Wilson's GS), b Bromley, Kent 11 Nov 1967. 5'11". RHB, SLA. Debut 1988. HS 52* v Middx (Lord's) 1990. BB 4-110 v Kent (Guildford) 1990. **RAL:** HS 2*.

LYNCH, Monte Alan (Ryden's S, Walton-on-Thames), b Georgetown, British Guiana 21 May 1958. 5'8". RHB, RM/OB. Debut 1977. Cap 1982. Benefit 1991. Guyana 1982-83. LOI: 3. Tours: SA 1983-84 (WI XI); P 1981-82 (Int). 1000 (7); most – 1714 (1985). HS 172* v Kent (Oval) 1989. BB 3-6 v Glam (Swansea) 1981. Awards: NWT 1; BHC 3. **NWT:** HS 129 v Durham (Oval) 1982. BB 1-11. **BHC:** HS 112* v Kent (Oval) 1987. **RAL:** HS 136 v Yorks (Bradford) 1985. BB 2-2 v Northants (Guildford) 1987 and v Sussex (Hove) 1990.

MEDLYCOTT, Keith Thomas (Parmiters GS, Wandsworth), b Whitechapel 12 May 1965. 5'11". RHB, SLA. Debut 1984 scoring 117* v CU (Banstead). Cap 1988. Natal B 1988-89. MCC Cricket Staff. Tour: WI 1989-90. HS 153 v Kent (Oval) 1987 – sharing Surrey record 7th-wkt stand of 262 with C.J.Richards. 50 wkts (3); most – 69 (1988). BB 8-52 v Sussex (Hove) 1988. **NWT:** HS 38 v Middx (Uxbridge) 1990. BB 1-45. **BHC:** HS 11 v Glos (Oval) 1989. BB 3-48 v Comb Us (Oxford) 1990. **RAL:** HS 44* v Leics (Oval) 1990. BB 4-18 v Warwks (Birmingham) 1989.

MURPHY, Anthony John (Xaverian C, Swansea U), b Manchester 6 Aug 1962. 6'0". RHB, RMF. Lancashire 1985-88. Surrey debut 1989. Cheshire 1984-85. Tour: WI 1986-87 (Lancs). HS 38 v Glos (Oval) 1989. 50 wkts (1): 65 (1989). BB 6-97 v Derbys (Derby) 1989. **NWT:** BB 2-34 v Hants (Oval) 1989. **BHC:** BB 2-36 v Hants (Oval) 1990. **RAL:** HS 3. BB 4-22 v Glos (Oval) 1989.

PETERS, Nicholas Howard (Sherborne S; West London IHE), b Guildford 21 Feb 1968. 6'2". RHB, RFM. Debut 1988. HS 25* v Leics (Oval) 1988. BB 6-31 v Warwks (Oval) 1988 (taking 10-67 in his fifth match). **NWT:** BB 2-28 v Essex (Chelmsford) 1988. **BHC:** HS 1*. BB 1-24. **RAL:** HS 4*. BB 2-16 v Middx (Oval) 1988.

ROBINSON, Jonathan David (Lancing C; West Sussex IHE), b Epsom 3 Aug 1966. Son of P.M.H. (L.C.Stevens' XI 1961). 5'10". LHB, RM. Debut 1988. HS 72 v Middx (Oval) 1990. BB 2-37 v Leics (Leicester) 1989. **BHC:** HS 2*. BB 2-41 v Yorks (Oval) 1990. **RAL:** HS 18* v Leics (Leicester) 1989. BB 1-13.

SARGEANT, Neil Fredrick (Whitmore HS), b Hammersmith 8 Nov 1965. 5'8". RHB, WK. Debut 1989. HS 18 v Ind (Oval) 1990. BAC HS 16 v Glos (Oval) 1989. **RAL:** HS 22 v Glos (Cheltenham) 1990.

SMITH, Andrew William (Sutton Manor S), b 30 May 1969. Son of W.A. (Surrey 1961-70). RHB, OB. No 1st XI appearances – joined staff 1990.

STEWART, Alec James (Tiffin S), b Merton 8 Apr 1963. Son of M.J. (Surrey and England 1954-72). 5'11". RHB, WK. Debut 1981. Cap 1985. **Tests:** 7 (1989-90 to 1990); HS 54 v NZ (Lord's) 1990. LOI: 13. Tour: WI 1989-90. 1000 runs (5); most – 1665 (1986). HS 206* v Essex (Oval) 1989. BB 1-7. Held 11 catches (equalling world f-c match record) v Leics (Leicester) 1989. Awards: NWT 1; BHC 2. **NWT:** HS 107* v Middx (Oval) 1988. **BHC:** HS 84* v Comb Us (Oxford) 1990. **RAL:** HS 125 v Lancs (Oval) 1990.

THORPE, Graham Paul (Weydon CS; Farnham C), b Farnham 1 Aug 1969. 5'11". LHB, RM. Debut 1988. Tour: Z 1989-90 (Eng A). 1000 runs (1): 1132 (1989). HS 154 v Kent (Oval) 1989. BB 2-31 v Essex (Oval) 1989. **NWT:** HS 74 v Northumb (Jesmond) 1989. **BHC:** HS 50* v Hants (Oval) 1990. BB 3-35 v Middx (Lord's) 1989. **RAL:** HS 85 v Leics (Oval) 1990 BB 1-13.

WAQAR YOUNIS (Government C, Vehari), b Vehari, Pakistan 16 Nov 1971. 6'0". RHB, RF. Multan 1987-88. United Bank 1988-90. Surrey debut/cap 1990. **Tests** (P): 5 (1989-90); HS 18 v A (Melbourne) 1989-90; BB 4-80 v I (Karachi) 1989-90. LOI (P): 23. Tour (P): A 1989-90. HS 51 United Bank v PIA (Lahore) 1989-90 Qaid-e-Azam Final. Sy HS 14 v Essex (Oval) 1990. 50 wkts (1): 57 (1990). BB 7-73 v Warwicks (Oval) 1990. **NWT:** BB 3-23 v Wilts (Trowbridge) 1990. **BHC:** HS 4 and BB 2-55 v Lancs (Manchester) 1990. **RAL:** HS 1*. BB 5-26 v Kent (Oval) 1990.

WARD, David Mark (Haling Manor HS), b Croydon 10 Feb 1961. 6'1". RHB, OB. Debut 1985. Cap 1990. 1000 runs (1) inc 2000 runs (1): 2072 (1990). HS 263 v Kent (Canterbury) 1990 – sharing in Surrey record 3rd-wkt stand of 413 with D.J.Bicknell. Award: NWT 1. **NWT:** HS 97 v Northumb (Jesmond) 1989. **BHC:** HS 46* v Yorks (Oval) 1990. **RAL:** HS 102* v Hants (Southampton) 1990.

DEPARTURES

CLINTON, Grahame Selvey (Chislehurst and Sidcup GS), b Sidcup, Kent 5 May 1953. 5'10". LHB, RM. Kent 1974-78. Surrey 1979-90 (cap 1980; benefit 1989). Rhodesia 1979-80. 1000 runs (7); most – 1292 (1990). HS 192 v Yorks (Oval) 1984. BB 2-8 K v P (Canterbury) 1978. Sy/BAC BB 2-77 v Warwks (Birmingham) 1980. Awards: BHC: 4. **NWT:** HS 146 v Kent (Canterbury) 1985. **BHC:** HS 121* v Kent (Oval) 1988. **RAL:** HS 105* v Yorks (Scarborough) 1981.

GRAY, Anthony Hollis (Malick SS), b Port-of-Spain, Trinidad 23 May 1963. 6'7". RHB, RF. Debut (NE Trinidad) 1983-84. Trinidad 1984-90. Surrey 1985-88 and 1990 (cap 1985). **Tests** (WI): 5 (1986-87); HS 12* and BB 4-39 v P (Faisalabad) 1986-87. LOI (WI): 19. Tours (WI): NZ 1986-87; P 1986-87; Z 1989-90 (WI B). HS 54* Trinidad v Leeward Is (Basseterre) 1985-86. Sy HS 35 v Glam (Oval) 1987. 50 wkts (2); most – 79 (1985). BB 8-40 v Yorks (Sheffield) 1985. **NWT:** HS 3 and BB 3-23 v Cheshire (Birkenhead) 1986. **RAL:** HS 24* v Essex (Chelmsford) 1986. BB 4-21 v Leics (Oval) 1986.

SURREY 1990

RESULTS SUMMARY

	Place	Won	Lost	Drew	Abandoned
Britannic Assurance Championship	9th	4	3	15	
All First-class Matches		4	3	17	
Refuge Assurance League	6th	9	6		1
NatWest Bank Trophy	2nd Round				
Benson and Hedges Cup	Quarter-Finalist				

BRITANNIC ASSURANCE CHAMPIONSHIP AVERAGES

BATTING AND FIELDING

Cap		M	I	NO	HS	Runs	Avge	100	50	Ct/St
1990	D.M.Ward	22	31	7	263	1843	76.79	6	3	26/2
1990	D.J.Bicknell	13	20	4	186	1199	74.93	5	5	2
1987	I.A.Greig	22	26	5	291	1130	53.80	2	4	16
–	R.I.Alikhan	11	16	2	138	726	51.85	2	4	3
1985	A.J.Stewart	12	21	6	100*	709	47.26	1	7	17
1980	G.S.Clinton	18	29	4	146	1092	43.68	1	6	5
1982	M.A.Lynch	22	29	4	104	1049	41.96	1	7	29
1989	M.P.Bicknell	19	15	7	50*	309	38.62	–	1	8
1990	M.A.Feltham	14	14	3	101	373	33.90	1	2	10
1990	Waqar Younis	14	9	7	14	56	28.00	–	–	4
–	G.P.Thorpe	16	24	4	86	537	26.85	–	3	8
1988	K.T.Medlycott	20	22	7	44	389	25.93	–	–	13
–	J.D.Robinson	7	9	0	72	151	16.77	–	1	1
–	N.M.Kendrick	11	12	4	52*	124	15.50	–	1	11
–	A.J.Murphy	12	6	3	4*	6	2.00	–	–	1

Also played: P.D.Atkins (1 match) 23, 0*; A.H.Gray (6 matches – cap 1985) 11, 11 (5 ct); N.F.Sargeant (2 matches) 1 (5 ct).

BOWLING

	O	M	R	W	Avge	Best	5wI	10wM
Waqar Younis	422	70	1357	57	23.80	7-73	3	1
M.P.Bicknell	597.5	137	1653	60	27.55	5-34	1	–
M.A.Feltham	334.4	59	1082	39	27.74	6-53	2	–
A.H.Gray	212.4	43	556	16	34.75	4-83	–	–
K.T.Medlycott	617.5	134	2020	53	38.11	7-92	3	–
A.J.Murphy	404.2	76	1367	30	45.56	5-67	2	–
N.M.Kendrick	273	50	987	17	58.05	4-110	–	–
I.A.Greig	199.1	19	805	12	67.08	3-60	–	–

Also bowled: R.I.Alikhan 20-1-83-1; D.J.Bicknell 9-1-20-0; M.A.Lynch 27-5-130-1; J.D.Robinson 118.3-21-393-6; A.J.Stewart 5-0-32-0; G.P.Thorpe 9-1-69-0.

The First-Class Averages (pp 166–181) give the records of Surrey players in all first-class matches (their other opponents being the Indians and Oxford U.), with the exception of:

M.P.Bicknell 20-16-8-50*-310-38.75-0-1-8ct. 640.1-149-1751-64-27.35-5/34-1-0.
K.T.Medlycott 22-25-9-44-410-25.62-0-0-14ct. 734.5-169-2307-59-39.10-7/92-3-0.
A.J.Stewart 14-24-6-100*-837-46.50-1-8-19ct. 5-0-32-0.
G.P.Thorpe 17-26-6-86-585-29.25-0-3-9ct. 23-7-99-1-99.00-1/30.

SURREY RECORDS

FIRST-CLASS CRICKET

Highest Total	For	811		v Somerset	The Oval	1899
	V	863		by Lancashire	The Oval	1990
Lowest Total	For	14		v Essex	Chelmsford	1983
	V	16		by MCC	Lord's	1872
Highest Innings	For	357*	R.Abel	v Somerset	The Oval	1899
	V	366	N.H.Fairbrother	for Lancashire	The Oval	1990

Highest Partnership for each Wicket

1st	428	J.B.Hobbs/A.Sandham	v Oxford U	The Oval	1926
2nd	371	J.B.Hobbs/E.G.Hayes	v Hampshire	The Oval	1909
3rd	413	D.J.Bicknell/D.M.Ward	v Kent	Canterbury	1990
4th	448	R.Abel/T.W.Hayward	v Yorkshire	The Oval	1899
5th	308	J.N.Crawford/F.C.Holland	v Somerset	The Oval	1908
6th	298	A. Sandham/H.S.Harrison	v Sussex	The Oval	1913
7th	262	C.J.Richards/K.T.Medlycott	v Kent	The Oval	1987
8th	205	I.A.Greig/M.P.Bicknell	v Lancashire	The Oval	1990
9th	168	E.R.T.Holmes/E.W.J.Brooks	v Hampshire	The Oval	1936
10th	173	A.Ducat/A.Sandham	v Essex	Leyton	1921

Best Bowling	For	10-43	T.Rushby	v Somerset	Taunton	1921
(Innings)	V	10-28	W.P.Howell	for Australians	The Oval	1899
Best Bowling	For	16-83	G.A.R.Lock	v Kent	Blackheath	1956
(Match)	V	15-57	W.P.Howell	for Australians	The Oval	1899

Most Runs – Season	3,246	T.W.Hayward	(av 72.13)	1906
Most Runs – Career	43,554	J.B.Hobbs	(av 49.72)	1905-1934
Most 100s – Season	(13	T.W.Hayward		1906
	(13	J.B.Hobbs		1925
Most 100s – Career	144	J.B.Hobbs		1905-1934
Most Wkts – Season	252	T.Richardson	(av 13.94)	1895
Most Wkts – Career	1,775	T.Richardson	(av 17.87)	1892-1904

LIMITED-OVERS CRICKET

Highest Total	NWT	313-5		v Northumb	Jesmond	1989
	BHC	331-5		v Hampshire	The Oval	1990
	RAL	304-6		v Warwicks	The Oval	1985
Lowest Total	NWT	74		v Kent	The Oval	1967
	BHC	89		v Notts	Nottingham	1984
	RAL	64		v Worcs	Worcester	1978
Highest Innings	NWT	146	G.S.Clinton	v Kent	Canterbury	1985
	BHC	121*	G.S.Clinton	v Kent	The Oval	1988
	RAL	136	M.A.Lynch	v Yorkshire	Bradford	1985
Best Bowling	NWT	7-33	R.D.Jackman	v Yorkshire	Harrogate	1970
	BHC	5-21	P.H.L.Wilson	v Comb Univs	The Oval	1979
	RAL	6-25	Intikhab Alam	v Derbyshire	The Oval	1974

SUSSEX

Formation of Present Club: 1 March 1839
Substantial Reorganisation: August 1857
Colours: Dark Blue, Light Blue and Gold
Badge: County Arms of Six Martlets
Championships: (0) Second 1902, 1903, 1932, 1933, 1934, 1953, 1981
NatWest Trophy/Gillette Cup Winners: (4) 1963, 1964, 1978, 1986
Benson and Hedges Cup Winners: (0) Semi-Finalists 1982
Sunday League Champions: (1) 1982
Match Awards: NWT 43; BHC 43

Secretary: N.Bett, County Ground, Eaton Road, Hove BN3 3AN (☎ 0273-732161)
Captain: P.W.G.Parker
Scorer: L.V.Chandler
1991 Beneficiary: A.C.S.Pigott

BUNTING, Rodney Alan (King Edward VII GS, King's Lynn), b East Winch, Norfolk, 25 Apr 1965. 6'5". RHB, RFM. Debut 1988 taking 5-86 v Glos (Bristol). Norfolk 1985-87 (cap 1986). HS 73 v CU (Hove) 1989. BAC HS 24* v Derbys (Hove) 1990. BB 5-44 v Warwks (Hove) 1988. **NWT:** HS 6. BB 1-30. **BHC:** HS 0*. BB 2-43 Minor C v Glam (Oxford) 1987. **RAL:** HS 5*. BB 2-8 v Glos (Bristol) 1988.

DODEMAIDE, Anthony Ian Christopher (St John's/Chisholm C; Footscray Institute), b Williamstown, Melbourne, Australia 5 Oct 1963. 6'2". RHB, RFM. Victoria 1983-90. Sussex debut/cap 1989. **Tests** (A): 8 (1987-88 to 1988-89); HS 50 and BB 6-58 v NZ (Melbourne) 1987-88. **LOI** (A): 12. Tour (Young Aus): Z 1985-86. 1000 runs (1): 1001 (1990). HS 112 v Somerset (Hove) 1990. 50 wkts (2); most – 65 (1989). BB 6-58 (Tests). Sx BB 6-106 v Lancs (Horsham) 1990. Award: NWT 1. **NWT:** HS 7. BB 6-9 v Ire (Downpatrick) 1990. **BHC:** HS 38 v Essex (Hove) 1989. BB 3-26 v Glam (Swansea) 1989. **RAL:** HS 40* v Warwks (Birmingham) 1989. BB 4-40 v Somerset (Hove) 1990.

DONELAN, Bradleigh Thomas Peter (Finchley Catholic HS), b Park Royal Hospital, Middx 3 Jan 1968. 6'1". RHB, OB. Debut 1989. MCC Cricket Staff. HS 53 v Warwks (Eastbourne) 1990. BB 3-51 v Worcs (Hove) 1989. **RAL:** HS 4. BB 1-23.

GOULD, Ian James (Westgate SS, Chippenham), b Slough, Bucks 19 Aug 1957. 5'8". LHB, WK. Middlesex 1975-80 (cap 1977). Auckland 1979-80. Sussex debut/cap 1981. Captain 1987. Benefit 1990. MCC Cricket Staff. **LOI:** 18. Tours: A 1982-83; P 1980-81 (Int); Z 1980-81 (Middx). HS 128 M v Worcs (Worcester) 1978. Sx HS 125 v Hants (Hove) 1989. BB 3-10 v Surrey (Oval) 1989. Awards: NWT 1; BHC 3. **NWT:** HS 88 v Yorks (Leeds) 1986. **BHC:** HS 72 v Kent (Hove) 1982. BB 1-0. **RAL:** HS 84* v Surrey (Oval) 1989.

GREENFIELD, Keith (Falmer HS), b Brighton 6 Dec 1968. 6'0". RHB, RM. Debut 1987. HS 102* v CU (Hove) 1990. BAC HS 38 v Leics (Leicester) 1990. **BHC:** HS 0. **RAL:** HS 22 v Northants (Hove) 1989.

HALL, James William (Chichester HS), b Chichester 30 Mar 1968. 6'3". RHB, OB. Debut 1990. 1000 runs (1): 1140 (1990 – debut season). HS 125 v Notts (Nottingham) 1990. **NWT:** HS 0.

HANLEY, Robin (Willingdon S; Eastbourne SFC), b Tonbridge, Kent 5 Jan 1968. 6'2". RHB. Debut 1990. HS 28 v Warwks (Eastbourne) 1990. **RAL:** HS 11 v Warwks (Eastbourne) 1990.

HANSFORD, Alan Roderick (Oakmeeds Community S; Haywards Heath SFC; Surrey U), b Burgess Hill 1 Oct 1968. 6'0". RHB, RM. Debut 1989 v CU (Hove) taking 4-46 and 4-25. HS 29 v Hants (Southampton) 1990. BB 5-79 v Hants (Hove) 1989. **NWT:** HS 5* and BB 2-48 v Middx (Lord's) 1989. **BHC:** HS 8*. BB 2-11 Comb Us v Surrey (Cambridge) 1989. **RAL:** HS 5*. BB 5-32 v Glos (Hove) 1989.

JONES, Adrian Nicholas (Seaford C), b Woking, Surrey 22 Jul 1961. 6'2". LHB, RFM. Sussex 1981-86 (cap 1986). Somerset 1987-90 (cap 1987). Border 1981-82. HS 43* Sm v Leics (Taunton) 1989. Sx HS 35 v Middx (Hove) 1984. 50 wkts (4); most – 71 (1989). BB 7-30 Sm v Hants (Southampton) 1988. Sx BB 5-29 v Glos (Hove) 1984. Awards: BHC 3. **NWT:** HS 7. BB 4-26 v Yorks (Leeds) 1986. **BHC:** HS 25 Sm v Essex (Taunton) 1989. BB 5-53 Sm v Notts (Taunton) 1989. **RAL:** HS 37 Sm v Surrey (Oval) 1989. BB 7-41 v Notts (Nottingham) 1986.

LENHAM, Neil John (Brighton C), b Worthing 17 Dec 1965. Son of L.J. (Sussex 1956-70). 5'11". RHB, RMF. Debut 1984. Cap 1990. 1000 runs (1): 1663 (1990). HS 123 v Somerset (Hove) 1990. BB 4-85 v Leics (Leicester) 1986. Award: BHC 1. **NWT:** HS 47 v Glam (Cardiff) 1990. BB 2-12 v Ire (Downpatrick) 1990. **BHC:** HS 82 v Somerset (Hove) 1986. BB 1-3. **RAL:** HS 78 v Middx (Lord's) 1990. BB 2-19 v Glos (Hove) 1989.

MOORES, Peter (King Edward VI S, Macclesfield), b Macclesfield, Cheshire 18 Dec 1962. 6'0". RHB, WK. Worcestershire 1983-84. Sussex debut 1985. Cap 1989. OFS 1988-89. HS 116 v Somerset (Hove) 1989. **NWT:** HS 20 v Derbys (Hove) 1988 and 20 v Berks (Hove) 1989. **BHC:** HS 76 v Middx (Hove) 1990. **RAL:** HS 34 v Derbys (Horsham) 1988.

NORTH, John Andrew (Chichester HS), b Slindon 19 Nov 1970. 5'9". RHB, RM. Debut 1990. HS 19* v Middx (Hove) 1990. BB 2-43 v Middx (Hove) and v CU (Hove) 1990. **BHC:** BB 1-48. **RAL:** HS 15* and BB 2-45 v Northant (Wellingborough) 1990.

PARKER, Paul William Giles (Collyer's GS; St Catharine's C, Cambridge), b Bulawayo, Rhodesia 15 Jan 1956. 5'10". RHB, RM. CU and Sussex debuts 1976. Blue 1976-77-78. Cap 1979. Captain 1988-. Benefit 1988. YC 1979. **Tests:** 1 (1981); HS 13 v A (Oval) 1981. 1000 runs (8); most – 1692 (1984). HS 215 CU v Essex (Cambridge) 1976. Sx HS 181 v SL (Hove) 1981. BAC HS 140 v Glos (Hove) 1984. BB 2-21 v Surrey (Guildford) 1984. Awards: NWT 4; BHC 4. **NWT:** HS 109 v Ire (Hove) 1985. BB 1-10. **BHC:** HS 85* v Kent (Canterbury) 1989 and v Minor C (Marlow) 1990. BB 2-3 v Minor C (Hove) 1987. **RAL:** HS 121* v Northants (Hastings) 1983. BB 1-2.

PIGOTT, Anthony Charles Shackleton (Harrow S), b Fulham, London 4 Jun 1958. 6'1". RHB, RFM. Debut 1978. Cap 1982. Benefit 1991. Wellington 1982-84. **Tests:** 1 (1983-84); HS 8* and BB 2-75 v NZ (Christchurch) 1983-84. Tours: NZ 1979-80 (DHR), 1983-84 (part). HS 104* v Warwks (Birmingham) 1986. 50 wkts (5); most – 74 (1988). BB 7-74 v Northants (Eastbourne) 1982. Hat-trick 1978 (his first f-c wkts). **NWT:** HS 53 v Derbys (Hove) 1988. BB 3-4 v Ire (Hove) 1985. **BHC:** HS 49* v Essex (Hove) 1989. BB 3-33 v Hants 1982 and v Somerset 1986. **RAL:** HS 51* v Northants (Hove) 1989. BB 5-24 v Lancs (Manchester) 1986.

REMY, Carlos Charles (St Aloyous C; Haringey Cricket C), b Castries, St Lucia 24 Jul 1968. 5'9". RHB, RM. Debut 1989. HS 4*. BB 4-63 v CU (Hove) 1990. BAC BB 1-22. **NWT:** HS 1. **RAL:** HS 12* v Leics (Leicester) 1990. BB 2-45 v Yorks (Hove) 1990.

SALISBURY, Ian David Kenneth (Moulton CS), b Northampton 21 Jan 1970. 5'11". RHB, LB. Debut 1989. MCC Cricket Staff. HS 68 v Derbys (Hove) 1990. BB 5-32 v Worcs (Worcester) 1990. **NWT:** HS 2*. **BHC:** HS 2. BB 1-60. **RAL:** HS 12* v Lancs (Manchester) 1989. BB 3-36 v Glam (Hove) 1990.

SMITH, David Mark (Battersea GS), b Balham, London 9 Jan 1956. 6'4". LHB, RM. Surrey 1973-83 and 1987-88 (cap 1980). Worcestershire 1984-86 (cap 1984). Sussex debut/cap 1989. **Tests:** 2 (1985-86); HS 47 v WI (P-of-S) 1985-86. LOI: 2. Tour: WI 1985-86. 1000 runs (5); most – 1305 (1989). HS 189* Wo v Kent (Worcester) 1984. Sx HS 184 v Notts (Eastbourne) 1989. BB 3-40 Sy v Sussex (Oval) 1976. Awards: NWT 3; BHC 3. **NWT:** HS 109 Wo v Lancs (Manchester) 1985. BB 3-39 Sy v Derbys (Ilkeston) 1976. **BHC:** HS 126 Wo v Warwks (Worcester) 1985. BB 4-29 Sy v Kent (Oval) 1980. **RAL:** HS 87* Sy v Hants (Oval) 1980. BB 2-21 Sy v Worcs (Byfleet) 1973.

SPEIGHT, Martin Peter (Hurstpierpoint C; Durham U), b Walsall, Staffs 24 Oct 1967. 5'9". RHB, WK. Debut 1986. Wellington 1989-90. 1000 runs (1): 1375 (1990). HS 131 v Glam (Hove) 1990. BB 1-2. Award: BHC 1. **NWT:** HS 48 v Leics (Hove) 1989. **BHC:** HS 83 Comb Us v Glos (Bristol) 1988. **RAL:** HS 77 v Derbys (Hove) 1990.

THRELFALL, Philip Walter (Barrow GS; Parkview S), b Barrow-in-Furness, Lancs 11 Feb 1967. 6'3". RHB, RMF. Debut 1988. Cumberland 1987. HS –. BB 3-45 v SL (Hove) 1990. BAC BB –.

WELLS, Alan Peter (Tideway CS, Newhaven), b Newhaven 2 Oct 1961. Younger brother of C.M. 6'0". RHB, RM. Debut 1981. Cap 1986. Border 1981-82. Tour: SA 1989-90 (Eng XI). 1000 runs (5); most – 1629 (1989). HS 161* v Kent (Hove) 1987. BB 3-67 v Worcs (Worcester) 1987. **NWT:** HS 86* v Leics (Hove) 1989. **BHC:** HS 74 v Middx (Hove) 1990. BB 1-17. **RAL:** HS 98 v Notts (Nottingham) 1990. BB 1-0.

WELLS, Colin Mark (Tideway CS, Newhaven), b Newhaven 3 Mar 1960. Elder brother of A.P. 5'11". RHB, RM. Debut 1979. Cap 1982. Border 1980-81. W Province 1984-85. LOI: 2. 1000 runs (6); most – 1456 (1987). HS 203 v Hants (Hove) 1984. 50 wkts (2); most – 59 (1984). BB 7-65 v Kent (Hove) 1989. Awards: BHC 3. **NWT:** HS 76 v Ire (Hove) 1985. BB 2-20 v Suffolk (Hove) 1979. **BHC:** HS 117 v Glam (Swansea) 1989. BB 4-21 v Middx (Lord's) 1980. **RAL:** HS 104* v Warwks (Hove) 1983. BB 4-15 v Worcs (Worcester) 1983.

NEWCOMERS

CORNFORD, Andrew Richard (Beacon S, Crowborough), b Crowborough 8 Oct 1970. Not related to W.L.Cornford (Sussex). RHB, RM.

DEAN, Jacob Winston, b Cuckfield 23 Aug 1970. RHB, SLA.

DEPARTURE

BABINGTON, A.M. – see GLOUCESTERSHIRE.

SUSSEX 1990

RESULTS SUMMARY

	Place	Won	Lost	Drew	Abandoned
Britannic Assurance Championship	17th	3	9	10	
All First-class Matches		3	11	11	
Refuge Assurance League	13th	5	9		2
NatWest Bank Trophy	2nd Round				
Benson and Hedges Cup	4th in Group B				

BRITANNIC ASSURANCE CHAMPIONSHIP AVERAGES

BATTING AND FIELDING

Cap		M	I	NO	HS	Runs	Avge	100	50	Ct/St
1990	N.J.Lenham	19	35	1	123	1499	44.08	4	7	6
1979	P.W.G.Parker	12	21	2	107	778	40.94	2	4	5
–	M.P.Speight	21	39	6	131	1349	40.87	2	11	13
1986	A.P.Wells	21	39	6	144*	1245	37.72	3	5	9
–	B.T.P.Donelan	9	13	6	53	211	30.14	–	1	3
1982	C.M.Wells	19	31	4	107	812	30.07	1	4	3
–	J.W.Hall	17	31	1	125	888	29.60	1	5	3
1989	A.I.C.Dodemaide	22	35	6	112	854	29.44	1	4	9
1989	D.M.Smith	8	14	2	71	324	27.00	–	2	2
–	I.D.K.Salisbury	18	23	10	68	313	24.07	–	1	13
1981	I.J.Gould	7	11	1	73	229	22.90	–	2	7
1989	P.Moores	22	35	3	106*	680	21.25	1	2	46/10
1982	A.C.S.Pigott	20	29	5	64*	451	18.79	–	4	10
–	K.Greenfield	2	4	0	38	74	18.50	–	–	1
–	A.R.Hansford	4	6	1	29	55	11.00	–	–	1
–	R.A.Bunting	13	13	5	24*	85	10.62	–	–	2
–	J.A.North	3	5	1	19*	41	10.25	–	–	1
–	R.Hanley	2	4	0	28	32	8.00	–	–	–

Also played: A.M.Babington (2 matches) 20, 8 (2 ct); C.C.Remy (1 match) 4*.

BOWLING

	O	M	R	W	Avge	Best	5wI	10wM
A.C.S.Pigott	516.1	88	1916	51	37.56	5-52	3	–
A.I.C.Dodemaide	681.1	112	2206	56	39.39	6-106	1	–
B.T.P.Donelan	258.4	50	853	19	44.89	3-79	–	–
I.D.K.Salisbury	535.1	103	1796	40	44.90	5-32	2	–
R.A.Bunting	298	55	1113	21	53.00	2-36	–	–
C.M.Wells	366	67	1195	17	70.29	3-48	–	–

Also bowled: A.M.Babington 43-7-166-2; I.J.Gould 5-0-18-0; K.Greenfield 0.3-0-8-0; A.R.Hansford 123.5-21-425-7; N.J.Lenham 62.5-11-231-2; J.A.North 49.2-10-147-3; P.W.G.Parker 8-0-59-0; C.C.Remy 17-0-91-1; A.P.Wells 29-4-144-1.

The First-Class Averages (pp 166–181) give the records of Sussex players in all first-class county matches (their other opponents being the New Zealanders, the Sri Lankans and Cambridge U.), with the exception of:
  P.W.G.Parker 14-24-4-107-892-44.60-2-5-7ct. 8-0-59-0.

SUSSEX RECORDS

FIRST-CLASS CRICKET

Highest Total	For	705-8d		v Surrey	Hastings	1902
	V	726		by Notts	Nottingham	1895
Lowest Total	For	⎰19		v Surrey	Godalming	1830
		⎱19		v Notts	Hove	1873
	V	18		by Kent	Gravesend	1867
Highest Innings	For	333	K.S.Duleepsinhji	v Northants	Hove	1930
	V	322	E.Paynter	for Lancashire	Hove	1937

Highest Partnership for each Wicket

1st	490	E.H.Bowley/J.G.Langridge	v	Middlesex	Hove	1933
2nd	385	E.H.Bowley/M.W.Tate	v	Northants	Hove	1921
3rd	298	K.S.Ranjitsinhji/E.H.Killick	v	Lancashire	Hove	1901
4th	326*	J.Langridge/G.Cox	v	Yorkshire	Leeds	1949
5th	297	J.H.Parks/H.W.Parks	v	Hampshire	Portsmouth	1937
6th	255	K.S.Duleepsinhji/M.W.Tate	v	Northants	Hove	1930
7th	344	K.S.Ranjitsinhji/W.Newham	v	Essex	Leyton	1902
8th	229*	C.L.A.Smith/G.Brann	v	Kent	Hove	1902
9th	178	H.W.Parks/A.F.Wensley	v	Derbyshire	Horsham	1930
10th	156	G.R.Cox/H.R.Butt	v	Cambridge U	Cambridge	1908

Best Bowling	For	10-48	C.H.G.Bland	v Kent	Tonbridge	1899
(Innings)	V	9-11	A.P.Freeman	for Kent	Hove	1922
Best Bowling	For	17-106	G.R.Cox	v Warwicks	Horsham	1926
(Match)	V	17-67	A.P.Freeman	for Kent	Hove	1922

Most Runs – Season	2,850	J.G.Langridge	(av 64.77)	1949
Most Runs – Career	34,152	J.G.Langridge	(av 37.69)	1928-1955
Most 100s – Season	12	J.G.Langridge		1949
Most 100s – Career	76	J.G.Langridge		1928-1955
Most Wkts – Season	198	M.W.Tate	(av 13.47)	1925
Most Wkts – Career	2,211	M.W.Tate	(av 17.41)	1912-1937

LIMITED-OVERS CRICKET

Highest Total	NWT	314-7		v Kent	Tunbridge W	1963
	BHC	305-6		v Kent	Hove	1982
	RAL	293-4		v Worcs	Horsham	1980
Lowest Total	NWT	49		v Derbyshire	Chesterfield	1969
	BHC	60		v Middlesex	Hove	1978
	RAL	61		v Derbyshire	Derby	1978
Highest Innings	NWT	141*	G.D.Mendis	v Warwicks	Hove	1980
	BHC	⎰117	R.D.V.Knight	v Surrey	The Oval	1977
		⎱117	C.M.Wells	v Glamorgan	Swansea	1989
	RAL	129	A.W.Greig	v Yorkshire	Scarborough	1976
Best Bowling	NWT	6-9	A.I.Dodemaide	v Ireland	Downpatrick	1990
	BHC	5-8	Imran Khan	v Northants	Northampton	1978
	RAL	7-41	A.N.Jones	v Notts	Nottingham	1986

WARWICKSHIRE

Formation of Present Club: 8 April 1882
Substantial Reorganisation: 19 January 1884
Colours: Dark Blue, Gold and Silver
Badge: Bear and Ragged Staff
Championships: (3) 1911, 1951, 1972
NatWest Trophy/Gillette Cup Winners: (3) 1966, 1968, 1989
Benson and Hedges Cup Winners: (0) Finalists 1984
Sunday League Champions: (1) 1980
Match Awards: NWT 39; BHC 40

Secretary: D.M.W.Heath, County Ground, Edgbaston, Birmingham, B5 7QU
(☎ 021-446 4422)
Captain: T.A.Lloyd
Scorer: A.Davies (home) and S.P.Austin (away)

ASIF DIN, Mohamed (Ladywood CS, Birmingham), b Kampala, Uganda 21 Sep 1960. 5'9½". RHB, LB. Debut 1981. Cap 1987. MCC Cricket Staff. 1000 (2); most – 1425 (1988). HS 158* v CU (Cambridge) 1988. BAC HS 131 v Northants (Northampton) 1988. BB 5-100 v Glam (Birmingham) 1982. Awards: NWT 2. **NWT:** HS 94* v Worcs (Birmingham) 1989. BB 5-40 v Herts (St Albans) 1990. **BHC:** HS 107 v Scot (Birmingham) 1988. BB 1-26. **RAL:** HS 113 v Somerset (W-s-M) 1990. BB 1-11.

BENJAMIN, Joseph Emmanuel (Cayon HS, St Kitts; Mount Pleasant S, Highgate, Birmingham), b Christ Church, St Kitts 2 Feb 1961. 6'2". RHB, RMF. Debut 1988. Staffordshire 1986-88. HS 41 v Surrey (Oval) 1990. BB 5-29 v CU (Cambridge) 1990. BAC BB 5-71 v Middx (Lord's) 1990. **NWT:** HS 19 and BB 2-37 Staffs v Glam (Stone) 1986. **BHC:** HS 20 v Worcs (Birmingham) 1990. BB 2-32 v Glos (Bristol) 1990. **RAL:** HS 24 v Lancs (Manchester) 1990. BB 2-29 v Kent (Birmingham) 1990.

BOOTH, Paul Antony (Hanley HS), b Huddersfield, Yorks 5 Sep 1965. 5'10". LHB, SLA. Yorkshire 1982-89. Warwickshire debut 1990. HS 60 v Somerset (Birmingham) 1990. BB 5-98 Y v Lancs (Manchester) 1988. Wa BB 4-55 v Yorks (Birmingham) 1990. **NWT:** HS 6*. **BHC:** HS 3* v Glam (Birmingham) 1990. BB 2-28 Y v Worcs (Bradford) 1985. **RAL:** BB 1-33.

DONALD, Allan Anthony (Grey College HS), b Bloemfontein, SA 20 Oct 1966. 6'2". RHB, RFM. OFS 1985-90. Warwickshire debut 1987. Cap 1989. 50 wkts (1): 86 (1989). BB 8-37 OFS v Transvaal (Johannesburg) 1986-87. Wa BB 7-66 v Middx (Birmingham) 1989. Award: NWT 1. **NWT:** HS 0. BB 5-12 v Wilts (Birmingham) 1989. **BHC:** HS 23* v Leics (Leicester) 1989. BB 4-28 v Scot (Perth) 1987. **RAL:** HS 18* v Middx (Lord's) 1988. BB 4-32 v Middx (Birmingham) 1989.

GREEN, Simon James (Old Swinford Hospital S), b Bloxwich, Staffs 19 Mar 1970. 6'2". RHB, LM. Debut 1988. HS 44 v SL (Birmingham) 1990. BAC HS 28 v Lancs (Nuneaton) 1988. **NWT:** HS 1. **BHC:** HS 0. **RAL:** HS 25 v Somerset (W-s-M) 1990.

HOLLOWAY, Piran Christopher Laity (Millfield S; Taunton S; now at Loughborough U), b Helston, Cornwall 1 Oct 1970. 5'8". LHB, WK. Debut 1988. HS 16 v Glam (Birmingham) 1988. **RAL:** HS 13 v Worcs (Worcester) 1988.

LLOYD, Timothy Andrew (Oswestry HS; Dorset CHE), b Oswestry, Salop 5 Nov 1956. 5'10". LHB, RM/OB. Debut 1977. Cap 1980. Captain 1988-. Benefit 1990. OFS 1978-80. Salop 1975. **Tests:** 1 (1984); HS 10* (rtd hurt) v WI (Birmingham) 1984. **LOI:** 3. Tour: Z 1984-85 (EC). 1000 runs (8); most – 1673 (1983). HS 208* v Glos (Birmingham) 1983. BB 3-62 v Surrey (Birmingham) 1985. Awards: NWT 3; BHC 2. **NWT:** HS 121 v Cambs (Birmingham) 1988. BB 1-4. **BHC:** HS 137* v Lancs (Birmingham) 1985. **RAL:** HS 90 v Kent (Birmingham) 1980. BB 1-42.

MOLES, Andrew James (Finham Park CS; Butts CHE), b Solihull 12 Feb 1961. 5'10". RHB, RM. Debut 1986. Cap 1987. GW 1986-89. 1000 runs (3); most – 1854 (1990). HS 230* GW v N Transvaal B (Verwoerdburg) 1988-89. Wa HS 224* v Glam (Swansea) 1990. BB 3-21 v OU (Oxford) 1987. BAC BB 3-50 v Essex (Chelmsford) 1987. Awards: NWT 1; BHC 1. **NWT:** HS 127 v Bucks (Birmingham) 1987. **BHC:** HS 72 v Scot (Perth) 1987. BB 1-11. **RAL:** HS 85 v Glos (Birmingham) 1986. BB 2-24 v Worcs (Worcester) 1987.

MUNTON, Timothy Alan (Sarson HS; King Edward VII Upper S), b Melton Mowbray, Leics 30 Jul 1965. 6'5". RHB, RMF. Debut 1985. Cap 1989. HS 38 v Yorks (Scarborough) 1987. 50 wkts (2); most – 78 (1990). BB 6-21 v Worcs (Birmingham) 1988. **NWT:** HS 1*. BB 3-36 v Kent (Canterbury) 1989. **BHC:** HS 13 v Leics (Leicester) 1989. BB 2-20 v Scot (Birmingham) 1989. **RAL:** HS 7*. BB 5-23 v Glos (Moreton) 1990.

OSTLER, Dominic Piers (Princethorpe C; Solihull TC), b Solihull 15 Jul 1970. 6'3". RHB, RM. Debut 1990. HS 71 v Kent (Birmingham) 1990. **NWT:** HS 4. **RAL:** HS 30 v Surrey (Oval) 1990.

PIERSON, Adrian Roger Kirshaw (Kent C, Canterbury; Hatfield Polytechnic), b Enfield, Middx 21 Jul 1963. 6'4". RHB, OB. Debut 1985. MCC Cricket Staff. HS 42* v Northants (Northampton) 1986. BB 6-82 v Derbys (Nuneaton) 1989. Award: BHC 1. **NWT:** HS 1*. BB 3-20 v Wilts (Birmingham) 1989. **BHC:** HS 11 v Minor C (Walsall) 1986. BB 3-34 v Lancs (Birmingham) 1988. **RAL:** HS 21* v Hants (Birmingham) 1987. BB 3-21 v Leics (Birmingham) 1988.

PIPER, Keith John (Haringey Cricket C), b Leicester 18 Dec 1969. 5'6". RHB, WK. Debut 1989. HS 111 v Somerset (Birmingham) 1990. **RAL:** HS 30 v Lancs (Manchester) 1990.

RATCLIFFE, Jason David (Sharman's Cross SS; Solihull SFC), b Solihull 19 Jun 1969. Son of D.P. (Warwks 1957-68). 6'4". RHB, RM. Debut 1988. HS 127* v CU (Cambridge) 1989. BAC HS 81* v Hants (Birmingham) 1990. BB 1-15. **NWT:** HS 59 v Wilts (Birmingham) 1989. **RAL:** HS 37 v Somerset (Birmingham) 1989. BB 1-8.

REEVE, Dermot Alexander (King George V S, Kowloon), b Kowloon, Hong Kong 2 Apr 1963. 6'0". RHB, RMF. Sussex 1983-87 (cap 1986). Warwickshire debut 1988. Cap 1989. Hong Kong 1982 (ICC Trophy). MCC Cricket Staff. 1000 runs (1): 1412 (1990). HS 202* v Northants (Northampton) 1990. 50 wkts (2); most – 55 (1984). BB 7-37 Sx v Lancs (Lytham) 1987. Wa BB 4-42 v Leics (Birmingham) 1990. Awards: NWT 3. **NWT:** HS 45 v Kent (Canterbury) 1989. BB 4-20 Sussex v Lancs (Lord's) 1986. **BHC:** HS 30* and BB 4-42 Sussex v Kent (Canterbury) 1987. **RAL:** HS 70* v Essex (Ilford) 1989. BB 5-23 v Essex (Birmingham) 1988.

SMALL, Gladstone Cleophas (Moseley S; Hall Green TC), b St George, Barbados 18 Oct 1961. 5'11". RHB, RFM. Debut 1979-80 (DHR XI in NZ). Warwickshire debut 1980. Cap 1982. S Australia 1985-86. **Tests:** 13 (1986 to 1990); HS 59 v A (Oval) 1989; BB 5-48 v A (Melbourne) 1986-87. LOI: 40. Tours: A 1986-87; WI 1989-90; NZ 1979-80 (DHR); P 1981-82 (Int). HS 70 v Lancs (Manchester) 1988. 50 wkts (6); most – 80 (1988). BB 7-15 v Notts (Birmingham) 1988. **NWT:** HS 33 v Surrey (Lord's) 1982. BB 3-22 v Glam (Cardiff) 1982. **BHC:** HS 22 v Kent (Canterbury) 1990. BB 4-22 v Glam (Birmingham) 1990. **RAL:** HS 40* v Essex (Ilford) 1984. BB 5-29 v Surrey (Birmingham) 1980.

SMITH, Gareth (Boldon CS; South Tyneside C), b Jarrow, Co Durham 20 Jul 1966. 6'1". RHB, RFM. Northamptonshire 1986-89. Warwickshire debut 1990. Dismissed S.M.Gavaskar with his second ball in f-c cricket. HS 30 v Sussex (Eastbourne) 1990. BB 6-72 Nh v Sussex (Hove) 1987. Wa BB 3-36 v Sussex (Eastbourne) 1990. **RAL:** HS 5 and BB 2-20 v Essex (Birmingham) 1990.

SMITH, Neil Michael Knight (Warwick S), b Birmingham 27 Jul 1967. Son of M.J.K. (Leics, Warwks and England 1951-75). 6'0". RHB, OB. Debut 1987. MCC Cricket Staff. HS 161 and BB 3-62 v Yorks (Leeds) 1989. **NWT:** HS 52 v Yorks (Leeds) 1990. BB 1-6. **BHC:** HS 30* v Worcs (Birmingham) 1990. BB 1-43. **RAL:** HS 38* and BB 3-36 v Hants (Birmingham) 1990.

SMITH, Paul Andrew (Heaton GS), b Jesmond, Northumb 15 Apr 1964. Son of K.D. sr (Leics 1950-51) and brother of K.D. jr (Warwks 1973-85). 6'2". RHB, RFM. Debut 1982. Cap 1986. MCC Cricket Staff. 1000 runs (2); most – 1508 (1986). HS 140 v Worcs (Worcester) 1989. BB 5-48 v Somerset (Birmingham) 1990. 2 hat-tricks: 1989, 1990. Award: BHC 1. **NWT:** HS 79 v Durham (Birmingham) 1986. BB 3-10 v Salop (Birmingham) 1984. **BHC:** HS 74 v Northants (Birmingham) 1989. BB 2-23 v Lancs (Manchester) 1987. **RAL:** HS 93* v Middx (Birmingham) 1989. BB 4-23 v Notts (Birmingham) 1983.

STEER, Ian Gary Samuel (St Edmund Campion S), b Aston, Birmingham 17 Aug 1970. 5'7". RHB, RM. No 1st XI appearances – joined staff 1990.

TWOSE, Roger Graham (King's C, Taunton), b Torquay, Devon 17 Apr 1968. Nephew of R.W.Tolchard (Leics and England 1965-83). 6'0". RHB, RM. Debut 1989. N Districts 1989-90. Devon 1988-89. MCC Cricket Staff. Debut 1989. HS 64* v Kent (Birmingham) 1990. BB 51 v Kent (Birmingham) 1990. BB 1-10. **NWT:** HS 56 Devon v Notts (Torquay) 1988. BB 1-31. **BHC:** HS 17 v Worcs (Birmingham) 1990. **RAL:** HS 40 v Surrey (Oval) 1990. BB 2-11 v Derbys (Derby) 1990.

WELCH, Graeme (Hetton CS), b Durham 21 Mar 1972. RHB, RM. No 1st XI appearances – joined staff 1990.

NEWCOMERS

BURNS, Michael (Walney CS), b Barrow-in-Furness, Lancs 2 Jun 1969. RHB, WK. Cumberland 1988-90.

WASIM KHAN (Josiah Mason SFC), b Birmingham 1971. LHB. Scored 171* for 2nd XI v Northants 1990.

DEPARTURES – see p 156.

WARWICKSHIRE 1990

RESULTS SUMMARY

	Place	Won	Lost	Drew	Abandoned
Britannic Assurance Championship	5th	7	7	8	
All First-class Matches		7	8	10	
Refuge Assurance League	14th	5	10		1
NatWest Bank Trophy	2nd Round				
Benson and Hedges Cup	4th in Group A				

BRITANNIC ASSURANCE CHAMPIONSHIP AVERAGES

BATTING AND FIELDING

Cap		M	I	NO	HS	Runs	Avge	100	50	Ct/St
1990	T.M.Moody	7	12	2	168	866	86.60	5	1	4
1989	D.A.Reeve	22	34	11	202*	1265	55.00	2	5	23
1987	A.J.Moles	22	42	8	224*	1669	49.08	3	10	12
1976	G.W.Humpage	11	18	3	74	552	36.80	–	5	28
–	J.E.Benjamin	12	11	6	41	169	33.80	–	–	4
–	D.P.Ostler	9	15	2	71	432	33.23	–	4	9
1986	P.A.Smith	12	20	4	117	520	32.50	1	3	1
–	N.M.K.Smith	7	9		83*	214	30.57	–	1	2
–	J.D.Ratcliffe	14	27	3	81*	689	28.70	–	3	7
1987	Asif Din	21	37	3	70	874	25.70	–	5	10
–	K.J.Piper	14	18	1	111	432	25.41	1	1	39/4
1972	A.I.Kallicharran	5	8	1	72	175	25.00	–	2	5
1980	T.A.Lloyd	15	27	1	101	646	24.84	1	4	7
–	P.A.Booth	7	12	0	60	177	14.75	–	1	2
–	R.G.Twose	4	6	0	51	88	14.66	–	1	3
–	A.R.K.Pierson	11	9	5	16*	57	14.25	–	–	1
1982	G.C.Small	12	18	2	55	212	13.25	–	1	3
1989	T.A.Munton	22	23	9	29*	121	8.64	–	–	9
1989	A.A.Donald	14	18	3	24*	118	7.86	–	–	

Also played: G.Smith (1 match) 30 (1 ct).

BOWLING

	O	M	R	W	Avge	Best	5wI	10wM
P.A.Smith	148.5	34	497	20	24.85	5-48	1	–
T.A.Munton	748.3	174	2086	75	27.81	5-33	2	–
D.A.Reeve	319.4	94	782	28	27.92	4-42	–	–
J.E.Benjamin	322.3	51	1036	34	30.47	5-71	3	–
G.C.Small	321.4	78	900	27	33.33	6-94	2	–
A.A.Donald	355.1	81	988	28	35.28	3-28	–	–
A.R.K.Pierson	302.4	55	965	25	38.60	5-101	1	–
P.A.Booth	214.2	70	495	12	41.25	4-55	–	–

Also bowled: Asif Din 133.2-24-569-6; G.W.Humpage 7-2-34-0; T.A.Lloyd 9-1-58-1; A.J.Moles 22-2-133-2; T.M.Moody 38-7-145-3; G.Smith 26.5-3-81-4; N.M.K.Smith 109.5-20-350-5; R.G.Twose 26-2-101-2.

The First-Class Averages (pp 166–181) give the records of Warwickshire players in all first-class county matches (their other opponents being the New Zealanders, the Sri Lankans and Cambridge U.), with the exception of G.C.Small, whose full county figures are as above, and:

T.A.Munton 24-24-9-29*-125-8.33-0-0-9ct. 790.1-184-2179-77-28.29-5/33-2-0.
D.A.Reeve 24-37-12-202*-1373-54.92-3-5-26ct. 364.4-108-900-33-27.27-4/42.

WARWICKSHIRE RECORDS

FIRST-CLASS CRICKET

Highest Total	For	657-6d		v	Hampshire	Birmingham	1899
	V	887		by	Yorkshire	Birmingham	1896
Lowest Total	For	16		v	Kent	Tonbridge	1913
	V	15		by	Hampshire	Birmingham	1922
Highest Innings	For	305*	F.R.Foster	v	Worcs	Dudley	1914
	V	322	I.V.A.Richards	for	Somerset	Taunton	1985

Highest Partnership for each Wicket

1st	377*	N.F.Horner/K.Ibadulla	v	Surrey	The Oval	1960
2nd	465*	J.A.Jameson/R.B.Kanhai	v	Glos	Birmingham	1974
3rd	327	S.P.Kinneir/W.G.Quaife	v	Lancashire	Birmingham	1901
4th	470	A.I.Kallicharran/G.W.Humpage	v	Lancashire	Southport	1982
5th	268	W.Quaife/W.G.Quaife	v	Essex	Leyton	1900
6th	220	H.E.Dollery/J.Buckingham	v	Derbyshire	Derby	1938
7th	250	H.E.Dollery/J.S.Ord	v	Kent	Maidstone	1953
8th	228	A.J.W.Croom/R.E.S.Wyatt	v	Worcs	Dudley	1925
9th	154	G.W.Stephens/A.J.W.Croom	v	Derbyshire	Birmingham	1925
10th	128	F.R.Santall/W.Sanders	v	Yorkshire	Birmingham	1930

Best Bowling	For	10-41	J.D.Bannister	v	Comb Servs	Birmingham	1959
(Innings)	V	10-36	H.Verity	for	Yorkshire	Leeds	1931
Best Bowling	For	15-76	S.Hargreave	v	Surrey	The Oval	1903
(Match)	V	17-92	A.P.Freeman	for	Kent	Folkestone	1932

Most Runs – Season	2,417	M.J.K.Smith	(av 60.42)	1959
Most Runs – Career	35,146	D.L.Amiss	(av 41.64)	1960-1987
Most 100s – Season	9	A.I.Kallicharran		1984
Most 100s – Career	78	D.L.Amiss		1960-1987
Most Wkts – Season	180	W.E.Hollies	(av 15.13)	1946
Most Wkts – Career	2,201	W.E.Hollies	(av 20.45)	1932-1957

LIMITED-OVERS CRICKET

Highest Total	NWT	392-5		v	Oxfordshire	Birmingham	1984
	BHC	308-4		v	Scotland	Birmingham	1988
	RAL	301-6		v	Essex	Colchester	1982
Lowest Total	NWT	109		v	Kent	Canterbury	1971
	BHC	96		v	Leics	Leicester	1972
	RAL	65		v	Kent	Maidstone	1979
Highest Innings	NWT	206	A.I.Kallicharran	v	Oxfordshire	Birmingham	1984
	BHC	137*	T.A.Lloyd	v	Lancashire	Birmingham	1985
	RAL	123*	J.A.Jameson	v	Notts	Nottingham	1973
Best Bowling	NWT	6-32	K.Ibadulla	v	Hampshire	Birmingham	1965
		6-32	A.I.Kallicharran	v	Oxfordshire	Birmingham	1984
	BHC	7-32	R.G.D.Willis	v	Yorkshire	Birmingham	1981
	RAL	6-20	N.Gifford	v	Northants	Birmingham	1985

WORCESTERSHIRE

Formation of Present Club: 11 March 1865
Colours: Dark Green and Black
Badge: Shield Argent a Fess between three Pears Sable
Championships: (5) 1964, 1965, 1974, 1988, 1989
NatWest Trophy/Gillette Cup Finalists: (3) 1963, 1966, 1988
Benson and Hedges Cup Finalists: (3) 1973, 1976, 1990
Sunday League Champions: (3) 1971, 1987, 1988
Match Awards: NWT 34; BHC 45

Secretary: Revd M.D.Vockins, County Ground, New Road, Worcester, WR2 4QQ
(☎ 0905-422694)
Captain: P.A.Neale
Scorer: J.W.Sewter

BENT, Paul (Worcester RGS), b Worcester 1 May 1965. 6'0". RHB, OB. Debut 1985. MCC Cricket Staff. HS 144 v Kent (Worcester) 1989. **RAL:** HS 36 v Sussex (Worcester) 1988.

BEVINS, Stuart Roy (Solihull S; Solihull TC), b Solihull, Warwks 8 Mar 1967. 5'6½". RHB, WK. Debut 1989. HS 10 v NZ (Worcester) 1990. BAC HS 6*. **BHC:** HS 0*.

BOTHAM, Ian Terence (Buckler's Mead SS, Yeovil), b Heswall, Cheshire 24 Nov 1955. 6'1". RHB, RM. Somerset 1974-86 (cap 1976; captain 1984-85; benefit 1984). Worcestershire debut/cap 1987. Queensland 1987-88. Wisden 1977. YC 1977. MCC Cricket Staff. **Tests:** 97 (1977 to 1989, 12 as captain); HS 208 v Ind (Oval) 1982; BB 8-34 v P (Lord's) 1978. LOI: 98. Tours: A 1978-79, 1979-80, 1982-83, 1986-87; WI 1980-81 (capt), 1985-86; NZ 1977-78, 1983-84; I 1979-80, 1981-82; P 1977-78, 1983-84; SL 1981-82. 1000 runs (4); most – 1530 (1985). Hit 80 sixes 1985 (f-c record). HS 228 Sm v Glos (Taunton) 1980. Wo HS 126* v Somerset (Taunton) 1987. Shared record Somerset 4th- and 8th-wkt stands of 310 (P.W.Denning) and 172 (I.V.A.Richards) respectively. 50 wkts (8) inc 100 wkts (1): 100 (1978). BB 8-34 (Tests). BAC BB 7-61 Sm v Glam (Cardiff) 1978. Wo BB 7-85 v Sussex (Hove) 1989. Hat-trick 1978 (MCC). Awards: NWT 4; BHC 8. **NWT:** HS 101 v Devon (Worcester) 1987. BB 5-51 v Lancs (Worcester) 1989. **BHC:** HS 138* v Glos (Bristol) 1990. BB 5-41 v Yorks (Worcester) 1988. **RAL:** HS 175* Sm v Northants (Wellingborough) 1986. BB 5-27 v Glos (Gloucester) 1987.

CURTIS, Timothy Stephen (Worcester RGS; Durham U; Magdalene C, Cambridge), b Chislehurst, Kent 15 Jan 1960. 5'11". RHB, LB. Debut 1979. Cap 1984. Cambridge U 1983 (blue). **Tests:** 5 (1988 to 1989); HS 41 v A (Birmingham) 1989. 1000 runs (7); most – 1731 (1990). HS 197* v Warwks (Worcester) 1990. Shared record Worcs 2nd-wkt stand of 287* with G.A.Hick v Glam (Neath) 1986. BB 2-58 CU v Notts (Cambridge) 1983. BAC BB 2-72 v Warwks (Worcester) 1987. Awards: NWT 5; BHC 2. **NWT:** HS 120 v Notts (Nottingham) 1988. BB 1-6. **BHC:** HS 97 v Warwks (Birmingham) 1990. **RAL:** HS 124 v Somerset (Taunton) 1990.

DILLEY, Graham Roy (Dartford West SS), b Dartford, Kent 18 May 1959. 6'3". LHB, RF. Kent 1977-86 (cap 1980). Worcestershire debut/cap 1987. Natal 1985-86. YC 1980. **Tests:** 41 (1979-80 to 1989); HS 56 v A (Leeds) 1981; BB 6-38 v NZ (Christchurch) 1987-88. LOI: 36. Tours: A 1979-80, 1986-87, 1987-88; SA 1989-90 (Eng XI); WI 1980-81; NZ 1983-84, 1987-88; I 1979-80, 1981-82; P 1983-84, 1987-88; SL 1981-82. HS 81 K v Northants (Northampton) 1979. Wo HS 45* v Glam (Worcester) 1990. 50 wkts (3); most – 64 (1982). BB 7-63 Natal v Transvaal (Johannesburg) 1985-86. BAC BB 6-43 v Leics (Worcester) 1987. 2 hat-tricks (Kent): 1985, 1986. Awards: NWT 1; BHC 1. **NWT:** HS 25 v Essex (Chelmsford) 1987. BB 5-29 K v Scot 1986 and 5-29 Wo v Middx 1988. **BHC:** HS 37* K v Hants (Canterbury) 1983. BB 4-14 K v Comb Us (Canterbury) 1981. **RAL:** HS 33 K v Northants (Northampton) 1982. BB 4-20 K v Glos (Canterbury) 1980.

D'OLIVEIRA, Damian Basil (Blessed Edward Oldcorne SS), b Cape Town, SA 19 Oct 1960. Son of B.L. (Worcs and England 1964-80). 5'9". RHB, OB. Debut 1982. Cap 1985. MCC Cricket Staff. Tour: Z 1984-85 (EC). 1000 runs (4); most – 1263 (1990). HS 155 v Lancs (Manchester) 1990. BB 2-17 v Glos (Bristol) 1986. Awards: NWT 2; BHC 2 **NWT:** HS 99 v Oxon (Worcester) 1986. BB 2-17 v Suffolk (Bury St E) 1990. **BHC:** HS 66 v Yorks (Leeds) 1986. BB 3-12 v Scot (Glasgow) 1986. **RAL:** HS 103 v Surrey (Worcester) 1985. BB 3-23 v Derbys (Derby) 1983.

GOFTON, Robert Paul (Wolfreton S, Hull), b Scarborough, Yorks 10 Sep 1968. 5'10". RHB, RM. MCC Cricket Staff. No 1st XI appearances – joined staff 1990.

HICK, Graeme Ashley (Prince Edward HS, Salisbury), b Salisbury, Rhodesia 23 May 1966. 6'3". RHB, OB. Zimbabwe 1983-86. Worcestershire debut 1984. Cap 1986. N Districts 1987-89. Wisden 1986. Tours (Z): E 1985; SL 1983-84. 1000 runs (6+1) inc 2000 runs (3); most – 2713 (1988); youngest to score 2000 (1986). 1019 runs before June 1988. HS 405* (Worcs record and 2nd-highest in UK f-c matches) v Somerset (Taunton) 1988. Shared in 4 record Worcs stands: 287* (2nd) with T.S.Curtis; 265 (6th) with S.J.Rhodes; 205 (7th) with P.J.Newport; and 177* (8th) with R.K.Illingworth. BB 5-37 v Glos (Worcester) 1990. Awards: NWT 2; BHC 6. **NWT:** HS 172* v Devon (Worcester) 1987. BB 4-54 v Hants (Worcester) 1988. **BHC:** HS 109 v Comb Us (Worcester) 1989. BB 3-36 v Warwks (Birmingham) 1990. **RAL:** HS 114* v Notts (Worcester) 1990. BB 4-42 v Sussex (Worcester) 1988.

ILLINGWORTH, Richard Keith (Salts GS), b Bradford, Yorks 23 Aug 1963. 5'11". RHB, SLA. Debut 1982. Cap 1986. Natal 1988-89. Tour: Z 1989-90 (Eng A). HS 120* v Warwks (Worcester) 1987. Shared record Worcs 8th-wkt stand of 177* with G.A.Hick v Somerset (Taunton) 1988. 50 wkts (3); most – 75 (1990). BB 7-50 v OU (Oxford) 1985. BAC BB 5-23 v Hants (Bournemouth) 1989. **NWT:** HS 22 v Northants (Northampton) 1984. BB 4-20 v Devon (Worcester) 1987. **BHC:** HS 36* v Kent (Worcester) 1990. BB 4-36 v Yorks (Bradford) 1985. **RAL:** HS 22 v Sussex (Hove) 1989. BB 5-24 v Somerset (Worcester) 1983.

LAMPITT, Stuart Richard (Kingswinford S; Dudley TC), b Wolverhampton, Staffs 29 Jul 1966. 5'11". RHB, RM. Debut 1985. Cap 1989. HS 46 v Warwks (Worcester) 1989. 50 wkts (1): 58 (1990). BB 5-32 v Kent (Worcester) 1990. Award: NWT 1. **NWT:** HS 9*. BB 5-22 v Suffolk (Bury St E) 1990. **BHC:** HS 41 v Glam (Worcester) 1990. BB 2-43 v Lancs (Lord's) 1990. **RAL:** HS 25* and BB 5-67 v Middx (Lord's) 1990.

LEATHERDALE, David Anthony (Pudsey Grangefield S), b Bradford, Yorks 26 Nov 1967. 5'10½". RHB, RM. Debut 1988. HS 70 v Lancs (Kidderminster) 1990. BB 1-12. **NWT:** HS 43 v Hants (Worcester) 1988. **RAL:** HS 62* v Kent (Folkestone) 1988.

LORD, Gordon John (Warwick S; Durham U), b Edgbaston, Birmingham 25 Apr 1961. 5'10". LHB, SLA. Warwickshire 1983-86. Worcestershire debut 1987. Cap 1990. 1000 runs (1): 1003 (1990). HS 199 Wa v Yorks (Birmingham) 1985. Wo HS 190 v Hants (Worcester) 1990. **NWT:** HS 0. **BHC:** HS 26 v Glos (Bristol) 1990. **RAL:** HS 103 Warwks v Derbys (Birmingham) 1985.

McEWAN, Steven Michael (Worcester RGS), b Worcester 5 May 1962. 6'1". RHB, RFM. Debut 1985. Cap 1989. HS 54 v Yorks (Worcester) 1990. 50 wkts (1): 52 (1989). BB 6-34 v Leics (Kidderminster) 1989. Hat-trick: 1990. **NWT:** HS 6 and BB 3-51 v Warwks (Birmingham) 1989. **BHC:** BB 2-53 v Notts (Nottingham) 1990. **RAL:** HS 18* v Yorks (Worcester) 1990. BB 4-35 v Derbys (Worcester) 1986.

NEALE, Phillip Anthony (Frederick Gough CS; John Leggott SFC; Leeds U), b Scunthorpe, Lincs 5 Jun 1954. 5'11". RHB, RM. Debut 1975. Cap 1978. Captain 1982-. Benefit 1988. Lincolnshire 1972. Wisden 1988. 1000 runs (8); most – 1706 (1984). HS 167 v Sussex (Kidderminster) 1988. BB 1-15. Awards: NWT 1; BHC 2. **NWT:** HS 98 v Cumberland (Worcester) 1988. **BHC:** HS 128 v Lancs (Manchester) 1980. **RAL:** HS 102 v Northants (Luton) 1982. BB 2-46 v Warwks (Worcester) 1976.

NEWPORT, Philip John (High Wycombe RGS; Portsmouth Polytechnic), b High Wycombe, Bucks 11 Oct 1962. 6'3". RHB, RFM. Debut 1982. Cap 1986. Boland 1987-88. Buckinghamshire 1981-82. **Tests:** 2 (1988 and 1989); HS 36 v A (Leeds) 1989; BB 4-87 v SL (Lord's) 1988. HS 98 v NZ (Worcester) 1990. BAC HS 96 v Essex (Worcester) 1990. Shared record Worcs 7th-wkt stand of 205 with G.A.Hick v Yorks (Worcester) 1988. 50 wkts (3); most – 93 (1988). BB 8-52 v Middx (Lord's) 1988. **NWT:** HS 25 v Northants (Northampton) 1984. BB 4-46 v Northants (Northampton) 1990. **BHC:** HS 28 v Kent (Worcester) 1990. BB 5-22 v Warwks (Birmingham) 1987. **RAL:** HS 26* v Leics (Leicester) 1987. BB 4-18 v Glam (Worcester) 1989.

RADFORD, Neal Victor (Athlone BHS, Johannesburg), b Luanshya, N Rhodesia 7 Jun 1957. Brother of W.R. (OFS). 5'11". RHB, RFM. Transvaal 1978-89. Lancashire 1980-84. Worcestershire debut/cap 1985. Wisden 1985. **Tests:** 3 (1986 to 1987-88); HS 12* v NZ (Lord's); BB 2-131 v I (Birmingham). LOI: 6. Tour: NZ 1987-88. HS 76* La v Derbys (Blackpool) 1981. Wo HS 66* v Sussex (Hove) 1989. 50 wkts (5) inc 100 wkts (2); most – 109 (1987). BB 9-70 v Somerset (Worcester) 1986. **NWT:** HS 37 v Essex (Chelmsford) 1987. BB 3-20 La v Middx 1981 and 3-20 Wo v Sussex 1986. **BHC:** HS 40 v Glam (Worcester) 1990. BB 4-25 v Northants (Northampton) 1988. **RAL:** HS 48* La v Glam (Cardiff) 1981. BB 5-32 v Warwks (Worcester) 1987.

RHODES, Steven John (Lapage Middle S; Carlton-Bolling S, Bradford), b Bradford, Yorks 17 Jun 1964. Son of W.E. (Notts 1961-64). 5'7". RHB, WK. Yorkshire 1981-84. Worcestershire debut 1985. Cap 1986. LOI 3. Tours: SL 1985-86 (Eng B); Z 1989-90 (Eng A). HS 108 v Derbys (Derby) 1988. Shared record Worcs 6th-wkt stand of 265 with G.A.Hick v Somerset (Taunton) 1988. Award: BHC 1. **NWT:** HS 61 v Derbys (Worcester) 1989. **BHC:** HS 51* v Warwks (Birmingham) 1987. **RAL:** HS 48* v Kent (Worcester) 1989.

STEMP, Richard David (Brittania HS, Rowley Regis), b Erdington, Birmingham 11 Dec 1967. 6'0" RHB, SLA. Debut 1990. HS 3* and BB 1-32 v Yorks (Worcester) 1990. **RAL:** HS 3*.

TOLLEY, Christopher Mark (King Edward VI C, Stourbridge; Loughborough U), b Kidderminster 30 Dec 1967. 5'9". RHB, LMF. Debut 1989. HS 37 v Kent (Worcester) 1989. BB 2-66 v Somerset (Worcester) 1990. Award: BHC 1. **BHC:** HS 77 Comb Us v Lancs (Cambridge) 1990. BB 1-12. **RAL:** HS 1*. BB 1-18.

WESTON, Martin John (Samuel Southall SS), b Worcester 8 Apr 1959. 6'1". RHB, RM. Debut 1979. Cap 1986. 1000 runs (1): 1061 (1984). HS 145* v Northants (Worcester) 1984. BB 4-24 v Warwks (Birmingham) 1988. Awards: NWT 1; BHC 1. **NWT:** HS 98 v Somerset (Taunton) 1990. BB 4-30 v Suffolk (Worcester) 1984. **BHC:** HS 99* v Notts (Nottingham) 1990. BB 2-27 v Yorks (Bradford) 1985. **RAL:** HS 109 v Somerset (Taunton) 1982. BB 4-11 v Hants (Worcester) 1984.

WESTON, William Philip Christopher (Durham S), b Durham 16 Jun 1973. 6'3". Son of Mike Weston (England RU). LHB, LM. No 1st XI appearances – joined staff 1990.

NEWCOMER

MOODY, Thomas Masson (Guildford GS, WA), b Adelaide, Australia 2 Oct 1965. 6'6½". RHB, RM. W Australia 1985-89. Warwickshire 1990 (cap 1990). **Tests** (A): 4 (1989-90); HS 106 v SL (Brisbane) 1989-90. BB 1-23. LOI (A): 6. Tour (A): E 1989. 1000 runs (1+1); most – 1175 (1988-89). HS 202 WA v Victoria (Perth) 1988-89. BAC HS 168 Wa v Derbys (Derby) 1990 (on BAC debut). Scored 147 v CU (Cambridge) 1990 on Warwks debut. Scored 26-minute 100 for Wa v Glam (Swansea) 1990. BB 4-30 A v Kent (Canterbury) 1989. BAC BB 1-7. **NWT:** HS 58 Wa v Herts (St Albans) 1990. BB 1-7. **BHC:** HS 41 Wa v Worcs (Birmingham) 1990. **RAL:** HS 64 Wa v Sussex (Eastbourne) 1990. BB 2-42 Wa v Northants (Birmingham) 1990.

COUNTY CAPS AWARDED IN 1990

Derbyshire	S.J.Base, I.R.Bishop
Essex	M.A.Garnham
Glamorgan	I.V.A.Richards
Gloucestershire	M.W.Alleyne
Hampshire	D.I.Gower, T.C.Middleton
Kent	R.P.Davis, M.V.Fleming
Lancashire	I.D.Austin
Leicestershire	C.C.Lewis
Middlesex	K.R.Brown, M.R.Ramprakash, M.A.Roseberry, P.C.R.Tufnell
Northamptonshire	C.E.L.Ambrose, N.A.Felton, A.Fordham, M.A.Robinson
Nottinghamshire	J.A.Afford, K.P.Evans
Somerset	A.N.Hayhurst
Surrey	D.J.Bicknell, C.K.Bullen, M.A.Feltham, Waqar Younis, D.M.Ward
Sussex	N.J.Lenham
Warwickshire	T.M.Moody
Worcestershire	G.J.Lord
Yorkshire	none

WORCESTERSHIRE 1990

RESULTS SUMMARY

	Place	Won	Lost	Drew	Abandoned
Britannic Assurance Championship	4th	7	1	14	
All First-class Matches		7	2	15	
Refuge Assurance League	10th	7	8		1
NatWest Bank Trophy	Quarter-Finalist				
Benson and Hedges Cup	Finalist				

BRITANNIC ASSURANCE CHAMPIONSHIP AVERAGES

BATTING AND FIELDING

Cap		M	I	NO	HS	Runs	Avge	100	50	Ct/St
1986	G.A.Hick	19	33	8	252*	2273	90.92	8	13	24
1984	T.S.Curtis	21	38	8	197*	1650	55.00	4	6	13
1990	G.J.Lord	12	23	2	190	983	46.80	3	5	4
1978	P.A.Neale	19	29	9	122	934	46.70	2	3	12
1986	S.J.Rhodes	21	24	10	96	653	46.64	–	5	59/8
1987	G.R.Dilley	10	8	4	45*	185	46.25	–	–	2
1985	D.B.D'Oliveira	21	32	2	155	1179	39.30	2	7	33
1987	I.T.Botham	12	17	1	113	576	36.00	1	4	7
1986	R.K.Illingworth	20	19	6	117	452	34.76	1	2	7
1986	P.J.Newport	19	15	5	96	318	31.80	–	2	5
–	P.Bent	6	10	0	79	315	31.50	–	2	–
–	D.A.Leatherdale	4	6	0	70	154	25.66	–	2	2
1989	S.M.McEwan	13	10	3	54	163	23.28	–	1	4
1985	N.V.Radford	10	6	1	43*	104	20.80	–	–	4
1989	S.R.Lampitt	21	22	5	45*	286	16.82	–	–	10
–	C.M.Tolley	6	6	1	29	79	15.80	–	–	2
1986	M.J.Weston	5	8	1	38*	80	11.42	–	–	1

Also played: S.R.Bevins (1 match) 6* (3 ct); R.D.Stemp (2 matches) 3*, 0* (1 ct).

BOWLING

	O	M	R	W	Avge	Best	5wI	10wM
R.K.Illingworth	804.5	261	1946	71	27.40	5-59	1	–
S.M.McEwan	310	61	970	32	30.31	3-31	–	–
S.R.Lampitt	539.3	96	1794	57	31.47	5-34	2	–
P.J.Newport	563.2	104	1806	57	31.68	6-73	3	–
I.T.Botham	174.4	34	546	17	32.11	4-65	–	–
G.A.Hick	208.5	41	645	20	32.25	5-37	1	–
G.R.Dilley	224.2	30	818	24	34.08	5-62	2	–
N.V.Radford	245	38	999	14	71.35	4-55	–	–

Also bowled: T.S.Curtis 5.3-1-43-0; D.B.D'Oliveira 11.3-1-80-2; R.D.Stemp 45-14-123-1; C.M.Tolley 88-14-326-5; M.J.Weston 7-1-23-0.

The First-Class Averages (pp 166–181) give the records of Worcestershire players in all first-class county matches (their other opponents being the New Zealanders and MCC), with the exception of:
R.K.Illingworth 22-22-6-117-532-33.25-1-3-7ct. 834.5-272-1998-74-27.00-5/59-1-0.
S.R.Lampitt 22-24-5-45*-356-18.73-0-0-10ct. 539.3-96-1794-57-31.47-5/34-2-0.

WORCESTERSHIRE RECORDS

FIRST-CLASS CRICKET

Highest Total	For 633		v	Warwicks	Worcester	1906
	V 701-4d		by	Leics	Worcester	1906
Lowest Total	For 24		v	Yorkshire	Huddersfield	1903
	V 30		by	Hampshire	Worcester	1903
Highest Innings	For 405*	G.A.Hick	v	Somerset	Taunton	1988
	V 331*	J.D.B.Robertson	for	Middlesex	Worcester	1949

Highest Partnership for each Wicket

1st	309	F.L.Bowley/H.K.Foster	v	Derbyshire	Derby	1901
2nd	287*	T.S.Curtis/G.A.Hick	v	Glamorgan	Neath	1986
3rd	314	M.J.Horton/T.W.Graveney	v	Somerset	Worcester	1962
4th	281	J.A.Ormrod/Younis Ahmed	v	Notts	Nottingham	1979
5th	393	E.G.Arnold/W.B.Burns	v	Warwicks	Birmingham	1909
6th	265	G.A.Hick/S.J.Rhodes	v	Somerset	Taunton	1988
7th	205	G.A.Hick/P.J.Newport	v	Yorkshire	Worcester	1988
8th	177*	G.A.Hick/R.K.Illingworth	v	Somerset	Taunton	1988
9th	181	J.A.Cuffe/R.D.Burrows	v	Glos	Worcester	1907
10th	119	W.B.Burns/G.A.Wilson	v	Somerset	Worcester	1906

Best Bowling	For	9-23	C.F.Root	v	Lancashire	Worcester	1931
(Innings)	V	10-51	J.Mercer	for	Glamorgan	Worcester	1936
Best Bowling	For	15-87	A.J.Conway	v	Glos	Moreton in M	1914
(Match)	V	17-212	J.C.Clay	for	Glamorgan	Swansea	1937

Most Runs – Season	2,654	H.H.I.Gibbons	(av 52.03)		1934
Most Runs – Career	33,490	D.Kenyon	(av 33.19)		1946-1967
Most 100s – Season	10	G.M.Turner			1970
	10	G.A.Hick			1988
Most 100s – Career	72	G.M.Turner			1967-1982
Most Wkts – Season	207	C.F.Root	(av 17.52)		1925
Most Wkts – Career	2,143	R.T.D.Perks	(av 23.73)		1930-1955

LIMITED-OVERS CRICKET

Highest Total	NWT	404-3		v	Devon	Worcester	1987
	BHC	314-5		v	Lancashire	Manchester	1980
	RAL	307-4		v	Derbyshire	Worcester	1975
Lowest Total	NWT	98		v	Durham	Chester-le-St	1968
	BHC	81		v	Leics	Worcester	1983
	RAL	86		v	Yorkshire	Leeds	1969
Highest Innings	NWT	172*	G.A.Hick	v	Devon	Worcester	1987
	BHC	143*	G.M.Turner	v	Warwicks	Birmingham	1976
	RAL	147	G.M.Turner	v	Sussex	Horsham	1980
Best Bowling	NWT	6-14	J.A.Flavell	v	Lancashire	Worcester	1963
	BHC	6-8	N.Gifford	v	Minor C (S)	High Wycombe	1979
	RAL	6-26	A.P.Pridgeon	v	Surrey	Worcester	1978

YORKSHIRE

Formation of Present Club: 8 January 1863
Substantial Reorganisation: 10 December 1891
Colours: Dark Blue, Light Blue and Gold
Badge: White Rose
Championships (since 1890): (29) 1893, 1896, 1898, 1900, 1901, 1902, 1905, 1908, 1912, 1919, 1922, 1923, 1924, 1925, 1931, 1932, 1933, 1935, 1937, 1938, 1939, 1946, 1959, 1960, 1962, 1963, 1966, 1967, 1968. **Joint:** (1) 1949
NatWest Trophy/Gillette Cup Winners: (2) 1965, 1969
Benson and Hedges Cup Winners: (1) 1987
Sunday League Champions: (1) 1983
Match Awards: NWT 25; BHC 49

Asst. Secretary: D. Ryder, Headingley Cricket Ground, Leeds, LS6 3BU
(☎ 0532-787394)
Captain: M.D.Moxon
Scorer: E.I.Lester (home) and J.T.Potter (away)
1991 Beneficiary: K.Sharp

BATTY, Jeremy David (Bingley GS; Horsforth C), b Bradford 15 May 1971. 6'1". RHB, OB. Debut 1989. HS 21 v Middx (Leeds) 1990. BB 5-118 v Lancs (Scarborough) 1989 (on debut).

BERRY, Philip John (Saltscar CS; Longlands CFE, Redcar), b Saltburn 28 Dec 1966. 6'0". RHB, OB. Debut 1986. HS 31* v Northants (Leeds) 1990. BB 2-35 v CU (Cambridge) 1988. BAC BB 1-10.

BLAKEY, Richard John (Rastrick GS), b Huddersfield 15 Jan 1967. 5'9". RHB, WK. Debut 1985. Cap 1987. YC 1987. Tours: WI 1986-87 (Yorks); Z 1989-90 (Eng A). 1000 runs (3); most – 1361 (1987). HS 221 Eng A v Z (Bulawayo) 1989-90. Y HS 204* v Glos (Leeds) 1987. BB 1-68. Award: BHC 1. **NWT:** HS 22 v Surrey (Oval) 1989. **BHC:** HS 79 v Surrey (Oval) 1990. **RAL:** HS 100* v Glos (Cheltenham) 1990.

BYAS, David (Scarborough C), b Kilham 26 Aug 1963. 6'4". LHB, RM. Debut 1986. HS 117 v Kent (Scarborough) 1989. BB 3-55 v Derbys (Chesterfield) 1990. **NWT:** HS 54 v Scot (Leeds) 1989. BB 1-23. **BHC:** HS 36 v Surrey (Oval) 1990. BB 2-38 v Somerset (Leeds) 1989. **RAL:** HS 69* v Surrey (Leeds) 1989. BB 3-19 v Notts (Leeds) 1989.

CARRICK, Phillip (Bramley SS; Intake SS; Park Lane CPE), b Armley 16 Jul 1952. 5'11½". RHB, SLA. Debut 1970. Cap 1976. Captain 1987-89. Benefit 1985. E Province 1976-77. N Transvaal 1982-83. Tours: SA 1975-76 (DHR); WI 1986-87 (Yorks – capt); SL 1977-78 (DHR). HS 131* v Northants (Northampton) 1980. 50 wkts (10); most – 79 (1975). BB 8-33 v CU (Cambridge) 1973. BAC BB 8-72 v Derbys (Scarborough) 1975. Awards: NWT 1; BHC 1. **NWT:** HS 54 v Sussex (Leeds) 1986. BB 3-8 v Norfolk (Leeds) 1990. **BHC:** HS 53 v Warwks (Leeds) 1985. BB 3-40 v Warwks (Birmingham) 1984. **RAL:** HS 48* Worcs (Scarborough) 1989. BB 4-13 v Derbys (Bradford) 1983.

CHAPMAN, Colin Anthony (Beckfoot GS, Bingley; Bradford & Ilkley Art C), b Bradford 8 Jun 1971. 5'8½" RHB, WK. Debut 1990. HS 20 v Middx (Uxbridge) 1990. **RAL:** HS 36* v Middx (Scarborough) 1990.

DOIDGE, Matthew James (Benton Park S, Rawdon), b Horsforth 2 Jul 1970. 6'0". LHB, SLA. Debut 1990. HS –.

FLETCHER, Stuart David (Reins Wood SS), b Keighley 8 Jun 1964. 5'10". RHB, RMF. Debut 1983. Cap 1988. HS 28* v Kent (Tunbridge Wells) 1984. 50 wkts (1): 59 (1988). BB 8-58 v Essex (Sheffield) 1988. Award: NWT 1. **NWT:** HS 16* v Surrey (Oval) 1989. BB 3-20 v Berks (Finchampstead) 1988. **BHC:** HS 15* v Lancs (Leeds) 1990. BB 4-34 v Scot (Glasgow) 1987. **RAL:** HS 8. BB 4-11 v Kent (Canterbury) 1988.

GOUGH, Darren (Priory CS, Lundwood), b Barnsley 18 Sep 1970. 5'11". RHB, RMF. Debut 1989. HS 24 v Leics (Sheffield) 1990. BB 4-68 v Middx (Leeds) 1990. **NWT:** BB 2-22 v Norfolk (Leeds) 1990. **RAL:** HS 17* v Hants (Leeds) 1990. BB 1-29.

GRAYSON, Adrian Paul (Bedale CS), b Ripon 31 Mar 1971. 6'1". RHB, SLA. Debut 1990. HS 44* v Somerset (Scarborough) 1990. BB 1-55.

HARTLEY, Peter John (Greenhead GS; Bradford C), b Keighley 18 Apr 1960. 6'0". RHB, RMF. Warwickshire 1982. Yorkshire debut 1985. Cap 1987. Tour: WI 1986-87 (Yorks). HS 127* v Lancs (Manchester) 1988. 50 wkts (1): 52 (1990). BB 6-57 v Warwks (Sheffield) 1990. Awards: NWT 1; BHC 1. **NWT:** HS 52 and BB 5-46 v Hants (Southampton) 1990. **BHC:** HS 29* v Notts (Nottingham) 1986. BB 5-43 v Scot (Leeds) 1986. **RAL:** HS 51 v Northants (Tring) 1990. BB 5-38 v Worcs (Worcester) 1990.

HOUSEMAN, Ian James (Harrogate GS, Loughborough U), b Harrogate 12 Oct 1969. 5'10". RHB, RFM. Debut 1989. HS 18 v Sussex (Middlesbrough) 1989. BB 2-26 v Ind (Leeds) 1990. BAC BB –.

JARVIS, Paul William (Bydales CS, Marske), b Redcar 29 Jun 1965. 5'10". RHB, RFM. Debut 1981 aged 16yr 75d (youngest Yorkshire player). Cap 1986. Tests: 6 (1987-88 to 1989); HS 29* and BB 4-107 v WI (Lord's) 1988. LOI: 5. Tours: SA 1989-90 (Eng XI); WI 1986-87 (Yorks); NZ 1987-88; P 1987-88. HS 59* v Notts (Nottingham) 1989. 50 wkts (3); most – 81 (1987). BB 7-55 v Surrey (Leeds) 1986. **NWT:** HS 16 v Somerset (Leeds) 1985. BB 4-41 v Leics (Leeds) 1987. **BHC:** HS 42 v Lancs (Leeds) 1990. BB 4-43 v Northants (Lord's) 1987. **RAL:** HS 29* v Somerset (Taunton) 1987. BB 6-27 v Somerset (Taunton) 1989.

KELLETT, Simon Andrew (Whitcliffe Mount S), b Mirfield 16 Oct 1967. 6'2". RHB. Debut 1989. HS 75* v Warwks (Sheffield) 1990. **BHC:** HS 45 v Surrey (Oval) 1990. **RAL:** HS 32 v Derbys (Leeds) 1990.

METCALFE, Ashley Anthony (Bradford GS; University C, London), b Horsforth 25 Dec 1963. 5'8". RHB, OB. Debut 1983 scoring 122 v Notts (Bradford). Cap 1986. YC 1986. OFS 1988-89. Tour: WI 1986-87 (Yorks). 1000 runs (5) inc 2000 runs (1): 2047 (1990). HS 216* v Middx (Leeds) 1988. BB 2-18 v Warwks (Scarborough) 1987. Awards: NWT 1; BHC 4 (all 1987). **NWT:** HS 127* v Warwks (Leeds) 1990. BB 2-44 v Wilts (Trowbridge) 1987. **BHC:** HS 94* v Warwks (Birmingham) 1987. **RAL:** HS 115* v Glos (Scarborough) 1984.

MOXON, Martyn Douglas (Holgate GS, Barnsley), b Barnsley 4 May 1960. 6'0". RHB, RM. Debut 1981 scoring 5 and 116 v Essex (Leeds). Cap 1984. Captain 1990-. GW 1982-84. Tests: 10 (1986 to 1989); HS 99 v NZ (Auckland) 1987-88. LOI: 8. Tours: A 1987-88; WI 1986-87 (Yorks); NZ 1987-88; I 1984-85; SL 1984-85, 1985-86 (Eng B). 1000 runs (6); most – 1633 (1990). HS 218* v Sussex (Eastbourne) 1990. BB 3-24 v Hants (Southampton) 1989. Awards: NWT 4; BHC 4. **NWT:** HS 107* v Warwks (Leeds) 1990. BB 2-19 v Norfolk (Leeds) 1990. **BHC:** HS

106* v Lancs (Manchester) 1986. BB 1-6. **RAL:** HS 105 v Somerset (Scarborough) 1990. BB 3-29 v Sussex (Hove) 1990.

PICKLES, Christopher Stephen (Whitcliffe Mount CS), b Mirfield 30 Jan 1966. 6'1". RHB, RM. Debut 1985. HS 66 v Somerset (Taunton) 1989. BB 4-92 v Northants (Northampton) 1989. **NWT:** HS 3. BB 1-41. **BHC:** HS 13* v Scot (Glasgow) 1987. BB 1-42. **RAL:** HS 19 v Surrey (Oval) 1989. BB 4-36 v Somerset (Scarborough) 1990.

PRIESTLEY, Iain Martin (Priesthorpe SS, Farsley), b Horsforth 25 Sep 1967. 6'3". RHB, RMF. Debut 1989. HS 23 v Northants (Northampton) 1989. BB 4-27 v Notts (Leeds) 1989 (on debut).

ROBINSON, Phillip Edward (Greenhead GS, Keighley), b Keighley 3 Aug 1963. 5'9". RHB, LM. Debut 1984. Cap 1988. 1000 runs (2); most – 1402 (1990). HS 150* v Derbys (Scarborough) 1990. BB 1-10. Award: BHC 1. **NWT:** HS 66 v Middx (Leeds) 1986. **BHC:** HS 73* v Hants (Southampton) 1990. **RAL:** HS 78* v Leics (Leicester) 1985.

SHARP, Kevin (Abbey Grange HS), b Leeds 6 Apr 1959. 5'9". LHB, OB. Debut 1976. Cap 1982. Benefit 1991. GW 1981-84. Tour: WI 1986-87 (Yorks); NZ 1979-80 (DHR). 1000 runs (1): 1445 (1984). HS 181 v Glos (Harrogate) 1986. BB 2-13 v Glam (Bradford) 1984. **NWT:** HS 50 v Leics (Leeds) 1987. BB 4-40 v Wilts (Trowbridge) 1987. **BHC:** HS 105* v Scot (Leeds) 1986. **RAL:** HS 114 v Essex (Chelmsford) 1985.

SHAW, Christopher (Crofton HS), b Hemsworth 17 Feb 1964. 6'1". RHB, RFM. Debut 1984. HS 31 v Notts (Sheffield) 1988. BB 6-64 v Lancs (Leeds) 1987. **NWT:** HS 6*. BB 4-29 v Middx (Leeds) 1988. **BHC:** HS 4*. BB 2-30 v Minor C (Leeds) 1988. **RAL:** HS 26 v Glam (Leeds) 1984. BB 5-41 v Hants (Bournemouth) 1984.

SIDEBOTTOM, Arnold (Broadway GS, Barnsley), b Barnsley 1 Apr 1954. 6'1". RHB, RMF. Debut 1973. Cap 1980. Benefit 1988. OFS 1981-84. Tests: 1 (1985); HS 2 and BB 1-65 v A (Nottingham) 1985. Tours: SA 1981-82 (SAB); WI 1986-87 (Yorks). HS 124 v Glam (Cardiff) 1977. 50 wkts (3); most – 68 (1989). BB 8-72 v Leics (Middlesbrough) 1986. Awards: NWT 1; BHC 2. **NWT:** HS 45 v Hants (Bournemouth) 1977. BB 5-27 v Glam (Leeds) 1987. **BHC:** HS 32 v Notts (Leeds) 1983. BB 5-27 v Worcs (Bradford) 1985. **RAL:** HS 52* v Northants (Middlesbrough) 1982. BB 4-22 v Worcs (Worcester) 1987.

WHITE, Craig (Flora Hill HS, Bendigo, Australia; Bendigo HS), b Morley Hall 16 Dec 1969. 6'0". RHB, OB. Debut 1990. Scored 209* and 115* for Yorks II v Worcs II (Worcester) 1990. HS 38 v Northants (Northampton) 1990. BB 5-74 v Surrey (Harrogate) 1990. **BHC:** HS 17* v Hants (Southampton) 1990. BB 1-31. **RAL:** HS 30* v Warwicks (Birmingham) 1990. BB 2-49 v Kent (Canterbury) 1990.

NEWCOMER

ROBINSON, Mark Andrew (Hull GS), b Hull 23 Nov 1966. 6'3". RHB, RFM. Northamptonshire 1987-90 (cap 1990). Canterbury 1988-89. HS 19* Nh v Essex (Chelmsford) 1988. Failed to score in 12 successive f-c innings 1990 – world record. BB 4-19 Nh v Glam (Wellingborough) 1988. **NWT:** HS 3*. BB 4-32 Nh v Somerset (Taunton) 1989. **BHC:** HS 1. BB 3-20 Nh v Scot (Glasgow) 1989. **RAL:** HS 2. BB 2-23 Nh v Derbys (Northampton) 1990.

DEPARTURE – see p 156

YORKSHIRE 1990

RESULTS SUMMARY

	Place	Won	Lost	Drew	Abandoned
Britannic Assurance Championship	10th	5	9	8	
All First-class Matches		5	9	10	
Refuge Assurance League	6th	9	6		1
NatWest Bank Trophy	Quarter-Finalist				
Benson and Hedges Cup	3rd in Group C				

BRITANNIC ASSURANCE CHAMPIONSHIP AVERAGES

BATTING AND FIELDING

Cap		M	I	NO	HS	Runs	Avge	100	50	Ct/St
1986	A.A.Metcalfe	21	40	3	194*	1854	50.10	6	6	10
1982	K.Sharp	8	12	5	53*	316	45.14	–	1	1
–	A.P.Grayson	4	7	4	44*	135	45.00	–	–	2
1988	P.E.Robinson	22	38	7	150*	1389	44.80	1	12	18
1984	M.D.Moxon	19	36	5	218*	1353	43.64	2	6	13
–	S.A.Kellett	14	25	2	75*	699	30.39	–	6	7
–	C.S.Pickles	15	21	7	57*	424	30.28	–	2	6
1973	D.L.Bairstow	5	6	0	61	179	29.83	–	1	9
1987	R.J.Blakey	22	39	7	111	928	29.00	1	5	41/8
–	D.Byas	17	27	3	83	693	28.87	–	5	19
1980	A.Sidebottom	2	4	0	38	104	26.00	–	–	1
1976	P.Carrick	18	22	2	64	515	25.75	–	3	7
1986	P.W.Jarvis	15	16	4	43*	212	17.66	–	–	2
1987	P.J.Hartley	16	14	1	75	215	16.53	–	1	7
–	C.White	8	9	1	38	106	13.25	–	–	3
–	C.A.Chapman	2	4	0	20	47	11.75	–	–	2
–	D.Gough	13	16	5	24	116	10.54	–	–	1
–	J.D.Batty	7	5	2	21	30	10.00	–	–	4
1988	S.D.Fletcher	10	13	3	19	39	3.90	–	–	3
–	P.J.Berry	2	4	1	31*	45	–	–	–	1

Also played: I.J.Houseman (2 matches) 0*.

BOWLING

	O	M	R	W	Avge	Best	5wI	10wM
P.Carrick	601	173	1570	46	34.13	5-49	3	–
S.D.Fletcher	268.5	58	936	27	34.66	5-94	1	–
P.J.Hartley	481.1	79	1754	48	36.54	6-57	2	–
P.W.Jarvis	405.2	68	1393	37	37.64	4-53	–	–
D.Gough	256.4	43	984	24	41.00	4-68	–	–
C.S.Pickles	296.1	59	1107	25	44.28	3-56	–	–
J.D.Batty	195	29	722	12	60.16	4-76	–	–

Also bowled: P.J.Berry 44.3-4-172-2; D.Byas 69-14-253-3; A.P.Grayson 63-13-227-1; I.J.Houseman 30-6-129-0; A.A.Metcalfe 9.1-0-88-0; M.D.Moxon 57-9-175-3; P.E.Robinson 3.3-0-28-1; A.Sidebottom 44-9-121-4; C.White 122-12-519-9.

The First-Class Averages (pp 166–181) give the records of Yorkshire players in all first-class county matches (their other opponents being the Indians and the Zimbabweans), with the exception of D.L.Bairstow, whose full county figures are as above, and:

R.J.Blakey 24-42-8-111-993-29.20-1-6-44ct/8st. Did not bowl.
M.D.Moxon 21-39-6-218*-1621-49.12-3-7-14ct. 57-9-175-3-58.33-1/10.

YORKSHIRE RECORDS

FIRST-CLASS CRICKET

Highest Total	For	887		v Warwicks	Birmingham	1896
	V	630		by Somerset	Leeds	1901
Lowest Total	For	23		v Hampshire	Middlesbrough	1965
	V	13		by Notts	Nottingham	1901
Highest Innings	For	341	G.H.Hirst	v Leics	Leicester	1905
	V	318*	W.G.Grace	for Glos	Cheltenham	1876

Highest Partnership for each Wicket

1st	555	P.Holmes/H.Sutcliffe	v Essex	Leyton	1932
2nd	346	W.Barber/M.Leyland	v Middlesex	Sheffield	1932
3rd	323*	H.Sutcliffe/M.Leyland	v Glamorgan	Huddersfield	1928
4th	312	D.Denton/G.H.Hirst	v Hampshire	Southampton	1914
5th	340	E.Wainwright/G.H.Hirst	v Surrey	The Oval	1899
6th	276	M.Leyland/E.Robinson	v Glamorgan	Swansea	1926
7th	254	W.Rhodes/D.C.F.Burton	v Hampshire	Dewsbury	1919
8th	292	R.Peel/Lord Hawke	v Warwicks	Birmingham	1896
9th	192	G.H.Hirst/S.Haigh	v Surrey	Bradford	1898
10th	149	G.Boycott/G.B.Stevenson	v Warwicks	Birmingham	1982

Best Bowling	For	10-10	H.Verity	v Notts	Leeds	1932
(Innings)	V	10-37	C.V.Grimmett	for Australians	Sheffield	1930
Best Bowling	For	17-91	H.Verity	v Essex	Leyton	1933
(Match)	V	17-91	H.Dean	for Lancashire	Liverpool	1913

Most Runs – Season	2,883	H.Sutcliffe	(av 80.08)		1932
Most Runs – Career	38,561	H.Sutcliffe	(av 50.20)		1919-1945
Most 100s – Season	12	H.Sutcliffe			1932
Most 100s – Career	112	H.Sutcliffe			1919-1945
Most Wkts – Season	240	W.Rhodes	(av 12.72)		1900
Most Wkts – Career	3,608	W.Rhodes	(av 16.00)		1898-1930

LIMITED-OVERS CRICKET

Highest Total	NWT	317-4		v Surrey	Lord's	1965
	BHC	317-5		v Scotland	Leeds	1986
	RAL	271-7		v Middlesex	Scarborough	1990
Lowest Total	NWT	76		v Surrey	Harrogate	1970
	BHC	111		v Notts	Nottingham	1989
	RAL	74		v Warwicks	Birmingham	1972
Highest Innings	NWT	146	G.Boycott	v Surrey	Lord's	1965
	BHC	142	G.Boycott	v Worcs	Worcester	1980
	RAL	119	J.H.Hampshire	v Leics	Hull	1971
Best Bowling	NWT	6-15	F.S.Trueman	v Somerset	Taunton	1965
	BHC	6-27	A.G.Nicholson	v Minor C (N)	Middlesbrough	1972
	RAL	7-15	R.A.Hutton	v Worcs	Leeds	1969

ESSEX – (continued from p 71)

NEWCOMER

SALIM MALIK (Government C, Lahore), b Lahore, Pakistan 16 Apr 1963. 5'9". RHB, RM. Lahore 1978-86. Habib Bank 1982-90. **Tests** (P): 57 (1981-82 to 1989-90); HS 119* v NZ (Karachi) 1984-85; BB 1-3. LOI (P): 117. Tours (P): Eng 1982, 1987; A 1981-82, 1983-84, 1989-90; WI 1987-88; NZ 1984-85, 1988-89; I 1983-84, 1986-87; SL 1984-85 (P U-23), 1985–86. HS 140* Pak U-23 v SL U-23 (Kandy) 1984-85. BB 5-19 Habib Bank v Karachi (Karachi) 1985-86.

DEPARTURES

HARDIE, Brian Ross (Larbert HS), b Stenhousemuir, Stirlingshire 14 Jan 1950. Brother of K.M. (Scot 1966-76). 5'11". RHB, RM. Scotland 1970-72. Essex 1973-90 (cap 1974; benefit 1983). 1000 runs (11); most – 1522 (1975). HS 162 v Warwks (Birmingham) 1975 and 162 v Somerset (Southend) 1985. BB 2-39 v Glam (Ilford) 1979. Awards: NWT 1; BHC 2. **NWT:** HS 110 v Notts (Lord's) 1985. BB 1-16. **BHC:** HS 119* v Sussex (Hove) 1986. **RAL:** HS 109 v Northants (Colchester) 1986. BB 1-4.

LILLEY, Alan William (Caterham HS, Ilford), b Ilford 8 May 1959. 5'11". RHB, RM. Essex 1978-90, scoring 22 and 100* v Notts (Nottingham) on debut; cap 1986. MCC Cricket Staff. HS 113* v Derbys (Chelmsford) 1989. BB 3-116 v Glam (Swansea) 1985. Awards: NWT 1; BHC 1. **NWT:** HS 113 v Northumb (Jesmond) 1986. BB 2-19 v Scot (Chelmsford) 1984. **BHC:** HS 119 v Comb Us (Chelmsford) 1979. BB 1-4. **RAL:** HS 60 v Northants (Chelmsford) 1980. BB 2-0 v Glos (Bristol) 1984. Appointed Essex Youth Cricket Development Officer 1990.

THOMAS, Kevin Oliver (Wanstead HS), b Mile End, London 20 Jun 1963. 6'3". RHB, RFM. Essex 1990. HS 2.

WAUGH, Mark Edward (E Hills HS), b Canterbury, Sydney, Australia 2 Jun 1965. Twin of S.R. (NSW, Somerset and Australia). 6'1". RHB, RM. NSW 1985-90. Essex debut 1988. Cap 1989. Wisden 1990. LOI (A): 8. Tours: Z 1985-86, 1987-88 (NSW). 1000 runs (2+1) in 2000 (1): 2072 (1990). HS 207* v Yorks (Middlesbrough) 1990. BB 5-37 v Northants (Chelmsford) 1990. Award: BHC 1. **NWT:** HS 47 v Hants (Chelmsford) 1990. **BHC:** HS 93 v Lancs (Chelmsford) 1989. BB 1-25. **RAL:** HS 112* v Glam (Neath) 1989. BB 3-37 v Yorks (Middlesbrough) 1990.

GLOUCESTERSHIRE – DEPARTURES (continued from p 82).

JARVIS, Kevin Bertram Sidney (Springhead S, Northfleet; Thames Polytechnic) b Dartford, Kent 23 Apr 1953. 6'3". RHB, RFM. Kent 1975-87 (cap 1977; benefit 1987). Gloucestershire 1988-90. Tours: WI 1982-83 (Int); SL 1977-78 (DHR). HS 32 v Hants (Portsmouth) 1989. 50 wkts (7); most – 81 (1981). BB 8-97 K v Worcs (Worcester) 1978. Gs BB 5-15 v Glam (Bristol) 1989. Hat-trick 1987 (Kent). Awards: NWT 1; BHC 1. **NWT:** HS 5*. BB 5-32 v Oxon (Oxford) 1989. **BHC:** HS 4*. BB 4-34 K v Worcs (Lord's) 1976. **RAL:** HS 11 v Somerset (Bath) 1989. BB 5-24 K v Notts (Nottingham) 1985.

OWEN, Paul Andrew (Bedford Modern S), b Regina, Canada 9 Jun 1969. 5'9". RHB, SLA. Gloucestershire 1990. Bedfordshire 1989. HS 1. BB 2-37 v Surrey (Cheltenham) 1990.

POOLEY, Malcolm William (Pool S), b Truro, Cornwall 27 Jul 1969. 5'10". RHB, RM. Gloucestershire 1988-90. Cornwall 1986-87. HS 38 v Middx (Lord's) 1988. BB 4-80 v Kent (Bristol) 1988. **BHC:** BB 2-30 v Surrey (Oval) 1989. **RAL:** HS 8. BB 3-37 v Glam (Newport) 1989.

STOVOLD, Andrew WILLIS- (Filton HS; Loughborough C), b Bristol 19 Mar 1953. Brother of M.W. (Glos 1979-82). 5'8". RHB, WK. Gloucestershire 1973-90 (cap 1976; benefit 1987). OFS 1974-76. Tour: SL 1986-87 (Glos). 1000 runs (8); most – 1671 (1983). HS 212* v Northants (Northampton) 1982. BB 1-0. Awards: NWT 4; BHC 9. **NWT:** HS 104* v Ire (Bristol) 1988. **BHC:** HS 123 v Comb Us (Oxford) 1982. **RAL:** HS 98* v Kent (Cheltenham) 1977.

TEDSTONE, Geoffrey Alan (Warwick S; St Paul's C, Cheltenham), b Southport, Lancs 19 Jan 1961. 5'7". RHB, WK, occ OB. Warwickshire 1982-88. Gloucestershire 1989-90. HS 67* Wa v CU (Cambridge) 1983. BAC HS 51 Wa v Northants (Birmingham) 1987. Gs HS 50 v Surrey (Oval) 1989. **NWT:** HS 55* Wa v Glos (Bristol) 1987. **RAL:** HS 31* Wa v Glam (Swansea) 1987.

LEICESTERSHIRE – DEPARTURES (continued from p 104)

FERRIS, George John Fitzgerald (Jennings SS, Antigua), b Urlings Village, Antigua 18 Oct 1964. 6'3". RHB, RF. Leeward Is 1982-89. Leicestershire 1983-90 (cap 1988). Tours (WI B): Z 1983-84, 1986-87. HS 36* v Hants (Leicester) 1988. 50 wkts (3); most – 62 (1988). BB 7-42 v Glam (Hinckley) 1983. Hat-trick 1983. Award: BHC 1. **NWT:** HS 2*. BB 2-47 v Yorks (Leeds) 1987. **BHC:** HS 1*. BB 5-28 v Warwks (Leicester) 1988. **RAL:** HS 13* v Worcs (Leicester) 1988. BB 4-24 v Lancs (Manchester) 1988.

TAYLOR, Leslie Brian (Heathfield HS), b Earl Shilton 25 Oct 1953. 6'3½". RHB, RFM. Leicestershire 1977-90 (cap 1981; benefit 1989). Natal 1981-84. **Tests:** 2 (1985); HS 1* and BB 2-34 v A (Oval). LOI: 2. Tours: SA 1981-82 (SAB); WI 1985-86; Z 1980-81 (Leics). HS 60 v Essex (Chelmsford) 1988. 50 wkts (4); most – 75 (1981). BB 7-28 v Derbys (Leicester) 1981. Hat-trick 1979. Award: NWT 1. **NWT:** HS 6*. BB 4-14 v Norfolk (Norwich) 1985. **BHC:** HS 5. BB 6-35 v Worcs (Worcester) 1982. **RAL:** HS 15* v Somerset (Taunton) 1980. BB 5-20 v Northants (Luton) 1989.

MIDDLESEX – DEPARTURES (continued from p 109)

BUTCHER, Roland Orlando (Shephalbury SS, Stevenage), b East Point, Barbados 14 Oct 1953. 5'8". UK resident since 1967. RHB, RM. Middlesex 1974-90 (cap 1979; benefit 1989). Barbados 1974-75. Tasmania 1982-83. MCC Cricket Staff. **Tests:** 3 (1980-81); HS 32 v WI (Kingston) 1980-81. LOI: 3. Tours: WI 1980-81, 1982-83 (Int); P 1981-82 (Int); Z 1980-81 (Middx). 1000 runs (4); most – 1326 (1984). HS 197 v Yorks (Lord's) 1982. BB 2-37 v Glos (Cheltenham) 1986. Awards: NWT 2; BHC 2. **NWT:** HS 65 v Surrey (Oval) 1988. BB 1-18. **BHC:** HS 85 v Surrey (Oval) 1983. **RAL:** HS 100 v Glos (Lord's) 1983.

HEMSTOCK, Jason Richard (King's GS, Grantham; Grantham CFE), b Grantham, Lincs 13 Dec 1970. 6'2". LHB, LM. No f-c appearances. **BHC:** BB 2-37 v Minor C (Lord's) 1990.

TAYLOR, N.R. – see HAMPSHIRE.

THURSFIELD, M.J. – see HAMPSHIRE.

NOTTINGHAMSHIRE – DEPARTURES (continued from p 120).

LAING, Dean Ralph (Jeppe BHS; Rand Afrikaans U), b Durban, SA 18 Sep 1970. 5'10". Nephew of K.R. Cooper (Natal). RHB, RM. Transvaal 1989-90. Nottinghamshire 1990. HS 59 Transvaal v W Province (Cape Town) 1989-90. Nt HS 2. BB 3-35 Transvaal B v W Province B (Verwoerdburg) 1989-90.

SAXELBY, Kevin (Magnus GS), b Worksop 23 Feb 1959. 6'2". RHB, RMF. Elder brother of M. (Notts). Nottinghamshire 1978-90 (cap 1984). HS 59* v Derbys (Chesterfield) 1982. 50 wkts (1): 50 (1983). BB 6-49 v Sussex (Nottingham) 1987. Award: BHC 1. **NWT:** HS 12 v Worcs (Worcester) 1983. BB 4-28 v Middx (Nottingham) 1984. **BHC:** HS 13* v Lancs (Nottingham) 1982. BB 5-21 v Minor C (Nottingham) 1988. **RAL:** HS 23* v Middx (Cleethorpes) 1983. BB 6-30 v Leics (Leicester) 1989. 2nd XI captain 1991.

WARWICKSHIRE – DEPARTURES (continued from p 140).

HUMPAGE, Geoffrey William (Golden Hillock CS), b Sparkhill, Birmingham 24 Apr 1954. 5'9". RHB, WK, RM. Warwickshire 1974-90 (cap 1976; benefit 1987). OFS 1981-82. Wisden 1984. LOI: 3. Tour: SA 1981-82 (SAB). 1000 runs (11); most – 1891 (1984). HS 254 v Lancs (Southport) 1982, adding 470 with A.I.Kallicharran (English 4th-wicket record). BB 2-13 v Glos (Birmingham) 1980. Awards: NWT 2; BHC 2. **NWT:** HS 77 v Salop (Birmingham) 1984. **BHC:** HS 100* v Scot (Birmingham) 1984. BB 2-43 v Worcs (Worcester) 1980. **RAL:** HS 109* v Glos (Birmingham) 1984. BB 4-53 v Glos (Moreton) 1979.

KALLICHARRAN, Alvin Isaac (Port Mourant CS), b Paidama, British Guiana 21 Mar 1949. Brother of D.I. (Trinidad). 5'4". LHB, OB. Guyana 1966-81. Warwickshire 1971-90 (cap 1972; benefit 1983). Queensland 1977-78. Transvaal 1981-84. OFS 1984-88 (capt 1984-85). Wisden 1982. **Tests** (WI): 66 (1971-72 to 1980-81, 9 as captain); scored 100* and 101 in first two innings (v NZ); HS 187 v I (Bombay) 1979-80; BB 2-16 v NZ (Christchurch) 1979-80. LOI (WI): 31. Tours (WI): E 1973, 1976, 1980; A 1975-76, 1979-80; SA (WI XI) 1982-83, 1983-84; NZ 1979-80; Ind/SL 1974-75, 1978-79 (capt); P 1973-74 (RW), 1974-75, 1980-81. 1000 runs (12+1) inc 2000 runs (2); most – 2301 (1984). HS 243* v Glam (Birmingham) 1983. Shared record English 4th-wkt stand of 470 with G.W.Humpage v Lancs (Southport) 1982. BB 5-45 Transvaal v W Province (Cape Town) 1982-83. Wa BB 4-48 v Derbys (Birmingham) 1978. Awards: NWT 5; BHC 4. **NWT:** HS 206 and BB 6-32 v Oxon (Birmingham) 1984. **BHC:** HS 122* v Northants (Northampton) 1984. **RAL:** HS 104 v Yorks (Leeds) 1989. BB 3-32 v Lancs (Birmingham) 1985.

MOODY. T.M. – see WORCESTERSHIRE.

YORKSHIRE – DEPARTURE (continued from p 151).

BAIRSTOW, David Leslie (Hanson GS, Bradford), b Horton, Bradford 1 Sep 1951. 5'9½". RHB, WK, RM. Yorkshire 1970 (cap 1973; captain 1984-86; benefit 1982; testimonial 1990). GW 1976-78 (capt 1977-78). **Tests:** 4 (1979 to 1980-81); HS 59 v I (Oval) on debut. LOI: 21. Tours: A 1978-79, 1979-80; WI 1980-81, 1986-87 (Yorks). 1000 runs (3); most – 1181 (1985). HS 145 v Middx (Scarborough) 1980. BB 3-25 v MCC (Scarborough) 1987. BAC BB 1-16. Held 11 catches (equalling world f-c match record) v Derbys (Scarborough) 1982. Awards: NWT 1; BHC 7. **NWT:** HS 92 v Worcs (Leeds) 1982. **BHC:** HS 103* v Derbys (Derby) 1981. **RAL:** HS 83* v Surrey (Oval) 1986.

HAPPILY, THIS YEAR THE COMMUNITY WILL BE OVER £14,000,000 BETTER OFF

This year, as in previous years, NatWest is taking an active role in the community. Over £14,000,000 has already been committed in various forms to a wide range of environmental, social, arts and sporting projects all over the country.

Cash donations, and the secondment of around 100 of our senior staff to help with the day to day running of community projects, are just two of the ways in which this money is put to good use.

If our contribution helps the community in which we live and work, then we at NatWest believe it's money well spent.

NatWest

UNIVERSITY MATCH RESULTS

Played: 145   Wins: Cambridge 54;   Oxford 46.   Drawn: 45.   Abandoned: 1.

This, the oldest surviving first-class fixture, dates from 1827 and, wartime interruptions apart, it has been played annually since 1838. With the exception of five matches played in the area of Oxford (1829, 1843, 1846, 1848 and 1850), all the fixtures have been played at Lord's.

1827	Drawn	1884	Oxford	1937	Oxford
1829	Oxford	1885	Cambridge	1938	Drawn
1836	Oxford	1886	Oxford	1939	Oxford
1838	Oxford	1887	Oxford	1946	Oxford
1839	Cambridge	1888	Drawn	1947	Drawn
1840	Cambridge	1889	Cambridge	1948	Oxford
1841	Cambridge	1890	Cambridge	1949	Cambridge
1842	Cambridge	1891	Cambridge	1950	Drawn
1843	Cambridge	1892	Oxford	1951	Oxford
1844	Drawn	1893	Cambridge	1952	Drawn
1845	Cambridge	1894	Oxford	1953	Cambridge
1846	Oxford	1895	Cambridge	1954	Drawn
1847	Cambridge	1896	Oxford	1955	Drawn
1848	Oxford	1897	Cambridge	1956	Drawn
1849	Cambridge	1898	Oxford	1957	Cambridge
1850	Oxford	1899	Drawn	1958	Cambridge
1851	Cambridge	1900	Drawn	1959	Oxford
1852	Oxford	1901	Drawn	1960	Drawn
1853	Oxford	1902	Cambridge	1961	Drawn
1854	Oxford	1903	Oxford	1962	Drawn
1855	Oxford	1904	Drawn	1963	Drawn
1856	Cambridge	1905	Cambridge	1964	Drawn
1857	Oxford	1906	Cambridge	1965	Drawn
1858	Oxford	1907	Cambridge	1966	Oxford
1859	Cambridge	1908	Oxford	1967	Drawn
1860	Cambridge	1909	Drawn	1968	Drawn
1861	Cambridge	1910	Oxford	1969	Drawn
1862	Cambridge	1911	Oxford	1970	Drawn
1863	Oxford	1912	Cambridge	1971	Drawn
1864	Oxford	1913	Cambridge	1972	Cambridge
1865	Oxford	1914	Oxford	1973	Drawn
1866	Oxford	1919	Oxford	1974	Drawn
1867	Cambridge	1920	Drawn	1975	Drawn
1868	Cambridge	1921	Cambridge	1976	Oxford
1869	Cambridge	1922	Cambridge	1977	Drawn
1870	Cambridge	1923	Oxford	1978	Drawn
1871	Oxford	1924	Cambridge	1979	Cambridge
1872	Cambridge	1925	Drawn	1980	Drawn
1873	Oxford	1926	Cambridge	1981	Drawn
1874	Oxford	1927	Cambridge	1982	Cambridge
1875	Oxford	1928	Drawn	1983	Drawn
1876	Cambridge	1929	Drawn	1984	Oxford
1877	Oxford	1930	Cambridge	1985	Drawn
1878	Cambridge	1931	Oxford	1986	Cambridge
1879	Cambridge	1932	Drawn	1987	Drawn
1880	Cambridge	1933	Drawn	1988	Abandoned
1881	Oxford	1934	Drawn	1989	Drawn
1882	Cambridge	1935	Cambridge	1990	Drawn
1883	Cambridge	1936	Cambridge		

OXFORD v CAMBRIDGE
145th UNIVERSITY MATCH

Played at Lord's, London, on 4 (no play), 5, 6 July.
Toss: Cambridge. Result: MATCH DRAWN.

OXFORD UNIVERSITY

D.A.Hagan c James b Jenkins	8	Second Innings Forfeited
*R.E.Morris c Turner b Jenkins	21	
P.D.Lunn b Shufflebotham	35	
G.J.Turner c Jenkins b Shufflebotham	36	
M.A.Crawley c Johnson b Buzza	55	
D.M.Curtis run out	27	
W.M.van der Merwe st Turner b Buzza	50	
P.S.Gerrans c James b Shufflebotham	16	
S.D.Weale not out	4	
I.M.Henderson not out	0	
†R.W.D.Trevelyan did not bat		
Extras (B3, LB12, NB2)	17	
Total (8 wickets declared)	269	

CAMBRIDGE UNIVERSITY

S.P.James		c Hagan b Crawley	56
R.Heap		b Crawley	37
†R.J.Turner		run out	7
*J.C.M.Atkinson	First Innings	b Crawley	7
M.J.Lowrey	Forfeited	not out	18
M.J.Morris		not out	9
R.A.Pyman			
D.H.Shufflebotham		did not bat	
R.H.J.Jenkins			
A.J.Buzza			
S.W.Johnson			
Extras		(B3, LB7, NB2)	12
Total		(4 wickets)	146

CAMBRIDGE	O	M	R	W	O	M	R	W	FALL OF WICKETS				
										OU	CU	OU	CU
Johnson	16	1	48	0					Wkt	1st	1st	2nd	2nd
Jenkins	20	2	68	2					1st	13	–	–	87
Pyman	18	7	63	0					2nd	41	–	–	110
Shufflebotham	19	5	60	3					3rd	95	–	–	111
Buzza	8	1	15	2					4th	108	–	–	118
OXFORD									5th	175	–	–	–
van der Merwe					14	2	23	0	6th	238	–	–	–
Henderson					5	0	21	0	7th	263	–	–	–
Gerrans					13	0	37	0	8th	265	–	–	–
Crawley					17	4	46	3	9th	–	–	–	–
Lunn					2	1	9	0	10th	–	–	–	–

Umpires: D.J.Constant and K.E.Palmer.

CAMBRIDGE UNIVERSITY

ARSCOTT, Jonathan Paul (Tonbridge S; Magdalene C), b Tooting, London 4 Jul 1970. 5'10". RHB, WK. Debut 1990. HS 43* v Glos (Cambridge) 1990.

ATKINSON, Jonathon Colin Mark (Millfield S; Downing C), b Butleigh Somerset 10 July 1968. Son of C.R.M. (Somerset 1960-67). 6'3". RHB, RMF. Somerset 1985-89. CU 1988-90; blue 1988-89-90; captain 1990. HS 79 Sm v Northants (W-s-M) 1985 (on debut). BB 2-80 Sm v Ind (Taunton) 1986. NWT: BB 1-16. BHC: HS 24 Comb Us v Glos (Bristol) 1988. RAL: HS 69 Sm v Warwks (Birmingham) 1989.

BUZZA, Alan Jan (Redruth CS; Loughborough U; Hughes Hall), b Beverley, Yorks 3 Mar 1966. 6'0". RHB, SLA. Debut 1989; blue 1989-90. HS 25* v Notts (Cambridge) 1989. BB 6-102 v Kent (Cambridge) 1989. Cornwall debut 1985. Rugby blue (captain 1989-90).

DYER, Geoffrey Barry Alexander (The Glasgow Academy; Emmanuel C), b Glasgow 14 May 1969. 5'10". RHB, OB. Debut 1990. HS 23 v Middx (Cambridge) 1990.

HEAP, Russell (Calday Grange GS; Ipswich S; Magdalene C), b Leeds, Yorks 6 Dec 1968. 5'10". RHB. Debut 1988; blue 1989-90. HS 63 v Sussex (Hove) 1990.

HOOPER, Anthony Mark (Latymer Upper S; St John's C), b Perivale, Middx 5 Sep 1967. 5'7". RHB, RM. Debut 1987; blue 1987. HS 89 v OU (Lord's) 1987.

HUTCHINSON, Gordon Michael (Shrewsbury S; Robinson C), b Welshpool, Montgomerys 10 Feb 1969. Brother of I.J.F. (Middx). 6'1". RHB, RM. Debut 1990. HS 29 v Notts (Cambridge) 1990.

JAMES, S.P. - see GLAMORGAN.

JENKINS, Rory Harry John (Oundle S; Downing C), b Leicester 29 Jun 1970. 6'2". RHB, RM. Debut 1990; blue 1990. HS 19* v Sussex (Hove) 1990. BB 5-100 v Middx (Cambridge) 1990.

JOHNSON, Simon Wolseley (Newcastle RGS; Magdalene C), b Newcastle upon Tyne, Northumb 29 Jan 1970. 6'2". RHB, RMF. Debut 1990; blue 1990. HS 14* v Warwks (Cambridge) 1990. BB 2-86 v Northants (Cambridge) 1990.

LOWREY, Mark John (Radley C; Homerton C), b Hampstead, London 13 Sep 1971. 5'8". RHB, OB. Debut 1990; blue 1990. HS 72 v Sussex (Hove) 1990. BB 2-13 v Northants (Cambridge) 1990.

MORRIS, Michael John (Cherwell S, Oxford; Pembroke C), b Melbourne, Australia 8 Mar 1969. 5'10". RHB. Debut 1989; blue 1990. HS 45 v Derbys (Cambridge) 1990.

POINTER, Graham Alan (St Dunstan's C; St John's C), b Lewisham, London 2 May 1967. 6'3½". RHB, LMF. Debut 1987; blue 1987-88. HS 33 v OU (Lord's) 1987. BB 3-31 v Yorks (Cambridge) 1988.

PYMAN, Richard Anthony (Harrow S; Pembroke C), b Changi, Singapore 17 Apr 1968. 5'10". RHB, RM. Debut 1988; blue 1989-90. HS 69 v Notts (Cambridge) 1989. BB 5-43 v OU (Lord's) 1989. Eton fives half-blue.

SHUFFLEBOTHAM, David Howell (Cefnsaeson CS, Neath; Neath Tertiary C; Magdalene C), b Neath, Glam 11 Mar 1968. 5'8". RHB, RM. Debut 1989 – in Varsity match; blue 1989-90. HS 29 v Glos (Cambridge) 1990. BB 3-60 v OU (Lord's) 1990.

TURNER, Robert Julian (Millfield S; Magdalene C), b Malvern, Worcs 25 Nov 1967. 6'1½". RHB, WK. Brother of S.J. (Somerset 1984-85). Debut 1988; blue 1988-89-90; captain 1991. HS 58 v Kent (Cambridge) 1989. **BHC:** HS 25* Comb Us v Surrey (Oxford) 1990.

CAMBRIDGE UNIVERSITY 1990

RESULTS SUMMARY

	Played	Won	Lost	Drew
All first-class matches	10	1	4	5

FIRST-CLASS AVERAGES

BATTING AND FIELDING

	M	I	NO	HS	Runs	Avge	100	50	Ct/St
S.P.James	10	19	1	116	723	40.16	3	4	7
J.P.Arscott	2	4	1	43*	75	25.00	–	–	–/2
M.J.Lowrey	10	18	2	72	363	22.68	–	2	1
R.Heap	10	19	2	63	376	22.11	–	2	3
J.C.M.Atkinson	10	19	2	72	360	21.17	–	2	6
R.J.Turner	8	9	0	38	287	20.50	–	–	6/4
D.H.Shufflebotham	8	9	3	29	121	20.16	–	–	1
G.B.A.Dyer	4	8	2	23	107	17.83	–	–	–
S.W.Johnson	6	6	4	14*	35	17.50	–	–	2
M.J.Morris	10	17	3	45	206	14.71	–	–	4
R.A.Pyman	9	12	1	23*	94	8.54	–	–	2
R.H.J.Jenkins	9	12	5	19*	58	8.28	–	–	1
A.J.Buzza	9	11	2	21	49	5.44	–	–	2

Also played: A.M.Hooper (2 matches) 0, 0, 5 (1 ct); G.M.Hutchinson (2 matches) 29, 2; G.A.Pointer (1 match) 7, 9.

BOWLING

	O	M	R	W	Avge	Best	5wI	10wM
M.J.Lowrey	151.2	33	483	10	48.30	2-13	–	–
A.J.Buzza	257	42	955	18	53.05	4-108	–	–
R.A.Pyman	285.4	76	870	15	58.00	2-29	–	–
R.H.J.Jenkins	281.4	41	959	15	63.93	5-100	1	–
D.H.Shufflebotham	139	20	538	6	89.66	3-60	–	–

Also bowled: J.C.M.Atkinson 23-3-101-1; S.W.Johnson 113-14-452-3; G.A.Pointer 17-3-67-0.

The following appeared in other first-class matches in 1990: J.C.M.Atkinson, A.J. Buzza, S.P.James, R.A.Pyman and R.J.Turner for Combined Universities v New Zealanders; S.P.James also appeared in 5 matches for Glamorgan.

OXFORD UNIVERSITY

ALMAER, Simon Ashley (Ilford CHS; St Catherine's C), b Wanstead, Essex 12 Jul 1969. 6'0". RHB, RM. Debut 1988; blue 1988-89. HS 67 v Lancs (Oxford) 1988.

CHAUHAN, Sanjay (AFBB School; Delhi U; Kent U; Worcester C), b Delhi, India 12 Dec 1966. Second cousin of C.P.S. (India). 5'10". RHB, OB. Debut 1989. HS 25 and BB 1-58 v Leics (Oxford) 1990.

CRAWLEY, M.A. – see NOTTINGHAMSHIRE.

CURTIS, David Michael (Falcon C, Salisbury; Cape Town U; St Anne's C), b Salisbury, Rhodesia 10 Apr 1965. 5'10". RHB, LB. Debut 1990; blue 1990. Zimbabwe U-25. HS 43 v Glam (Oxford) 1990. Rugby blue.

DAVIES, Henry Richard (St Dunstan's C; Christ Church), b Camberwell, London 2 Sep 1970. 5'10". LHB, OB. Debut 1990. HS 24 and BB 3-93 v Hants (Oxford) 1990 – on debut.

GERRANS, Philip Simon (Daramalau C; Canberra U; Worcester C), b Melbourne, Australia 14 Oct 1959. 6'0". RHB, RSM. Debut 1990; blue 1990. HS 39 v Lancs (Oxford) 1990. BB 3-86 v Surrey (Oxford) 1990. Golf blue.

HAGAN, David Andrew (Trinity S, Leamington Spa; St Edmund Hall and Linacre C), b Wide Open, Northumb 25 Jun 1966. 5'9". RHB, OB. Debut 1985; blue 1986-88-89-90. HS 88 v Lancs (Oxford) 1986.

HENDERSON, Iain Mark (Laxton S, Oundle; Pembroke C), b Glapthorn, Northants 8 Sep 1967. 6'1". RHB, RMF. Debut 1987; blue 1987-89-90. HS 44 v Surrey (Oxford) 1990. BB 3-48 v Glos (Oxford) 1987.

KILBORN, Michael John (Farrer HS; U of NSW; St John's C), b Gunnedah, Australia 20 Sep 1962. 6'2". RHB, RM. Debut 1986; blue 1986-87-88; captain 1988. HS 95 v Lancs (Oxford) 1990. BB 3-37 v Hants (Oxford) 1988.

LUNN, Peter Daniel (Gosford Hill S, Kidlington; Abingdon S; New C), b Oxford 16 Apr 1970. 5'11". RHB, LB. Debut 1989; blue 1989-90. HS 61 v Surrey (Oxford) 1989. BB 1-34.

McGRADY, John Ewart (Ryton CS; St Catherine's C), b Ryton, Co Durham 30 Apr 1968. 5'10". RHB, WK. Debut 1990. HS 14 v Hants (Oxford) 1990.

MORRIS, Russell Edward (Dyffryn Conwy S, Llanrwst; Oriel C), b St Asaph, Flintshire, 8 Jun 1967. 5'8". RHB, RM. Debut 1987; blue 1987-89-90; captain 1990. HS 96 v Surrey (Oxford) 1990. Soccer blue.

RUSSELL, Mark John (Medina HS, IOW; Pembroke C), b Lincoln 18 Nov 1970. 5'10". RHB, RSM. Debut 1990. HS 4.

TREVELYAN, Robert William Dixey (Marlborough C; Pembroke C; Alexandria U), b Folkestone, Kent 28 Nov 1970. 5'10". RHB, WK. Debut 1990; blue 1990. HS 0.

TURNER, Graeme John (St Stithian's; Cape Town U; St Anne's C), b Bulawayo, Rhodesia 5 Aug 1964. 6'2". LHB, OB. W Province 1984-86. N Transvaal B 1986-88. SADF 1988-89. OU debut 1990; blue 1990; captain 1991. HS 69* WP B v Natal B (Cape Town) 1985-86. OU HS 59 v Hants (Oxford) 1990. BB 4-94 SADF v Boland (Windhoek) 1988-89. OU BB 3-100 v Lancs (Oxford) 1990.

VAN DER MERWE, Willem Mare (Grey C, Bloemfontein; Cape Town U; St Anne's C), b Rustenburg, SA 20 Jul 1960. 6'4". LHB, RMF. OFS 1978-84. W Province 1985-87. SADF but 1990; blue 1990. HS 96 OFS v N ransvaal B (Welkom) 1984-85.

OU HS 84 v Hants (Oxford) 1990. BB 5-35 WP B v Boland (Cape Town) 1985-86. OU BB 1-44. Rugby for WP and blue. Award: BHC 1. **BHC:** HS 27 and BB 2-34 v Yorks (Leeds) 1990.

WEALE, Simon David (Westminster City S; Keble C), b Knightsbridge, London 16 Sep 1967. 6'2". RHB, SLA. Debut 1986; blue 1987-88-90. HS 76 v CU (Lord's) 1987. BB 3-130 v Lancs (Oxford) 1988.

WINCHESTER, Angus Lewis Charles (Rugby S; St Catherine's C), b Newcastle upon Tyne, Northumb 28 Nov 1969. RHB, RM. Debut 1990. HS 0*.

OXFORD UNIVERSITY 1990

RESULTS SUMMARY

	Played	Won	Lost	Drew
All first-class matches	9	0	0	9

FIRST-CLASS AVERAGES

BATTING AND FIELDING

	M	I	NO	HS	Runs	Avge	100	50	Ct/St
M.A.Crawley	9	10	3	105*	620	88.57	2	5	8
W.M.van der Merwe	7	7	3	84	272	68.00	–	3	4
M.J.Kilborn	5	6	1	95	279	55.80	–	2	4
I.M.Henderson	6	4	3	44	46	46.00	–	–	2
R.E.Morris	8	10	1	96	370	41.11	–	4	1
P.D.Lunn	8	10	4	44*	184	30.66	–	–	1
G.J.Turner	8	10	0	59	258	25.80	–	2	4
D.M.Curtis	4	4	0	43	89	22.25	–	–	–
H.R.Davies	4	4	2	24	36	18.00	–	–	–
D.A.Hagan	9	12	0	47	175	14.58	–	–	2
P.S.Gerrans	8	7	0	39	95	13.57	–	–	3
S.D.Weale	5	4	2	13	24	12.00	–	–	–

Also played: S.A.Almaer (1 match) 4 (2 ct); S.Chauhan (3 matches) 25, 4; J.E.McGrady (6 matches) 14, 1 (2 st); M.J.Russell (4 matches) 4, 4, 2 (1 ct); R.W.D.Trevelyan (3 matches) 0 (2 ct); A.L.C.Winchester (1 match) 0*.

BOWLING

	O	M	R	W	Avge	Best	5wI	10wM
M.A.Crawley	190.2	30	673	17	39.58	6-92	1	–
G.J.Turner	177.2	36	680	10	68.00	3-100	–	–
P.S.Gerrans	181	31	618	9	68.66	3-86	–	–
I.M.Henderson	105.2	9	469	6	78.16	3-102	–	–

Also bowled: S.Chauhan 15-1-58-1; D.M.Curtis 1-0-8-0; H.R.Davies 54-6-261-3; P.D.Lunn 23-4-92-2; W.M.van der Merwe 112-23-341-3; S.D.Weale 50-8-251-1; A.L.C.Winchester 13-0-81-0.

The following appeared in other first-class matches in 1990: M.A.Crawley, P.S.Gerrans, M.J.Kilborn, R.E.Morris, G.J.Turner and W.M.van der Merwe for Combined Universities v New Zealanders; M.A.Crawley also appeared in one match for Lancashire.

FIRST-CLASS CRICKET

Highest Total	For	703-9d	v Sussex	Hove	1890
	V	730-3	by W Indians	Cambridge	1950
Lowest Total	For	30	v Yorkshire	Cambridge	1928
	V	32	by Oxford U	Lord's	1878
Highest Innings	For	254* K.S.Duleepsinhji	v Middlesex	Cambridge	1927
	V	304* E.de C.Weekes	for W Indians	Cambridge	1950

Highest Partnership for each Wicket

1st	349	J.G.Dewes/D.S.Sheppard	v Sussex	Hove	1950
2nd	429*	J.G.Dewes/G.H.G.Doggart	v Essex	Cambridge	1949
3rd	284	E.T.Killick/G.C.Grant	v Essex	Cambridge	1929
4th	275	R.de W.K.Winlaw/J.H.Human	v Essex	Cambridge	1934
5th	220	R.Subba Row/F.C.M.Alexander	v Notts	Nottingham	1953
6th	245	J.L.Bryan/C.T.Ashton	v Surrey	The Oval	1921
7th	289	G.Goonesena/G.W.Cook	v Oxford U	Lord's	1957
8th	145	H.Ashton/A.E.R.Gilligan	v F Foresters	Cambridge	1920
9th	200	G.W.Cook/C.S.Smith	v Lancashire	Liverpool	1957
10th	177	A.E.R.Gilligan/J.H.Naumann	v Sussex	Hove	1919

Best Bowling	For	10-69	S.M.J.Woods	v C.I.T's XI†	Cambridge	1890
(Innings)	V	10-38	S.E.Butler	for Oxford U	Lord's	1871
Best Bowling	For	15-88	S.M.J.Woods	v C.I.T's XI†	Cambridge	1890
(Match)	V	15-95	S.E.Butler	for Oxford U	Lord's	1871

Most Runs – Season	1,581	D.S.Sheppard	(av 79.05)	1952
Most Runs – Career	4,310	J.M.Brearley	(av 38.48)	1961-1968
Most 100s – Season	7	D.S.Sheppard		1952
Most 100s – Career	14	D.S.Sheppard		1950-1952
Most Wkts – Season	80	O.S.Wheatley	(av 17.63)	1958
Most Wkts – Career	208	G.Goonesena	(av 21.82)	1954-1957

UNIVERSITY MATCH RECORDS

Highest Total	432-9d		1936
Lowest Total	39		1858
Highest Innings	211	G.Goonesena	1957
Best Bowling (Innings)	8-44	G.E.Jeffery	1873
Best Bowling (Match)	13-73	A.G.Steel	1878
Hat-Tricks	F.C.Cobden (1870), A.G.Steel (1879), P.H.Morton		
	(1880), J.F.Ireland (1911), R.G.H.Lowe (1926)		
Match Double	No instance		

†C.I.Thornton's XI

OXFORD UNIVERSITY RECORDS

FIRST-CLASS CRICKET

Highest Total	For	651		v Sussex	Hove	1895
	V	679-7d		by Australians	Oxford	1938
Lowest Total	For	12		v MCC	Oxford	1877
	V	24		by MCC	Oxford	1846
Highest Innings	For	281	K.J.Key	v Middlesex	Chiswick Park	1887
	V	338	W.W.Read	for Surrey	The Oval	1888

Highest Partnership for each Wicket

1st	338	T.Bowring/H.Teesdale	v Gentlemen	Oxford	1908
2nd	226	W.G.Keighley/H.A.Pawson	v Cambridge U	Lord's	1947
3rd	273	F.C.de Saram/N.S.M.Innes†	v Glos	Oxford	1934
4th	276	P.G.T.Kingsley/N.M.Ford	v Surrey	The Oval	1930
5th	256*	A.A.Baig/C.A.Fry	v F Foresters	Oxford	1959
6th	270	D.R.Walsh/S.A.Westley	v Warwicks	Oxford	1969
7th	340	K.J.Key/H.Philipson	v Middlesex	Chiswick Park	1887
8th	160	H.Philipson/A.C.M.Croome	v MCC	Lord's	1889
9th	157	H.M.G-Wells‡/C.K.H.Hill-Wood	v Kent	Oxford	1928
10th	149	F.H.Hollins/B.A.Collins	v MCC	Oxford	1901

Best Bowling	For	10-38	S.E.Butler	v Cambridge U	Lord's	1871
(Innings)	V	10-49	W.G.Grace	for MCC	Oxford	1886
Best Bowling	For	15-65	B.J.T.Bosanquet	v Sussex	Oxford	1900
(Match)	V	16-225	J.E.Walsh	for Leics	Oxford	1953

Most Runs – Season	1,307	Nawab of Pataudi, sr	(av 93.35)	1931
Most Runs – Career	3,319	N.S.Mitchell-Innes	(av 47.41)	1934-1937
Most 100s – Season	6	Nawab of Pataudi, sr		1931
Most 100s – Career	9	A.M.Crawley		1927-1930
	9	Nawab of Pataudi, sr		1928-1931
	9	N.S.Mitchell-Innes		1934-1937
	9	M.P.Donnelly		1946-1947
Most Wkts – Season	70	I.A.R.Peebles	(av 18.15)	1930
Most Wkts – Career	182	R.H.B.Bettington	(av 19.38)	1920-1923

UNIVERSITY MATCH RECORDS

Highest Total	503		1900
Lowest Total	32		1878
Highest Innings	238*	Nawab of Pataudi, sr	1931
Best Bowling (Innings)	10-38	S.E.Butler	1871
Best Bowling (Match)	15-95	S.E.Butler	1871
Hat-Trick	No instance		
Match Doubles	160 and 11-66	P.R.le Couteur	1910
	149 and 10-93	G.J.Toogood	1985

†N.S.Mitchell-Innes   ‡H.M.Garland-Wells

1990 FIRST-CLASS AVERAGES

These averages include performances in all first-class matches played in the British Isles in 1990.

'Cap' denotes the season in which the player was awarded a 1st XI cap by the county he represented in 1990.

Team abbreviations: CU – Cambridge University; D – Derbyshire; E – England; Ex – Essex; Gm – Glamorgan; Gs – Gloucestershire; H – Hampshire; Ind – India(ns); Ire – Ireland; K – Kent; La – Lancashire; Le – Leicestershire; M – Middlesex; MC – Minor Counties; MCC – Marylebone Cricket Club; Nh – Northamptonshire; Nt – Nottinghamshire; NZ – New Zealand(ers); OU – Oxford University; Sc – Scotland; SL – Sri Lankans; Sm – Somerset; Sy – Surrey; Sx – Sussex; T – Test & County Cricket Board XI; Us – Combined (Oxbridge) Universities; W – World XI; Wa – Warwickshire; Wo – Worcestershire; Y – Yorkshire; Z – Zimbabweans.

† Left-handed batsman.

BATTING AND FIELDING

	Cap	M	I	NO	HS	Runs	Avge	100	50	Ct/St
Adams, C.J. (D)	—	23	34	4	111*	932	31.06	2	5	25
Afford, J.A. (Nt)	1990	22	22	7	5	16	1.06	–	–	7
Agnew, J.P. (Le)	1984	22	26	5	46*	257	12.23	–	–	5
†Ahangama F.S. (SL)	—	1	–	–	–	–	–	–	–	–
Alikhan, R.I. (Sy)	—	11	16	2	138	726	51.85	2	4	3
Alleyne, M.W. (Gs)	1990	13	21	0	256	854	40.66	2	3	11
Allott, P.J.W. (La)	1981	13	6	2	55*	114	28.50	–	1	10
Almaer, S.A. (OU)	—	1	1	0	4	4	4.00	–	–	2
†Ambrose, C.E.L. (Nh)	1990	15	18	5	55*	203	15.61	–	1	1
Andrew, S.J.W. (Ex)	—	18	16	7	35	119	13.22	–	–	1
Anthony, H.A.G. (Gm)	—	6	8	0	39	127	15.87	–	–	–
†Arnold, K.A. (MC)	—	1	–	–	–	–	–	–	–	2
Arnott, K.J. (Z)	—	1	2	0	2	2	1.00	–	–	–
Arscott, J.P. (CU)	—	2	4	1	43*	75	25.00	–	–	–/2
Asif Din (Wa)	1987	22	39	4	100*	974	27.82	1	5	10
Atapattu, M.S. (SL)	—	6	8	4	74*	241	60.25	–	2	7
Atherton, M.A. (La/MCC/E)	1989	20	31	4	191	1924	71.25	7	12	24
Athey, C.W.J. (Gs)	1985	23	35	7	131	1474	52.64	3	9	18
Atkins, P.D. (Sy)	—	1	2	1	23	23	23.00	–	–	–
Atkinson, J.C.M. (CU/Us)	—	11	21	2	72	374	19.68	–	2	7
†Austin, I.D. (La)	1990	13	15	6	58	276	30.66	–	1	–
Ayling, J.R. (H)	—	9	11	3	62*	368	46.00	–	3	2
Aymes, A.N. (H)	—	5	8	4	75*	317	79.25	–	3	9/3
Azharuddin, M. (Ind)	—	9	11	1	179	770	77.00	3	3	3
†Babington, A.M. (Sx)	—	3	2	0	20	28	14.00	–	–	2
Bailey, R.J. (Nh)	1985	23	39	8	204*	1987	64.09	7	9	16
Bainbridge, P. (Gs)	1981	20	28	3	152	1107	44.28	2	5	4
Bairstow, D.L. (Y/W)	1973	6	6	0	61	179	29.83	–	1	13
Bakker, P.-J. (H)	1989	16	9	4	20	95	19.00	–	–	3
Ball, M.C.J. (Gs)	—	4	5	0	15	39	7.80	–	–	4
Barnes, S.N. (Gs)	—	10	9	2	12*	23	3.28	–	–	3
Barnett, K.J. (D)	1982	24	39	6	141	1648	49.93	5	9	14
Bartlett, R.J. (Sm)	—	1	2	0	73	85	42.50	–	1	–
Barwick, S.R. (Gm)	1987	5	2	2	2*	2	–	–	–	–
Base, S.J. (D)	1990	13	13	2	58	215	19.54	–	2	4
Bastien, S. (Gm)	—	12	9	3	12	47	7.83	–	–	–
Batty, J.D. (Y)	—	7	5	2	21	30	10.00	–	–	4
Bee, A. (Sc)	—	1	1	1	29*	29	–	–	–	–

	Cap	M	I	NO	HS	Runs	Avge	100	50	Ct/St
Bell, R.M. (Gs)	—	2	2	1	0*	0	0.00	–	–	–
Benjamin, J.E. (Wa)	—	15	14	7	41	188	26.85	–	–	4
Benjamin, W.K.M. (Le)	1989	12	15	2	101*	437	33.61	1	4	3
Benson, J.D.R. (Le)	—	18	27	6	106	725	34.52	1	3	12
†Benson, M.R. (K/MCC)	1981	16	25	1	159	1171	48.79	5	5	5
Bent, P. (Wo)	—	7	12	0	79	346	28.83	–	2	–
Berry, P.J. (Y)	—	2	4	3	31*	45	–	–	–	1
Bevins, S.R. (Wo)	—	2	3	1	10	17	8.50	–	–	6
†Bicknell, D.J. (Sy)	1990	15	23	4	186	1317	69.31	5	6	2
Bicknell, M.P. (Sy/T)	1989	21	16	8	50*	310	38.75	–	1	8
Bishop, I.R. (D)	1990	13	16	4	103*	333	27.75	1	–	2
Blakey, R.J. (Y/T)	1987	25	43	9	111	1033	30.38	1	6	45/9
Boon, T.J. (Le)	1986	24	45	4	138	1539	37.53	2	11	13
†Booth, P.A. (Wa)	—	10	16	2	60	240	17.14	–	2	3
Botham, I.T. (Wo)	1987	13	18	1	113	595	35.00	1	4	7
Bowler, P.D. (D)	1989	22	39	5	210	1428	42.00	3	7	17
Bracewell, J.G. (NZ)	—	8	8	3	40*	169	33.80	–	–	5
Bramhall, S. (La)	—	2	3	2	1*	1	1.00	–	–	2/1
Brandes, E.A. (Z)	—	2	3	1	22	40	20.00	–	–	1
†Brent, J.P. (Z)	—	2	4	2	34*	101	50.50	–	–	–
Briant, G.A. (Z)	—	2	3	0	69	109	36.33	–	1	1
Briers, N.E. (Le)	1981	24	44	4	176	1996	49.90	5	11	7
†Broad, B.C. (Nt)	1984	22	43	2	227*	2226	54.29	9	3	7
Brown, A.M. (D)	—	8	12	2	139*	413	41.30	1	1	7
Brown, G.K. (MC)	—	1	2	1	103	192	192.00	1	1	–
Brown, K.R. (M)	1990	24	36	8	200*	1505	53.75	5	8	30
Brown, S.J. (Nh)	—	4	2	1	4*	6	6.00	–	–	2
Bunting, R.A. (Sx)	—	15	13	5	24*	85	10.62	–	–	2
Burn, P. (MC)	—	1	2	1	47*	47	47.00	–	–	–
†Burns, N.D. (Sm)	1987	24	34	10	166	951	39.62	1	5	43/1
Butchart, I.P. (Z)	—	3	5	1	71	115	28.75	–	1	–
†Butcher, A.R. (Gm)	1987	23	41	5	151*	2116	58.77	6	15	8
Butcher, I.P. (Gs)	—	12	19	4	102	513	34.20	1	2	4
Butcher, R.O. (M)	1979	2	4	2	32	83	41.50	–	–	3
Buzza, A.J. (CU/Us)	—	10	12	3	21	49	5.44	–	–	3
†Byas, D. (Y)	—	19	29	4	83	704	28.16	–	5	21
†Cann, M.J. (Gm)	—	6	10	0	64	206	20.60	–	2	2
Capel, D.J. (Nh)	1986	18	29	6	123	1092	47.47	3	7	16
Carrick, P. (Y)	1976	18	22	2	64	515	25.75	–	3	7
Chapman, C.A. (Y)	—	2	4	0	20	47	11.75	–	–	2
Chauhan, S. (OU)	—	3	2	0	25	29	14.50	–	–	–
†Childs, J.H. (Ex)	1986	23	16	5	26	123	11.18	–	–	7
†Clinton, G.S. (Sy)	1980	20	32	4	146	1292	46.14	1	8	6
Cohen, M.F. (Ire)	—	1	2	0	60	75	37.50	–	1	–
Connor, C.A. (H)	1988	22	10	4	46	148	24.66	–	–	10
Cook, G. (Nh)	1975	9	12	1	87	287	26.09	–	1	2
Cook, N.G.B. (Nh)	1987	19	19	8	30	143	13.00	–	–	10
Cook, S.J. (Sm)	1989	24	41	7	313*	2608	76.70	9	11	10
†Cooper, K.E. (Nt)	1980	21	26	6	35*	227	11.35	–	–	9
Cork, D.G. (D)	—	2	2	1	7	9	9.00	–	–	–
Cottey, P.A. (Gm)	—	20	35	5	156	1001	33.36	3	4	12
Cowans, N.G. (M/MCC)	1984	18	17	7	46*	127	12.70	–	–	3
Cowdrey, C.S. (K)	1979	13	24	6	107*	733	40.72	3	2	9
Cowdrey, G.R. (K)	1988	22	39	6	135	1576	47.75	3	8	9
Cowley, N.G. (Gm)	—	14	17	4	76	536	41.23	–	6	9

	Cap	M	I	NO	HS	Runs	Avge	100	50	Ct/St
†Cox, R.M.F. (H)	—	4	7	2	104*	220	44.00	1	—	3
Crawley, J.P. (La)	—	3	1	—	76*	103	51.50	—	1	1
Crawley, M.A. (OU/Us/La)	—	11	14	3	105*	762	69.27	2	5	9
Croft, R.D.B. (Gm)	—	16	26	11	91*	672	44.80	—	4	2
Crowe, J.J. (NZ)	—	8	15	4	132	493	44.81	1	2	6
Crowe, M.D. (NZ)	—	9	13	3	123*	537	53.70	1	5	5
Curran, K.M. (Gs)	1985	23	33	8	144*	1267	50.68	3	5	15
Curtis, D.M. (OU)	—	4	4	0	43	89	22.25	—	—	—
Curtis, T.M. (Wo)	1984	22	39	8	197*	1731	55.83	4	7	13
Dale, A. (Gm)	—	9	14	0	92	229	16.35	—	1	6
†Davies, H.R. (OU)	—	4	4	2	24	36	18.00	—	—	1
Davies, M. (Gm)	—	1	1	1	5*	5	—	—	—	—
Davis, R.P. (K)	1990	24	32	3	59	504	17.37	—	2	27
Davis, W.W. (Nh)	1987	9	7	1	47	101	16.83	—	—	2
DeFreitas, P.A.J. (La/E)	1989	18	20	3	102	660	38.82	2	2	7
Dennis, S.J. (Gm)	—	14	8	1	6	23	3.28	—	—	3
Derrick, J. (Gm)	1988	1	1	1	28*	28	—	—	—	—
De Silva, P.A. (SL)	—	6	12	4	221*	563	70.37	1	3	10
De Villiers, P.S. (K)	—	12	15	3	37	264	22.00	—	—	6
†Dilley, G.R. (Wo)	1987	10	8	4	45*	185	46.25	—	—	2
Dobson, M.C. (K)	—	1	2	0	6	6	3.00	—	—	—
Dodemaide, A.I.C. (Sx)	1989	24	38	8	112	1001	33.36	2	4	9
†Doidge, M.J. (Y)	—	1	—	—	—	—	—	—	—	—
D'Oliveira, D.B. (Wo)	1985	23	35	2	155	1263	38.27	2	7	33
Dolphin, D.F. (Z)	—	2	1	0	25	25	25.00	—	—	1
Donald, A.A. (Wa)	1989	16	22	6	25*	148	9.25	—	—	4
Donelan, B.T.P. (Sx)	—	11	13	6	·53	211	30.14	—	1	4
Downton, P.R. (M)	1981	16	24	2	63	587	26.68	—	4	42/3
Dube, L.E. (Z)	—	2	2	1	0	1	1.00	—	—	1
Duers, K.G. (Z)	—	2	1	1	11*	11	—	—	—	—
Dunlop, A.R. (Ire)	—	1	1	0	56	56	56.00	—	1	1
Dyer, G.B.A. (CU)	—	4	8	2	23	107	17.83	—	—	—
Ealham, M.A. (K)	—	2	2	1	13*	13	13.00	—	—	1
†Ellison, R.M. (K)	1983	15	19	7	81	473	39.41	—	3	6
Emburey, J.E. (M)	1977	23	32	7	111*	702	28.08	1	2	33
Evans, K.P. (Nt)	1990	15	25	9	100*	738	46.12	1	4	13
Evans, R.A. (MC)	—	1	1	1	4*	4	—	—	—	—
Evans, R.J. (Nt)	—	3	5	2	21*	37	12.33	—	—	1
†Fairbrother, N.H. (La/E)	1985	22	32	7	366	1740	69.60	4	9	20
Farbrace, P. (M)	—	8	8	2	79	124	20.66	—	1	17/2
Feltham, M.A. (Sy)	1990	15	16	3	101	379	29.15	1	2	11
†Felton, N.A. (Nh)	1990	22	39	2	122	1538	41.56	4	9	19
Ferris, G.J.F. (Le)	1988	6	6	0	35	104	17.33	—	1	1
Field-Buss, M.G. (Nt)	—	3	2	0	0	0	0.00	—	—	—
†Fitton, J.D. (La)	—	15	13	5	25*	133	16.62	—	—	3
Fleming, M.V. (K)	1990	19	32	6	102	980	37.69	1	5	6
Fletcher, S.D. (Y)	1988	11	13	3	19	39	3.90	—	—	3
Flower, G.W. (Z)	—	2	4	1	65	97	32.33	—	1	4*
†Folland, N.A. (MC)	—	1	2	0	82	108	54.00	—	1	—
Folley, I. (La)	1987	3	2	1	47*	52	52.00	—	—	—
Fordham, A. (Nh)	1990	24	42	2	206*	1767	44.17	4	9	22
Foster, N.A. (Ex)	1983	22	22	2	101	530	26.50	1	2	13
Fothergill, A.R. (MC)	—	1	1	0	3	3	3.00	—	—	—
†Fowler, G. (La)	1981	21	35	6	126	938	32.34	2	2	13
Franklin, T.J. (NZ)	—	11	17	1	103	731	45.68	2	5	3
Fraser, A.R.C. (M/E)	1988	15	13	2	92	214	19.45	—	1	3

	Cap	M	I	NO	HS	Runs	Avge	100	50	Ct/St
French, B.N. (Nt)	1980	22	34	9	105*	506	20.24	1	–	46/11
Frost, M. (Gm)	–	20	18	8	12	42	4.20	–	–	2
Gallian, J.E.R. (La)	–	1	1	1	17*	17	–	–	–	–
Garnham, M.A. (Ex)	1990	24	28	7	84*	615	29.28	–	2	48/2
Gatting, M.W. (M)	1977	23	37	7	170*	1704	56.80	4	9	20
Gerrans, P.S. (OU/Us)	–	9	9	0	39	102	11.33	–	–	4
†Gidley, M.I. (Le)	–	5	5	1	73	113	28.25	–	1	2
Goldsmith, S.C. (D)	–	12	17	1	51	267	16.68	–	1	9
Gooch, G.A. (Ex/E)	1975	18	30	3	333	2746	101.70	12	8	16
Gough, D. (Y)	–	14	17	6	24	123	11.18	–	–	1
†Gould, I.J. (Sx)	1981	8	12	2	73	235	23.50	–	2	8
Govan, J.W. (Nh)	–	3	4	0	17	41	10.25	–	–	–
†Gower, D.I. (H/E)	1990	20	32	5	157*	1263	46.77	3	3	17
Graveney, D.A. (Gs)	1976	13	13	4	46*	107	11.88	–	–	7
Gray, A.H. (Sy)	1985	7	2	0	11	22	11.00	–	–	3
Grayson, P.A. (Y)	–	5	8	4	44*	145	36.25	–	–	2
†Greatbatch, M.J. (NZ/W)	–	11	16	3	168*	744	57.23	2	4	7
Green, S.J. (Wa)	–	1	2	0	44	44	22.00	–	–	–
Greenfield, K. (Sx)	–	3	6	2	102*	230	57.50	1	1	3
Greenidge, C.G. (W)	–	1	2	0	23	23	11.50	–	–	1
Greensword, S. (MC)	–	1	1	0	1	1	1.00	–	–	–
Greig, I.A. (Sy)	1987	24	29	6	291	1259	54.73	2	5	16
Griffith, F.A. (D)	–	1	1	0	1	1	1.00	–	–	–
†Gurusinha, A.P. (SL)	–	3	6	3	58	138	46.00	–	1	–
†Hadlee, Sir R.J. (NZ)	–	5	6	0	90	204	34.00	–	2	4
Hagan, D.A. (OU)	–	9	12	0	47	175	14.58	–	–	2
Haggo, D.J. (Sc)	–	1	1	0	34	34	34.00	–	–	–/2
Hall, J.W. (Sx)	–	20	37	2	125	1140	32.57	2	5	6
Hallett, J.C. (Sm)	–	3	1	0	0	0	–	–	0.00	–
Hanley, R. (Sx)	–	2	4	0	28	32	8.00	–	–	–
Hansford, A.R. (Sx)	–	4	6	1	29	55	11.00	–	–	1
Harden, R.J. (Sm)	1989	24	31	7	104*	1460	60.83	3	12	18
Hardie, B.R. (Ex)	1974	12	17	7	125	728	72.80	2	4	11
†Hardy, J.J.E. (Sm)	1987	9	16	5	91	361	32.81	–	1	6
Harper, R.A. (W)	–	1	1	0	17	17	17.00	–	–	1
†Harrison, G.D. (Ire)	–	1	1	0	1	1	1.00	–	–	–
Hartley, P.J. (Y)	1987	17	15	1	75	218	15.57	–	1	8
Hathurusinghe, U.C. (SL)	–	5	10	0	136	385	38.50	1	1	1
†Hawkes, C.J. (Le)	–	1	2	1	3	5	5.00	–	–	1
Hayhurst, A.N. (Sm)	1990	22	35	8	170	1559	57.74	4	8	9
Haynes, D.L. (M)	1989	23	39	5	255*	2346	69.00	8	7	14
Heap, R. (CU)	–	10	19	2	63	376	22.11	–	2	3
Hegg, W.K. (La/MCC)	1989	21	22	6	100*	674	42.12	1	3	49/2
Hemmings, E.E. (Nt/E)	1980	17	20	5	83	333	22.20	–	2	2
Henderson, I.M. (OU)	–	6	4	3	44	46	46.00	–	–	2
†Henry, O. (Sc)	–	1	1	0	23	23	23.00	–	–	–
Hepworth, P.N. (Le)	–	4	8	2	55*	185	30.83	–	1	4
Hick, G.A. (Wo)	1986	21	35	9	252*	2347	90.26	8	14	26
†Hinks, S.G. (K)	1985	24	43	0	234	1588	36.93	4	6	8
Hirwani, N.D. (Ind)	–	9	5	3	15*	17	8.50	–	–	3
Hodgson, G.D. (Gs)	–	24	40	4	126	1320	36.66	2	10	12
Holmes, G.C. (Gm)	1985	10	15	4	125*	465	42.27	1	2	2
Hooper, A.M. (CU)	–	2	3	0	5	5	1.66	–	–	1
Houseman, I.J. (Y)	–	3	1	0	0*	0	–	–	–	–
Hughes, D.P. (La)	1970	18	17	7	57	237	23.70	–	1	13

	Cap	M	I	NO	HS	Runs	Avge	100	50	Ct/St
Hughes, J.G. (Nh)	—	4	7	0	2	4	0.57	–	–	–
Hughes, S.P. (M)	1981	17	18	5	23*	111	8.53	–	–	3
Humpage, G.W. (Wa)	1976	13	22	4	74	628	34.88	–	5	30
Hussain, N. (Ex/T)	1989	16	23	3	197	752	37.60	1	2	16
Hutchinson, G.M. (CU)	—	2	2	0	29	31	15.50	–	–	–
Igglesden, A.P. (K)	1989	14	17	9	24	105	13.12	–	–	5
Illingworth, R.K. (Wo/T)	1986	23	22	6	117	532	33.25	1	3	7
†Ilott, M.C. (Ex)	—	9	10	2	42*	123	15.37	–	–	1
Irani, R. (La)	—	1	–	–	–	–	–	–	–	–
Jackson, P.B. (Ire)	—	1	1	0	59	59	59.00	–	1	–/1
†James, K.D. (H)	1989	1	2	1	104*	154	154.00	1	1	–
James, S.P. (CU/Us/Gm)	—	16	31	2	131*	1000	34.48	4	5	11
James, W.R. (Z)	—	3	6	1	52	143	28.60	–	1	4
Jarvis, K.B.S. (Gs)	—	2	2	2	1*	1	–	–	–	–
Jarvis, M.P.(Z)	—	1	1	1	1*	1	–	–	–	–
Jarvis, P.W. (Y)	1986	15	16	4	43*	212	17.66	–	–	2
†Jayasuriya, S.T. (SL)	—	6	9	2	105*	345	49.28	1	2	5
Jean-Jacques, M. (D)	—	12	13	5	25	107	13.37	–	–	2
Jenkins, R.H.J. (CU)	—	9	12	5	19*	58	8.28	–	–	1
Jesty, T.E. (La)	1989	17	24	6	98	785	43.61	–	7	6
Johnson, P. (Nt/T)	1986	23	43	3	165*	1518	37.95	3	9	14
Johnson, S.W. (CU)	—	6	6	4	14*	35	17.50	–	–	2
Jones, A.H. (NZ)	—	10	16	3	121*	692	53.23	1	5	3
†Jones, A.N. (Sm)	1987	22	9	5	41	100	25.00	–	–	6
Joseph, L.A. (H)	—	6	5	4	69*	152	152.00	–	1	1
†Kallicharran, A.I. (Wa)	1972	7	10	1	72	221	24.55	–	2	5
Kapil Dev (Ind)	—	9	12	2	110	377	37.70	1	2	3
Kelleher, D.J.M. (K)	—	5	8	0	44	101	12.62	–	–	2
Kellett, S.A. (Y)	—	16	28	3	75*	774	30.96	–	6	8
Kendrick, N.M. (Sy)	—	13	12	4	52*	124	15.50	–	1	14
Kilborn, M.J. (OU/Us)	—	6	8	1	95	309	44.14	–	2	5
Krikken, K.M. (D)	—	22	29	2	77*	488	18.07	–	2	60/3
Kuiper, A.P. (D)	—	12	17	0	68	407	23.94	–	2	10
Kumble, A. (Ind)	—	7	5	2	35*	63	21.00	–	–	1
Kuruppu, D.S.B.P. (SL)	—	5	10	1	56*	259	28.77	–	2	7/1
Labrooy, G.F. (SL)	—	4	6	0	69	121	20.16	–	1	1
Laing, D.R. (Nt)	—	1	1	0	2	2	2.00	–	–	–
Lamb, A.J. (Nh/E)	1978	17	29	4	235	1596	63.84	6	5	9
Lampitt, S.R. (Wo/T)	1989	23	24	5	45*	356	18.73	–	–	11
Larkins, W. (Nh)	1976	15	25	0	207	701	28.04	2	2	8
Lawrence, D.V. (Gs/MCC)	1985	23	24	3	35	163	7.76	–	–	7
Leatherdale, D.A. (Wo)	—	4	6	0	70	154	25.66	–	2	2
Lefebvre, R.P. (Sm)	—	17	16	3	53	214	16.46	–	1	8
Lenham, N.J. (Sx)	1990	22	41	1	123	1663	41.57	4	9	6
Lester, T.A. (MC)	—	1	1	0	4	4	4.00	–	–	–
Lewis, C.C. (Le/E)	1990	17	26	5	189*	697	33.19	1	2	15
Lewis, D.A. (Ire)	—	1	1	0	6	6	6.00	–	–	1
Lewis, J.J.B. (Ex)	—	1	1	1	116*	116	–	–	1	–
Lilley, A.W. (Ex)	1986	1	1	0	1	1	1.00	–	–	–
†Llong, N.J. (K)	—	1	–	–	–	–	–	–	–	1
Lloyd, G.D. (La)	—	14	20	2	96	796	44.22	–	8	9
†Lloyd, T.A. (Wa)	1980	15	27	1	101	646	24.84	1	4	7
†Lloyds, J.W. (Gs)	1985	24	34	12	93	839	38.13	–	4	16
†Lord, G.J. (Wo)	1990	13	24	2	190	1003	45.59	3	5	4
Lowrey, M.J. (CU)	—	10	18	2	72	363	22.68	–	2	1
Lunn, P.D. (OU)	—	8	10	4	44*	184	30.66	–	–	1

170

	Cap	M	I	NO	HS	Runs	Avge	100	50	Ct/St
Lynch, M.A. (Sy)	1982	24	32	5	104	1227	45.44	1	9	30
McCrum, P. (Ire)	—	1	1	0	0	0	0.00	–	–	–
McEwan, S.M. (Wo)	1989	15	12	5	54	164	23.42	–	1	5
McGrady, J.E. (OU)	—	6	2	0	14	15	7.50	–	–	–/2
†McKnight, C.T. (Sc)	—	1	1	0	0	0	0.00	–	–	1
†Madurasinghe, A.W.R. (SL)	—	4	3	1	28*	43	21.50	–	–	1
Mahanama, R.S. (SL)	—	6	10	0	114	494	49.40	2	2	10
Maher, B.J.M. (D)	1987	1	–	–	–	–	–	–	–	–
Mahmood, M. (Sc)	—	1	1	0	3	3	3.00	–	–	1
Malcolm, D.E. (D/E)	1989	16	13	5	20*	76	9.50	–	–	–
Mallender, N.A. (Sm)	1987	20	10	3	87*	177	25.28	–	1	3
Manjrekar, S.V. (Ind)	—	11	17	3	158*	814	58.14	2	6	6
Marsh, S.A. (K)	1986	24	35	8	114*	911	33.74	1	5	49/5
Marshall, M.D. (H)	1981	18	24	3	117	962	45.80	2	6	7
Martin, P.J. (La)	—	10	7	3	21	44	11.00	–	–	5
Martindale, D.J.R. (Nt)	—	17	28	3	138	751	30.04	2	2	5
Maru, R.J. (H)	1986	25	20	2	59	520	28.88	–	3	30
Maynard, M.P. (Gm)	1987	23	41	7	125*	1501	44.14	2	11	15
Medlycott, K.T. (Sy/T)	1988	23	25	9	44	410	25.62	–	–	14
Mendis, G.D. (La)	1986	21	35	6	180	1551	53.48	4	8	16
Merrick, T.A. (K)	—	7	8	2	35	66	11.00	–	–	1
Metcalfe, A.A. (Y)	1986	23	44	4	194*	2047	51.17	6	7	10
Metson, C.P. (Gm)	1987	23	27	5	50*	352	16.00	–	1	59
Middleton, T.C. (H)	1990	18	29	3	127	1238	47.61	5	5	9
Mike, G.W. (Nt)	—	4	5	1	18*	45	11.25	–	–	4
Milburn, E.T. (Gs)	—	2	4	2	35	49	24.50	–	–	–
Miller, G. (D)	1976	14	14	8	47*	233	38.83	–	–	7
Millmow, J.P. (NZ)	—	5	1	1	2*	2	–	–	–	2
†Millns, D.J. (Le)	—	9	10	5	10*	23	4.60	–	–	3
Moir, J.D. (Sc)	—	1	1	0	12	12	12.00	–	–	1
Moles, A.J. (Wa)	1987	24	46	8	224*	1854	48.78	4	10	12
Mongia, N.R. (Ind)	—	8	11	4	63*	269	38.42	–	2	9/3
Moody, T.M. (Wa)	1990	9	15	2	168	1163	89.46	7	1	4
Moores, P. (Sx)	1989	25	36	4	106*	694	21.68	1	2	53/10
More, K.S. (Ind)	—	9	11	2	95	295	32.77	–	2	17/1
†Morris, H. (Gm)	1986	25	46	5	160*	2276	55.51	10	10	14
Morris, J.E. (D/MCC/E)	1986	21	33	6	157*	1459	54.03	6	6	12
Morris, M.J. (CU)	—	10	17	3	45	206	14.71	–	–	4
Morris, R.E. (OU/Us)	—	9	12	1	96	498	45.27	–	6	1
Morrison, D.K. (NZ)	—	9	6	2	6	14	3.50	–	–	3
Mortensen, O.H. (D)	1986	12	11	9	5*	20	10.00	–	–	5
Moseley, E.A. (W)	—	1	–	–	–	–	–	–	–	–
Moxon, M.D. (Y/MCC)	1984	22	40	6	218*	1633	48.02	3	7	14
Mudassar Nazar (W)	—	1	2	1	107*	136	136.00	1	–	–
Mullally, A.D. (Le)	—	19	18	6	29	113	9.41	–	–	4
Munton, T.A. (Wa/T)	1989	25	24	9	29*	125	8.33	–	–	9
Murphy, A.J. (Sy)	—	12	6	3	4*	6	2.00	–	–	1
Neale, P.A. (Wo)	1978	21	32	10	122	976	44.36	2	3	12
Nelson, A.N. (Ire)	—	1	1	1	23*	23	–	–	–	–
Nelson, N. (Ire)	—	1	1	0	0	0	0.00	–	–	–
Newell, M. (Nt)	1987	15	27	2	112	851	34.04	1	6	4
Newport, P.J. (Wo)	1986	21	18	6	98	424	35.33	–	3	6
Nicholas, M.C.J. (H)	1982	23	35	10	104	895	35.80	1	5	9
†Nixon, P.A. (Le)	—	19	23	8	46	411	27.40	–	–	49/1
Noon, W.M. (Nh)	—	3	3	0	2	6	2.00	–	–	5/1

	Cap	M	I	NO	HS	Runs	Avge	100	50	Ct/St
North, J.A. (Sx)	—	4	5	1	19*	41	10.25	–	–	1
O'Gorman, T.J.G. (D)	—	7	12	1	100	448	40.72	1	4	4
Ostler, D.P. (Wa)	—	11	19	2	71	510	30.00	–	5	9
Owen, P.A. (Gs)	—	3	2	0	1	2	1.00	–	–	–
Parker, P.W.G. (Sx/MCC)	1979	15	25	4	107	985	46.90	2	6	8
Parks, R.J. (H)	1982	20	21	10	36*	216	19.63	–	–	49/4
Parore, A.C. (NZ)	—	7	6	1	43	131	26.20	–	–	14/1
†Parsons, G.J. (Le)	1984	10	13	3	20	112	11.20	–	–	4
Patel, M.M. (K)	—	9	12	5	41*	104	14.85	–	–	2
Patterson, B.M.W. (Sc)	—	1	1	0	60	60	60.00	–	1	3
Patterson, B.P. (La)	1987	10	4	1	4*	5	1.66	–	–	2
†Patterson, T.J.T. (Ire)	—	1	1	0	84	84	84.00	–	1	1
†Penberthy, A.L. (Nh)	—	12	17	3	101*	435	31.07	1	3	8
†Penn, C. (K)	1987	7	6	2	23*	66	16.50	–	–	2
Philip, I.L. (Sc)	—	1	1	0	100	100	100.00	1	–	–
†Pick, R.A. (Nt)	1987	17	16	6	35	204	20.40	–	–	6
Pickles, C.S. (Y)	—	16	22	8	57*	478	34.14	–	3	6
Pierson, A.R.K. (Wa)	—	11	9	5	16*	57	14.25	–	–	1
Pigott, A.C.S. (Sx)	1982	21	29	5	64*	451	18.79	–	4	10
Piper, K.J. (Wa)	—	16	21	1	111	461	23.05	1	1	40/4
Pointer, G.A. (CU)	—	1	2	0	9	16	8.00	–	–	–
†Pollard, P.R. (Nt)	—	7	13	0	72	277	21.30	–	1	5
Pook, R.N. (Gm)	—	1	2	1	0*	0	0.00	–	–	–
†Pooley, J.C. (M)	—	1	2	0	13	21	10.50	–	–	1
Pooley, M.W. (Gs)	—	1	–	–	–	–	–	–	–	–
Potter, L. (Le)	1988	23	38	5	109*	1080	32.72	1	7	23
Prabhakar, M. (Ind)	—	10	14	3	76	296	26.90	–	2	4
Prichard, P.J. (Ex)	1986	22	32	3	245	1407	48.51	5	4	9
†Priest, M.W. (NZ)	—	9	11	3	72	345	43.12	–	3	6
Pringle, C. (NZ/W)	—	5	1	0	6	6	6.00	–	–	4
Pringle, D.R. (Ex)	1982	17	15	2	84	443	34.07	–	3	9
Pycroft, A.J. (Z)	—	3	5	1	55	120	30.00	–	1	2
Pyman, R.A. (CU/Us)	—	10	14	2	23*	98	8.16	–	–	2
Radford, N.V. (Wo)	1985	12	8	1	43*	118	16.85	–	–	6
Raju, S.L.V. (Ind)	—	6	6	2	40*	105	26.25	–	–	–
†Raman, W.V. (Ind)	—	8	15	2	127	623	47.92	1	7	6
Ramanayake, C.P.H. (SL)	—	4	4	4	9*	25	–	–	–	–
Ramprakash, M.R. (M)	1990	24	42	10	146*	1541	48.15	5	6	6
Randall, D.W. (Nt)	1973	15	28	1	178	987	36.55	2	5	14
Ratcliffe, J.D. (Wa)	—	16	31	3	81*	780	27.85	–	3	7
Rea, M.P. (Ire)	—	1	2	1	22	43	43.00	–	–	1
Reeve, D.A. (Wa/MCC)	1989	25	38	12	202*	1412	54.30	3	5	26
Remy, C.C. (Sx)	—	2	1	1	4*	4	–	–	–	1
Rhodes, S.J. (Wo)	1986	22	25	10	96	672	44.80	–	5	61/8
Richards, I.V.A. (Gm)	1990	18	28	5	164*	1425	61.95	7	3	8
Richardson, R.B. (W)	—	1	2	0	65	107	53.50	–	1	1
Ripley, D. (Nh)	1987	21	28	6	109*	656	29.81	1	2	28/6
Roberts, A.R. (Nh)	—	2	3	0	5	5	1.66	–	–	1
Roberts, B. (D)	1986	24	38	7	124*	1108	35.74	2	4	23
Roberts, M.J. (MC)	—	1	2	0	85	86	43.00	–	1	–
Roberts, M.L. (Gm)	—	4	5	1	25	79	19.75	–	–	10
Robertson, C.M. (Z)	—	3	6	1	125	168	33.60	1	–	1
†Robinson, J.D. (Sy)	—	8	10	0	72	175	17.50	–	1	1
Robinson, M.A. (Nh)	1990	19	16	10	1*	3	0.50	–	–	5
Robinson, P.E. (Y)	1988	23	39	7	150*	1402	43.81	1	12	20

	Cap	M	I	NO	HS	Runs	Avge	100	50	Ct/St
Robinson, R.T. (Nt)	1983	23	45	5	220*	1747	43.67	4	8	12
Roebuck, P.M. (Sm)	1978	18	28	5	201*	1134	49.30	2	6	7
Romaines, P.W. (Gs)	1983	7	11	2	95	295	32.77	–	2	2
Rose, G.D. (Sm)	1988	24	29	11	97*	1000	55.55	–	8	13
Roseberry, M.A. (M)	1990	24	44	4	135*	1593	39.82	3	11	23
Russell, A.B. (Sc)	—	1	1	0	47	47	47.00	–	–	–
Russell, M.J. (OU)	—	4	3	0	4	10	3.33	–	–	1
†Russell, R.C. (Gs/E)	1985	17	23	2	120	794	37.80	2	3	45/1
Rutherford, K.R. (NZ)	—	8	13	5	68*	376	47.00	–	1	7
Sadiq, Z.A. (D)	—	1	1	0	0	0	0.00	–	–	3
Salisbury, I.D.K. (Sx)	—	20	23	10	68	313	24.07	–	1	13
Sargeant, N.F. (Sy)	—	3	2	0	18	19	9.50	–	–	6/1
Saxelby, K. (Nt)	1984	5	6	0	20	42	7.00	–	–	3
†Saxelby, M. (Nt)	—	8	15	4	73	335	30.45	–	2	3
Scott, C.W. (Nt)	1988	3	3	2	67*	111	111.00	–	1	1
†Scott, R.J. (H)	—	6	10	2	71	144	18.00	–	1	4
†Seymour, A.C. (Ex)	—	3	5	2	89	131	43.66	–	1	1
†Shah, A.H. (Z)	—	3	3	0	185	215	71.66	1	–	–
Shahid, N. (Ex/T)	—	19	29	7	125	1003	45.59	1	6	22
Sharma, C. (W)	—	1	–	–	–	–	–	–	–	–
Sharma, S.K. (Ind)	—	9	7	3	38	132	33.00	–	–	2
†Sharp, K. (Y)	1982	9	13	5	53*	318	39.75	–	1	1
Shastri, R.J. (Ind)	—	9	11	1	187	644	64.40	4	1	6
Shine, K.J. (H)	—	7	1	1	24*	24	—	–	–	1
Shufflebotham, D.H. (CU)	—	8	9	3	29	121	20.16	–	–	1
Sidebottom, A. (Y)	1980	3	4	0	38	104	26.00	–	–	1
Sidhu, N.S. (Ind)	—	9	17	3	142	639	45.64	2	4	1
Sleep, P.R. (W)	—	1	1	0	42	42	42.00	–	–	1
Small, G.C. (Wa/E)	1982	15	22	4	55	296	16.44	–	1	4
Smith, B.F. (Le)	—	2	2	1	15*	19	19.00	–	–	1
Smith, C.L. (H)	1981	22	38	7	148	1886	60.83	4	12	14
†Smith, D.M. (Sx)	1989	9	16	2	71	353	25.21	–	2	2
Smith, G. (Wa)	—	1	1	0	30	30	30.00	–	–	1
Smith, I. (Gm)	—	7	10	2	112*	328	41.00	1	2	1
Smith, I.D.S. (NZ)	—	6	4	1	34	65	21.66	–	–	5
Smith, N.M.K. (Wa)	—	10	14	2	83*	370	30.83	–	1	4
Smith, P.A. (Wa)	1986	12	20	4	117	520	32.50	1	3	1
Smith, R.A. (H/E)	1985	18	30	8	181	1454	66.09	6	7	11
†Snedden, M.C. (NZ)	—	7	6	3	21*	38	12.66	–	–	3
Speak, N.J. (La)	—	6	9	0	138	409	45.44	1	3	3
Speight, M.P. (Sx)	—	23	41	7	131	1375	40.44	2	11	14
Stanworth, J. (La)	1989	2	–	–	–	–	–	–	–	3
Stemp, R.D. (Wo)	—	2	2	3	3*	3	—	–	–	1
Stephenson, F.D. (Nt)	1988	20	35	7	121	807	28.82	1	4	5
Stephenson, J.P. (Ex/T)	1989	25	41	8	202*	1887	57.18	4	13	16
Stewart, A.J. (Sy/E)	1985	17	29	6	100*	984	42.78	1	9	24
Storie, A.C. (Sc)	—	1	1	0	32	32	32.00	–	–	1
Stovold, A.W. (Gs)	1976	2	4	0	74	104	26.00	–	1	4
Such, P.M. (Ex)	—	11	5	3	27	44	22.00	–	–	2
Swallow, I.G. (Sm)	—	23	17	7	32	187	18.70	–	–	12
Swan, R.G. (Sc)	—	1	1	0	9	9	9.00	–	–	–
Tavaré, C.J. (Sm)	1989	24	32	4	219	1638	58.50	3	12	16
†Taylor, C.W. (M)	—	2	2	1	13	13	13.00	–	–	–
Taylor, L.B. (Le)	1981	1	–	–	–	–	–	–	–	–
Taylor, N.R. (M/MC)	—	2	2	0	0	0	0.00	–	–	1

173

	Cap	M	I	NO	HS	Runs	Avge	100	50	Ct/St
Taylor, N.R. (K)	1982	22	37	5	204	1979	61.84	7	10	9
Tedstone, G.A. (Gs)	—	6	5	0	23	88	16.60	–	–	9/1
Tendulkar, S.R. (Ind)	—	11	19	4	119*	945	63.00	2	6	5
Terry, V.P. (H)	1983	22	35	3	165	1332	41.62	5	4	24
†Thomas, D.R. (MC)	—	1	1	0	27	27	27.00	–	–	1
Thomas, J.G. (Nh)	—	12	13	3	48	152	15.20	–	–	9
Thomas, K.O. (Ex)	—	1	1	0	2	2	2.00	–	–	–
Thomson, S.A. (NZ)	—	5	5	4	20	32	32.00	–	–	5
†Thorpe, G.P. (Sy/T)	—	18	28	6	86	608	27.63	–	3	9
Threlfall, P.W. (Sx)	—	1								
Thursfield, M.J. (M)	—	2								
†Tillekeratne, H.P. (SL)	—	5	9	2	109*	349	49.85	2	–	7/2
Titchard, S.P. (La)	—	3	5	0	80	129	25.80	–	1	–
Tolley, C.M. (Wo)	—	6	6	1	29	79	15.80	–	–	2
Topley, T.D. (Ex)	1988	9	6	2	23*	78	19.50	–	–	6
Townsend, G.T.J. (Sm)	—	2	4	1	15	21	7.00	–	–	3
Traicos, A.J. (Z)	—	2	1	0	1	1	1.00	–	–	5
Tremlett, T.M. (H)	1983	8	5	3	78	143	71.50	–	1	1
Trevelyan, R.W.D. (OU)	—	3	1	0	0	0	0.00	–	–	2
Trump, H.R.J. (Sm)	—	7	5	1	4*	11	2.75	–	–	3
Tufnell, P.C.R. (M/MCC)	1990	23	22	9	37	283	21.76	–	–	8
†Turner, G.J. (OU/Us)	—	9	12	0	59	298	24.83	–	2	5
Turner, I.J. (H)	—	5	3	1	14	15	7.50	–	–	2
Turner, R.J. (CU/Us)	—	9	16	0	38	302	18.87	–	–	8/4
†Twose, R.G. (Wa)	—	6	10	1	64*	241	26.77	–	3	3
Udal, S.D. (H)	—	7	6	2	28*	79	19.75	–	–	2
†Van der Merwe, W.M. (OU/Us)	—	8	9	3	84	310	51.66	–	3	6
Vengsarkar, D.B. (Ind)	—	10	14	4	83*	576	57.60	–	6	4
Walsh, C.A. (Gs)	1985	20	20	3	63*	464	27.29	–	3	6
Waqar Younis (Sy)	1990	14	9	7	14	56	28.00	–	–	4
Ward, D.M. (Sy)	1990	24	34	7	263	2072	76.74	7	3	32/3
Ward, T.R. (K)	1989	15	28	1	175	863	31.96	2	5	14
Warke, S.J.S. (Ire)	—	1	2	1	100*	104	104.00	1	–	1
Warner, A.E. (D)	1987	14	19	2	59	160	9.41	–	1	2
†Wasim Akram (La)	1989	8	11	0	32	135	12.27	–	–	4
Wassan, A.S. (Ind)	—	9	3	1	24	47	23.50	–	–	–
Waterton, S.N.V. (La)	—	1	1	0	3	3	3.00	–	–	4
Watkin, S.L. (Gm/MCC)	1989	24	25	8	25*	187	11.00	–	–	6
Watkinson, M. (La)	1987	19	23	2	138	754	35.90	1	4	8
Watson, W. (NZ)	—	2	1	1	17*	17	—	–	–	–
Waugh, M.E. (Ex)	1989	22	33	6	207*	2072	76.74	8	8	18
Weale, S.D. (OU)	—	5	4	2	13	24	12.00	–	–	1
Weekes, P.N. (M)	—	3	3	0	51	75	25.00	–	1	3
Wells, A.P. (Sx)	1986	24	44	7	144*	1611	43.54	4	7	12
Wells, C.M. (Sx)	1982	20	33	5	113*	933	33.32	2	4	5
Wells, V.J. (K)	—	8	15	0	58	352	23.46	–	2	8
Weston, M.J. (Wo)	1986	6	10	1	38*	90	10.00	–	–	1
Whitaker, J.J. (Le)	1986	24	45	6	124*	1767	45.30	4	8	14
White, C. (Y)	—	10	11	2	38	127	14.11	–	–	4
Whitney, M.R. (W)	—	1								
Whitticase, P. (Le)	1987	5	7	2	11*	39	7.80	–	–	13
Wickremansinghe, G.P. (SL)	—	3	2	0	17	17	8.50	–	–	–
Wijegunawardene, K.I.W. (SL)	—	4	1	0	0	0	0.00	–	–	5
Wijetunge, P.K. (SL)	—	4	1	1	5*	5	—	–	–	3
†Wild, D.J. (Nh)	1986	2	4	0	43	80	20.00	–	–	–

174

	Cap	M	I	NO	HS	Runs	Avge	100	50	Ct/St
Willey, P. (Le)	1984	22	40	6	177	1150	33.82	2	5	10
Williams, N.F. (M/E)	1984	21	24	3	55*	448	21.33	–	2	4
†Williams, R.C.J. (Gs)	–	8	4	50*	132	33.00	–	1	27/4
Williams, R.G. (Nh)	1979	17	26	5	96	566	26.95	–	4	6
Winchester, A.L.C. (OU)	–	1	1	1	0*	0	–	–	–	–
†Wood, J.R. (H)	–	2	2	0	17	28	14.00	–	–	1
†Wren, T.N. (K)	–	5	5	2	16	23	7.66	–	–	2
Wright, A.J. (Gs)	1987	23	38	3	112	911	26.02	1	5	23
†Wright, J.G. (NZ)	–	9	15	2	121	653	50.23	1	5	2
Yates, G. (La)	–	5	4	2	106	165	82.50	1	–	1

BOWLING

(See BATTING and FIELDING section for details of caps and teams.)

	Cat	O	M	R	W	Avge	Best	5 wI	10 wM
Adams, C.J.	OB	14	1	56	2	28.00	1-5	–	–
Afford, J.A.	SLA	688	209	1944	42	46.28	4-137	–	–
Agnew, J.P.	RFM	612	108	2196	59	37.22	5-54	5	–
Ahangama, F.S.	RMF	1.3	0	4	0	–	–	–	–
Alikhan, R.I.	OB	20	1	83	1	83.00	1-12	–	–
Alleyne, M.W.	RM	112	29	391	16	24.43	3 23	–	–
Allott, P.J.W.	RFM	266	77	730	18	40.55	4-23	–	–
Ambrose, C.E.L.	RF	503.4	127	1413	61	23.16	7-89	5	1
Andrew, S.J.W.	RMF	503	75	1897	46	41.23	5-55	1	–
Anthony, H.A.G.	RF	142.4	32	466	12	38.83	3-95	–	–
Arnold, K.A.	RMF	28	6	113	1	113.00	1-113	–	–
Asif Din	LB	159.1	30	635	10	63.50	3-17	–	–
Atapattu, M.S.		4	0	21	0	–	–	–	–
Atherton, M.A.	LB	433.3	104	1398	45	31.06	6-78	3	–
Athey, C.W.J.	RM	50.5	10	145	2	72.50	2-13	–	–
Atkinson, J.C.M.	RMF	23	3	101	1	101.00	1-27	–	–
Austin, I.D.	RM	245	76	662	12	55.16	3-42	–	–
Ayling, J.R.	RM	181.2	46	572	11	52.00	2-48	–	–
Babington, A.M.	RFM	63	7	256	3	85.33	2-109	–	–
Bailey, R.J.	OB	168.2	29	604	11	54.90	3-82	–	–
Bainbridge, P.	RM	162.4	30	515	11	46.81	3-23	–	–
Bakker, P.-J.	RMF	436.2	90	1439	37	38.89	5-101	1	–
Ball, M.C.J.	OB	62	15	201	3	67.00	2-37	–	–
Barnes, S.N.	RM	207	45	602	16	37.62	4-51	–	–
Barnett, K.J.	LB	293.3	54	757	26	29.11	4-28	–	–
Barwick, S.R.	RMF	158.4	43	441	9	49.00	3-29	–	–
Base, S.J.	RMF	414.3	68	1402	35	40.05	6-105	2	–
Bastien, S.	RMF	317.1	57	1187	39	30.43	6-75	2	–
Batty, J.D.	OB	195	29	722	12	60.16	4-76	–	–
Bee, A.	RMF	28	11	73	0	–	–	–	–
Bell, R.M.	RM	44	7	114	3	38.00	2-38	–	–
Benjamin, J.E.	RMF	388.3	68	1205	43	28.02	5-29	4	–
Benjamin, W.K.M.	RFM	284.3	63	858	28	30.64	5-73	2	–
Benson, J.D.R.	RM	39.5	3	157	1	157.00	1-83	–	–
Benson, M.R.	OB	8	2	46	1	46.00	1-14	–	–
Berry, P.J.	OB	44.3	4	172	2	86.00	1-48	–	–
Bicknell, D.J.	LM	9	1	20	0	–	–	–	–
Bicknell, M.P.	RFM	671.1	157	1827	67	27.26	5-34	1	–
Bishop, I.R.	RF	407.3	94	1124	59	19.05	6-71	3	–

175

	Cat	O	M	R	W	Avge	Best	5 wI	10 wM
Boon, T.J.	RM	6.5	0	39	0	–	–	–	–
Booth, P.A.	SLA	250.5	75	636	13	48.92	4-55	–	–
Botham, I.T.	RMF	194.4	38	614	21	29.23	4-65	–	–
Bowler, P.D.	OB	11	0	81	1	81.00	1-48	–	–
Bracewell, J.G.	OB	383.3	102	1120	34	32.94	7-120	2	1
Brandes, E.A.	RFM	49.2	12	165	7	23.57	4-35	–	–
Brent, J.P.	RM	26	6	79	2	39.50	2-28	–	–
Brown, G.K.	OB	9	1	39	1	39.00	1-39	–	–
Brown, K.R.	RSM	16	4	65	1	65.00	1-16	–	–
Brown, S.J.	LFM	73	17	250	6	41.66	1-11	–	–
Bunting, R.A.	RFM	360	62	1314	26	50.53	2-36	–	–
Burns, N.D.	SLA	0.3	0	8	0	–	–	–	–
Butchart, I.P.	RM	41	7	156	2	78.00	1-39	–	–
Butcher, A.R.	LM	25.3	2	153	1	153.00	1-16	–	–
Butcher, R.O.	RSM	2	0	2	0	–	–	–	–
Buzza, A.J.	SLA	287	47	1086	23	47.21	4-87	–	–
Byas, D.	RM	96	19	358	4	89.50	3-55	–	–
Cann, M.J.	OB	35	3	162	1	162.00	1-39	–	–
Capel, D.J.	RMF	234	51	711	25	28.44	5-74	1	–
Carrick, P.	SLA	601	173	1570	46	34.13	5-49	3	–
Chauhan, S.	OB	15	1	58	1	58.00	1-58	–	–
Childs, J.H.	SLA	655.5	211	1590	27	58.88	4-56	–	–
Connor, C.A.	RFM	510.1	88	1789	47	38.06	5-96	1	–
Cook, N.G.B.	SLA	527.1	167	1364	40	34.10	5-44	2	–
Cook, S.J.	OB	8	0	42	2	21.00	2-25	–	–
Cooper, K.E.	RFM	703.4	153	2203	54	40.79	5-56	3	–
Cork, D.G.	RFM	39	8	123	2	61.50	1-4	–	–
Cottey, P.A.		18	0	116	1	116.00	1-49	–	–
Cowans, N.G.	RF	460	124	1247	39	31.97	5-67	1	–
Cowdrey, C.S.	RM	61	12	192	4	48.00	2-20	–	–
Cowdrey, G.R.	RM	6.3	1	44	0	–	–	–	–
Cowley, N.G.	OB	316.3	64	900	12	75.00	3-84	–	–
Cox, R.M.F.	OB	1	0	1	0	–	–	–	–
Crawley, M.A.	RM	224.5	38	750	20	37.50	6-92	1	–
Croft, R.D.B.	OB	397.1	83	1335	28	47.67	3-10	–	–
Crowe, M.D.	RM	8	3	20	0	–	–	–	–
Curran, K.M.	RMF	598.3	111	1961	64	30.64	5-63	1	–
Curtis, D.M.	LB	1	0	8	0	–	–	–	–
Curtis, T.S.	LB	5.3	1	43	0	–	–	–	–
Dale, A.	RM	90	13	338	7	48.28	3-21	–	–
Davies, H.R.	OB	54	6	261	3	87.00	3-93	–	–
Davies, M.	SLA	8	1	16	0	–	–	–	–
Davis, R.P.	SLA	908.1	221	2844	73	38.95	6-40	5	1
Davis, W.W.	RF	237.5	28	812	13	62.46	3-28	–	–
DeFreitas, P.A.J.	RFM	489.3	109	1440	40	36.00	6-39	2	–
Dennis, S.J.	LFM	322	61	1071	22	48.68	5-76	1	–
Derrick, J.	RM	9	2	58	0	–	–	–	–
De Silva, P.A.	RM	25	3	81	2	40.50	2-25	–	–
De Villiers, P.S.	RFM	304.5	58	992	25	39.68	6-70	1	–
Dilley, G.R.	RF	224.2	30	818	24	34.08	5-62	2	–
Dobson, M.C.	SLA	3.1	1	7	0	–	–	–	–
Dodemaide, A.I.C.	RFM	763.1	130	2457	61	40.27	6-106	1	–
Doidge, M.J.	SLA	24	5	106	0	–	–	–	–
D'Oliveira, D.B.	OB	11.3	1	80	2	40.00	2-23	–	–
Dolphin, D.F.	SLA	39	10	134	1	134.00	1-29	–	–

	Cat	O	M	R	W	Avge	Best	5 wI	10 wM
Donald, A.A.	RF	391	89	1089	29	37.55	3-28	–	–
Donelan, B.T.P.	OB	304.4	56	1000	20	50.00	3-79	–	–
Downton, P.R.	OB	1.1	0	4	1	4.00	1-4	–	–
Dube, L.E.	RFM	25	4	107	0	–	–	–	–
Duers, K.G.	RM	74	17	266	5	53.20	2-63	–	–
Dunlop, A.R.	OB	10	0	37	0	–	–	–	–
Ealham, M.A.	RMF	34.2	5	120	3	40.00	2-33	–	–
Ellison, R.M.	RMF	291.5	51	963	19	50.68	4-76	–	–
Emburey, J.E.	OB	942.3	275	1957	61	32.08	5-32	2	–
Evans, K.P.	RMF	356	78	1232	34	36.23	4-50	–	–
Evans, R.A.	OB	28	1	147	2	73.50	2-147	–	–
Evans, R.J.	RM	6	1	24	0	–	–	–	–
Fairbrother, N.H.	LM	7	0	29	0	–	–	–	–
Feltham, M.A.	RMF	349.4	61	1150	40	28.75	6-53	2	–
Felton, N.A.	OB	19	1	113	1	113.00	1-48	–	–
Ferris, G.J.F.	RF	138.2	29	482	12	40-16	4-44	–	–
Field-Buss, M.G.	OB	48.5	16	99	3	33.00	3-14	–	–
Fitton, J.D.	OB	454.4	91	1447	14	103.35	3-69	–	–
Fleming, M.V.	RM	394.5	94	1072	22	48.72	3-65	–	–
Fletcher, S.D.	RMF	292.5	60	1035	29	35.68	5-94	1	–
Flower, G.W.	SLA	29.5	4	101	3	33.66	2-33	–	–
Folley, I.	SLA	114.1	18	397	6	66.16	2-18	–	–
Fordham, A.	RM	10	0	43	1	43.00	1-25	–	–
Foster, N.A.	RFM	819.2	175	2502	94	26.61	6-32	6	1
Fowler, G.	RM	4.1	2	33	1	33.00	1-33	–	–
Fraser, A.R.C.	RFM	596	144	1533	57	26.89	6-30	4	–
Frost, M.	RMF	557.1	74	2047	59	34.69	5-40	2	1
Gallian, J.E.R.	RM	21	8	65	1	65.00	1-50	–	–
Gatting, M.W.	RM	56	21	138	7	19.71	4-2	–	–
Gerrans, P.S.	RM	208	40	695	12	57.91	3-86	–	–
Gidley, M.I.	OB	94	27	309	1	309.00	1-54	–	–
Goldsmith, S.C.	RM	128	22	383	7	54.71	2-105	–	–
Gooch, G.A.	RM	66	19	220	1	220.00	1-26	–	–
Gough, D.	RMF	279.4	49	1037	28	37.03	4-68	–	–
Gould, I.J.	RM	5.4	0	19	0	–	–	–	–
Govan, J.W.	OB	47	14	142	5	28.40	2-12	–	–
Graveney, D.A.	SLA	485.4	136	1189	31	38.35	5-45	3	1
Gray, A.H.	RF	239.5	43	666	19	35.05	4-83	–	–
Grayson, A.P.	SLA	80	19	270	1	270.00	1-55	–	–
Greenfield, K.	RM	0.3	0	8	0	–	–	–	–
Greensword, S.	RM	19	6	52	0	–	–	–	–
Greig, I.A.	RMF	216.1	21	858	13	66.00	3-60	–	–
Griffith, F.A.	RM	11	2	20	1	20.00	1-20	–	–
Gurusinha, A.P.	RM	40	8	113	5	22.60	3-38	–	–
Hadlee, Sir R.J.	RFM	201.5	39	586	24	24.41	5-27	2	–
Hallett, J.C.	RMF	65.5	9	238	6	39.66	2-40	–	–
Hansford, A.R.	RM	123.5	21	425	7	60.71	3-91	–	–
Harden, R.J.	SLA	67	6	276	6	46.00	2-39	–	–
Hardie, B.R.	RM	1	0	16	0	–	–	–	–
Harper, R.A.	OB	33.4	8	104	5	20.80	4-68	–	–
Harrison, G.D.	RFM	43.2	11	113	9	12.55	9-113	1	–
Hartley, P.J.	RMF	491	80	1781	52	34.25	6-57	2	–
Hathurusinghe, U.C.	RMF	21.1	8	58	3	19.33	2-3	–	–
Hawkes, C.J.	SLA	14	3	40	0	–	–	–	–
Hayhurst, A.N.	RM	321.2	50	1087	17	63.94	3-58	–	–

177

	Cat	O	M	R	W	Avge	Best	5 wI	10 wM
Haynes, D.L.	LB	35	7	113	2	56.50	1-18	–	–
Hemmings, E.E.	OB	688.2	197	1844	51	36.15	6-58	2	–
Henderson, I.M.	RMF	105.2	9	469	6	78.16	3-102	–	–
Henry, O.	SLA	32.4	3	106	2	53.00	2-54	–	–
Hick, G.A.	OB	208.5	41	645	20	32.25	5-37	1	–
Hinks, S.G.	RM	15	2	60	2	30.00	1-15	–	–
Hirwani, N.D.	LB	399.2	59	1280	31	41.29	5-117	1	–
Holmes, G.C.	RM	42	10	132	4	33.00	1-6	–	–
Houseman, I.J.	RFM	50	9	198	2	99.00	2-26	–	–
Hughes, D.P.	SLA	280.4	61	918	24	38.25	4-25	–	–
Hughes, J.G.	RM	66	12	293	3	97.66	2-57	–	–
Hughes, S.P.	RFM	386.2	73	1287	33	39.00	5-101	1	–
Humpage, G.W.	RM	9	3	35	0	–	–	–	–
Hussain, N.	LB	12	2	62	0	–	–	–	–
Igglesden, A.P.	RF	326	47	1150	32	35.93	4-79	–	–
Illingworth, R.K.	SLA	875.5	280	2122	75	28.29	5-59	1	–
Ilott, M.C.	LMF	322.1	65	1036	31	33.41	5-34	2	–
Irani, R.	RM	22	7	73	2	36.50	1-12	–	–
James, K.D.	LMF	28	8	74	1	74.00	1-43	–	–
Jarvis, K.B.S.	RFM	34	3	142	3	47.33	2-31	–	–
Jarvis, M.P.	LM	30	7	101	2	50.50	2-61	–	–
Jarvis, P.W.	RFM	405.2	68	1393	37	37.64	4-53	–	–
Jayasuriya, S.T.	SLA	7	1	18	1	18.00	1-14	–	–
Jean-Jacques, M.	RMF	300	42	1106	25	44.24	6-60	1	–
Jenkins, R.H.J.	RM	281.4	41	959	15	63.93	5-100	1	–
Jesty, T.E.	RM	8	3	27	1	27.00	1-20	–	–
Johnson, P.	RM	1	0	1	0	–	–	–	–
Johnson, S.W.	RMF	113	14	452	3	150.66	2-86	–	–
Jones, A.H.	OB	26	4	87	3	29.00	1-1	–	–
Jones, A.N.	RFM	572.4	92	2055	56	36.69	6-75	2	–
Joseph, L.A.	RFM	102	16	462	7	66.00	2-28	–	–
Kapil Dev	RFM	246.4	59	744	13	57.23	2-28	–	–
Kelleher, D.J.M.	RMF	112.5	20	398	7	56.85	3-148	–	–
Kendrick, N.M.	SLA	348	66	1194	25	47.76	4-110	–	–
Kuiper, A.P.	RM	125.3	29	393	12	32.75	4-69	–	–
Kumble, A.	LB	212	40	660	14	47.14	6-49	1	–
Labrooy, G.F.	RFM	111	13	440	16	27.50	5-97	1	–
Laing, D.R.	RM	5	1	21	0	–	–	–	–
Lampitt, S.R.	RMF	565.3	98	1889	58	32.56	5-34	2	–
Larkins, W.	RM	10	1	45	0	–	–	–	–
Lawrence, D.V.	RF	497.3	53	1979	58	34.12	5-51	2	–
Lefebvre, R.P.	RMF	506.1	137	1281	31	41.32	5-30	1	–
Lenham, N.J.	RMF	95	19	317	5	63.40	2-26	–	–
Lewis, C.C.	RFM	536.2	102	1697	56	30.30	6-55	2	1
Lewis, D.A.	RM	11	0	55	0	–	–	–	–
Lilley, A.W.	RM	1	0	7	0	–	–	–	–
Llong, N.J.	OB	7	1	24	0	–	–	–	–
Lloyd, G.D.	RM	3.1	0	29	0	–	–	–	–
Lloyd, T.A.	RM/OB	9	1	58	1	58.00	1-58	–	–
Lloyds, J.W.	OB	382.5	60	1429	25	57.16	4-11	–	–
Lowrey, M.J.	OB	151.2	33	483	10	48.30	2-13	–	–
Lunn, P.D.	LB	23	4	92	2	46.00	1-34	–	–
Lynch, M.A.	OB	27	5	130	1	130.00	1-43	–	–
McCrum, P.	RFM	12	3	28	0	–	–	–	–

	Cat	O	M	R	W	Avge	Best	5 wI	10 wM
McEwan, S.M.	RFM	375.2	75	1189	38	31.28	3-31	–	–
McKnight, C.T.	SLA	23	5	72	3	24.00	3-48	–	–
Madurasinghe, A.W.R.	OB	176.2	28	560	21	26.66	5-108	1	–
Mahmood, M.	OB	31	9	103	4	25.75	3-63	–	–
Malcolm, D.E.	RF	518.2	99	1688	52	32.46	5-46	2	–
Mallender, N.A.	RFM	553.2	116	1585	51	31.07	5-46	2	–
Marsh, S.A.	RSM	8.4	0	36	2	18.00	2-20	–	–
Marshall, M.D.	RF	554.2	142	1381	72	19.18	7-47	4	2
Martin, P.J.	RFM	275.3	52	868	22	39.45	4-68	–	–
Maru, R.J.	SLA	851.1	219	2420	66	36.66	6-97	2	–
Maynard, M.P.	RM	29	2	184	0	–	–	–	–
Medlycott, K.T.	SLA	748.5	170	2382	61	39.04	7-92	3	–
Merrick, T.A.	RFM	184.3	45	488	17	28.70	4-66	–	–
Metcalfe, A.A.	OB	9.1	0	88	0	–	–	–	–
Middleton, T.C.	SLA	5	0	29	0	–	–	–	–
Mike, G.W.	RMF	60.2	10	263	2	131.50	1-59	–	–
Milburn, E.T.	RM	32.3	4	150	3	50.00	3-43	–	–
Miller, G.	OB	461	114	1308	35	37.37	6-45	1	–
Millmow, J.P.	RFM	105	14	391	11	35.54	3-66	–	–
Millns, D.J.	RMF	206.4	36	662	31	21.35	6-63	2	–
Moir, J.D.	RM	26.3	8	76	1	76.00	1-76	–	–
Moles, A.J.	RM	22	2	133	2	66.50	2-56	–	–
Moody, T.M.	RM	59	15	212	3	70.66	1-7	–	–
More, K.S.		8	0	54	0	–	–	–	–
Morris, H.	RM	6	0	62	0	–	–	–	–
Morris, J.E.	RM	27	0	170	1	170.00	1-17	–	–
Morrison, D.K.	RFM	234.4	36	889	21	42.33	4-64	–	–
Mortensen, O.H.	RFM	316.2	91	785	35	22.42	4-22	–	–
Moseley, E.A.	RFM	21	3	58	1	58.00	1-36	–	–
Moxon, M.D.	RM	57	9	175	3	58.33	1-10	–	–
Mullally, A.D.	LFM	487.2	117	1446	38	38.05	4-59	–	–
Munton, T.A.	RMF	827.1	199	2254	78	28.89	5-33	2	–
Murphy, A.J.	RMF	404.2	76	1367	30	45.56	5-67	2	–
Nelson, A.N.	RFM	33	8	74	1	74.00	1-74	–	–
Nelson, N.	RM	15	0	51	0	–	–	–	–
Newell, M.	LB	8.2	3	35	1	35.00	1-22	–	–
Newport, P.J.	RFM	626.2	116	2001	63	31.76	6-54	4	–
Nicholas, M.C.J.	RM	69.2	9	276	2	138.00	1-7	–	–
North, J.A.	RM	83.1	17	236	6	39.33	2-43	–	–
Owen, P.A.	SLA	57	7	239	4	59.75	2-37	–	–
Parker, P.W.G.	RM	8	0	59	0	–	–	–	–
Parsons, G.J.	RMF	304.5	77	963	35	27.51	6-75	2	–
Patel, M.M.	SLA	297.5	72	836	20	41.80	6-57	2	1
Patterson, B.P.	RF	281.4	45	1015	29	35.00	4-52	–	–
Penberthy, A.L.	RM	207.4	29	791	22	35.95	4-91	–	–
Penn, C.	RFM	186	35	636	11	57.81	3-45	–	–
Pick, R.A.	RMF	494.5	83	1657	51	32.49	7-128	1	1
Pickles, C.S.	RM	325.1	72	1163	28	41.53	3-56	–	–
Pierson, A.R.K.	OB	302.4	55	965	25	38.60	5-101	1	–
Pigott, A.C.S.	RFM	541	94	1997	54	36.98	5-52	3	–
Pointer, G.A.	LMF	17	3	67	0	–	–	–	–
Pook, R.N.	RM	8	3	19	0	–	–	–	–
Pooley, J.C.	OB	2	0	11	0	–	–	–	–
Pooley, M.W.	RM	16	1	67	2	33.50	2-51	–	–

179

	Cat	O	M	R	W	Avge	Best	5 wI	10 wM
Potter, L.	SLA	181	40	623	7	89.00	2-2	–	–
Prabhakar, M.	RMF	281	47	994	16	62.12	4-74	–	–
Prichard, P.J.		1.4	0	11	0	–	–	–	–
Priest, M.W.	SLA	312.4	90	907	14	64.78	3-35	–	–
Pringle, C.	RMF	149	32	483	10	48.30	2-49	–	–
Pringle, D.R.	RMF	358.3	91	994	34	29.23	5-66	–	–
Pyman, R.A.	RM	308.4	81	938	15	62.53	2-29	–	–
Radford, N.V.	RFM	302	49	1195	18	66.38	4-55	–	–
Raju, S.L.V.	SLA	182.3	41	528	9	58.66	4-73	–	–
Raman, W.V.	SLA	15	2	72	1	72.00	1-44	–	–
Ramanayake, C.P.H.	RMF	133	12	510	12	42.50	3-96	–	–
Ramprakash, M.R.	RM	41	7	164	2	82.00	1-17	–	–
Reeve, D.A.	RMF	377.4	111	940	33	28.48	4-42	–	–
Remy, C.C.	RM	54	6	224	5	44.80	4-63	–	–
Richards, I.V.A.	OB	137	26	426	5	85.20	2-27	–	–
Roberts, A.R.	LB	63	14	207	3	69.00	2-123	–	–
Roberts, B.	RM	19	5	52	3	17.33	1-0	–	–
Robinson, J.D.	RM	146.3	28	476	7	68.00	2-84	–	–
Robinson, M.A.	RFM	559.1	104	1889	40	47.22	3-47	–	–
Robinson, P.E.	LM	3.3	0	28	1	28.00	1-10	–	–
Roebuck, P.M.	RM/LB	182.3	42	529	8	66.12	2-34	–	–
Romaines, P.W.	OB	6	0	30	1	30.00	1-30	–	–
Rose, G.D.	RM	571.4	99	1951	53	36.81	5-52	1	–
Roseberry, M.A.	RM	22	5	115	2	57.50	1-41	–	–
Russell, A.B.	RM	6	1	23	1	23.00	1-23	–	–
Rutherford, K.R.	RM	42	3	196	0	–	–	–	–
Salisbury, I.D.K.	LB	601.1	113	2075	42	49.40	5-32	2	–
Saxelby, K.	RMF	91	19	319	7	45.57	4-92	–	–
Saxelby, M.	RM	61.4	9	270	3	90.00	1-21	–	–
Scott, R.J.	RM	36.4	5	165	5	33.00	2-5	–	–
Shah, A.H.	RM	75	19	193	5	38.60	2-46	–	–
Shahid, N.	LB	111.2	18	454	7	64.85	3-91	–	–
Sharma, C.	RFM	13	0	69	0	–	–	–	–
Sharma, S.K.	RM	229	36	873	13	67.15	2-53	–	–
Shastri, R.J.	SLA	199.2	30	607	7	86.71	2-80	–	–
Shine, K.J.	RMF	156.4	30	552	14	39.42	4-52	–	–
Shufflebotham, D.H.	RM	139	20	538	6	89.66	3-60	–	–
Sidebottom, A.	RMF	60.5	11	190	4	47.50	3-54	–	–
Sleep, P.R.	LB	19	1	110	3	36.66	2-47	–	–
Small, G.C.	RFM	425.4	105	1194	32	37.18	6-94	2	–
Smith, C.L.	OB	28	9	97	5	19.40	3-35	–	–
Smith, G.	LFM	26.5	3	81	4	20.25	3-36	–	–
Smith, I.	RM	39	3	181	1	181.00	1-43	–	–
Smith, N.M.K.	OB	177.5	37	535	7	76.42	2-76	–	–
Smith, P.A.	RFM	148.5	34	497	20	24.85	5-48	1	–
Smith, R.A.	LB	0.3	0	5	0	–	–	–	–
Snedden, M.C.	RFM	231.5	56	633	23	27.52	5-63	1	–
Speak, N.J.	RM/OB	5	0	26	1	26.00	1-26	–	–
Stemp, R.D.	SLA	45	14	123	1	123.00	1-32	–	–
Stephenson, F.D.	RFM	610.4	94	2098	54	38.85	6-84	2	–
Stephenson, J.P.	RM	123	28	485	5	97.00	1-16	–	–
Stewart, A.J.	RSM	5	0	32	0	–	–	–	–
Such, P.M.	OB	272.4	67	715	20	35.75	3-34	–	–
Swallow, I.G.	OB	689.1	161	2174	34	63.94	3-88	–	–
Tavaré, C.J.	RSM	17.2	0	162	0	–	–	–	–

	Cat	O	M	R	W	Avge	Best	5 wI	10 wM
Taylor, C.W.	LFM	47.5	7	139	6	23.16	5-33	1	–
Taylor, L.B.	RFM	9	1	34	0	–	–	–	–
Taylor, N.R. (M/MC)	RM	37	7	131	4	32.75	3-44	–	–
Taylor, N.R. (K)	OB	21	5	57	1	57.00	1-19	–	–
Tedstone, G.A.	OB	2	1	1	0	–	–	–	–
Tendulkar, S.R.	RM	79	12	268	3	89.33	3-79	–	–
Terry, V.P.	RM	1	0	19	0	–	–	–	–
Thomas, D.R.	RFM	15	1	65	0	–	–	–	–
Thomas, J.G.	RF	305.2	51	1171	29	40.37	7-75	1	–
Thomas, K.O.	RFM	18.2	3	81	0	–	–	–	–
Thomson, S.A.	RMF	106.2	18	435	5	87.00	2-84	–	–
Thorpe, G.P.	RM	23	7	99	1	99.00	1-30	–	–
Threlfall, P.W.	RMF	30	8	89	5	17.80	3-45	–	–
Thursfield, M.J.	RM	42	11	130	2	65.00	1-24	–	–
Tolley, C.M.	LMF	88	14	326	5	65.20	2-66	–	–
Topley, T.D.	RMF	223	34	713	22	32.40	4-67	–	–
Traicos, A.J.	OB	84	22	186	4	46.50	3-43	–	–
Tremlett, T.M.	RMF	120.5	30	393	10	39.30	3-33	–	–
Trump, H.R.J.	OB	164	41	520	9	57.77	3-58	–	–
Tufnell, P.C.R.	SLA	1036.5	281	2635	74	35.60	6-79	2	–
Turner, G.J.	OB	212.2	39	819	10	81.90	3-100	–	–
Turner, I.J.	SLA	148.2	39	424	9	47.11	2-60	–	–
Twose, R.G.	RM	53	12	185	4	46.25	1-10	–	–
Udal, S.D.	OB	238.3	46	900	22	40.90	4-139	–	–
Van der Merwe, W.M.	RMF	131	27	399	3	133.00	1-44	–	–
Walsh, C.A.	RF	612.1	107	2022	72	28.08	8-58	3	1
Waqar Younis	RF	422	70	1357	57	23.80	7-73	3	1
Ward, T.R.	OB	53	6	225	4	56.25	2-48	–	–
Warner, A.E.	RFM	393.3	67	1330	33	40.30	3-56	–	–
Wasim Akram	LFM	204	44	640	16	40.00	3-76	–	–
Wassan, A.S.	RFM	207.3	24	886	18	49.22	6-89	1	–
Watkin, S.L.	RMF	796.1	137	2712	69	39.30	5-100	1	–
Watkinson, M.	RMF	508.2	122	1578	47	33.57	5-65	3	–
Watson, W.	RMF	54	10	177	3	59.00	2-67	–	–
Waugh, M.E.	RM	191	33	771	12	64.25	5-37	1	–
Weale, S.D.	SLA	50	8	251	1	251.00	1-119	–	–
Weekes, P.N.	OB	80	17	264	4	66.00	2-115	–	–
Wells, A.P.	RM	39	8	169	3	56.33	2-25	–	–
Wells, C.M.	RM	374	68	1237	17	72.76	3-48	–	–
Wells, V.J.	RM	85	19	257	12	21.41	5-43	1	–
Weston, M.J.	RM	21	3	74	1	74.00	1-32	–	–
White, C.	OB	159	23	608	13	46.76	5-74	1	–
Whitney, M.R.	LFM	27	5	97	5	19.40	3-46	–	–
Wickremansinghe, G.P.	RFM	79	17	251	6	41.83	3-95	–	–
Wijegunawardene, K.I.W.	RFM	87.3	13	318	9	35.33	2-30	–	–
Wijetunge, P.K.	SLA	129.4	24	438	12	36.50	4-133	–	–
Wild, D.J.	RM	21.5	6	74	1	74.00	1-32	–	–
Willey, P.	OB	421.4	119	1091	23	47.43	2-7	–	–
Williams, N.F.	RFM	530.1	98	1618	54	29.96	7-61	2	–
Williams, R.G.	OB	432.3	119	1204	31	38.83	4-94	–	–
Winchester, A.L.C.	RM	13	0	81	0	–	–	–	–
Wren, T.N.	LM	122	14	489	6	81.50	2-78	–	–
Wright, A.J.	RM	0.5	0	7	0	–	–	–	–
Yates, G.	OB	167	38	420	8	52.50	4-94	–	–

LEADING CURRENT PLAYERS

The leading career records of players currently registered for first-class county cricket. All figures are to the end of the 1990 English season.

BATTING
(Qualification: 100 innings)

	Runs	Avge
G.A.Hick	15080	64.17
M.Azharuddin	6837	55.13
I.V.A.Richards	32033	50.20
S.J.Cook	15394	48.25
A.J.Lamb	24634	48.11
M.W.Gatting	24455	47.85
M.A.Atherton	5429	47.62
G.A.Gooch	31363	46.46
T.M.Moody	5239	45.95
D.L.Haynes	17126	45.66
R.A.Smith	10841	43.71
C.L.Smith	16475	43.12
A.J.Moles	8118	42.95
R.J.Shastri	9839	41.86
M.R.Ramprakash	3335	41.17
N.H.Fairbrother	10226	41.06
M.R.Benson	13224	40.94
R.J.Bailey	10847	40.93
R.T.Robinson	16989	40.83
D.M.Ward	4179	40.57
D.I.Gower	22258	40.24
T.S.Curtis	11771	39.90
J.J.Whitaker	9884	39.69
M.D.Moxon	12180	39.16
C.J.Tavaré	21519	38.56
D.J.Bicknell	3703	38.17
A.J.Stewart	9166	38.03
J.E.Morris	9798	37.83
B.C.Broad	17368	37.75
M.P.Maynard	6855	37.66
P.M.Roebuck	16719	37.57
D.W.Randall	25727	37.55
N.R.Taylor (Kent)	12309	37.41

BOWLING
(Qualification: 100 wickets)

	Wkts	Avge
M.D.Marshall	1396	18.22
I.R.Bishop	237	21.28
O.H.Mortensen	330	22.70
C.E.L.Ambrose	251	22.77
F.D.Stephenson	393	22.92
C.A.Walsh	776	23.23
A.A.Donald	338	23.68
N.G.Cowans	576	23.84
T.M.Tremlett	449	23.96
A.R.C.Fraser	309	24.00
N.A.Foster	767	24.15
A.Sidebottom	595	24.42
T.A.Merrick	250	24.52
Wasim Akram	273	25.06
P.J.W.Allott	638	25.31
T.D.Topley	272	25.46
N.V.Radford	793	25.60
K.M.Curran	311	25.75
J.E.Emburey	1217	25.76
D.R.Pringle	626	26.10
S.J.Base	250	26.37
M.P.Bicknell	258	26.39
P-J.Bakker	162	26.60
T.A.Munton	254	26.65
I.T.Botham	1082	26.81
G.R.Dilley	611	27.02
P.J.Newport	423	27.04
P.A.J.DeFreitas	413	27.24
K.E.Cooper	704	27.29
T.E.Jesty	585	27.47
J.N.Maguire	334	27.52
P.W.Jarvis	405	27.58
R.M.Ellison	395	27.64

WICKET-KEEPING

	Total	Ct	St
P.R.Downton	767	679	88
B.N.French	760	677	83
R.J.Parks	687	617	70
I.J.Gould	603	536	67
D.E.East	533	480	53
R.C.Russell	502	430	72
S.J.Rhodes	416	376	42
D.Ripley	312	264	48
C.P.Metson	287	265	22

FIELDING

	Ct
G.A.Gooch	427
I.V.A.Richards	413
C.J.Tavaré	362
J.E.Emburey	357
M.W.Gatting	346
C.W.J.Athey	332
D.W.Randall	329
I.T.Botham	324
D.P.Hughes	321

FIRST-CLASS CAREER RECORDS
Compiled by Geoffrey Saulez

The following career records are for all players who appeared in first-class cricket during the 1990 season and are complete to the end of that season. Some players who did not appear for their counties in 1990, but remain registered, are also included.

BATTING AND FIELDING

'1000' denotes instances of scoring 1000 runs in a season. Where such aggregates have been achieved outside the UK, they are shown after a plus sign.

	M	I	NO	HS	Runs	Avge	100	1000	Ct/St
Adams, C.J.	31	46	5	111*	1214	29.60	2	–	36
Afford, J.A.	78	70	31	22*	124	3.17	–	–	22
Agnew, J.P.	218	232	49	90	2118	11.57	–	–	39
Ahangama, F.S.	19	12	4	34*	83	10.37	–	–	4
Alikhan, R.I.	80	136	12	138	3427	27.63	2	–	44
Alleyne, M.W.	77	118	17	256	2896	28.67	4	–	68/1
Allott, P.J.W.	236	254	62	88	3297	17.17	–	–	130
Almaer, S.A.	15	24	1	67	441	19.17	–	–	6
Ambrose, C.E.L.	66	89	21	59	1116	16.41	–	–	13
Andrew, S.J.W.	75	48	25	35	224	9.73	–	–	16
Anthony, H.A.G.	11	15	0	39	174	11.60	–	–	5
Arnold, K.A.	2	–	–	–	–	–	–	–	3
Arnott, K.J.	16	29	5	70	542	22.58	–	–	10
Arscott, J.P.	2	4	1	43*	75	25.00	–	–	0/2
Asif Din	181	294	42	158*	7559	29.99	6	2	98
Atapattu, M.S.	12	17	5	74*	559	46.58	–	–	9
Atherton, M.A.	77	129	15	191	5429	47.62	16	3	65
Athey, C.W.J.	342	567	56	184	17585	34.41	35	8	332/2
Atkins, P.D.	10	18	3	114*	471	31.40	1	–	3
Atkinson, J.C.M.	41	64	5	79	1316	22.30	–	–	19
Austin, I.D.	31	40	11	64	704	24.27	–	–	3
Ayling, J.R.	28	44	7	88*	1079	29.16	–	–	7
Aymes, A.N.	8	10	5	75*	399	79.80	–	–	23/3
Azharuddin, M.	96	141	17	226	6837	55.13	23	0+2	78
Babington, A.M.	60	61	26	20	224	6.40	–	–	21
Bailey, R.J.	188	313	48	224*	10847	40.93	26	7	134
Bainbridge, P.	257	424	60	169	12353	33.93	22	8	110
Bairstow, D.L.	459	647	119	145	13961	26.44	10	3	961/138
Bakker, P-J.	53	41	16	22	247	9.88	–	–	7
Ball, M.C.J.	14	14	3	17*	72	6.54	–	–	9
Barnes, S.N.	10	9	2	12*	23	3.28	–	–	3
Barnett, A.A.	1	1	0	10	10	10.00	–	–	–
Barnett, K.J.	290	465	40	239*	15826	37.23	32	8	186
Bartlett, R.J.	38	62	5	117*	1327	23.28	2	–	27
Barwick, S.R.	143	137	57	30	629	7.86	–	–	30
Base, S.J.	77	96	26	58	834	11.91	–	–	26
Bastien, S.	20	17	7	36*	105	10.50	–	–	1
Batty, J.D.	8	7	3	21	34	8.50	–	–	4
Bee, A.	2	2	0	29*	40	–	–	–	1
Bell, R.M.	2	2	1	0*	0	0.00	–	–	–
Benjamin, J.E.	22	18	8	41	213	21.30	–	–	6
Benjamin, W.K.M.	100	118	29	101*	2094	23.52	1	–	43
Benson, J.D.R.	23	36	6	106	838	27.93	1	–	13
Benson, M.R.	207	354	27	162	13224	40.44	34	9	96

	M	I	NO	HS	Runs	Avge	100	1000	Ct/St
Bent, P.	24	41	1	144	1001	25.02	1	–	1
Berry, P.J.	7	7	6	31*	76	76.00	–	–	6
Bevins, S.R.	4	5	2	10	28	9.33	–	–	13
Bicknell, D.J.	64	112	15	186	3703	38.17	10	2	25
Bicknell, M.P.	81	79	26	50*	776	14.64	–	–	26
Bishop, I.R.	62	86	29	103*	909	15.94	1	–	13
Blakey, R.J.	109	179	23	221	5092	32.64	6	3	162/13
Boden, D.J.P.	1	–	–	–	–	–	–	–	1
Boiling, J.	4	6	3	15	38	12.66	–	–	1
Boon, T.J.	162	269	34	144	7484	31.84	8	5	80
Booth, P.A.	33	45	11	60	433	12.73	–	–	10
Botham, I.T.	359	551	39	228	17436	34.05	34	4	324
Bowler, P.D.	80	141	12	210	4754	36.85	10	3	54/1
Bracewell, J.G.	149	208	40	110	4354	25.91	4	–	125
Bramhall, S.	2	3	2	1*	1	1.00	–	–	2/1
Brandes, E.A.	26	36	6	31	295	9.83	–	–	13
Brent, J.P.	3	5	2	34*	101	33.66	–	–	–
Briant, G.A.	2	3	0	69	109	36.33	–	–	1
Briers, N.E.	287	462	44	201*	13120	31.38	19	7	113
Broad, B.C.	276	492	32	227*	17368	37.75	37	8	158
Brown, A.M.	14	22	3	139*	668	35.15	1	–	12
Brown, G.K.	2	4	1	103	209	69.66	1	–	2
Brown, K.R.	87	134	23	200*	4099	36.92	8	1	105
Brown, S.J.	15	14	6	25*	70	8.75	–	–	6
Bullen, C.K.	29	34	6	65	626	22.35	–	–	26
Bunting, R.A.	34	36	11	73	260	10.40	–	–	4
Burn, P.	1	2	1	47*	47	47.00	–	–	–
Burns, N.D.	98	144	30	166	3290	28.85	3	–	202/17
Butchart, I.P.	43	68	10	82	1083	18.67	–	–	36
Butcher, A.R.	374	638	57	216*	20773	35.75	42	11	169
Butcher, I.P.	124	201	16	139	5480	29.62	11	2	87
Butcher, R.O.	277	428	43	197	12021	31.22	17	4	290/1
Butler, K.A.	1	1	1	10*	10	–	–	–	–
Buzza, A.J.	17	17	5	25*	86	7.16	–	–	6
Byas, D.	54	88	7	117	2140	26.41	2	–	48
Cann, M.J.	40	62	5	138	1579	27.70	3	–	15
Capel, D.J.	216	327	52	134	8384	30.48	10	3	100
Carrick, P.	400	509	88	131*	9325	22.14	3	–	186
Chapman, C.A.	2	4	0	20	47	11.75	–	–	2
Chauhan, S.	6	6	0	25	51	8.50	–	–	2
Childs, J.H.	282	258	121	34*	1161	8.47	–	–	92
Clarke, A.R.	26	37	9	68	406	14.50	–	–	7
Cleal, M.W.	15	19	1	30	165	9.16	–	–	4
Clinton, G.S.	270	450	53	192	13118	33.04	20	7	96
Cobb, R.A.	122	195	15	91	4388	24.37	–	1	73
Cohen, M.F.	8	14	0	60	234	16.71	–	–	4
Connor, C.A.	128	100	33	46	614	9.16	–	–	39
Cook, G.	460	793	65	203	23277	31.97	37	12	419/3
Cook, N.G.B.	302	318	83	75	2757	11.73	–	–	178
Cook, S.J.	205	359	40	313*	15394	48.25	43	2+2	111
Cooper, K.E.	270	279	67	46	2139	10.08	–	–	85
Cork, D.G.	2	2	1	7	9	9.00	–	–	–
Cottey, P.A.	48	79	2	156	1845	26.73	3	1	22
Cowans, N.G.	197	199	50	66	1345	9.02	–	–	54
Cowdrey, C.S.	294	447	68	159	12048	31.78	21	4	289

	M	I	NO	HS	Runs	Avge	100	1000	Ct/St
Cowdrey, G.R.	81	128	17	145	3543	31.91	5	1	43
Cowley, N.G.	271	375	62	109*	7309	23.35	2	1	105
Cox, R.M.F.	4	7	2	104*	220	44.00	1	–	3
Crawley, J.P.	3	3	1	76*	103	51.50	–	–	1
Crawley, M.A.	26	37	6	140	1331	42.93	3	–	17
Croft, R.D.B.	21	34	13	91*	801	38.14	–	–	3
Crowe, J.J.	160	269	31	159	8503	35.72	17	0+1	171
Crowe, M.D.	196	321	50	242*	15512	57.23	54	2+4	184
Curran, K.M.	168	259	45	144*	7883	36.83	18	5	97
Curtis, D.M.	4	4	0	43	89	22.25	–	–	–
Curtis, T.S.	200	341	46	197*	11771	39.90	20	7	109
Dale, A.	13	22	1	92	363	17.28	–	–	6
Davies, H.R.	4	4	2	24	36	18.00	–	–	–
Davies, M.	1	1	1	5*	5	–	–	–	1
Davis, R.P.	72	86	22	67	925	14.45	–	–	60
Davis, W.W.	173	215	58	77	2211	14.08	–	–	57
DeFreitas, P.A.J.	127	172	19	113	3321	21.70	4	–	40
Dennis, S.J.	101	98	29	53*	666	9.65	–	–	26
Derrick, J.	93	122	35	78*	1969	22.63	–	–	39
De Silva, P.A.	60	91	11	221*	3493	43.66	9	–	40
De Villiers, P.S.	43	59	20	46*	672	17.23	–	–	24
Dilley, G.R.	221	238	87	81	2241	14.84	–	–	72
Dobson, M.C.	8	12	1	52	143	13.00	–	–	–
Dodemaide, A.I.C.	117	180	42	112	4042	29.28	2	1	61
Doidge, M.J.	1	–	–	–	–	–	–	–	–
D'Oliveira, D.B.	181	287	19	155	7465	27.85	8	4	153
Dolphin, D.F.	4	4	2	25	40	20.00	–	–	–
Donald, A.A.	96	120	43	40	843	10.94	–	–	21
Donelan, B.T.P.	20	22	9	53	252	19.38	–	–	8
Downton, P.R.	309	399	74	126*	8081	24.86	6	1	679/88
Dube, L.E.	2	1	0	1	1	1.00	–	–	–
Duers, K.G.	26	25	15	15*	89	8.90	–	–	8
Dunlop, A.R.	1	1	0	56	56	56.00	–	–	1
Dyer, G.B.A.	4	8	2	23	107	17.83	–	–	–
Ealham, M.A.	4	5	2	45	69	23.00	–	–	–
East, D.E.	190	254	32	134	4553	20.50	4	–	480/53
Ellcock, R.M.	42	46	12	45*	398	11.70	–	–	8
Ellison, R.M.	168	232	56	108	4216	23.95	1	–	62
Emburey, J.E.	399	502	102	133	9132	22.83	4	–	357
Evans, K.P.	55	81	19	100*	1647	26.56	1	–	51
Evans, R.A.	1	1	1	4*	4	–	–	–	–
Evans, R.J.	6	9	3	50*	112	18.66	–	–	4
Fairbrother, N.H.	184	290	41	366	10226	41.06	20	7	111
Farbrace, P.	16	20	5	79	317	21.13	–	–	35/4
Feltham, M.A.	88	105	27	101	1714	21.97	1	–	41
Felton, N.A.	144	245	12	173*	7104	30.48	12	3	76
Ferris, G.J.F.	94	105	44	36*	745	12.21	–	–	13
Field-Buss, M.G.	7	9	2	34*	68	9.71	–	–	1
Fitton, J.D.	36	41	12	44	519	17.89	–	–	10
Fleming, M.V.	27	44	9	102	1184	33.82	1	–	7
Fletcher, S.D.	94	80	29	28*	366	7.17	–	–	20
Flower, G.W.	4	7	1	65	184	30.66	–	–	4
Folland, N.A.	1	2	0	82	108	54.00	–	–	–
Folley, I.	136	158	49	69	1465	13.44	–	–	58
Fordham, A.	55	97	11	206*	3077	35.77	6	1	43

	M	I	NO	HS	Runs	Avge	100	1000	Ct/St
Foster, N.A.	188	221	52	101	3269	19.34	1	–	92
Fothergill, A.R.	1	1	0	3	3	3.00	–	–	–
Fowler, G.	244	411	23	226	14227	36.66	32	8	134/5
Franklin, T.J.	119	201	16	181	6618	35.77	15	–	68
Fraser, A.G.J.	5	5	3	19*	51	25.50	–	–	–
Fraser, A.R.C.	94	104	26	92	962	12.33	–	–	12
French, B.N.	302	400	80	105*	6146	19.20	1	–	677/83
Frost, M.	33	31	9	12	64	2.90	–	–	4
Gallian, J.E.R.	1	1	1	17*	17	–	–	–	–
Garnham, M.A.	122	164	34	100	3401	26.16	1	–	258/28
Gatting, M.W.	386	601	90	258	24455	47.85	58	12+1	346
Gerrans, P.S.	9	9	0	39	102	11.33	–	–	4
Gidley, M.I.	6	6	1	73	128	25.60	–	–	3
Goldsmith, S.C.	49	81	6	89	1763	23.50	–	1	32
Gooch, G.A.	431	732	57	333	31363	46.46	82	14+1	427
Gough, D.	16	19	7	24	134	11.16	–	–	4
Gould, I.J.	297	399	63	128	8756	26.05	4	–	536/67
Govan, J.W.	8	11	1	17	80	8.00	–	–	4
Gower, D.I.	379	609	56	228	22258	40.24	46	10	239/1
Graveney, D.A.	383	487	142	119	6109	17.70	2	–	201
Gray, A.H.	94	94	15	54*	909	11.50	–	–	41
Grayson, A.P.	5	8	4	44*	145	36.25	–	–	2
Greatbatch, M.J.	84	144	19	202*	4793	38.34	10	–	69
Green, S.J.	4	7	0	44	91	13.00	–	–	2
Greenfield, K.	10	18	2	102*	396	24.75	1	–	7
Greenidge, C.G.	506	860	72	273*	36434	46.23	90	15+2	508
Greensword, S.	43	74	8	84*	1095	16.59	–	–	30
Greig, I.A.	233	308	46	291	7691	29.35	8	2	145
Griffith, F.A.	11	18	1	37	208	12.23	–	–	6
Gurusinha, A.P.	40	60	9	118	2244	44.00	7	–	36
Hadlee, Sir R.J.	342	473	93	210*	12052	31.71	14	2	198
Hagan, D.A.	40	65	4	88	1242	20.36	–	–	18
Haggo, D.J.	4	6	0	45	115	19.16	–	–	5/3
Hall, J.W.	20	37	2	125	1140	32.57	2	1	6
Hallett, J.C.	3	1	0	0	0	0.00	–	–	–
Hanley, R.	2	4	0	28	32	8.00	–	–	–
Hansford, A.R.	9	10	3	29	108	15.42	–	–	3
Harden, R.J.	111	173	28	115*	5160	35.58	9	2	65
Hardie, B.R.	378	608	79	162	18103	34.22	27	11	349
Hardy, J.J.E.	130	217	29	119	5828	31.00	4	1	79
Harper, R.A.	164	210	34	234	5523	31.38	8	–	206
Harrison, G.D.	8	13	1	86	315	26.25	–	–	1
Hartley, P.J.	84	91	22	127*	1572	22.78	1	–	32
Hathurusinghe, U.C.	23	37	3	136	963	28.32	1	–	13
Hawkes, C.J.	1	2	1	3	5	5.00	–	–	1
Hayhurst, A.N.	64	98	14	170	2744	32.66	5	1	20
Haynes, D.L.	247	421	46	255*	17126	45.66	38	2+3	145/1
Heap, R.	20	36	4	63	669	20.90	–	–	11
Hegg, W.K.	86	122	19	130	2272	22.05	2	–	208/26
Hemmings, E.E.	456	595	137	127*	9003	19.65	1	–	188
Henderson, I.M.	21	23	6	44	186	10.94	–	–	5
Henry, O.	96	147	29	125	3230	27.37	4	–	104
Hepworth, P.N.	13	22	2	55*	380	19.00	–	–	4
Hick, G.A.	168	269	34	405*	15080	64.17	54	6+1	189

	M	I	NO	HS	Runs	Avge	100	1000	Ct/St
Hinks, S.G.	145	253	13	234	7294	30.39	11	3	90
Hirwani, N.D.	48	48	23	17	191	7.64	–	–	20
Hodgson, G.D.	27	44	4	126	1380	34.50	2	1	12
Holloway, P.C.L.	3	5	0	16	40	8.00	–	–	8/1
Holmes, G.C.	202	327	50	182	7956	28.72	11	3	84
Hooper, A.M.	7	10	0	89	122	12.20	–	–	1
Houseman, I.J.	4	2	1	18	18	18.00	–	–	–
Hughes, D.P.	439	578	106	153	10308	21.83	8	2	321
Hughes, J.G.	4	7	0	2	4	0.57	–	–	–
Hughes, S.P.	174	188	61	53	1498	11.79	–	–	41
Humpage, G.W.	351	574	76	254	18098	36.34	29	11	671/72
Hussain, N.	48	73	10	197	2520	40.00	5	–	48
Hutchinson, G.M.	2	2	0	29	31	15.50	–	–	–
Hutchinson, I.J.F.	13	22	3	201*	779	41.00	3	–	14
Igglesden, A.P.	68	76	28	41	502	10.45	–	–	20
Illingworth, R.K.	195	208	54	120*	3186	20.68	3	–	87
Ilott, M.C.	16	15	6	42*	151	16.77	–	–	2
Irani, R.	1	–	–	–	–	–	–	–	–
Jackson, P.B.	10	14	3	59	244	22.18	–	–	16/5
James, K.D.	93	123	24	162	2956	29.85	5	–	28
James, S.P.	41	71	4	151*	2168	32.35	7	1	25
James, W.R.	7	12	2	52	223	22.30	–	–	10
Jarvis, K.B.S.	260	199	87	32	403	3.59	–	–	59
Jarvis, M.P.	24	32	8	28	174	7.25	–	–	6
Jarvis, P.W.	124	143	45	59*	1408	14.36	–	–	34
Jayasuriya, S.T.	31	46	9	207*	1762	47.62	5	–	14
Jean-Jacques, M.	46	57	13	73	546	12.40	–	–	11
Jenkins, R.H.J.	9	12	5	19*	58	8.28	–	–	1
Jesty, T.E.	489	775	105*	248	21790	32.52	34	10	265/1
Johnson, P.	169	280	26	165*	8645	34.03	17	4	119/1
Johnson, S.W.	6	6	4	14*	35	17.50	–	–	2
Jones, A.H.	96	163	26	181*	5690	41.53	8	0+1	61
Jones, A.N.	137	120	51	43*	814	11.79	–	–	40
Joseph, L.A.	21	20	6	69*	347	24.78	–	–	7
Kallicharran, A.I.	505	834	86	243*	32650	43.64	87	12+1	323
Kapil Dev	239	341	36	193	9824	32.20	14	–	169
Kelleher, D.J.M.	33	41	5	53*	526	14.61	–	–	8
Kellett, S.A.	18	31	3	75*	779	27.82	–	–	9
Kendrick, N.M.	17	16	6	52*	149	14.90	–	–	18
Kilborn, M.J.	31	49	4	95	1275	28.33	–	–	23
Krikken, K.M.	27	39	5	77*	596	17.52	–	–	65/4
Kuiper, A.P.	111	176	23	161*	5058	33.05	5	–	76
Kumble, A.	12	13	4	58	215	23.88	–	–	3
Kuruppu, D.S.B.P.	38	63	7	201*	2037	36.37	4	–	41/10
Labrooy, G.F.	24	24	5	69	360	18.94	–	–	7
Laing, D.R.	10	15	1	59	210	15.00	–	–	4
Lamb, A.J.	362	604	92	294	24634	48.11	66	9	274
Lampitt, S.R.	47	47	11	46	577	16.02	–	–	22
Larkins, W.	399	693	42	252	22278	34.22	49	11	234
Lawrence, D.V.	160	177	34	65*	1376	9.62	–	–	40
Leatherdale, D.A.	21	29	2	70	502	18.59	–	–	18
Lefebvre, R.P.	17	16	3	53	214	16.46	–	–	8
Lenham, N.J.	89	151	16	123	4203	31.13	6	1	33
Lester, T.A.	1	1	0	4	4	4.00	–	–	–
Lewis, C.C.	51	75	10	189*	1460	22.46	1	–	39

	M	I	NO	HS	Runs	Avge	100	1000	Ct/St
Lewis, D.A.	3	5	0	42	76	15.20	–	–	1
Lewis, J.J.B.	1	1	1	116*	116	–	1	–	1
Lilley, A.W.	120	190	15	113*	4495	25.68	3	–	67
Llong, N.J.	1	–	–	–	–	–	–	–	1
Lloyd, G.D.	22	34	3	117	1260	40.64	3	–	12
Lloyd, T.A.	267	471	41	208*	15180	35.30	29	8	132
Lloyds, J.W.	243	373	58	132*	9876	31.35	10	3	208
Longley, J.I.	4	8	0	17	42	5.25	–	–	–
Lord, G.J.	73	118	10	199	2988	27.66	5	1	19
Lowrey, M.J.	10	18	2	72	363	22.68	–	–	1
Lunn, P.D.	16	21	5	61	431	26.93	–	–	2
Lynch, M.A.	267	426	51	172*	13570	36.18	30	7	252
McCrum, P.	1	1	0	0	0	0.00	–	–	–
McEwan, S.M.	55	35	16	54	348	18.31	–	–	17
McGrady, J.E.	6	2	0	14	15	7.50	–	–	0/2
McKnight, C.T.	1	1	0	0	0	0.00	–	–	1
MacLeay, K.H.	90	112	18	114*	2295	24.41	2	–	62
Madurasinghe, A.W.R.	26	29	9	51	353	17.65	–	–	13
Maguire, J.N.	99	122	37	65*	840	9.88	–	–	34
Mahanama, R.S.	40	63	9	114	1968	36.44	2	–	27
Maher, B.J.M.	127	199	35	126	3662	22.32	4	–	280/14
Mahmood, M.	1	1	0	3	3	3.00	–	–	1
Malcolm, D.E.	85	91	29	51	530	8.54	–	–	15
Mallender, N.A.	258	282	89	88	2985	15.46	–	–	91
Manjrekar, S.V.	58	86	15	278	3857	54.32	10	–	30
Marsh, S.A.	127	178	36	120	3686	25.95	3	–	258/19
Marshall, M.D.	324	411	53	117	8757	24.46	6	–	118
Martin, P.J.	12	9	3	21	64	10.66	–	–	6
Martindale, D.J.R.	54	84	9	138	1857	24.76	4	–	23
Maru, R.J.	170	153	40	74	1842	16.30	–	–	170
Maynard, M.P.	123	207	25	191*	6855	37.66	11	5	105
Medlycott, K.T.	122	153	36	153	3060	26.15	2	–	84
Mendis, G.D.	320	558	55	209*	18798	37.37	36	11	132/1
Merrick, T.A.	69	88	17	74*	1061	14.94	–	–	26
Metcalfe, A.A.	141	245	15	216*	8473	36.83	21	5	50
Metson, C.P.	119	158	37	96	2021	16.70	–	–	265/22
Middleton, T.C	36	59	7	127	1878	36.11	5	1	25
Mike, G.W.	5	7	2	56*	116	23.20	–	–	4
Milburn, E.T.	5	8	4	35	86	21.50	–	–	2
Miller, G.	383	548	94	130	12027	26.49	2	–	309
Millmow, J.P.	32	22	11	16*	89	8.09	–	–	9
Millns, D.J.	24	25	11	10*	59	4.21	–	–	9
Moir, J.D.	2	3	1	15	28	14.00	–	–	1
Moles, A.J.	118	214	25	230*	8118	42.95	20	3	88
Mongia, N.R.	14	21	6	101*	584	38.93	1	–	23/4
Moody, T.M.	76	123	9	202	5239	45.95	16	1+1	37
Moores, P.	92	130	17	116	2368	20.95	2	–	182/21
More, K.S.	93	121	27	101*	2824	30.04	3	–	179/45
Morris, H.	161	274	28	160*	8664	35.21	19	4	85
Morris, J.E.	170	283	24	191	9798	37.83	23	5	76
Morris, M.J.	16	26	5	45	281	13.38	–	–	8
Morris, R.E.	27	41	3	96	873	22.97	–	–	5
Morrison, D.K.	63	59	25	36	270	7.94	–	–	23
Mortensen, O.H.	111	129	70	74*	560	9.49	–	–	35

	M	I	NO	HS	Runs	Avge	100	1000	Ct/St
Moseley, E.A.	64	83	15	70*	1259	18.51	–	–	17
Moxon, M.D.	196	336	25	218*	12180	39.16	25	6	159
Mudassar Nazar	217	353	33	241	14075	43.98	42	0+4	139
Mullally, A.D.	35	30	10	34	177	8.85	–	–	9
Munton, T.A.	98	97	38	38	473	8.01	–	–	26
Murphy, A.J.	48	46	18	38	109	3.89	–	–	8
Neale, P.A.	337	546	88	167	16879	36.85	28	8	127
Nelson, A.N.	3	5	2	23*	56	18.66	–	–	1
Nelson, N.	1	1	0	0	0	0.00	–	–	1
Newell, M.	99	174	24	203*	4470	29.80	6	1	90/1
Newport, P.J.	142	154	49	98	2735	26.04	–	–	45
Nicholas, M.C.J.	278	457	61	206*	13123	33.13	28	7	176
Nixon, P.A.	25	30	11	46	498	26.21	–	–	61/3
Noon, W.M.	4	5	0	37	43	8.60	–	–	8/2
North, J.A.	4	5	1	19*	41	10.25	–	–	1
O'Gorman, T.J.G.	22	39	4	124	1081	30.88	3	–	13
Ostler, D.P.	11	19	2	71	510	30.00	–	–	9
Owen, P.A.	3	2	0	1	2	1.00	–	–	–
Parker, P.W.G.	316	540	75	215	16557	35.60	40	8	220
Parks, R.J.	248	274	79	89	3775	19.35	–	–	617/70
Parore, A.C.	13	15	1	45	248	17.71	–	–	32/3
Parsons, G.J.	236	309	71	76	4512	18.95	–	–	72
Patel, M.M.	10	13	5	41*	107	13.37	–	–	3
Patterson, B.M.W.	3	4	0	100	259	64.75	1	–	8
Patterson, B.P.	132	132	49	29	505	6.08	–	–	24
Patterson, T.J.T.	2	2	0	84	107	53.50	–	–	2
Penberthy, A.L.	16	25	3	101*	510	23.18	1	–	12
Penn, C.	98	114	30	115	1648	19.61	1	–	45
Peters, N.H.	16	18	8	25*	101	10.10	–	–	7
Philip, I.L.	5	7	0	145	344	49.14	2	–	4
Pick, R.A.	99	99	28	63	1094	15.40	–	–	23
Pickles, C.S.	41	51	17	66	921	27.08	–	–	20
Pierson, A.R.K.	52	58	25	42*	372	11.27	–	–	16
Pigott, A.C.S.	198	241	51	104*	3941	20.74	1	–	105
Piper, K.J.	28	36	3	111	669	20.27	1	–	66/5
Pointer, G.A.	16	25	5	33	234	11.70	–	–	1
Pollard, P.R.	39	69	1	153	1901	27.95	3	1	34
Pook, R.N.	2	3	1	6	6	3.00	–	–	3
Pooley, J.C.	2	3	0	14	35	11.66	–	–	1
Pooley, M.W.	12	16	6	38	155	15.50	–	–	4
Potter, L.	164	264	32	165*	6762	29.14	7	2	147
Prabhakar, M.	76	100	23	229*	3545	46.03	10	–	26
Prichard, P.J.	147	230	27	245	7001	34.48	8	3	88
Priest, M.W.	38	61	11	92*	1565	31.30	–	–	22
Priestley, I.M.	2	4	2	23	25	12.50	–	–	1
Pringle, C.	11	11	3	33	120	15.00	–	–	8
Pringle, D.R.	241	339	61	128	7454	26.81	8	–	127
Pringle, N.J.	25	44	6	79	662	17.42	–	–	14
Pycroft, A.J.	67	120	14	133	4047	38.17	5	–	58
Pyman, R.A.	21	27	5	69	320	14.54	–	–	6
Radford, N.V.	217	218	49	76*	2722	16.10	–	–	113
Raju, S.L.V.	36	36	12	52*	403	16.79	–	–	18
Raman, W.V.	60	92	14	313	3769	48.32	6	0+1	41
Ramanayake, C.P.H.	35	41	10	68	476	15.35	–	–	9

	M	I	NO	HS	Runs	Avge	100	1000	Ct/St
Ramprakash, M.R.	62	103	22	146*	3335	41.17	6	2	28
Randall, D.W.	442	754	69	237	25727	37.55	46	12	329
Ratcliffe, J.D.	29	55	7	127*	1382	28.79	1	–	14
Ren, M.P.	4	8	1	53	153	21.85	–	–	–
Reeve, D.A.	146	179	50	202*	4185	32.44	5	1	101
Remy, C.C.	3	2	1	4*	4	4.00	–	–	1
Rhodes, S.J.	156	197	69	108	3969	31.00	1	–	374/42
Richards, I.V.A.	454	708	50	322	33033	50.20	109	13+3	413/1
Richardson, R.B.	118	194	14	194	7312	40.62	21	0+1	114
Ripley, D.	135	171	38	134*	2882	21.66	4	–	264/48
Roberts, A.R.	4	6	1	8*	27	5.40	–	–	2
Roberts, B.	204	331	32	184	9102	30.44	13	3	165/1
Roberts, M.J.	1	2	0	85	86	43.00	–	–	–
Roberts, M.L.	8	8	1	25	93	13.28	–	–	14/1
Robertson, C.M.	18	32	1	125	433	13.96	1	–	8
Robinson, J.D.	18	26	4	72	405	18.40	–	–	4
Robinson, M.A.	65	68	32	19*	72	2.00	–	–	14
Robinson, P.E.	108	176	24	150*	5375	35.36	5	2	76
Robinson, R.T.	271	474	58	220*	16989	40.83	39	8	168
Roebuck, P.M.	318	523	78	221*	16719	37.57	32	9	158
Romaines, P.W.	170	304	23	186	8085	28.77	13	3	67
Rose, G.D.	85	105	29	97*	2206	29.02	–	1	38
Roseberry, M.A.	71	116	16	135	3227	32.27	4	1	50
Russell, A.B.	4	5	0	51	122	24.40	–	–	5
Russell, M.J.	4	3	0	4	10	3.33	–	–	1
Russell, R.C.	196	264	62	128*	5312	26.29	3	–	430/72
Rutherford, K.R.	108	179	18	317	6581	40.87	18	–	84
Sadiq, Z.A.	8	12	0	64	213	17.75	–	–	5
Salisbury, I.D.K.	31	33	14	68	375	19.73	–	–	17
Sargeant, N.F.	6	5	1	18	45	11.25	–	–	10/2
Saxelby, K.	136	137	42	59*	1112	11.70	–	–	31
Saxelby, M.	9	17	5	73	371	30.91	–	–	3
Scott, C.W.	61	72	18	78	1263	23.38	–	–	132/9
Scott, R.J.	27	46	4	107*	917	21.83	1	–	20
Seymour, A.C.	4	6	3	89	164	54.66	–	–	1
Shah, A.H.	29	47	3	185	1078	24.50	2	–	12
Shahid, N.	26	38	9	125	1258	43.37	1	1	28
Sharma, C.	74	82	25	72*	1653	29.00	–	–	40
Sharma, S.K.	49	47	16	76	1137	36.67	–	–	13
Sharp, K.	218	361	38	181	9962	30.84	14	1	107
Shastri, R.J.	193	280	45	200*	9839	41.86	24	1+1	113
Shaw, C.	61	58	27	31	340	10.96	–	–	9
Shine, K.J.	9	3	2	26*	53	53.00	–	–	1
Shufflebotham, D.H.	9	10	3	29	149	21.28	–	–	1
Sidebottom, A.	227	262	61	124	4490	22.33	1	–	62
Sidhu, N.S.	67	102	6	286	3769	39.26	11	–	22
Sleep, P.R.	147	240	39	146*	6796	33.81	13	–	86
Small, G.C.	226	291	66	70	3335	14.82	–	–	65
Smith, B.F.	2	2	1	15*	19	19.00	–	–	1
Smith, C.L.	253	439	57	217	16475	43.12	41	9	172
Smith, D.M.	258	408	79	189*	11823	35.93	23	5	157
Smith, G.	10	11	2	30	90	10.00	–	–	3
Smith, I.	52	68	11	116	1429	25.07	3	–	17
Smith, I.D.S.	162	228	37	173	5090	26.64	6	–	360/31

	M	I	NO	HS	Runs	Avge	100	1000	Ct/St
Smith, N.M.K.	22	30	5	161	677	29.08	1	–	7
Smith, P.A.	159	259	32	140	6534	28.78	4	2	45
Smith, R.A.	180	303	55	209*	10841	43.71	27	5	114
Snedden, M.C.	118	124	29	69	1792	18.86	–	–	55
Speak, N.J.	13	23	1	138	644	29.27	1	–	9
Speight, M.P.	46	77	9	131	2230	32.79	2	1	36
Stanley, N.A.	11	18	2	75	450	28.12	–	–	4
Stanworth, J.	37	38	11	50*	236	8.74	–	–	54/8
Stemp, R.D.	2	2	2	3*	3	–	–	–	1
Stephenson, F.D.	96	154	17	165	3575	26.09	4	1	43
Stephenson, J.P.	104	178	21	202*	5740	36.56	9	2	60
Stewart, A.J.	168	272	31	206*	9166	38.03	16	5	209/6
Storie, A.C.	46	76	12	106	1382	21.59	1	–	30
Stovold, A.W.	354	630	35	212*	17705	29.75	20	8	289/45
Such, P.M.	103	86	33	27	171	3.22	–	–	41
Swallow, I.G.	84	99	25	114	1483	20.04	1	–	40
Swan, R.G.	11	17	1	77	359	22.43	–	–	7
Tavaré, C.J.	374	623	65	219	21519	38.56	39	14	361
Taylor, C.W.	2	2	1	13	13	13.00	–	–	–
Taylor, L.B.	218	199	86	60	1061	9.38	–	–	53
Taylor, N.R. (M/MCo)	2	2	0	0	0	0.00	–	–	1
Taylor, N.R. (K)	220	379	50	204	12309	37.41	30	7	119
Tedstone, G.A.	50	67	9	67*	935	16.12	–	–	82/14
Tendulkar, S.R.	29	47	8	119*	2143	54.94	4	–	9
Tennant, L.	4	4	2	12*	16	8.00	–	–	1
Terry, V.P.	196	327	33	190	10271	34.93	22	7	219
Thomas, D.R.	1	1	0	27	27	27.00	–	–	–
Thomas, J.G.	180	241	42	110	3213	16.14	2	–	71
Thomas, K.O.	1	1	0	2	2	2.00	–	–	–
Thomson, S.A.	29	45	14	84	1029	33.19	–	–	14
Thorpe, G.P.	41	66	13	154	2040	38.49	3	1	26
Threlfall, P.W.	2	–	–	–	–	–	–	–	–
Thursfield, M.J.	2	–	–	–	–	–	–	–	–
Tillekeratne, H.P.	36	52	15	128*	1662	44.91	6	–	37/2
Titchard, S.P.	3	5	0	80	129	25.80	–	–	–
Tolley, C.M.	11	12	3	37	199	22.11	–	–	2
Topley, T.D.	80	94	22	66	1116	15.50	–	–	44
Townsend, G.T.J.	2	4	1	15	21	7.00	–	–	3
Traicos, A.J.	113	154	60	43	1123	11.94	–	–	100
Tremlett, T.M.	206	249	66	102*	3862	21.10	1	–	73
Trevelyan, R.W.D.	3	1	0	0	0	0.00	–	–	2
Trump, H.R.J.	30	31	4	48	167	6.18	–	–	16
Tufnell, P.C.R.	63	60	21	37	434	11.12	–	–	28
Turner, G.J.	34	59	5	69*	1392	24.85	–	–	25
Turner, I.J.	6	5	2	14	24	8.00	–	–	2
Turner, R.J.	25	41	5	58	710	19.72	–	–	24/11
Twose, R.G.	19	34	6	64*	777	27.75	–	–	10
Udal, S.D.	8	6	2	28*	79	19.75	–	–	2
Van der Merwe, W.M.	44	67	15	96	1274	24.50	–	–	14
Vengsarkar, D.B.	240	360	48	210	16095	51.58	50	0+5	163
Walker, A.	90	85	44	41*	589	14.36	–	–	35
Walsh, C.A.	200	236	61	63*	2343	13.38	–	–	54
Waqar Younis	38	38	17	51	323	15.38	–	–	7
Ward, D.M.	80	122	19	263	4179	40.57	10	1	87/3

191

	M	I	NO	HS	Runs	Avge	100	1000	Ct/St
Ward, T.R.	50	89	7	175	2542	31.00	3	1	36
Warke, S.J.S.	9	16	2	144*	705	50.35	2	–	5
Warner, A.E.	129	182	35	91	2544	17.30	–	–	32
Wasim Akram	84	108	17	123	1953	21.46	2	–	28
Wassan, A.S.	26	17	5	53	238	19.83	–	–	11
Waterton, S.N.V.	41	48	10	58*	757	19.92	–	–	79/15
Watkin, S.L.	67	74	20	31	436	8.07	–	–	16
Watkinson, M.	159	232	31	138	4952	24.63	2	–	81
Watson, W.	54	42	18	27*	201	8.37	–	–	13
Waugh, M.E.	94	150	23	207*	6848	53.92	23	2+1	107
Weale, S.D.	20	24	2	76	392	17.81	–	–	3
Weekes, P.N.	3	3	0	51	75	25.00	–	–	3
Wells, A.P.	190	315	53	161*	9232	35.23	14	5	100
Wells, C.M.	256	408	62	203	11567	33.43	20	6	82
Wells, V.J.	11	21	1	58	395	19.75	–	–	10
Weston, M.J.	149	239	20	145*	5279	24.10	3	1	71
Whitaker, J.J.	180	286	37	200*	9884	39.69	23	7	116
White, C.	10	11	2	38	127	14.11	–	–	4
Whitney, M.R.	83	79	29	28*	254	5.08	–	–	40
Whitticase, P.	101	134	31	71	2281	22.14	–	–	240/9
Wickremasinghe, G.P.	6	6	0	17	24	4.00	–	–	1
Wijegunawardene, K.I.W.	20	19	8	16	86	7.81	–	–	9
Wijetunge, P.K.	10	9	6	7	20	6.66	–	–	5
Wild, D.J.	119	167	21	144	3688	25.26	5	–	40
Willey, P.	547	900	116	227	24144	30.79	44	10	229
Williams, N.F.	153	171	40	69*	2777	21.19	–	–	35
Williams, R.C.J.	8	8	4	50*	132	33.00	–	–	27/4
Williams, R.G.	274	433	62	175*	11564	31.16	17	6	98
Winchester, A.L.C.	1	1	1	0*	0	–	–	–	–
Wood, J.R.	14	20	2	96	616	34.22	–	–	7
Wren, T.N.	5	5	2	16	23	7.66	–	–	2
Wright, A.J.	161	278	17	161	6969	26.70	8	3	110
Wright, J.G.	346	597	43	192	23413	42.26	55	6+2	185
Yates, G.	5	4	2	106	165	82.50	1	–	1

BOWLING

'100wS' denotes instances of taking 100 or more wickets in a season.

	Runs	Wkts	Avge	Best	5wI	10wM	100wS
Adams, C.J.	56	2	28.00	1-5	–	–	–
Afford, J.A.	6484	188	34.48	6-81	7	1	–
Agnew, J.P.	19485	666	29.25	9-70	37	6	1
Ahangama, F.S.	1311	68	19.27	7-30	2	1	–
Alikhan, R.I.	231	5	46.20	2-19	–	–	–
Alleyne, M.W.	1529	37	41.32	4-48	–	–	–
Allott, P.J.W.	16149	638	25.31	8-48	30	–	–
Ambrose, C.E.L.	5716	251	22.77	8-45	13	3	–
Andrew, S.J.W.	6148	193	31.85	7-92	5	–	–
Anthony, H.A.G.	894	31	28.83	5-40	1	–	–
Arnold, K.A.	221	6	36.83	5-57	1	–	–
Asif Din	3956	68	58.17	5-100	1	–	–
Atapattu, M.S.	93	5	18.60	3-19	–	–	–
Atherton, M.A.	3993	96	41.59	6-78	3	–	–

192

	Runs	Wkts	Avge	Best	5wI	10wM	100wS
Athey, C.W.J.	1966	41	47.95	3-3	–	–	–
Atkinson, J.C.M.	639	6	106.50	2-80	–	–	–
Austin, I.D.	1610	54	29.81	5-79	1	–	–
Ayling, J.R.	1670	58	28.79	4-57	–	–	–
Azharuddin, M.	281	4	70.25	2-33	–	–	–
Babington, A.M.	4671	135	34.60	5-37	2	–	–
Bailey, R.J.	1618	35	46.22	3-27	–	–	–
Bainbridge, P.	9985	273	36.57	8-53	7	–	–
Bairstow, D.L.	308	9	34.22	3-25	–	–	–
Bakker, P-J.	4310	162	26.60	7-31	7	–	–
Ball, M.C.J.	795	23	34.56	4-53	–	–	–
Barnes, S.N.	602	16	37.62	4-51	–	–	–
Barnett, A.A.	65	0	–	–	–	–	–
Barnett, K.J.	4578	113	40.51	6-115	1	–	–
Bartlett, R.J.	145	4	36.25	1-9	–	–	–
Barwick, S.R.	10537	314	33.55	8-42	9	1	–
Base, S.J.	6593	250	26.37	7-60	10	1	–
Bastien, S.	1678	51	32.90	6-75	3	–	–
Batty, J.D.	915	20	45.75	5-118	1	–	–
Bee, A.	128	2	64.00	2-20	–	–	–
Bell, R.M.	114	3	38.00	2-38	–	–	–
Benjamin, J.E.	1763	57	30.92	5-29	4	–	–
Benjamin, W.K.M.	7102	285	24.91	7-54	17	2	–
Benson, J.D.R.	201	2	100.50	1-44	–	–	–
Benson, M.R.	424	4	106.00	2-55	–	–	–
Berry. P.J.	401	7	57.28	2-35	–	–	–
Bicknell, D.J.	113	1	113.00	1-73	–	–	–
Bicknell, M.P.	6810	258	26.39	9-45	8	–	–
Bishop, I.R.	5044	237	21.28	6-39	13	1	–
Blakey, R.J.	68	1	68.00	1-68	–	–	–
Boden, D.J.P.	26	4	6.50	4-11	–	–	–
Boiling, J.	202	5	40.40	3-40	–	–	–
Boon, T.J.	329	6	54.83	3-40	–	–	–
Booth, P.A.	2153	48	44.85	5-98	1	–	–
Botham, I.T.	29011	1082	26.81	8-34	56	8	1
Bowler, P.D.	893	11	81.18	2-1	–	–	–
Bracewell, J.G.	13919	522	26.66	8-81	33	9	–
Brandes, E.A.	2272	73	31.12	6-59	4	–	–
Brent, J.P.	99	3	33.00	2-28	–	–	–
Briers, N.E.	988	32	30.87	4-29	–	–	–
Broad, B.C.	1036	16	64.75	2-14	–	–	–
Brown, G.K.	39	1	39.00	1-39	–	–	–
Brown, K.R.	129	4	32.25	2-7	–	–	–
Brown, S.J.	814	25	32.56	3-20	–	–	–
Bullen, C.K.	1030	34	30.29	6-119	1	–	–
Bunting, R.A.	2787	72	38.70	5-44	3	–	–
Burns, N.D.	8	0	–	–	–	–	–
Butchart, I.P.	2052	62	33.09	5-65	1	–	–
Butcher, A.R.	5388	139	38.76	6-48	1	–	–
Butcher, I.P.	43	1	43.00	1-2	–	–	–
Butcher, R.O.	182	4	45.50	2-37	–	–	–
Buzza, A.J.	1842	43	42.83	6-102	1	–	–
Byas, D.	598	10	59.80	3-55	–	–	–
Cann, M.J.	920	14	65.71	3-30	–	–	–
Capel, D.J.	12009	363	33.08	7-46	11	–	–

193

	Runs	Wkts	Avge	Best	5wI	10wM	100wS
Carrick, P.	28878	963	29.98	8-33	43	5	–
Chauhan, S.	59	1	59.00	1-58	–	–	–
Childs, J.H.	21366	708	30.17	9-56	38	8	–
Clarke, A.R.	1872	53	35.32	5-60	2	–	–
Cleal, M.W.	909	26	34.96	4-41	–	–	–
Clinton, G.S.	201	4	50.25	2-8	–	–	–
Cobb, R.A.	49	0	–	–	–	–	–
Connor, C.A.	10634	339	31.36	7-31	9	1	–
Cook, G.	806	15	53.73	3-47	–	–	–
Cook, N.G.B.	22447	788	28.48	7-63	30	3	–
Cook, S.J.	81	3	27.00	2-25	–	–	–
Cooper, K.E.	19215	704	27.29	8-44	25	1	1
Cork, D.G.	123	2	61.50	1-4	–	–	–
Cottey, P.A.	122	1	122.00	1-49	–	–	–
Cowans, N.G.	13732	576	23.84	6-31	23	1	–
Cowdrey, C.S.	7962	200	39.81	5-46	2	–	–
Cowdrey, G.R.	530	9	58.88	1-5	–	–	–
Cowley, N.G.	14879	437	34.04	6-48	5	–	–
Cox, R.M.F.	1	0	–	–	–	–	–
Crawley, M.A.	1572	27	58.22	6-92	1	–	–
Croft, R.D.B.	1647	29	56.79	3-10	–	–	–
Crowe, J.J.	48	1	48.00	1-10	–	–	–
Crowe, M.D.	3739	116	32.23	5-18	4	–	–
Curran, K.M.	8009	311	25.75	7-47	10	4	–
Curtis, D.M.	8	0	–	–	–	–	–
Curtis, T.S.	424	7	60.57	2-58	–	–	–
Dale, A.	467	9	51.88	3-21	–	–	–
Davies, H.R.	261	3	87.00	3-93	–	–	–
Davies, M.	16	0	–	–	–	–	–
Davis, R.P.	6870	169	40.65	6-40	6	1	–
Davis, W.W.	16613	582	28.54	7-52	28	7	–
DeFreitas, P.A.J.	11251	413	27.24	7-21	23	2	–
Dennis, S.J.	8328	251	33.17	5-35	7	–	–
Derrick, J.	5147	136	37.84	6-54	2	–	–
De Silva, P.A.	588	11	53.45	2-16	–	–	–
De Villiers, P.S.	3771	150	25.14	6-47	7	–	–
Dilley, G.R.	16515	611	27.02	7-63	33	3	–
Dobson, M.C.	424	8	53.00	2-20	–	–	–
Dodemaide, A.I.C.	11096	319	34.78	6-58	8	–	–
Doidge, M.J.	106	0	–	–	–	–	–
D'Oliveira, D.B.	1003	25	40.12	2-17	–	–	–
Dolphin, D.F.	286	5	57.20	3-59	–	–	–
Donald, A.A.	8007	338	23.68	8-37	15	1	–
Donelan, B.T.P.	1633	34	48.02	3-51	–	–	–
Downton, P.R.	9	1	9.00	1-4	–	–	–
Dube, L.E.	107	0	–	–	–	–	–
Duers, K.G.	2242	68	32.97	8-102	2	–	–
Dunlop, A.R.	37	0	–	–	–	–	–
Ealham, M.A.	238	4	59.50	2-33	–	–	–
East, D.E.	17	0	–	–	–	–	–
Ellcock, R.M.	3191	109	29.27	5-35	1	–	–
Ellison, R.M.	10920	395	27.64	7-75	14	2	–
Emburey, J.E.	31360	1217	25.76	7-27	59	9	1
Evans, K.P.	3404	94	36.21	4-50	–	–	–

194

	Runs	Wkts	Avge	Best	5wI	10wM	100wS
Evans, R.A.	147	2	73.50	2-147	–	–	–
Evans, R.J.	97	3	32.33	3-40	–	–	–
Fairbrother, N.H.	423	5	84.60	2-91	–	–	–
Feltham, M.A.	7066	232	30.45	6-53	6	–	–
Felton, N.A.	186	2	93.00	1-48	–	–	–
Ferris, G.J.F.	7355	286	25.71	7-42	9	1	–
Field-Buss, M.G.	227	10	22.70	4-33	–	–	–
Fitton, J.D.	3065	57	53.77	6-59	3	–	–
Fleming, M.V.	1517	28	54.17	3-65	–	–	–
Fletcher, S.D.	7201	214	33.64	8-58	4	–	–
Flower, G.W.	175	4	43.75	2-33	–	–	–
Folley, I.	8890	284	31.30	7-15	10	1	–
Fordham, A.	49	1	49.00	1-25	–	–	–
Foster, N.A.	18529	767	24.15	8-107	42	7	1
Fowler, G.	265	8	33.12	2-34	–	–	–
Franklin, T.J.	51	1	51.00	1-21	–	–	–
Fraser, A.G.J.	247	9	27.44	3-46	–	–	–
Fraser, A.R.C.	7416	309	24.00	7-77	15	2	–
French, B.N.	22	0	–	–	–	–	–
Frost, M.	3052	84	36.33	5-40	3	1	–
Gallian, J.E.R.	65	1	65.00	1-50	–	–	–
Gatting, M.W.	4329	154	28.11	5-34	2	–	–
Gerrans, P.S.	695	12	57.91	3-86	–	–	–
Gidley, M.I.	332	2	166.00	1-23	–	–	–
Goldsmith, S.C.	545	8	68.12	2-105	–	–	–
Gooch, G.A.	7339	213	34.45	7-14	3	–	–
Gough, D.	1210	34	35.58	4-68	–	–	–
Gould, I.J.	365	7	52.14	3-10	–	–	–
Govan, J.W.	614	25	24.56	5-54	1	–	–
Gower, D.I.	223	4	55.75	3-47	–	–	–
Graveney, D.A.	23953	829	28.89	8-85	36	7	–
Gray, A.H.	7888	359	21.97	8-40	18	4	–
Grayson, A.P.	270	1	270.00	1-55	–	–	–
Greatbatch, M.J.	8	0	–	–	–	–	–
Greenfield, K.	19	0	–	–	–	–	–
Greenidge, C.G.	472	17	27.76	5-49	1	–	–
Greensword, S.	1002	29	34.55	3-22	–	–	–
Greig, I.A.	12597	409	30.79	7-43	10	2	–
Griffith, F.A.	519	16	32.43	4-47	–	–	–
Gurusinha, A.P.	701	36	19.47	5-54	1	–	–
Hadlee, Sir R.J.	26998	1490	18.11	9-52	102	18	2
Hagan, D.A.	31	0	–	–	–	–	–
Hallett, J.C.	238	6	39.66	2-40	–	–	–
Hansford, A.R.	910	27	33.70	5-79	1	–	–
Harden, R.J.	799	16	49.93	2-7	–	–	–
Hardie, B.R.	254	3	84.66	2-39	–	–	–
Hardy, J.J.E.	26	0	–	–	–	–	–
Harper, R.A.	12540	458	27.37	6-57	19	2	–
Harrison, G.D.	381	18	21.16	9-113	2	–	–
Hartley, P.J.	7332	208	35.25	6-57	6	–	–
Hathurusinghe, U.C.	851	32	26.59	4-59	–	–	–
Hawkes, C.J.	40	0	–	–	–	–	–
Hayhurst, A.N.	2731	66	41.37	4-27	–	–	–
Haynes, D.L.	196	6	32.66	1-2	–	–	–

195

	Runs	Wkts	Avge	Best	5wI	10wM	100wS
Hegg, W.K.	7	0	–	–	–	–	–
Hemmings, E.E.	38747	1325	29.24	10-175	64	14	–
Henderson, I.M.	1547	25	61.88	3-48	–	–	–
Henry, O.	8154	358	22.77	7-22	19	3	–
Hick, G.A.	4192	116	36.13	5-37	3	1	–
Hinks, S.G.	367	8	45.87	2-18	–	–	–
Hirwani, N.D.	6136	195	31.46	8-61	15	3	–
Holmes, G.C.	3963	88	45.03	5-38	2	–	–
Houseman, I.J.	259	2	129.50	2-26	–	–	–
Hughes, D.P.	19613	650	30.17	7-24	20	2	–
Hughes, J.G.	293	3	97.66	2-57	–	–	–
Hughes, S.P.	12527	418	29.96	7-35	9	–	–
Humpage, G.W.	553	13	42.53	2-13	–	–	–
Hussain, N.	110	0	–	–	–	–	–
Igglesden, A.P.	6511	232	28.06	6-34	10	2	–
Illingworth, R.K.	13509	427	31.63	7-50	15	4	–
Ilott, M.C.	1512	44	34.36	5-34	2	–	–
Irani, R.	73	2	36.50	1-12	–	–	–
James, K.D.	5093	164	31.05	6-22	7	–	–
Jarvis, K.B.S.	19998	674	29.67	8-97	20	3	–
Jarvis, M.P.	2043	61	33.49	5-74	2	–	–
Jarvis, P.W.	11172	405	27.58	7-55	18	3	–
Jayasuriya, S.T.	417	14	29.78	2-8	–	–	–
Jean-Jacques, M.	3460	98	35.30	8-77	2	1	–
Jenkins, R.H.J.	959	15	63.93	5-100	1	–	–
Jesty, T.E.	16075	585	27.47	7-75	19	–	–
Johnson, P.	418	3	139.33	1-9	–	–	–
Johnson, S.W.	452	3	150.66	2-86	–	–	–
Jones, A.H.	1079	28	38.53	4-28	–	–	–
Jones, A.N.	10480	340	30.82	7-30	10	1	–
Joseph, L.A.	1565	46	34.02	4-43	–	–	–
Kallicharran, A.I.	4030	84	47.97	5-45	1	–	–
Kapil Dev	20017	728	27.49	9-83	35	3	–
Kelleher, D.J.M.	2486	74	33.59	6-109	2	–	–
Kendrick, N.M.	1430	32	44.68	4-110	–	–	–
Kilborn, M.J.	312	6	52.00	3-37	–	–	–
Krikken, K.M.	40	0	–	–	–	–	–
Kuiper, A.P.	4351	160	27.19	6-55	4	–	–
Kumble, A.	1131	38	29.76	6-49	2	–	–
Labrooy, G.F.	2380	70	34.00	7-71	5	–	–
Laing, D.R.	551	15	36.73	3-35	–	–	–
Lamb, A.J.	164	6	27.33	1-1	–	–	–
Lampitt, S.R.	2710	92	29.45	5-32	4	–	–
Larkins, W.	1852	42	44.09	5-59	1	–	–
Lawrence, D.V.	14172	423	33.50	7-47	16	–	–
Leatherdale, D.A.	20	1	20.00	1-12	–	–	–
Lefebvre, R.P.	1281	31	41.32	5-30	1	–	–
Lenham, N.J.	954	21	45.42	4-85	–	–	–
Lewis, C.C.	4188	150	27.92	6-22	7	2	–
Lewis, D.A.	88	1	88.00	1-33	–	–	–
Lilley, A.W.	565	8	70.62	3-116	–	–	–
Llong, N.J.	24	0	–	–	–	–	–
Lloyd, G.D.	84	0	–	–	–	–	–
Lloyd, T.A.	1358	17	79.88	3-62	–	–	–
Lloyds, J.W.	11293	299	37.76	7-88	12	1	–

	Runs	Wkts	Avge	Best	5wI	10wM	100wS
Lord, G.J.	61	0	–	–	–	–	–
Lowrey, M.J.	483	10	48.30	2-13	–	–	–
Lunn, P.D.	383	3	127.66	1-34	–	–	–
Lynch, M.A.	1246	25	49.84	3-6	–	–	–
McCrum, P.	28	0	–	–	–	–	–
McEwan, S.M.	4069	139	29.27	6-34	3	–	–
McKnight, C.T.	72	3	24.00	3-48	–	–	–
MacLeay, K.H.	7070	248	28.50	6-93	6	–	–
Madurasinghe, A.W.R.	1969	63	31.25	5-19	3	1	–
Maguire, J.N.	9193	334	27.52	7-46	18	3	–
Mahanama, R.S.	3	0	–	–	–	–	–
Maher, B.J.M.	234	4	58.50	2-69	–	–	–
Mahmood, M.	103	4	25.75	3-63	–	–	–
Malcolm, D.E.	7853	260	30.20	6-68	6	1	–
Mallender, N.A.	18721	666	28.10	7-27	18	3	–
Manjrekar, S.V.	212	3	70.66	1-4	–	–	–
Marsh, S.A.	73	2	36.50	2-20	–	–	–
Marshall, M.D.	25443	1396	18.22	8-71	82	13	2
Martin, P.J.	1001	23	43.52	4-68	–	–	–
Martindale, D.J.R.	8	0	–	–	–	–	–
Maru, R.J.	13453	422	31.87	8-41	14	1	–
Maynard, M.P.	417	4	104.25	3-21	–	–	–
Medlycott, K.T.	9814	308	31.86	8-52	16	5	–
Mendis, G.D.	158	1	158.00	1-65	–	–	–
Merrick, T.A.	6131	250	24.52	7-45	14	2	–
Metcalfe, A.A.	293	4	73.25	2-18	–	–	–
Middleton, T.C.	103	2	51.50	1-13	–	–	–
Mike, G.W.	370	4	92.50	2-62	–	–	–
Milburn, E.T.	278	5	55.60	3-43	–	–	–
Miller, G.	24854	888	27.98	8-70	39	7	–
Millmow, J.P.	2434	86	28.30	6-13	3	1	–
Millns, D.J.	1744	58	30.06	6-63	2	–	–
Moir, J.D.	139	3	46.33	2-47	–	–	–
Moles, A.J.	1517	33	45.96	3-21	–	–	–
Moody, T.M.	1146	32	35.81	4-30	–	–	–
Moores, P.	16	0	–	–	–	–	–
More, K.S.	73	0	–	–	–	–	–
Morris, H.	323	2	161.50	1-6	–	–	–
Morris, J.E.	710	4	177.50	1-13	–	–	–
Morris, R.E.	16	0	–	–	–	–	–
Morrison, D.K.	5817	177	32.86	7-82	7	–	–
Mortensen, O.H.	7494	330	22.70	6-27	13	1	–
Moseley, E.A.	5440	223	24.39	6-23	7	–	–
Moxon, M.D.	1440	26	55.38	3-24	–	–	–
Mudassar Nazar	5221	152	34.34	6-32	2	–	–
Mullally, A.D.	3054	75	40.72	4-59	–	–	–
Munton, T.A.	6771	254	26.65	6-21	7	–	–
Murphy, A.J.	4643	128	36.27	6-97	4	–	–
Neale, P.A.	283	1	283.00	1-15	–	–	–
Nelson, A.N.	237	10	23.70	5-27	1	–	–
Nelson, N.	51	0	–	–	–	–	–
Newell, M.	282	7	40.28	2-38	–	–	–
Newport, P.J.	11439	423	27.04	8-52	23	3	–
Nicholas, M.C.J.	2819	66	42.71	6-37	2	–	–
North, J.A.	236	6	39.33	2-43	–	–	–

	Runs	Wkts	Avge	Best	5wI	10wM	100wS
Owen, P.A.	239	4	59.75	2-37	–	–	–
Parker, P.W.G.	658	11	59.81	2-21	–	–	–
Parks, R.J.	166	0	–	–	–	–	..
Parsons, G.J.	16792	551	30.47	9-72	16	1	–
Patel, M.M.	870	21	41.42	6-57	2	1	–
Patterson, B.P.	11040	403	27.39	7-24	20	2	–
Patterson, T.J.T.	96	3	32.00	2-54	–	–	–
Penberthy, A.L.	953	25	38.12	4-91	–	–	–
Penn, C.	7693	226	34.03	7-70	9	–	–
Peters, N.H.	1246	40	31.15	6-31	1	1	–
Pick, R.A.	8075	240	33.64	7-128	6	2	–
Pickles, C.S.	2783	63	44.17	4-92	–	–	–
Pierson, A.R.K.	3474	81	42.88	6-82	3	–	–
Pigott, A.C.S.	15961	537	29.72	7-74	22	1	–
Pointer, G.A.	1298	17	76.35	3-31	–	–	–
Pollard, P.R.	5	0	–	–	–	–	–
Pook, R.N.	19	0	–	–	–	–	–
Pooley, J.C.	11	0	–	–	–	–	–
Pooley, M.W.	564	15	37.60	4-80	–	–	–
Potter, L.	3708	98	37.83	4-52	–	–	–
Prabhakar, M.	5545	191	29.03	6-36	8	1	–
Prichard, P.J.	151	0	–	–	–	–	–
Priest, M.W.	3785	102	37.10	9-95	4	2	–
Priestley, I.M.	119	4	29.75	4-27	–	–	–
Pringle, C.	1048	33	31.75	4-56	–	–	–
Pringle, D.R.	16343	626	26.10	7-18	22	3	–
Pringle, N.J.	551	5	110.20	2-35	–	–	–
Pycroft, A.J.	52	1	52.00	1-0	–	–	–
Pyman, R.A.	1537	28	54.89	5-43	1	–	–
Radford, N.V.	20355	793	25.66	9-70	39	6	2
Raju, S.L.V.	3233	122	26.50	6-52	3	–	–
Raman, W.V.	2791	79	35.32	6-29	4	1	–
Ramanayake, C.P.H.	3060	101	30.29	7-21	2	–	–
Ramprakash, M.R.	278	2	139.00	1-17	–	–	–
Randall, D.W.	386	12	32.16	3-15	–	–	–
Ratcliffe, J.D.	82	1	82.00	1-15	–	–	–
Reeve, D.A.	8581	307	27.95	7-37	5	–	–
Remy, C.C.	257	6	42.83	4-63	–	–	–
Richards, I.V.A.	9350	210	44.52	5-88	1	–	–
Richardson, R.B.	160	5	32.00	5-40	1	–	–
Ripley, D.	89	2	44.50	2-89	–	–	–
Roberts, A.R.	364	5	72.80	2-123	–	–	–
Roberts, B.	2948	89	33.12	5-68	1	–	–
Robinson, J.D.	701	13	53.92	2-37	–	–	–
Robinson, M.A.	5193	151	34.39	4-19	–	–	–
Robinson, P.E.	189	1	189.00	1-10	–	–	–
Robinson, R.T.	211	2	105.50	1-22	–	–	–
Roebuck, P.M.	3225	63	51.19	6-50	1	–	–
Romaines, P.W.	247	4	61.75	3-42	–	–	–
Rose, G.D.	6015	211	28.50	6-41	4	–	–
Roseberry, M.A.	248	4	62.00	1-1	–	–	–
Russell, A.B.	46	1	46.00	1-23	–	–	–;
Russell, R.C.	19	0	–	–	–	–	–
Rutherford, K.R.	803	16	50.18	5-72	1	–	–

	Runs	Wkts	Avge	Best	5wI	10wM	100wS
Salisbury, I.D.K.	3007	57	52.75	5-32	2	–	–
Saxelby, K.	9705	300	32.35	6-49	6	1	–
Saxelby, M.	320	5	64.00	2-25	–	–	–
Scott, C.W.	10	0	–	–	–	–	–
Scott, R.J.	257	5	51.40	2-5	–	–	–
Shah, A.H.	741	13	57.00	2-22	–	–	–
Shahid, N.	780	15	52.00	3-91	–	–	–
Sharma, C.	6545	234	27.97	7-83	13	1	–
Sharma, S.K.	3937	99	39.76	8-76	2	–	–
Sharp, K.	887	12	73.91	2-13	–	–	–
Shastri, R.J.	14609	426	34.29	9-101	14	3	–
Shaw, C.	4101	123	33.34	6-64	3	–	–
Shine, K.J.	640	17	37.64	4-52	–	–	–
Shufflebotham, D.H.	572	7	81.71	3-60	–	–	–
Sidebottom, A.	14532	595	24.42	8-72	23	3	–
Sidhu, N.S.	36	0	–	–	–	–	–
Sleep, P.R.	12582	324	38.83	8-133	8	–	–
Small, G.C.	18373	656	28.00	7-15	27	2	–
Smith, C.L.	2622	50	52.44	5-69	1	–	–
Smith, D.M.	1541	30	51.36	3-40	–	–	–
Smith, G.	633	21	30.14	6-72	1	–	–
Smith, I.	2294	48	47.79	3-48	–	–	–
Smith, I.D.S.	38	0	–	–	–	–	–
Smith, N.M.K.	1134	22	51.54	3-62	–	–	–
Smith, P.A.	6823	183	37.28	5-48	2	–	–
Smith, R.A.	520	9	57.77	2-11	–	–	–
Snedden, M.C.	9918	387	25.62	8-73	15	2	–
Speak, N.J.	26	1	26.00	1-26	–	–	–
Speight, M.P.	2	1	2.00	1-2	–	–	–
Stemp, R.D.	123	1	123.00	1-32	–	–	–
Stephenson, F.D.	9011	393	22.92	8-47	25	6	1
Stephenson, J.P.	1390	30	46.33	3-22	–	–	–
Stewart, A.J.	295	3	98.33	1-7	–	–	–
Storie, A.C.	71	0	–	–	–	–	–
Stovold, A.W.	218	4	54.50	1-0	–	–	–
Such, P.M.	7086	227	31.21	6-123	6	–	–
Swallow, I.G.	5444	98	55.55	7-95	1	–	–
Swan, R.G.	0	0	–	–	–	–	–
Tavaré, C.J.	687	5	137.40	1-3	–	–	–
Taylor, C.W.	139	6	23.16	5-33	1	–	–
Taylor, L.B.	14648	581	25.21	7-28	18	1	–
Taylor, N.R. (M/MCo)	131	4	32.75	3-44	–	–	–
Taylor, N.R. (K)	865	16	54.06	2-20	–	–	–
Tedstone, G.A.	1	0	–	–	–	–	–
Tendulkar, S.R.	437	3	145.66	3-79	–	–	–
Tennant, L.	110	3	36.66	1-0	–	–	–
Terry, V.P.	58	0	–	–	–	–	–
Thomas, D.R.	65	0	–	–	–	–	–
Thomas, J.G.	15366	497	30.91	7-75	16	1	–
Thomas, K.O.	81	0	–	–	–	–	–
Thomson, S.A.	1810	47	38.51	5-49	1	–	–
Thorpe, G.P.	381	9	42.33	2-31	–	–	–
Threlfall, P.W.	120	5	24.00	3-45	–	–	–
Thursfield, M.J.	130	2	65.00	1-24	–	–	–

	Runs	Wkts	Avge	Best	5wI	10wM	100wS
Tillekeratne, H.P.	130	3	43.33	1-9	–	–	–
Tolley, C.M.	464	6	77.33	2-66	–	–	–
Topley, T.D.	6927	272	25.46	7-75	11	2	–
Traicos, A.J.	8927	265	33.68	6-66	7	–	–
Tremlett, T.M.	10759	449	23.96	6-53	11	–	–
Trump, H.R.J.	2341	58	40.36	4-17	–	–	–
Tufnell, P.C.R.	6720	192	35.00	6-60	6	–	–
Turner, G.J.	975	18	54.16	4-94	–	–	–
Turner, I.J.	472	13	36.30	3-20	–	–	–
Twose, R.G.	472	6	78.66	1-10	–	–	–
Udal, S.D.	921	22	41.86	4-139	–	–	–
Van der Merwe, W.M.	3388	130	26.06	5-35	4	–	–
Vengsarkar, D.B.	126	1	126.00	1-31	–	–	–
Walker, A.	6461	212	30.47	6-50	2	–	–
Walsh, C.A.	18029	776	23.23	9-72	44	9	1
Waqar Younis	3295	119	27.68	7-73	7	2	–
Ward, D.M.	31	0	–	–	–	–	–
Ward, T.R.	386	5	77.20	2-48	–	–	–
Warner, A.E.	8488	260	32.64	5-27	2	–	–
Wasim Akram	6842	273	25.06	7-42	20	4	–
Wassan, A.S.	2798	91	30.74	7-36	6	2	–
Watkin, S.L.	6809	217	31.37	8-59	11	3	–
Watkinson, M.	11135	341	32.65	7-25	17	–	–
Watson, W.	4377	147	29.77	7-60	6	–	–
Waugh, M.E.	2544	62	41.03	5-37	1	–	–
Weale, S.D.	1459	15	97.26	3-130	–	–	–
Weekes, P.N.	264	4	66.00	2-115	–	–	–
Wells, A.P.	575	8	71.87	3-67	–	–	–
Wells, C.M.	12443	364	34.18	7-65	6	–	–
Wells, V.J.	369	14	26.35	5-43	1	–	–
Weston, M.J.	2998	78	38.43	4-24	–	–	–
Whitaker, J.J.	168	1	168.00	1-41	–	–	–
White, C.	608	13	46.76	5-74	1	–	–
Whitney, M.R.	7680	284	27.04	7-89	13	–	–
Whitticase, P.	7	0	–	–	–	–	–
Wickremasinghe, G.P.	417	7	59.57	3-95	–	–	–
Wijegunawardene, K.I.W.	1328	50	26.56	6-42	1	–	–
Wijetunge, P.K.	981	38	25.81	7-51	1	–	–
Wild, D.J.	2910	66	44.09	4-4	–	–	–
Willey, P.	22959	751	30.57	7-37	26	3	–
Williams, N.F.	11479	394	29.13	7-55	10	1	–
Williams, R.G.	12380	368	33.64	7-73	9	–	–
Winchester, A.L.C.	81	0	–	–	–	–	–
Wood, J.R.	21	1	21.00	1-5	–	–	–
Wren, T.N.	489	6	81.50	2-78	–	–	–
Wright, A.J.	37	1	37.00	1-16	–	–	–
Wright, J.G.	339	2	169.50	1-4	–	–	–
Yates, G.	420	8	52.50	4-94	–	–	–

LIMITED-OVERS INTERNATIONALS CAREER RECORDS

These career records for players contracted to play county cricket in 1991 are complete to 1 November 1990 and have been compiled by **Philip Bailey**.

BATTING AND FIELDING

	M	I	NO	HS	Runs	Avge	100	50	Ct/St
Allott, P.J.W.	13	6	1	8	15	3.00	–	–	2
Ambrose, C.E.L.	37	18	10	26*	124	15.50	–	–	12
Atherton, M.A.	2	2	0	59	66	33.00	–	1	2
Athey, C.W.J.	31	30	3	142*	848	31.40	2	4	16
Azharuddin, M.	106	96	19	108*	2661	34.55	3	10	40
Bailey, R.J.	4	4	2	43*	137	68.50	–	–	1
Barnett, K.J.	1	1	0	84	84	84.00	–	1	–
Benson, M.R.	1	1	0	24	24	24.00	–	–	–
Bishop, I.R.	26	11	7	33*	73	18.25	–	–	7
Botham, I.T.	98	89	12	72	1730	22.46	–	7	30
Broad, B.C.	34	34	0	106	1361	40.02	1	11	10
Butcher, A.R.	1	1	0	14	14	14.00	–	–	–
Capel, D.J.	23	19	2	50*	327	19.23	–	1	6
Cook, N.G.B.	3	–	–	–	–	–	–	–	2
Cowans, N.G.	23	8	3	4*	13	2.60	–	–	5
Cowdrey, C.S.	3	3	1	46*	51	25.50	–	–	–
DeFreitas, P.A.J.	52	36	14	33	355	16.13	–	–	12
Dilley, G.R.	36	18	8	31*	114	11.40	–	–	4
Dodemaide, A.I.C.	12	8	5	30	84	28.00	–	–	4
Downton, P.R.	28	20	5	44*	242	16.13	–	–	26/3
Ellison, R.M.	14	12	4	24	86	10.75	–	–	2
Emburey, J.E.	58	43	10	34	471	14.27	–	–	19
Fairbrother, N.H.	11	11	2	54	232	25.77	–	2	5
Foster, N.A.	48	25	12	24	150	11.53	–	–	12
Fowler, G.	26	26	2	81*	744	31.00	–	4	4/2
Fraser, A.R.C.	13	3	3	4*	7	–	–	–	–
French, B.N.	13	8	3	9*	34	6.80	–	–	13/3
Gatting, M.W.	85	82	17	115*	2049	31.52	1	9	22
Gooch, G.A.	85	83	5	142	3305	42.37	8	19	30
Gould, I.J.	18	14	2	42	155	12.91	–	–	15/3
Gower, D.I.	109	106	8	158	3110	31.73	7	12	42
Haynes, D.L.	174	173	23	152*	6471	43.14	16	36	40
Hemmings, E.E.	28	8	4	4*	15	3.75	–	–	4
Hussain, N.	2	2	1	15*	17	17.00	–	–	1
Jarvis, P.W.	5	2	1	5*	5	5.00	–	–	–
Jesty, T.E.	10	10	4	52*	127	21.16	–	1	5
Lamb, A.J.	99	95	16	118	3306	41.84	4	21	26
Larkins, W.	18	17	0	124	427	25.11	1	–	4
Lewis, C.C.	7	2	0	7	13	6.50	–	–	1
Lloyd, T.A.	3	3	0	49	101	33.66	–	–	–
Lynch, M.A.	3	3	0	6	8	2.66	–	–	1
MacLeay, K.H.	16	13	2	41	139	12.63	–	–	2
Maguire, J.N.	23	11	5	14*	42	7.00	–	–	2
Malcolm, D.E.	2	1	0	4	4	4.00	–	–	–

	M	I	NO	HS	Runs	Avge	100	50	Ct/St
Marshall, M.D.	113	62	16	66	781	16.97	–	2	12
Moody, T.M.	13	13	2	89	281	25.54	–	2	4
Moxon, M.D.	8	8	0	70	174	21.75	–	1	5
Pringle, D.R.	26	21	9	49*	369	30.75	–	–	7
Radford, N.V.	6	3	2	0*	0	0.00	–	–	2
Randall, D.W.	49	45	5	88	1067	26.67	–	5	25
Rhodes, S.J.	3	2	1	8	9	9.00	–	–	3
Richards, I.V.A.	179	160	24	189*	6501	47.80	11	44	99
Robinson, R.T.	26	26	0	83	597	22.96	–	3	6
Russell, R.C.	17	12	6	50	210	35.00	–	1	12/4
Shastri, R.J.	123	101	18	102	2391	28.80	2	14	34
Small, G.C.	40	17	8	18*	59	6.55	–	–	2
Smith, C.L.	4	4	0	70	109	27.25	–	1	–
Smith, D.M.	2	2	1	10*	15	15.00	–	–	–
Smith, R.A.	20	19	3	128	691	43.18	2	4	9
Stewart, A.J.	13	11	1	61	194	19.40	–	1	5
Tavaré, C.J.	29	28	2	83*	720	27.69	–	4	7
Thomas, J.G.	3	3	2	1*	1	1.00	–	–	–
Walsh, C.A.	88	27	11	18	129	8.06	–	–	12
Waqar Younis	23	8	4	20*	38	9.50	–	–	2
Wasim Akram	97	68	14	86	763	14.12	–	1	18
Waugh, M.E.	8	7	0	42	145	20.71	–	–	3
Wells, C.M.	2	2	0	17	22	11.00	–	–	–
Whitaker, J.J.	2	2	1	44*	48	48.00	–	–	1
Willey, P.	26	24	1	64	538	23.39	–	5	4

BOWLING

	Balls	Runs	Wkts	Avge	4w	Best
Allott, P.J.W.	819	552	15	36.80	–	3-41
Ambrose, C.E.L.	2021	1219	65	18.75	6	5-17
Athey, C.W.J.	6	10	0	–	–	–
Azharuddin, M.	540	468	12	39.00	–	3-19
Bailey, R.J.	36	25	0	–	–	–
Bishop, I.R.	1339	858	46	18.65	5	5-27
Botham, I.T.	5269	3511	118	29.75	1	4-56
Broad, B.C.	6	6	0	–	–	–
Capel, D.J.	1038	805	17	47.35	–	3-38
Cook, N.G.B.	144	95	5	19.00	–	2-18
Cowans, N.G.	1282	913	23	39.69	–	3-44
Cowdrey, C.S.	52	55	2	27.50	–	1-3
DeFreitas, P.A.J.	2944	1923	60	32.05	1	4-35
Dilley, G.R.	2043	1291	48	26.89	3	4-23
Dodemaide, A.I.C.	655	360	20	18.00	1	5-21
Ellison, R.M.	696	510	12	42.50	–	3-42
Emburey, J.E.	3281	2226	75	29.68	2	4-37
Foster, N.A.	2627	1836	59	31.11	–	3-20
Fraser, A.R.C.	712	457	10	45.70	–	2-25
Gatting, M.W.	386	334	10	33.40	–	3-32
Gooch, G.A.	1598	1203	31	38.80	–	3-19
Gower, D.I.	5	14	0	–	–	–
Haynes, D.L.	30	24	0	–	–	–
Hemmings, E.E.	1464	1045	32	32.65	1	4-52
Jarvis, P.W.	287	187	6	31.16	1	4-33

	Balls	Runs	Wkts	Avge	4w	Best
Jesty, T.E.	108	93	1	93.00	–	1-23
Lamb, A.J.	6	3	0	–	–	–
Larkins, W.	12	21	0	–	–	–
Lewis, C.C.	324	282	8	35.25	–	3-54
MacLeay, K.H.	857	626	15	41.73	1	6-39
Maguire, J.N.	1009	769	19	40.47	–	3-61
Malcolm, D.E.	132	76	3	25.33	–	2-19
Marshall, M.D.	5993	3412	137	24.90	5	4-23
Moody, T.M.	102	81	1	81.00	–	1-21
Pringle, D.R.	1439	1079	23	46.91	–	3-21
Radford, N.V.	348	230	2	115.00	–	1-32
Randall, D.W.	2	2	1	2.00	–	1-2
Richards, I.V.A.	5542	4144	118	35.11	3	6-41
Shastri, R.J.	5756	4025	114	35.50	2	4-38
Small, G.C.	2195	1528	45	33.95	1	4-31
Smith, C.L.	36	28	2	14.00	–	2-8
Tavaré, C.J.	12	3	0	–	–	–
Thomas, J.G.	156	144	3	48.00	–	2-59
Walsh, C.A.	4659	2977	101	29.47	5	5-1
Waqar Younis	1050	688	37	18.59	4	6-26
Wasim Akram	4833	3073	130	23.63	5	5-21
Willey, P.	1031	659	13	50.69	–	3-33

TEST CAREER RECORDS

(To the end of the 1990 season)

ENGLAND

BATTING AND FIELDING

	Tests	I	NO	HS	Runs	Avge	100	50	Ct/St
Allott, P.J.W.	13	18	3	52*	213	14.20	–	1	4
Atherton, M.A.	8	15	0	151	808	53.86	2	6	7
Athey, C.W.J.	23	41	1	123	919	22.97	1	4	13
Bailey, R.J.	4	8	0	43	119	14.87	–	–	–
Barnett, K.J.	4	7	0	80	207	29.57	–	2	1
Benson, M.R.	1	2	0	30	51	25.50	–	–	–
Botham, I.T.	97	154	5	208	5119	34.35	14	22	112
Broad, B.C.	25	44	2	162	1661	39.54	6	6	10
Butcher, A.R.	1	2	0	20	34	17.00	–	–	–
Capel, D.J.	15	25	1	98	374	15.58	–	2	6
Childs, J.H.	2	4	4	2*	2	–	–	–	1
Cook, N.G.B.	15	25	4	31	179	8.52	–	–	5

	Tests	I	NO	HS	Runs	Avge	100	50	Ct/St
Cowans, N.G.	19	29	7	36	175	7.95	–	–	9
Cowdrey, C.S.	6	8	1	38	101	14.42	–	–	5
Curtis, T.S.	5	9	0	41	140	15.55	–	–	3
DeFreitas, P.A.J.	17	25	1	40	301	12.54	–	–	5
Dilley, G.R.	41	58	19	56	521	13.35	–	2	10
Downton, P.R.	30	48	8	74	785	19.62	–	4	70/5
Ellison, R.M.	11	16	1	41	202	13.46	–	–	2
Emburey, J.E.	60	89	18	75	1540	21.69	–	8	33
Fairbrother, N.H.	7	9	1	33*	64	8.00	–	–	4
Foster, N.A.	28	43	7	39	410	11.38	–	–	7
Fowler, G.	21	37	0	201	1307	35.32	3	8	10
Fraser, A.R.C.	8	9	1	29	61	7.62	–	–	–
French, B.N.	16	21	4	59	308	18.11	–	1	38/1
Gatting, M.W.	68	117	14	207	3870	37.57	9	18	51
Gooch, G.A.	81	147	5	333	5910	41.61	12	33	82
Gower, D.I.	109	189	15	215	7674	44.10	16	37	72
Greig, I.A.	2	4	0	14	26	6.50	–	–	–
Hemmings, E.E.	15	20	4	95	383	23.93	–	2	4
Hussain, N.	3	5	0	35	100	20.00	–	–	1
Igglesden, A.P.	1	1	1	2*	2	–	–	–	1
Jarvis, P.W.	6	9	2	29*	109	15.57	–	–	–
Lamb, A.J.	67	118	10	139	3981	36.86	13	14	64
Larkins, W.	10	19	1	54	352	19.55	–	1	7
Lawrence, D.V.	1	1	0	4	4	4.00	–	–	–
Lewis, C.C.	3	3	0	32	36	12.00	–	–	4
Lloyd, T.A.	1	1	1	10*	10	–	–	–	–
Malcolm, D.E.	11	14	6	15*	63	7.87	–	–	1
Maynard, M.P.	1	2	0	10	13	6.50	–	–	–
Morris, J.E.	3	5	2	32	71	23.66	–	–	3
Moxon, M.D.	10	17	1	99	455	28.43	–	3	10
Newport, P.J.	2	3	0	36	70	23.33	–	–	1
Parker, P.W.G.	1	2	0	13	13	6.50	–	–	–
Pigott, A.C.S.	1	2	1	8*	12	12.00	–	–	1
Pringle, D.R.	21	36	3	63	512	15.51	–	1	7
Radford, N.V.	3	4	1	12*	21	7.00	–	–	–
Randall, D.W.	47	79	5	174	2470	33.37	7	12	31
Robinson, R.T.	29	49	5	175	1601	36.38	4	6	8
Russell, R.C.	17	26	5	128*	690	32.85	1	3	49/5
Sidebottom, A.	1	1	0	2	2	2.00	–	–	–
Small, G.C.	13	18	6	59	221	18.41	–	1	5
Smith, C.L.	8	14	1	91	392	30.15	–	2	5
Smith, D.M.	2	4	0	47	80	20.00	–	–	–
Smith, R.A.	18	34	8	143	1397	53.73	4	10	8
Stephenson, J.P.	1	2	0	25	36	18.00	–	–	–
Stewart, A.J.	7	13	1	54	317	26.41	–	1	7
Tavaré, C.J.	31	56	2	149	1755	32.50	2	12	20
Terry, V.P.	2	3	0	8	16	5.33	–	–	2
Thomas, J.G.	5	10	4	31*	83	13.83	–	–	–
Whitaker, J.J.	1	1	0	11	11	11.00	–	–	1
Willey, P.	26	50	6	102*	1184	26.90	2	5	3
Williams, N.F.	1	1	0	38	38	38.00	–	–	–

BOWLING

	Balls	Runs	Wkts	Avge	Best	5wI	10wM
Allott, P.J.W.	2225	1084	26	41.69	6-61	1	–
Atherton, M.A.	276	212	1	212.00	1-60	–	–
Barnett, K.J.	36	32	0	–	–	–	–
Botham, I.T.	21281	10633	376	28.27	8-34	27	4
Broad, B.C.	6	4	0	–	–	–	–
Butcher, A.R.	12	9	0	–	–	–	–
Capel, D.J.	2000	1064	21	50.66	3-88	–	–
Childs, J.H.	516	183	3	61.00	1-13	–	–
Cook, N.G.B.	4174	1689	52	32.48	6-65	4	1
Cowans, N.G.	3452	2003	51	39.27	6-77	2	–
Cowdrey, C.S.	399	309	4	77.25	2-65	–	–
Curtis, T.S.	18	7	0	–	–	–	–
DeFreitas, P.A.J.	3550	1713	38	45.07	5-53	2	–
Dilley, G.R.	8192	4107	138	29.76	6-38	6	–
Ellison, R.M.	2264	1048	35	29.94	6-77	3	1
Emburey, J.E.	14227	5105	138	36.99	7-78	6	–
Fairbrother, N.H.	12	9	0	–	–	–	–
Foster, N.A.	6081	2797	88	31.78	8-107	5	1
Fowler, G.	18	11	0	–	–	–	–
Fraser, A.R.C.	2248	944	36	26.22	5-28	3	–
Gatting, M.W.	752	317	4	79.25	1-14	–	–
Gooch, G.A.	1803	717	15	47.80	2-12	–	–
Gower, D.I.	36	20	1	20.00	1-1	–	–
Greig, I.A.	188	114	4	28.50	4-53	–	–
Hemmings, E.E.	3999	1626	37	43.94	6-58	1	–
Igglesden, A.P.	222	146	3	48.66	2-91	–	–
Jarvis, P.W.	1347	708	14	50.57	4-107	–	–
Lamb, A.J.	30	23	1	23.00	1-6	–	–
Lawrence, D.V.	216	111	3	37.00	2-74	–	–
Lewis, C.C.	636	408	9	45.33	3-76	–	–
Malcolm, D.E.	2606	1448	42	34.47	6-77	3	1
Moxon, M.D.	48	30	0	–	–	–	–
Newport, P.J.	549	339	9	37.66	4-87	–	–
Pigott, A.C.S.	102	75	2	37.50	2-75	–	–
Pringle, D.R.	3750	1807	48	37.64	5-95	2	–
Radford, N.V.	678	351	4	87.75	2-131	–	–
Randall, D.W.	16	3	0	–	–	–	–
Robinson, R.T.	6	0	0	–	–	–	–
Sidebottom, A.	112	65	1	65.00	1-65	–	–
Small, G.C.	3033	1447	46	31.45	5-48	2	–
Smith, C.L.	102	39	3	13.00	2-31	–	–
Tavaré, C.J.	30	11	0	–	–	–	–
Thomas, J.G.	774	504	10	50.40	4-70	–	–
Willey, P.	1091	456	7	65.14	2-73	–	–
Williams, N.F.	246	148	2	74.00	2-148	–	–

AUSTRALIA

BATTING AND FIELDING

	Tests	I	NO	HS	Runs	Avge	100	50	Ct/St
Alderman, T.M.	35	46	19	23	169	6.25	–	–	22
Boon, D.C.	48	88	7	200	3186	39.33	8	14	49
Border, A.R.	115	199	36	205	8701	53.38	23	48	125
Campbell, G.D.	4	4	0	6	10	2.50	–	–	1
Dodemaide, A.I.C.	8	12	3	50	171	19.00	–	1	6
Healy, I.A.	21	29	2	52	529	19.59	–	1	55/2
Hughes, M.G.	23	28	5	72*	449	19.52	–	2	8
Jones, D.M.	34	59	8	216	2637	51.70	9	9	19
Lawson, G.F.	46	68	12	74	894	15.96	–	4	10
McDermott, C.J.	24	33	3	36	339	11.30	–	–	6
Marsh, G.R.	33	66	3	138	2129	33.79	4	9	27
Matthews, C.D.	3	5	0	32	54	10.80	–	–	1
Matthews, G.R.J.	21	34	6	130	1031	36.82	3	4	13
Moody, T.M.	4	6	0	106	234	39.00	1	1	3
O'Donnell, S.P.	6	10	3	48	206	29.42	–	–	4
Rackemann, C.G.	11	12	4	15*	43	5.37	–	–	2
Reid, B.A.	18	22	10	13	75	6.25	–	–	4
Sleep, P.R.	14	21	1	90	483	24.15	–	3	4
Taylor, M.A.	15	27	2	219	1618	64.72	6	8	20
Taylor, P.L.	10	15	3	87	383	31.91	–	2	10
Veletta, M.R.J.	8	11	0	39	207	18.81	–	–	12
Waugh, S.R.	39	60	10	177*	1983	39.66	3	13	30

BOWLING

	Balls	Runs	Wkts	Avge	Best	5wI	10wM
Alderman, T.M.	9152	4083	153	26.68	6-128	13	1
Boon, D.C.	12	5	0	–	–	–	–
Border, A.R.	2719	1022	29	35.24	7-46	1	1
Campbell, G.D.	951	503	13	38.69	3-79	–	–
Dodemaide, A.I.C.	1861	803	28	28.67	6-58	1	–
Hughes, M.G.	5336	2689	88	30.55	8-87	5	1
Jones, D.M.	174	55	1	55.00	1-5	–	–
Lawson, G.F.	11118	5501	180	30.56	8-112	11	2
McDermott, C.J.	5027	2735	80	34.18	8-141	3	–
Matthews, C.D.	570	313	6	52.16	3-95	–	–
Matthews, G.R.J.	3500	1707	39	43.76	5-103	2	1
Moody, T.M.	234	53	1	53.00	1-23	–	–
O'Donnell, S.P.	940	504	6	84.00	3-37	–	–
Rackemann, C.G.	2546	1028	39	26.35	6-86	3	1
Reid, B.A.	4051	1836	62	29.61	4-53	–	–
Sleep, P.R.	2982	1397	31	45.06	5-72	1	–
Taylor, P.L.	1891	873	24	36.37	6-78	1	–
Waugh, S.R.	3638	1800	43	41.86	5-69	2	–

WEST INDIES

BATTING AND FIELDING

	Tests	I	NO	HS	Runs	Avge	100	50	Ct/St
Ambrose, C.E.L.	20	30	7	44	332	14.43	–	–	5
Arthurton, K.L.T.	5	8	2	37	105	17.50	–	–	2
Baptiste, E.A.E.	10	11	1	87*	233	23.30	–	1	2
Best, C.A.	6	9	1	164	320	40.00	1	1	7
Bishop, I.R.	8	12	6	30*	124	20.66	–	–	1
Dujon, P.J.L.	68	96	11	139	2994	35.22	5	14	218/5
Greenidge, C.G.	100	170	15	223	7134	46.02	18	34	93
Harper, R.A.	24	31	3	74	532	19.00	–	3	35
Haynes, D.L.	89	153	17	184	5711	41.99	14	31	56
Hooper, C.L.	19	31	1	100*	710	23.66	1	3	13
Logie, A.L.	40	61	6	130	1919	34.89	2	10	42
Marshall, M.D.	68	88	9	92	1457	18.44	–	8	25
Moseley, E.A.	2	4	0	26	35	8.75	–	–	1
Patterson, B.P.	18	23	11	21*	90	7.50	–	–	3
Richards, I.V.A.	111	166	10	291	7990	51.21	24	38	116
Richardson, R.B.	49	83	7	194	3515	46.25	10	13	60
Walsh, C.A.	37	48	17	30*	302	9.74	–	–	4

BOWLING

	Balls	Runs	Wkts	Avge	Best	5wI	10wM
Ambrose, C.E.L.	4487	1948	80	24.35	8-45	2	1
Arthurton, K.L.T.	84	38	0	–	–	–	–
Baptiste, E.A.E.	1362	563	16	35.18	3-31	–	–
Best, C.A.	24	19	0	–	–	–	–
Bishop, I.R.	1795	789	37	21.32	6-87	2	–
Greenidge, C.G.	26	4	0	–	–	–	–
Harper, R.A.	3645	1252	45	27.82	6-57	1	–
Haynes, D.L.	18	8	1	8.00	1-2	–	–
Hooper, C.L.	1276	575	7	82.14	2-42	–	–
Logie, A.L.	7	4	0	–	–	–	–
Marshall, M.D.	15221	6831	329	20.76	7-22	22	4
Moseley, E.A.	522	261	6	43.50	2-70	–	–
Patterson, B.P.	2972	1844	60	30.73	5-24	3	–
Richards, I.V.A.	5002	1857	32	58.03	2-17	–	–
Richardson, R.B.	54	12	0	–	–	–	–
Walsh, C.A.	7177	3201	134	23.88	6-62	5	1

NEW ZEALAND

BATTING AND FIELDING

	Tests	I	NO	HS	Runs	Avge	100	50	Ct/St
Bracewell, J.G.	41	60	11	110	1001	20.42	1	4	31
Cairns, C.L.	1	2	0	28	29	14.50	–	–	–
Crowe, J.J.	39	65	4	128	1601	26.24	3	6	41
Crowe, M.D.	51	83	7	188	3384	44.52	11	12	48
Franklin, T.J.	15	25	1	101	569	23.70	1	3	8
Greatbatch, M.J.	14	21	4	146*	917	53.94	2	4	5
Hadlee, Sir R.J.	86	134	19	151*	3124	27.16	2	15	39
Horne, P.A.	3	5	0	27	59	11.80	–	–	1
Jones, A.H.	17	30	4	170*	1190	45.76	2	5	13
Morrison, D.K.	16	20	8	27*	70	5.83	–	–	4
Parore, A.C.	1	2	1	20	32	32.00	–	–	4/1
Patel, D.N.	8	16	0	62	274	17.12	–	1	2
Priest, M.W.	1	1	0	26	26	26.00	–	–	–
Rutherford, K.R.	22	34	3	107*	524	16.90	1	3	14
Smith, I.D.S.	55	75	16	173	1588	26.91	2	5	143/8
Snedden, M.C.	25	30	8	33*	327	14.86	–	–	7
Thomson, S.A.	1	2	1	43*	65	65.00	–	–	1
Vance, R.H.	4	7	0	68	207	29.57	–	1	–
Watson, W.	3	3	1	8*	13	6.50	–	–	2
Wright, J.G.	71	126	6	185	4377	36.47	10	18	34

BOWLING

	Balls	Runs	Wkts	Avge	Best	5wI	10wM
Bracewell, J.G.	8403	3653	102	35.81	6-32	4	1
Cairns, C.L.	72	60	0	–	–	–	–
Crowe, J.J.	18	9	0	–	–	–	–
Crowe, M.D.	1239	607	13	46.69	2-25	–	–
Greatbatch, M.J.	6	0	0	–	–	–	–
Hadlee, Sir R.J.	21918	9611	431	22.29	9-52	36	9
Jones, A.H.	156	90	1	90.00	1-40	–	–
Morrison, D.K.	3053	1826	49	37.26	5-69	4	–
Patel, D.N.	427	210	1	210.00	1-80	–	–
Priest, M.W.	72	26	1	26.00	1-26	–	–
Rutherford, K.R.	244	150	1	150.00	1-38	–	–
Smith, I.D.S.	18	5	0	–	–	–	–
Snedden, M.C.	4775	2199	58	37.91	5-68	1	–
Thomson, S.A.	165	122	2	61.00	2-92	–	–
Watson, W.	659	314	4	78.50	2-51	–	–
Wright, J.G.	30	5	0	–	–	–	–

INDIA

BATTING AND FIELDING

	Tests	I	NO	HS	Runs	Avge	100	50	Ct/St
Ankola, S.A.	1	1	0	6	6	6.00	–	–	–
Arshad Ayub	13	19	4	57	257	17.13	–	1	2
Arun Lal	16	29	1	93	729	26.03	–	6	13
Azharuddin, M.	40	60	3	199	2953	51.80	10	10	31
Gursharan Singh	1	1	0	18	18	18.00	–	–	2
Hirwani, N.D.	13	17	10	17	45	6.42	–	–	5
Kapil Dev	109	158	13	163	4521	31.17	7	23	54
Kumble, A.	1	1	0	2	2	2.00	–	–	–
Maninder Singh	34	38	12	15	99	3.80	–	–	9
Manjrekar, S.V.	15	24	2	218	1067	48.50	3	5	11
More, K.S.	34	46	10	73	924	25.66	–	5	68/15
Prabhakar, M.	12	20	6	95	621	44.35	–	4	3
Raju, S.L.V.	2	3	1	31	55	27.50	–	–	1
Raman, W.V.	6	10	1	96	303	33.66	–	3	3
Razdan, V.	2	2	1	6	6	6.00	–	–	–
Sharma, G.	4	3	1	10*	11	5.50	–	–	1
Sharma, S.K.	2	3	1	38	56	28.00	–	–	1
Shastri, R.J.	72	109	14	187	3372	35.49	10	11	35
Sidhu, N.S.	17	28	2	116	792	30.46	2	4	2
Srikkanth, K.	39	64	3	123	1927	31.59	2	12	33
Tendulkar, S.R.	10	15	1	119*	577	41.21	1	4	5
Vengsarkar, D.B.	110	175	22	166	6703	43.81	17	33	74
Wassan, A.S.	4	5	1	53	94	23.50	–	1	1

BOWLING

	Balls	Runs	Wkts	Avge	Best	5wI	10wM
Ankola, S.A.	180	128	2	64.00	1-35	–	–
Arshad Ayub	3663	1438	41	35.07	5-50	3	–
Arun Lal	16	7	0	–	–	–	–
Azharuddin, M.	6	8	0	–	–	–	–
Hirwani, N.D.	3752	1765	57	30.96	8-61	3	1
Kapil Dev	23037	11199	371	30.18	9-83	21	2
Kumble, A.	360	170	3	56.66	3-105	–	–
Maninder Singh	7816	3143	81	38.80	7-27	3	2
Manjrekar, S.V.	6	7	0	–	–	–	–
More, K.S.	12	12	0	–	–	–	–
Prabhakar, M.	2907	1580	30	52.66	6-132	2	–
Raju, S.L.V.	276	113	3	37.66	3-86	–	–
Raman, W.V.	258	66	2	33.00	1-7	–	–
Razdan, V.	240	141	5	28.20	5-79	1	–
Sharma, G.	1085	353	9	39.22	4-88	–	–
Sharma, S.K.	414	247	6	41.16	3-37	–	–
Shastri, R.J.	15103	5914	143	41.35	5-75	2	–
Sidhu, N.S.	6	9	0	–	–	–	–
Srikkanth, K.	210	108	0	–	–	–	–
Tendulkar, S.R.	30	25	0	–	–	–	–
Vengsarkar, D.B.	47	36	0	–	–	–	–
Wassan, A.S.	712	504	10	50.40	4-108	–	1

PAKISTAN

BATTING AND FIELDING

	Tests	I	NO	HS	Runs	Avge	100	50	Ct/St
Aamer Malik	12	15	3	117	486	40.50	2	2	13/1
Aaqib Javed	2	2	0	0	0	0.00	–	–	1
Abdul Qadir	63	74	10	61	1022	15.96	–	3	15
Akram Raza	1	–	–	–	–	–	–	–	1
Ijaz Ahmed	16	21	0	122	637	30.33	2	2	14
Imran Khan	82	118	22	136	3541	36.88	6	15	28
Javed Miandad	104	158	18	280*	7891	56.36	22	38	86/1
Mansoor Akhtar	19	29	3	111	655*	25.19	1	3	9
Mushtaq Ahmed	1	2	0	4	4	2.00	–	–	–
Nadeem Abbasi	3	2	0	36	46	23.00	–	–	6
Nadeem Ghauri	1	1	0	0	0	0.00	–	–	–
Naved Anjum	1	1	0	12	12	12.00	–	–	–
Ramiz Raja	31	49	3	122	1390	30.21	2	9	21
Salim Jaffer	10	10	4	9	22	3.66	–	–	1
Salim Malik	57	79	14	119*	2718	41.81	7	15	43
Salim Yousuf	28	39	5	91*	977	28.73	–	5	73/11
Shahid Mahboob	1	–	–	–	–	–	–	–	–
Shahid Saeed	1	1	0	12	12	12.00	–	–	–
Shoaib Mohammad	29	42	3	203*	1611	41.30	4	8	16
Tausif Ahmed	31	35	18	35*	284	16.70	–	–	8
Waqar Younis	5	6	1	18	43	8.60	–	–	–
Wasim Akram	32	39	6	123	665	20.25	1	3	11
Zakir Khan	2	2	2	9*	9	–	–	–	1

BOWLING

	Balls	Runs	Wkts	Avge	Best	5wI	10wM
Aamer Malik	126	73	1	73.00	1-0	–	–
Aaqib Javed	541	262	3	87.33	2-47	–	–
Abdul Qadir	16592	7458	230	32.42	9-56	15	5
Akram Raza	108	58	0	–	–	–	–
Ijaz Ahmed	12	3	0	–	–	–	–
Imran Khan	19290	8188	358	22.87	8-58	23	6
Javed Miandad	1470	682	17	40.11	3-74	–	–
Mushtaq Ahmed	288	141	1	141.00	1-72	–	–
Nadeem Ghauri	48	20	0	–	–	–	–
Naved Anjum	306	149	4	37.25	2-57	–	–
Salim Jaffer	1931	887	25	35.48	5-40	1	–
Salim Malik	254	101	5	20.20	1-3	–	–
Shahid Mahboob	294	131	2	65.50	2-131	–	–
Shahid Saeed	90	43	0	–	–	–	–
Shoaib Mohammad	198	89	4	22.25	2-8	–	–
Tausif Ahmed	7508	2831	92	30.77	6-45	3	–
Waqar Younis	846	461	10	46.10	4-80	–	–
Wasim Akram	7017	2967	111	26.72	6-62	8	2
Zakir Khan	444	259	5	51.80	3-80	–	–

SRI LANKA

BATTING AND FIELDING

	Tests	I	NO	HS	Runs	Avge	100	50	Ct/St
Ahangama, F.S.	3	3	1	11	11	5.50	–	–	1
Anurasiri, S.D.	4	5	2	8	13	4.33	–	–	–
De Silva, E.A.R.	7	11	3	50	146	18.25	–	1	4
De Silva, P.A.	17	31	2	167	974	33.58	3	3	9
Gurusinha, A.P.	9	15	2	116*	414	31.84	1	–	6
Kuruppu, D.S.B.P.	3	5	1	201*	294	73.50	1	–	1
Labrooy, G.F.	5	8	2	42	81	13.50	–	–	1
Madugalle, R.S.	21	39	4	103	1029	29.40	1	7	9
Madurasinghe, A.W.R.	1	2	0	4	6	3.00	–	–	–
Mahanama, R.S.	6	10	0	85	243	24.30	–	1	3
Ramanayake, C.P.H.	4	7	3	10*	27	6.75	–	–	2
Ranatunga, A.	26	46	2	135*	1621	36.84	2	12	14
Ranatunga, D.	2	3	0	45	87	29.00	–	–	1
Ratnayake, R.J.	15	25	4	56	277	13.19	–	1	6
Ratnayeke, J.R.	22	38	6	93	807	25.21	–	5	1
Samarasekera, M.A.R.	2	3	0	57	75	25.00	–	1	3
Silva, S.A.R.	9	16	2	111	353	25.21	2	–	33/1
Tillekeratne, H.P.	1	2	0	6	6	3.00	–	–	5
Warnaweera, K.P.J.	1	2	0	3	3	1.50	–	–	–
Wickremasinghe, A.G.D.	1	1	0	2	2	2.00	–	–	3

BOWLING

	Balls	Runs	Wkts	Avge	Best	5wI	10wM
Ahangama, F.S.	801	348	18	19.33	5-52	1	–
Anurasiri, S.D.	486	159	5	31.80	4-71	–	–
De Silva, E.A.R.	1440	639	4	159.75	1-10	–	–
De Silva, P.A.	234	134	3	44.66	2-65	–	–
Gurusinha, A.P.	254	172	7	24.57	2-25	–	–
Labrooy, G.F.	1297	778	14	55.57	5-133	1	–
Madugalle, R.S.	84	38	0	–	–	–	–
Madurasinghe, A.W.R.	96	41	0	–	–	–	–
Mahanama, R.S.	6	3	0	–	–	–	–
Ramanayake, C.P.H.	674	396	6	66.00	2-81	–	–
Ranatunga, A.	1555	688	11	62.54	2-17	–	–
Ratnayake, R.J.	3153	1701	49	34.71	6-66	3	–
Ratnayeke, J.R.	3833	1972	56	35.21	8-83	4	–
Samarasekera, M.A.R.	192	104	3	34.66	2-38	–	–
Warnaweera, K.P.J.	51	26	1	26.00	1-26	–	–

CRICKET RECORDS
FIRST-CLASS MATCHES

UPDATED TO THE END OF THE 1990 SEASON

TEAM RECORDS
Highest Innings Totals

1107	Victoria v New South Wales	Melbourne	1926-27
1059	Victoria v Tasmania	Melbourne	1922-23
951-7d	Sind v Baluchistan	Karachi	1973-74
918	New South Wales v South Australia	Sydney	1900-01
912-8d	Holkar v Mysore	Indore	1945-46
910-6d	Railways v Dera Ismail Khan	Lahore	1964-65
903-7d	England v Australia	The Oval	1938
887	Yorkshire v Warwickshire	Birmingham	1896
863	Lancashire v Surrey	The Oval	1990
860-6d	Tamil Nadu v Goa	Panaji	1988-89
849	England v West Indies	Kingston	1929-30

There have been 25 instances of a team scoring 800 runs or more in an innings, the most recent being by Lancashire (above). Tamil Nadu's total of 860-6d was boosted to 912 by 52 penalty runs.

Highest Second Innings Total

770	New South Wales v South Australia	Adelaide	1920-21

Highest Fourth Innings Total

654-5	England v South Africa	Durban	1938-39

Highest Match Aggregate

2376	Maharashtra v Bombay	Poona	1948-49

Record Margin of Victory

Innings and 851 runs	Railways v Dera Ismail Khan	Lahore	1964-65

Most Runs in a Day

721	Australians v Essex	Southend	1948

Most Hundreds in an Innings

6	Holkar v Mysore	Indore	1945-46
5	New South Wales v South Australia	Sydney	1900-01
5	Australia v West Indies	Kingston	1954-55

Lowest Innings Totals

12	†Oxford University v MCC and Ground	Oxford	1877
12	Northamptonshire v Gloucestershire	Gloucester	1907
13	Auckland v Canterbury	Auckland	1877-78
13	Nottinghamshire v Yorkshire	Nottingham	1901
14	Surrey v Essex	Chelmsford	1983
15	MCC v Surrey	Lord's	1839

15	†Victoria v MCC	Melbourne	1903-04
15	†Northamptonshire v Yorkshire	Northampton	1908
15	Hampshire v Warwickshire	Birmingham	1922

†Batted one man short

There have been 26 instances of a team being dismissed for under 20, the most recent being by Surrey in 1983 (above).

Lowest Match Aggregate by One Team

| 34 (16 and 18) Border v Natal | East London | 1959-60 |

Lowest Completed Match Aggregate by Both Teams

| 105 | MCC v Australians | Lord's | 1878 |

Fewest Runs in an Uninterrupted Day's Play

| 95 | Australia (80) v Pakistan (15-2) | Karachi | 1956-57 |

Tied Matches

Before 1948 a match was considered to be tied if the scores were level after the fourth innings, even if the side batting last had wickets in hand when play ended. Law 22 was amended in 1948 and since then a match has been tied only when the scores are level after the fourth innings has been completed. There have been 48 tied first-class matches, five of which would not have qualified under the current law. The most recent are:

| Peshawar (263-9d/249) v Bahawalpur (325-8c/187) | Bahawalpur | 1988-89 |
| Wellington (398/250-4d) v Canterbury (381/267) | Wellington | 1988-89 |

BATTING RECORDS
Highest Individual Innings

499	Hanif Mohammad	Karachi v Bahawalpur	Karachi	1958-59
452*	D.G.Bradman	New South Wales v Queensland	Sydney	1929-30
443*	B.B.Nimbalkar	Maharashtra v Kathiawar	Poona	1948-49
437	W.H.Ponsford	Victoria v Queensland	Melbourne	1927-28
429	W.H.Ponsford	Victoria v Tasmania	Melbourne	1922-23
428	Aftab Baloch	Sind v Baluchistan	Karachi	1973-74
424	A.C.MacLaren	Lancashire v Somerset	Taunton	1895
405*	G.A.Hick	Worcestershire v Somerset	Taunton	1988
385	B.Sutcliffe	Otago v Canterbury	Christchurch	1952-53
383	C.W.Gregory	New South Wales v Queensland	Brisbane	1906-07
369	D.G.Bradman	South Australia v Tasmania	Adelaide	1935-36
366	N.H.Fairbrother	Lancashire v Surrey	The Oval	1990
365*	C.Hill	South Australia v NSW	Adelaide	1900-01
365*	G.St A.Sobers	West Indies v Pakistan	Kingston	1957-58
364	L.Hutton	England v Australia	The Oval	1938
359*	V.M.Merchant	Bombay v Maharashtra	Bombay	1943-44
359	R.B.Simpson	New South Wales v Queensland	Brisbane	1963-64
357*	R.Abel	Surrey v Somerset	The Oval	1899
357	D.G.Bradman	South Australia v Victoria	Melbourne	1935-36
356	B.A.Richards	S Australia v W Australia	Perth	1970-71
355*	G.R.Marsh	W Australia v S Australia	Perth	1989-90
355	B.Sutcliffe	Otago v Auckland	Dunedin	1949-50
352	W.H.Ponsford	Victoria v New South Wales	Melbourne	1926-27
350	Rashid Israr	Habib Bank v National Bank	Lahore	1976-77

There have been 104 triple hundreds in first-class cricket, W.V.Raman (313) and Arjan Kripal Singh (302*) for Tamil Nadu v Goa at Panaji in 1988-89 providing the only instance of two batsmen scoring 300 in the same innings.

Most Hundreds in Successive Innings

6	C.B.Fry	Sussex and Rest of England	1901
6	D.G.Bradman	South Australia and D.G.Bradman's XI	1938-39
6	M.J.Procter	Rhodesia	1970-71

Two Double Hundreds in a Match

244	202*	A.E.Fagg	Kent v Essex	Colchester	1938

Triple Hundreds and Hundreds in a Match

333	123	G.A.Gooch	England v India	Lord's	1990

Double Hundred and Hundred in a Match Most Times

4	Zaheer Abbas	Gloucestershire	1976-81

Two Hundreds in a Match Most Times

8	Zaheer Abbas	Gloucestershire and PIA	1976-82
7	W.R.Hammond	Gloucestershire, England and MCC	1927-45

Most Hundreds in a Season

18	D.C.S.Compton	1947
16	J.B.Hobbs	1925

Most Hundreds in a Career

(The season in which his 100th hundred was scored is given in brackets)

197	J.B.Hobbs (1923)	117	D.G.Bradman (1947-48)
170	E.H.Hendren (1928-29)	109	I.V.A.Richards (1988-89)
167	W.R.Hammond (1935)	108	Zaheer Abbas (1982-83)
153	C.P.Mead (1927)	107	A.Sandham (1935)
151	G.Boycott (1977)	107	M.C.Cowdrey (1973)
149	H.Sutcliffe (1932)	104	T.W.Hayward (1913)
145	F.E.Woolley (1929)	103	J.H.Edrich (1977)
129	L.Hutton (1951)	103	G.M.Turner (1982)
126	W.G.Grace (1895)	102	G.E.Tyldesley (1934)
123	D.C.S.Compton (1952)	102	L.E.G.Ames (1950)
122	T.W.Graveney (1964)	102	D.L.Amiss (1986)

Most Runs in a Season

Runs			I	NO	HS	Avge	100	Season
3816	D.C.S.Compton	Middlesex	50	8	246	90.85	18	1947
3539	W.J.Edrich	Middlesex	52	8	267*	80.43	12	1947
3518	T.W.Hayward	Surrey	61	8	219	66.37	13	1906

The feat of scoring 3000 runs in a season has been achieved on 28 occasions, the most recent instance being by W.E.Alley (3019) in 1961. The highest aggregate in a season since 1969, when the number of County Championship matches was substantially reduced, is 2746 by G.A.Gooch in 1990.

1000 Runs in a Season Most Times

28   W.G.Grace (Gloucestershire), F.E.Woolley (Kent)

Highest Batting Average in a Season

(Qualification: 12 innings)

Avge			I	NO	HS	Runs	100	Season
115.66	D.G.Bradman	Australians	26	5	278	2429	13	1938
102.53	G.Boycott	Yorkshire	20	5	175*	1538	6	1979
102.00	W.A.Johnston	Australians	17	16	28*	102	–	1953
101.70	G.A.Gooch	Essex	30	3	333	2746	12	1990
100.12	G.Boycott	Yorkshire	30	5	233	2503	13	1971

Fastest Hundred Against Genuine Bowling

35 min   P.G.H.Fender   Surrey v Northamptonshire   Northampton   1920

Fastest Double Hundred

113 min   R.J.Shastri   Bombay v Baroda   Bombay   1984-85

Fastest Triple Hundred

181 min   D.C.S.Compton   MCC v NE Transvaal   Benoni   1948-49

Most Sixes in an Innings

15	J.R.Reid	Wellington v N Districts	Wellington	1962-63
13	Majid Khan	Pakistanis v Glamorgan	Swansea	1967
13	C.G.Greenidge	D.H.Robins' XI v Pakistanis	Eastbourne	1974
13	C.G.Greenidge	Hampshire v Sussex	Southampton	1975
13	G.W.Humpage	Warwickshire v Lancashire	Southport	1982
13	R.J.Shastri	Bombay v Baroda	Bombay	1984-85

Most Sixes in a Match

17   W.J.Stewart   Warwickshire v Lancashire   Blackpool   1959

Most Sixes in a Season

80   I.T.Botham   Somerset and England   1985

Most Boundaries in an Innings

68   P.A.Perrin   Essex v Derbyshire   Chesterfield   1904

Most Runs off One Over Without No-Balls

36	G.St A.Sobers	Nottinghamshire v Glamorgan	Swansea	1968
36	R.J.Shastri	Bombay v Baroda	Bombay	1984-85

Both batsmen hit all six balls of an over (bowled by M.A.Nash and Tilak Raj respectively) for six.

Most Runs in a Day

345   C.G.Macartney   Australians v Nottinghamshire   Nottingham   1921

There have been 18 instances of a batsman scoring 300 or more runs in a day, the most recent being by N.H.Fairbrother (311*) for Lancashire v Surrey at The Oval in 1990.

Highest Partnerships

First Wicket
561	Waheed Mirza/Mansoor Akhtar	Karachi W v Quetta	Karachi	1976-77
555	P.Holmes/H.Sutcliffe	Yorkshire v Essex	Leyton	1932
554	J.T.Brown/J.Tunnicliffe	Yorkshire v Derbys	Chesterfield	1898

Second Wicket
465*	J.A.Jameson/R.B.Kanhai	Warwickshire v Glos	Birmingham	1974
455	K.V.Bhandarkar/B.B.Nimbalkar	Maha'tra v Kathiawar	Poona	1948-49
451	D.G.Bradman/W.H.Ponsford	Australia v England	The Oval	1934

Third Wicket
456	Khalid Irtiza/Aslam Ali	United Bank v Multan	Karachi	1975-76
451	Mudassar Nazar/Javed Miandad	Pakistan v India	Hyderabad	1982-83
445	P.E.Whitelaw/W.N.Carson	Auckland v Otago	Dunedin	1936-37
434	J.B.Stollmeyer/G.E.Gomez	Trinidad v Br Guiana	Port-of-Spain	1946-47
424*	W.J.Edrich/D.C.S.Compton	Middlesex v Somerset	Lord's	1948

Fourth Wicket
577	V.S.Hazare/Gul Mahomed	Baroda v Holkar	Baroda	1946-47
574*	C.L.Walcott/F.M.M.Worrell	Barbados v Trinidad	Port-of-Spain	1945-46
502*	F.M.M.Worrell/J.D.C.Goddard	Barbados v Trinidad	Bridgetown	1943-44
470	A.I.Kallicharran/G.W.Humpage	Warwickshire v Lancs	Southport	1982

Fifth Wicket
405	S.G.Barnes/D.G.Bradman	Australia v England	Sydney	1946-47
397	W.Bardsley/C.Kelleway	NSW v S Australia	Sydney	1920-21
393	E.G.Arnold/W.B.Burns	Worcs v Warwickshire	Birmingham	1909

Sixth Wicket
487*	G.A.Headley/C.C.Passailaigue	Jamaica v Tennyson's	Kingston	1931-32
428	W.W.Armstrong/M.A.Noble	Australians v Sussex	Hove	1902
411	R.M.Poore/E.G.Wynyard	Hampshire v Somerset	Taunton	1899

Seventh Wicket
347	D.St E.Atkinson/C.C.Depeiza	W Indies v Australia	Bridgetown	1954-55
344	K.S.Ranjitsinhji/W.Newham	Sussex v Essex	Leyton	1902

Eighth Wicket
433	A.Sims/V.T.Trumper	Australians v C'bury	Christchurch	1913-14
292	R.Peel/Lord Hawke	Yorkshire v Warwicks	Birmingham	1896

Ninth Wicket
283	J.Chapman/A.Warren	Derbys v Warwicks	Blackwell	1910
251	J.W.H.T.Douglas/S.N.Hare	Essex v Derbyshire	Leyton	1921

Tenth Wicket
307	A.F.Kippax/J.E.H.Hooker	NSW v Victoria	Melbourne	1928-29
249	C.T.Sarwate/S.N.Banerjee	Indians v Surrey	The Oval	1946
235	F.E.Woolley/A.Fielder	Kent v Worcs	Stourbridge	1909

Most Runs in a Career

	Career	I	NO	HS	Runs	Avge	100
J.B.Hobbs	1905-34	1315	106	316*	61237	50.65	197
F.E.Woolley	1906-38	1532	85	305*	58969	40.75	145
E.H.Hendren	1907-38	1300	166	301*	57611	50.80	170
C.P.Mead	1905-36	1340	185	280*	55061	47.67	153
W.G.Grace	1865-1908	1493	105	344	54896	39.55	126
W.R.Hammond	1920-51	1005	104	336*	50551	56.10	167
H.Sutcliffe	1919-45	1088	123	313	50138	51.95	149
G.Boycott	1962-86	1014	162	261*	48426	56.83	151
T.W.Graveney	1948-71/72	1223	159	258	47793	44.91	122
T.W.Hayward	1893-1914	1138	96	315*	43551	41.79	104
D.L.Amiss	1960-87	1139	126	262*	43423	42.86	102
M.C.Cowdrey	1950-76	1130	134	307	42719	42.89	107
A.Sandham	1911-37/38	1000	79	325	41284	44.82	107
L.Hutton	1934-60	814	91	364	40140	55.51	129
M.J.K.Smith	1951-75	1091	139	204	39832	41.84	69
W.Rhodes	1898-1930	1528	237	267*	39802	30.83	58
J.H.Edrich	1956-78	979	104	310*	39790	45.47	103
R.E.S.Wyatt	1923-57	1141	157	232	39405	40.04	85
D.C.S.Compton	1936-64	839	88	300	38942	51.85	123
G.E.Tyldesley	1909-36	961	106	256*	38874	45.46	102
J.T.Tyldesley	1895-1923	994	62	295*	37897	40.60	86
K.W.R.Fletcher	1962-88	1167	170	228*	37665	37.77	63
J.W.Hearne	1909-36	1025	116	285*	37252	40.98	96
L.E.G.Ames	1926-51	951	95	295	37248	43.51	102
D.Kenyon	1946-67	1159	59	259	37002	33.63	74
W.J.Edrich	1934-58	964	92	267*	36965	42.39	86
J.M.Parks	1949-76	1227	172	205*	36673	34.76	51
D.Denton	1894-1920	1163	70	221	36479	33.37	69
C.G.Greenidge	1970-90	860	72	273*	36434	46.23	90
G.H.Hirst	1891-1929	1215	151	341	36323	34.13	60
A.Jones	1957-83	1168	72	204*	36049	32.89	56
W.G.Quaife	1894-1928	1203	185	255*	36012	35.37	72
R.E.Marshall	1945/46-72	1053	59	228*	35725	35.94	68
G.Gunn	1902-32	1061	82	220	35208	35.96	62

BOWLING RECORDS

All Ten Wickets in an Innings

This feat has been achieved on 72 occasions at first-class level.

Three Times: A.P.Freeman (1929, 1930, 1931)
Twice: V.E.Walker (1859, 1865); H.Verity (1931, 1932); J.C.Laker (1956)

Instances since 1945:

W.E.Hollies	Warwickshire v Notts	Birmingham	1946
J.M.Sims	East v West	Kingston on Thames	1948
J.K.R.Graveney	Gloucestershire v Derbyshire	Chesterfield	1949
T.E.Bailey	Essex v Lancashire	Clacton	1949
R.Berry	Lancashire v Worcestershire	Blackpool	1953
S.P.Gupte	President's XI v Combined XI	Bombay	1954-55
J.C.Laker	Surrey v Australians	The Oval	1956
K.Smales	Nottinghamshire v Glos	Stroud	1956
G.A.R.Lock	Surrey v Kent	Blackheath	1956
J.C.Laker	England v Australia	Manchester	1956

P.M.Chatterjee	Bengal v Assam	Jorhat	1956-57
J.D.Bannister	Warwicks v Combined Services	Birmingham	1959
A.J.G.Pearson	Cambridge U v Leicestershire	Loughborough	1961
N.I.Thomson	Sussex v Warwickshire	Worthing	1964
P.J.Allan	Queensland v Victoria	Melbourne	1965-66
I.J.Brayshaw	Western Australia v Victoria	Perth	1967-68
Shahid Mahmood	Karachi Whites v Khairpur	Karachi	1969-70
E.E.Hemmings	International XI v W Indians	Kingston	1982-83
P.Sunderam	Rajasthan v Vidarbha	Jodhpur	1985-86
S.T.Jefferies	Western Province v OFS	Cape Town	1987-88
Imran Adil	Bahawalpur v Faisalabad	Faisalabad	1989-90

Most Wickets in a Match

| 19 | J.C.Laker | England v Australia | Manchester | 1956 |

Most Wickets in a Season

Wkts		Season	Matches	Overs	Mdns	Runs	Avge
304	A.P.Freeman	1928	37	1976.1	423	5489	18.05
298	A.P.Freeman	1933	33	2039	651	4549	15.26

The feat of taking 250 wickets in a season has been achieved on 12 occasions, the last instance being by A.P.Freeman in 1933. 200 or more wickets in a season have been taken on 59 occasions, the last being by G.A.R.Lock (212 wickets, average 12.02) in 1957.

The highest aggregates of wickets taken in a season since the reduction of the County Championship matches in 1969 are as follows:

Wkts		Season	Matches	Overs	Mdns	Runs	Avge
134	M.D.Marshall	1982	22	822	225	2108	15.73
131	L.R.Gibbs	1971	23	1024.1	295	2475	18.89

Since 1969 there have been 44 instances of bowlers taking 100 wickets in a season, the last being by F.D.Stephenson (125 wickets, average 18.31) in 1988.

Most Hat-Tricks in a Career

7	D.V.P.Wright
6	T.W.J.Goddard, C.W.L.Parker
5	S.Haigh, V.W.C.Jupp, A.E.G.Rhodes, F.A.Tarrant

Most Wickets in a Career

	Career	Runs	Wkts	Avge	100w
W.Rhodes	1898-1930	69993	4187	16.71	23
A.P.Freeman	1914-36	69577	3776	18.42	17
C.W.L.Parker	1903-35	63817	3278	19.46	16
J.T.Hearne	1888-1923	54352	3061	17.75	15
T.W.J.Goddard	1922-52	59116	2979	19.84	16
W.G.Grace	1865-1908	51545	2876	17.92	10
A.S.Kennedy	1907-36	61034	2874	21.23	15
D.Shackleton	1948-69	53303	2857	18.65	20
G.A.R.Lock	1946-70/71	54709	2844	19.23	14
F.J.Titmus	1949-82	63313	2830	22.37	16
M.W.Tate	1912-37	50571	2784	18.16	13+1
G.H.Hirst	1891-1929	51282	2739	18.72	15
C.Blythe	1899-1914	42136	2506	16.81	14

	Career	Runs	Wkts	Avge	100w
D.L.Underwood	1963-87	49993	2465	20.28	10
W.E.Astill	1906-39	57783	2431	23.76	9
J.C.White	1909-37	43759	2356	18.57	14
W.E.Hollies	1932-57	48656	2323	20.94	14
F.S.Trueman	1949-69	42154	2304	18.29	12
J.B.Statham	1950-68	36995	2260	16.36	13
R.T.D.Perks	1930-55	53770	2233	24.07	16
J.Briggs	1879-1900	35430	2221	15.95	12
D.J.Shepherd	1950-72	47302	2218	21.32	12
E.G.Dennett	1903-26	42571	2147	19.82	12
T.Richardson	1892-1905	38794	2104	18.43	10
T.E.Bailey	1945-67	48170	2082	23.13	9
R.Illingworth	1951-83	42023	2072	20.28	10
F.E.Woolley	1906-38	41066	2068	19.85	8
N.Gifford	1960-88	48731	2068	23.56	4
G.Geary	1912-38	41339	2063	20.03	11
D.V.P.Wright	1932-57	49307	2056	23.98	10
J.A.Newman	1906-30	51111	2032	25.15	9
A.Shaw	1864-97	24579	2027†	12.12	9
S.Haigh	1895-1913	32091	2012	15.94	11

†Excluding one wicket for which no analysis is available

ALL-ROUND RECORDS

The 'Double'

3000 runs and 100 wickets: J.H.Parks (1937)
2000 runs and 200 wickets: G.H.Hirst (1906)
2000 runs and 100 wickets: F.E.Woolley (4), J.W.Hearne (3), W.G.Grace (2), G.H.Hirst (2), W.Rhodes (2), T.E.Bailey, D.E.Davies, G.L.Jessop, V.W.C.Jupp, James Langridge, F.A.Tarrant, C.L.Townsend, L.F.Townsend
1000 runs and 200 wickets: M.W.Tate (3), A.E.Trott (2), A.S.Kennedy
Most Doubles: W.Rhodes (16), G.H.Hirst (14), V.W.C.Jupp (10)
Double in debut season: D.B.Close (1949) – aged 18, he is the youngest to achieve this feat

The feat of scoring 1000 runs and taking 100 wickets in a season has been achieved on 305 occasions, R.J.Hadlee (1984) and F.D.Stephenson (1988) being the only players to complete the 'double' since the reduction of Championship matches in 1969.

WICKET-KEEPING RECORDS

Most Dismissals in an Innings

8 (8ct)	A.T.W.Grout	Queensland v W Australia	Brisbane	1959-60
8 (8ct)	D.E.East	Essex v Somerset	Taunton	1985

Most Dismissals in a Match

12 (8ct, 4st)	E.Pooley	Surrey v Sussex	The Oval	1868
12 (9ct, 3st)	D.Tallon	Queensland v NSW	Sydney	1938-39
12 (9ct, 3st)	H.B.Taber	NSW v South Australia	Adelaide	1968-69

Most Catches in a Match

11	A.Long	Surrey v Sussex	Hove	1964
11	R.W.Marsh	W Australia v Victoria	Perth	1975-76
11	D.L.Bairstow	Yorkshire v Derbyshire	Scarborough	1982
11	W.K.Hegg	Lancashire v Derbyshire	Chesterfield	1989
11	A.J.Stewart	Surrey v Leicestershire	Leicester	1989

Most Dismissals in a Season

128 (79ct, 49st)   L.E.G.Ames   1929

Most Dismissals in a Career

	Career	Dismissals	Ct	St
R.W.Taylor	1960-88	**1649**	1473	176
J.T.Murray	1952-75	**1527**	1270	257
H.Strudwick	1902-27	**1497**	1242	255
A.P.E.Knott	1964-85	**1344**	1211	133
F.H.Huish	1895-1914	**1310**	933	377
B.Taylor	1949-73	**1294**	1083	211
D.Hunter	1889-1909	**1253**	906	347
H.R.Butt	1890-1912	**1228**	953	275
J.H.Board	1891-1914/15	**1207**	852	355
H.Elliott	1920-47	**1206**	904	302
J.M.Parks	1949-76	**1181**	1088	93
R.Booth	1951-70	**1126**	948	178
L.E.G.Ames	1926-51	**1121**	703	418
D.L.Bairstow	1970-90	**1099**	961	138
G.Duckworth	1923-47	**1096**	753	343
H.W.Stephenson	1948-64	**1082**	748	334
J.G.Binks	1955-75	**1071**	895	176
T.G.Evans	1939-69	**1066**	816	250
A.Long	1960-80	**1046**	922	124
G.O.Dawkes	1937-61	**1043**	895	148
R.W.Tolchard	1965-83	**1037**	912	125
W.L.Cornford	1921-47	**1017**	675	342

FIELDING RECORDS

Most Catches in an Innings

| 7 | M.J.Stewart | Surrey v Northamptonshire | Northampton | 1957 |
| 7 | A.S.Brown | Gloucestershire v Nottinghamshire | Nottingham | 1966 |

Most Catches in a Match

| 10 | W.R.Hammond | Gloucestershire v Surrey | Cheltenham | 1928 |

Most Catches in a Season

| 78 | W.R.Hammond | (1928) | 77 | M.J.Stewart | (1957) |

Most Catches in a Career

1018	F.E.Woolley	(1906-38)	784	J.G.Langridge	(1928-55)
887	W.G.Grace	(1865-1908)	764	W.Rhodes	(1898-1930)
830	G.A.R.Lock	(1946-70/71)	758	C.A.Milton	(1948-74)
819	W.R.Hammond	(1920-51)	754	E.H.Hendren	(1907-38)
813	D.B.Close	(1949-86)			

TEST CRICKET RECORDS

(UPDATED TO THE END OF THE 1990 SEASON)

TEAM RECORDS

HIGHEST INNINGS TOTALS

903-7d	England v Australia	The Oval	1938
849	England v West Indies	Kingston	1929-30
790-3d	West Indies v Pakistan	Kingston	1957-58
758-8d	Australia v West Indies	Kingston	1954-55
729-6d	Australia v England	Lord's	1930
708	Pakistan v England	The Oval	1987
701	Australia v England	The Oval	1934
699-5	Pakistan v India	Lahore	1989-90
695	Australia v England	The Oval	1930
687-8d	West Indies v England	The Oval	1976
681-8d	West Indies v England	Port-of-Spain	1953-54
676-7	India v Sri Lanka	Kanpur	1986-87
674-6	Pakistan v India	Faisalabad	1984-85
674	Australia v India	Adelaide	1947-48
668	Australia v West Indies	Bridgetown	1954-55
659-8d	Australia v England	Sydney	1946-47
658-8d	England v Australia	Nottingham	1938
657-8d	Pakistan v West Indies	Bridgetown	1957-58
656-8d	Australia v England	Manchester	1964
654-5	England v South Africa	Durban	1938-39
653-4d	England v India	Lord's	1990
652-7d	England v India	Madras	1984-85
652-8d	West Indies v England	Lord's	1973
652	Pakistan v India	Faisalabad	1982-83
650-6d	Australia v West Indies	Bridgetown	1964-65

The highest innings for other countries are:

622-9d	South Africa v Australia	Durban	1969-70
553-7d	New Zealand v Australia	Brisbane	1985-86
491-7d	Sri Lanka v England	Lord's	1984

LOWEST INNINGS TOTALS

26	New Zealand v England	Auckland	1954-55
30	South Africa v England	Port Elizabeth	1895-96
30	South Africa v England	Birmingham	1924
35	South Africa v England	Cape Town	1898-99
36	Australia v England	Birmingham	1902
36	South Africa v Australia	Melbourne	1931-32
42	Australia v England	Sydney	1887-88
42	New Zealand v Australia	Wellington	1945-46
42	India v England	Lord's	1974
43	South Africa v England	Cape Town	1888-89
44	Australia v England	The Oval	1896
45	England v Australia	Sydney	1886-87
45	South Africa v Australia	Melbourne	1931-32
47	South Africa v England	Cape Town	1888-89
47	New Zealand v England	Lord's	1958

The lowest innings for other countries are:

53	West Indies v Pakistan	Faisalabad	1986-87
62	Pakistan v Australia	Perth	1981-82
93	Sri Lanka v New Zealand	Wellington	1982-83

BATTING RECORDS
HIGHEST INDIVIDUAL INNINGS

365*	G.St A.Sobers	WI v P	Kingston	1957-58
364	L.Hutton	E v A	The Oval	1938
337	Hanif Mohammad	P v WI	Bridgetown	1957-58
336*	W.R.Hammond	E v NZ	Auckland	1932-33
334	D.G.Bradman	A v E	Leeds	1930
333	G.A.Gooch	E v I	Lord's	1990
325	A.Sandham	E v WI	Kingston	1929-30
311	R.B.Simpson	A v E	Manchester	1964
310*	J.H.Edrich	E v NZ	Leeds	1965
307	R.M.Cowper	A v E	Melbourne	1965-66
304	D.G.Bradman	A v E	Leeds	1934
302	L.G.Rowe	WI v E	Bridgetown	1973-74
299*	D.G.Bradman	A v SA	Adelaide	1931-32
291	I.V.A.Richards	WI v E	The Oval	1976
287	R.E.Foster	E v A	Sydney	1903-04
285*	P.B.H.May	E v WI	Birmingham	1957
280*	Javed Miandad	P v I	Hyderabad	1982-83
278	D.C.S.Compton	E v P	Nottingham	1954
274	R.G.Pollock	SA v A	Durban	1969-70
274	Zaheer Abbas	P v E	Birmingham	1971
271	Javed Miandad	P v NZ	Auckland	1988-89
270*	G.A.Headley	WI v E	Kingston	1934-35
270	D.G.Bradman	A v E	Melbourne	1936-37
268	G.N.Yallop	A v P	Melbourne	1983-84
266	W.H.Ponsford	A v E	The Oval	1934
262*	D.L.Amiss	E v WI	Kingston	1973-74
261	F.M.M.Worrell	WI v E	Nottingham	1950
260	C.C.Hunte	WI v P	Kingston	1957-58
260	Javed Miandad	P v E	The Oval	1987
259	G.M.Turner	NZ v WI	Georgetown	1971-72
258	T.W.Graveney	E v WI	Nottingham	1957
258	S.M.Nurse	WI v NZ	Christchurch	1968-69
256	R.B.Kanhai	WI v I	Calcutta	1958-59
256	K.F.Barrington	E v A	Manchester	1964
255*	D.J.McGlew	SA v NZ	Wellington	1952-53
254	D.G.Bradman	A v E	Lord's	1930
251	W.R.Hammond	E v A	Sydney	1928-29
250	K.D.Walters	A v NZ	Christchurch	1976-77
250	S.F.A.F.Bacchus	WI v I	Kanpur	1978-79

The highest individual innings for other countries are:

| 236* | S.M.Gavaskar | I v WI | Madras | 1983-84 |
| 201* | D.S.B.P.Kuruppu | SL v NZ | Colombo (CCC) | 1986-87 |

MOST RUNS IN A SERIES

Runs			Series	M	I	NO	HS	Avge	100	50
974	D.G.Bradman	A v E	1930	5	7	0	334	139.14	4	–
905	W.R.Hammond	E v A	1928-29	5	9	1	251	113.12	4	–
839	M.A.Taylor	A v E	1989	6	11	1	219	83.90	2	5
834	R.N.Harvey	A v SA	1952-53	5	9	0	205	92.66	4	3
829	I.V.A.Richards	WI v E	1976	4	7	0	291	118.42	3	2
827	C.L.Walcott	WI v A	1954-55	5	10	0	155	82.70	5	2
824	G.St A.Sobers	WI v P	1957-58	5	8	2	365*	137.33	3	3
810	D.G.Bradman	A v E	1936-37	5	9	0	270	90.00	3	1
806	D.G.Bradman	A v SA	1931-32	5	5	1	299*	201.50	4	–
779	E.de C.Weekes	WI v I	1948-49	5	7	0	194	111.28	4	2
774	S.M.Gavaskar	I v WI	1970-71	4	8	3	220	154.80	4	3
761	Mudassar Nazar	P v I	1982-83	6	8	2	231	126.83	4	1
758	D.G.Bradman	A v E	1934	5	8	0	304	94.75	2	1
753	D.C.S.Compton	E v SA	1947	5	8	0	208	94.12	4	2
752	G.A.Gooch	E v I	1990	3	6	0	333	125.33	3	2

RECORD WICKET PARTNERSHIPS

1st	413	V.Mankad/Pankaj Roy	I v NZ	Madras	1955-56
2nd	451	W.H.Ponsford/D.G.Bradman	A v E	The Oval	1934
3rd	451	Mudassar Nazar/Javed Miandad	P v I	Hyderabad	1982-83
4th	411	P.B.H.May/M.C.Cowdrey	E v WI	Birmingham	1957
5th	405	S.G.Barnes/D.G.Bradman	A v E	Sydney	1946-47
6th	346	J.H.W.Fingleton/D.G.Bradman	A v E	Melbourne	1936-37
7th	347	D.St E.Atkinson/C.C.Depeiza	WI v A	Bridgetown	1954-55
8th	246	L.E.G.Ames/G.O.B.Allen	E v NZ	Lord's	1931
9th	190	Asif Iqbal/Intikhab Alam	P v E	The Oval	1967
10th	151	B.F.Hastings/R.O.Collinge	NZ v P	Auckland	1972-73

WICKET PARTNERSHIPS OF OVER 300

451	2nd	W.H.Ponsford/D.G.Bradman	A v E	The Oval	1934
451	3rd	Mudassar Nazar/Javed Miandad	P v I	Hyderabad	1982-83
446	2nd	C.C.Hunte/G.St A.Sobers	WI v P	Kingston	1957-58
413	1st	V.Mankad/Pankaj Roy	I v NZ	Madras	1955-56
411	4th	P.B.H.May/M.C.Cowdrey	E v WI	Birmingham	1957
405	5th	S.G.Barnes/D.G.Bradman	A v E	Sydney	1946-47
399	4th	G.St A.Sobers/F.M.M.Worrell	WI v E	Bridgetown	1959-60
397	3rd	Qasim Omar/Javed Miandad	P v SL	Faisalabad	1985-86
388	4th	W.H.Ponsford/D.G.Bradman	A v E	Leeds	1934
387	1st	G.M.Turner/T.W.Jarvis	NZ v WI	Georgetown	1971-72
382	2nd	L.Hutton/M.Leyland	E v A	The Oval	1938
382	1st	W.M.Lawry/R.B.Simpson	A v WI	Bridgetown	1964-65
370	3rd	W.J.Edrich/D.C.S.Compton	E v SA	Lord's	1947
369	2nd	J.H.Edrich/K.F.Barrington	E v NZ	Leeds	1965
359	1st	L.Hutton/C.Washbrook	E v SA	Jo'burg	1948-49
351	2nd	G.A.Gooch/D.I.Gower	E v A	The Oval	1985
350	4th	Mushtaq Mohammad/Asif Iqbal	P v NZ	Dunedin	1972-73
347	7th	D.St E.Atkinson/C.C.Depeiza	WI v A	Bridgetown	1954-55
346	6th	J.H.W.Fingleton/D.G.Bradman	A v E	Melbourne	1936-37
344*	2nd	S.M.Gavaskar/D.B.Vengsarkar	I v WI	Calcutta	1978-79
341	3rd	E.J.Barlow/R.G.Pollock	SA v A	Adelaide	1963-64
338	3rd	E.de C.Weekes/F.M.M.Worrell	WI v E	Pt-of-Spain	1953-54
336	4th	W.M.Lawry/K.D.Walters	A v WI	Sydney	1968-69
331	2nd	R.T.Robinson/D.I.Gower	E v A	Birmingham	1985
329	1st	G.R.Marsh/M.A.Taylor	A v E	Nottingham	1989

223

323	1st	J.B.Hobbs/W.Rhodes	E v A	Melbourne	1911-12
319	3rd	A.Melville/A.D.Nourse	SA v E	Nottingham	1947
316†	3rd	G.R.Viswanath/Yashpal Sharma	I v E	Madras	1981-82
308	7th	Waqar Hassan/Imtiaz Ahmed	P v NZ	Lahore	1955-56
308	3rd	R.D.Richardson/I.V.A.Richards	WI v A	St John's	1983-84
308	3rd	G.A.Gooch/A.J.Lamb	E v I	Lord's	1990
303	3rd	I.V.A.Richards/A.I.Kallicharran	WI v E	Nottingham	1976
301	2nd	A.R.Morris/D.G.Bradman	A v E	Leeds	1948

†415 runs were added for this wicket in two separate partnerships. D.B.Vengsarkar retired hurt and was replaced by Yashpal Sharma after 99 runs had been added.

4000 RUNS IN TESTS

Runs		I	M	I	NO	HS	Avge	100	50
10122	S.M.Gavaskar	I	125	214	16	236*	51.12	34	45
8701	A.R.Border	A	115	199	36	205	53.38	23	48
8114	G.Boycott	E	108	193	23	246*	47.72	22	42
8032	G.St A.Sobers	WI	93	160	21	365*	57.78	26	30
7990	I.V.A.Richards	WI	111	166	10	291	51.21	24	38
7891	Javed Miandad	P	104	158	18	280*	56.36	22	38
7674	D.I.Gower	E	109	189	15	215	44.10	16	37
7624	M.C.Cowdrey	E	114	188	15	182	44.06	22	38
7515	C.H.Lloyd	WI	110	175	14	242*	46.67	19	39
7249	W.R.Hammond	E	85	140	16	336*	58.45	22	24
7134	C.G.Greenidge	WI	100	170	15	223	46.02	18	34
7110	G.S.Chappell	A	87	151	19	247*	53.86	24	31
6996	D.G.Bradman	A	52	80	10	334	99.94	29	13
6971	L.Hutton	E	79	138	15	364	56.67	19	33
6806	K.F.Barrington	E	82	131	15	256	58.67	20	35
6703	D.B.Vengsarkar	I	110	175	22	166	43.81	17	33
6227	R.B.Kanhai	WI	79	137	6	256	47.53	15	28
6149	R.N.Harvey	A	79	137	10	205	48.41	21	24
6080	G.R.Viswanath	I	91	155	10	222	41.93	14	35
5910	G.A.Gooch	E	81	147	5	333	41.61	12	33
5807	D.C.S.Compton	E	78	131	15	278	50.06	17	28
5711	D.L.Haynes	WI	89	153	17	184	41.99	14	31
5410	J.B.Hobbs	E	61	102	7	211	56.94	15	28
5357	K.D.Walters	A	74	125	14	250	48.26	15	33
5345	I.M.Chappell	A	75	136	10	196	42.42	14	26
5234	W.M.Lawry	A	67	123	12	210	47.15	13	27
5138	J.H.Edrich	E	77	127	9	310*	43.54	12	24
5119	I.T.Botham	E	97	154	5	208	34.35	14	22
5062	Zaheer Abbas	P	78	124	11	274	44.79	12	20
4882	T.W.Graveney	E	79	123	13	258	44.38	11	20
4869	R.B.Simpson	A	62	111	7	311	46.81	10	27
4737	I.R.Redpath	A	66	120	11	171	43.45	8	31
4555	H.Sutcliffe	E	54	84	9	194	60.73	16	23
4537	P.B.H.May	E	66	106	9	285*	46.77	13	22
4521	Kapil Dev	I	109	158	13	163	31.17	7	23
4502	E.R.Dexter	E	62	102	8	205	47.89	9	27
4455	E.de C.Weekes	WI	48	81	5	207	58.61	15	19
4415	K.J.Hughes	A	70	124	6	213	37.41	9	22
4399	A.I.Kallicharran	WI	66	109	10	187	44.43	12	21
4389	A.P.E.Knott	E	95	149	15	135	32.75	5	30
4378	M.Amarnath	I	69	113	10	138	42.50	11	24
4377	J.G.Wright	NZ	71	126	6	185	36.47	10	18
4334	R.C.Fredericks	WI	59	109	7	169	42.49	8	26
4114	Mudassar Nazar	P	76	116	8	231	38.09	10	17

MOST HUNDREDS

34	S.M.Gavaskar	I	22	G.Boycott	E
29	D.G.Bradman	A	22	M.C.Cowdrey	E
26	G.St A.Sobers	WI	22	W.R.Hammond	E
24	G.S.Chappell	A	22	Javed Miandad	P
24	I.V.A.Richards	WI	21	R.N.Harvey	A
23	A.R.Border	A	20	K.F.Barrington	E

BOWLING RECORDS

MOST WICKETS IN AN INNINGS

10-53	J.C.Laker	E v A	Manchester	1956
9-28	G.A.Lohmann	E v SA	Johannesburg	1895-96
9-37	J.C.Laker	E v A	Manchester	1956
9-52	R.J.Hadlee	NZ v A	Brisbane	1985-86
9-56	Abdul Qadir	P v E	Lahore	1987-88
9-69	J.M.Patel	I v A	Kanpur	1959-60
9-83	Kapil Dev	I v WI	Ahmedabad	1983-84
9-86	Sarfraz Nawaz	P v A	Melbourne	1978-79
9-95	J.M.Noreiga	WI v I	Port-of-Spain	1970-71
9-102	S.P.Gupte	I v WI	Kanpur	1958-59
9-103	S.F.Barnes	E v SA	Johannesburg	1913-14
9-113	H.J.Tayfield	SA v E	Johannesburg	1956-57
9-121	A.A.Mailey	A v E	Melbourne	1920-21

MOST WICKETS IN A TEST

19-90	J.C.Laker	E v A	Manchester	1956
17-159	S.F.Barnes	E v SA	Johannesburg	1913-14
16-136	N.D.Hirwani	I v WI	Madras	1987-88
16-137	R.A.L.Massie	A v E	Lord's	1972
15-28	J.Briggs	E v SA	Cape Town	1888-89
15-45	G.A.Lohmann	E v SA	Port Elizabeth	1895-96
15-99	C.Blythe	E v SA	Leeds	1907
15-104	H.Verity	E v A	Lord's	1934
15-123	R.J.Hadlee	NZ v A	Brisbane	1985-86
15-124	W.Rhodes	E v A	Melbourne	1903-04

MOST WICKETS IN A SERIES

Wkts			Series	M	Balls	Runs	Avge	5 wI	10 wM
49	S.F.Barnes	E v SA	1913-14	4	1356	536	10.93	7	3
46	J.C.Laker	E v A	1956	5	1703	442	9.60	4	2
44	C.V.Grimmett	A v SA	1935-36	5	2077	642	14.59	5	3
42	T.M.Alderman	A v E	1981	6	1950	893	21.26	4	—
41	R.M.Hogg	A v E	1978-79	6	1740	527	12.85	5	2
41	T.M.Alderman	A v E	1989	6	1616	712	17.36	6	1
40	Imran Khan	P v I	1982-83	6	1339	558	13.95	4	2
39	A.V.Bedser	E v A	1953	5	1591	682	17.48	5	1
39	D.K.Lillee	A v E	1981	6	1870	870	22.30	2	1
38	M.W.Tate	E v A	1924-25	5	2528	881	23.18	5	1
37	W.J.Whitty	A v SA	1910-11	5	1395	632	17.08	2	—
37	H.J.Tayfield	SA v E	1956-57	5	2280	636	17.18	4	1
36	A.E.E.Vogler	SA v E	1909-10	5	1349	783	21.75	4	1
36	A.A.Mailey	A v E	1920-21	5	1465	946	26.27	4	2
35	G.A.Lohmann	E v SA	1895-96	3	520	203	5.80	4	2
35	B.S.Chandrasekhar	I v E	1972-73	5	1747	662	18.91	4	—
35	M.D.Marshall	WI v E	1988	5	1219	443	12.65	3	1

200 WICKETS IN TESTS

Wkts			M	Balls	Runs	Avge	5wI	10wM
431	Sir R.J.Hadlee	NZ	86	21918	9611	22.29	36	9
376	I.T.Botham	E	97	21281	10633	28.27	27	4
371	Kapil Dev	I	109	23037	11199	30.18	21	2
358	Imran Khan	P	82	19290	8188	22.87	23	6
355	D.K.Lillee	A	70	18467	8493	23.92	23	7
329	M.D.Marshall	WI	68	15221	6831	20.76	22	4
325	R.G.D.Willis	E	90	17357	8190	25.20	16	–
309	L.R.Gibbs	WI	79	27115	8989	29.09	18	2
307	F.S.Trueman	E	67	15178	6625	21.57	17	3
297	D.L.Underwood	E	86	21862	7674	25.83	17	6
266	B.S.Bedi	I	67	21364	7637	28.71	14	1
259	J.Garner	WI	58	13169	5433	20.97	7	–
252	J.B.Statham	E	70	16056	6261	24.84	9	1
249	M.A.Holding	WI	60	12680	5898	23.68	13	2
248	R.Benaud	A	63	19108	6704	27.03	16	1
246	G.D.McKenzie	A	60	17681	7328	29.78	16	3
242	B.S.Chandrasekhar	I	58	15963	7199	29.74	16	2
236	A.V.Bedser	E	51	15918	5876	24.89	15	5
235	G.St A.Sobers	WI	93	21599	7999	34.03	6	–
230	Abdul Qadir	P	63	16592	7458	32.42	15	5
228	R.R.Lindwall	A	61	13650	5251	23.03	12	–
216	C.V.Grimmett	A	37	14513	5231	24.21	21	7
202	A.M.E.Roberts	WI	47	11136	5174	25.61	11	2
202	J.A.Snow	E	49	12021	5387	26.66	8	1
200	J.R.Thomson	A	51	10535	5601	28.00	8	–

HAT-TRICKS

F.R.Spofforth	Australia v England	Melbourne	1878-79
W.Bates	England v Australia	Melbourne	1882-83
J.Briggs	England v Australia	Sydney	1891-92
G.A.Lohmann	England v South Africa	Port Elizabeth	1895-96
J.T.Hearne	England v Australia	Leeds	1899
H.Trumble	Australia v England	Melbourne	1901-02
H.Trumble	Australia v England	Melbourne	1903-04
T.J.Matthews (2)*	Australia v South Africa	Manchester	1912
M.J.C.Allom†	England v New Zealand	Christchurch	1929-30
T.W.J.Goddard	England v South Africa	Johannesburg	1938-39
P.J.Loader	England v West Indies	Leeds	1957
L.F.Kline	Australia v South Africa	Cape Town	1957-58
W.W.Hall	West Indies v Pakistan	Lahore	1958-59
G.M.Griffin	South Africa v England	Lord's	1960
L.R.Gibbs	West Indies v Australia	Adelaide	1960-61
P.J.Petherick	New Zealand v Pakistan	Lahore	1976-77
C.A.Walsh‡	West Indies v Australia	Brisbane	1988-89
M.G.Hughes‡	Australia v West Indies	Perth	1988-89

*Hat-trick in each innings   †Four wickets in five balls

‡Involving both innings

WICKET-KEEPING RECORDS

MOST DISMISSALS IN AN INNINGS

7	Wasim Bari	Pakistan v New Zealand	Auckland	1978-79
7	R.W.Taylor	England v India	Bombay	1979-80
6	A.T.W.Grout	Australia v South Africa	Johannesburg	1957-58
6	D.T.Lindsay	South Africa v Australia	Johannesburg	1966-67
6	J.T.Murray	England v India	Lord's	1967
6†	S.M.H.Kirmani	India v New Zealand	Christchurch	1975-76
6	R.W.Marsh	Australia v England	Brisbane	1982-83
6	S.A.R.Silva	Sri Lanka v India	Colombo (SSC)	1985-86

†Including one stumping

MOST STUMPINGS IN AN INNINGS

5	K.S.More	India v West Indies	Madras	1987-88

MOST DISMISSALS IN A TEST

10	R.W.Taylor	England v India	Bombay	1979-80
9†	G.R.A.Langley	Australia v England	Lord's	1956
9	D.A.Murray	West Indies v Australia	Melbourne	1981-82
9	R.W.Marsh	Australia v England	Brisbane	1982-83
9	S.A.R.Silva	Sri Lanka v India	Colombo (SSC)	1985-86
9†	S.A.R.Silva	Sri Lanka v India	Colombo (PSS)	1985-86

†Including one stumping

MOST DISMISSALS IN A SERIES

28	R.W.Marsh	Australia v England	1982-83
26 (inc 3st)	J.H.B.Waite	South Africa v New Zealand	1961-62
26	R.W.Marsh	Australia v West Indies (6 Tests)	1975-76
24 (inc 2st)	D.L.Murray	West Indies v England	1963
24	D.T.Lindsay	South Africa v Australia	1966-67
24 (inc 3st)	A.P.E.Knott	England v Australia (6 Tests)	1970-71

100 DISMISSALS IN TESTS

Total			Tests	Ct	St
355	R.W.Marsh	Australia	96	343	12
269	A.P.E.Knott	England	95	250	19
228	Wasim Bari	Pakistan	81	201	27
223†	P.J.L.Dujon	West Indies	68	218	5
219	T.G.Evans	England	91	173	46
198	S.M.H.Kirmani	India	88	160	38
189	D.L.Murray	West Indies	62	181	8
187	A.T.W.Grout	Australia	51	163	24
174	R.W.Taylor	England	57	167	7
151	I.D.S.Smith	New Zealand	55	143	8
141	J.H.B.Waite	South Africa	50	124	17
130	W.A.S.Oldfield	Australia	54	78	52
114†	J.M.Parks	England	46	103	11

†Including two catches taken in the field

FIELDING RECORDS
(Excluding Wicket-Keepers)

MOST CATCHES IN AN INNINGS

5	V.Y.Richardson	Australia v South Africa	Durban	1935-36
5	Yajurvindra Singh	India v England	Bangalore	1976-77
5	M.Azharuddin	India v Pakistan	Karachi	1989-90

MOST CATCHES IN A TEST

7	G.S.Chappell	Australia v England	Perth	1974-75
7	Yajurvindra Singh	India v England	Bangalore	1976-77

MOST CATCHES IN A SERIES

15	J.M.Gregory	Australia v England	1920-21

100 CATCHES IN TESTS

Total			Tests
125	A.R.Border	Australia	115
122	G.S.Chappell	Australia	87
120	M.C.Cowdrey	England	114
116	I.V.A.Richards	West Indies	111
112	I.T.Botham	England	97
110	R.B.Simpson	Australia	62
110	W.R.Hammond	England	85
109	G.St A.Sobers	West Indies	93
108	S.M.Gavaskar	India	125
105	I.M.Chappell	Australia	75

MOST TEST APPEARANCES

England	M.C.Cowdrey	114
Australia	A.R.Border	115
South Africa	J.H.B.Waite	50
West Indies	I.V.A.Richards	111
New Zealand	R.J.Hadlee	86
India	S.M.Gavaskar	125
Pakistan	Javed Miandad	104
Sri Lanka	A.Ranatunga	26

MOST CONSECUTIVE TEST APPEARANCES

112	A.R.Border	Australia	March 1979 to March 1990
106	S.M.Gavaskar	India	January 1975 to February 1987

MOST MATCHES BETWEEN APPEARANCES

104	Younis Ahmed	November 1969 to February 1987
103	D.Shackleton	November 1951 to June 1963

SUMMARY OF ALL TEST MATCHES

To end of 1990 season in England

		Tests	E	A	SA	WI	NZ	I	P	SL	Tied	Drawn
						Won by						
England	v Australia	269	88	101	–	–	–	–	–	–	–	80
	v South Africa	102	46	–	18	–	–	–	–	–	–	38
	v West Indies	99	22	–	–	41	–	–	–	–	–	36
	v New Zealand	69	31	–	–	–	4	–	–	–	–	34
	v India	78	31	–	–	–	–	11	–	–	–	36
	v Pakistan	47	13	–	–	–	–	–	5	–	–	29
	v Sri Lanka	3	2	–	–	–	–	–	–	0	–	1
Australia	v South Africa	53	–	29	11	–	–	–	–	–	–	13
	v West Indies	67	–	28	–	22	–	–	–	–	1	16
	v New Zealand	26	–	10	–	–	6	–	–	–	–	10
	v India	45	–	20	–	–	–	8	–	–	1	16
	v Pakistan	34	–	12	–	–	–	–	9	–	–	13
	v Sri Lanka	4	–	3	–	–	–	–	–	0	–	1
South Africa	v New Zealand	17	–	–	9	–	2	–	–	–	–	6
West Indies	v New Zealand	24	–	–	–	8	4	–	–	–	–	12
	v India	62	–	–	–	26	–	6	–	–	–	30
	v Pakistan	25	–	–	–	9	–	–	6	–	–	10
New Zealand	v India	31	–	–	–	–	6	12	–	–	–	13
	v Pakistan	29	–	–	–	–	3	–	10	–	–	16
	v Sri Lanka	6	–	–	–	–	4	–	–	0	–	2
India	v Pakistan	44	–	–	–	–	–	4	7	–	–	33
	v Sri Lanka	7	–	–	–	–	–	2	–	1	–	4
Pakistan	v Sri Lanka	9	–	–	–	–	–	–	5	1	–	3
		1150	233	203	38	106	29	43	42	2	2	452

	Tests	Won	Lost	Drawn	Tied	Toss Won
England	667	233	180	254	–	330
Australia	498	203	144	149	2	250
South Africa	172	38	77	57	–	80
West Indies	277	106	66	104	1	145
New Zealand	202	29	80	93	–	100
India	267	43	91	132	1	132
Pakistan	188	42	42	104	–	98
Sri Lanka	29	2	16	11	–	15

SUMMARY OF ALL LIMITED-OVERS INTERNATIONALS

To 1 November 1990

		Matches	E	A	I	NZ	P	SL	WI	B	C	EA	Z	Tied	NR
England	v Australia	47	24	21	–	–	–	–	–	–	–	–	–	1	1
	v India	22	12	–	10	–	–	–	–	–	–	–	–	–	–
	v New Zealand	29	14	–	–	12	–	–	–	–	–	–	–	–	3
	v Pakistan	29	19	–	–	–	10	–	–	–	–	–	–	–	–
	v Sri Lanka	8	7	–	–	–	–	1	–	–	–	–	–	–	–
	v West Indies	39	14	–	–	–	–	–	23	–	–	–	–	–	2
	v Canada	1	1	–	–	–	–	–	–	–	0	–	–	–	–
	v East Africa	1	1	–	–	–	–	–	–	–	–	0	–	–	–
Australia	v India	33	–	18	12	–	–	–	–	–	–	–	–	–	3
	v New Zealand	43	–	29	–	12	–	–	–	–	–	–	–	–	2
	v Pakistan	33	–	15	–	–	16	–	–	–	–	–	–	–	2
	v Sri Lanka	20	–	15	–	–	–	3	–	–	–	–	–	–	2
	v West Indies	53	–	17	–	–	–	–	35	–	–	–	–	1	–
	v Bangladesh	1	–	1	–	–	–	–	–	0	–	–	–	–	–
	v Canada	1	–	1	–	–	–	–	–	–	0	–	–	–	–
	v Zimbabwe	4	–	3	–	–	–	–	–	–	–	–	1	–	–
India	v New Zealand	28	–	–	16	12	–	–	–	–	–	–	–	–	–
	v Pakistan	34	–	–	10	–	22	–	–	–	–	–	–	–	2
	v Sri Lanka	20	–	–	14	–	–	5	–	–	–	–	–	–	1
	v West Indies	33	–	–	6	–	–	–	27	–	–	–	–	–	–
	v Bangladesh	1	–	–	1	–	–	–	–	0	–	–	–	–	–
	v East Africa	1	–	–	1	–	–	–	–	–	–	0	–	–	–
	v Zimbabwe	4	–	–	4	–	–	–	–	–	–	–	0	–	–
N Zealand	v Pakistan	20	–	–	–	11	8	–	–	–	–	–	–	–	1
	v Sri Lanka	19	–	–	–	15	–	4	–	–	–	–	–	–	–
	v West Indies	13	–	–	–	1	–	–	11	–	–	–	–	–	1
	v Bangladesh	1	–	–	–	1	–	–	–	0	–	–	–	–	–
	v East Africa	1	–	–	–	1	–	–	–	–	–	0	–	–	–
	v Zimbabwe	2	–	–	–	2	–	–	–	–	–	–	0	–	–
Pakistan	v Sri Lanka	28	–	–	–	–	22	5	–	–	–	–	–	–	1
	v West Indies	48	–	–	–	–	13	–	35	–	–	–	–	–	–
	v Bangladesh	2	–	–	–	–	2	–	–	0	–	–	–	–	–
	v Canada	1	–	–	–	–	1	–	–	–	0	–	–	–	–
Sri Lanka	v West Indies	11	–	–	–	–	–	1	10	–	–	–	–	–	–
	v Bangladesh	2	–	–	–	–	–	2	–	0	–	–	–	–	–
W Indies	v Zimbabwe	2	–	–	–	–	–	–	2	–	–	–	0	–	–
		635	92	120	74	67	94	21	143	0	0	0	1	2	21

	Matches	Won	Lost	Tied	NR
England	176	92	77	1	6
Australia	235	120	103	2	10
India	176	74	96	–	6
New Zealand	156	67	82	–	7
Pakistan	195	94	95	–	6
Sri Lanka	108	21	83	–	4
West Indies	199	143	52	1	3
Bangladesh	7	–	7	–	–
Canada	3	–	3	–	–
East Africa	3	–	3	–	–
Zimbabwe	12	1	11	–	–

LIMITED-OVERS INTERNATIONALS RECORDS

Compiled by Philip Bailey to 1 November 1990

TEAM RECORDS

Highest Innings Totals

360-4 (50 overs)	West Indies v Sri Lanka	Karachi	1987-88
338-4 (50 overs)	New Zealand v Bangladesh	Sharjah	1989-90
338-5 (50 overs)	Pakistan v Sri Lanka	Swansea	1983
334-4 (60 overs)	England v India	Lord's	1975
333-8 (45 overs)	West Indies v India	Jamshedpur	1983-84
333-9 (60 overs)	England v Sri Lanka	Taunton	1983
332-3 (50 overs)	Australia v Sri Lanka	Sharjah	1989-90
330-6 (60 overs)	Pakistan v Sri Lanka	Nottingham	1975

Highest Total Batting Second

298-6 (54.5 overs)	New Zealand v England	Leeds	1990

Highest Match Aggregate

626-14 (120 overs)	Pakistan v Sri Lanka	Swansea	1983

Lowest Totals
(Excluding abbreviated matches)

45 (40.3 overs)	Canada v England	Manchester	1979
55 (28.3 overs)	Sri Lanka v West Indies	Sharjah	1986-87
63 (25.5 overs)	India v Australia	Sydney	1980-81
64 (35.5 overs)	New Zealand v Pakistan	Sharjah	1985-86
70 (25.2 overs)	Australia v England	Birmingham	1977
70 (26.3 overs)	Australia v New Zealand	Adelaide	1985-86

Lowest Match Aggregate

91-12 (54.2 overs)	England v Canada	Manchester	1979

Largest Margins of Victory

232 runs	Australia beat Sri Lanka	Adelaide	1984-85
206 runs	New Zealand beat Australia	Adelaide	1985-86
202 runs	England beat India	Lord's	1975
10 wickets	India beat East Africa	Leeds	1975
10 wickets	New Zealand beat India	Melbourne	1980-81
10 wickets	West Indies beat Zimbabwe	Birmingham	1983
10 wickets	India beat Sri Lanka	Sharjah	1983-84
10 wickets	West Indies beat New Zealand	Port-of-Spain	1984-85
10 wickets	Pakistan beat New Zealand	Sharjah	1985-86
10 wickets	West Indies beat New Zealand	Christchurch	1986-87

Tied Matches

Australia	222-9	West Indies	222-5	Melbourne	1983-84
India	212-6	Pakistan	212-7	Hyderabad	1986-87
	(Match awarded to India for losing fewer wickets)				
Pakistan	229-7	Australia	229-8	Lahore	1988-89
	(Match awarded to Pakistan for losing fewer wickets)				
England	226-5	Australia	226-8	Nottingham	1989

BATTING RECORDS

Highest Individual Innings

189*	I.V.A.Richards	West Indies v England	Manchester	1984
181	I.V.A.Richards	West Indies v Sri Lanka	Karachi	1987-88
175*	Kapil Dev	India v Zimbabwe	Tunbridge Wells	1983
171*	G.M.Turner	New Zealand v East Africa	Birmingham	1975
158	D.I.Gower	England v New Zealand	Brisbane	1982-83
153*	I.V.A.Richards	West Indies v Australia	Melbourne	1979-80
152*	D.L.Haynes	West Indies v India	Georgetown	1988-89

Hundred on debut

103	D.L.Amiss	England v Australia	Manchester	1972
148	D.L.Haynes	West Indies v Australia	St John's	1977-78

Highest Partnership For Each Wicket

1st	212	G.R.Marsh/D.C.Boon	A v I	Jaipur	1986-87
2nd	221	C.G.Greenidge/I.V.A.Richards	WI v I	Jamshedpur	1983-84
3rd	224*	D.M.Jones/A.R.Border	A v SL	Adelaide	1984-85
4th	173	D.M.Jones/S.R.Waugh	A v P	Perth	1986-87
5th	152	I.V.A.Richards/C.H.Lloyd	WI v SL	Brisbane	1984-85
6th	144	Imran Khan/Shahid Mahboob	P v SL	Leeds	1983
7th	115	P.J.L.Dujon/M.D.Marshall	WI v P	Gujranwala	1986-87
8th	117	D.L.Houghton/I.P.Butchart	Z v NZ	Hyderabad (Ind)	1987-88
9th	126*	Kapil Dev/S.M.H.Kirmani	I v Z	Tunbridge Wells	1983
10th	106*	I.V.A.Richards/M.A.Holding	WI v E	Manchester	1984

Most Runs in a Career

		I	NO	HS	Runs	Avge	100	50
I.V.A.Richards	WI	160	24	189*	6501	47.80	11	44
D.L.Haynes	WI	173	23	152*	6471	43.14	16	36
Javed Miandad	P	162	32	119*	5610	43.15	6	38
A.R.Border	A	195	29	127*	5263	31.70	3	33
C.G.Greenidge	WI	119	12	133*	4981	46.55	11	31
D.M.Jones	A	98	19	121	3857	48.82	6	28
R.B.Richardson	WI	123	17	110	3795	35.80	3	30
K.Srikkanth	I	125	3	123	3541	29.02	4	22
D.B.Vengsarkar	I	120	19	105	3508	34.73	1	23

BOWLING RECORDS

Most Wickets in an Innings

7-51	W.W.Davis	West Indies v Australia	Leeds	1983
6-14	G.J.Gilmour	Australia v England	Leeds	1975
6-14	Imran Khan	Pakistan v India	Sharjah	1984-85
6-15	C.E.H.Croft	West Indies v England	Kingston	1980-81
6-26	Waqar Younis	Pakistan v Sri Lanka	Sharjah	1989-90
6-29	B.P.Patterson	West Indies v India	Nagpur	1987-88
6-39	K.H.MacLeay	Australia v India	Nottingham	1983
6-41	I.V.A.Richards	West Indies v India	Delhi	1989-90

Hat-Tricks

Jalaluddin	Pakistan v Australia	Hyderabad	1982-83
B.A.Reid	Australia v New Zealand	Sydney	1985-86
C.Sharma	India v New Zealand	Nagpur	1987-88
Wasim Akram	Pakistan v West Indies	Sharjah	1989-90
Wasim Akram	Pakistan v Australia	Sharjah	1989-90

Most Wickets in a Career

		Balls	Runs	Wkts	Avge	Best	4w
Kapil Dev	I	7941	4977	185	26.90	5-43	2
Imran Khan	P	6337	4063	165	24.62	6-14	4
R.J.Hadlee	NZ	6182	3407	158	21.56	5-25	6
J. Garner	WI	5330	2752	146	18.84	5-31	5
M.A.Holding	WI	5473	3034	142	21.36	5-26	6
E.J.Chatfield	NZ	6065	3621	140	25.86	5-34	4
M.D.Marshall	WI	5993	3412	137	24.90	4-23	5
Abdul Qadir	P	4948	3340	131	25.49	5-44	6
Wasim Akram	P	4833	3072	130	23.63	5-21	5
I.T.Botham	E	5269	3511	118	29.75	4-56	1
I.V.A.Richards	WI	5542	4144	118	35.11	6-41	3
M.C.Snedden	NZ	4519	3235	114	28.37	4-34	1
R.J.Shastri	I	5756	4025	114	35.30	4-38	2
Mudassar Nazar	P	4855	3431	111	30.90	5-28	2
D.K.Lillee	A	3593	2145	103	20.82	5-34	6
C.A.Walsh	WI	4659	2977	101	29.47	5-1	5

WICKET-KEEPING RECORDS

Most Dismissals in an Innings

5 (5 ct)	R.W.Marsh	Australia v England	Leeds	1981
5 (5 ct)	R.G.de Alwis	Sri Lanka v Australia	Colombo (PSS)	1982-83
5 (5 ct)	S.M.H.Kirmani	India v Zimbabwe	Leicester	1983
5 (3 ct, 2 st)	S.Viswanath	India v England	Sydney	1984-85
5 (3 ct, 2 st)	K.S.More	India v New Zealand	Sharjah	1987-88

Most Dismissals in a Career

P.J.L.Dujon	West Indies	188 (170 ct, 18 st) in 155 matches

FIELDING RECORDS

Most Catches in an Innings

4	Salim Malik	Pakistan v New Zealand	Sialkot	1984-85
4	S.M.Gavaskar	India v Pakistan	Sharjah	1984-85

Most Catches in a Career

I.V.A.Richards	West Indies	99 in 179 matches
A.R.Border	Australia	96 in 210 matches

ALL-ROUND RECORDS

1000 Runs and 100 Dismissals

I.T.Botham	England	1730 runs	118 wickets
P.J.L.Dujon	West Indies	1785 runs	188 dismissals (170 ct, 18 st)
R.J.Hadlee	New Zealand	1749 runs	158 wickets
Imran Khan	Pakistan	3051 runs	165 wickets
Kapil Dev	India	3087 runs	185 wickets
R.W.Marsh	Australia	1225 runs	124 dismissals (120 ct, 4 st)
Mudassar Nazar	Pakistan	2624 runs	111 wickets
I.V.A.Richards	West Indies	6501 runs	118 wickets
R.J.Shastri	India	2391 runs	114 wickets

ENGLAND v WEST INDIES
1928 to 1990

Captains

Season	England	West Indies	P	E	WI	D
1928	A.P.F.Chapman	R.K.Nunes	3	3	–	–
1929-30	Hon. F.S.G.Calthorpe	E.L.G.Hoad[1]	4	1	1	2
1933	D.R.Jardine[2]	G.C.Grant	3	2	–	1
1934-35	R.E.S.Wyatt	G.C.Grant	4	1	2	1
1939	W.R.Hammond	R.S.Grant	3	1	–	2
1947-48	G.O.B.Allen[3]	J.D.C.Goddard[4]	4	–	2	2
1950	N.W.D.Yardley[5]	J.D.C.Goddard	4	1	3	–
1953-54	L.Hutton	J.B.Stollmeyer	5	2	2	1
1957	P.B.H.May	J.D.C.Goddard	5	3	–	2
1959-60	P.B.H.May[6]	F.C.M.Alexander	5	1	–	4
1963	E.R.Dexter	F.M.M.Worrell	5	1	3	1
1966	M.C.Cowdrey[7]	G.S.Sobers	5	1	3	1
1967-68	M.C.Cowdrey	G.S.Sobers	5	1	–	4
1969	R.Illingworth	G.S.Sobers	3	2	–	1
1973	R.Illingworth	R.B.Kanhai	3	–	2	1
1973-74	M.H.Denness	R.B.Kanhai	5	1	1	3
1976	A.W.Greig	C.H.Lloyd	5	–	3	2
1980	I.T.Botham	C.H.Lloyd[8]	5	–	1	4
1980-81	I.T.Botham	C.H.Lloyd	4	–	2	2
1984	D.I.Gower	C.H.Lloyd	5	–	5	–
1985-86	D.I.Gower	I.V.A.Richards	5	–	5	–
1988	J.E.Emburey[9]	I.V.A.Richards	5	–	4	1
1989-90	G.A.Gooch[10]	I.V.A.Richards[11]	4	1	2	1

	P	E	WI	D
Lord's	13	4	4	5
Manchester	11	3	5	3
The Oval	12	4	6	2
Nottingham	6	–	3	3
Birmingham	4	1	1	2
Leeds	8	2	5	1
Bridgetown	10	1	4	5
Port-of-Spain	14	4	5	5
Georgetown	7	1	2	4
Kingston	11	2	4	5
St John's	3	–	2	1
In England	54	14	24	16
In West Indies	45	8	17	20
Totals	99	22	41	36

The following deputised for the official captain:
[1]N.Betancourt (2nd), M.P.Fernandes (3rd), R.K.Nunes (4th). [2]R.E.S.Wyatt (3rd). [3]K.Cranston (1st). [4]G.A.Headley (1st), G.E.Gomez (2nd). [5]F.R.Brown (4th). [6]M.C.Cowdrey (4th and 5th). [7]M.J.K.Smith (1st), D.B.Close (5th). [8]I.V.A. Richards (5th). [9]M.W.Gatting (1st), C.S.Cowdrey (4th), G.A.Gooch (5th). [10] A.J.Lamb (4th and 5th). [11]D.L.Haynes (3rd).

HIGHEST INNINGS TOTALS

England	in England	619-6d	Nottingham	1957
	in West Indies	849	Kingston	1929-30
West Indies	in England	687-8d	The Oval	1976
	in West Indies	681-8d	Port-of-Spain	1953-54

LOWEST INNINGS TOTALS

England	in England	71	Manchester	1976
	in West Indies	103	Kingston	1934-35
West Indies	in England	86	The Oval	1957
	in West Indies	102	Bridgetown	1934-35

HIGHEST MATCH AGGREGATE

| 1815 for 34 wickets | | Kingston | 1929-30 |

LOWEST MATCH AGGREGATE

| 309 for 29 wickets | | Bridgetown | 1934-35 |

HIGHEST INDIVIDUAL INNINGS

England	in England	285*	P.B.H.May	Birmingham	1957
		258	T.W.Graveney	Nottingham	1957
		203	D.L.Amiss	The Oval	1976
		202*	L.Hutton	The Oval	1950
	in West Indies	325	A.Sandham	Kingston	1929-30
		262*	D.L.Amiss	Kingston	1973-74
		205*	E.H.Hendren	Port-of-Spain	1929-30
		205	L.Hutton	Kingston	1953-54
West Indies	in England	291	I.V.A.Richards	The Oval	1976
		261	F.M.M.Worrell	Nottingham	1950
		232	I.V.A.Richards	Nottingham	1976
		223	C.G.Greenidge	Manchester	1984
		214*	C.G.Greenidge	Lord's	1984
		209*	B.F.Butcher	Nottingham	1966
	in West Indies	302	L.G.Rowe	Bridgetown	1973-74
		270*	G.A.Headley	Kingston	1934-35
		226	G.St A.Sobers	Bridgetown	1959-60
		223	G.A.Headley	Kingston	1929-30
		220	C.L.Walcott	Bridgetown	1953-54
		209	C.A.Roach	Georgetown	1929-30
		206	E.de C.Weekes	Port-of-Spain	1953-54

181 hundreds have been scored in this series: England 85, West Indies 96.

HUNDRED IN EACH INNINGS

West Indies	134	101	C.G.Greenidge	Manchester	1976
	114	112	G.A.Headley	Georgetown	1929-30
	106	107	G.A.Headley	Lord's	1939

CARRIED BAT THROUGH INNINGS

| England | 202* | (344) | L.Hutton | The Oval | 1950 |
| West Indies | 191* | (372) | F.M.M.Worrell | Nottingham | 1957 |

HIGHEST AGGREGATE OF RUNS IN A SERIES

England	in England	489 (av 97.80)	P.B.H.May	1957
	in West Indies	693 (av 115.50)	E.H.Hendren	1929-30
West Indies	in England	829 (av 118.42)	I.V.A.Richards	1976
	in West Indies	709 (av 101.28)	G.St A.Sobers	1959-60

RECORD WICKET PARTNERSHIPS – ENGLAND

1st	212	C.Washbrook (102), R.T.Simpson (94)	Nottingham	1950
2nd	266	P.E.Richardson (126), T.W.Graveney (258)	Nottingham	1957
3rd	264	L.Hutton (165*), W.R.Hammond (138)	The Oval	1939
4th	411	P.B.H.May (285*), M.C.Cowdrey (154)	Birmingham	1957
5th	130*	C.Milburn (126*), T.W.Graveney (30*)	Lord's	1966
6th	163	A.W.Greig (148), A.P.E.Knott (87)	Bridgetown	1973-74
7th	197	M.J.K.Smith (96), J.M.Parks (101*)	Port-of-Spain	1959-60
8th	217	T.W.Graveney (165), J.T.Murray (112)	The Oval	1966
9th	109	G.A.R.Lock (89), P.I.Pocock (13)	Georgetown	1967-68
10th	128	K.Higgs (63), J.A.Snow (59*)	The Oval	1966

RECORD WICKET PARTNERSHIPS – WEST INDIES

1st	298	C.G.Greenidge (149), D.L.Haynes (167)	St John's	1989-90
2nd	287*	C.G.Greenidge (214*), H.A.Gomes (92*)	Lord's	1984
3rd	338	E.de C.Weekes (206), F.M.M.Worrell (167)	Port-of-Spain	1953-54
4th	399	G.St A.Sobers (226), F.M.M.Worrell (197*)	Bridgetown	1959-60
5th	265	S.M.Nurse (137), G.St A.Sobers (174)	Leeds	1966
6th	274*	G.St A.Sobers (163*), D.A.J.Holford (105*)	Lord's	1966
7th	155*†	G.St A.Sobers (150*), B.D.Julien (121)	Lord's	1973
8th	99	C.A.McWatt (54), J.K.Holt (48*)	Georgetown	1953-54
9th	150	E.A.E.Baptiste (87*), M.A.Holding (69)	Birmingham	1984
10th	67*	M.A.Holding (58*), C.E.H.Croft (17*)	St John's	1980-81

†231 runs were added for this wicket; G.St A.Sobers retired ill and was succeeded by K.D.Boyce after 155 had been scored.

HAT-TRICK

England		P.J.Loader	Leeds	1957

BEST INNINGS BOWLING ANALYSIS

England	in England	8-103	I.T.Botham	Lord's	1984
	in West Indies	8-86	A.W.Greig	Port-of-Spain	1973-74
West Indies	in England	8-92	M.A.Holding	The Oval	1976
	in West Indies	8-45	C.E.L.Ambrose	Bridgetown	1989-90

BEST MATCH BOWLING ANALYSIS

England	in England	12-119	F.S.Trueman	Birmingham	1963
	in West Indies	13-156	A.W.Greig	Port-of-Spain	1973-74
West Indies	in England	14-149	M.A.Holding	The Oval	1976
	in West Indies	11-229	W.Ferguson	Port-of-Spain	1947-48

HIGHEST AGGREGATE OF WICKETS IN A SERIES

England	in England	34 (av 17.47)	F.S.Trueman	1963
	in West Indies	27 (av 18.66)	J.A.Snow	1967-68
West Indies	in England	35 (av 12.65)	M.D.Marshall	1988
	in West Indies {	27 (av 16.14)	J.Garner	1985-86
		27 (av 17.65)	M.D.Marshall	1985-86

ENGLAND v SRI LANKA

1982 to 1988

		Captains		P	E	SL	D
Season	England		Sri Lanka				
1981-82	K.W.R.Fletcher		B.Warnapura	1	1	–	–
1984	D.I.Gower		L.R.D.Mendis	1	–	–	1
1988	G.A.Gooch		R.S.Madugalle	1	1	–	–
		At Lord's		2	1	–	1
		At PSS, Colombo		1	1	–	–
		Totals		3	2	–	1

HIGHEST INNINGS TOTALS

England	in England	429	Lord's	1988
	in Sri Lanka	223	Colombo (PSS)	1981-82
Sri Lanka	in England	491-7d	Lord's	1984
	in Sri Lanka	218	Colombo (PSS)	1981-82

LOWEST INNINGS TOTALS

England	in England	370	Lord's	1984
	in Sri Lanka	223	Colombo (PSS)	1981-82
Sri Lanka	in England	194	Lord's	1988
	in Sri Lanka	175	Colombo (PSS)	1981-82

HIGHEST INDIVIDUAL INNINGS

England	in England	107	A.J.Lamb	Lord's	1984
	in Sri Lanka	89	D.I.Gower	Colombo (PSS)	1981-82
Sri Lanka	in England	190	S.Wettimuny	Lord's	1984
	in Sri Lanka	77	R.L.Dias	Colombo (PSS)	1981-82

RECORD WICKET PARTNERSHIPS – ENGLAND

1st	73	G.A.Gooch (36), R.T.Robinson (34*)	Lord's	1988
2nd	131	G.A.Gooch (75), R.C.Russell (94)	Lord's	1988
3rd	85	B.C.Broad (86), D.I.Gower (55)	Lord's	1984
4th	87	K.J.Barnett (66), A.J.Lamb (63)	Lord's	1988
5th	38	A.J.Lamb (63), R.A.Smith (31)	Lord's	1988
6th	87	A.J.Lamb (107), R.M.Ellison (41)	Lord's	1984
7th	49	A.J.Lamb (107), P.R.Downton (10)	Lord's	1984
8th	9	R.W.Taylor (31*), P.J.W.Allott (3)	Colombo (PSS)	1981-82
9th	37	P.J.Newport (26), N.A.Foster (14*)	Lord's	1988
10th	9	N.A.Foster (14*), D.V.Lawrence (4)	Lord's	1988

RECORD WICKET PARTNERSHIPS – SRI LANKA

1st	43	D.S.B.P.Kuruppu (25), S.A.R.Silva (16)	Lord's	1988
2nd	83	B.Warnapura (38), R.L.Dias (77)	Colombo (PSS)	1981-82
3rd	101	S.Wettimuny (190), R.L.Dias (32)	Lord's	1984
4th	148	S.Wettimuny (190), A.Ranatunga (84)	Lord's	1984
5th	150	S.Wettimuny (190), L.R.D.Mendis (111)	Lord's	1984
6th	138	S.A.R.Silva (102*), L.R.D.Mendis (94)	Lord's	1984
7th	59	L.R.D.Mendis (21), J.R.Ratnayeke (59*)	Lord's	1988
8th	27*	A.L.F.De Mel (20*), J.R.Ratnayeke (5*)	Lord's	1984
9th	12	J.R.Ratnayeke (32), G.F.Labrooy (9*)	Lord's	1988
10th	64	J.R.Ratnayeke (59*), G.F.Labrooy (42)	Lord's	1988

BEST INNINGS BOWLING ANALYSIS

England	in England	6-90	I.T.Botham	Lord's	1984
	in Sri Lanka	6-33	J.E.Emburey	Colombo (PSS)	1981-82
Sri Lanka	in England	4-98	V.B.John	Lord's	1984
	in Sri Lanka	4-70	A.L.F.De Mel	Colombo (PSS)	1981-82

BEST MATCH BOWLING ANALYSIS

England	in England	7-164	P.J.Newport	Lord's	1988
	in Sri Lanka	8-95	D.L.Underwood	Colombo (PSS)	1981-82
Sri Lanka	in England	4-98	V.B.John	Lord's	1984
	in Sri Lanka	5-103	A.L.F.De Mel	Colombo (PSS)	1981-82

TOURS PROGRAMME

1991
West Indies to England
Sri Lanka to England

1991-92
India to Australia*
West Indies to Australia
Sri Lanka to Pakistan
England to New Zealand
ICC World Cup in A and NZ
Sri Lanka to India

1992
Pakistan to England
Australia to Sri Lanka*

1992-93
West Indies to Australia
England to India
Pakistan to Australia*
England to Sri Lanka*
Australia to New Zealand
India to West Indies
Pakistan to West Indies

1993
Australia to England
New Zealand to Sri Lanka*

1993-94
England to West Indies*
New Zealand to Australia
India to Pakistan
Sri Lanka to Australia
India to Sri Lanka
Pakistan to New Zealand
Australia to Pakistan*

1994
India to England*
New Zealand to England

1994-95
England to Australia
West Indies to India*
West Indies to New Zealand
Pakistan to India
Australia to West Indies*

1995-96
Sri Lanka to India
Pakistan to Australia*
West Indies to Australia*
England to New Zealand
New Zealand to West Indies

*unconfirmed

FIRST-CLASS UMPIRES 1991

BALDERSTONE, John Christopher (Paddock Council S, Huddersfield), b Longwood, Huddersfield, Yorks 16 Nov 1940. RHB, SLA. Yorkshire 1961-69. Leicestershire 1971-86 (cap 1973; testimonial 1984). Tests: 2 (1976); HS 35 v WI (Leeds) 1976; BB 1-80. Tour: Z 1980-81 (Leics). 1000 runs (11); most – 1482 (1982). Hat-trick 1976. HS 181* Leics v Glos (Leicester) 1984. BB 6-25 Leics v Hants (Southampton) 1978. F-c career: 390 matches; 19,034 runs @ 34.11, 32 hundreds; 310 wickets @ 26.32; 210 ct. Soccer for Huddersfield Town, Carlisle United, Doncaster Rovers and Queen of the South. Appointed 1988.

BIRD, Harold Dennis ('Dickie') (Raley SM, Barnsley), b Barnsley, Yorks 19 Apr 1933. RHB, RM. Yorkshire 1956-59. Leicestershire 1960-64 (cap 1960). MBE 1986. 1000 runs (1): 1028 (1960). HS 181 Yorks v Glam (Bradford) 1959. F-c career: 93 matches; 3314 runs @ 20.71, 2 hundreds. Appointed 1970. Umpired 44 Tests (1973 to 1990). Officiated in 1987 Reliance World Cup in India and Pakistan. Completed 100 'internationals' (Tests and LOI) 1988.

BOND, John David ('Jack') (Bolton S), b Kearsley, Lancs 6 May 1932. RHB, LB. Lancashire 1955-72 (cap 1955; captain 1968-72; coach 1973; manager 1980-86; benefit 1970). Nottinghamshire 1974 (captain/coach 1974). 1000 (2); most – 2125 (1963). HS 157 Lancs v Hants (Manchester) 1962. Test selector 1974. F-c career: 362 matches; 12,125 runs @ 25.90, 14 hundreds; 222 ct. Appointed 1988.

BURGESS, Graham Iefvion (Millfield S), b Glastonbury, Somerset 5 May 1943. RHB, RM. Somerset 1966-79 (cap 1968; testimonial 1977). HS 129 v Glos (Taunton) 1973. BB 7-43 (13-75 match) v OU (Oxford) 1975. F-c career: 252 matches; 7,129 runs @ 18.90, 2 hundreds; 474 wickets @ 28.57. Appointed 1991.

CONSTANT, David John, b Bradford-on-Avon, Wilts 9 Nov 1941. LHB, SLA. Kent 1961-63. Leicestershire 1965-68. HS 80 Leics v Glos (Bristol) 1966. F-c career: 61 matches; 1517 runs @ 19.20; 1 wicket @ 36.00. Appointed 1969. Umpired 36 Tests (1971 to 1988). Represented Gloucestershire at bowls 1984-86.

*DUDLESTON, Barry (Stockport S), b Bebington, Cheshire 16 Jul 1945. RHB, SLA. Leicestershire 1966-80 (cap 1969; benefit 1980). Gloucestershire 1981-83. Rhodesia 1976-80. 1000 (8); most – 1374 (1970). HS 202 Leics v Derbys (Leicester) 1979. BB 4-6 Leics v Surrey (Leicester) 1972. F-c career: 295 matches; 14,747 runs @ 32.48, 32 hundreds; 47 wickets @ 29.04. Appointed 1984.

HAMPSHIRE, John Harry (Oakwood THS, Rotherham), b Thurnscoe, Yorks 10 Feb 1941. RHB, LB. Son of J. (Yorks 1937); brother of A.W. (Yorks 1975). Yorkshire 1961-81 (cap 1963; benefit 1976; captain 1979-80). Derbyshire 1982-84 (cap 1982). Tasmania 1967-69, 1977-79. Tests: 8 (1969 to 1975); 403 runs @ 26.86, HS 107 v WI (Lord's) 1969 on debut (only England player to score hundred at Lord's on debut in Tests). Tours: Aus 1970-71; SA 1972-73 (DHR), 1974-75 (DHR); WI 1964-65 (Cavs); NZ 1970-71; Pak 1967-68 (Cwlth XI); SL 1969-70; Z 1980-81 (Leics XI). 1000 runs (15); most – 1596 (1978). HS 183 Yorks v Sussex (Hove) 1971. BB 7-52 Yorks v Glam (Cardiff) 1963. F-c career: 577 matches; 28,059 runs @ 34.55, 43 hundreds; 30 wickets @ 54.56; 445 ct. Appointed 1985. Umpired 7 Tests (1989 to 1990), including 4 in Pakistan 1989-90.

HARRIS, John Henry, b Taunton, Somerset 13 Feb 1936. LHB, RFM. Somerset 1952-59. Suffolk 1960-62. Devon 1975. HS 41 v Worcs (Taunton) 1957. BB 3-29 v Worcs (Bristol) 1959. F-c career: 15 matches; 154 runs @ 11.00; 19 wickets @ 32.57. Appointed 1983.

HASSAN, Basharat (City HS, Nairobi), b Nairobi, Kenya 24 March 1944. RHB, RM, WK. Debut 1963-64 (East African XI). Nottinghamshire 1966-85 (cap 1970; benefit 1978). 1000 runs (5); most – 1395 (1970). HS 182* v Glos (Nottingham) 1977. BB 3-33 v Lancs (Manchester) 1976. F-c career: 332 matches; 14,394 runs @ 29.07, 15 hundreds; 6 wickets @ 67.83; 309 dismissals (308 ct, 1 st). Appointed 1989.

*HOLDER, John Wakefield (Combermere S, Barbados), b St George, Barbados 19 Mar 1945. RHB, RFM. Hampshire 1968-72. Hat-trick 1972. HS 33 v Sussex (Hove) 1971. BB 7-79 v Glos (Gloucester) 1972. F-c career: 47 matches; 374 runs @ 10.68; 139 wickets @ 24.56. Appointed 1983. Umpired 9 Tests (1988 to 1990), including 4 in Pakistan 1989-90.

JONES, Allan Arthur (St John's C, Horsham), b Horley, Surrey 9 Dec 1947. RHB RFM. Sussex 1966-69. Somerset 1970-75 (cap 1972). Northern Transvaal 1972-73. Middlesex 1976-79 (cap 1976). Orange Free State 1976-77. Glamorgan 1980-81. HS 33 Middx v Kent (Canterbury) 1978. BB 9-51 Somerset v Sussex (Hove) 1972. F-c career: 214 matches; 799 runs @ 5.39; 549 wickets @ 28.07. Appointed 1985.

JULIAN, Raymond (Wigston SM), b Cosby, Leics 23 Aug 1936. RHB, WK. Leicestershire 1953-71 (cap 1961). HS 51 v Worcs (Worcester) 1962. F-c career: 192 matches; 2581 runs @ 9.73; 421 dismissals (382 ct, 39 st). Appointed 1972.

*KITCHEN, Mervyn John (Backwell SM, Nailsea), b Nailsea, Somerset 1 Aug 1940. LHB, RM. Somerset 1960-79 (cap 1966; testimonial 1973). Tour: Rhodesia 1972-73 (Int W). 1000 runs (7); most – 1730 (1968). HS 189 v Pakistanis (Taunton) 1967. BB 1-4. F-c career: 354 matches; 15,230 runs @ 26.25, 17 hundreds; 2 wickets @ 54.50. Appointed 1982. Umpired 1 Test (1990).

LEADBEATER, Barrie (Harehills SS), b Harehills, Leeds, Yorks 14 Aug 1943. RHB, RM. Yorkshire 1966-79 (cap 1969; joint benefit with G.A.Cope 1980). Tour: WI 1969-70 (DN). HS 140* v Hants (Portsmouth) 1976. F-c career: 147 matches; 5373 runs @ 25.34, 1 hundred; 1 wicket @ 5.00. Appointed 1981.

LYONS, Kevin James (Lady Mary's HS), b Cardiff, Glam 18 Dec 1946. RHB, RM. Glamorgan 1967-77. Tour: WI 1969-70 (Glam). HS 92 v CU (Cambridge) 1972. F-c career: 62 matches; 1673 runs @ 19.68; 2 wickets @ 126.00. Appointed 1985.

*MEYER, Barrie John (Boscombe SS), b Bournemouth, Hants 21 Aug 1932. RHB, WK. Gloucestershire 1957-71 (cap 1958; benefit 1971). HS 63 v Indians (Cheltenham) 1959, 63 v OU (Bristol) 1962, and 63 v Sussex (Bristol) 1964. F-c career: 406 matches; 5367 runs @ 14.16; 826 dismissals (707 ct, 119 st). Soccer for Bristol Rovers, Plymouth Argyle, Newport County and Bristol City. Appointed 1973. Umpired 22 Tests (1978 to 1990).

OSLEAR, Donald Osmund, b Cleethorpes, Lincs 3 Mar 1929. No first-class appearances. Appointed 1975. Umpired 5 Tests (1980 to 1984).

*PALMER, Kenneth Ernest (Southbroom SM, Devizes), b Winchester, Hants 22 Apr 1937. RHB, RFM. Brother of R. (below) and father of G.V. (Somerset 1982-88). Somerset 1955-69 (cap 1958; testimonial 1968). Tours: WI 1963-64 (Cavs); Pak 1963-64 (Cwlth XI). **Tests:** 1 (1964-65; while coaching in South Africa); 10 runs; 1 wicket. 1000 runs (1): 1036 (1961). 100 wickets (4); most – 139 (1963). HS 125* v Northants (Northampton) 1961. BB 9-57 v Notts (Nottingham) 1963. F-c career: 314 matches; 7,761 runs @ 20.64, 2 hundreds; 866 wickets @ 21.34. Appointed 1972. Umpired 18 Tests (1978 to 1989).

PALMER, Roy (Southbroom SM), b Devizes, Wilts 12 Jul 1942. RHB, RFM. Brother of K.E. (above). Somerset 1965-70. HS 84 v Leics (Taunton) 1967. BB 6-45 v Middx (Lord's) 1967. F-c career: 74 matches; 1037 runs @ 13.29; 172 wickets @ 31.62. Appointed 1980.

PLEWS, Nigel Trevor, b Nottingham 5 Sep 1934. Former policeman (Fraud Squad). No first-class appearances. Appointed 1982. Umpired 5 Tests (1988 and 1990).

*SHEPHERD, David Robert (Barnstaple GS; St Luke's C, Exeter), b Bideford, Devon 27 Dec 1940. RHB, RM. Gloucestershire 1965-79 (cap 1969; joint benefit with J.Davey 1978). Scored 108 on debut (v OU). Devon 1959-64. 1000 runs (2); most – 1079 (1970). HS 153 v Middx (Bristol) 1968. F-c career: 282 matches; 10,672 runs @ 24.47, 12 hundreds; 2 wickets @ 53.00. Appointed 1981. Umpired 11 Tests (1985 to 1990). Officiated in 1987 Reliance World Cup in India and Pakistan.

TOLCHARD, Raymond Charles (Malvern C), b Torquay, Devon 13 Oct 1953. Brother of J.G. (Leics and Devon) and R.W. (Leics, Devon and England 1965-83). LHB. Devon 1975-84. No first-class appearances. Appointed 1991.

WHITE, Robert Arthur (Chiswick GS), b Fulham, London 6 Oct 1936. LHB, OB. Middlesex 1958-65 (cap 1963). Nottinghamshire 1966-80 (cap 1966; benefit 1974). 1000 runs (1): 1355 (1963). HS 116* Notts v Surrey (Oval) 1967. BB 7-41 Notts v Derbys (Ilkeston) 1971. F-c career: 413 matches; 12,452 runs @ 23.18, 5 hundreds; 693 wickets @ 30.50. Appointed 1983.

WHITEHEAD, Alan Geoffrey Thomas, b Butleigh, Somerset 28 Oct 1940. LHB, SLA. Somerset 1957-61. HS 15 v Hants (Southampton) 1959, and 15 v Leics (Leicester) 1960. BB 6-74 v Sussex (Eastbourne) 1959. F-c career: 38 matches; 137 runs @ 5.70; 67 wickets @ 34.41. Appointed 1970. Umpired 5 Tests (1982 to 1987).

WIGHT, Peter Bernard, b Georgetown, British Guiana 25 Jun 1930. RHB, OB. Brother of G.L. (West Indies 1949-53), H.A. and N. (all British Guiana). British Guiana 1950-51. Somerset 1953-65 (cap 1954; benefit 1963). Canterbury 1963-64. 1000 runs (10); most – 2375 (1960). HS 222* v Kent (Taunton) 1959. BB 6-29 v Derbys (Chesterfield) 1957. F-c career: 333 matches 17,773 runs @ 33.09, 28 hundreds; 68 wickets @ 33.26. Appointed 1966.

RESERVE LIST

Dr D.FAWKNER-CORBETT, M.J.HARRIS, V.A.HOLDER, J.SIMMONS, G.A.STICKLEY.

*On Test Match and Texaco Trophy Panel for 1991
See page 63 for key to abbreviations.

PRINCIPAL FIXTURES 1991

Includes Sunday play

Saturday 13 April

*Fenners: Cambridge Us v Lancs
The Parks: Oxford U v Hants

Tuesday 16 April

Lord's: MCC v Middx (Four days)
Fenners: Cambridge U v Northants

Wednesday 17 April

The Parks: Oxford U v Glam

Friday 19 April

Fenners: Cambridge U v Essex

Sunday 21 April

Refuge Assurance League
Cardiff: Glam v Northants
Bristol: Glos v Middx
Southampton: Hants v Yorks
Old Trafford: Lancs v Notts
Leicester: Leics v Derbys
The Oval: Surrey v Somerset
Edgbaston: Warwicks v Sussex
Worcester: Worcs v Kent

Tuesday 23 April

Benson & Hedges Cup
Derby: Derbys v Northants
Bristol: Glos v Combined Us
Southampton: Hants v Notts
Canterbury: Kent v Leics
Taunton: Somerset v Middx
The Oval: Surrey v Essex
Trowbridge: Minor Counties v Glam
Forfar: Scotland v Lancs

Thursday 25 April

Benson & Hedges Cup
Old Trafford: Lancs v Kent
Lord's: Middx v Surrey
Trent Bridge: Notts v Yorks
Hove: Sussex v Leics
Edgbaston: Warwicks v Essex
Worcester: Worcs v Glos
The Parks: Combined Us v Derbys
Trowbridge: Minor Counties v Hants

Saturday 27 April

Britannic Assurance Championship
(Four days)
Derby: Derbys v Northants
Chelmsford: Essex v Surrey
*Southampton: Hants v Kent
Leicester: Leics v Glam
Lord's: Middx v Yorks
Taunton: Somerset v Sussex
Edgbaston: Warwicks v Lancs
*Worcester: Worcs v Glos
Other Match
The Parks: Oxford U v Notts

Sunday 28 April

Refuge Assurance League
Chelmsford: Essex v Yorks
Old Trafford: Lancs v Northants
Leicester: Leics v Glam
Lord's: Middx v Surrey
Trent Bridge: Notts v Warwicks
Taunton: Somerset v Sussex

Thursday 2 May

Benson & Hedges Cup
Chelmsford: Essex v Middx
Bristol: Glos v Northants
Southampton: Hants v Glam
Canterbury: Kent v Sussex
Leicester: Leics v Scotland
Edgbaston: Warwicks v Somerset
Headingley: Yorks v Minor Counties
Fenners: Combined Us v Worcs

Saturday 4 May

Benson & Hedges Cup
Cardiff: Glam v Notts
Leicester: Leics v Lancs
Lord's: Middx v Warwicks
Northampton: Northants v Combined Us

†Taunton: Somerset v Surrey
†Hove: Sussex v Scotland
Worcester: Worcs v Derbys
Headingley: Yorks v Hants

†*Reserve day Sunday*

Sunday 5 May

Refuge Assurance League
Derby: Derbys v Hants
Chelmsford: Essex v Leics
Cardiff: Glam v Notts
Bristol: Glos v Worcs
Canterbury: Kent v Warwicks
Lord's: Middx v Northants

Tuesday 7 May

Benson & Hedges Cup
Derby: Derbys v Glos
Chelmsford: Essex v Somerset
Cardiff: Glam v Yorks
Old Trafford: Lancs v Sussex
Northampton: Northants v Worcs
Trent Bridge: Notts v Minor Counties
The Oval: Surrey v Warwicks
Glasgow (Hamilton Crescent):
    Scotland v Kent

Thursday 9 May

Britannic Assurance Championship
(Four days)
Bristol: Glos v Hants
Lord's: Middx v Sussex
Northampton: Northants v Essex
Trent Bridge: Notts v Leics
Taunton: Somerset v Glam
The Oval: Surrey v Kent
Worcester: Worcs v Lancs
Headingley: Yorks v Warwicks
Other Match
Fenners: Cambridge U v Derbys

Sunday 12 May

Refuge Assurance League
Southampton: Hants v Kent
Northampton: Northants v Leics
Trent Bridge: Notts v Essex
Taunton: Somerset v Glam
The Oval: Surrey v Glos
Hove: Sussex v Middx
Worcester: Worcs v Lancs
Headingley: Yorks v Warwicks
Tourist Match
Arundel: Lavinia, Duchess of
    Norfolk's XI v West Indians (One
    day)

Tuesday 14 May

Tourist Match
Bristol: Glos v West Indians (One
    day)

Wednesday 15 May

Tourist Match
Worcester: Worcs v West Indians
Other Matches
Fenners: Cambridge U v Middx
The Parks: Oxford U v Glos

Thursday 16 May

Britannic Assurance Championship
(Four days)
Swansea: Glam v Warwicks
Folkestone: Kent v Essex
Old Trafford: Lancs v Derbys
Northampton: Northants v Leics
Hove: Sussex v Hants
Headingley: Yorks v Notts

Saturday 18 May

Tourist Match
*Lord's: Middx v West Indians
Other Match
Fenners: Cambridge U v Surrey

Sunday 19 May

Refuge Assurance League
Derby: Derbys v Lancs
Swansea: Glam v Warwicks
Bournemouth: Hants v Somerset
Folkestone: Kent v Essex
Leicester: Leics v Yorks
Northampton: Northants v Worcs
Hove: Sussex v Glos

Wednesday 22 May

Britannic Assurance Championship
Derby: Derbys v Somerset
Chelmsford: Essex v Warwicks
Cardiff: Glam v Northants
Trent Bridge: Notts v Kent
The Oval: Surrey v Lancs
Hove: Sussex v Middx
Sheffield: Yorks v Glos

Other Match
Fenners: Cambridge U v Leics

Thursday 23 May

TEXACO TROPHY
Edgbaston: ENGLAND v WEST INDIES
(First One-day International)

Saturday 25 May

TEXACO TROPHY
Old Trafford: ENGLAND v WEST INDIES
(Second One-day International)
Britannic Assurance Championship
Cardiff: Glam v Sussex
Bournemouth: Hants v Surrey
Canterbury: Kent v Derbys
Leicester: Leics v Notts
Taunton: Somerset v Middx
Edgbaston: Warwicks v Glos
Headingley: Yorks v Northants
Other Match
The Parks: Oxford U v Worcs

Sunday 26 May

Refuge Assurance League
Swansea: Glam v Sussex
Swindon: Glos v Hants
Canterbury: Kent v Derbys
Leicester: Leics v Notts
Taunton: Somerset v Middx
The Oval: Surrey v Essex
Edgbaston: Warwicks v Worcs
Headingley: Yorks v Northants

Monday 27 May

TEXACO TROPHY
Lord's: ENGLAND v WEST INDIES
(Third One-day International)

Wednesday 29 May

Benson & Hedges Cup
Quarter-Finals
Tourist Match
Taunton or The Oval: Somerset or Surrey v West Indians

Friday 31 May

Britannic Assurance Championship
Bristol: Glos v Essex
Old Trafford: Lancs v Sussex

Lord's: Middx v Kent
Northampton: Northants v Derbys
Trent Bridge: Notts v Hants
Edgbaston: Warwicks v Yorks
Worcester: Worcs v Glam

Saturday 1 June

Tourist Match
*Leicester: Leics v West Indians

Sunday 2 June

Refuge Assurance League
Chesterfield: Derbys v Yorks
Pontypridd: Glam v Essex
Old Trafford: Lancs v Sussex
Southgate: Middx v Kent
Northampton: Northants v Hants
Edgbaston: Warwicks v Somerset
Worcester: Worcs v Surrey

Tuesday 4 June

Britannic Assurance Championship
Ilford: Essex v Leics
Swansea: Glam v Somerset
Bristol: Glos v Middx
Basingstoke: Hants v Lancs
Tunbridge Wells: Kent v Warwicks
Northampton: Northants v Worcs
The Oval: Surrey v Notts
Other Match
The Parks: Oxford U v Yorks

Thursday 6 June

CORNHILL INSURANCE TEST MATCH
Headingley: ENGLAND v WEST INDIES (First Test Match)

Friday 7 June

Britannic Assurance Championship
Chesterfield: Derbys v Glam
Ilford: Essex v Worcs
Southampton: Hants v Glos
Tunbridge Wells: Kent v Sussex
Uxbridge: Middx v Leics
Edgbaston: Warwicks v Somerset

Friday 7 June

Other Match
The Parks: Oxford U v Lancs

Sunday 9 June

Refuge Assurance League
Chesterfield: Derbys v Surrey
Ilford: Essex v Worcs
Moreton-in-Marsh: Glos v Northants
Basingstoke: Hants v Sussex
Old Trafford: Lancs v Glam
Uxbridge: Middx v Leics
Trent Bridge: Notts v Somerset

Tuesday 11 June

Harrogate: Tilcon Trophy (Three days)

Wednesday 12 June

Benson & Hedges Cup
Semi-Finals
Tourist Match
Derby or Southport: Derbys or Lancs
   v West Indies

Friday 14 June

Britannic Assurance Championship
Cardiff: Glam v Middx
Gloucester: Glos v Notts
Leicester: Leics v Surrey
Hove: Sussex v Worcs
Harrogate: Yorks v Kent

Saturday 15 June

Tourist Match
*Northampton: Northants v West
   Indians

Sunday 16 June

Refuge Assurance League
Checkley: Derbys v Somerset
Chelmsford: Essex v Hants

Cardiff: Glam v Middx
Gloucester: Glos v Notts
Leicester: Leics v Surrey
Hove: Sussex v Worcs
Edgbaston: Warwicks v Lancs
Scarborough: Yorks v Kent

Tuesday 18 June

Britannic Assurance Championship
Gloucester: Glos v Derbys
Leicester: Leics v Lancs
Bath: Somerset v Hants
Coventry: Warwicks v Sussex

Worcester: Worcs v Notts
Other Matches
Fenners: Cambridge U v Glam
The Parks: Oxford U v Kent

Thursday 20 June

**CORNHILL INSURANCE TEST
MATCH**
*Lord's: ENGLAND v WEST
   INDIES (Second Test Match)

Friday 21 June

Britannic Assurance Championship
Derbys: Derbys v Surrey
*Neath: Glam v Leics
Old Trafford: Lancs v Kent
*Northampton: Northants v Hants
Trent Bridge: Notts v Warwicks
Bath: Somerset v Essex
Horsham: Sussex v Essex
Sheffield: Yorks v Middx

Saturday 22 June

*Dublin (Malahide): Ireland v Scotland
   (Three days)

Sunday 23 June

Refuge Assurance League
Old Trafford: Lancs v Kent
Trent Bridge: Notts v Middx
Bath: Somerset v Glos
Horsham: Sussex v Essex
Edgbaston: Warwicks v Surrey
Sheffield: Yorks v Worcs

Wednesday 26 June

NatWest Bank Trophy
First Round
Bedford: Beds v Worcs
Reading: Berks v Hants
Exmouth: Devon v Essex
Bournemouth: Dorset v Lancs
Darlington: Durham v Glam
Bristol: Glos v Norfolk
Bishop's Stortford: Herts v Derbys
Dublin (Castle Ave): Ireland v Middx
Canterbury: Kent v Cambs
Leicester: Leics v Shrops
Trent Bridge: Notts v Lincs
Edinburgh (Myreside): Scotland v
   Sussex

Bath: Somerset v Bucks
Stone: Staffs v Northants
The Oval: Surrey v Oxon
Edgbaston: Warwicks v Yorks
Tourist Match
The Parks: Oxbridge v West.Indians
(Two days)

Friday 28 June

Britannic Assurance Championship
Liverpool: Lancs v Glam
Lord's: Middx v Essex
Luton: Northants v Glos
The Oval: Surrey v Somerset
Edgbaston: Warwicks v Derbys
Worcester: Worcs v Leics
Tourist Match
Trowbridge: League Cricket
Conference v West Indians
(One day)

Saturday 29 June

Tourist Match
*Southampton: Hants v West Indians
Other Match
*Hove: Sussex v Cambridge U

Sunday 30 June

Refuge Assurance League
Chelmsford: Essex v Derbys
Canterbury: Kent v Glos
Luton: Northants v Somerset
The Oval: Surrey v Notts
Worcester: Worcs v Leics
Headingley: Yorks v Glam

Tuesday 2 July

Britannic Assurance Championship
Chelmsford: Essex v Hants
Cardiff: Glam v Notts
Maidstone: Kent v Northants
Hinckley: Leics v Glos
Taunton: Somerset v Lancs
Arundel: Sussex v Surrey
Edgbaston: Warwicks v Middx
Headingley: Yorks v Worcs
Other Match
Lord's: Oxford U v Cambridge U

Thursday 4 July

CORNHILL INSURANCE TEST MATCH
Trent Bridge: ENGLAND v WEST INDIES (Third Test Match)

Friday 5 July

Britannic Assurance Championship
Derby: Derbys v Sussex
Southampton: Hants v Yorks
Maidstone: Kent v Glamorgan
Leicester: Leics v Northants
The Oval: Surrey v Essex

Sunday 7 July

Refuge Assurance League
Derby: Derbys v Sussex
Chelmsford: Essex v Warwicks
Southampton: Hants v Worcs
Maidstone: Kent v Glam
Leicester: Leics v Lancs
Lord's: Middx v Yorks
Tring: Northants v Surrey
Other Match
Taunton: Somerset v Glos
(Centenary Challenge) (One day)

Wednesday 10 July

Tourist Match
Darlington: Minor Counties v West Indians (Two days)

Thursday 11 July

NatWest Bank Trophy
Second Round
Luton or Worcester: Beds or Worcs v Durham or Glam
Reading or Southampton: Berks or Hants v Dorset or Lancs
Bristol or Lakenham: Glos or Norfolk v Notts or Lincs
Glasgow (Titwood) or Hove: Scotland or Sussex v Devon or Essex
Taunton or Marlow: Somerset or Bucks v Ireland or Middx
Burton (Ind Coope) or Northampton: Staffs or Northants v Leics or Shrops
The Oval or Oxford (Christ Church College): Surrey or Oxon v Kent or Cambs
Edgbaston or Headingley: Warwicks or Yorks v Herts or Derbys

Saturday 13 July

Lord's: *Benson & Hedges Cup Final*
Tourist Match
Downpatrick: Ireland v West Indians
(One day)

Sunday 14 July

Refuge Assurance League
Matches involving B & H Cup Finalists
to be re-arranged
Canterbury: Kent v Leics
Trent Bridge: Notts v Hants
Taunton: Somerset v Lancs
The Oval: Surrey v Sussex
Edgbaston: Warwicks v Middx
Worcester: Worcs v Derbys
Scarborough: Yorks v Glos

Monday 15 July

Tourist Match
Brecon: Wales v West Indians
(One day)

Tuesday 16 July

Britannic Assurance Championship
Southend: Essex v Kent
Portsmouth: Hants v Worcs
Uxbridge: Middx v Northants
Trent Bridge: Notts v Lancs
Guildford: Surrey v Glos
Hove: Sussex v Somerset
Scarborough: Yorks v Derbys
Tourist Match
Swansea: Glam v West Indians

Friday 19 July

Britannic Assurance Championship
Southend: Essex v Somerset
Cheltenham: Glos v Glam
Portsmouth: Hants v Warwicks
Uxbridge: Middx v Lancs
Wellingborough School: Northants v
Notts
Guildford: Surrey v Yorks
Hove: Sussex v Leics
Kidderminster: Worcs v Derbys

Saturday 20 July

Tourist Match
*Canterbury: Kent v West Indians

Sunday 21 July

Refuge Assurance League
Southend: Essex v Somerset
Cheltenham: Glos v Derbys
Portsmouth: Hants v Warwicks
Lord's: Middx v Lancs
Wellingborough School: Northants v
Notts
The Oval: Surrey v Yorks
Hove: Sussex v Leics
Worcester: Worcs v Glam

Tuesday 23 July

Britannic Assurance Championship
Chesterfield: Derbys v Hants
Cardiff: Glam v Essex
Cheltenham: Glos v Sussex
Old Trafford: Lancs v Warwicks
Northampton: Northants v Somerset
Worksop: Notts v Yorks
Worcester: Worcs v Kent

Wednesday 24 July

Tourist Match
Wolverhampton: England Amateur
XI v Sri Lankans (One day)

Thursday 25 July

**CORNHILL INSURANCE TEST
MATCH**
Edgbaston: ENGLAND v WEST
INDIES (Fourth Test Match)

Friday 26 July

Britannic Assurance Championship
Cheltenham: Glos v Worcs
*Leicester: Leics v Warwicks
Lord's: Middx v Notts
Taunton: Somerset v Kent
The Oval: Surrey v Glam
Tourist Match
Hartlepool: Durham v Sri Lankans
(One day)

Saturday 27 July

Tourist Match
*Headingley: Yorks v Sri Lankans

Sunday 28 July

Refuge Assurance League
Derby: Derbys v Northants
Cheltenham: Glos v Essex
Southampton: Hants v Lancs
Taunton: Somerset v Kent
The Oval: Surrey v Glam
Hove: Sussex v Notts

Tuesday 30 July

Tourist Match
Swansea or Worcester: Glam or
Worcs v Sri Lankans

Wednesday 31 July

NatWest Bank Trophy
Quarter-Finals
Tourist Match
Trent Bridge or Bristol: Notts or
Glos v West Indians
Other Match
Jesmond: England XI v Rest of the
World XI (One day)

Thursday 1 August

Jesmond: England XI v Rest of the
World XI (One day)

Friday 2 August

Britannic Assurance Championship
Canterbury: Kent v Surrey
Old Trafford: Lancs v Yorks
Lord's: Middx v Hants
Weston-s-Mare: Somerset v Leics
Eastbourne: Sussex v Northants
Worcester: Worcs v Warwicks
Tourist Match
Derby: Derbys v Sri Lankans

Saturday 3 August

Tourist Match
*Chelmsford: Essex v West Indians

Sunday 4 August

Refuge Assurance League
Swansea: Glam v Glos
Canterbury: Kent v Surrey
Old Trafford: Lancs v Yorks
Lord's: Middx v Hants
Trent Bridge: Notts v Worcs
Weston-s-Mare: Somerset v Leics

Eastbourne: Sussex v Northants
Edgbaston: Warwicks v Derbys

Tuesday 6 August

Britannic Assurance Championship
Derby: Derbys v Essex
Canterbury: Kent v Hants
Lytham: Lancs v Northants
Leicester: Leics v Yorks
Weston-s-Mare: Somerset v Worcs
Eastbourne: Sussex v Notts
Edgbaston: Warwicks v Surrey
Tourist Match
Bristol: Glos v Sri Lankans
Other Match
Lord's: England Under-19 v Australia
Under-19 (First Youth One-day
International)

Thursday 8 August

**CORNHILL INSURANCE TEST
MATCH**
*The Oval: ENGLAND v WEST
INDIES (Fifth Test Match)
Other Match
Trent Bridge: England Under-19 v
Australia Under-19 (Second Youth
One-day International)

Friday 9 August

Britannic Assurance Championship
Swansea: Glam v Hants
Bristol: Glos v Lancs
Leicester: Leics v Kent
Lord's: Middx v Derbys
Northampton: Northants v Warwicks
Trent Bridge: Notts v Essex
Middlesbrough: Yorks v Sussex

Saturday 10 August

Tourist Match
*Taunton: Somerset v Sri Lankans

Sunday 11 August

Refuge Assurance League
Ebbw Vale: Glam v Hants
Bristol: Glos v Lancs
Leicester: Leics v Warwicks
Lord's: Middx v Derbys
Peterborough: Northants v Essex
Trent Bridge: Notts v Kent
Middlesbrough: Yorks v Sussex

Monday 12 or Tuesday 13 August

Bain Clarkson Trophy
Semi-Finals (One day)

Wednesday 14 August

NatWest Bank Trophy
Semi-Finals
Tourist Match
†Old Trafford: England 'A' v Sri
    Lankans (One day)

Thursday 15 August

Tourist Match
†Old Trafford: England 'A' v Sri
    Lankans (One day)

† *Or at another venue if Lancashire in
    NWT semi-finals*

Friday 16 August

Britannic Assurance Championship
Derby: Derbys v Lancs
Colchester: Essex v Northants
Bournemouth: Hants v Leics
Trent Bridge: Notts v Somerset
Worcester: Worcs v Surrey
Headingley: Yorks v Glam
Other Match
Leicester: England Under-19 v
    Australia Under-19 (First Youth
    Test Match) (Four days)

Saturday 17 August

Tourist Match
*Hove: Sussex v Sri Lankans

Sunday 18 August

Refuge Assurance League
Derby: Derbys v Glam
Colchester: Essex v Middx
Bournemouth: Hants v Leics
Canterbury: Kent v Northants
Old Trafford: Lancs v Surrey
Edgbaston: Warwicks v Glos
Worcester: Worcs v Somerset
Scarborough: Yorks v Notts

Tuesday 20 August

Britannic Assurance Championship
Derby: Derbys v Leics

Colchester: Essex v Yorks
Bournemouth: Hants v Sussex
Dartford or Canterbury: Kent v Glos
Blackpool: Lancs v Worcs
The Oval: Surrey v Middx
Edgbaston: Warwicks v Glam

Thursday 22 August

**CORNHILL INSURANCE TEST
MATCH**
Lord's: ENGLAND v SRI LANKA

Friday 23 August

Britannic Assurance Championship
Old Trafford: Lancs v Essex
Northampton: Northants v Surrey
Trent Bridge: Notts v Derbys
Taunton: Somerset v Yorks
Worcester: Worcs v Middx

Sunday 25 August

Refuge Assurance League
Old Trafford: Lancs v Essex
Leicester: Leics v Glos
Northampton: Northants v Warwicks
Trent Bridge: Notts v Derbys
Taunton: Somerset v Yorks
The Oval: Surrey v Hants
Hove: Sussex v Kent
Worcester: Worcs v Middx

Tuesday 27 August

Chelmsford: England Under-19 v
    Australia Under-19 (Second Youth
    Test Match) (Four days)

Wednesday 28 August

Britannic Assurance Championship
(Four days)
Abergavenny: Glam v Glos
Southampton: Hants v Somerset
Canterbury: Kent v Middx
Old Trafford: Lancs v Notts
Leicester: Leics v Derbys
Northampton: Northants v Yorks
The Oval: Surrey v Sussex
Edgbaston: Warwicks v Worcs
Other Match
Scarborough: Michael Parkinson's
    International Match (Three days)

Saturday 31 August

Scarborough: Scarborough Festival
Trophy (Three days)

Sunday 1 September

Refuge Assurance Cup
Semi-Finals

Tuesday 3 September

Britannic Assurance Championship
(Four days)
Chelmsford: Essex v Derbys
Bristol: Glos v Northants
Trent Bridge: Notts v Middx
The Oval: Surrey v Hants
Hove: Sussex v Kent
Worcester: Worcs v Somerset
Scarborough: Yorks v Lancs

Saturday 7 September

Lord's: *NatWest Bank Trophy Final*
Reserve days Sunday and Monday
Hove: Seeboard Trophy (Three days)
Scarborough: Yorks v The
Yorkshiremen (One day)

Sunday 8 September

Scarborough: Michael Parkinson's XI
v Yorks (One day)

Monday 9 September

Old Trafford: England Under-19 v
Australia Under-19 (Third Youth
Test Match) (Four days)
Bain Clarkson Trophy Final (One day)

Tuesday 10 September

Britannic Assurance Championship
(Four days)
Derby: Derbys v Notts
Cardiff: Glam v Worcs
Bristol: Glos v Somerset
Leicester: Leics v Essex
Lord's: Middx v Surrey
Edgbaston: Warwicks v Northants

Sunday 15 September

Old Trafford: *Refuge Assurance Cup
Final*

Tuesday 17 September

Britannic Assurance Championship
(Four days)
Chesterfield: Derbys v Yorks
Chelmsford: Essex v Middx
Southampton: Hants v Glam
Canterbury: Kent v Leics
Old Trafford: Lancs v Surrey
Trent Bridge: Notts v Worcs
Taunton: Somerset v Warwicks
Hove: Sussex v Glos

Sunday 22 September

Britannic Assurance Challenge (One
day)
Britannic Assurance Champions v
1990-91 Sheffield Shield Winners

Monday 23 September

Britannic Assurance Challenge (Four
days)
Britannic Assurance Champions v
1990-91 Sheffield Shield Winners

SECOND XI FIXTURES 1991

(R)   Rapid Cricketline Championship (*Three days*)
(BC) Bain Clarkson Trophy (*One day*)

APRIL			
Wed 24	(R)	Chesterfield	Derbyshire v Warwickshire
Sat 27		Hove	Sussex v England Under 19 (Four days)
Tue 30	(BC)	Old Trafford	Lancashire v Leicestershire
	(R)	Southgate	Middlesex v Northamptonshire

MAY

Wed 1	(R)	Old Trafford	Lancashire v Leicestershire
	(R)	The Oval	Surrey v Worcestershire
	(R)	Hastings	Sussex v Glamorgan
	(R)	Mitchells and Butlers	Warwickshire v Hampshire
Thu 2	(BC)	Derby	Derbyshire v Nottinghamshire
	(BC)	Maidstone	Kent v MCC Young Cricketers
Mon 6	(BC)	Ilkeston (Shipley Hall)	Derbyshire v Leicestershire
	(BC)	Old Trafford	Lancashire v Yorkshire
	(BC)	Edgbaston	Warwickshire v Somerset
Tue 7	(R)	Chesterfield	Derbyshire v Somerset
	(BC)	Swansea	Glamorgan v Warwickshire
	(BC)	Finchley	Middlesex v Essex
	(BC)	Eastbourne	Sussex v Kent
Wed 8	(R)	Swansea	Glamorgan v Surrey
	(R)	Uppingham	Leicestershire v Northamptonshire
	(R)	Shireoaks (Steetley)	Nottinghamshire v Worcestershire
	(R)	Hove	Sussex v Lancashire
Thu 9	(BC)	Moreton-in-Marsh	Gloucestershire v Warwickshire
Mon 13	(BC)	Sidley	Sussex v MCC Young Cricketers
Tue 14	(R)	Chelmsford	Essex v Somerset
	(R)	Horsham	Sussex v Northamptonshire
	(BC)	Chesterfield	Derbyshire v Lancashire
	(BC)	Southampton	Hampshire v Worcestershire
	(BC)	Clipstone	Nottinghamshire v Yorkshire
	(BC)	The Oval	Surrey v Kent
	(BC)	Edgbaston	Warwickshire v Glamorgan
Wed 15	(R)	Chesterfield	Derbyshire v Lancashire
	(R)	Bristol	Gloucestershire v Worcestershire
	(R)	Hinckley	Leicestershire v Hampshire
	(R)	Trent Bridge	Nottinghamshire v Yorkshire
	(R)	The Oval	Surrey v Kent
	(R)	Nuneaton (Griff & Coton)	Warwickshire v Glamorgan
Mon 20	(BC)	Newbury Park	Essex v Kent
	(BC)	Leicester	Leicestershire v Northamptonshire
	(BC)	Worthington Simpson	Nottinghamshire v Lancashire
	(BC)	The Oval	Surrey v Middlesex
	(BC)	Coventry & North Warwicks	Warwickshire v Gloucestershire
Tue 21	(R)	Harrow	Middlesex v Hampshire
	(R)	Northampton	Northamptonshire v Essex
	(BC)	Leicester	Leicestershire v Lancashire
	(BC)	Worcester	Worcestershire v Somerset
Wed 22	(R)	Belper Meadow	Derbyshire v Glamorgan
	(R)	Bristol	Gloucestershire v Yorkshire
	(R)	Market Harborough	Leicestershire v Kent
	(R)	Worcester	Worcestershire v Somerset
Mon 27	(BC)	Bristol	Gloucestershire v Glamorgan
	(BC)	Eastbourne	Sussex v Surrey
	(BC)	Bradford	Yorkshire v Leicestershire
Tue 28	(R)	Colchester	Essex v Derbyshire
	(R)	Oundle School	Northamptonshire v Kent
	(R)	Eastbourne	Sussex v Surrey
	(BC)	Worksop College	Nottinghamshire v Leicestershire
	(BC)	Yeovil (Westlands)	Somerset v Glamorgan

Wed 29	(R)	Uxbridge (RAF Vine Lane)	Middlesex v Lancashire
	(R)	North Perrott	Somerset v Glamorgan
	(R)	Bradford	Yorkshire v Warwickshire
Thu 30	(BC)	Kidderminster	Worcestershire v Gloucestershire
Fri 31	(BC)	Colchester	Essex v Surrey

JUNE

Mon 3	(BC)	Maidstone	Kent v Surrey
	(BC)	Taunton	Somerset v Hampshire
	(BC)	Bingley	Yorkshire v Northamptonshire
Tue 4	(R)	Maidstone	Kent v Warwickshire
	(R)	Cheltenham (Dowty Arle Court)	Gloucestershire v Essex
	(R)	Old Trafford	Lancashire v Northamptonshire
	(R)	Hinckley	Leicestershire v Glamorgan
	(R)	Taunton	Somerset v Hampshire
	(R)	Banstead	Surrey v Derbyshire
	(R)	Worcester	Worcestershire v Sussex
	(BC)	Richmond	Middlesex v MCC Young Cricketers
	(BC)	Sheffield (Bawtry Road)	Yorkshire v Nottinghamshire
Fri 7	(BC)	Trent Bridge	Nottinghamshire v Northamptonshire
	(BC)	Winscombe	Somerset v Gloucestershire
	(BC)	Worcester	Worcestershire v Hampshire
Mon 10	(BC)	Bournemouth	Hampshire v Gloucestershire
	(BC)	Ealing	Middlesex v Sussex
	(BC)	Northampton	Northamptonshire v Leicestershire
	(BC)	The Oval	Surrey v MCC Young Cricketers
	(BC)	Worcester	Worcestershire v Warwickshire
Tue 11	(R)	Bournemouth	Hampshire v Gloucestershire
	(R)	Sittingbourne	Kent v Derbyshire
	(R)	Teddington (Lensbury Club)	Middlesex v Sussex
	(R)	Old Northamptonians	Northamptonshire v Surrey
	(R)	Worthington Simpson	Nottinghamshire v Essex
	(R)	Glastonbury	Somerset v Leicestershire
	(BC)	Bridgend	Glamorgan v Worcestershire
	(BC)	Todmorden	Yorkshire v Lancashire
Wed 12	(R)	Abergavenny	Glamorgan v Worcestershire
	(R)	Todmorden	Yorkshire v Lancashire
Mon 17	(BC)	Chesterfield	Derbyshire v Yorkshire
	(BC)	Ilford	Essex v MCC Young Cricketers
	(BC)	Llanelli	Glamorgan v Somerset
	(BC)	The Oval	Surrey v Sussex
Tue 18	(R)	Chelmsford	Essex v Leicestershire
	(R)	Southampton	Hampshire v Yorkshire
	(R)	Canterbury	Kent v Middlesex
	(R)	Crosby (Northern)	Lancashire v Gloucestershire
	(R)	Oundle School	Northamptonshire v Worcestershire
	(R)	Hove	Sussex v Warwickshire
		The Oval	Surrey v England Under 19
Wed 19	(R)	Worksop	Nottinghamshire v Somerset
Fri 21	(BC)	Canterbury	Kent v Middlesex
	(BC)	Southampton	Hampshire v Warwickshire
Mon 24	(BC)	Chelmsford	Essex v Middlesex
	(BC)	Swansea	Glamorgan v Gloucestershire
	(BC)	Southampton	Hampshire v Somerset
	(BC)	Headingley	Yorkshire v Derbyshire

Tue 25	(R)	Chelmsford	Essex v Middlesex
	(R)	BP Llandarcy	Glamorgan v Gloucestershire
	(R)	Blackpool	Lancashire v Kent
	(R)	Northampton	Northamptonshire v Nottinghamshire
	(R)	Taunton	Somerset v Sussex
	(R)	Harrogate	Yorkshire v Derbyshire
Wed 26	(R)	Portsmouth	Hampshire v Surrey
	(R)	Stratford-upon-Avon	Warwickshire v Leicestershire

JULY

Mon 1	(BC)	Banbury	Northamptonshire v Nottinghamshire
Tue 2	(R)	Southampton	Hampshire v Northamptonshire
	(R)	Lydney	Gloucestershire v Nottinghamshire
	(R)	Old Trafford	Lancashire v Glamorgan
	(R)	The Oval	Surrey v Yorkshire
	(R)	Worcester	Worcestershire v Essex
	(BC)	Birkbeck College	Middlesex v Kent
Wed 3	(R)	Knowle & Dorridge	Warwickshire v Middlesex
	(BC)	Norbury	MCC Young Cricketers v Kent
Fri 5	(BC)	Northampton	Northamptonshire v Derbyshire
	(BC)	Bristol	Gloucestershire v Worcestershire
Mon 8	(BC)	Norbury	MCC Young Cricketers v Surrey
	(BC)	Farnsfield	Nottinghamshire v Derbyshire
	(BC)	Taunton	Somerset v Worcestershire
	(BC)	Lewes Priory	Sussex v Essex
	(BC)	Edgbaston	Warwickshire v Hampshire
Tue 9	(R)	Chelmsford	Essex v Warwickshire
	(BC)	Bristol	Gloucestershire v Hampshire
	(BC)	Maidstone	Kent v Sussex
	(BC)	Leicester	Leicestershire v Nottinghamshire
	(BC)	Harrow	Middlesex v Surrey
	(BC)	Bedford Modern School	Northamptonshire v Lancashire
	(BC)	Stourbridge	Worcestershire v Glamorgan
Wed 10	(R)	Derby	Derbyshire v Middlesex
	(R)	Cardiff	Glamorgan v Nottinghamshire
	(R)	Maidstone	Kent v Sussex
	(R)	Old Trafford	Lancashire v Hampshire
	(R)	Oakham	Leicestershire v Gloucestershire
	(R)	York	Yorkshire v Somerset
Mon 15	(BC)	Panteg	Glamorgan v Hampshire
	(BC)	Leicester	Leicestershire v Derbyshire
	(BC)	Northampton	Northamptonshire v Yorkshire
	(BC)	The Oval	Surrey v Essex
Tue 16	(R)	Gloucester (Tuffley Park)	Gloucestershire v Derbyshire
	(R)	Ebbw Vale	Glamorgan v Hampshire
	(R)	Canterbury	Kent v Essex
	(R)	Northampton	Northamptonshire v Yorkshire
	(R)	Worcester (Flagge Meadow)	Worcestershire v Middlesex
	(R)	Old Trafford	Lancashire v Nottinghamshire
Wed 17	(R)	Liverpool	Lancashire v Nottinghamshire
	(R)	Leicester	Leicestershire v Surrey
Fri 19	(BC)	Gloucester (Tuffley Park)	Gloucestershire v Somerset
	(BC)	Canterbury	Kent v Essex
	(BC)	Old Edwardians	Warwickshire v Worcestershire

Mon 22	(BC)	Heanor	Derbyshire v Northamptonshire
	(BC)	Southampton	Hampshire v Glamorgan
	(BC)	Norbury	MCC Young Cricketers v Sussex
Tue 23	(R)	Chelmsford	Essex v Glamorgan
	(R)	Bristol	Gloucestershire v Kent
	(R)	Wellingborough School	Northamptonshire v Somerset
	(R)	Worksop College	Nottinghamshire v Surrey
	(R)	Studley	Warwickshire v Lancashire
	(R)	Marske-by-Sea	Yorkshire v Worcestershire
	(BC)	Hove	Sussex v Middlesex
Wed 24	(R)	Heanor	Derbyshire v Sussex
	(R)	Richmond	Middlesex v Leicestershire
Fri 26	(BC)	Norbury	MCC Young Cricketers v Essex
	(BC)	Old Trafford	Lancashire v Northamptonshire
Mon 29	(BC)	Southend	Essex v Sussex
	(BC)	Old Trafford	Lancashire v Derbyshire
	(BC)	Market Harborough	Leicestershire v Yorkshire
	(BC)	Norbury	MCC Young Cricketers v Middlesex
	(BC)	Bristol Imperial	Somerset v Warwickshire
Tue 30	(R)	Southend	Essex v Sussex
	(R)	Bournemouth	Hampshire v Nottinghamshire
	(R)	Dartford	Kent v Worcestershire
	(R)	Market Harborough	Leicestershire v Yorkshire
	(R)	Clevedon	Somerset v Warwickshire
	(R)	Oxted	Surrey v Middlesex
Wed 31	(R)	Oundle School	Northamptonshire v Derbyshire

AUGUST

Tue 6	(R)	Chelmsford	Essex v Lancashire
	(R)	Southampton	Hampshire v Kent
	(R)	Ammanford	Glamorgan v Northamptonshire
	(R)	Southgate	Middlesex v Nottinghamshire
	(R)	Taunton	Somerset v Gloucestershire
	(R)	Guildford	Surrey v Warwickshire
	(R)	Worcester	Worcestershire v Leicestershire
	(R)	Headingley	Yorkshire v Sussex
Mon 12	(BC)		Bain Clarkson Trophy
or Tue 13			Semi Finals
Tue 13	(R)	Oxted	Surrey v Essex
Wed 14	(R)	Usk	Glamorgan v Yorkshire
	(R)	Collingham	Nottinghamshire v Sussex
	(R)	Weston (Devonshire Road)	Somerset v Middlesex
	(R)	Walmley	Warwickshire v Gloucestershire
	(R)	Halesowen	Worcestershire v Derbyshire
Tue 20	(R)	Cheltenham (Dowty Arle Court)	Gloucestershire v Northamptonshire
	(R)	Guildford	Surrey v Somerset
	(R)	Hove	Sussex v Hampshire
	(R)	Barnt Green	Worcestershire v Lancashire
	(R)	Elland	Yorkshire v Essex
Wed 21	(R)	Cardiff	Glamorgan v Kent
	(R)	Leamington Spa	Warwickshire v Nottinghamshire
Tue 27	(R)	Derby	Derbyshire v Leicestershire
	(R)	Bristol	Gloucestershire v Surrey

Wed 28	(R)	Bournemouth	Hampshire v Essex
	(R)	Taunton	Somerset v Lancashire
	(R)	Shireoaks (Steetley)	Nottinghamshire v Kent
	(R)	Worcester	Worcestershire v Warwickshire
	(R)	Headingley	Yorkshire v Middlesex

SEPTEMBER

Tue 3	(R)	Derby	Derbyshire v Hampshire
	(R)	Harrow	Middlesex v Glamorgan
	(R)	Horsham	Sussex v Gloucestershire
Wed 4	(R)	Folkestone	Kent v Yorkshire
	(R)	Leicester	Leicestershire v Nottinghamshire
	(R)	Moseley	Warwickshire v Northamptonshire
Mon 9	(BC)		Bain Clarkson Trophy Final
			(Reserve Day Tuesday 10)
Wed 11	(R)	Southampton	Hampshire v Worcestershire
	(R)	Canterbury	Kent v Somerset
	(R)	Crosby (Northern)	Lancashire v Surrey
	(R)	Enfield	Middlesex v Gloucestershire
	(R)	Trent Bridge	Nottinghamshire v Derbyshire
	(R)	Hove	Sussex v Leicestershire

YOUNG CRICKETER OF THE YEAR

Every September since 1950 the Cricket Writers' Club have selected their best young cricketer of the season. In 1986 their ballot resulted in a dead heat for the first time. Only five of their selections have ended their first-class careers without a Test cap.

1950	R.Tattersall	1971	J.Whitehouse
1951	P.B.H.May	1972	D.R.Owen-Thomas
1952	F.S.Trueman	1973	M.Hendrick
1953	M.C.Cowdrey	1974	P.H.Edmonds
1954	P.J.Loader	1975	A.Kennedy
1955	K.F.Barrington	1976	G.Miller
1956	B.Taylor	1977	I.T.Botham
1957	M.J.Stewart	1978	D.I.Gower
1958	A.C.D.Ingleby-Mackenzie	1979	P.W.G.Parker
1959	G.Pullar	1980	G.R.Dilley
1960	D.A.Allen	1981	M.W.Gatting
1961	P.H.Parfitt	1982	N.G.Cowans
1962	P.J.Sharpe	1983	N.A.Foster
1963	G.Boycott	1984	R.J.Bailey
1964	J.M.Brearley	1985	D.V.Lawrence
1965	A.P.E.Knott	1986	A.A.Metcalfe / J.J.Whitaker
1966	D.L.Underwood		
1967	A.W.Greig	1987	R.J.Blakey
1968	R.M.H.Cottam	1988	M.P.Maynard
1969	A.Ward	1989	N.Hussain
1970	C.M.Old	1990	M.A.Atherton

A QUEEN ANNE PRESS BOOK

© Queen Anne Press 1991

First published in Great Britain in 1991 by
Queen Anne Press, a division of
Macdonald & Co (Publishers) Ltd
Orbit House
1 New Fetter Lane
London EC4A 1AR
A member of the Maxwell Macmillan Pergamon Publishing Corporation

Cover photograph: Robin Smith (Hampshire and England)
                  by Adrian Murrell (All-Sport)

ISBN 0-356-19683-6 (Paperback)
ISBN 0-356-20162-7 (Hardback)

British Library Cataloguing in Publication Data

Playfair cricket annual. – 1991
    1. Cricket – Serials
    I. Frindall, Bill
    796.35'8'05

Typeset by BP Integraphics, Bath, Avon
Printed and bound in Great Britain by
BPCC Hazell Books
Aylesbury, Bucks, England
Member of BPCC Ltd.